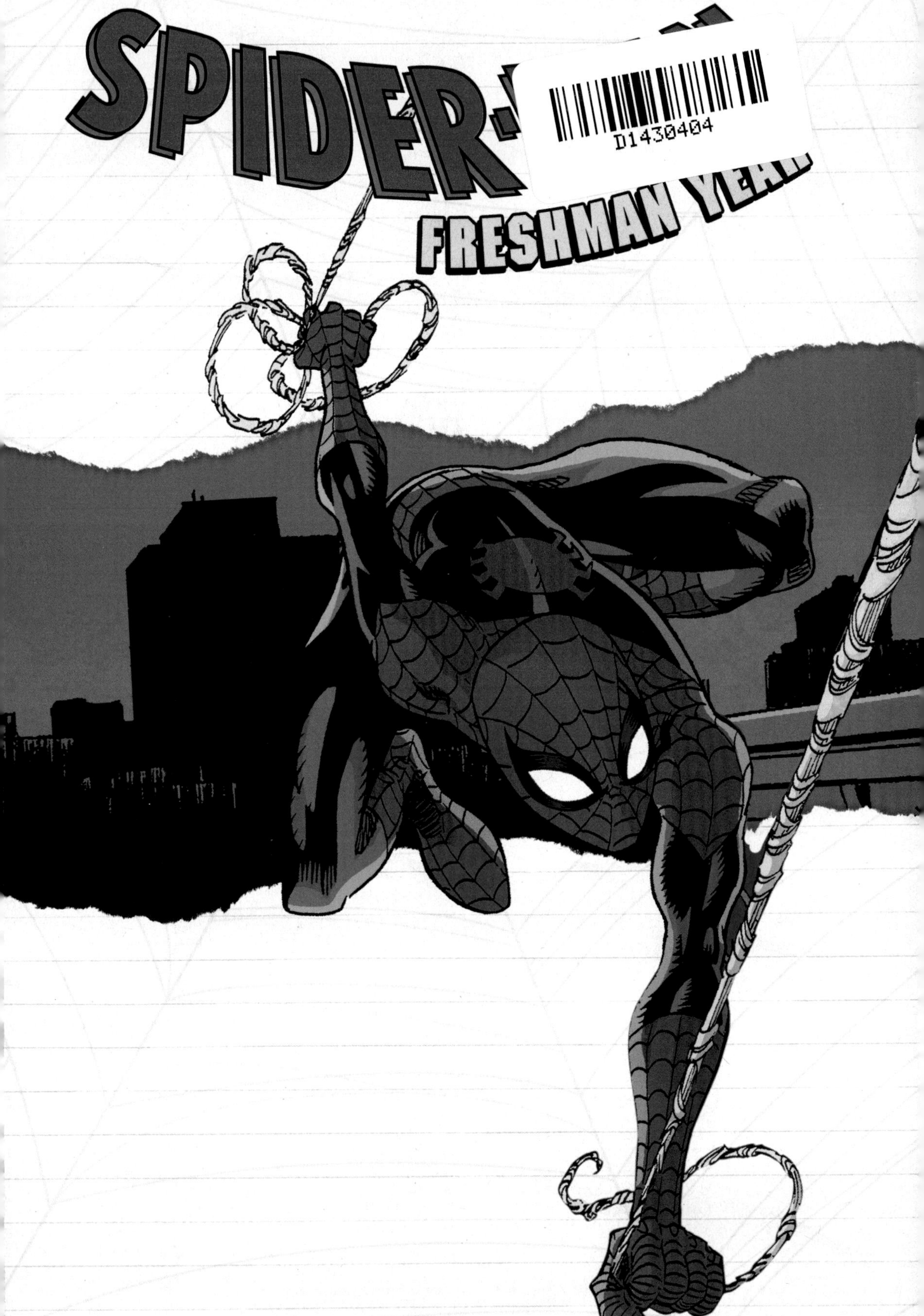
SPIDER-
FRESHMAN YEA

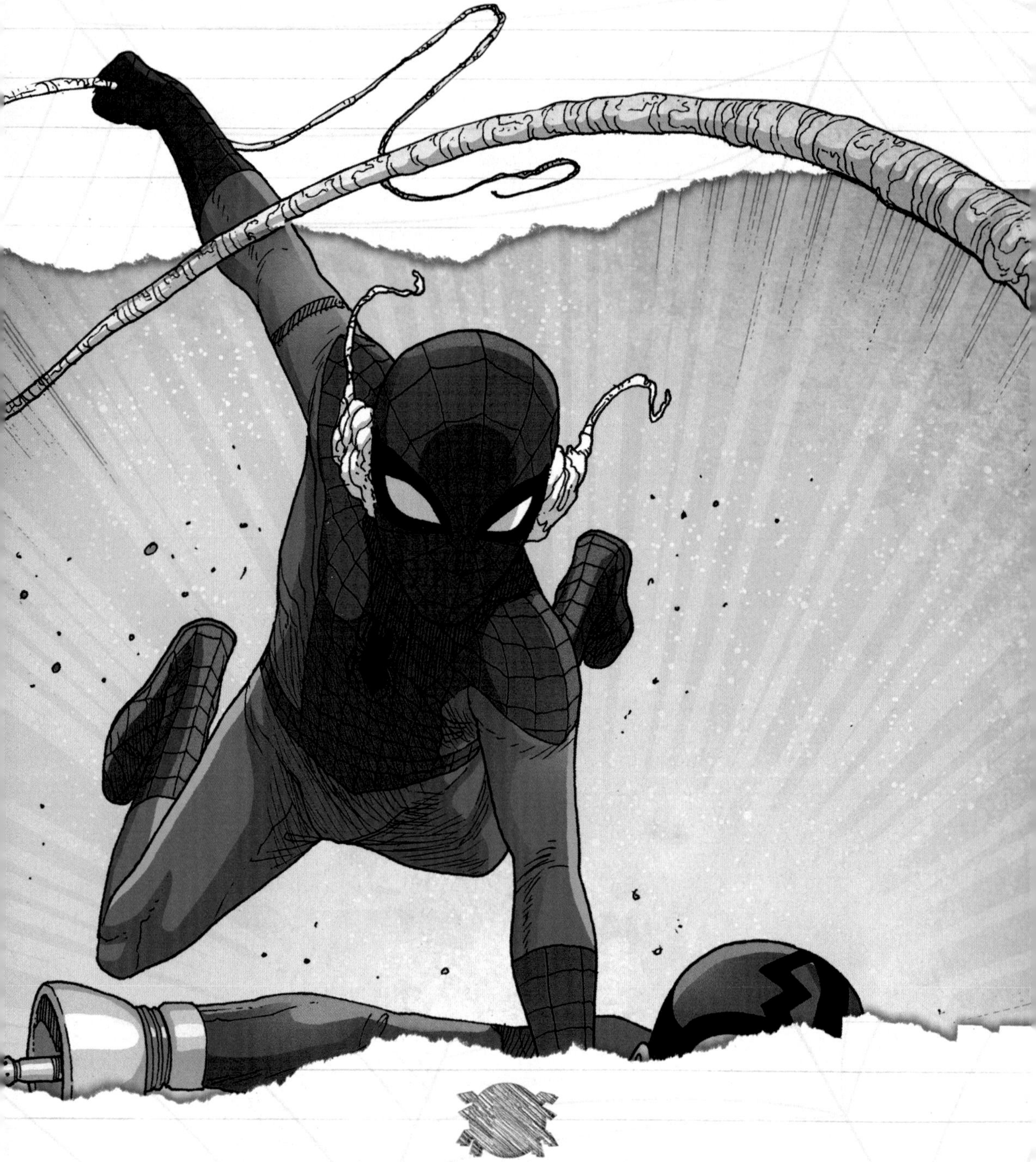

COLLECTION EDITOR JENNIFER GRÜNWALD
ASSISTANT EDITOR DANIEL KIRCHHOFFER
ASSOCIATE MANAGER, TALENT RELATIONS LISA MONTALBANO
VP PRODUCTION & SPECIAL PROJECTS JEFF YOUNGQUIST
BOOK DESIGNER YOUSSIF BAYOR
MANAGER & SENIOR DESIGNER ADAM DEL RE
LEAD DESIGNER JAY BOWEN
SVP PRINT, SALES & MARKETING DAVID GABRIEL
EDITOR IN CHIEF C.B. CEBULSKI

SPIDEY: FRESHMAN YEAR. Contains material originally published in magazine form as SPIDEY (2015) #1-12 and SPIDER-MAN: MASTER PLAN (2017) #1. First printing 2023. ISBN 978-1-302-95185-6. Published by MARVEL WORLDWIDE, INC., a subsidiary of MARVEL ENTERTAINMENT, LLC. OFFICE OF PUBLICATION: 1290 Avenue of the Americas, New York, NY 10104. **Printed in Canada.** KEVIN FEIGE, Chief Creative Officer; DAN BUCKLEY, President, Marvel Entertainment; DAVID BOGART, Associate Publisher & SVP of Talent Affairs; TOM BREVOORT, VP, Executive Editor; NICK LOWE, Executive Editor, VP of Content, Digital Publishing; DAVID GABRIEL, VP of Print & Digital Publishing; SVEN LARSEN, VP of Licensed Publishing; MARK ANNUNZIATO, VP of Planning & Forecasting; JEFF YOUNGQUIST, VP of Production & Special Projects; ALEX MORALES, Director of Publishing Operations; DAN EDINGTON, Director of Editorial Operations; RICKEY PURDIN, Director of Talent Relations; JENNIFER GRÜNWALD, Director of Production & Special Projects; SUSAN CRESPI, Production Manager; STAN LEE, Chairman Emeritus. For information regarding advertising in Marvel Comics or on Marvel.com, please contact Vit DeBellis, Custom Solutions & Integrated Advertising Manager, at vdebellis@marvel.com. For Marvel subscription inquiries, please call 888-511-5480. **Manufactured between 9/29/2023 and 10/31/2023 by SOLISCO PRINTERS, SCOTT, QC, CANADA.**

10 9 8 7 6 5 4 3 2 1

SPIDER-MAN
FRESHMAN YEAR

ROBBIE THOMPSON
WRITER

SPIDEY #1-3

NICK BRADSHAW
ARTIST

JIM CAMPBELL WITH
RACHELLE ROSENBERG (#3)
COLOR ARTISTS

NICK BRADSHAW &
JIM CAMPBELL
COVER ART

SPIDEY #4-7

ANDRÉ LIMA ARAÚJO
ARTIST

RACHELLE ROSENBERG (#4) &
JIM CAMPBELL (#5-7) WITH
JAVA TARTAGLIA (#5)
COLOR ARTISTS

NICK BRADSHAW &
JIM CAMPBELL (#4, #6);
ANDRÉ LIMA ARAÚJO &
JIM CAMPBELL (#5); AND
KHARY RANDOLPH &
EMILIO LOPEZ (#7)
COVER ART

SPIDEY #8-12 & SPIDER-MAN: MASTER PLAN

NATHAN STOCKMAN
ARTIST

JIM CAMPBELL
COLOR ARTIST

KHARY RANDOLPH & **EMILIO LOPEZ** (#8-12) AND
NATHAN STOCKMAN & **JIM CAMPBELL** (SPIDER-MAN: MASTER PLAN)
COVER ART

VC's **TRAVIS LANHAM**
LETTERER

DEVIN LEWIS
ASSOCIATE EDITOR

DARREN SHAN &
MARK BASSO
EDITORS

NICK LOWE
EXECUTIVE EDITOR

SPIDER-MAN CREATED BY **STAN LEE** & **STEVE DITKO**

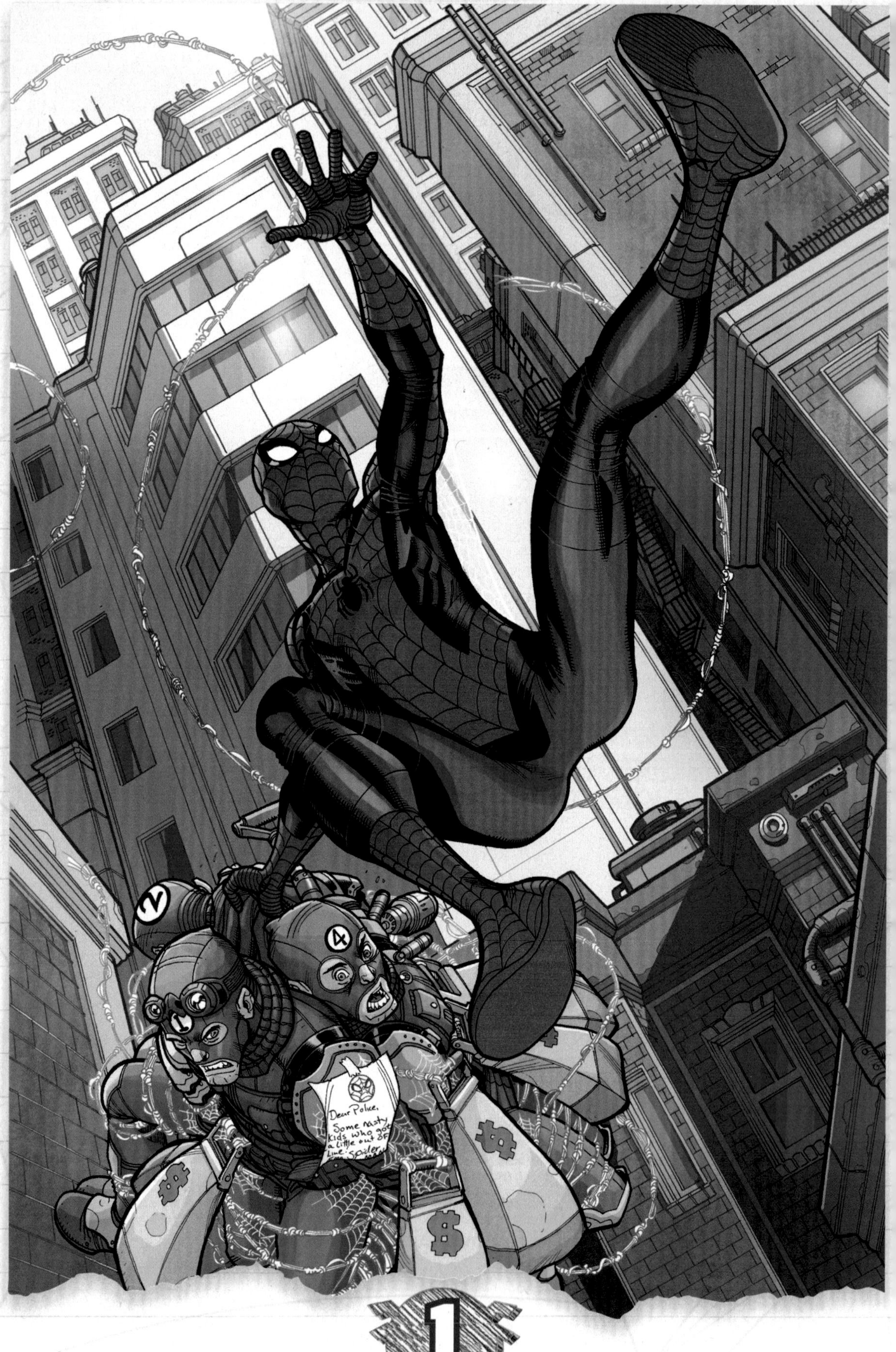
Dear Police,
Some nasty kids who got a little out of line.
Spider

1

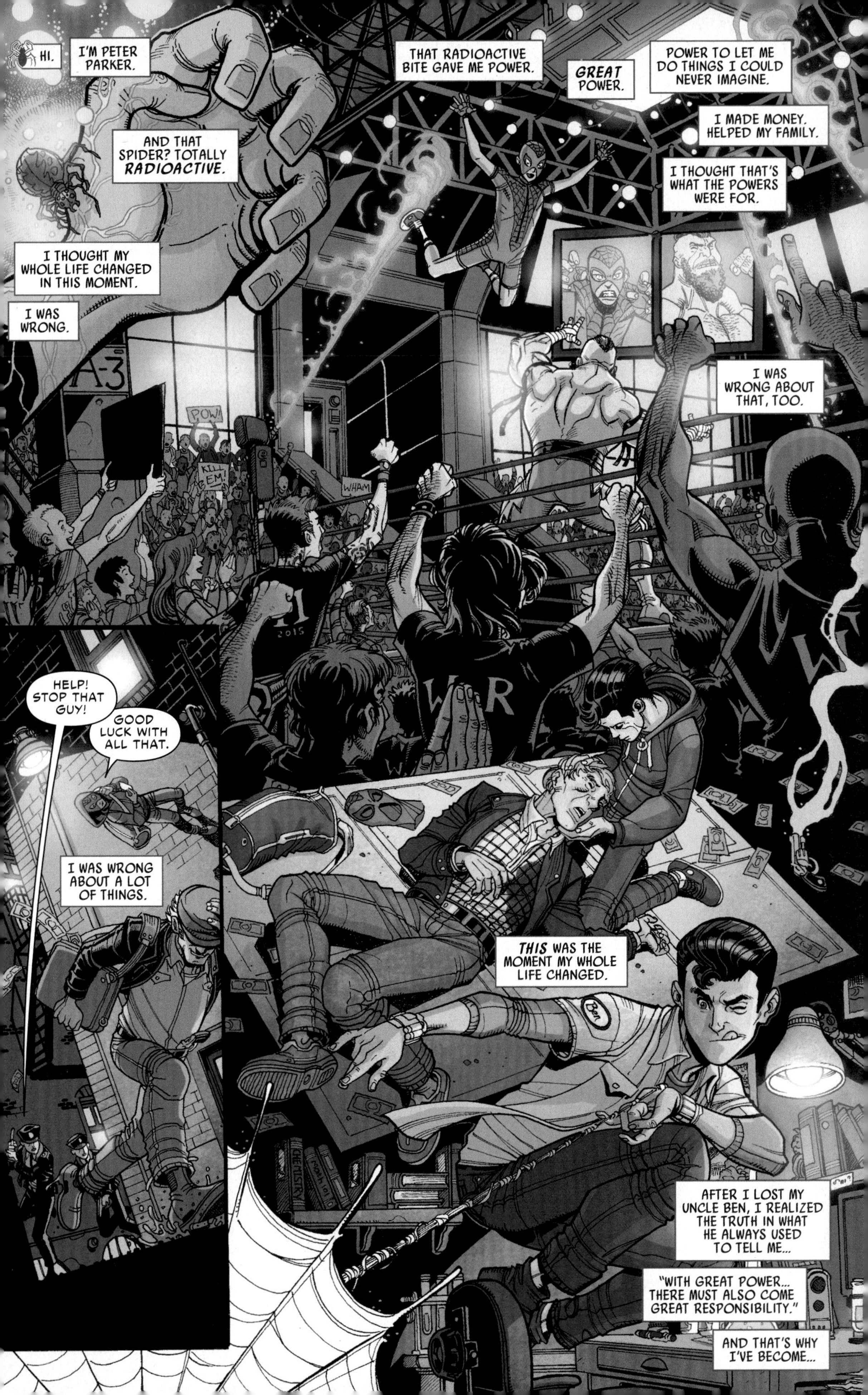
HI.
I'M PETER PARKER.
AND THAT SPIDER? TOTALLY RADIOACTIVE.
I THOUGHT MY WHOLE LIFE CHANGED IN THIS MOMENT.
I WAS WRONG.
THAT RADIOACTIVE BITE GAVE ME POWER.
GREAT POWER.
POWER TO LET ME DO THINGS I COULD NEVER IMAGINE.
I MADE MONEY. HELPED MY FAMILY.
I THOUGHT THAT'S WHAT THE POWERS WERE FOR.
I WAS WRONG ABOUT THAT, TOO.
A-3
POW!
KILL 'EM!
WHAM
HELP! STOP THAT GUY!
GOOD LUCK WITH ALL THAT.
I WAS WRONG ABOUT A LOT OF THINGS.
THIS WAS THE MOMENT MY WHOLE LIFE CHANGED.
Ben
AFTER I LOST MY UNCLE BEN, I REALIZED THE TRUTH IN WHAT HE ALWAYS USED TO TELL ME...
"WITH GREAT POWER... THERE MUST ALSO COME GREAT RESPONSIBILITY."
AND THAT'S WHY I'VE BECOME...

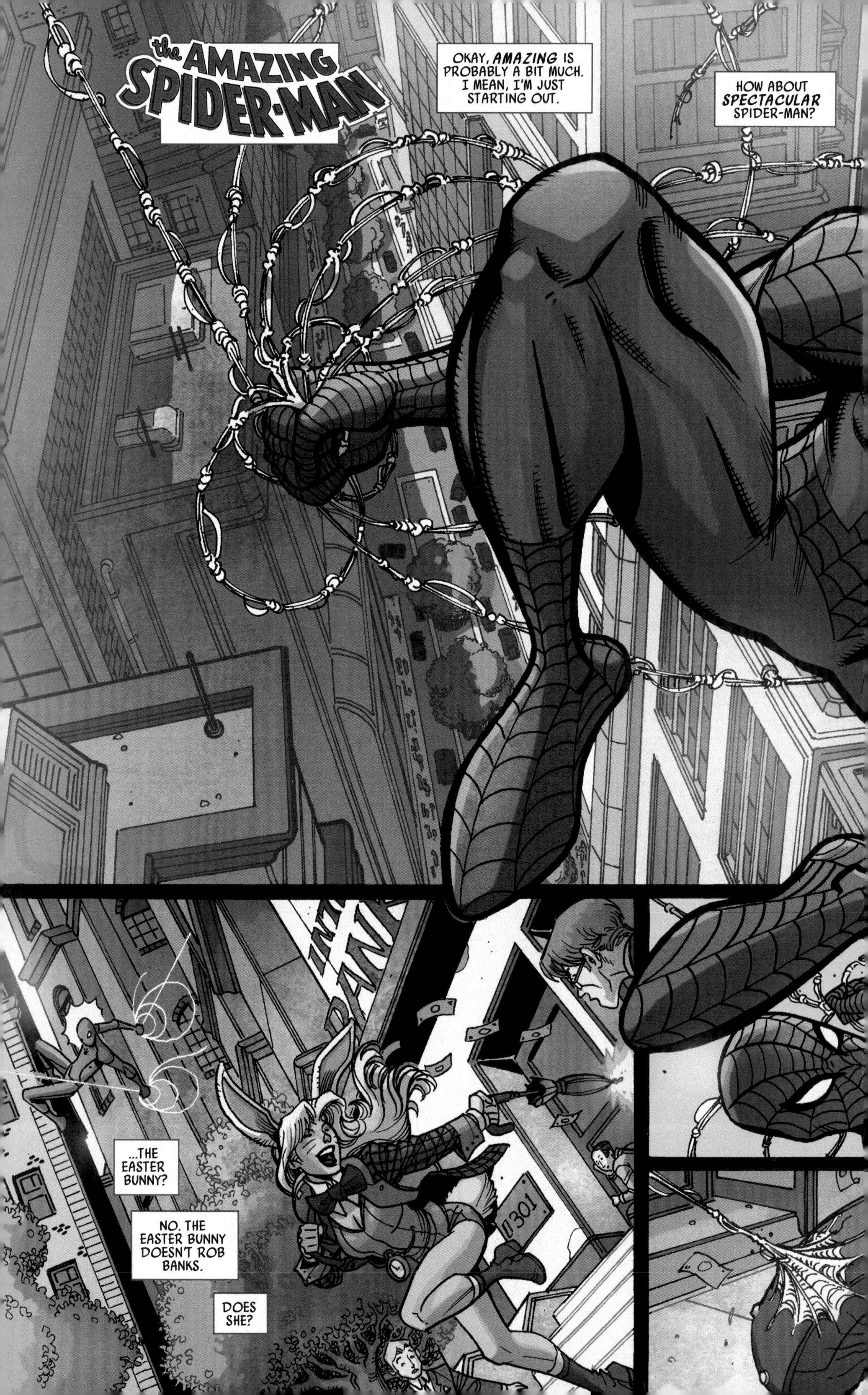
the AMAZING SPIDER-MAN
OKAY, AMAZING IS PROBABLY A BIT MUCH. I MEAN, I'M JUST STARTING OUT.
HOW ABOUT SPECTACULAR SPIDER-MAN?
...THE EASTER BUNNY?
NO, THE EASTER BUNNY DOESN'T ROB BANKS.
DOES SHE?
1301

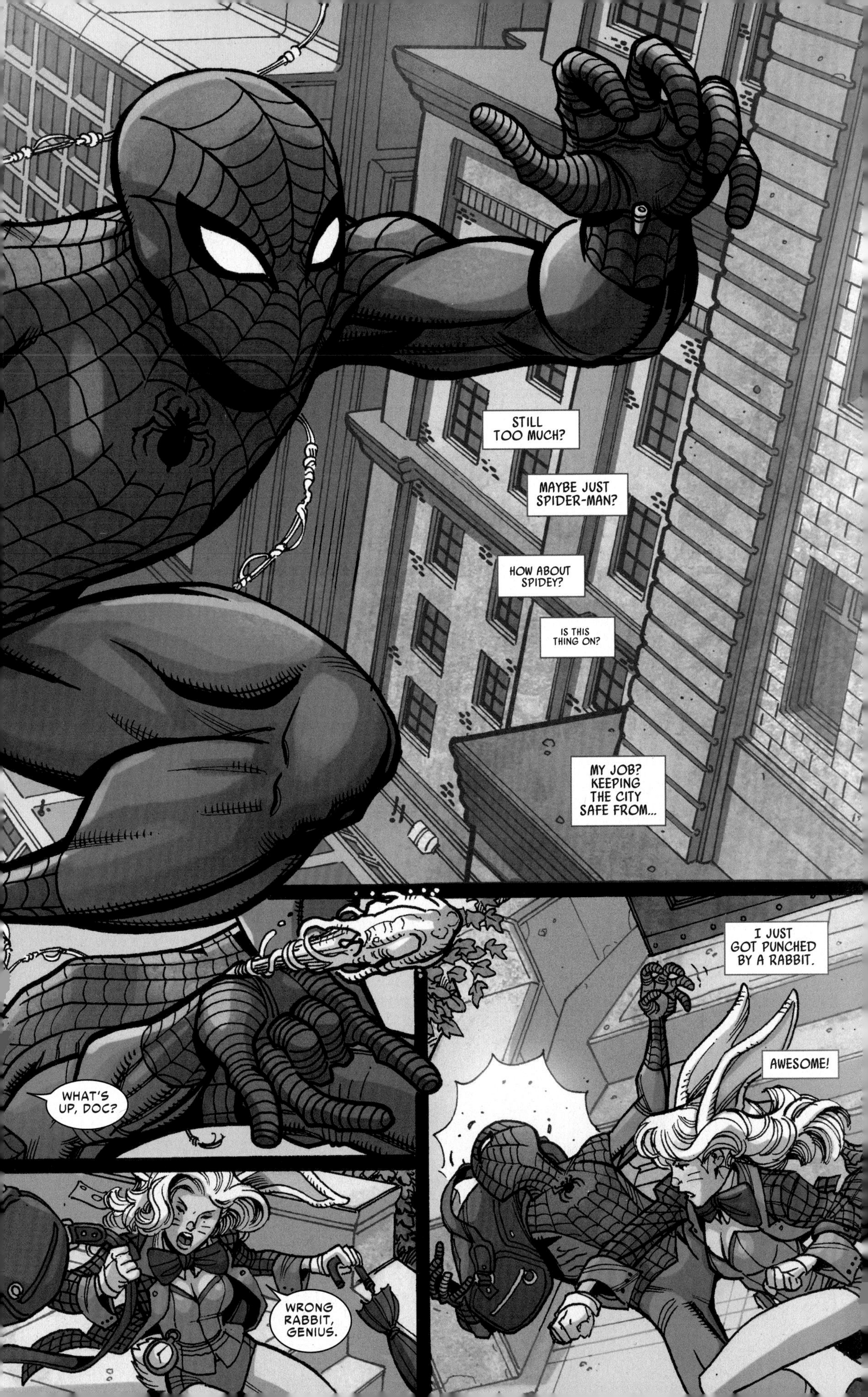
STILL TOO MUCH?
MAYBE JUST SPIDER-MAN?
HOW ABOUT SPIDEY?
IS THIS THING ON?
MY JOB? KEEPING THE CITY SAFE FROM...
WHAT'S UP, DOC?
I JUST GOT PUNCHED BY A RABBIT.
AWESOME!
WRONG RABBIT, GENIUS.

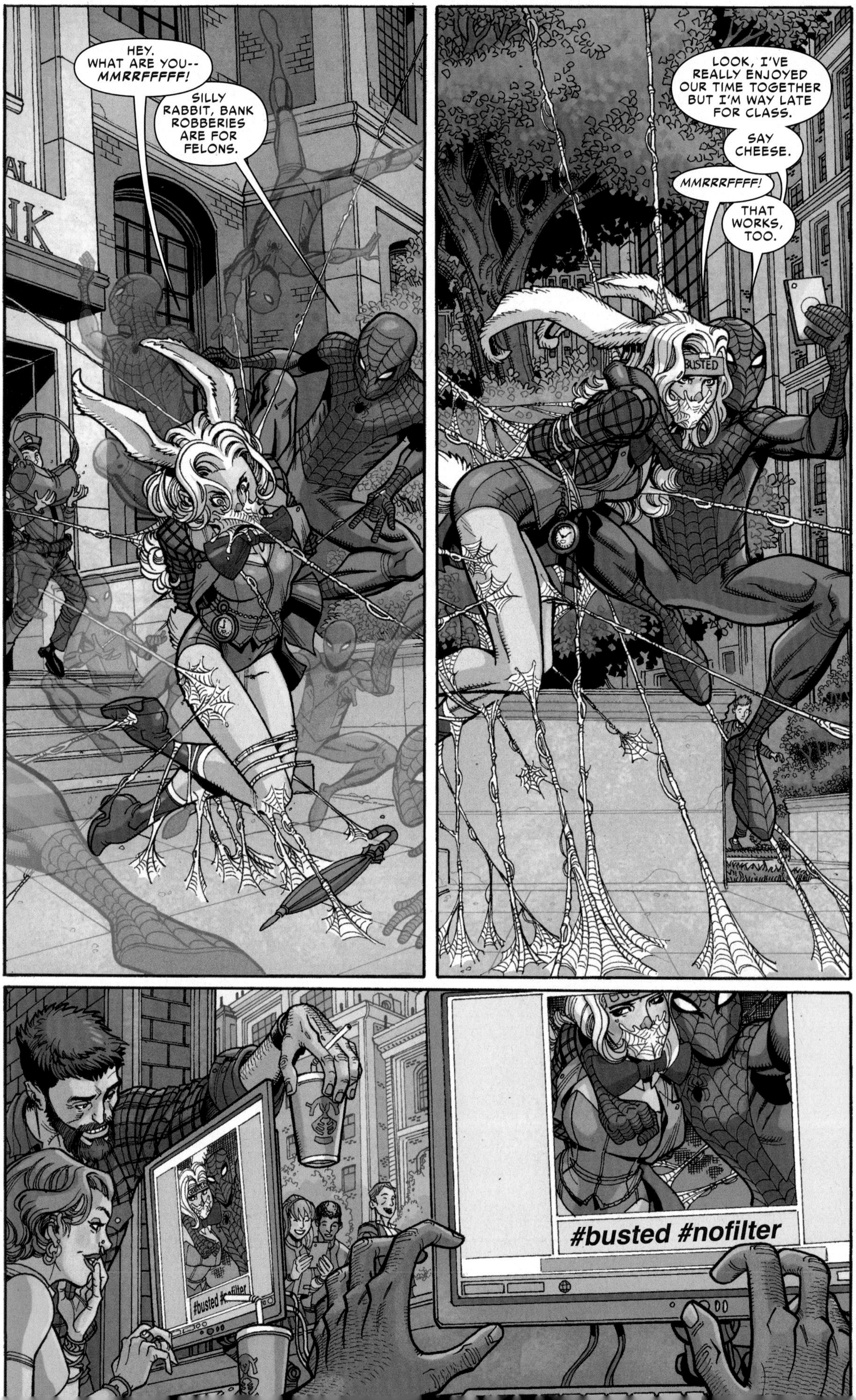
HEY. WHAT ARE YOU-- MMRRFFFFF!
SILLY RABBIT, BANK ROBBERIES ARE FOR FELONS.
LOOK, I'VE REALLY ENJOYED OUR TIME TOGETHER BUT I'M WAY LATE FOR CLASS.
SAY CHEESE.
MMRRRFFFF!
THAT WORKS, TOO.
BUSTED
#busted #nofilter

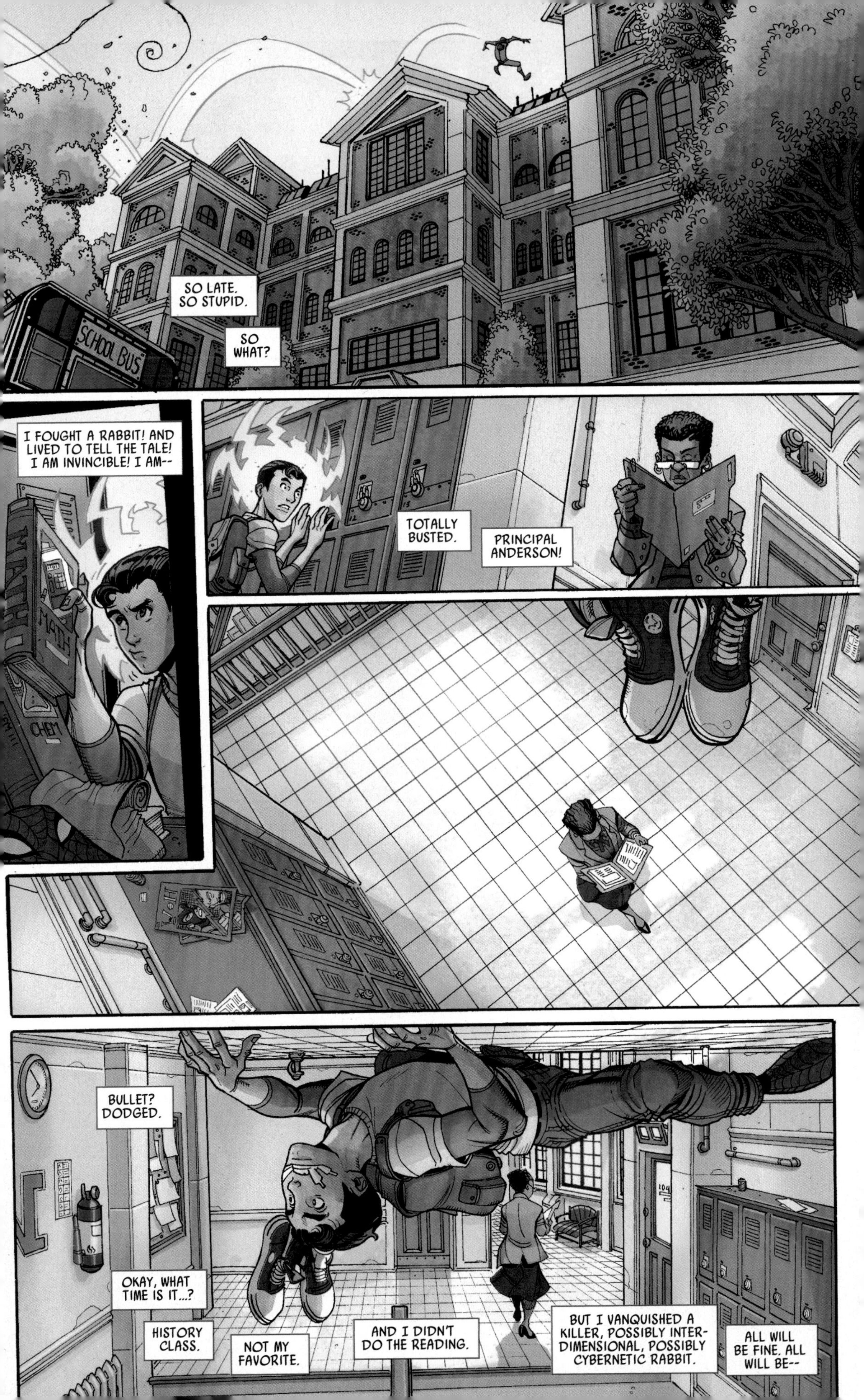
SO LATE. SO STUPID.
SO WHAT?
SCHOOL BUS
I FOUGHT A RABBIT! AND LIVED TO TELL THE TALE! I AM INVINCIBLE! I AM--
MATH
CHEM
TOTALLY BUSTED.
PRINCIPAL ANDERSON!
BULLET? DODGED.
OKAY, WHAT TIME IS IT...?
HISTORY CLASS.
NOT MY FAVORITE.
AND I DIDN'T DO THE READING.
BUT I VANQUISHED A KILLER, POSSIBLY INTER-DIMENSIONAL, POSSIBLY CYBERNETIC RABBIT.
ALL WILL BE FINE. ALL WILL BE--

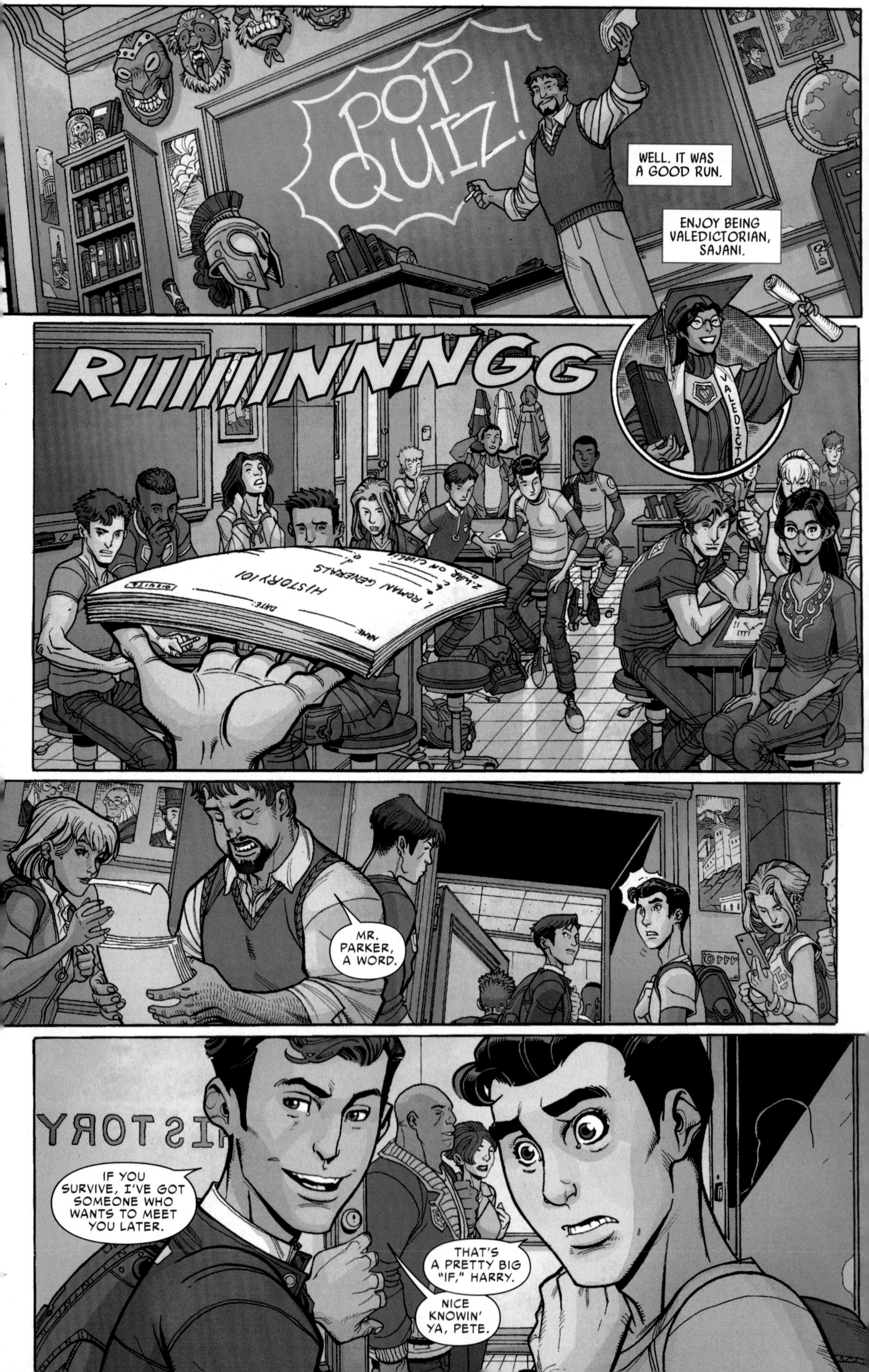
POP QUIZ!
WELL. IT WAS A GOOD RUN.
ENJOY BEING VALEDICTORIAN, SAJANI.
VALEDICTO
RIIIIIINNNNGG
NAME:
DATE:
HISTORY 101
1. ROMAN GENERALS
2. WAR ON CIVILIANS
MR. PARKER, A WORD.
HISTORY
IF YOU SURVIVE, I'VE GOT SOMEONE WHO WANTS TO MEET YOU LATER.
THAT'S A PRETTY BIG "IF," HARRY.
NICE KNOWIN' YA, PETE.

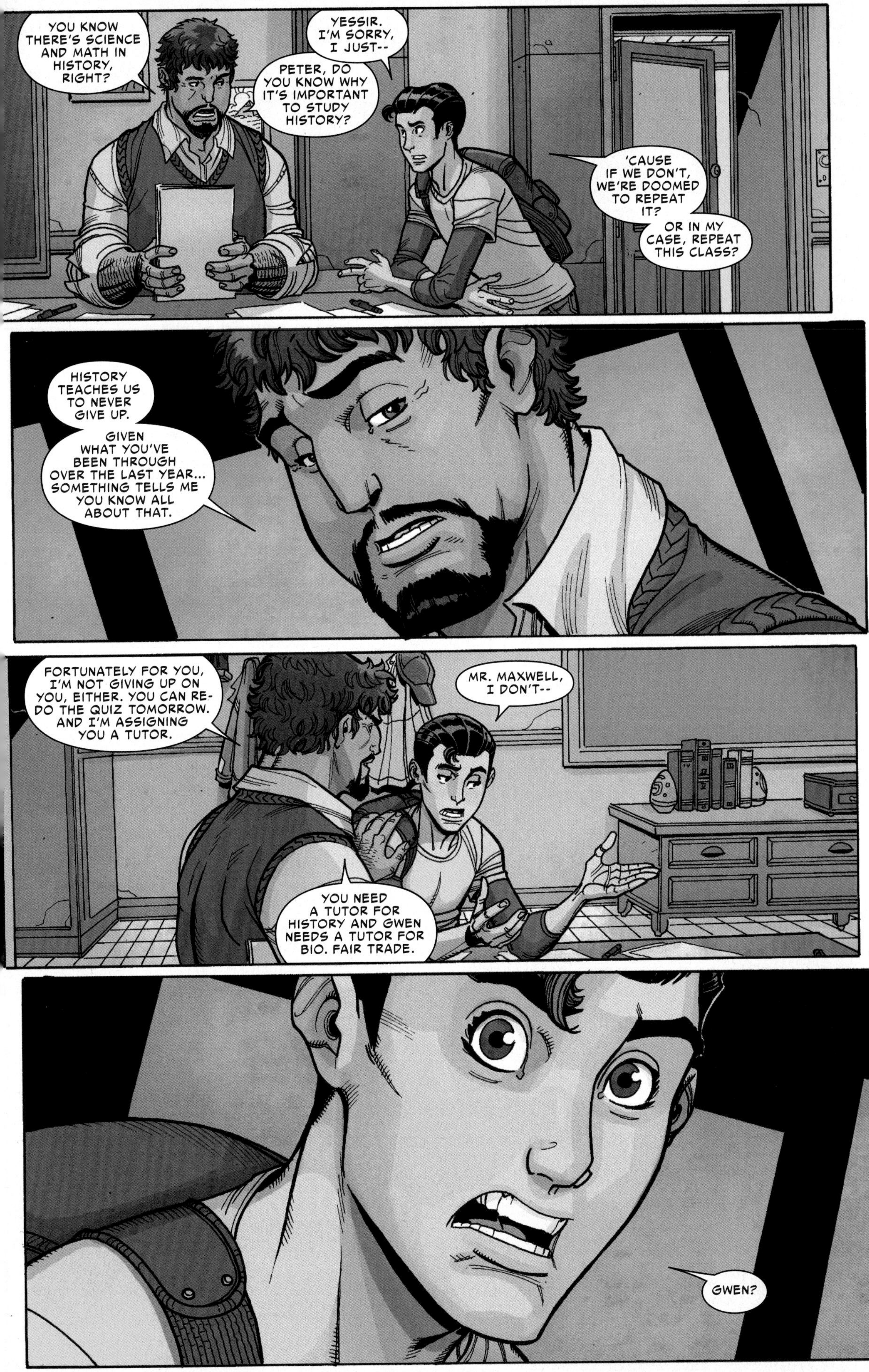
YOU KNOW THERE'S SCIENCE AND MATH IN HISTORY, RIGHT?
YESSIR. I'M SORRY, I JUST--
PETER, DO YOU KNOW WHY IT'S IMPORTANT TO STUDY HISTORY?
'CAUSE IF WE DON'T, WE'RE DOOMED TO REPEAT IT?
OR IN MY CASE, REPEAT THIS CLASS?
HISTORY TEACHES US TO NEVER GIVE UP.
GIVEN WHAT YOU'VE BEEN THROUGH OVER THE LAST YEAR... SOMETHING TELLS ME YOU KNOW ALL ABOUT THAT.
FORTUNATELY FOR YOU, I'M NOT GIVING UP ON YOU, EITHER. YOU CAN RE-DO THE QUIZ TOMORROW. AND I'M ASSIGNING YOU A TUTOR.
MR. MAXWELL, I DON'T--
YOU NEED A TUTOR FOR HISTORY AND GWEN NEEDS A TUTOR FOR BIO. FAIR TRADE.
GWEN?

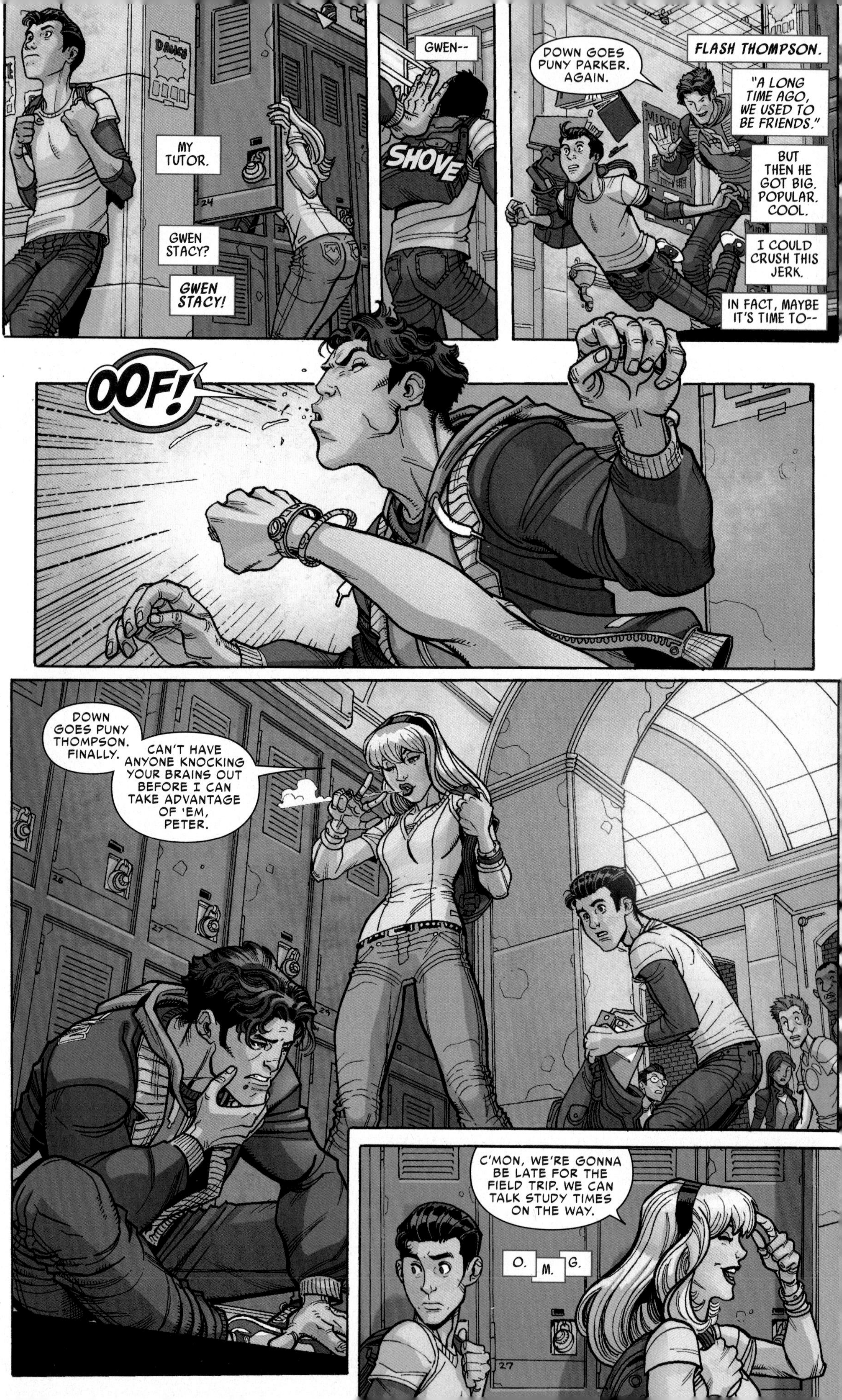
MY TUTOR.
GWEN STACY?
GWEN STACY!
GWEN--
SHOVE
DOWN GOES PUNY PARKER. AGAIN.
FLASH THOMPSON.
"A LONG TIME AGO, WE USED TO BE FRIENDS."
BUT THEN HE GOT BIG. POPULAR. COOL.
I COULD CRUSH THIS JERK.
IN FACT, MAYBE IT'S TIME TO--
OOF!
DOWN GOES PUNY THOMPSON. FINALLY.
CAN'T HAVE ANYONE KNOCKING YOUR BRAINS OUT BEFORE I CAN TAKE ADVANTAGE OF 'EM, PETER.
C'MON, WE'RE GONNA BE LATE FOR THE FIELD TRIP. WE CAN TALK STUDY TIMES ON THE WAY.
O. M. G.

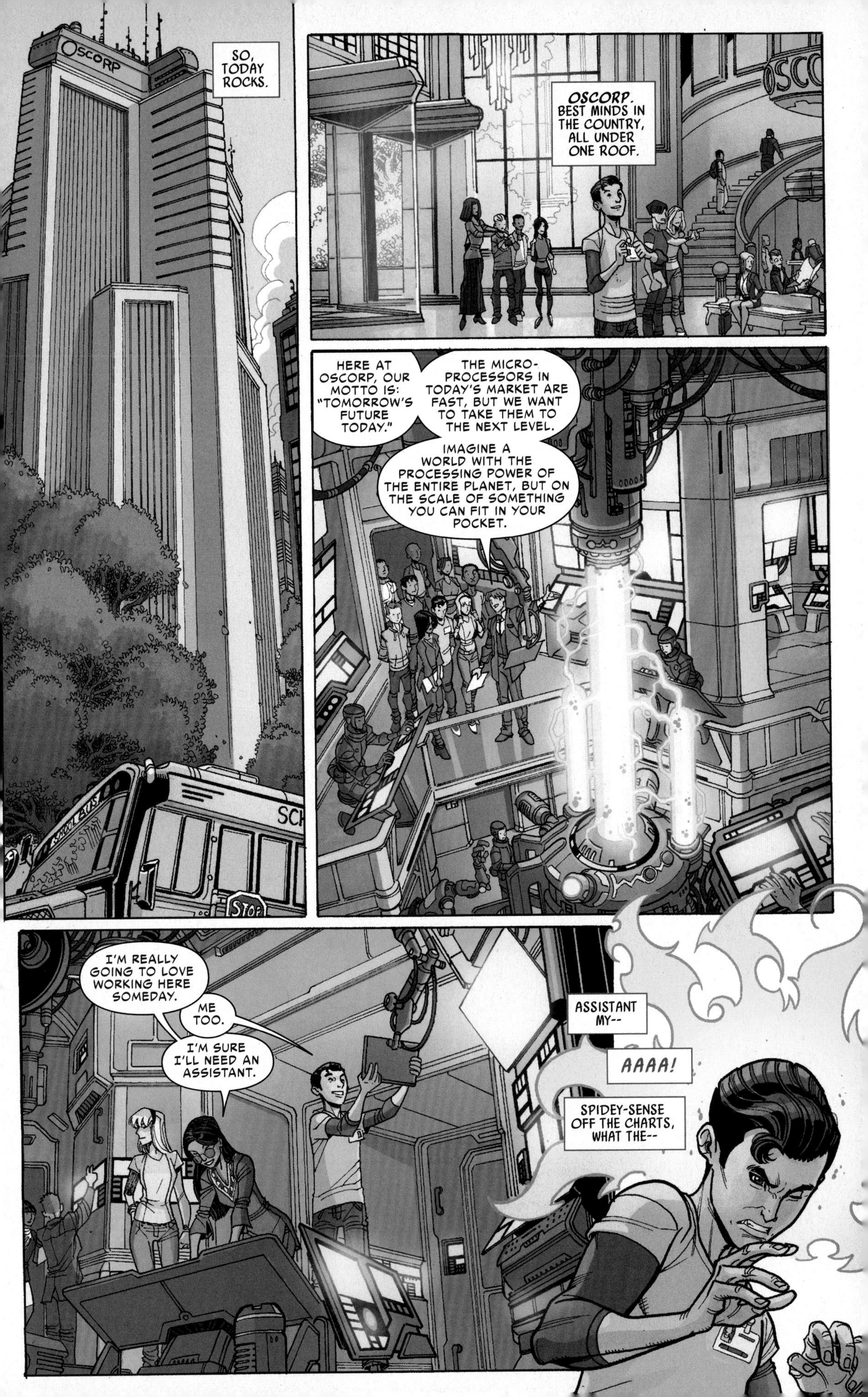
SO, TODAY ROCKS.
OSCORP
OSCORP. BEST MINDS IN THE COUNTRY, ALL UNDER ONE ROOF.
HERE AT OSCORP, OUR MOTTO IS: "TOMORROW'S FUTURE TODAY."
THE MICRO-PROCESSORS IN TODAY'S MARKET ARE FAST, BUT WE WANT TO TAKE THEM TO THE NEXT LEVEL.
IMAGINE A WORLD WITH THE PROCESSING POWER OF THE ENTIRE PLANET, BUT ON THE SCALE OF SOMETHING YOU CAN FIT IN YOUR POCKET.
I'M REALLY GOING TO LOVE WORKING HERE SOMEDAY.
ME TOO.
I'M SURE I'LL NEED AN ASSISTANT.
ASSISTANT MY--
AAAA!
SPIDEY-SENSE OFF THE CHARTS, WHAT THE--

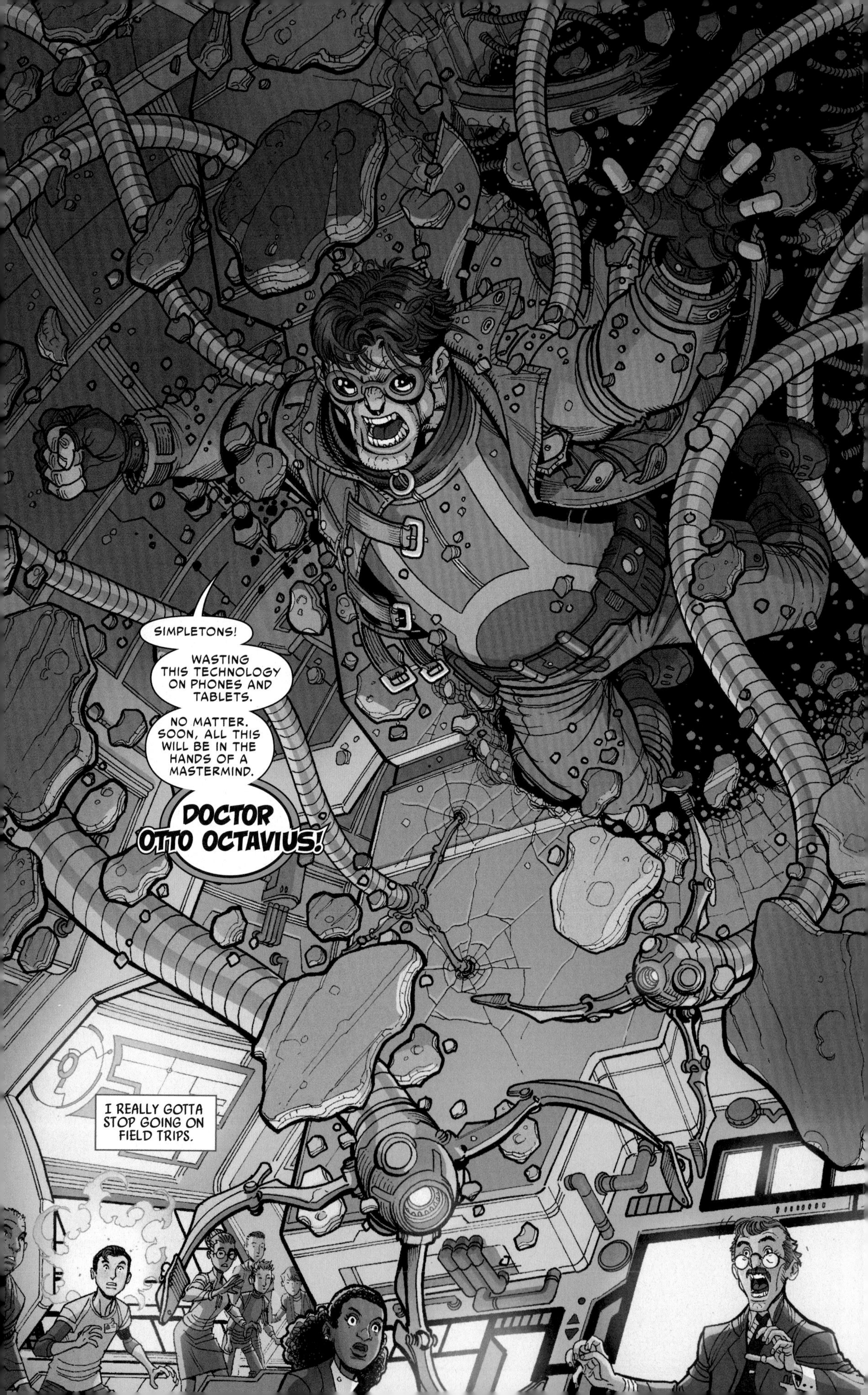
SIMPLETONS!
WASTING THIS TECHNOLOGY ON PHONES AND TABLETS.
NO MATTER. SOON, ALL THIS WILL BE IN THE HANDS OF A MASTERMIND.
DOCTOR OTTO OCTAVIUS!
I REALLY GOTTA STOP GOING ON FIELD TRIPS.

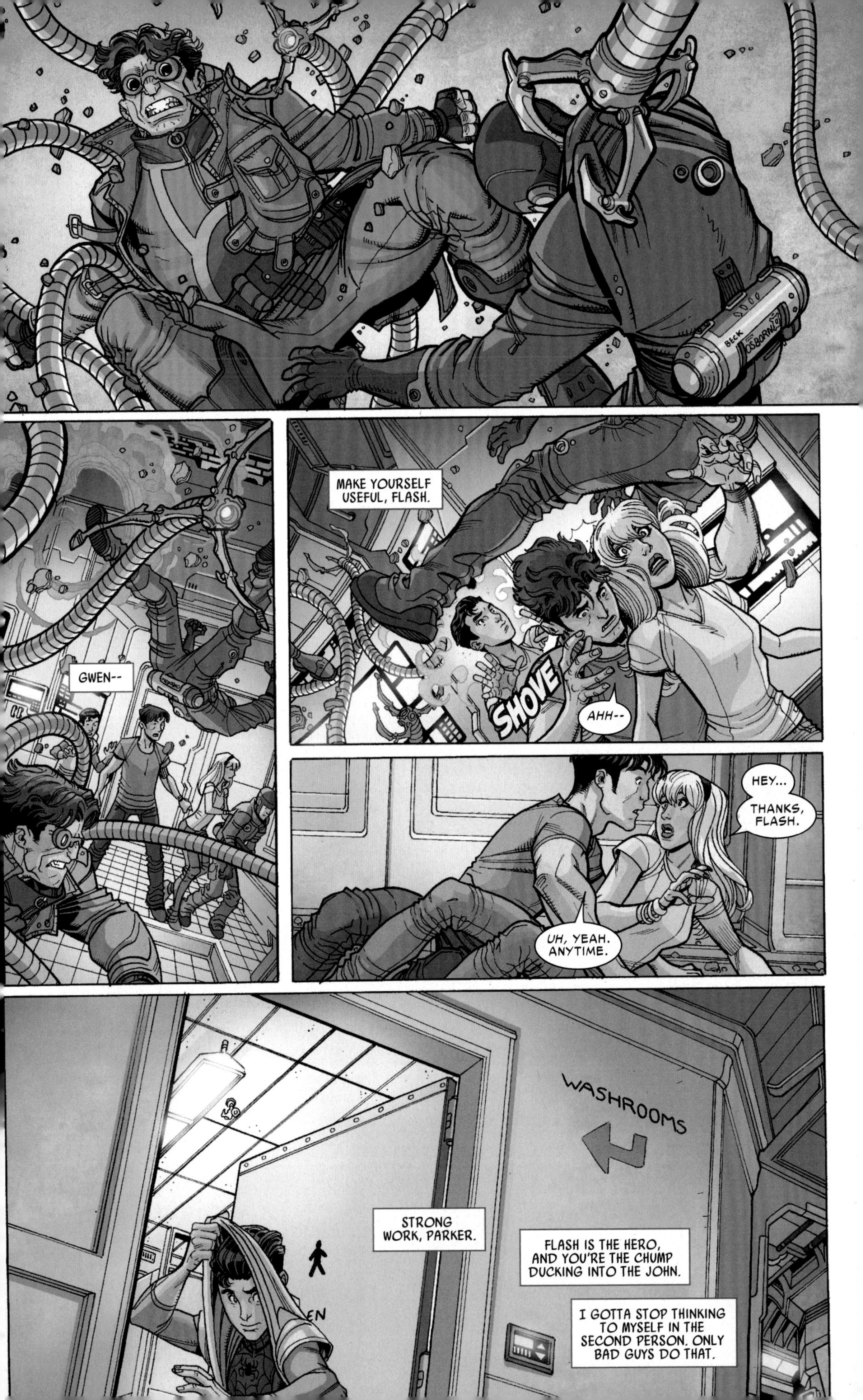
BECK
OSBORN
GWEN--
MAKE YOURSELF USEFUL, FLASH.
SHOVE
AHH--
HEY...
THANKS, FLASH.
UH, YEAH. ANYTIME.
WASHROOMS
STRONG WORK, PARKER.
FLASH IS THE HERO, AND YOU'RE THE CHUMP DUCKING INTO THE JOHN.
I GOTTA STOP THINKING TO MYSELF IN THE SECOND PERSON. ONLY BAD GUYS DO THAT.

I HAVE TO GET BACK OUT THERE. DOC OCK IS NOTHING BUT TROUBLE.

DOORS ARE LOCKED. BUT THE VENTS LEAD BACK INTO THE LAB.

SORRY FOR THE DAMAGE, FUTURE EMPLOYER!

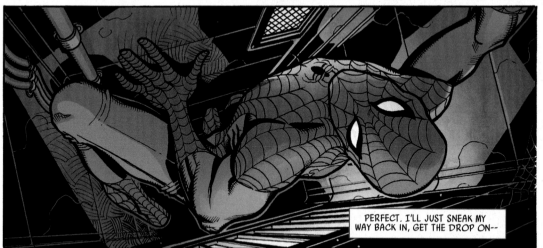

PERFECT. I'LL JUST SNEAK MY WAY BACK IN, GET THE DROP ON--

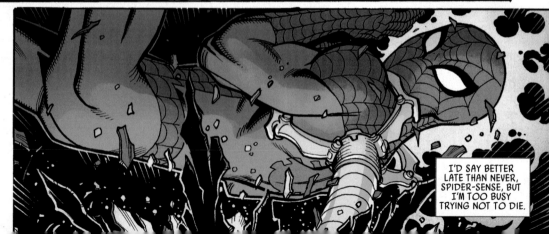

I'D SAY BETTER LATE THAN NEVER, SPIDER-SENSE, BUT I'M TOO BUSY TRYING NOT TO DIE.

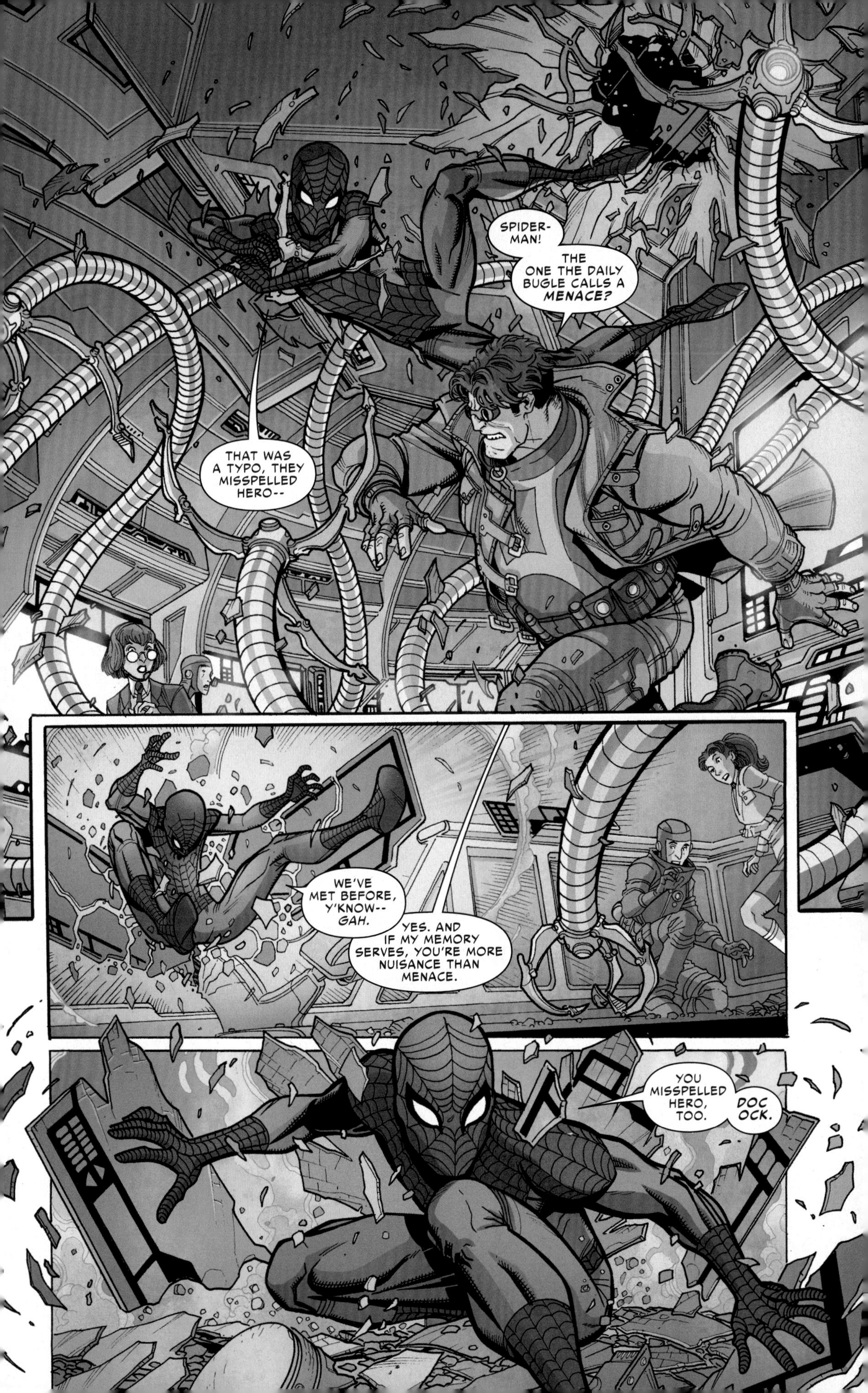

SPIDER-MAN!
THE ONE THE DAILY BUGLE CALLS A MENACE?
THAT WAS A TYPO, THEY MISSPELLED HERO--
WE'VE MET BEFORE, Y'KNOW-- GAH.
YES. AND IF MY MEMORY SERVES, YOU'RE MORE NUISANCE THAN MENACE.
YOU MISSPELLED HERO, TOO.
DOC OCK.

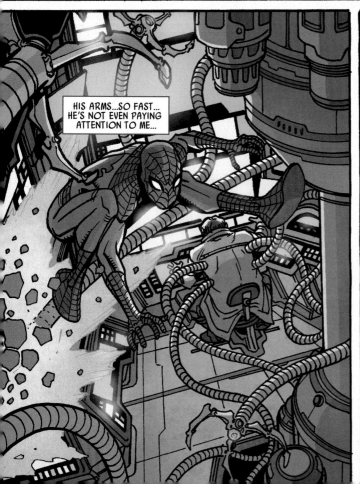

HIS ARMS...SO FAST... HE'S NOT EVEN PAYING ATTENTION TO ME...

WHAM

ANOTHER DULLARD, WHO THINKS A TIRED WIT CAN OUTMATCH MY SUPERIOR INTELLECT.

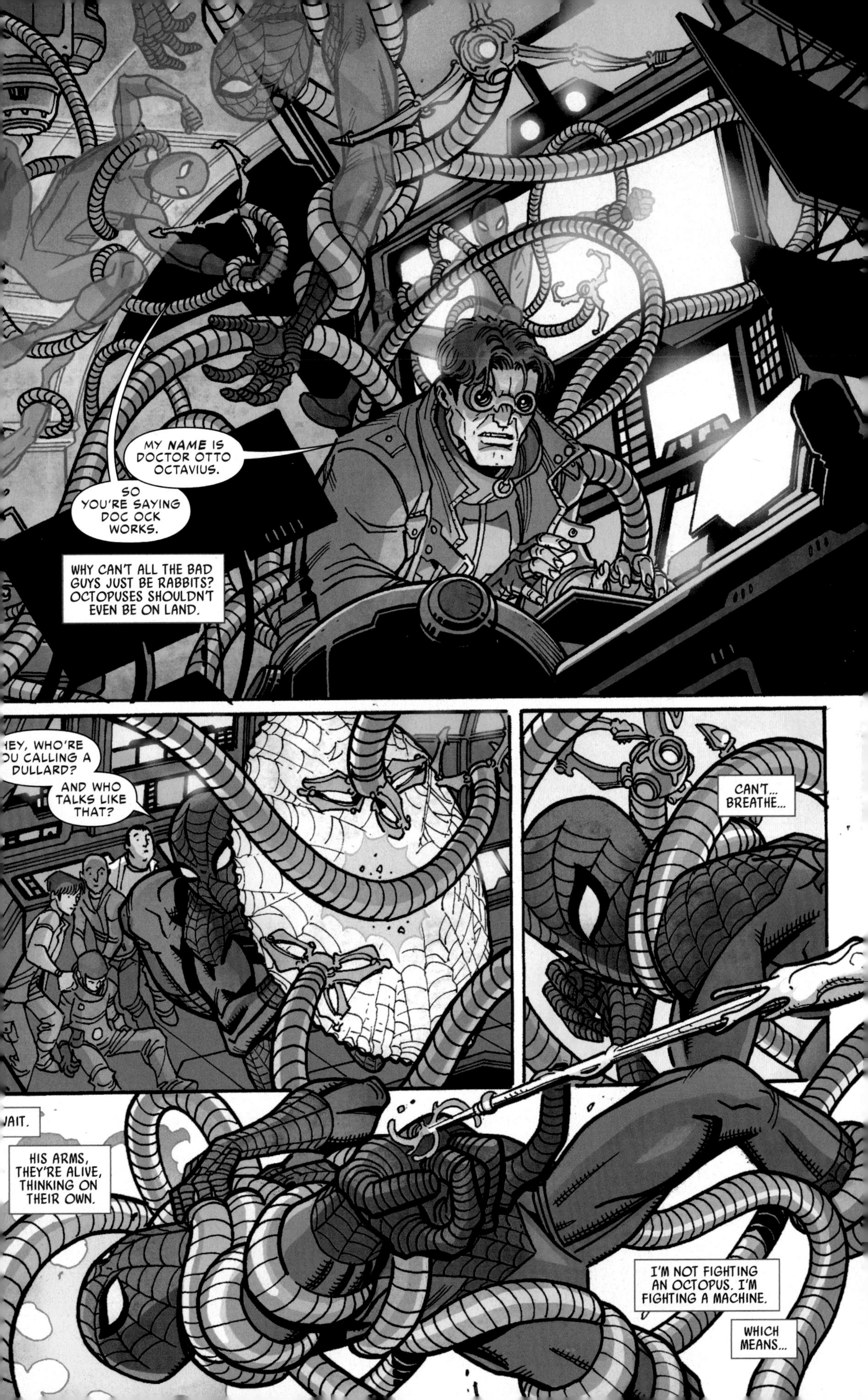
MY NAME IS DOCTOR OTTO OCTAVIUS.
SO YOU'RE SAYING DOC OCK WORKS.
WHY CAN'T ALL THE BAD GUYS JUST BE RABBITS? OCTOPUSES SHOULDN'T EVEN BE ON LAND.
HEY, WHO'RE OU CALLING A DULLARD?
AND WHO TALKS LIKE THAT?
CAN'T... BREATHE...
AIT.
HIS ARMS, THEY'RE ALIVE, THINKING ON THEIR OWN.
I'M NOT FIGHTING AN OCTOPUS. I'M FIGHTING A MACHINE.
WHICH MEANS...

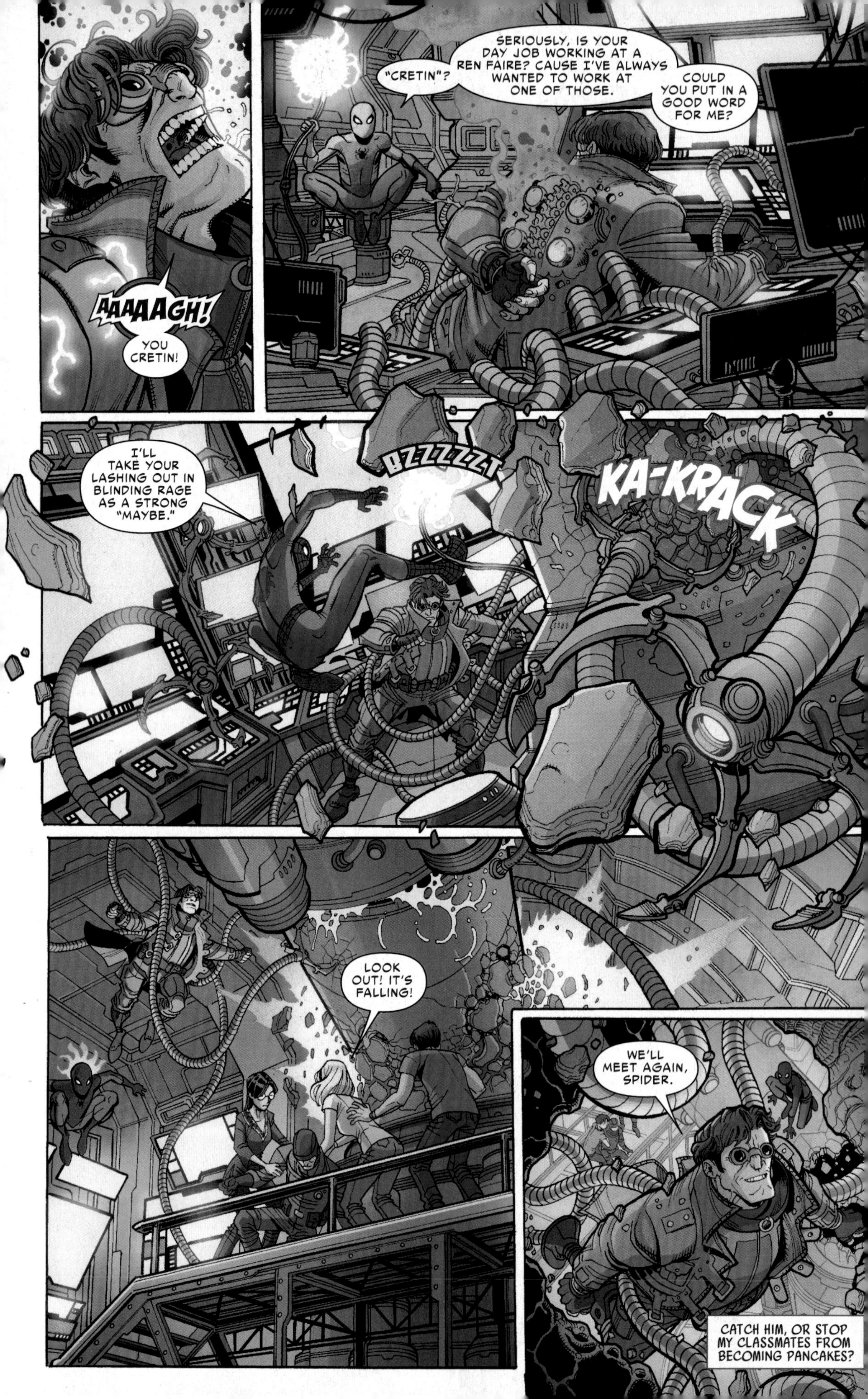
AAAAAGH!
YOU CRETIN!
"CRETIN"?
SERIOUSLY, IS YOUR DAY JOB WORKING AT A REN FAIRE? CAUSE I'VE ALWAYS WANTED TO WORK AT ONE OF THOSE.
COULD YOU PUT IN A GOOD WORD FOR ME?
I'LL TAKE YOUR LASHING OUT IN BLINDING RAGE AS A STRONG "MAYBE."
BZZZZZT
KA-KRACK
LOOK OUT! IT'S FALLING!
WE'LL MEET AGAIN, SPIDER.
CATCH HIM, OR STOP MY CLASSMATES FROM BECOMING PANCAKES?

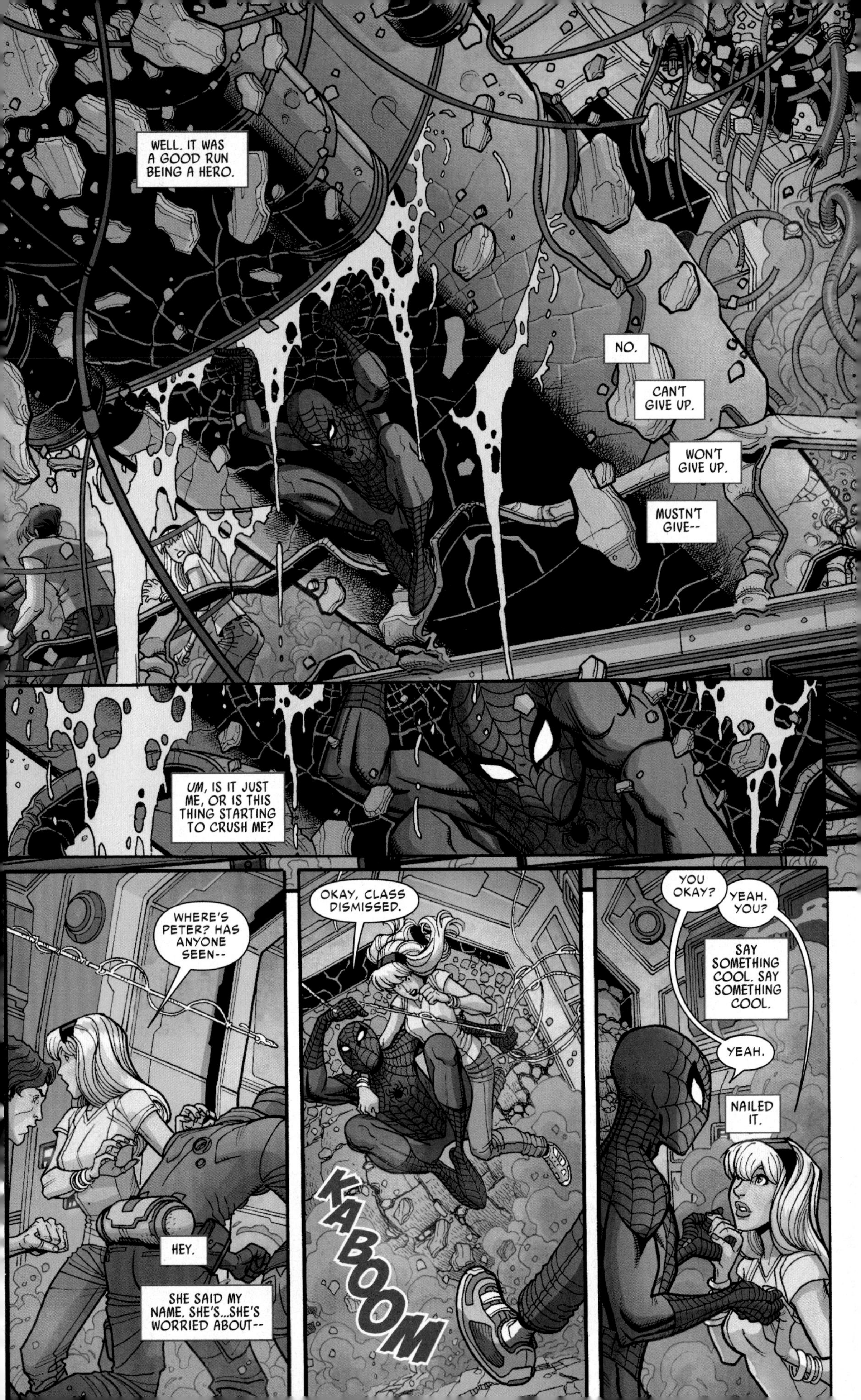
WELL. IT WAS A GOOD RUN BEING A HERO.
NO.
CAN'T GIVE UP.
WON'T GIVE UP.
MUSTN'T GIVE--
UM, IS IT JUST ME, OR IS THIS THING STARTING TO CRUSH ME?
WHERE'S PETER? HAS ANYONE SEEN--
HEY.
SHE SAID MY NAME. SHE'S...SHE'S WORRIED ABOUT--
OKAY, CLASS DISMISSED.
KABOOM
YOU OKAY?
YEAH. YOU?
SAY SOMETHING COOL. SAY SOMETHING COOL.
YEAH.
NAILED IT.

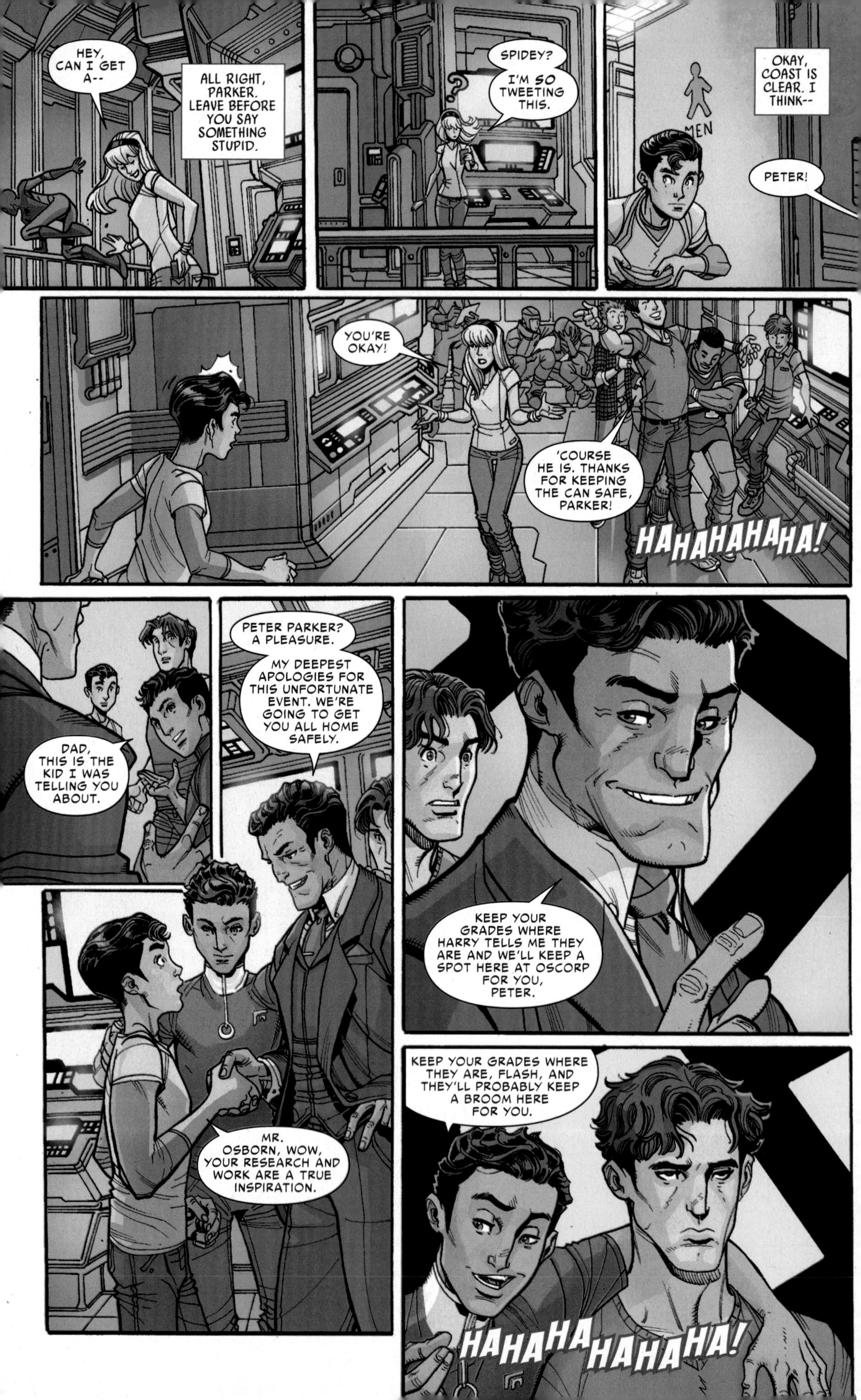
HEY, CAN I GET A--
ALL RIGHT, PARKER. LEAVE BEFORE YOU SAY SOMETHING STUPID.
SPIDEY?
I'M SO TWEETING THIS.
MEN
OKAY, COAST IS CLEAR. I THINK--
PETER!
YOU'RE OKAY!
'COURSE HE IS. THANKS FOR KEEPING THE CAN SAFE, PARKER!
HAHAHAHAHAHA!
DAD, THIS IS THE KID I WAS TELLING YOU ABOUT.
PETER PARKER? A PLEASURE.
MY DEEPEST APOLOGIES FOR THIS UNFORTUNATE EVENT. WE'RE GOING TO GET YOU ALL HOME SAFELY.
KEEP YOUR GRADES WHERE HARRY TELLS ME THEY ARE AND WE'LL KEEP A SPOT HERE AT OSCORP FOR YOU, PETER.
MR. OSBORN, WOW, YOUR RESEARCH AND WORK ARE A TRUE INSPIRATION.
KEEP YOUR GRADES WHERE THEY ARE, FLASH, AND THEY'LL PROBABLY KEEP A BROOM HERE FOR YOU.
HAHAHA HAHAHA!

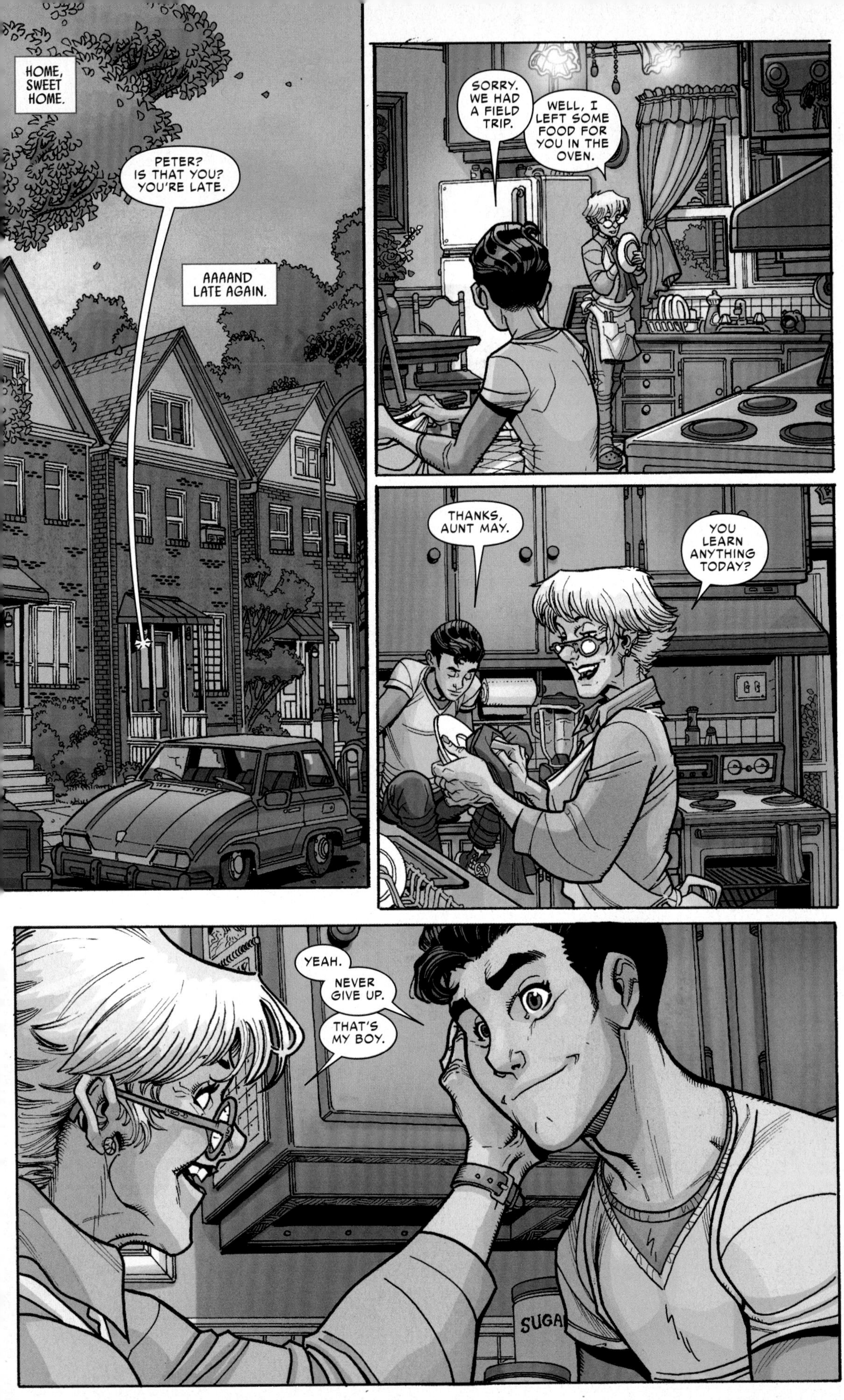
HOME, SWEET HOME.
PETER? IS THAT YOU? YOU'RE LATE.
AAAAND LATE AGAIN.
SORRY. WE HAD A FIELD TRIP.
WELL, I LEFT SOME FOOD FOR YOU IN THE OVEN.
THANKS, AUNT MAY.
YOU LEARN ANYTHING TODAY?
YEAH.
NEVER GIVE UP.
THAT'S MY BOY.
SUGA

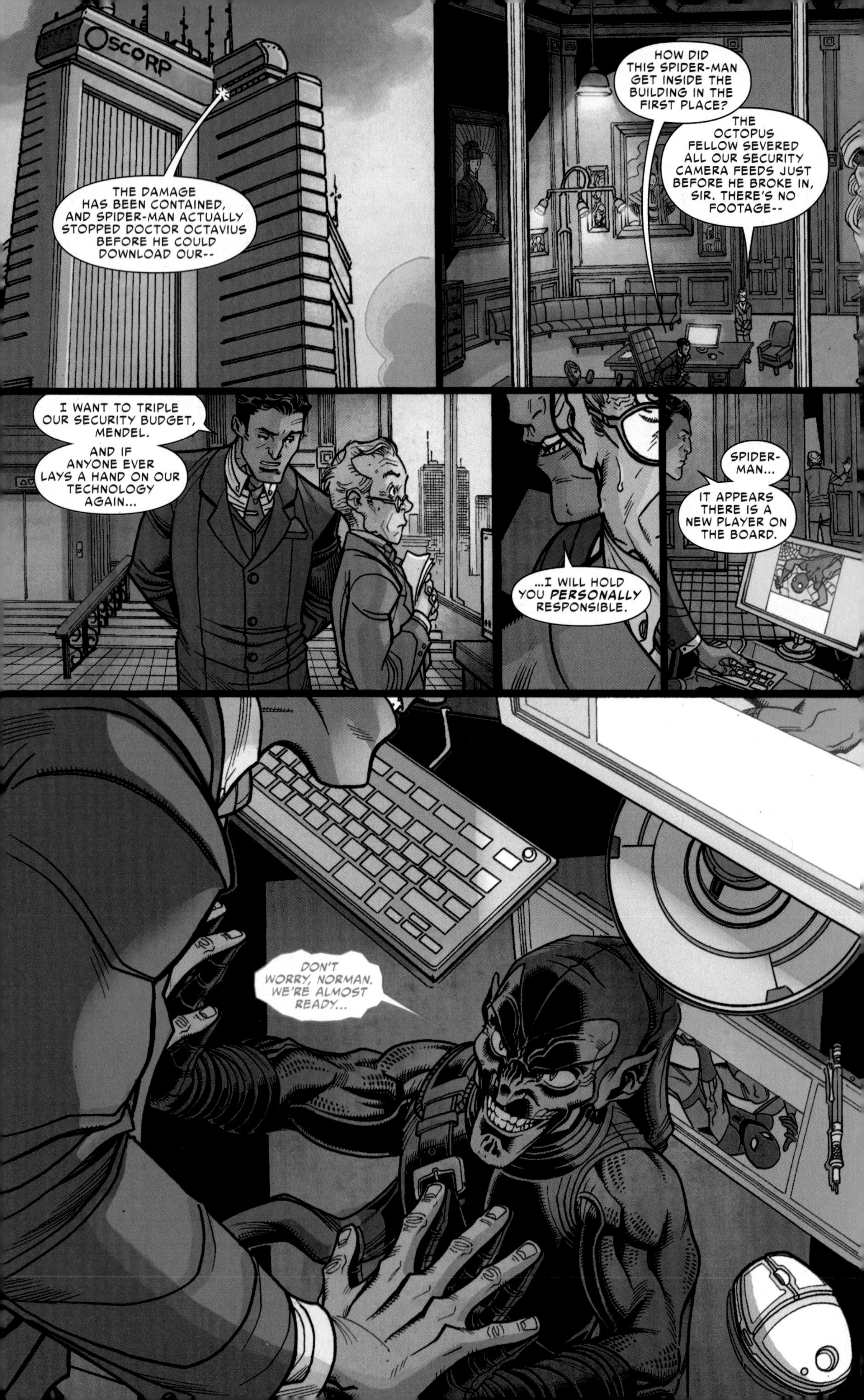
OSCORP
THE DAMAGE HAS BEEN CONTAINED, AND SPIDER-MAN ACTUALLY STOPPED DOCTOR OCTAVIUS BEFORE HE COULD DOWNLOAD OUR--
HOW DID THIS SPIDER-MAN GET INSIDE THE BUILDING IN THE FIRST PLACE?
THE OCTOPUS FELLOW SEVERED ALL OUR SECURITY CAMERA FEEDS JUST BEFORE HE BROKE IN, SIR. THERE'S NO FOOTAGE--
I WANT TO TRIPLE OUR SECURITY BUDGET, MENDEL.
AND IF ANYONE EVER LAYS A HAND ON OUR TECHNOLOGY AGAIN...
...I WILL HOLD YOU PERSONALLY RESPONSIBLE.
SPIDER-MAN...
IT APPEARS THERE IS A NEW PLAYER ON THE BOARD.
DON'T WORRY, NORMAN. WE'RE ALMOST READY...

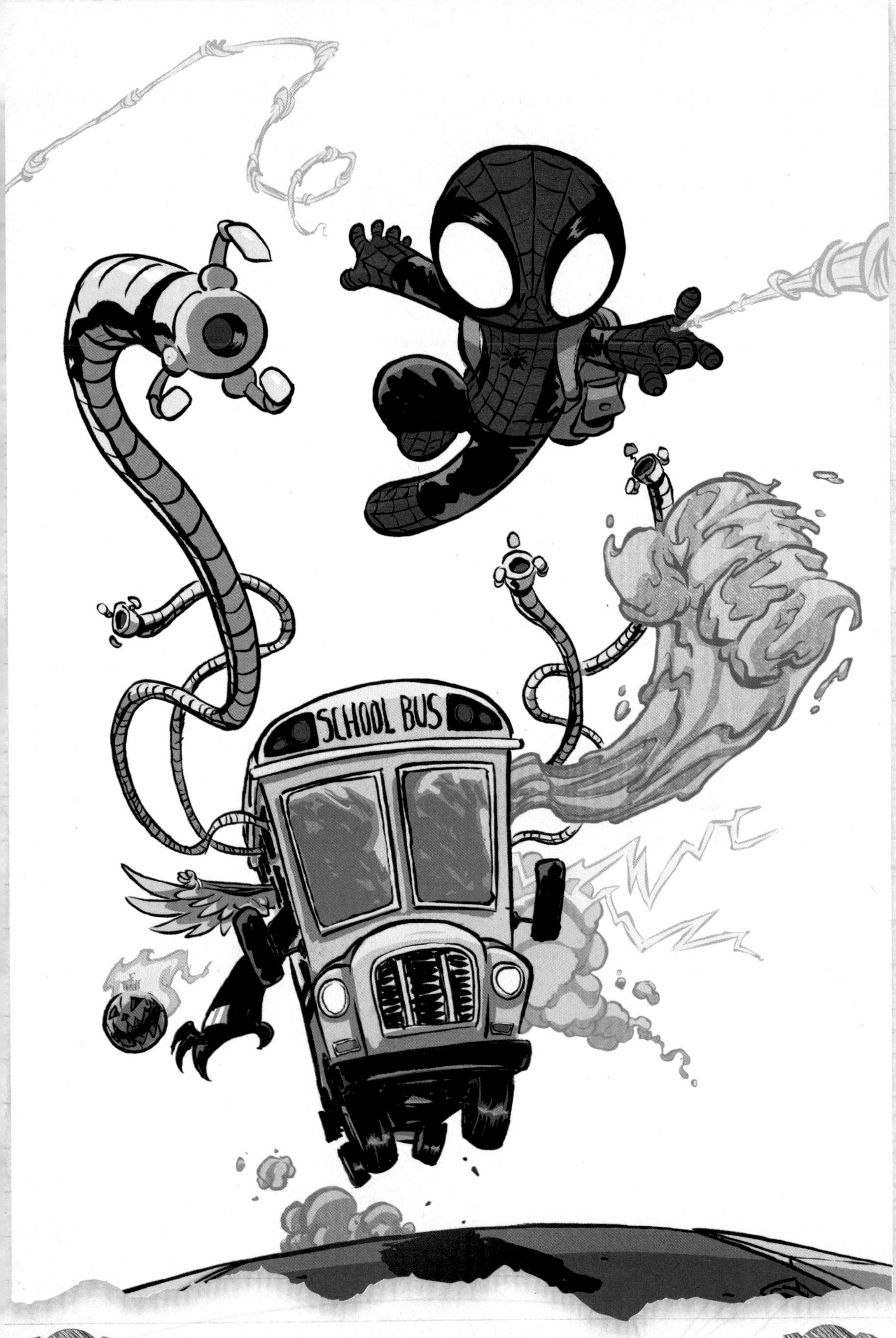
SCHOOL BUS

SKOTTIE YOUNG
1 VARIANT

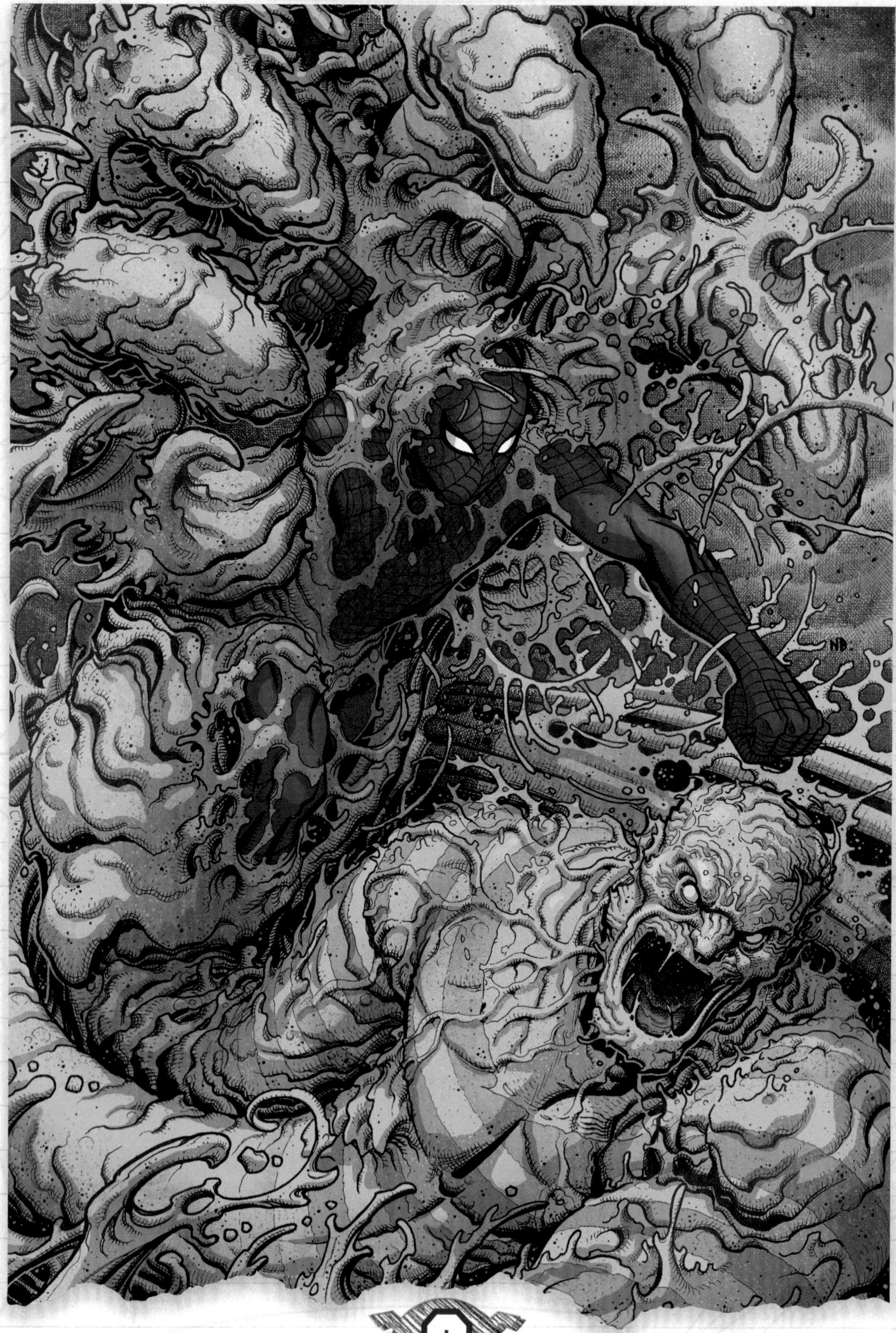

2

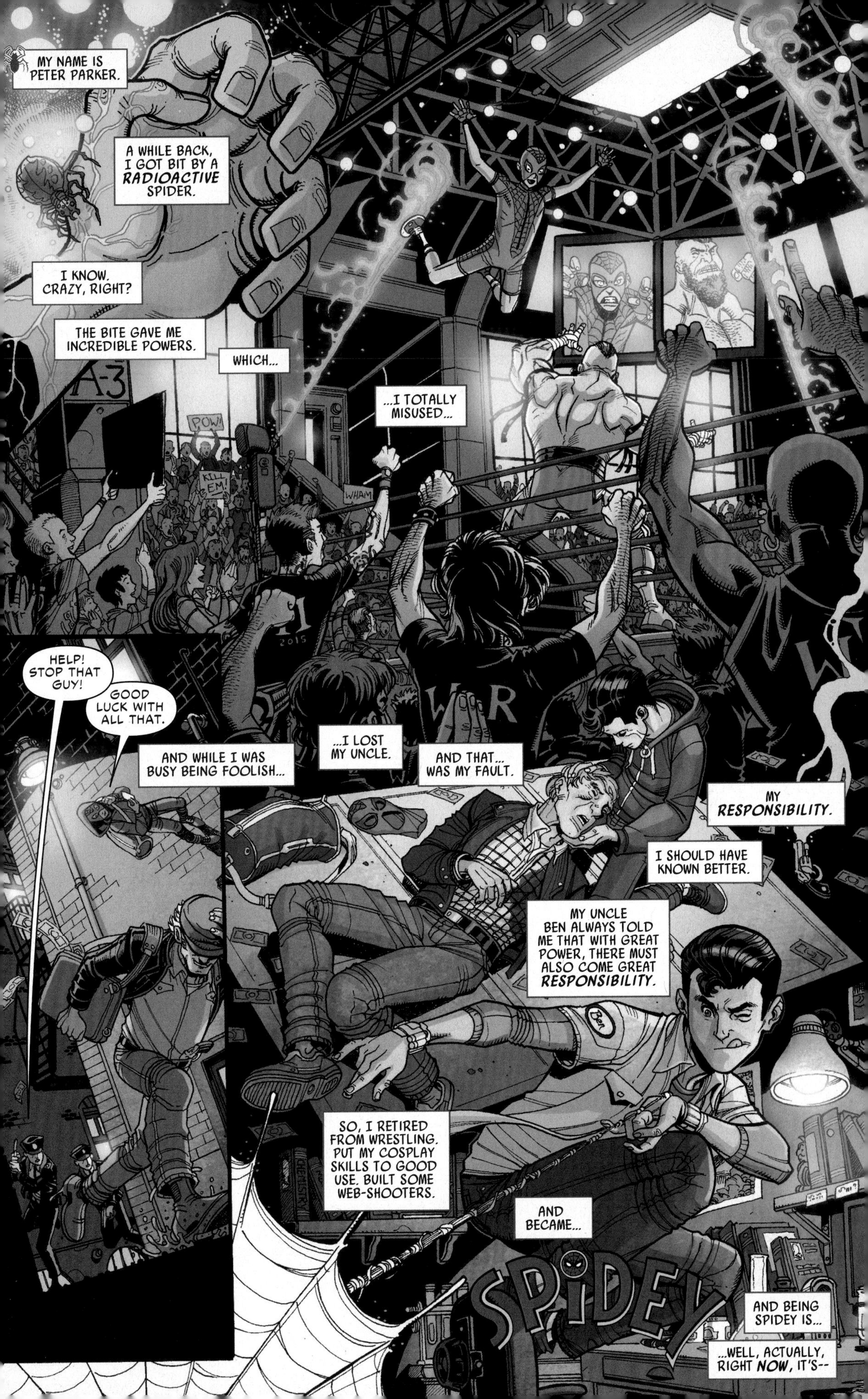
MY NAME IS PETER PARKER.
A WHILE BACK, I GOT BIT BY A RADIOACTIVE SPIDER.
I KNOW. CRAZY, RIGHT?
THE BITE GAVE ME INCREDIBLE POWERS.
WHICH...
...I TOTALLY MISUSED...
A-3
POW!
KILL 'EM!
WHAM
HELP! STOP THAT GUY!
GOOD LUCK WITH ALL THAT.
AND WHILE I WAS BUSY BEING FOOLISH...
...I LOST MY UNCLE.
AND THAT... WAS MY FAULT.
MY RESPONSIBILITY.
I SHOULD HAVE KNOWN BETTER.
MY UNCLE BEN ALWAYS TOLD ME THAT WITH GREAT POWER, THERE MUST ALSO COME GREAT RESPONSIBILITY.
BEN
SO, I RETIRED FROM WRESTLING. PUT MY COSPLAY SKILLS TO GOOD USE. BUILT SOME WEB-SHOOTERS.
AND BECAME...
SPIDEY
AND BEING SPIDEY IS...
...WELL, ACTUALLY, RIGHT NOW, IT'S--

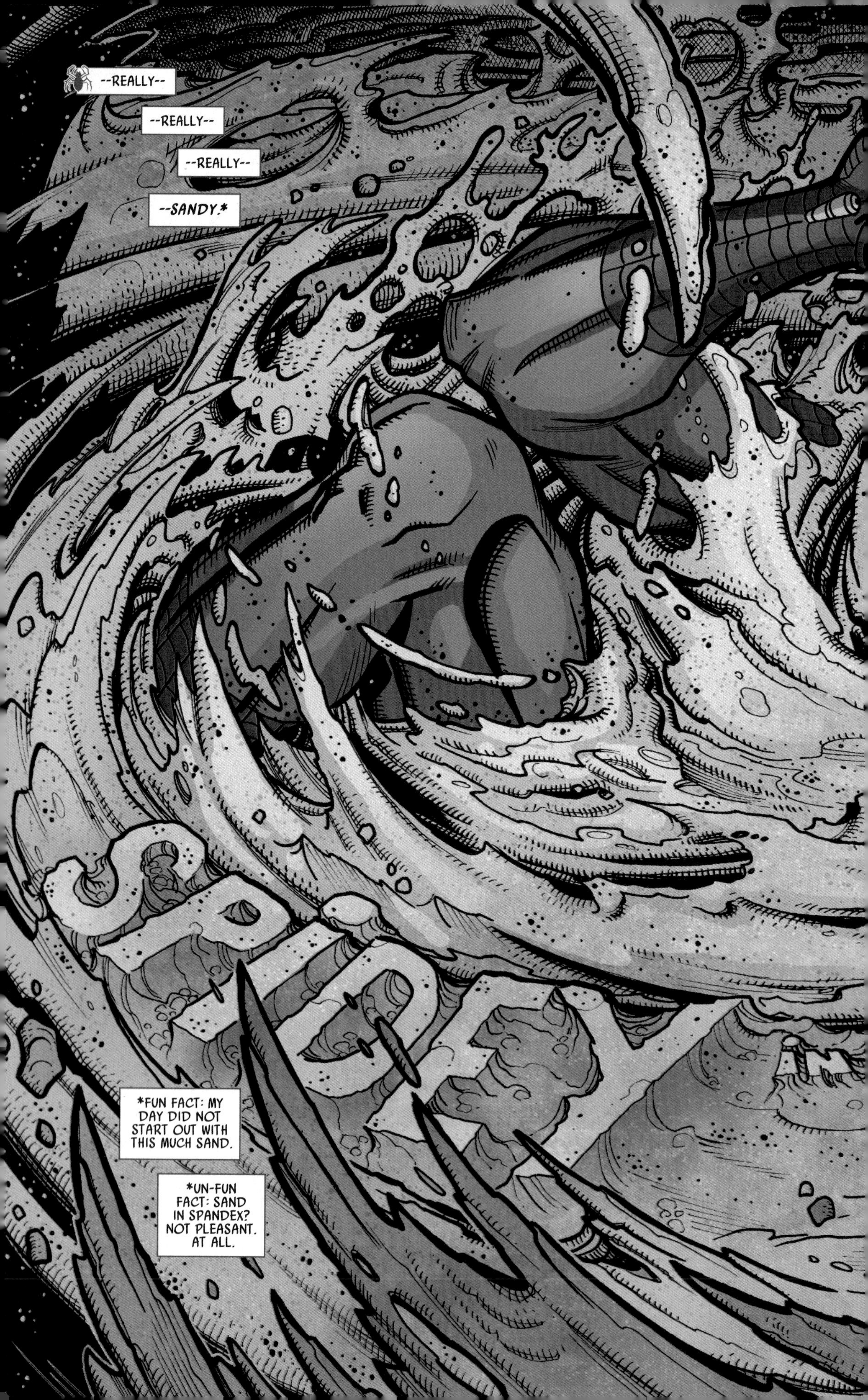
--REALLY--
--REALLY--
--REALLY--
--SANDY.*
*FUN FACT: MY DAY DID NOT START OUT WITH THIS MUCH SAND.
*UN-FUN FACT: SAND IN SPANDEX? NOT PLEASANT. AT ALL.

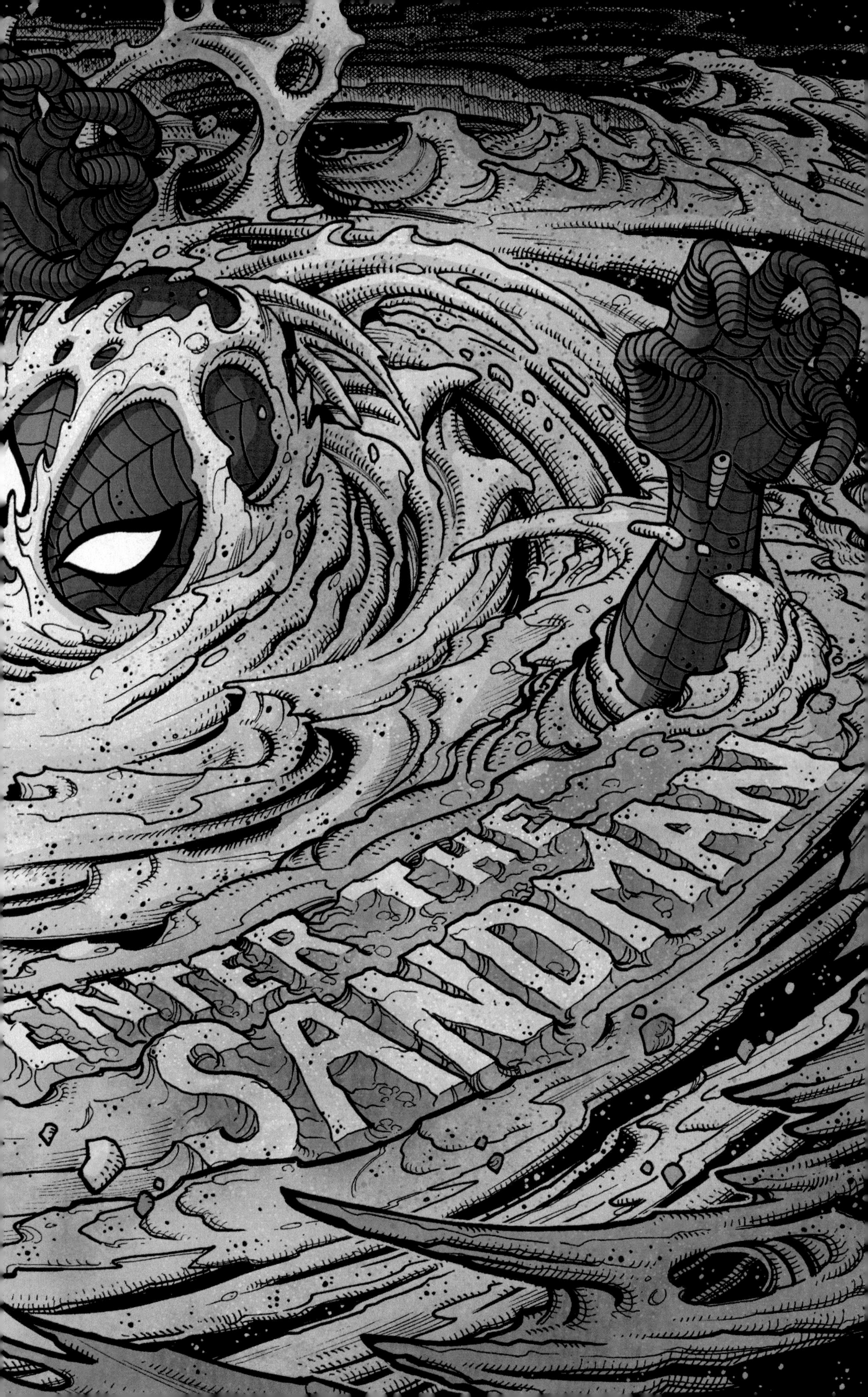

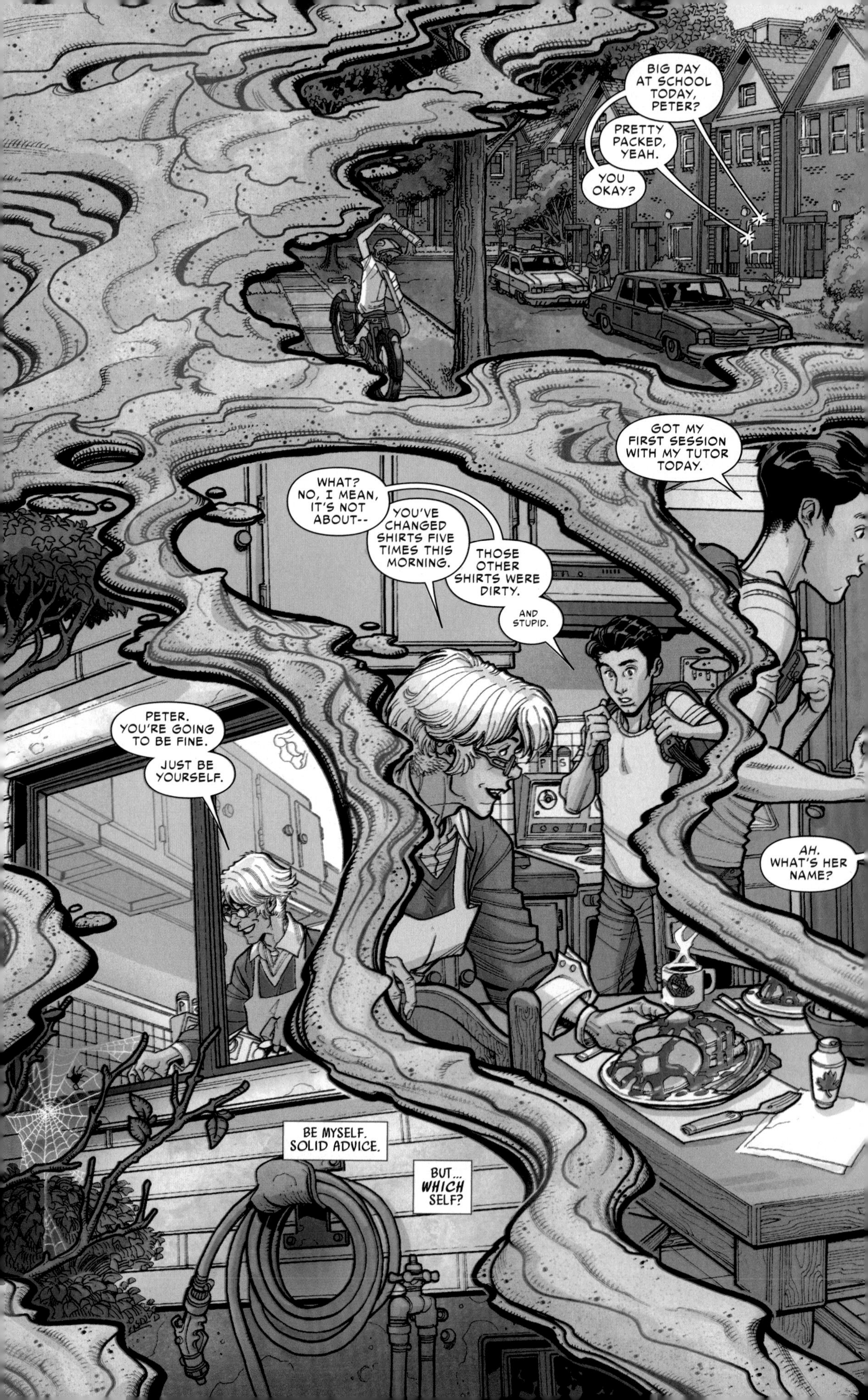
BIG DAY AT SCHOOL TODAY, PETER?
PRETTY PACKED, YEAH.
YOU OKAY?
GOT MY FIRST SESSION WITH MY TUTOR TODAY.
AH. WHAT'S HER NAME?
WHAT? NO, I MEAN, IT'S NOT ABOUT--
YOU'VE CHANGED SHIRTS FIVE TIMES THIS MORNING.
THOSE OTHER SHIRTS WERE DIRTY.
AND STUPID.
PETER. YOU'RE GOING TO BE FINE.
JUST BE YOURSELF.
BE MYSELF. SOLID ADVICE.
BUT... WHICH SELF?

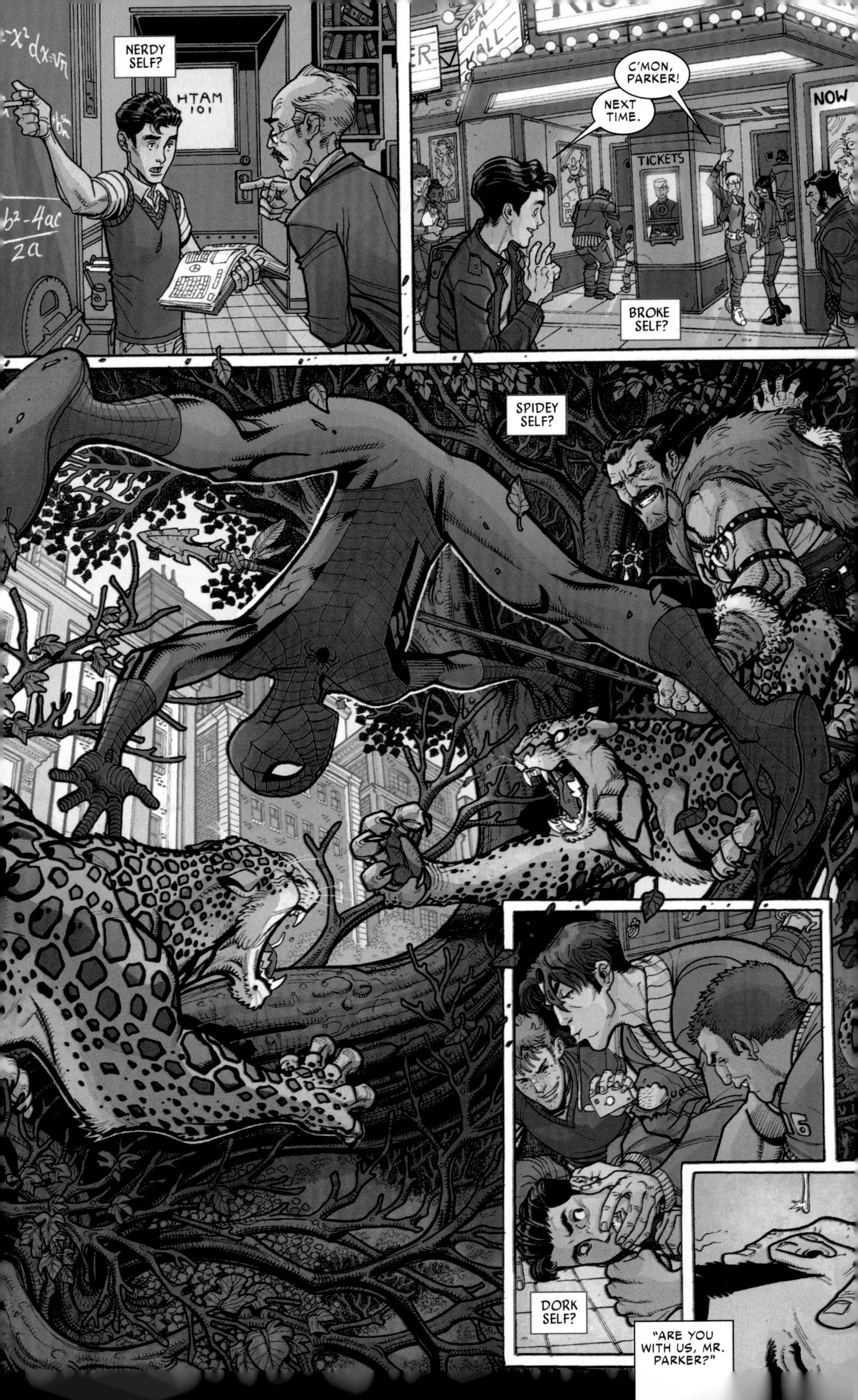

NERDY SELF?
HTAM 101
C'MON, PARKER!
NEXT TIME.
TICKETS
NOW
BROKE SELF?
SPIDEY SELF?
DORK SELF?
"ARE YOU WITH US, MR. PARKER?"

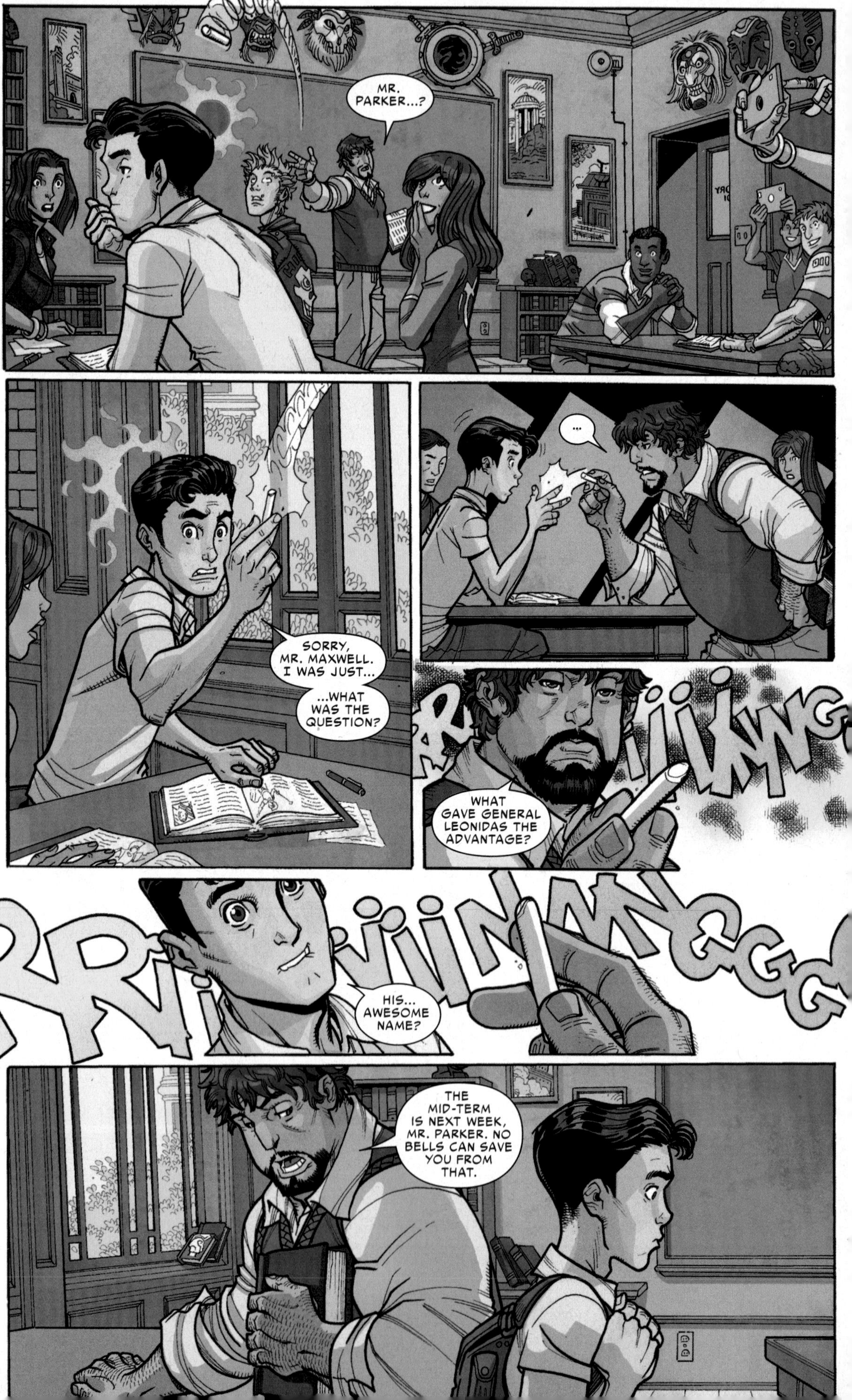
MR. PARKER...?
SORRY, MR. MAXWELL. I WAS JUST...
...WHAT WAS THE QUESTION?
...
WHAT GAVE GENERAL LEONIDAS THE ADVANTAGE?
RRIIIINNNGGG
HIS... AWESOME NAME?
THE MID-TERM IS NEXT WEEK, MR. PARKER. NO BELLS CAN SAVE YOU FROM THAT.

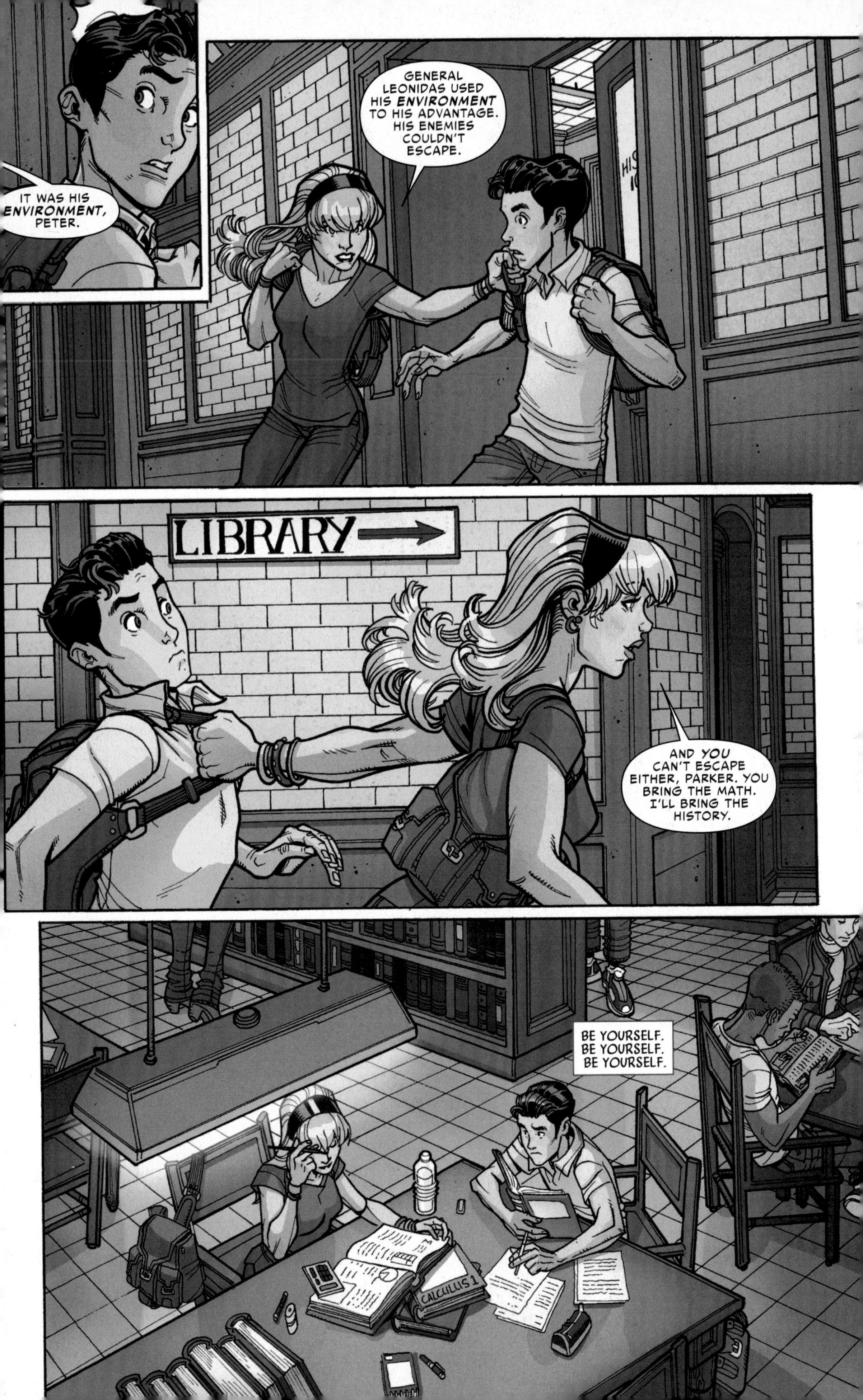
GENERAL LEONIDAS USED HIS ENVIRONMENT TO HIS ADVANTAGE. HIS ENEMIES COULDN'T ESCAPE.
IT WAS HIS ENVIRONMENT, PETER.
LIBRARY
AND YOU CAN'T ESCAPE EITHER, PARKER. YOU BRING THE MATH. I'LL BRING THE HISTORY.
BE YOURSELF. BE YOURSELF. BE YOURSELF.
CALCULUS 1

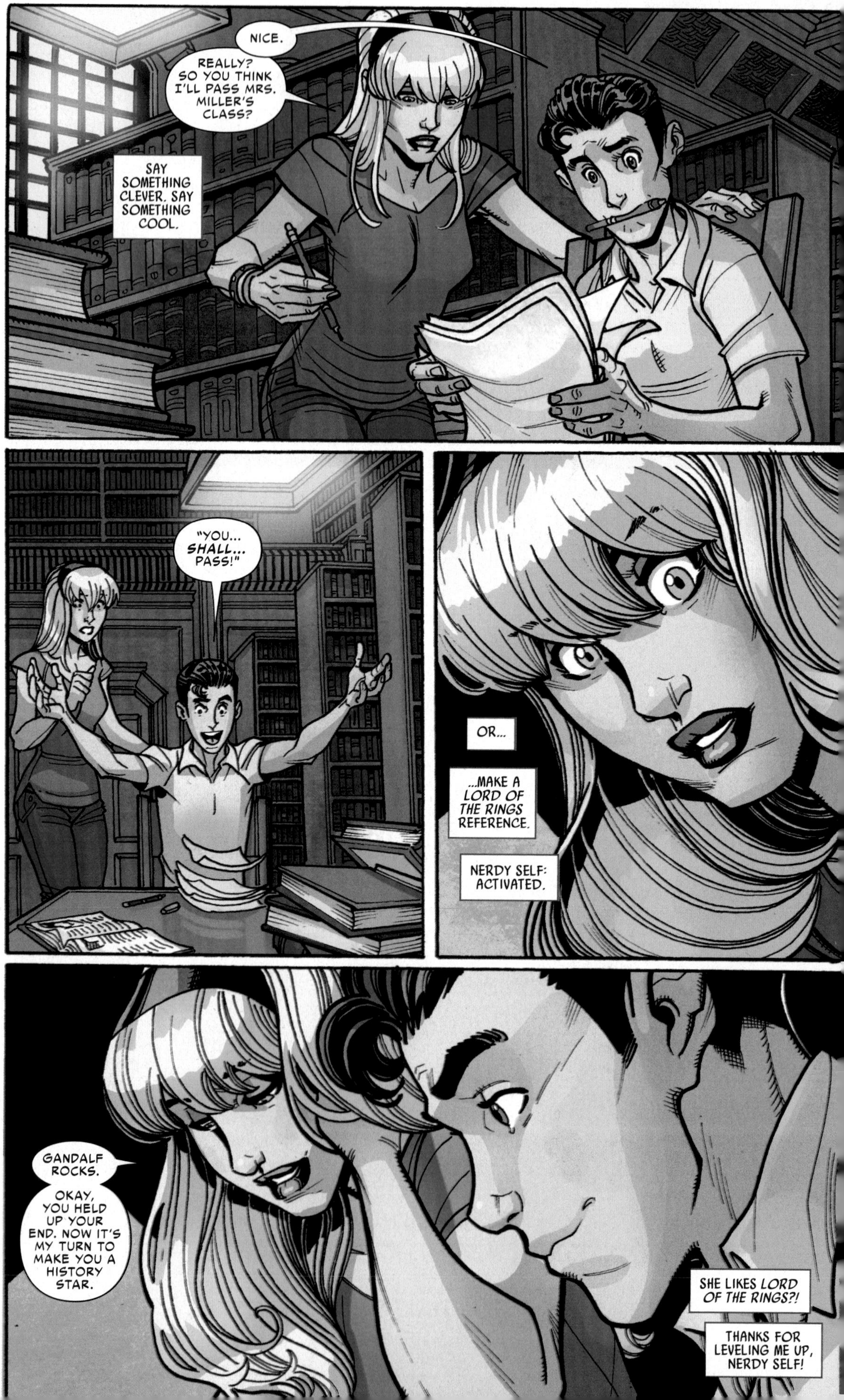
NICE.
REALLY? SO YOU THINK I'LL PASS MRS. MILLER'S CLASS?
SAY SOMETHING CLEVER. SAY SOMETHING COOL.
"YOU... SHALL... PASS!"
OR...
...MAKE A LORD OF THE RINGS REFERENCE.
NERDY SELF: ACTIVATED.
GANDALF ROCKS.
OKAY, YOU HELD UP YOUR END. NOW IT'S MY TURN TO MAKE YOU A HISTORY STAR.
SHE LIKES LORD OF THE RINGS?!
THANKS FOR LEVELING ME UP, NERDY SELF!

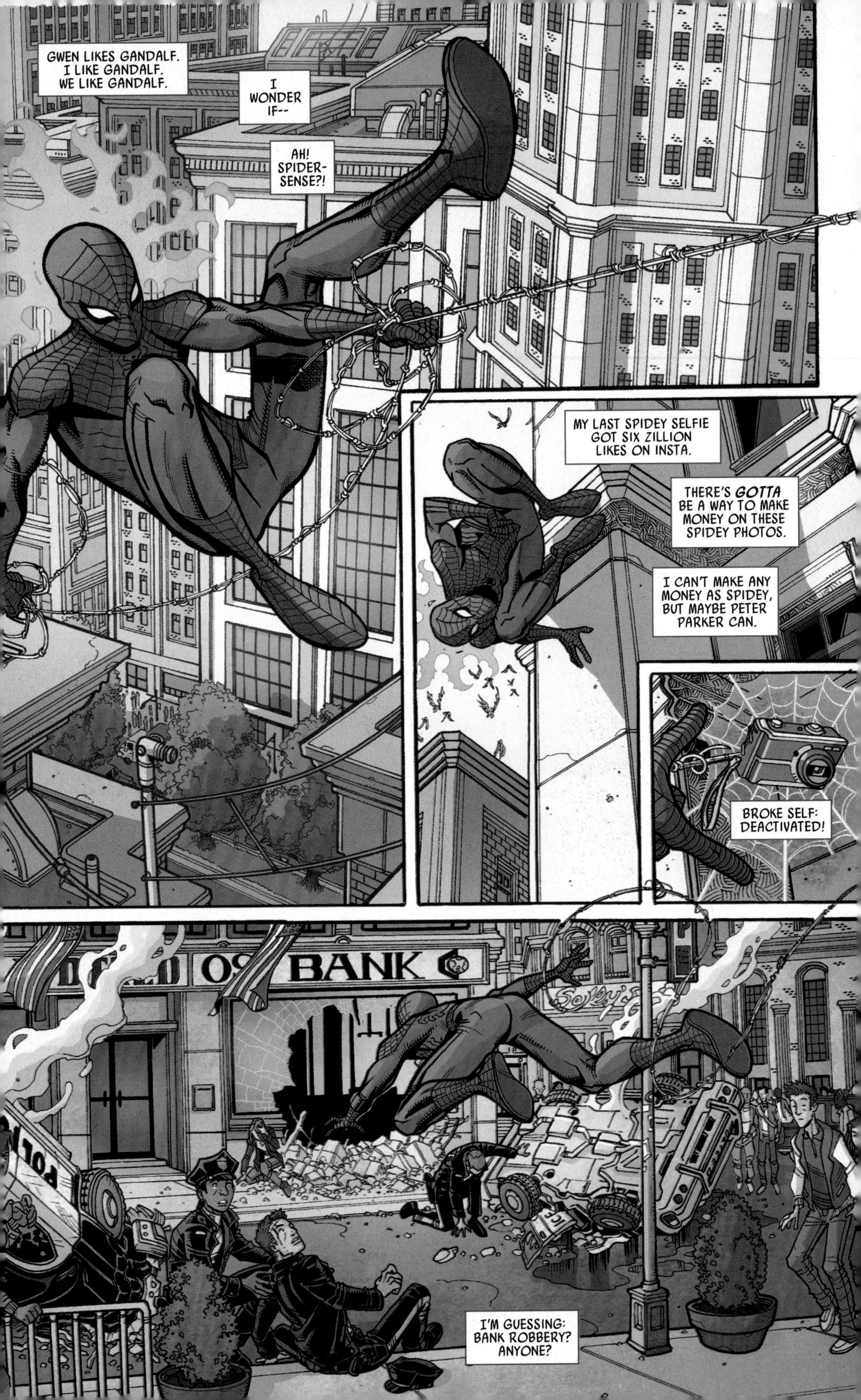
GWEN LIKES GANDALF. I LIKE GANDALF. WE LIKE GANDALF.
I WONDER IF--
AH! SPIDER-SENSE?!
MY LAST SPIDEY SELFIE GOT SIX ZILLION LIKES ON INSTA.
THERE'S GOTTA BE A WAY TO MAKE MONEY ON THESE SPIDEY PHOTOS.
I CAN'T MAKE ANY MONEY AS SPIDEY, BUT MAYBE PETER PARKER CAN.
BROKE SELF: DEACTIVATED!
OS BANK
I'M GUESSING: BANK ROBBERY? ANYONE?

LIGHTS OUT.

THAT'S NOT GOOD.

LOOKS LIKE I MISSED THE PARTY.

WAIT...

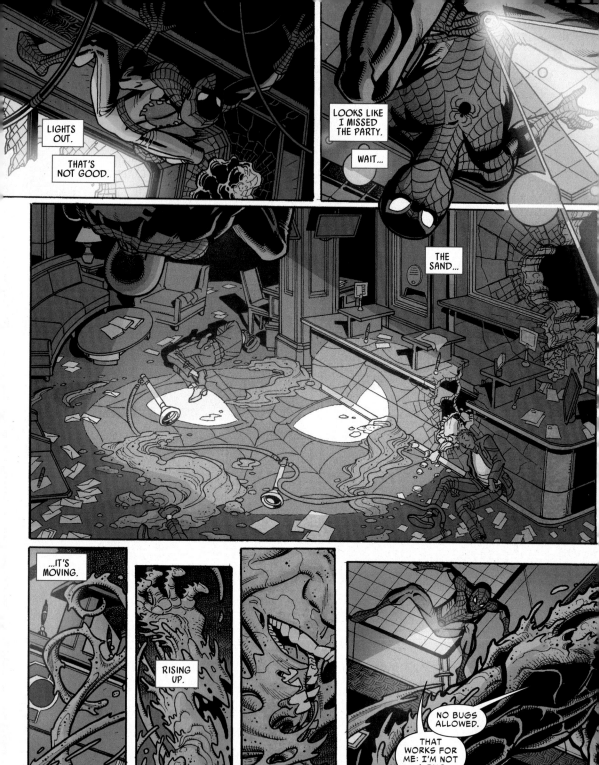

THE SAND...

...IT'S MOVING.

RISING UP.

WHICH MEANS--

NO BUGS ALLOWED.

THAT WORKS FOR ME: I'M NOT A BUG.

I'M A--

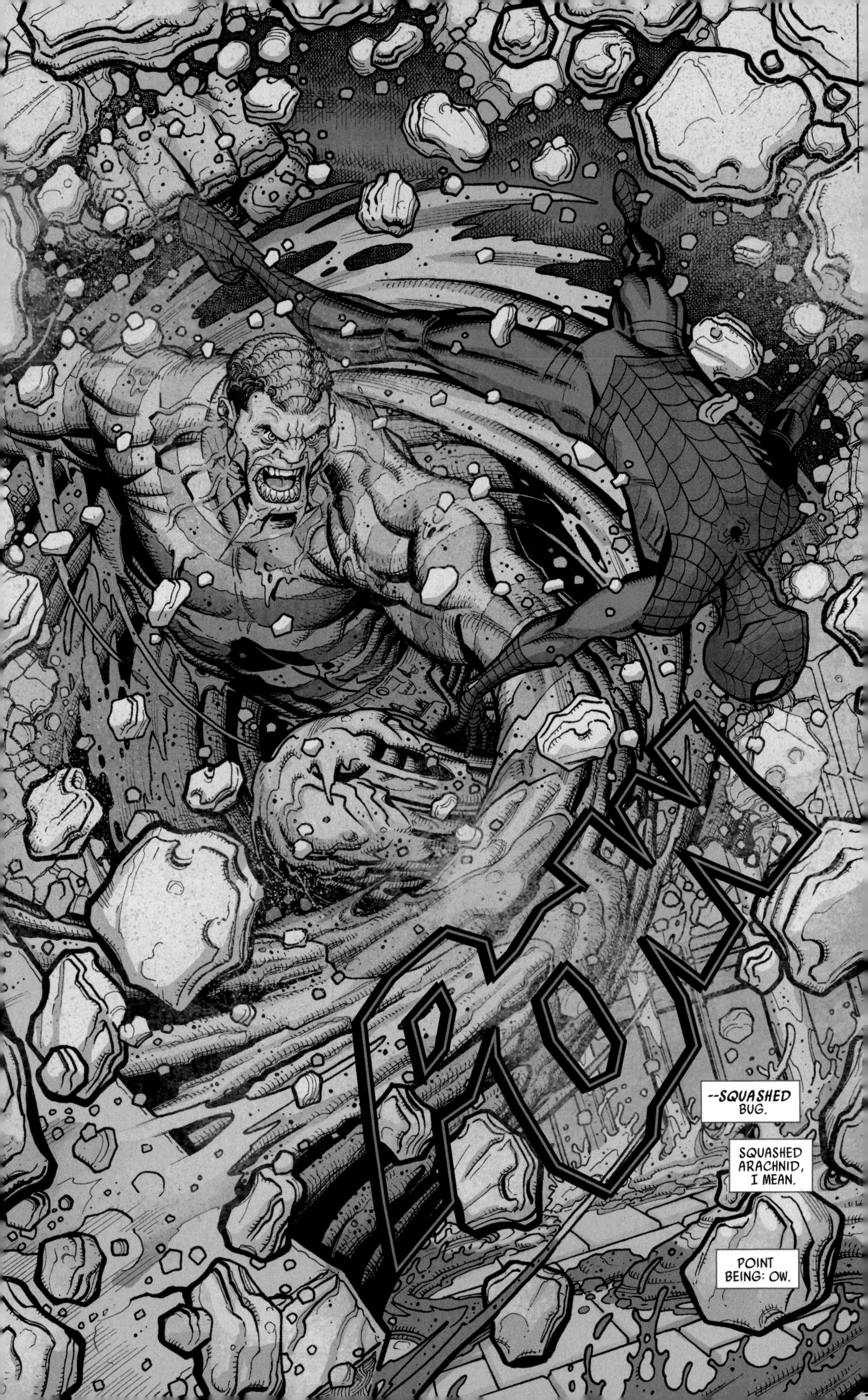
--SQUASHED BUG.
SQUASHED ARACHNID, I MEAN.
POINT BEING: OW.

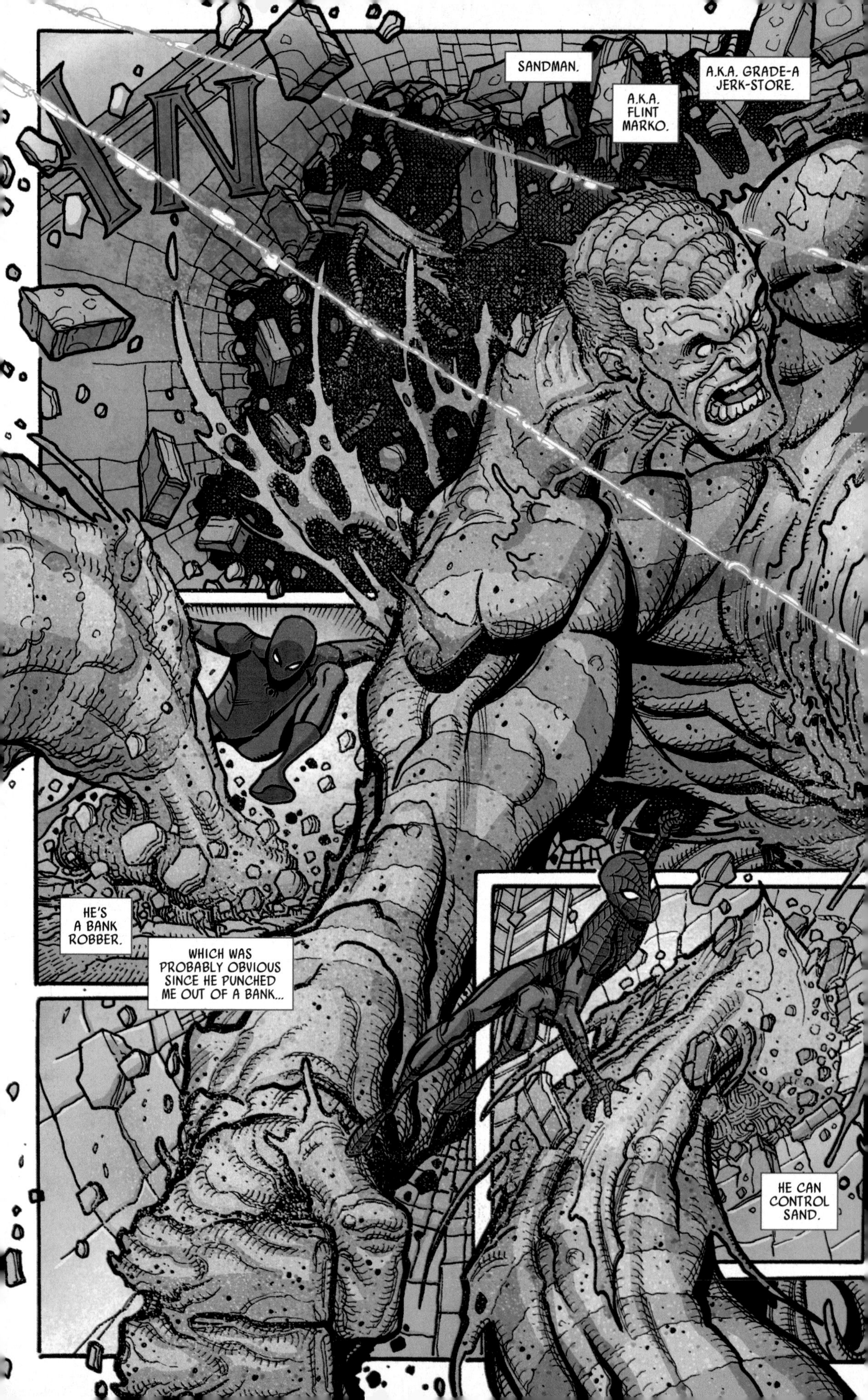
SANDMAN.
A.K.A. FLINT MARKO.
A.K.A. GRADE-A JERK-STORE.
HE'S A BANK ROBBER.
WHICH WAS PROBABLY OBVIOUS SINCE HE PUNCHED ME OUT OF A BANK...
HE CAN CONTROL SAND.

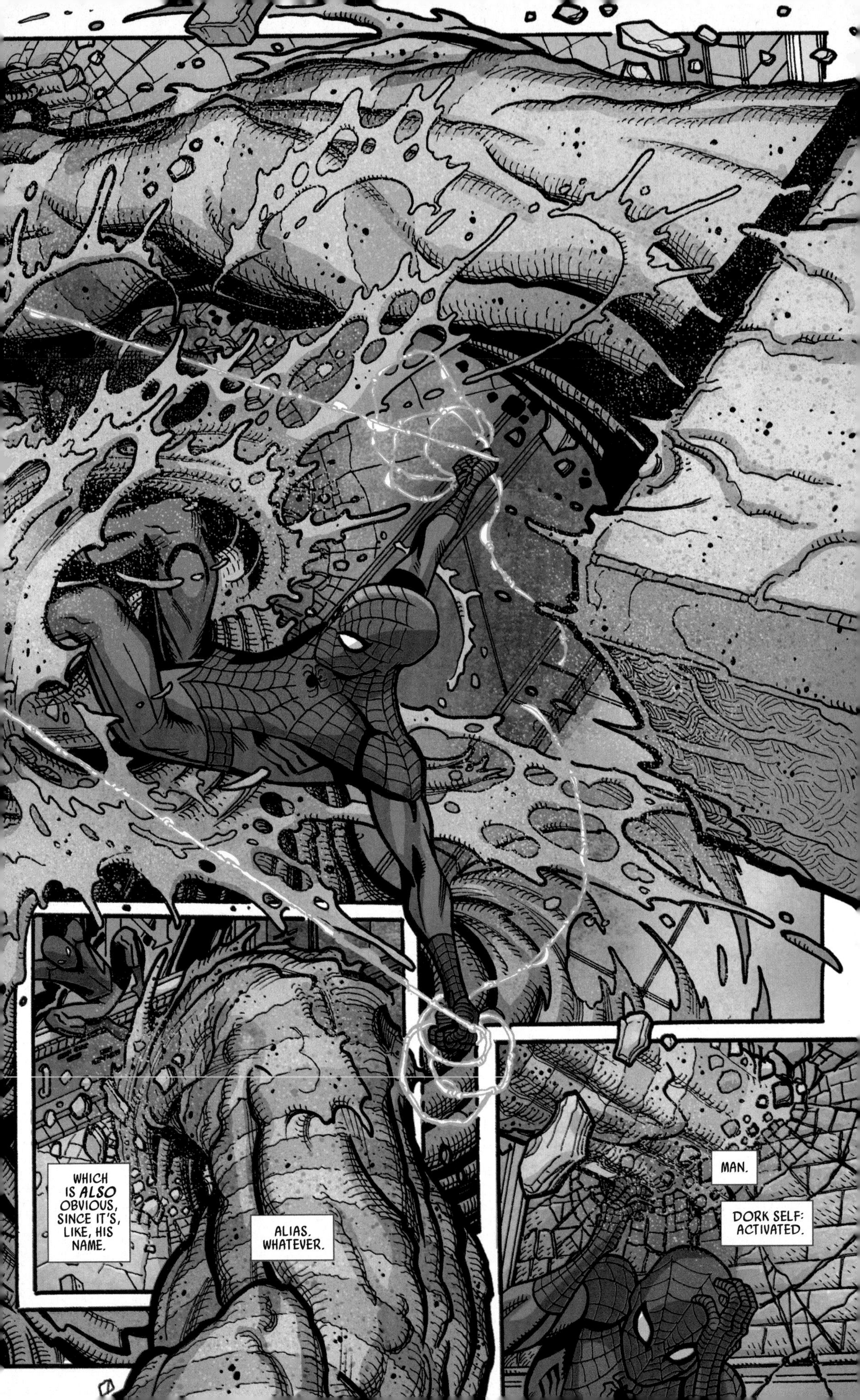
WHICH IS ALSO OBVIOUS, SINCE IT'S, LIKE, HIS NAME.
ALIAS. WHATEVER.
MAN.
DORK SELF: ACTIVATED.

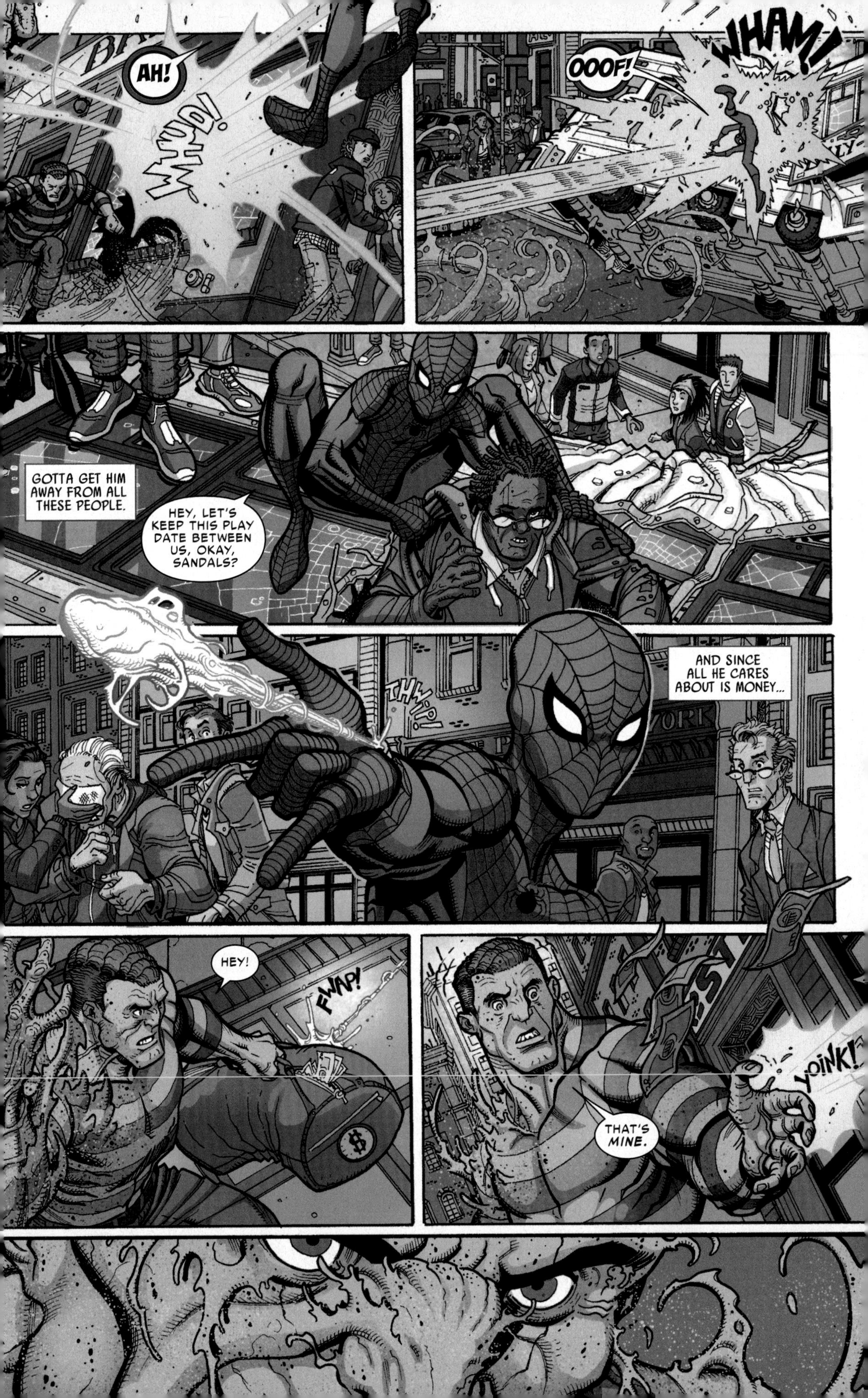
AH!
WHUD!
OOOF!
WHAM!
GOTTA GET HIM AWAY FROM ALL THESE PEOPLE.
HEY, LET'S KEEP THIS PLAY DATE BETWEEN US, OKAY, SANDALS?
THWIP!
AND SINCE ALL HE CARES ABOUT IS MONEY...
HEY!
FWAP!
THAT'S MINE.
YOINK!

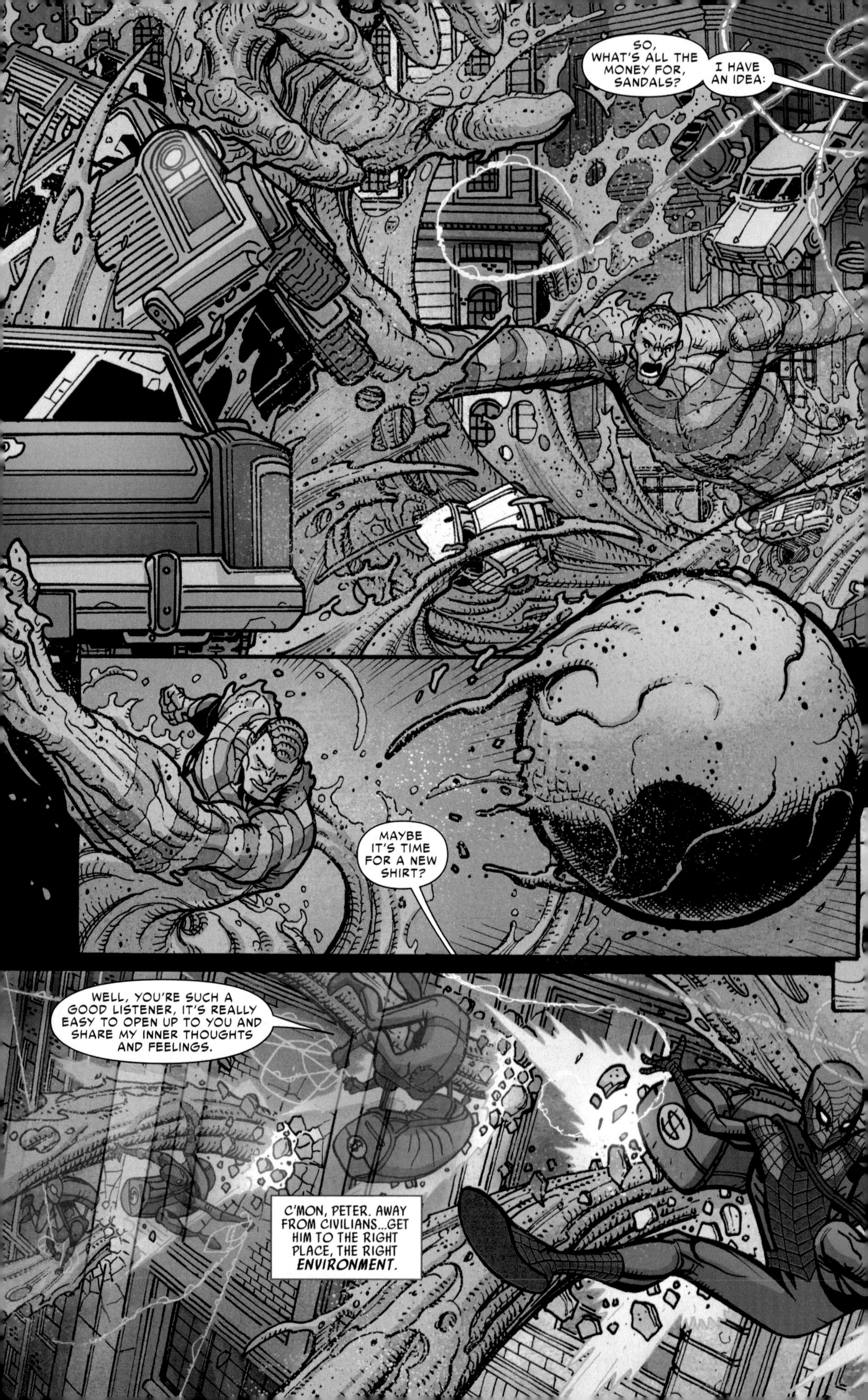
SO, WHAT'S ALL THE MONEY FOR, SANDALS?
I HAVE AN IDEA:
MAYBE IT'S TIME FOR A NEW SHIRT?
WELL, YOU'RE SUCH A GOOD LISTENER, IT'S REALLY EASY TO OPEN UP TO YOU AND SHARE MY INNER THOUGHTS AND FEELINGS.
C'MON, PETER. AWAY FROM CIVILIANS...GET HIM TO THE RIGHT PLACE, THE RIGHT ENVIRONMENT.

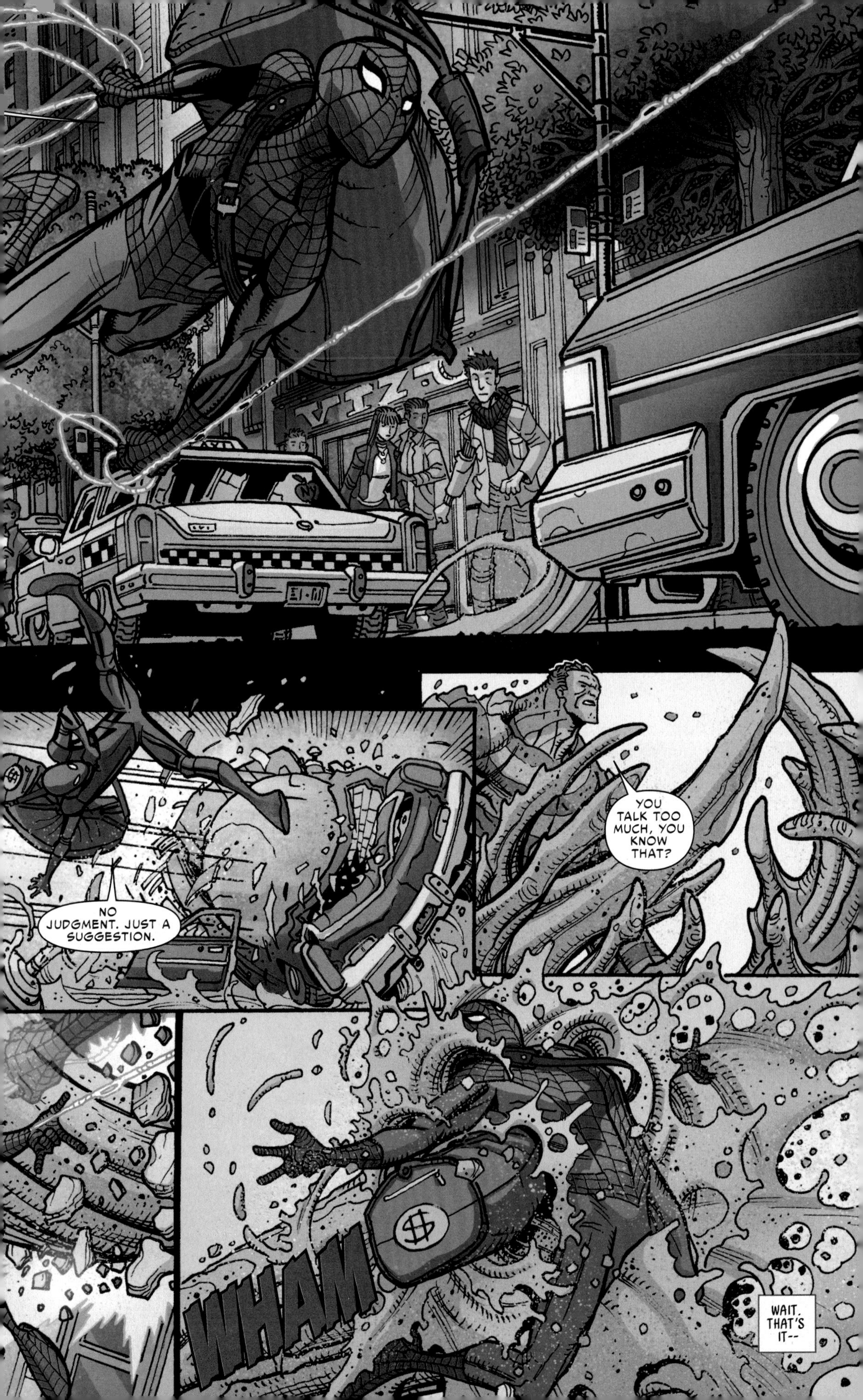
NO JUDGMENT. JUST A SUGGESTION.
YOU TALK TOO MUCH, YOU KNOW THAT?
WHAM
WAIT. THAT'S IT--

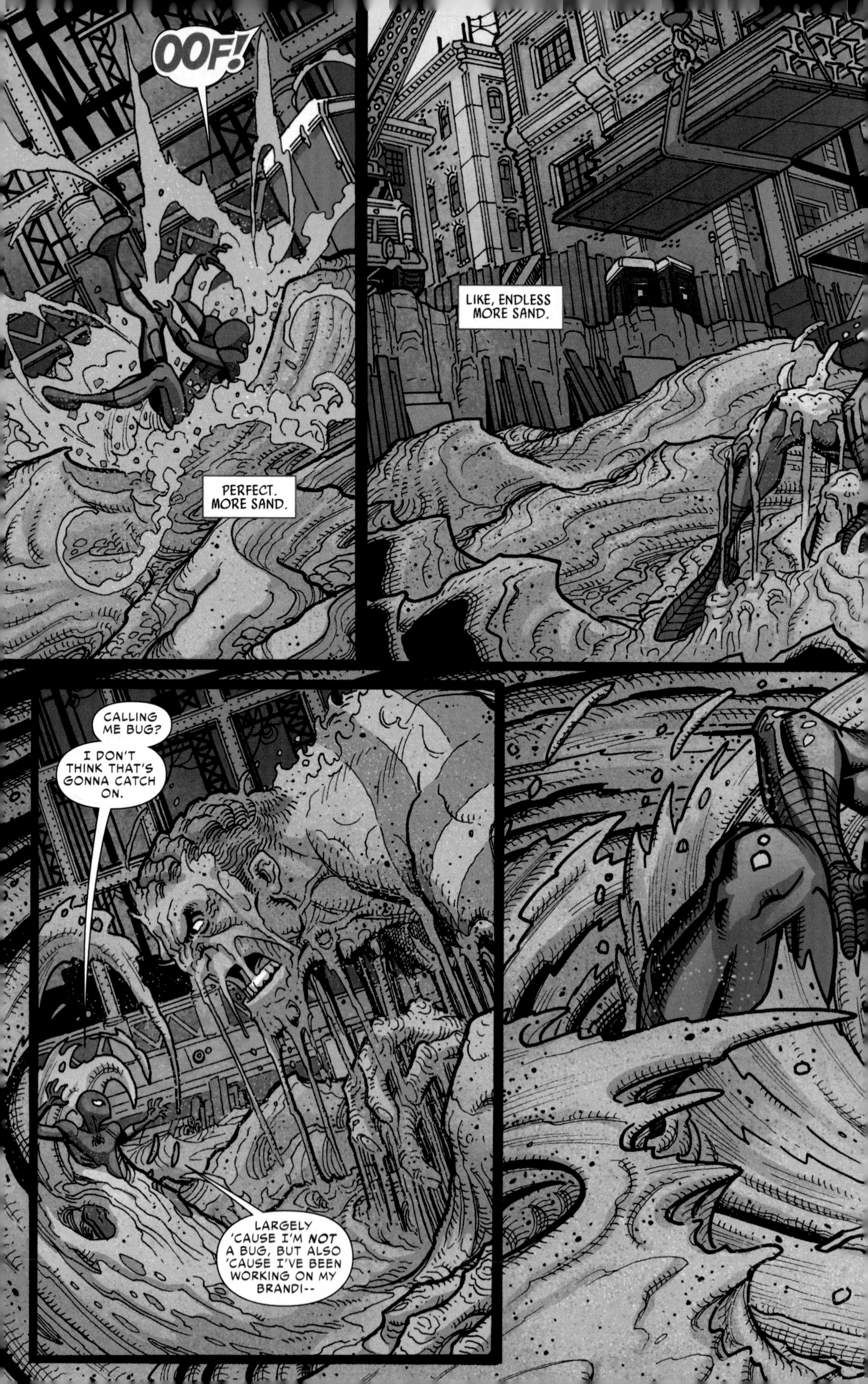
OOF!
PERFECT. MORE SAND.
LIKE, ENDLESS MORE SAND.
CALLING ME BUG?
I DON'T THINK THAT'S GONNA CATCH ON.
LARGELY 'CAUSE I'M NOT A BUG, BUT ALSO 'CAUSE I'VE BEEN WORKING ON MY BRANDI--

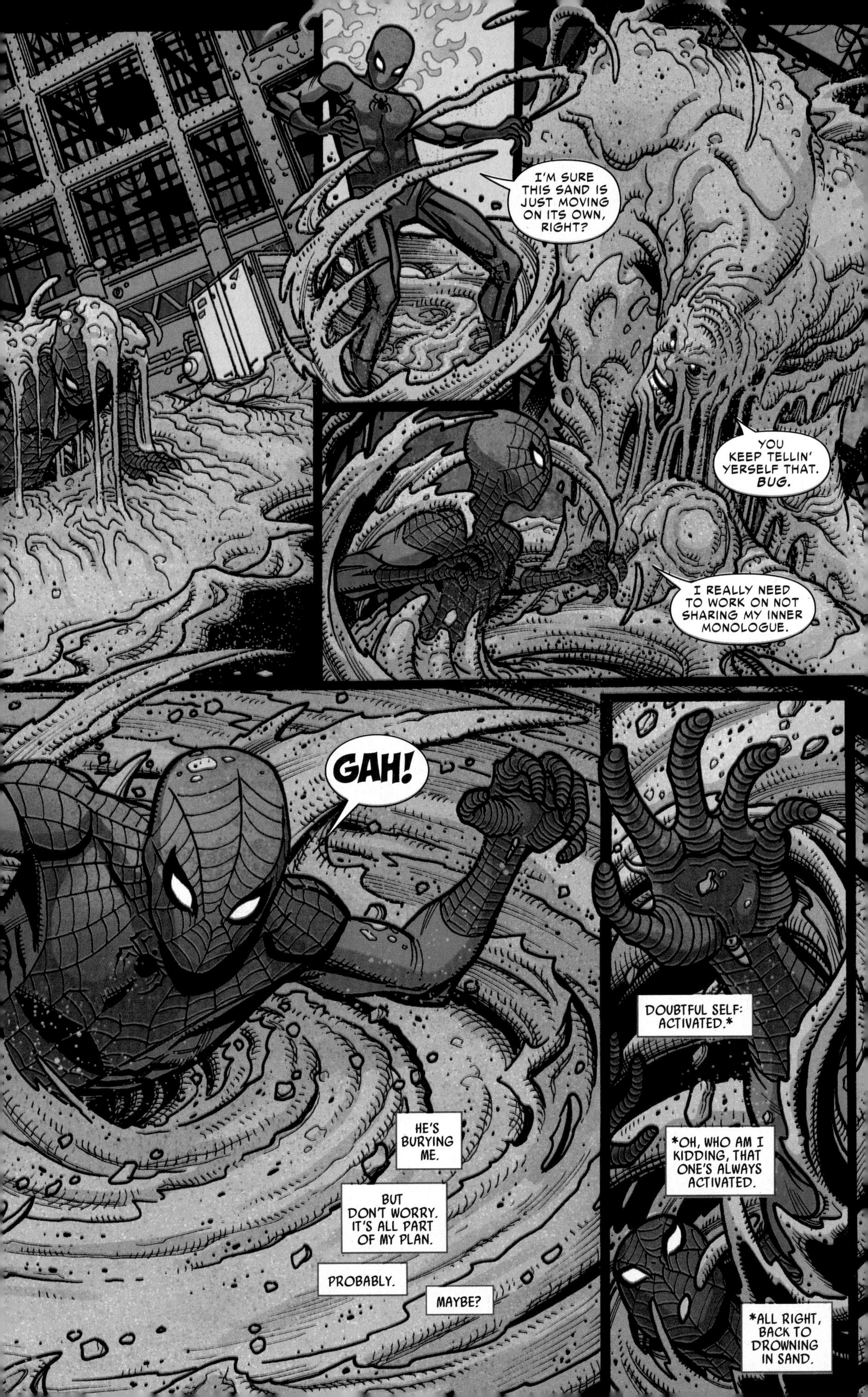
I'M SURE THIS SAND IS JUST MOVING ON ITS OWN, RIGHT?
YOU KEEP TELLIN' YERSELF THAT. BUG.
I REALLY NEED TO WORK ON NOT SHARING MY INNER MONOLOGUE.
GAH!
HE'S BURYING ME.
BUT DON'T WORRY. IT'S ALL PART OF MY PLAN.
PROBABLY.
MAYBE?
DOUBTFUL SELF: ACTIVATED.*
*OH, WHO AM I KIDDING, THAT ONE'S ALWAYS ACTIVATED.
*ALL RIGHT, BACK TO DROWNING IN SAND.

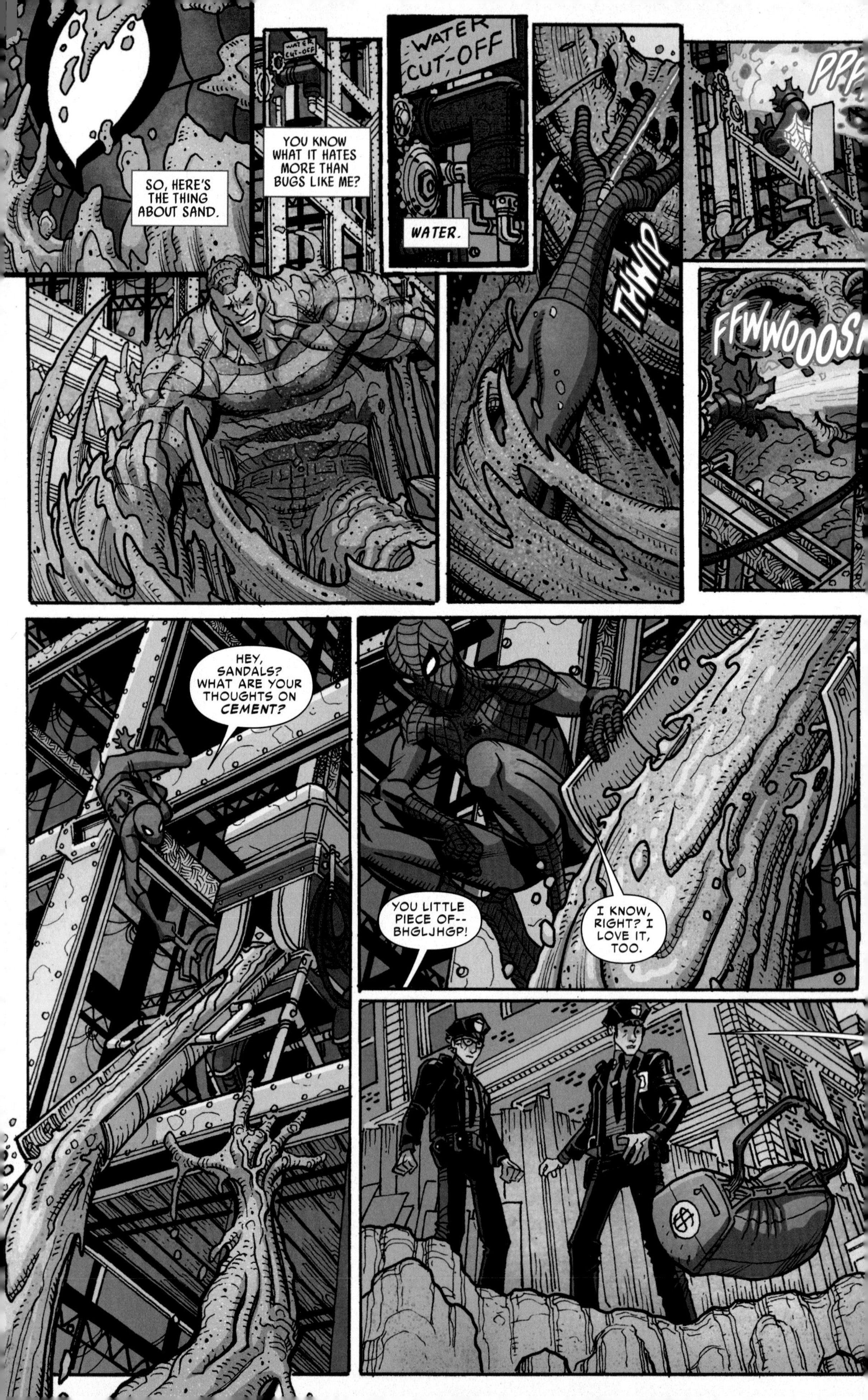
SO, HERE'S THE THING ABOUT SAND.
WATER CUT-OFF
YOU KNOW WHAT IT HATES MORE THAN BUGS LIKE ME?
WATER CUT-OFF
WATER.
THWIP
PPF
FFWWOOOS
HEY, SANDALS? WHAT ARE YOUR THOUGHTS ON CEMENT?
YOU LITTLE PIECE OF-- BHGLJHGP!
I KNOW, RIGHT? I LOVE IT, TOO.

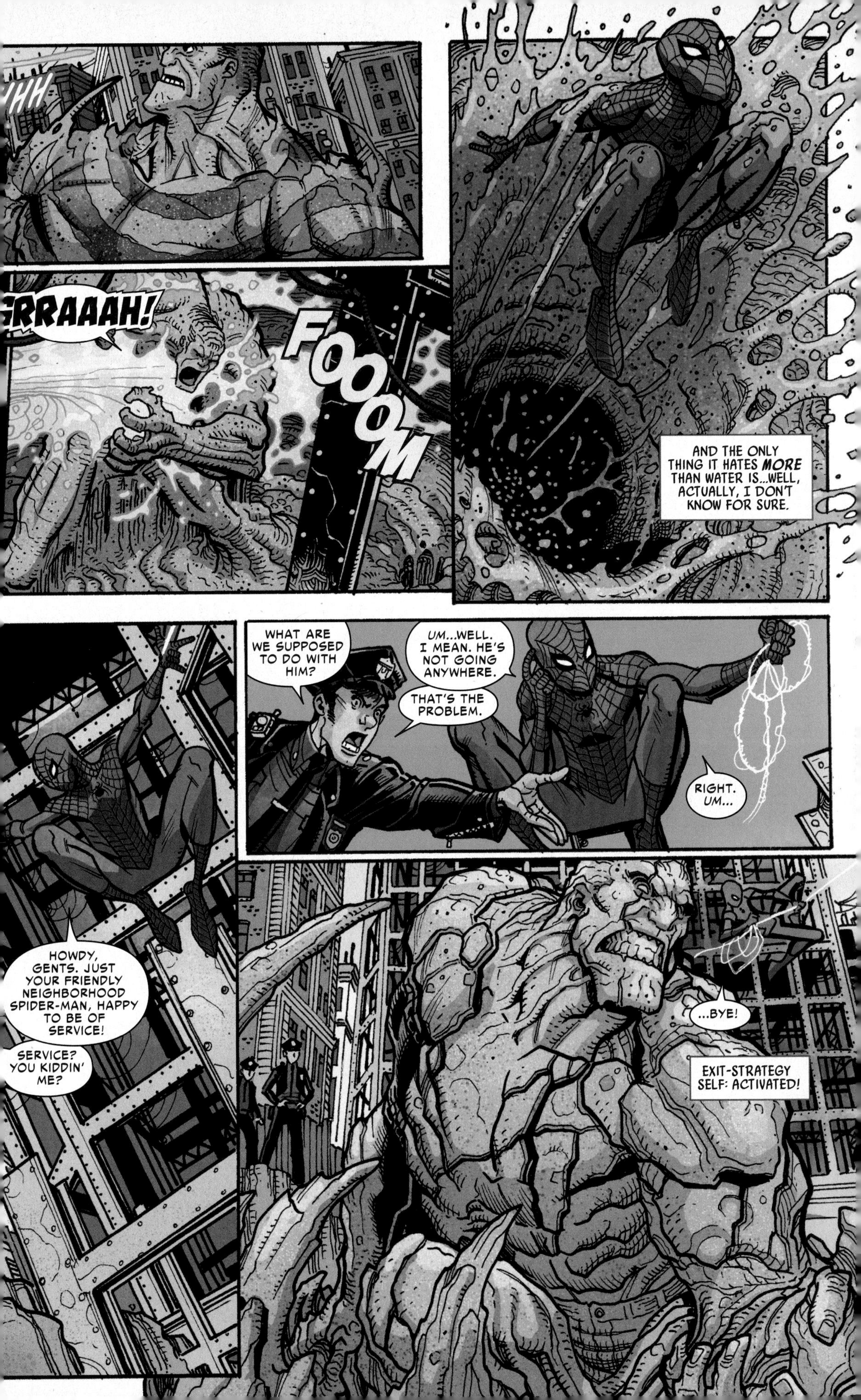

HHH
RRAAAH!
FOOOM
AND THE ONLY THING IT HATES MORE THAN WATER IS...WELL, ACTUALLY, I DON'T KNOW FOR SURE.
HOWDY, GENTS. JUST YOUR FRIENDLY NEIGHBORHOOD SPIDER-MAN, HAPPY TO BE OF SERVICE!
SERVICE? YOU KIDDIN' ME?
WHAT ARE WE SUPPOSED TO DO WITH HIM?
UM...WELL. I MEAN. HE'S NOT GOING ANYWHERE.
THAT'S THE PROBLEM.
RIGHT. UM...
...BYE!
EXIT-STRATEGY SELF: ACTIVATED!

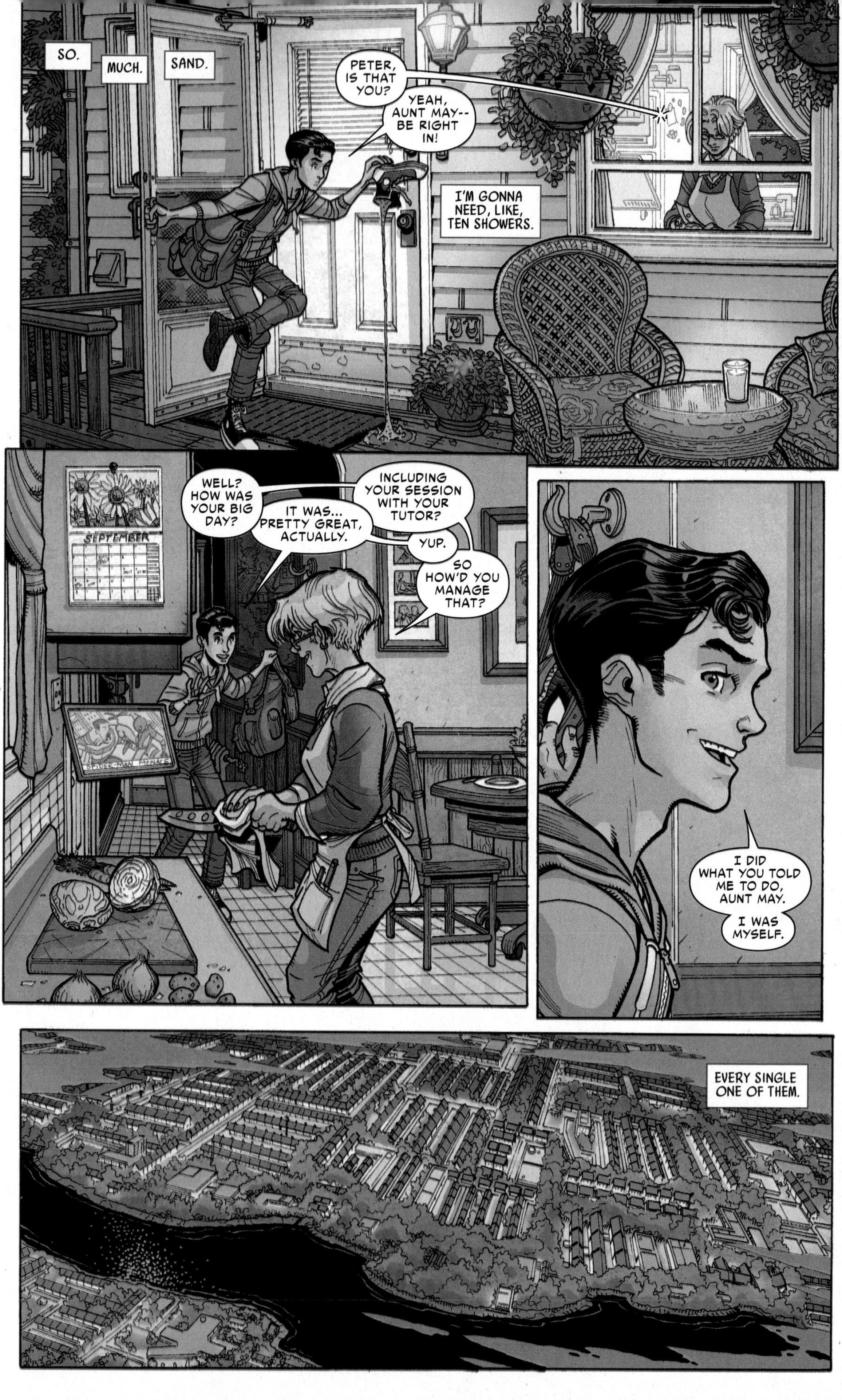
SO.
MUCH.
SAND.
PETER, IS THAT YOU?
YEAH, AUNT MAY-- BE RIGHT IN!
I'M GONNA NEED, LIKE, TEN SHOWERS.
WELL? HOW WAS YOUR BIG DAY?
IT WAS... PRETTY GREAT, ACTUALLY.
INCLUDING YOUR SESSION WITH YOUR TUTOR?
YUP.
SO HOW'D YOU MANAGE THAT?
I DID WHAT YOU TOLD ME TO DO, AUNT MAY.
I WAS MYSELF.
EVERY SINGLE ONE OF THEM.

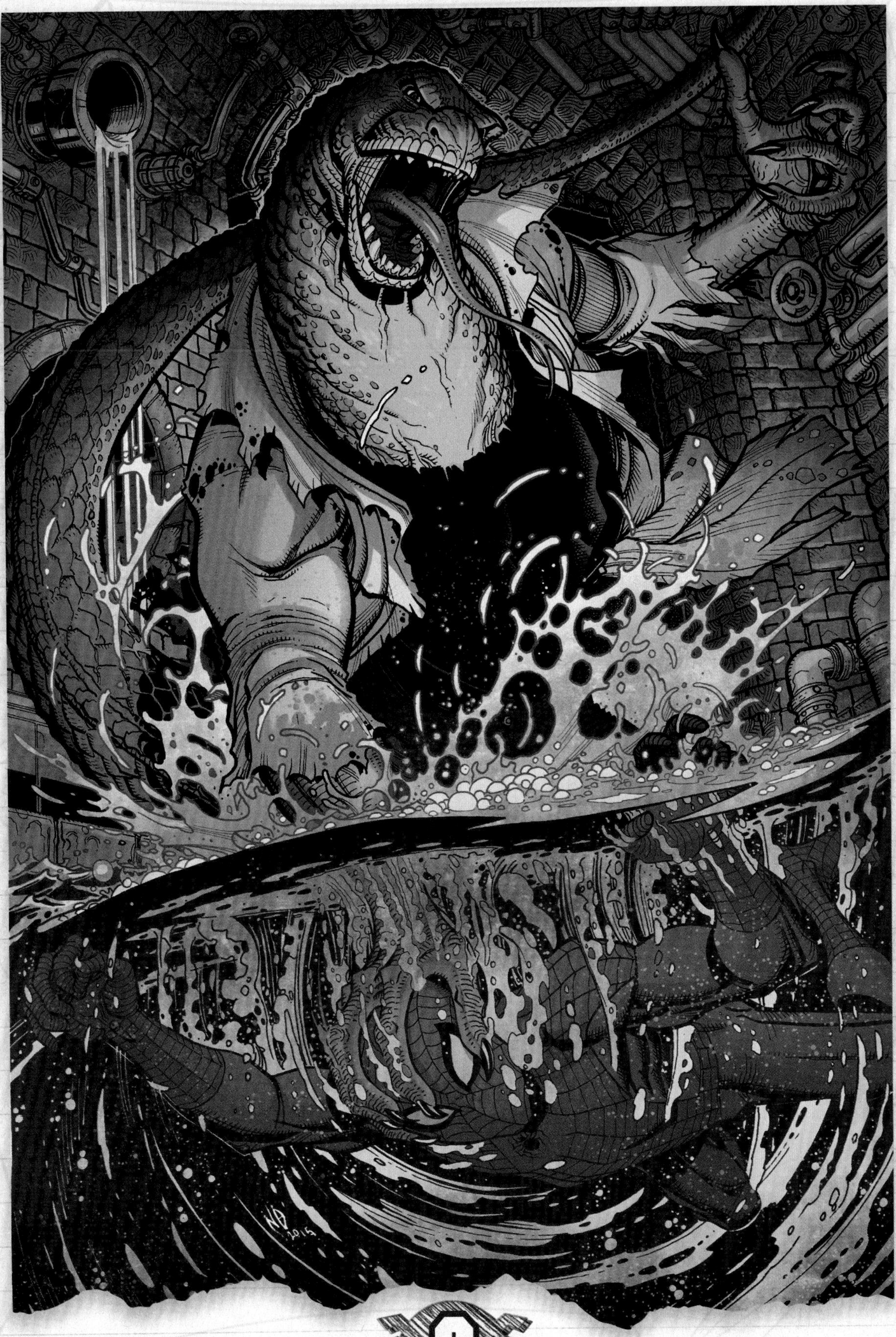

3

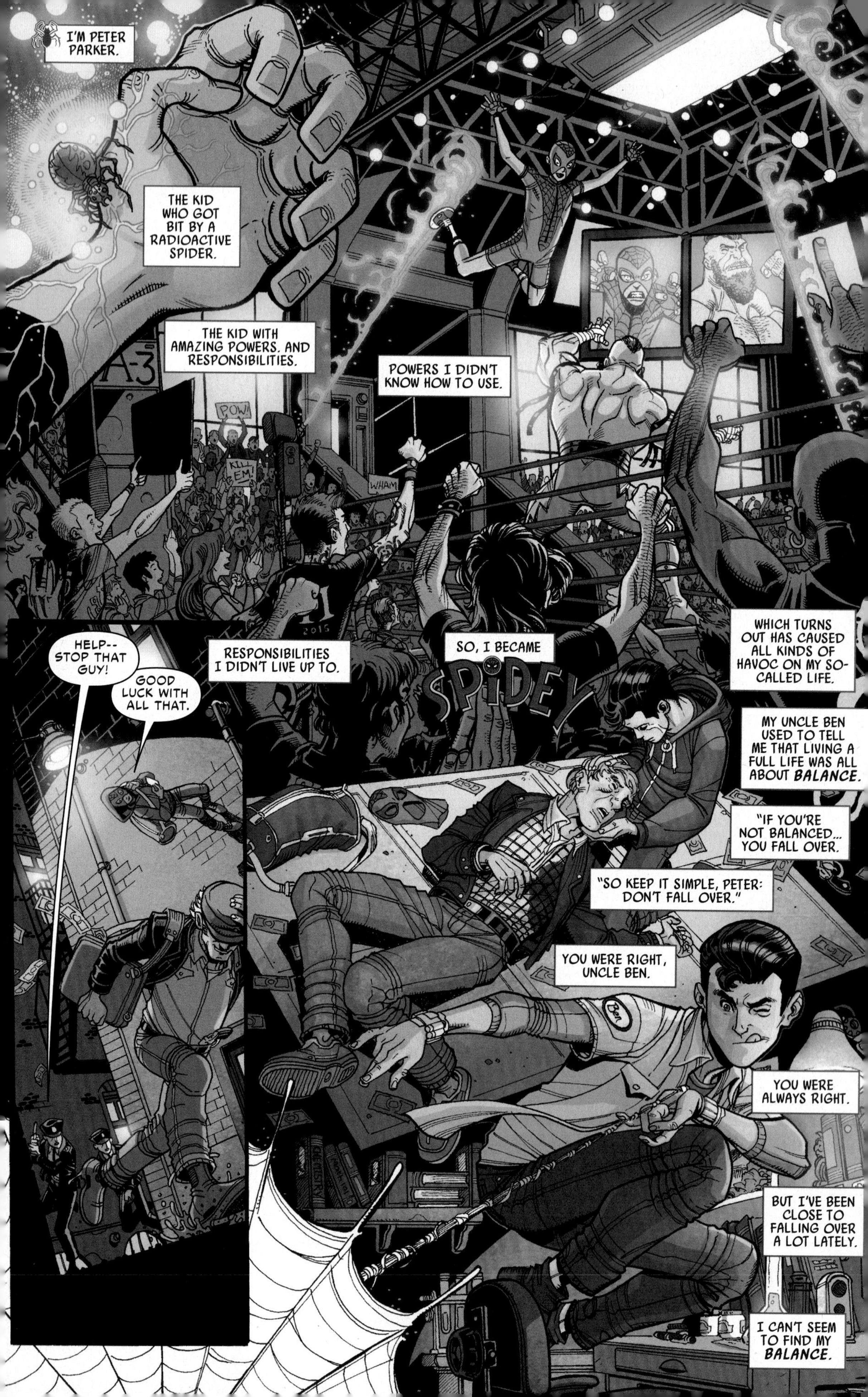
I'M PETER PARKER.
THE KID WHO GOT BIT BY A RADIOACTIVE SPIDER.
THE KID WITH AMAZING POWERS. AND RESPONSIBILITIES.
POWERS I DIDN'T KNOW HOW TO USE.
POW!
KILL 'EM!
WHAM
RESPONSIBILITIES I DIDN'T LIVE UP TO.
SO, I BECAME
SPIDEY
WHICH TURNS OUT HAS CAUSED ALL KINDS OF HAVOC ON MY SO-CALLED LIFE.
HELP-- STOP THAT GUY!
GOOD LUCK WITH ALL THAT.
MY UNCLE BEN USED TO TELL ME THAT LIVING A FULL LIFE WAS ALL ABOUT ***BALANCE***.
"IF YOU'RE NOT BALANCED... YOU FALL OVER.
"SO KEEP IT SIMPLE, PETER: DON'T FALL OVER."
YOU WERE RIGHT, UNCLE BEN.
Ben
YOU WERE ALWAYS RIGHT.
BUT I'VE BEEN CLOSE TO FALLING OVER A LOT LATELY.
I CAN'T SEEM TO FIND MY ***BALANCE***.

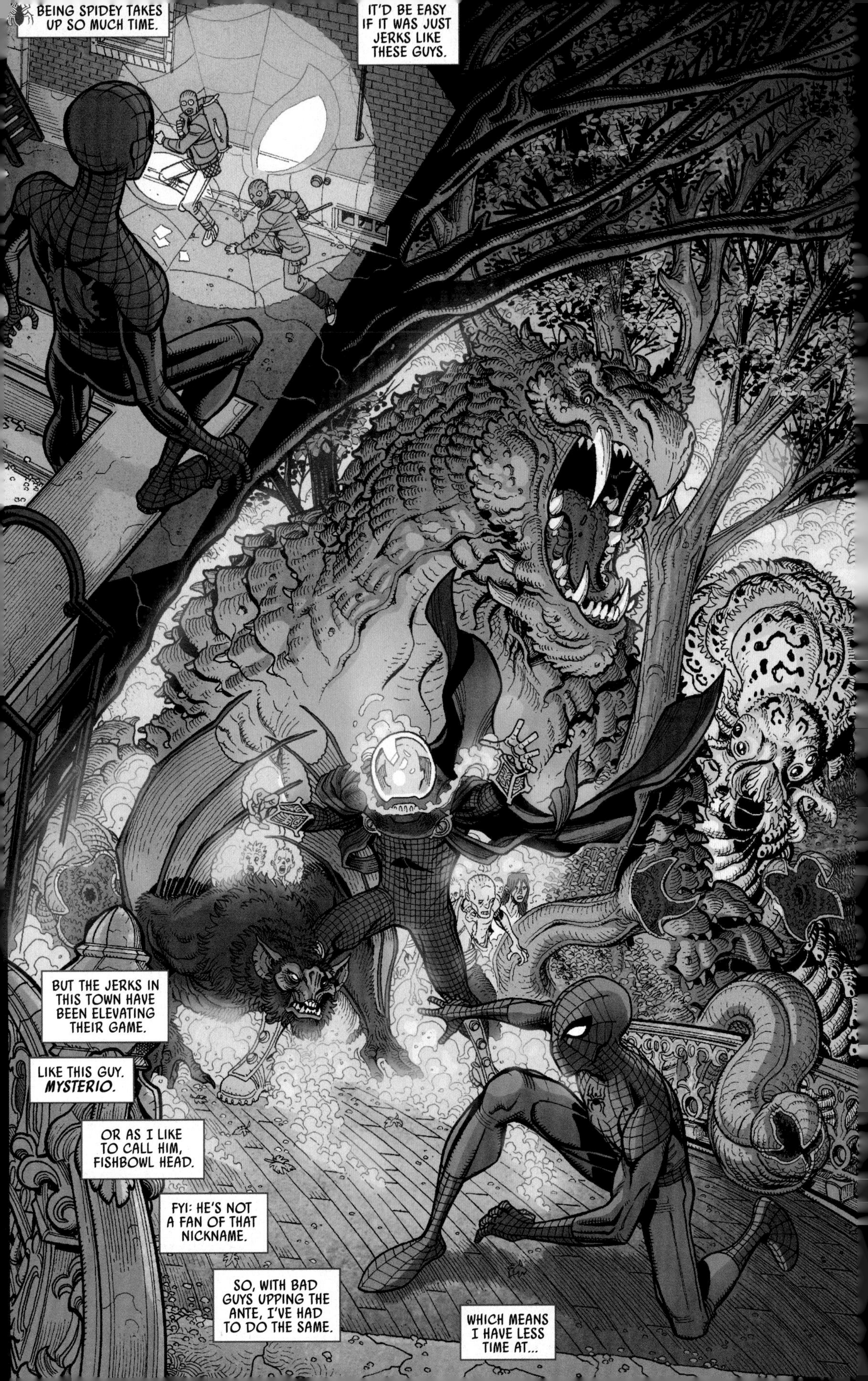
BEING SPIDEY TAKES UP SO MUCH TIME.
IT'D BE EASY IF IT WAS JUST JERKS LIKE THESE GUYS.
BUT THE JERKS IN THIS TOWN HAVE BEEN ELEVATING THEIR GAME.
LIKE THIS GUY. *MYSTERIO.*
OR AS I LIKE TO CALL HIM, FISHBOWL HEAD.
FYI: HE'S NOT A FAN OF THAT NICKNAME.
SO, WITH BAD GUYS UPPING THE ANTE, I'VE HAD TO DO THE SAME.
WHICH MEANS I HAVE LESS TIME AT...

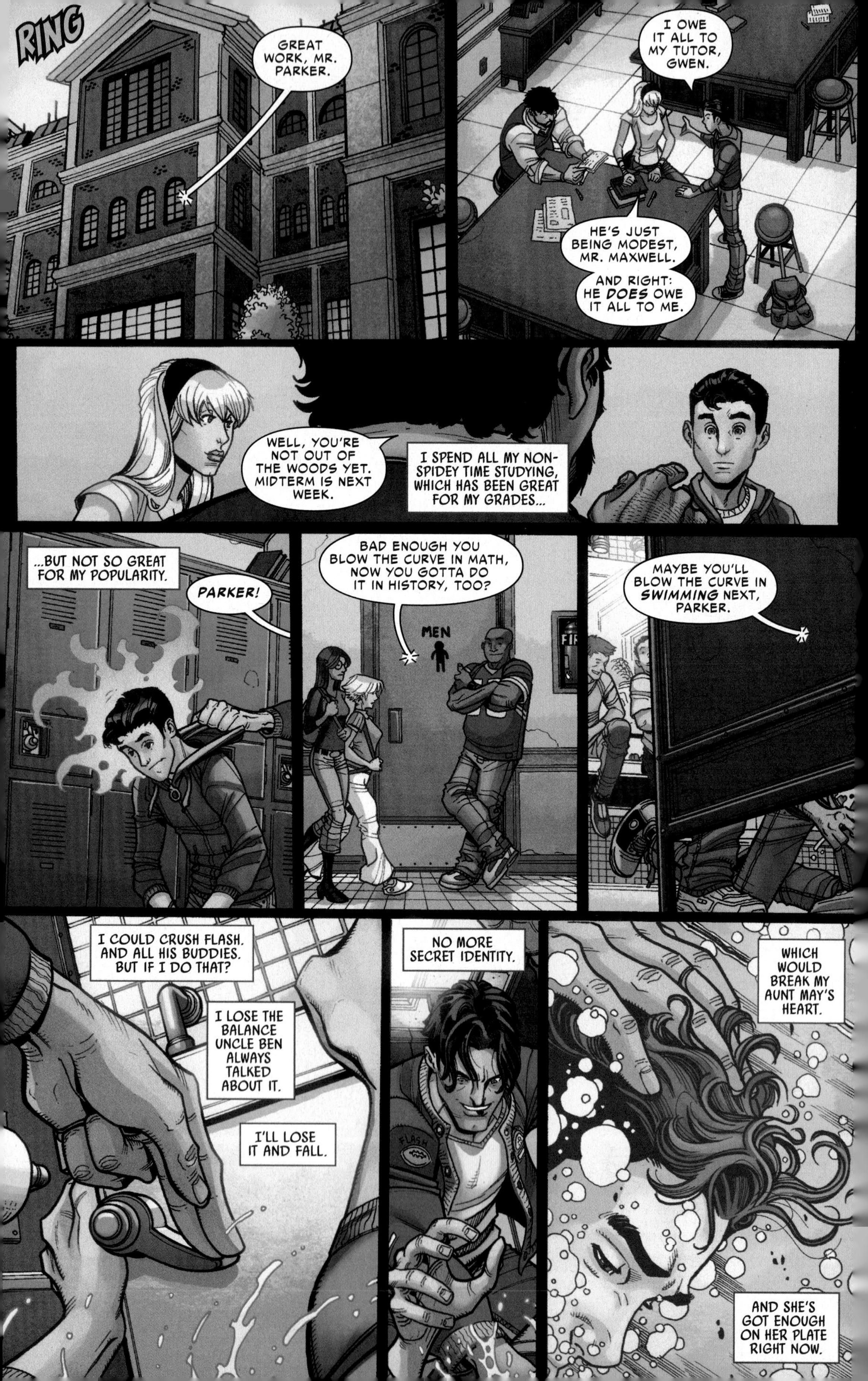
RING
GREAT WORK, MR. PARKER.
I OWE IT ALL TO MY TUTOR, GWEN.
HE'S JUST BEING MODEST, MR. MAXWELL.
AND RIGHT: HE DOES OWE IT ALL TO ME.
WELL, YOU'RE NOT OUT OF THE WOODS YET. MIDTERM IS NEXT WEEK.
I SPEND ALL MY NON-SPIDEY TIME STUDYING, WHICH HAS BEEN GREAT FOR MY GRADES...
...BUT NOT SO GREAT FOR MY POPULARITY.
PARKER!
BAD ENOUGH YOU BLOW THE CURVE IN MATH, NOW YOU GOTTA DO IT IN HISTORY, TOO?
MEN
MAYBE YOU'LL BLOW THE CURVE IN SWIMMING NEXT, PARKER.
I COULD CRUSH FLASH. AND ALL HIS BUDDIES. BUT IF I DO THAT?
I LOSE THE BALANCE UNCLE BEN ALWAYS TALKED ABOUT IT.
I'LL LOSE IT AND FALL.
NO MORE SECRET IDENTITY.
WHICH WOULD BREAK MY AUNT MAY'S HEART.
AND SHE'S GOT ENOUGH ON HER PLATE RIGHT NOW.

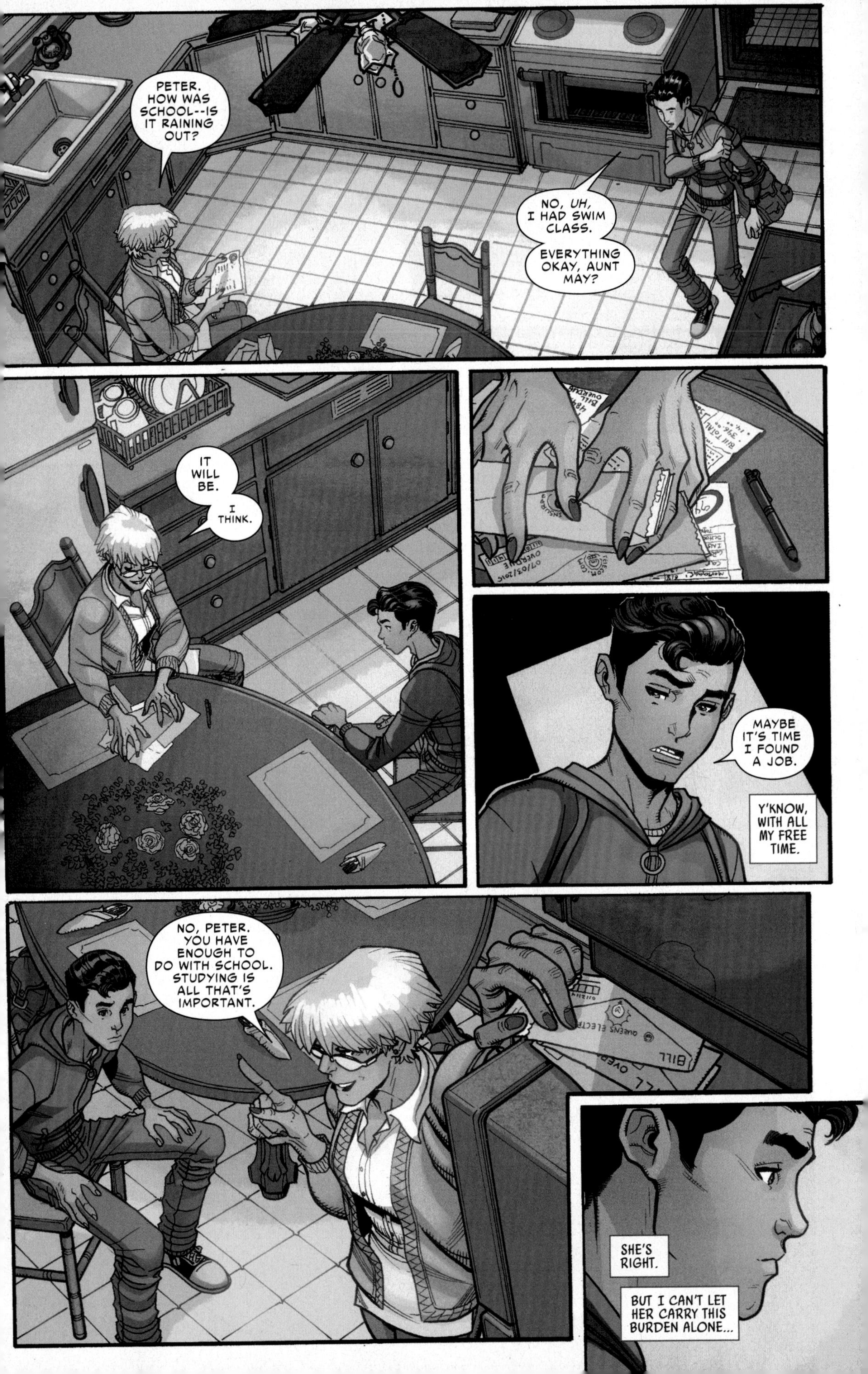
PETER. HOW WAS SCHOOL--IS IT RAINING OUT?
NO, UH, I HAD SWIM CLASS.
EVERYTHING OKAY, AUNT MAY?
IT WILL BE.
I THINK.
MAYBE IT'S TIME I FOUND A JOB.
Y'KNOW, WITH ALL MY FREE TIME.
NO, PETER. YOU HAVE ENOUGH TO DO WITH SCHOOL. STUDYING IS ALL THAT'S IMPORTANT.
SHE'S RIGHT.
BUT I CAN'T LET HER CARRY THIS BURDEN ALONE...

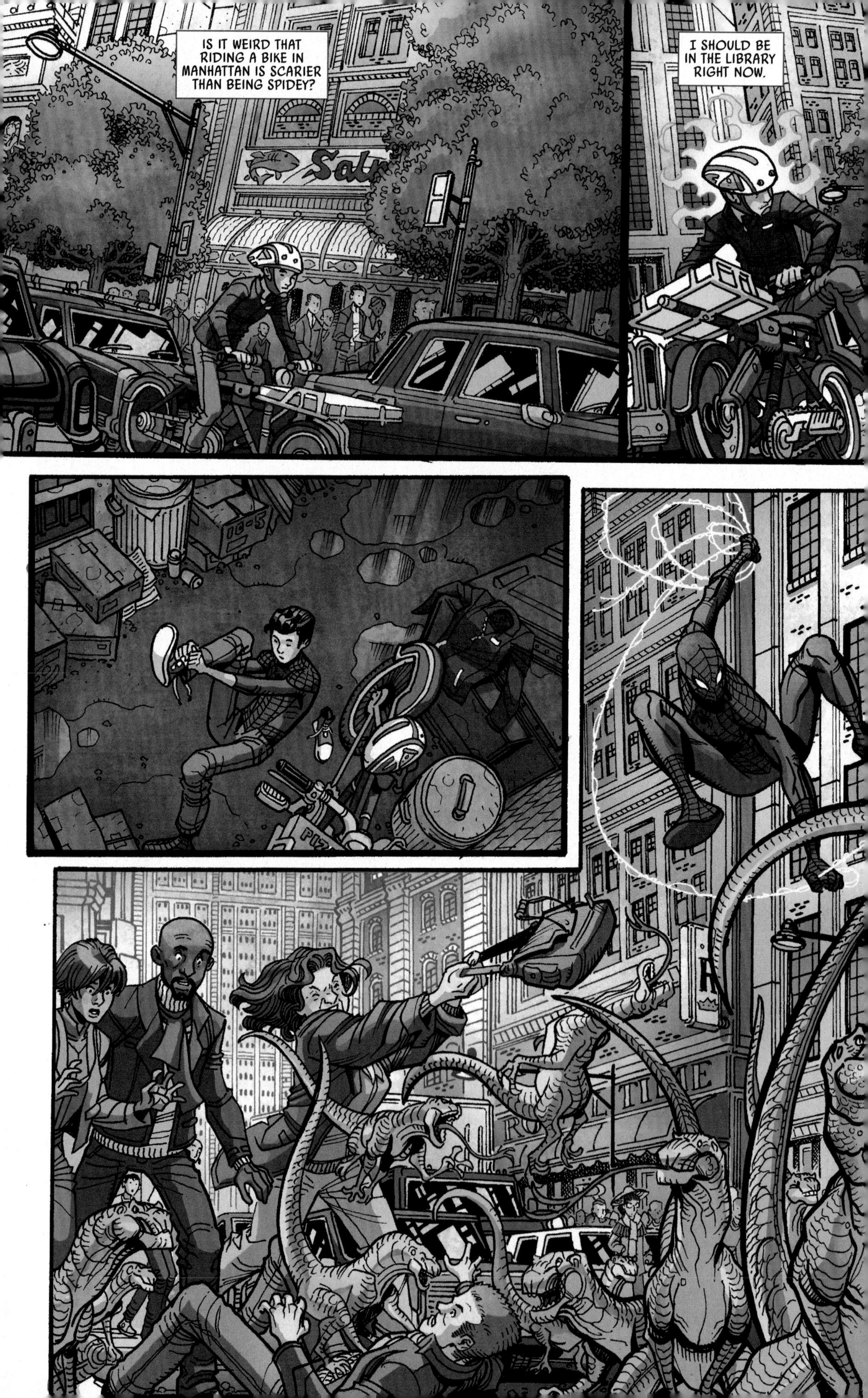
IS IT WEIRD THAT RIDING A BIKE IN MANHATTAN IS SCARIER THAN BEING SPIDEY?
I SHOULD BE IN THE LIBRARY RIGHT NOW.

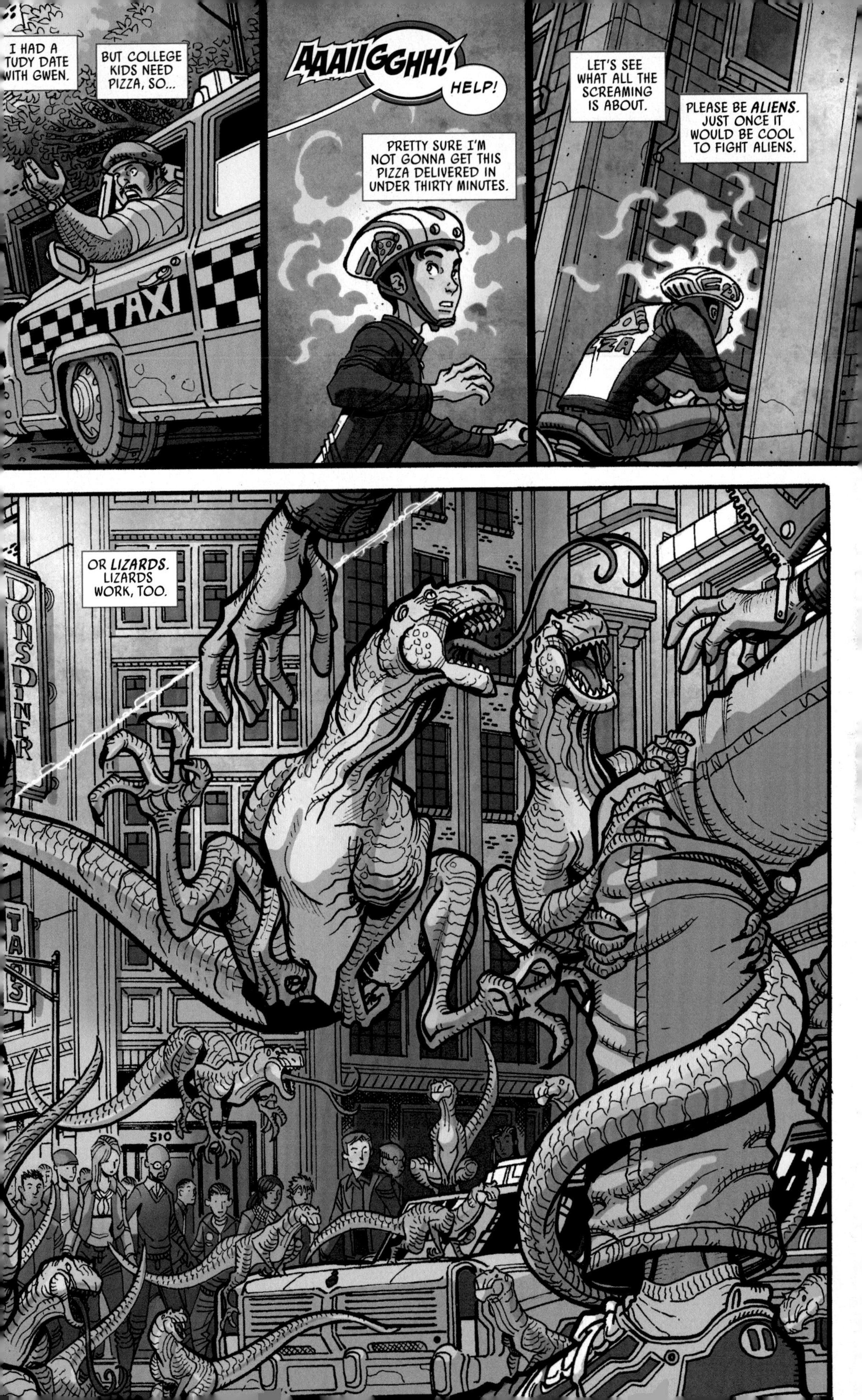
I HAD A
TUDY DATE
WITH GWEN.
BUT COLLEGE
KIDS NEED
PIZZA, SO...
AAAIIGGHH!
HELP!
PRETTY SURE I'M
NOT GONNA GET THIS
PIZZA DELIVERED IN
UNDER THIRTY MINUTES.
LET'S SEE
WHAT ALL THE
SCREAMING
IS ABOUT.
PLEASE BE ALIENS.
JUST ONCE IT
WOULD BE COOL
TO FIGHT ALIENS.
OR LIZARDS.
LIZARDS
WORK, TOO.

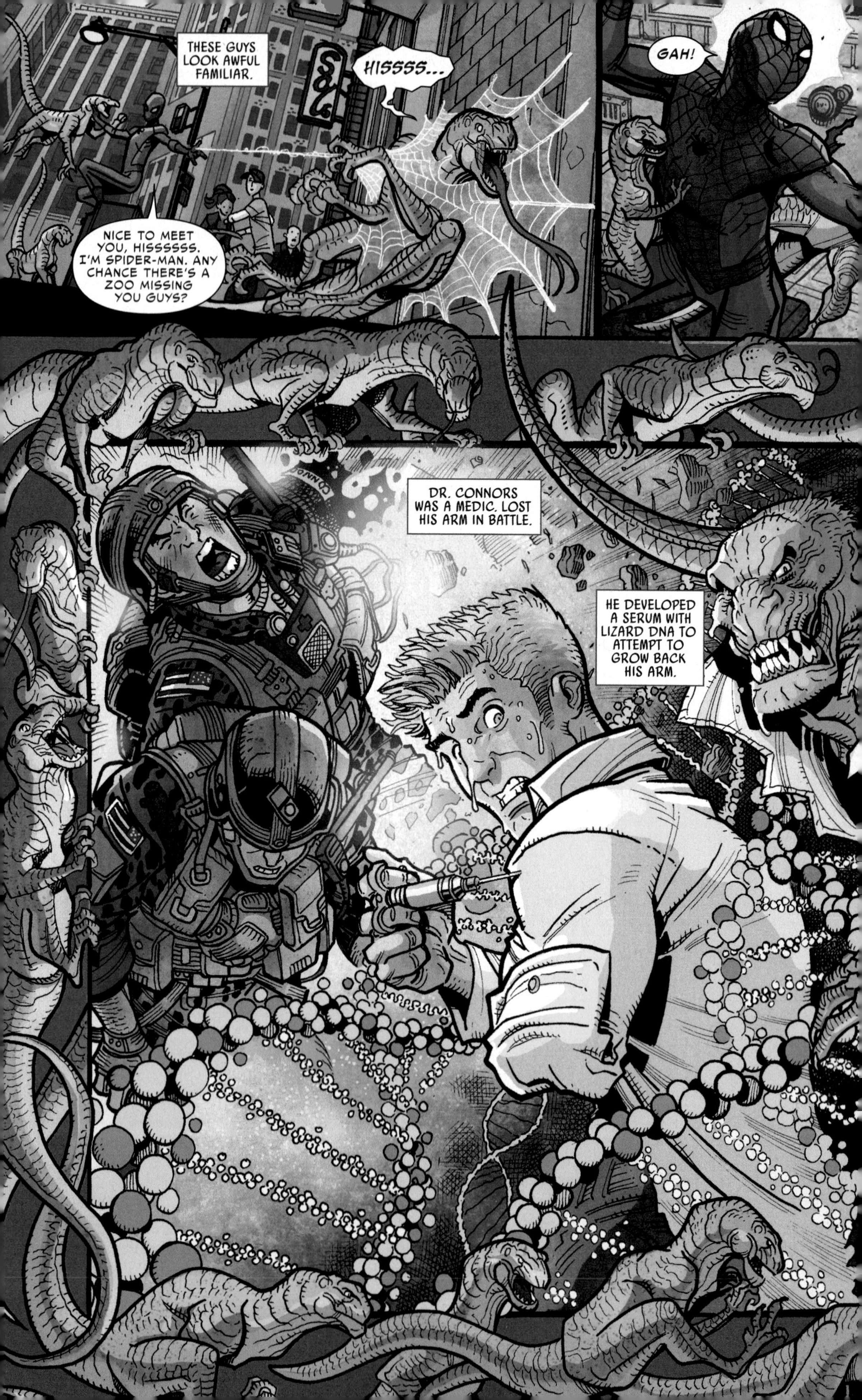
THESE GUYS LOOK AWFUL FAMILIAR.
HISSSS...
NICE TO MEET YOU, HISSSSSS. I'M SPIDER-MAN. ANY CHANCE THERE'S A ZOO MISSING YOU GUYS?
GAH!
DR. CONNORS WAS A MEDIC. LOST HIS ARM IN BATTLE.
HE DEVELOPED A SERUM WITH LIZARD DNA TO ATTEMPT TO GROW BACK HIS ARM.

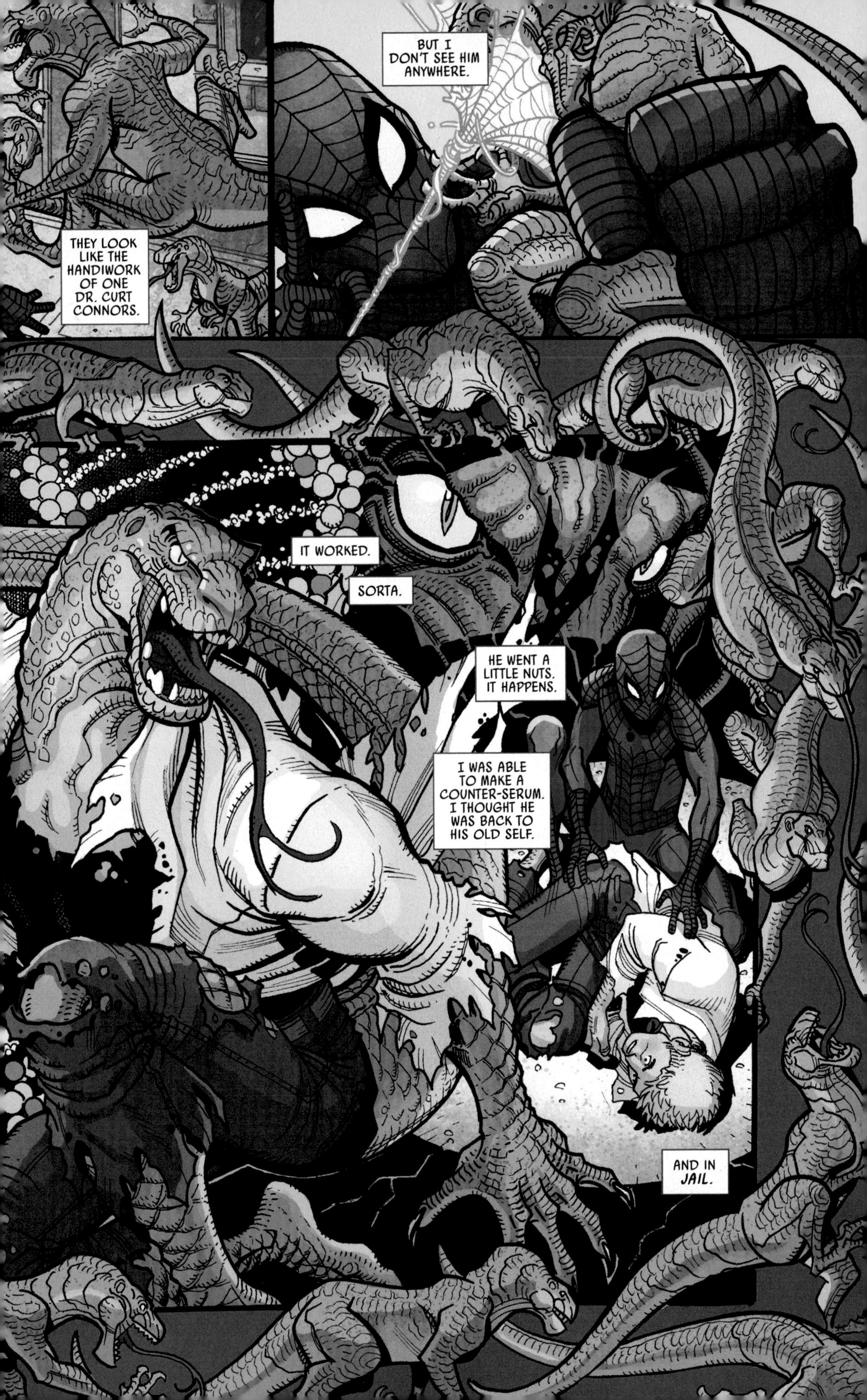
THEY LOOK LIKE THE HANDIWORK OF ONE DR. CURT CONNORS.
BUT I DON'T SEE HIM ANYWHERE.
IT WORKED.
SORTA.
HE WENT A LITTLE NUTS. IT HAPPENS.
I WAS ABLE TO MAKE A COUNTER-SERUM. I THOUGHT HE WAS BACK TO HIS OLD SELF.
AND IN JAIL.

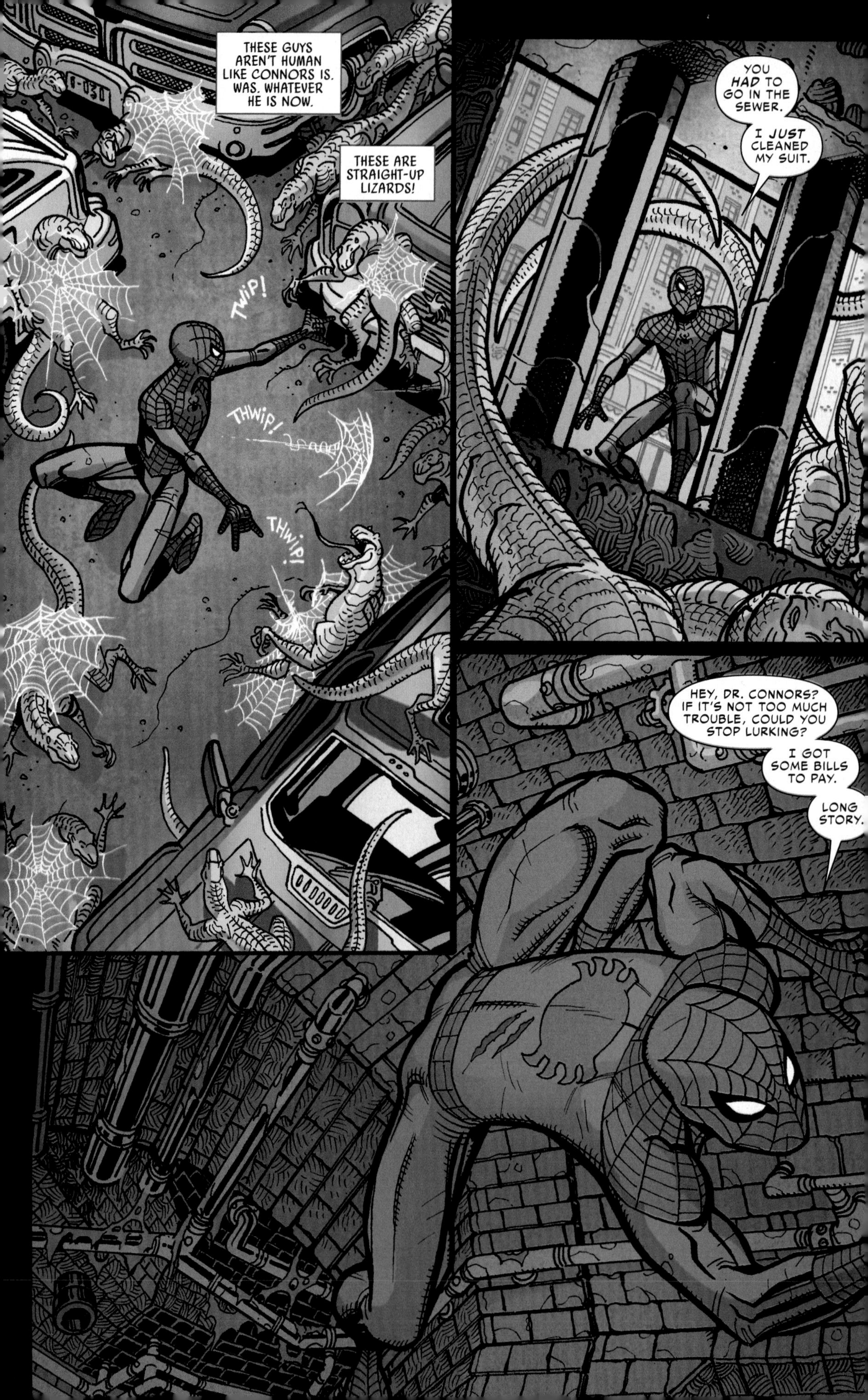
THESE GUYS AREN'T HUMAN LIKE CONNORS IS. WAS. WHATEVER HE IS NOW.
THESE ARE STRAIGHT-UP LIZARDS!
THWIP!
THWIP!
THWIP!
YOU HAD TO GO IN THE SEWER.
I JUST CLEANED MY SUIT.
HEY, DR. CONNORS? IF IT'S NOT TOO MUCH TROUBLE, COULD YOU STOP LURKING?
I GOT SOME BILLS TO PAY.
LONG STORY.

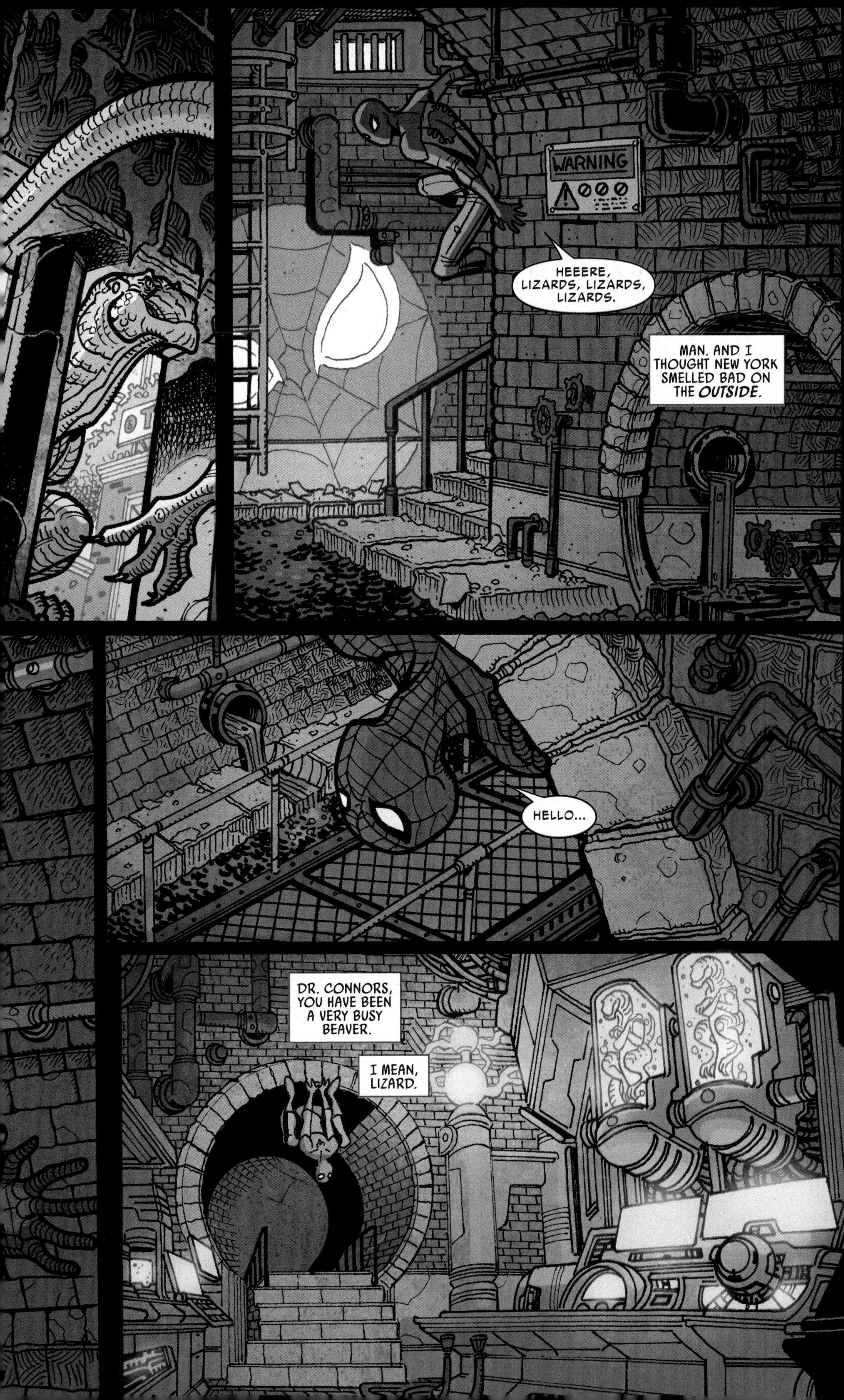
WARNING
HEEERE, LIZARDS, LIZARDS, LIZARDS.
MAN. AND I THOUGHT NEW YORK SMELLED BAD ON THE *OUTSIDE.*
HELLO...
DR. CONNORS, YOU HAVE BEEN A VERY BUSY BEAVER.
I MEAN, LIZARD.

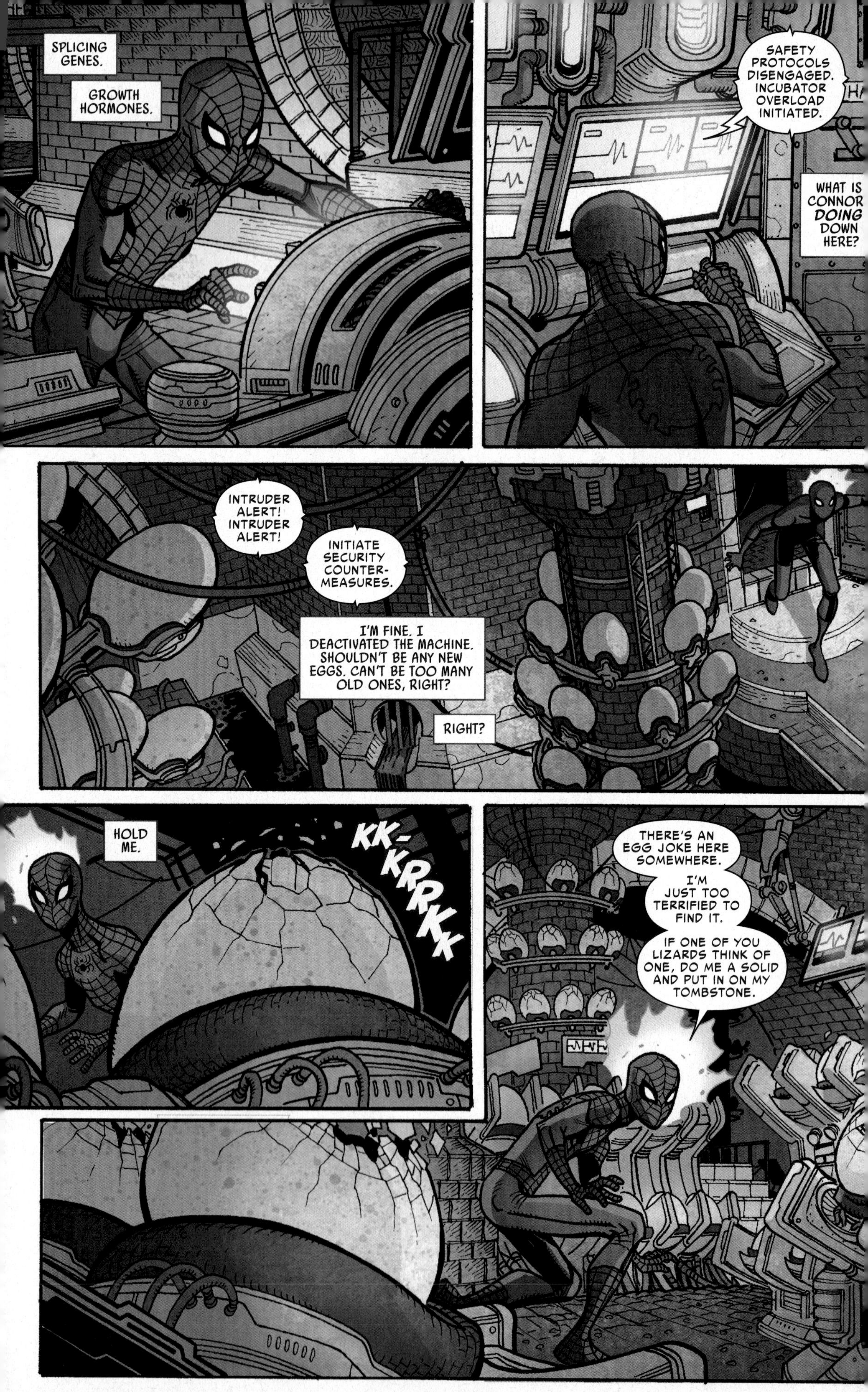

SPLICING GENES.
GROWTH HORMONES.
SAFETY PROTOCOLS DISENGAGED. INCUBATOR OVERLOAD INITIATED.
WHAT IS CONNOR DOING DOWN HERE?
INTRUDER ALERT! INTRUDER ALERT!
INITIATE SECURITY COUNTER-MEASURES.
I'M FINE. I DEACTIVATED THE MACHINE. SHOULDN'T BE ANY NEW EGGS. CAN'T BE TOO MANY OLD ONES, RIGHT?
RIGHT?
HOLD ME.
KK-KRRKK
THERE'S AN EGG JOKE HERE SOMEWHERE.
I'M JUST TOO TERRIFIED TO FIND IT.
IF ONE OF YOU LIZARDS THINK OF ONE, DO ME A SOLID AND PUT IN ON MY TOMBSTONE.

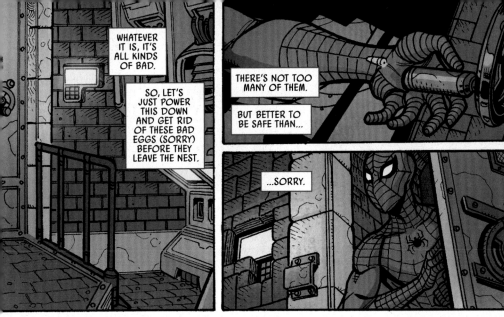

WHATEVER IT IS, IT'S ALL KINDS OF BAD.

SO, LET'S JUST POWER THIS DOWN AND GET RID OF THESE BAD EGGS (SORRY) BEFORE THEY LEAVE THE NEST.

THERE'S NOT TOO MANY OF THEM.

BUT BETTER TO BE SAFE THAN...

...SORRY.

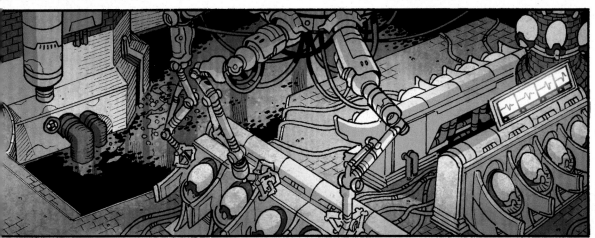

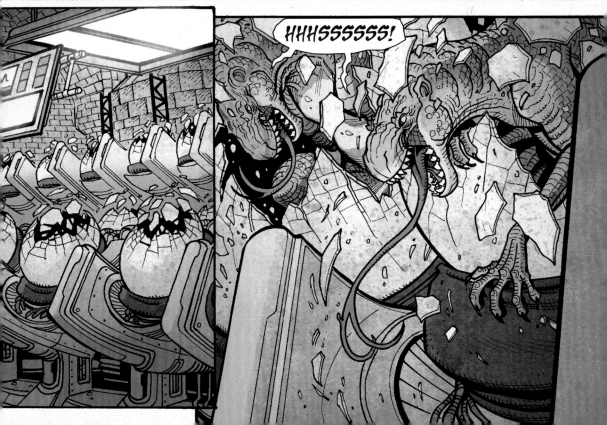

HHHSSSSSS!

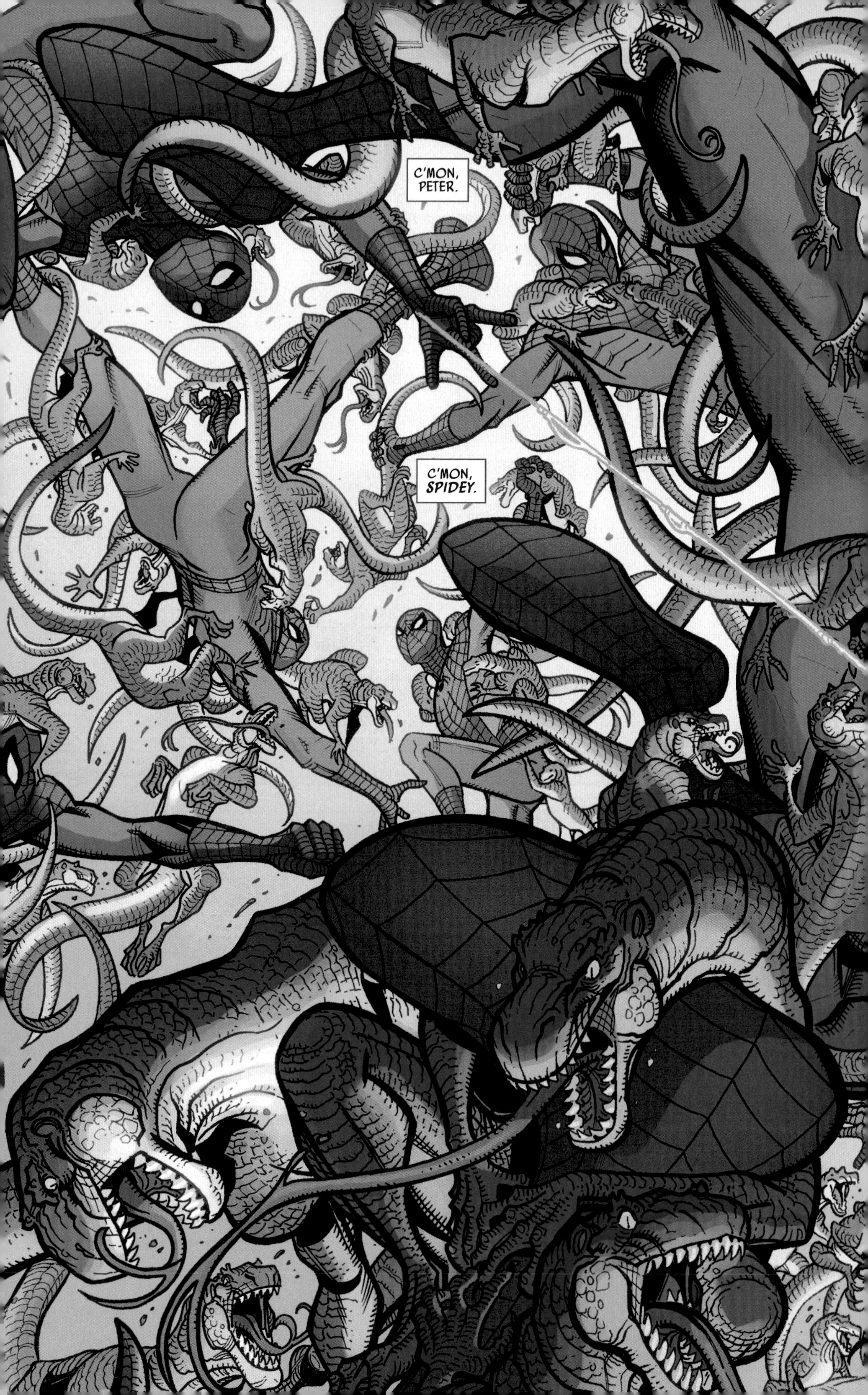
C'MON, PETER.
C'MON, SPIDEY.

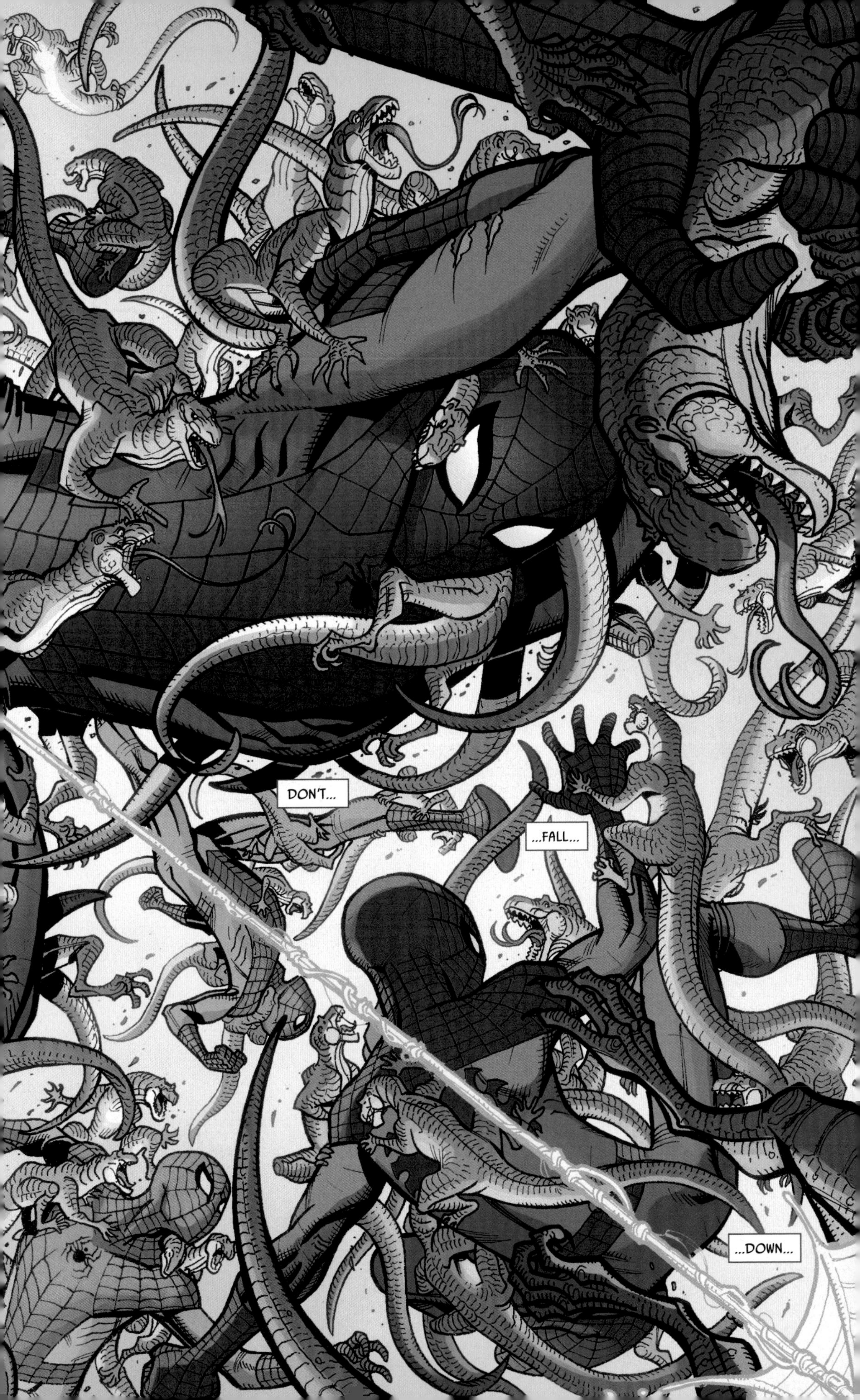
DON'T...
...FALL...
...DOWN...

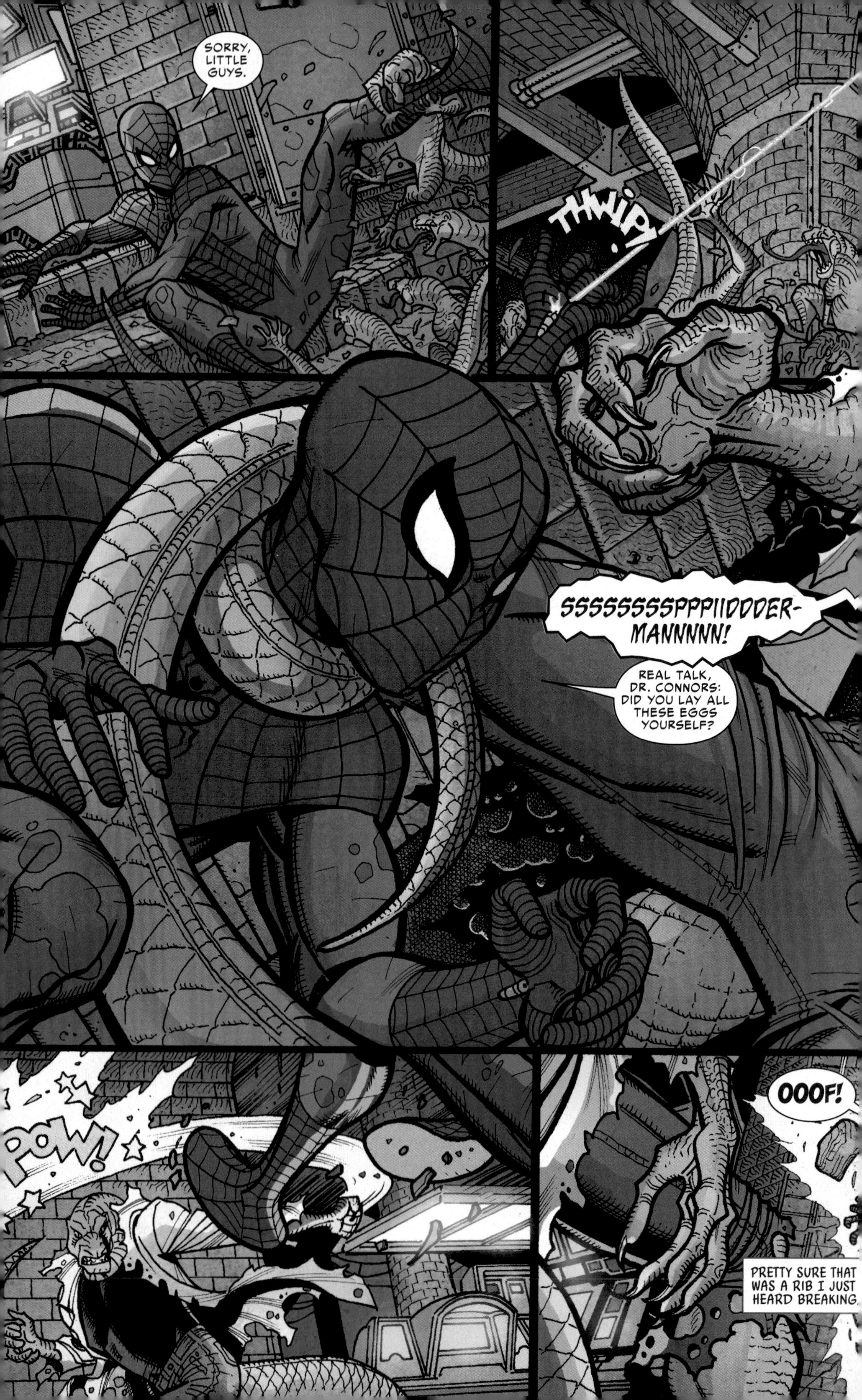
SORRY, LITTLE GUYS.
THWIP!
SSSSSSSSPPPIIDDDER-MANNNNN!
REAL TALK, DR. CONNORS: DID YOU LAY ALL THESE EGGS YOURSELF?
POW!
OOOF!
PRETTY SURE THAT WAS A RIB I JUST HEARD BREAKING.

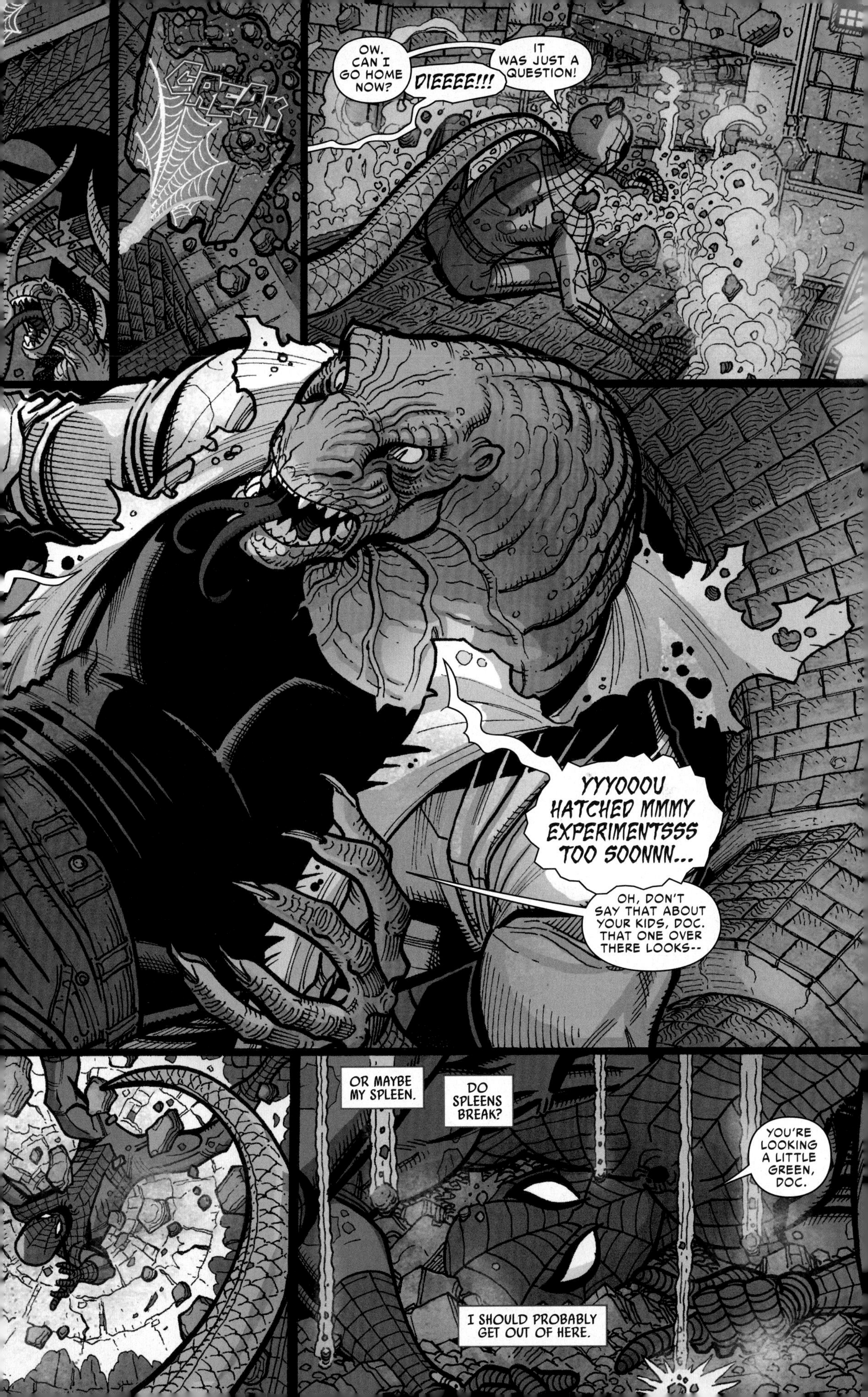
CREAK
OW. CAN I GO HOME NOW?
DIEEEE!!!
IT WAS JUST A QUESTION!
YYYOOOU HATCHED MMMY EXPERIMENTSSS TOO SOONNN...
OH, DON'T SAY THAT ABOUT YOUR KIDS, DOC. THAT ONE OVER THERE LOOKS--
OR MAYBE MY SPLEEN.
DO SPLEENS BREAK?
YOU'RE LOOKING A LITTLE GREEN, DOC.
I SHOULD PROBABLY GET OUT OF HERE.

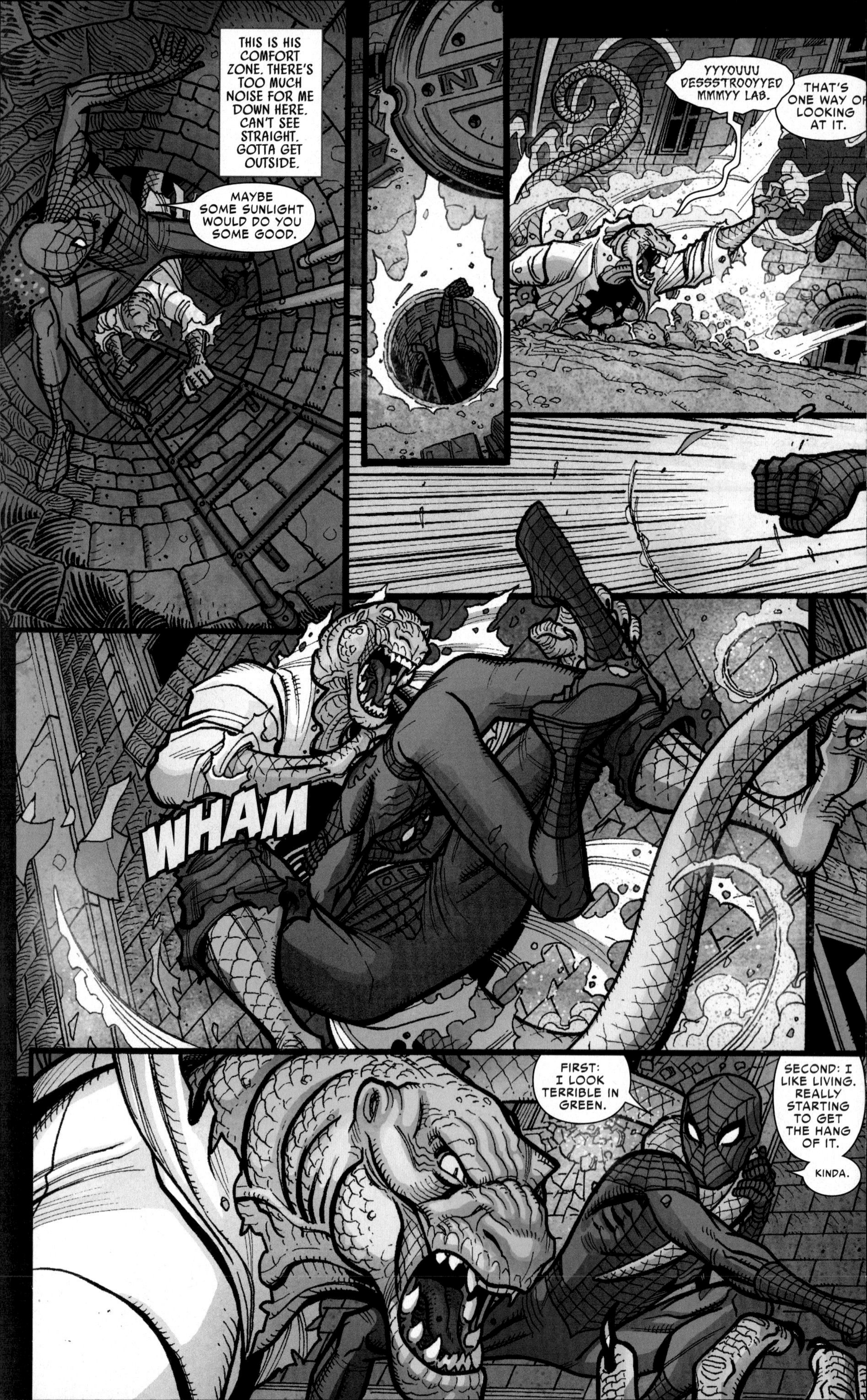
THIS IS HIS COMFORT ZONE. THERE'S TOO MUCH NOISE FOR ME DOWN HERE. CAN'T SEE STRAIGHT. GOTTA GET OUTSIDE.
MAYBE SOME SUNLIGHT WOULD DO YOU SOME GOOD.
YYYOUUU DESSSTROOYYED MMMYY LAB.
THAT'S ONE WAY OF LOOKING AT IT.
WHAM
FIRST: I LOOK TERRIBLE IN GREEN.
SECOND: I LIKE LIVING. REALLY STARTING TO GET THE HANG OF IT.
KINDA.

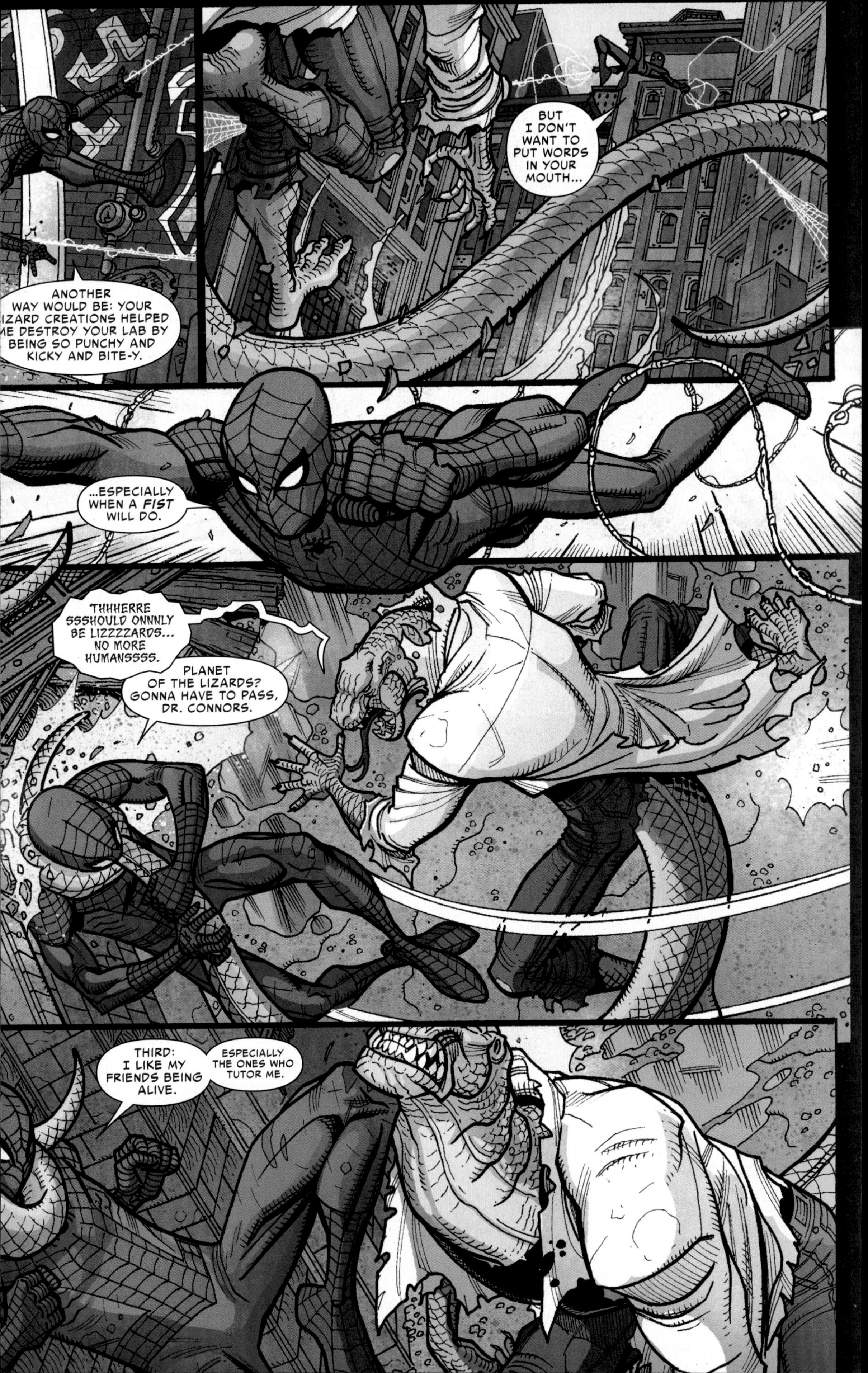
BUT I DON'T WANT TO PUT WORDS IN YOUR MOUTH...
ANOTHER WAY WOULD BE: YOUR LIZARD CREATIONS HELPED ME DESTROY YOUR LAB BY BEING SO PUNCHY AND KICKY AND BITE-Y.
...ESPECIALLY WHEN A FIST WILL DO.
THHHERRE SSSHOULD ONNNLY BE LIZZZZARDS... NO MORE HUMANSSSS.
PLANET OF THE LIZARDS? GONNA HAVE TO PASS, DR. CONNORS.
THIRD: I LIKE MY FRIENDS BEING ALIVE.
ESPECIALLY THE ONES WHO TUTOR ME.

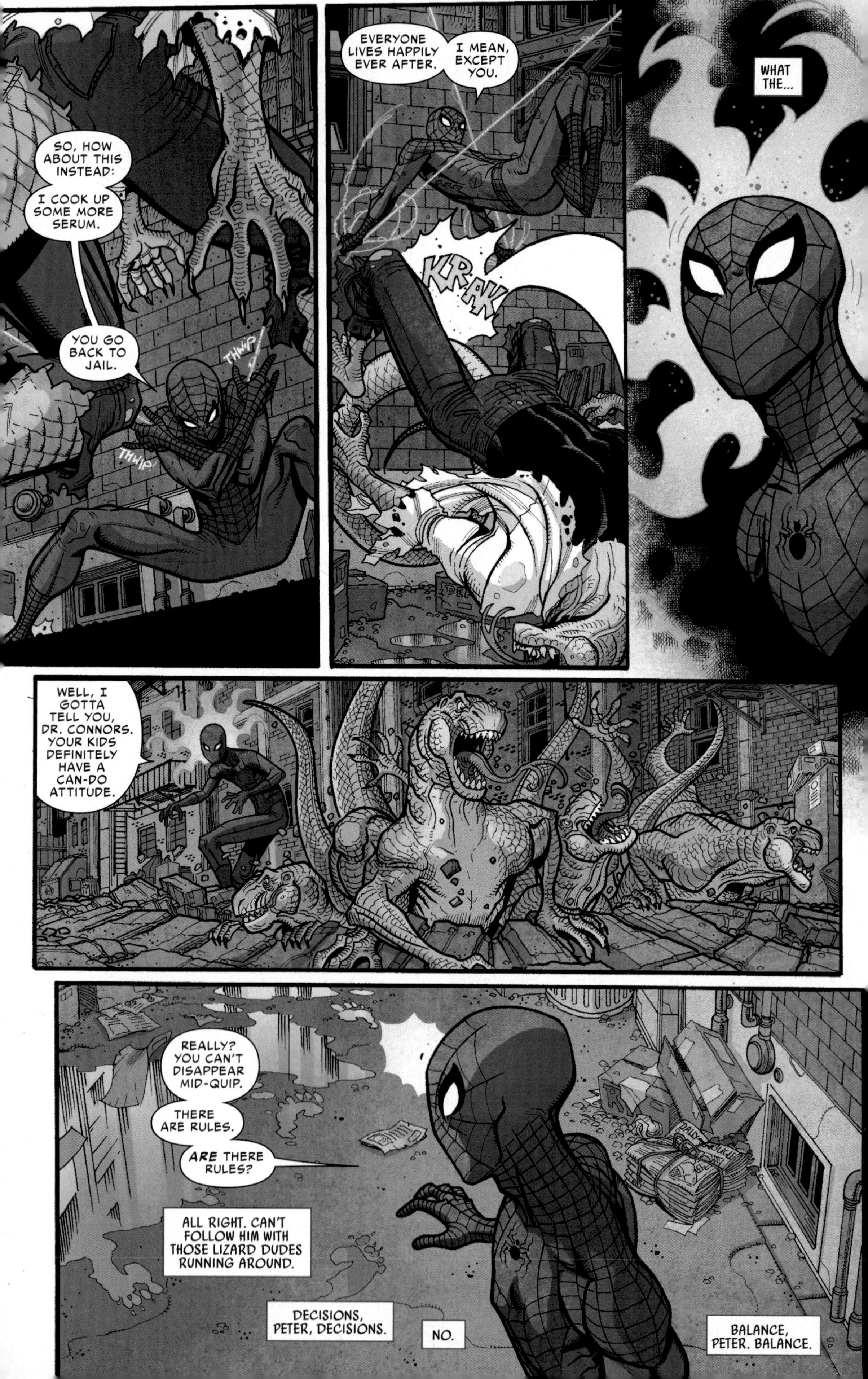
SO, HOW ABOUT THIS INSTEAD:
I COOK UP SOME MORE SERUM.
YOU GO BACK TO JAIL.
THWIP
THWIP!
EVERYONE LIVES HAPPILY EVER AFTER.
I MEAN, EXCEPT YOU.
KRAK
WHAT THE...
WELL, I GOTTA TELL YOU, DR. CONNORS. YOUR KIDS DEFINITELY HAVE A CAN-DO ATTITUDE.
REALLY? YOU CAN'T DISAPPEAR MID-QUIP.
THERE ARE RULES.
ARE THERE RULES?
ALL RIGHT. CAN'T FOLLOW HIM WITH THOSE LIZARD DUDES RUNNING AROUND.
DECISIONS, PETER, DECISIONS.
NO.
BALANCE, PETER. BALANCE.

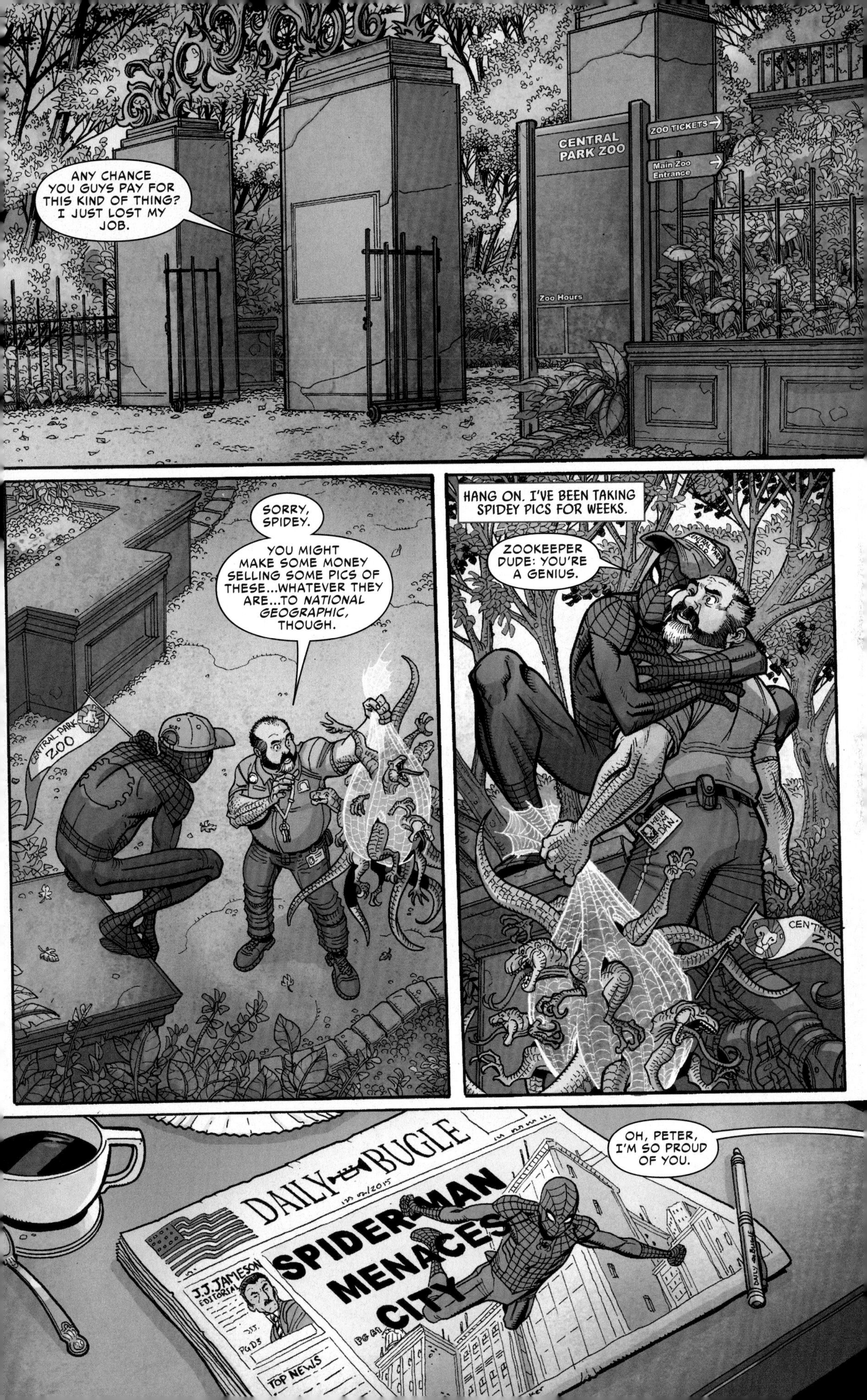
CENTRAL PARK ZOO
ZOO TICKETS
Main Zoo Entrance
Zoo Hours
ANY CHANCE YOU GUYS PAY FOR THIS KIND OF THING? I JUST LOST MY JOB.
SORRY, SPIDEY.
YOU MIGHT MAKE SOME MONEY SELLING SOME PICS OF THESE...WHATEVER THEY ARE...TO NATIONAL GEOGRAPHIC, THOUGH.
CENTRAL PARK ZOO
HANG ON. I'VE BEEN TAKING SPIDEY PICS FOR WEEKS.
ZOOKEEPER DUDE: YOU'RE A GENIUS.
CENTRAL ZOO
DAILY BUGLE
SPIDER-MAN MENACES CITY
J.J. JAMESON EDITORIAL
TOP NEWS
OH, PETER, I'M SO PROUD OF YOU.

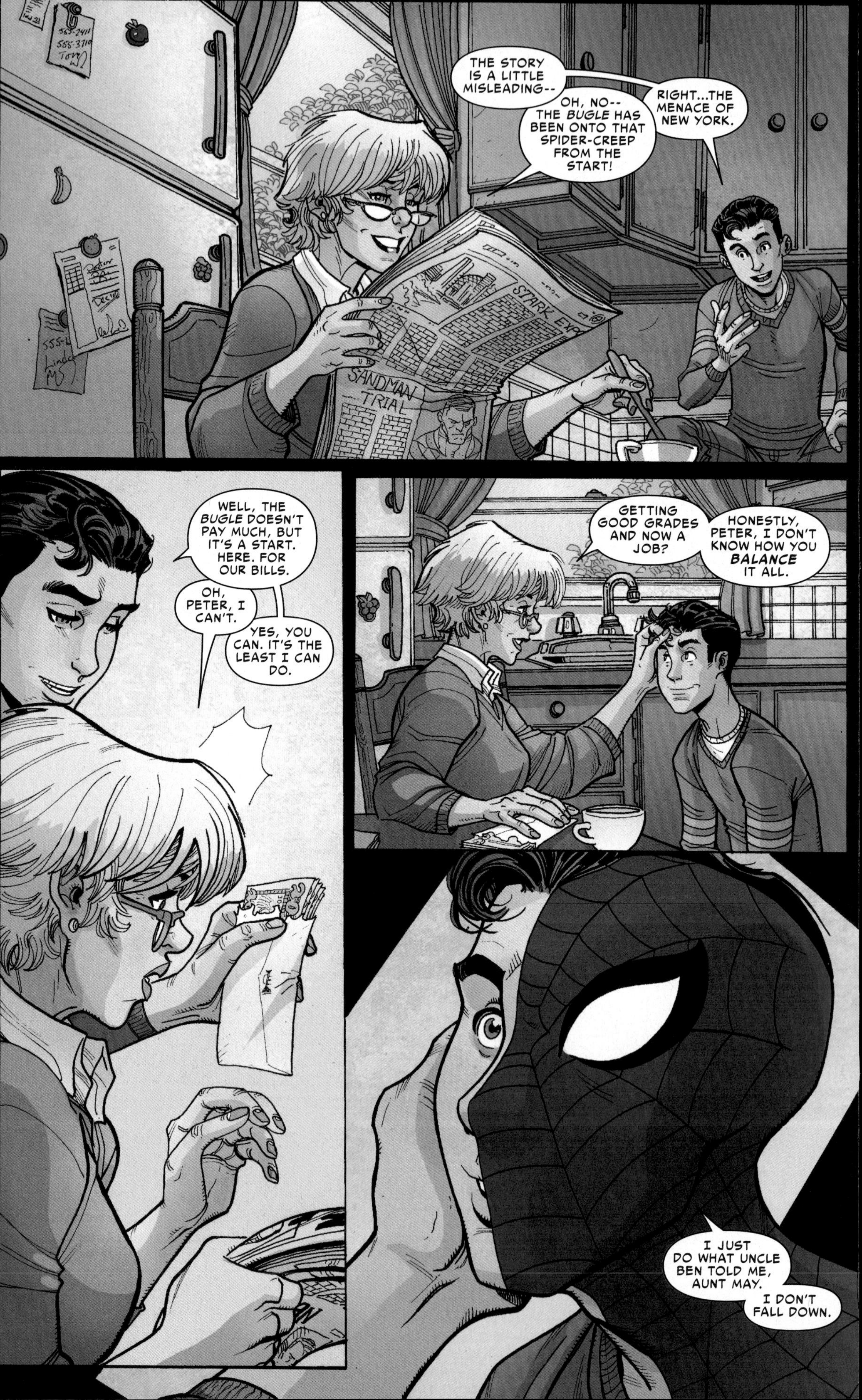
THE STORY IS A LITTLE MISLEADING--
OH, NO-- THE BUGLE HAS BEEN ONTO THAT SPIDER-CREEP FROM THE START!
RIGHT...THE MENACE OF NEW YORK.
SANDMAN TRIAL
STARK EXPO
WELL, THE BUGLE DOESN'T PAY MUCH, BUT IT'S A START. HERE. FOR OUR BILLS.
OH, PETER, I CAN'T.
YES, YOU CAN. IT'S THE LEAST I CAN DO.
GETTING GOOD GRADES AND NOW A JOB?
HONESTLY, PETER, I DON'T KNOW HOW YOU BALANCE IT ALL.
I JUST DO WHAT UNCLE BEN TOLD ME, AUNT MAY.
I DON'T FALL DOWN.

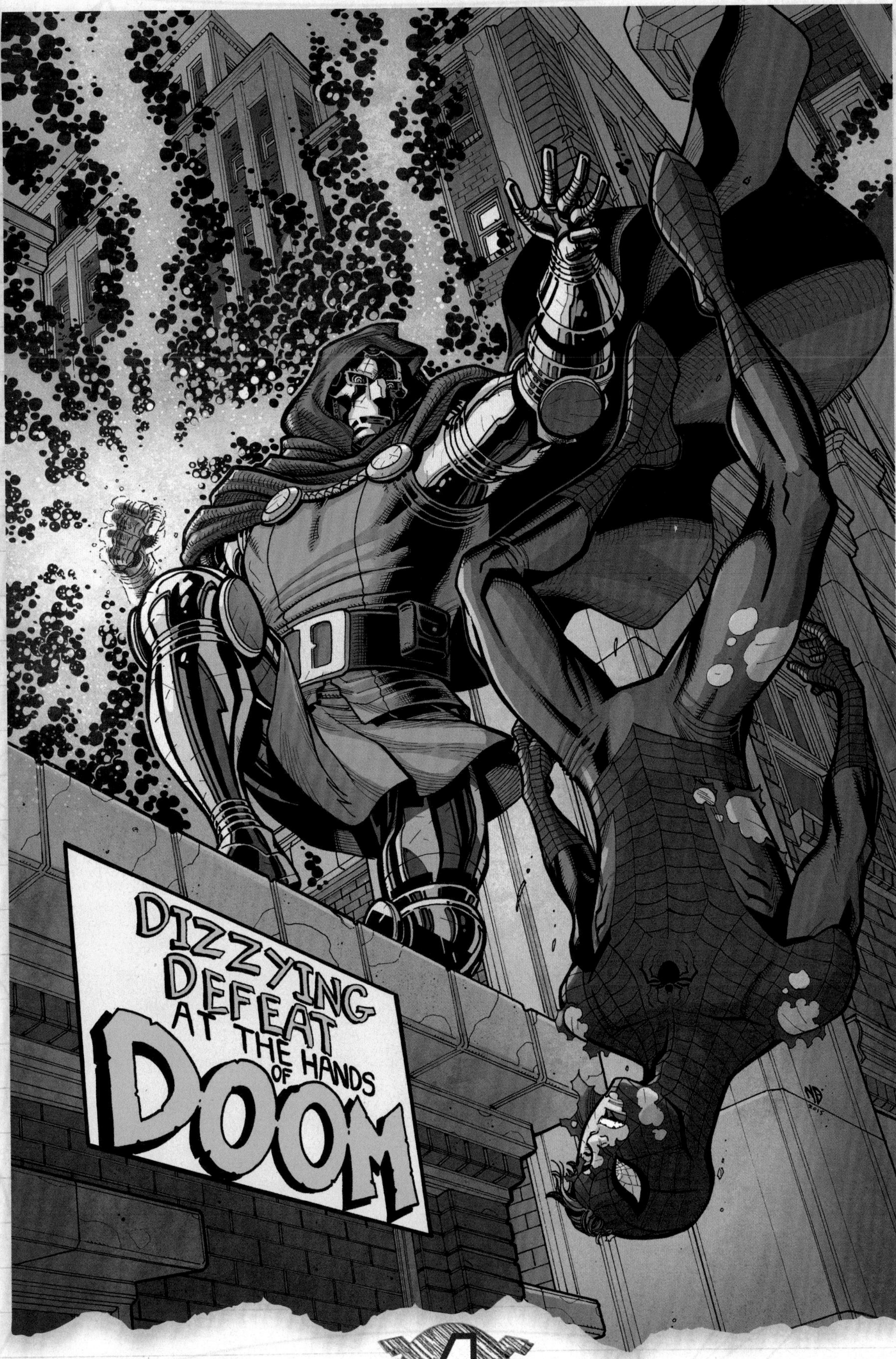
DIZZYING DEFEAT AT THE HANDS OF DOOM

4

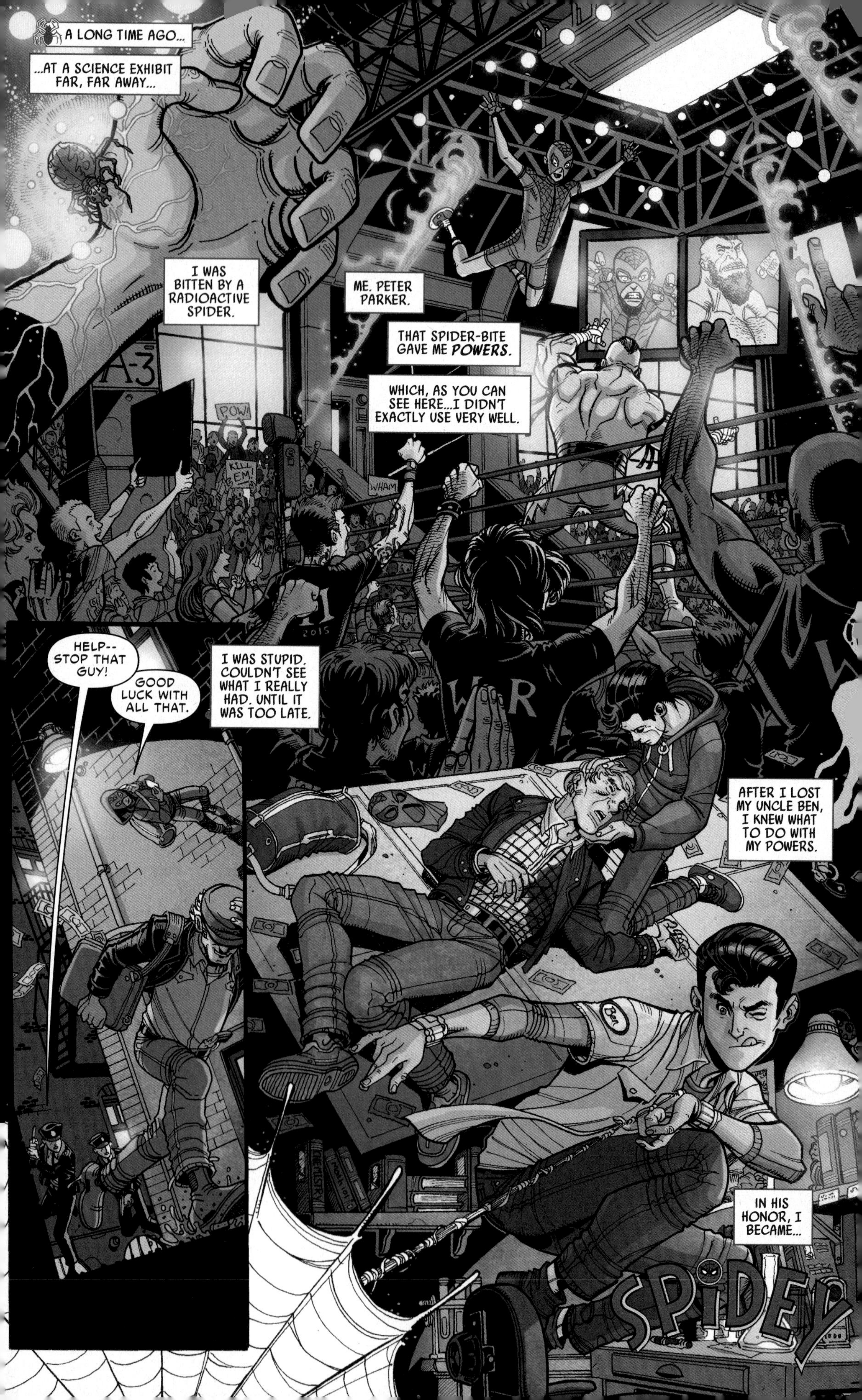
A LONG TIME AGO...
...AT A SCIENCE EXHIBIT FAR, FAR AWAY...
I WAS BITTEN BY A RADIOACTIVE SPIDER.
ME. PETER PARKER.
THAT SPIDER-BITE GAVE ME POWERS.
WHICH, AS YOU CAN SEE HERE...I DIDN'T EXACTLY USE VERY WELL.
POW!
KILL 'EM!
WHAM
HELP-- STOP THAT GUY!
GOOD LUCK WITH ALL THAT.
I WAS STUPID. COULDN'T SEE WHAT I REALLY HAD. UNTIL IT WAS TOO LATE.
AFTER I LOST MY UNCLE BEN, I KNEW WHAT TO DO WITH MY POWERS.
IN HIS HONOR, I BECAME...
SPIDEY

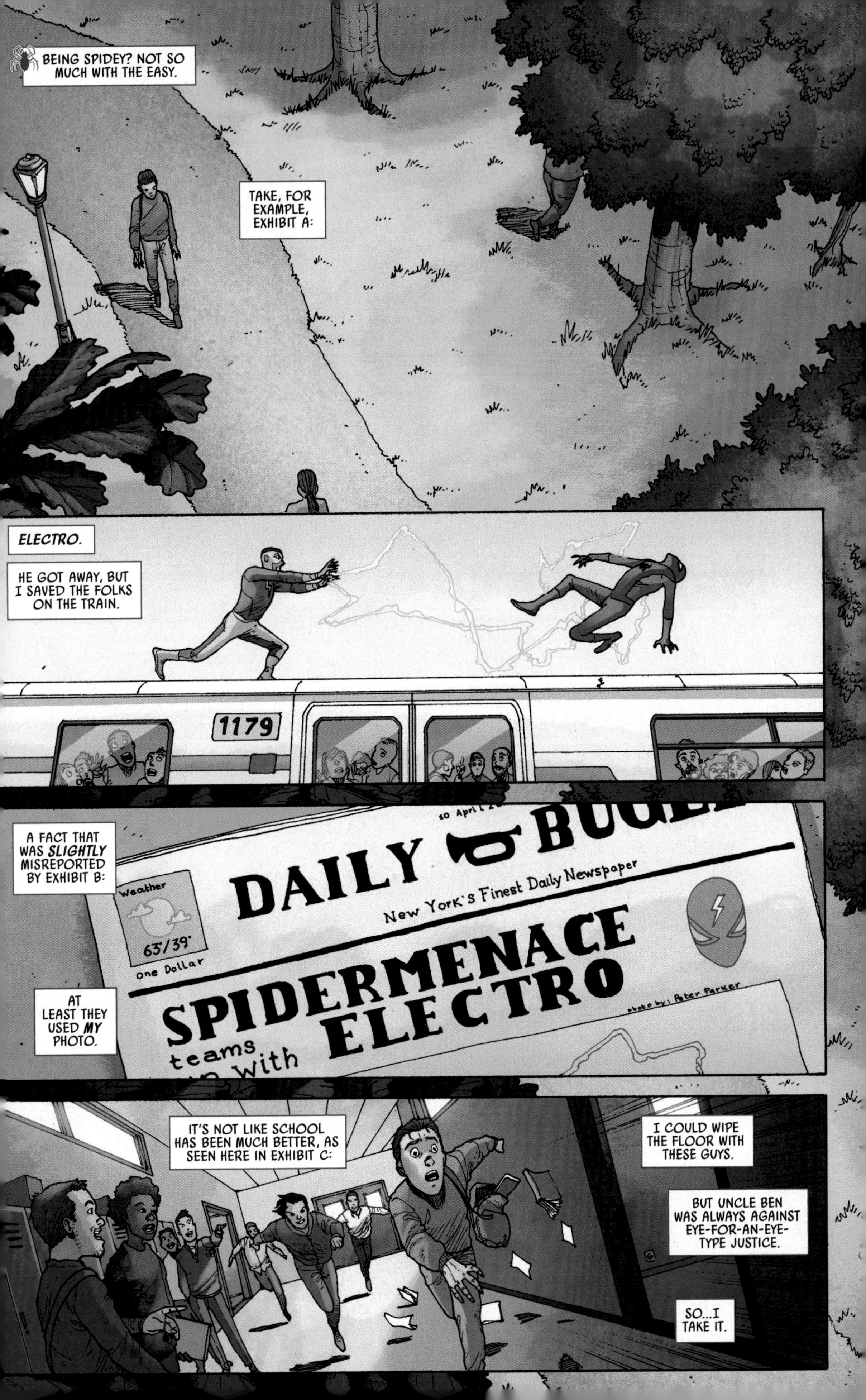
BEING SPIDEY? NOT SO MUCH WITH THE EASY.
TAKE, FOR EXAMPLE, EXHIBIT A:
ELECTRO.
HE GOT AWAY, BUT I SAVED THE FOLKS ON THE TRAIN.
1179
A FACT THAT WAS SLIGHTLY MISREPORTED BY EXHIBIT B:
DAILY BUGLE
New York's Finest Daily Newspaper
Weather
63/39°
One Dollar
SPIDERMENACE teams up with ELECTRO
photo by: Peter Parker
AT LEAST THEY USED MY PHOTO.
IT'S NOT LIKE SCHOOL HAS BEEN MUCH BETTER, AS SEEN HERE IN EXHIBIT C:
I COULD WIPE THE FLOOR WITH THESE GUYS.
BUT UNCLE BEN WAS ALWAYS AGAINST EYE-FOR-AN-EYE-TYPE JUSTICE.
SO...I TAKE IT.

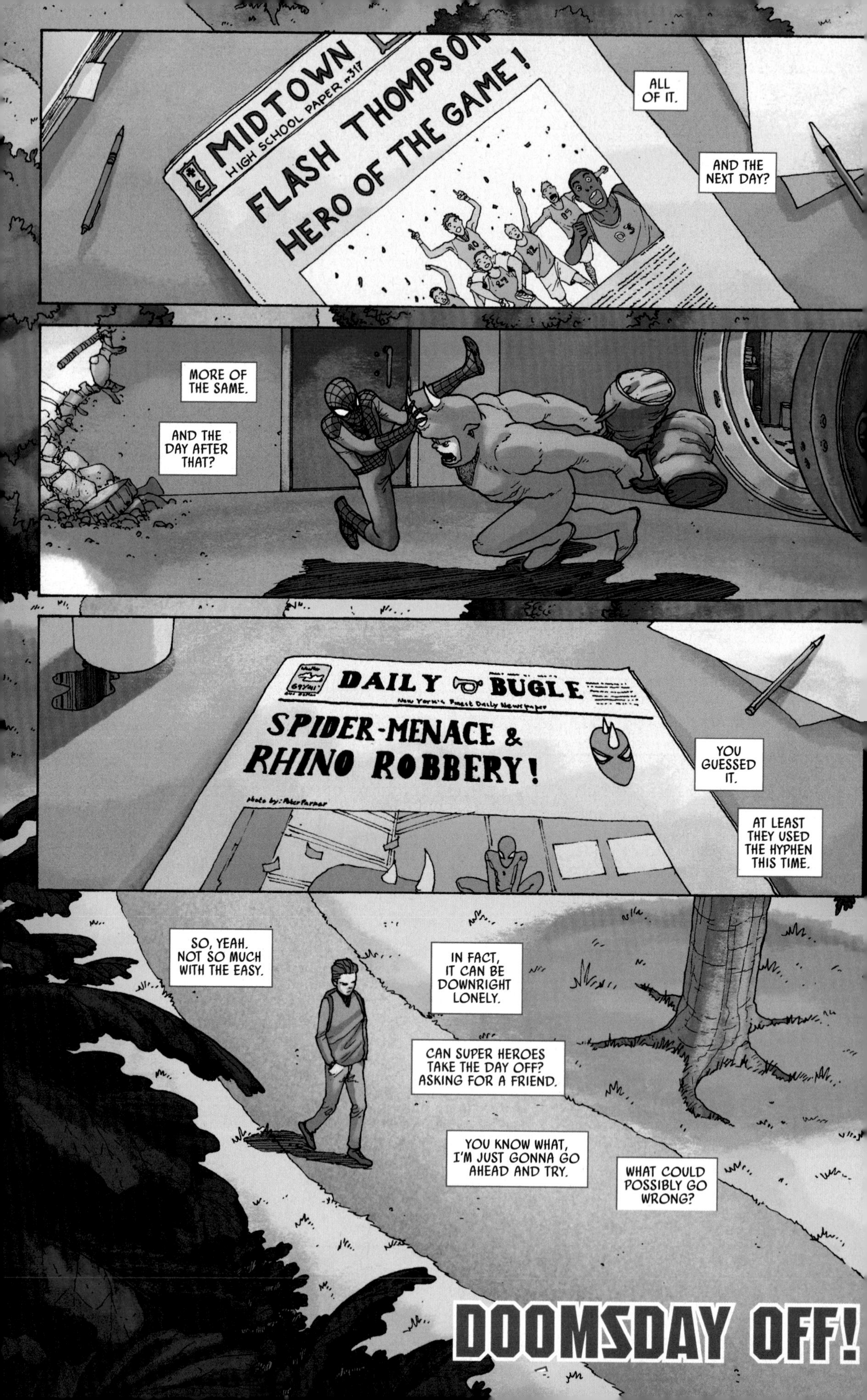
MIDTOWN
HIGH SCHOOL PAPER #317
FLASH THOMPSON HERO OF THE GAME!
ALL OF IT.
AND THE NEXT DAY?
MORE OF THE SAME.
AND THE DAY AFTER THAT?
DAILY BUGLE
SPIDER-MENACE & RHINO ROBBERY!
YOU GUESSED IT.
AT LEAST THEY USED THE HYPHEN THIS TIME.
SO, YEAH. NOT SO MUCH WITH THE EASY.
IN FACT, IT CAN BE DOWNRIGHT LONELY.
CAN SUPER HEROES TAKE THE DAY OFF? ASKING FOR A FRIEND.
YOU KNOW WHAT, I'M JUST GONNA GO AHEAD AND TRY.
WHAT COULD POSSIBLY GO WRONG?
DOOMSDAY OFF!

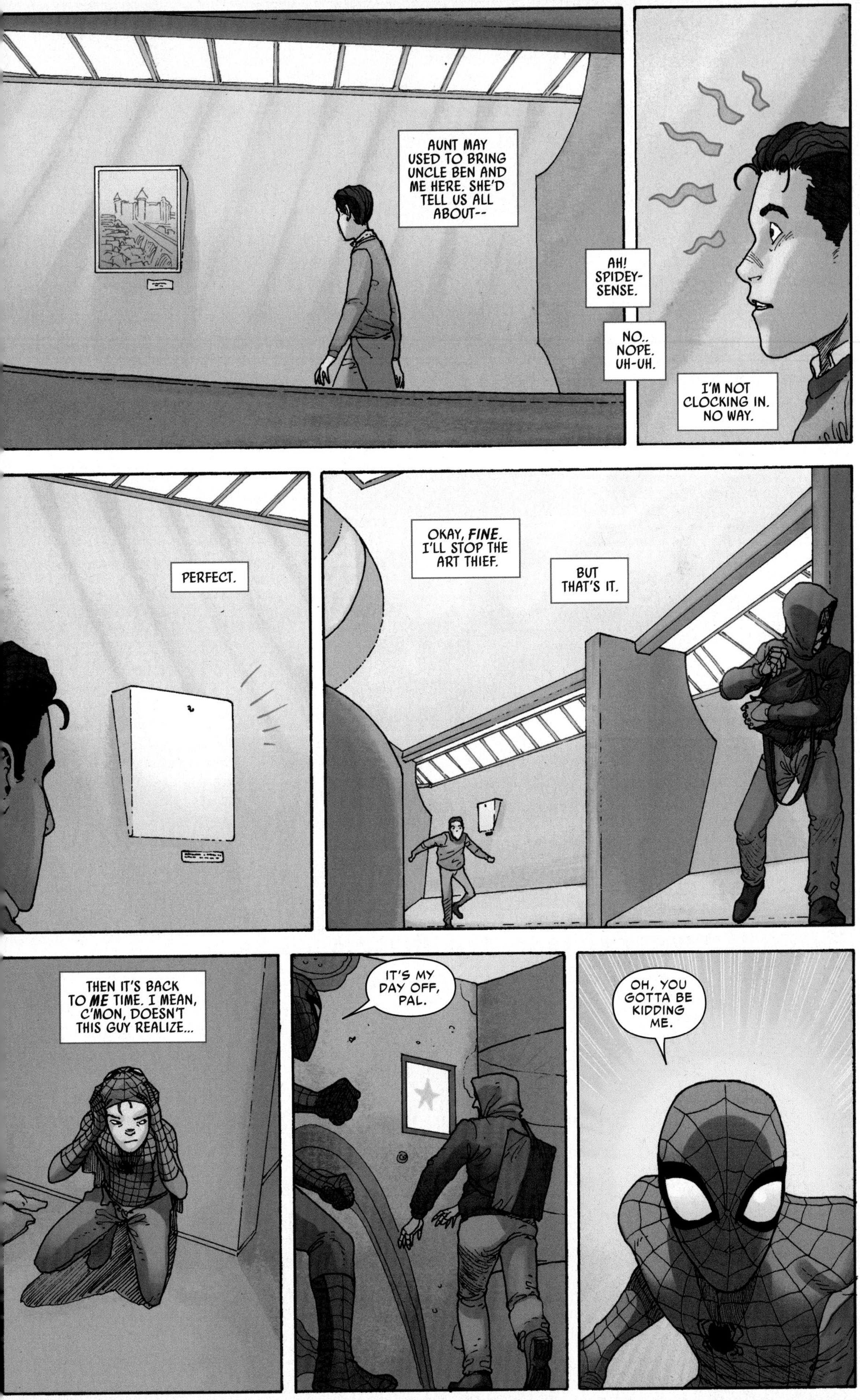
AUNT MAY USED TO BRING UNCLE BEN AND ME HERE. SHE'D TELL US ALL ABOUT--
AH! SPIDEY-SENSE.
NO.. NOPE. UH-UH.
I'M NOT CLOCKING IN. NO WAY.
PERFECT.
OKAY, FINE. I'LL STOP THE ART THIEF.
BUT THAT'S IT.
THEN IT'S BACK TO ME TIME. I MEAN, C'MON, DOESN'T THIS GUY REALIZE...
IT'S MY DAY OFF, PAL.
OH, YOU GOTTA BE KIDDING ME.

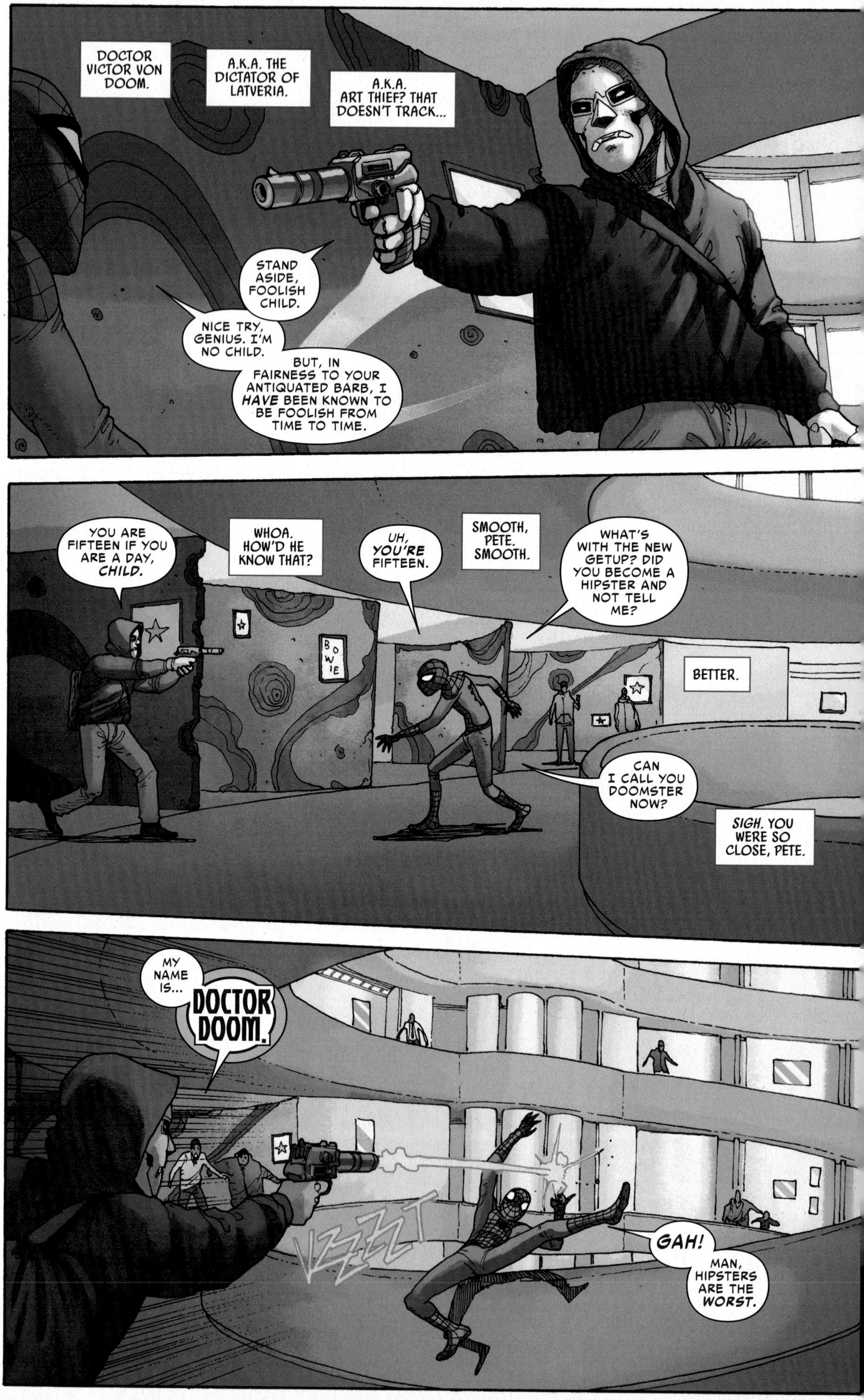
DOCTOR VICTOR VON DOOM.
A.K.A. THE DICTATOR OF LATVERIA.
A.K.A. ART THIEF? THAT DOESN'T TRACK...
STAND ASIDE, FOOLISH CHILD.
NICE TRY, GENIUS. I'M NO CHILD.
BUT, IN FAIRNESS TO YOUR ANTIQUATED BARB, I *HAVE* BEEN KNOWN TO BE FOOLISH FROM TIME TO TIME.
YOU ARE FIFTEEN IF YOU ARE A DAY, *CHILD*.
WHOA. HOW'D HE KNOW THAT?
UH, *YOU'RE* FIFTEEN.
SMOOTH, PETE. SMOOTH.
WHAT'S WITH THE NEW GETUP? DID YOU BECOME A HIPSTER AND NOT TELL ME?
BETTER.
CAN I CALL YOU DOOMSTER NOW?
SIGH. YOU WERE SO CLOSE, PETE.
MY NAME IS... DOCTOR DOOM.
VZZZZT
GAH!
MAN, HIPSTERS ARE THE *WORST*.

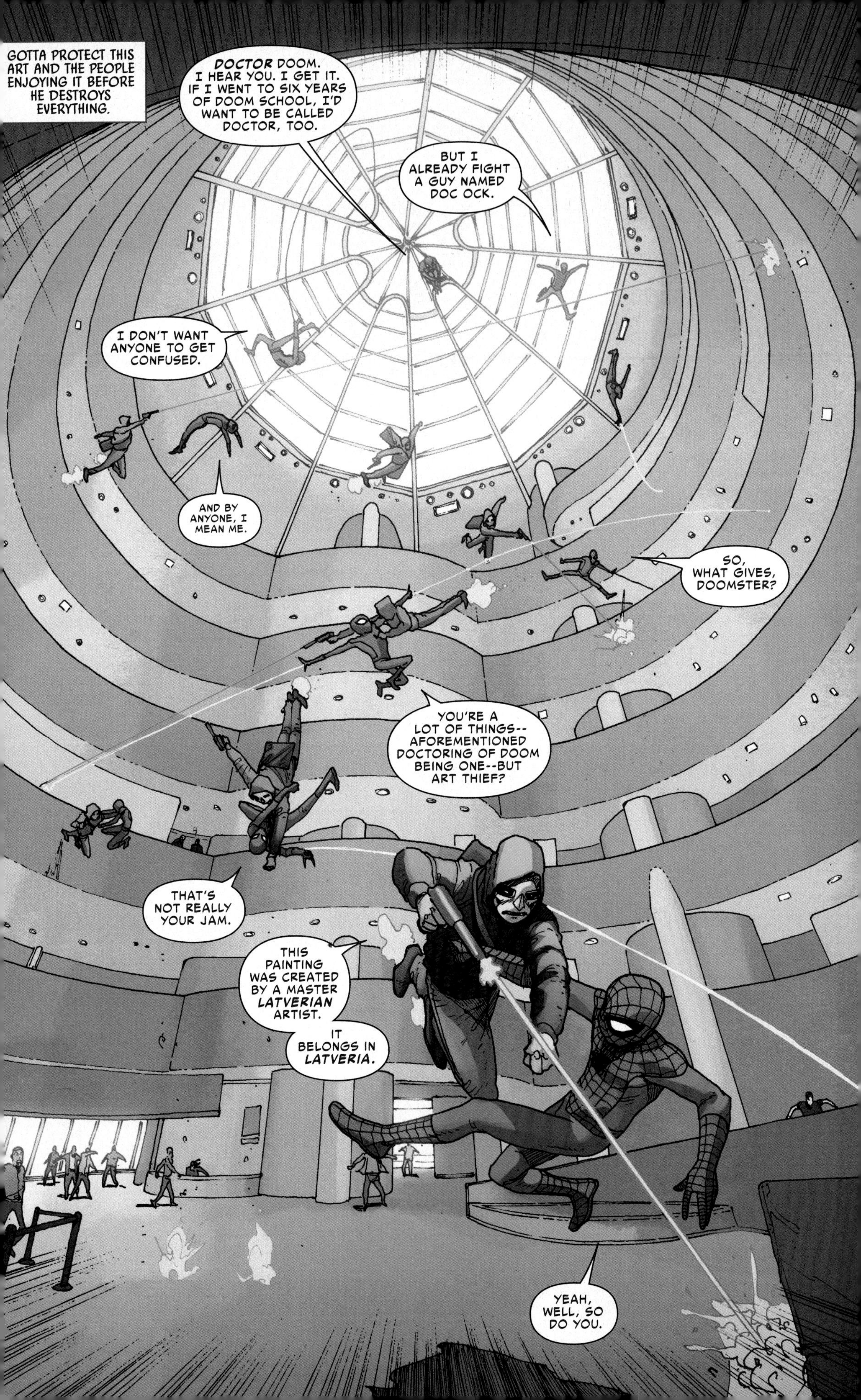
GOTTA PROTECT THIS ART AND THE PEOPLE ENJOYING IT BEFORE HE DESTROYS EVERYTHING.
DOCTOR DOOM. I HEAR YOU. I GET IT. IF I WENT TO SIX YEARS OF DOOM SCHOOL, I'D WANT TO BE CALLED DOCTOR, TOO.
BUT I ALREADY FIGHT A GUY NAMED DOC OCK.
I DON'T WANT ANYONE TO GET CONFUSED.
AND BY ANYONE, I MEAN ME.
SO, WHAT GIVES, DOOMSTER?
YOU'RE A LOT OF THINGS-- AFOREMENTIONED DOCTORING OF DOOM BEING ONE--BUT ART THIEF?
THAT'S NOT REALLY YOUR JAM.
THIS PAINTING WAS CREATED BY A MASTER LATVERIAN ARTIST.
IT BELONGS IN LATVERIA.
YEAH, WELL, SO DO YOU.

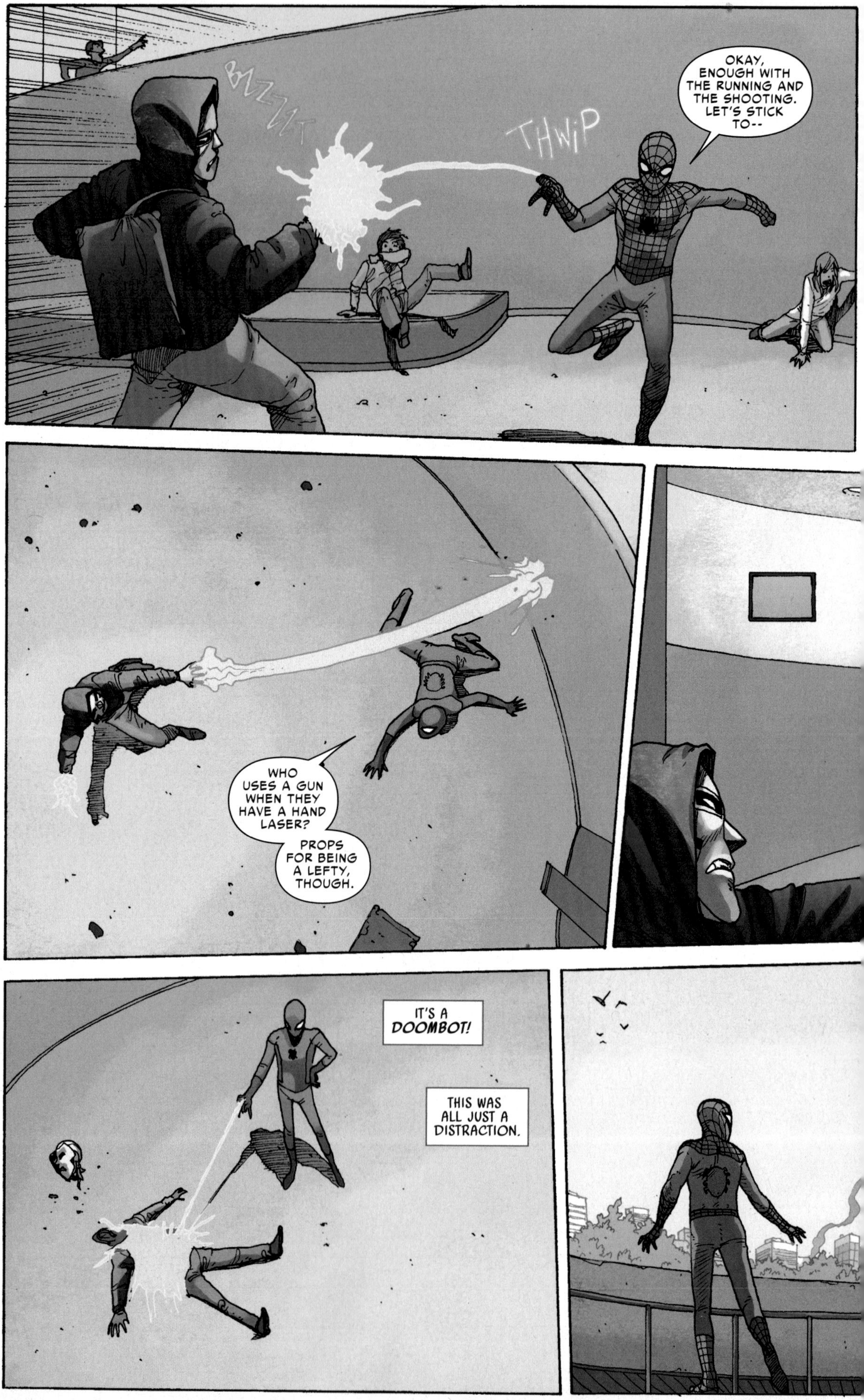
BAZZZZT
THWIP
OKAY, ENOUGH WITH THE RUNNING AND THE SHOOTING. LET'S STICK TO--
WHO USES A GUN WHEN THEY HAVE A HAND LASER?
PROPS FOR BEING A LEFTY, THOUGH.
IT'S A *DOOMBOT!*
THIS WAS ALL JUST A DISTRACTION.

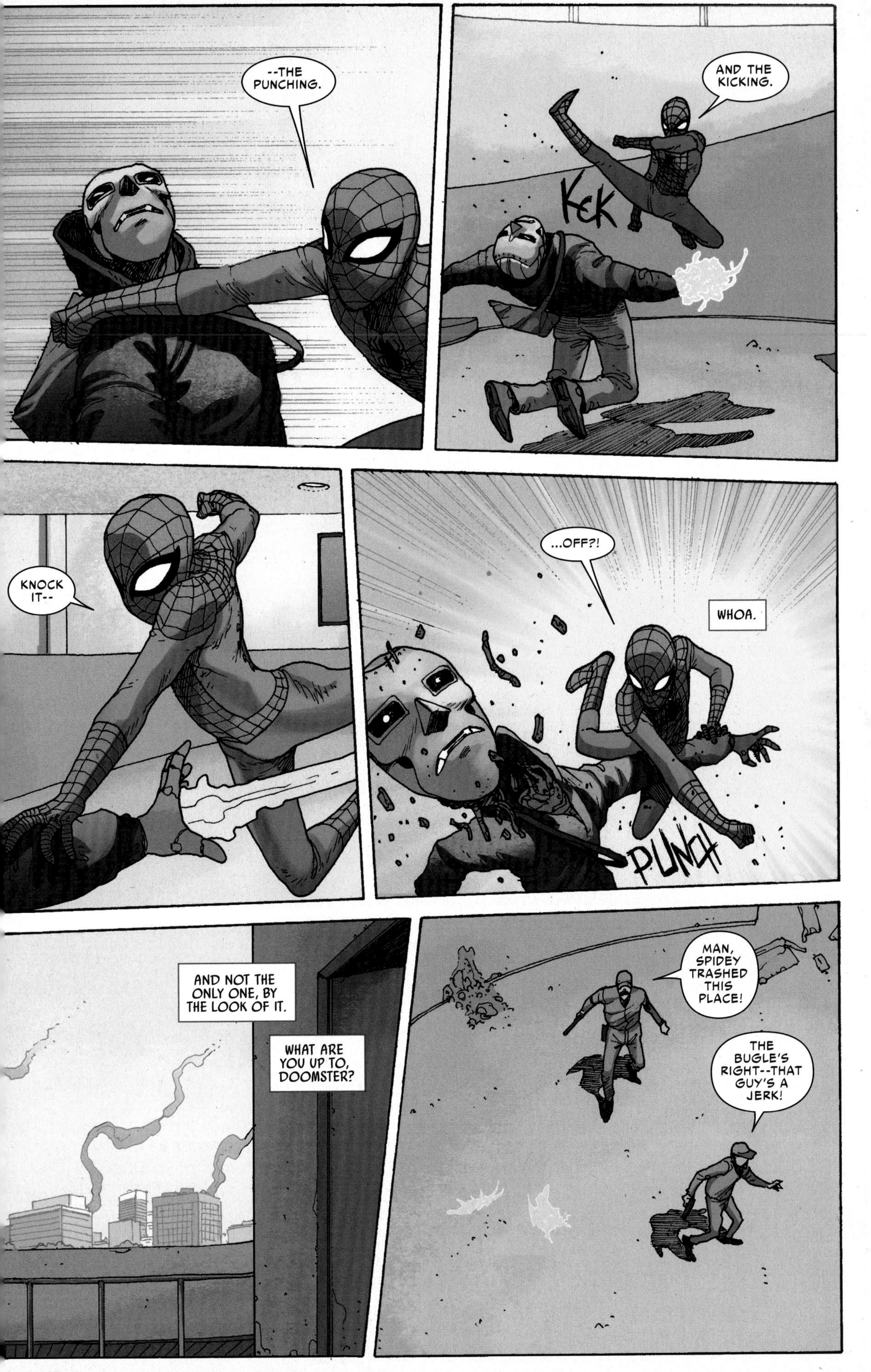
--THE PUNCHING.
AND THE KICKING.
KICK
KNOCK IT--
...OFF?!
WHOA.
PUNCH
AND NOT THE ONLY ONE, BY THE LOOK OF IT.
WHAT ARE YOU UP TO, DOOMSTER?
MAN, SPIDEY TRASHED THIS PLACE!
THE BUGLE'S RIGHT--THAT GUY'S A JERK!

I NEED EYES. LIKE... EVERYWHERE.

HERE WE GO.

CEBULSKI'S TVs

THE BEST TVS IN AMERICA

COMIC

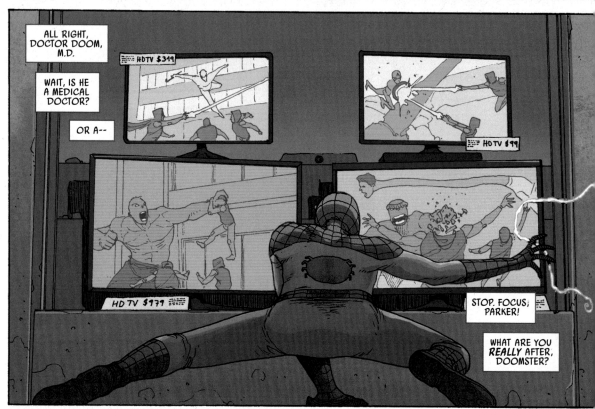

ALL RIGHT, DOCTOR DOOM, M.D.

WAIT, IS HE A MEDICAL DOCTOR?

OR A--

HDTV $349

HDTV $199

HD TV $979

STOP. FOCUS, PARKER!

WHAT ARE YOU *REALLY* AFTER, DOOMSTER?

POWER.

NEWS UPDATE: POWER OUTAGE IN BROOKLYN. NEWS U

I'M BETTING IT'S LESS "POWER OUTAGE" AND MORE POWER THEFT-AGE.

THAT'S MORE DOOM'S STYLE.

AND YES, I KNOW THEFT-AGE ISN'T A THING. NEITHER IS DOOMSTER. WORK WITH ME, PEOPLE!

HDTV $979

SO DOOM IS STEALING POWER. WHY?

ONE WAY TO FIND OUT...

--THE POWER IS OUT AND THE PLANT HAS GONE INTO LOCKDOWN MODE--

--SOURCES ARE TELLING ME THEY'RE LOOKING FOR A MANUAL OVERRIDE BUT--

PLEASE LET THERE BE NO RADIATION. PLEASE LET THERE BE NO RADIATION. PLEASE LET THERE BE NO RADIATION. PLEASE LET THERE BE NO --

BINGO.

LIGHT AT THE END OF THE HOPEFULLY-NOT-RADIOACTIVE TUNNEL.

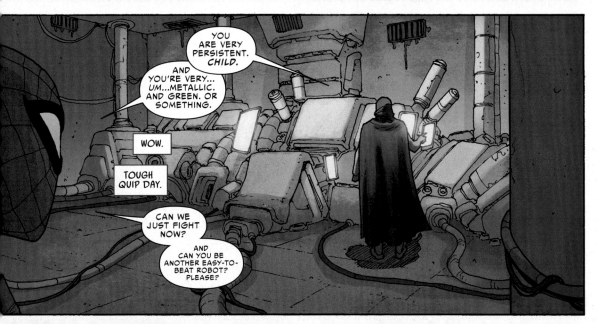

YOU ARE VERY PERSISTENT, CHILD.

AND YOU'RE VERY... UM...METALLIC. AND GREEN. OR SOMETHING.

WOW.

TOUGH QUIP DAY.

CAN WE JUST FIGHT NOW?

AND CAN YOU BE ANOTHER EASY-TO-BEAT ROBOT? PLEASE?

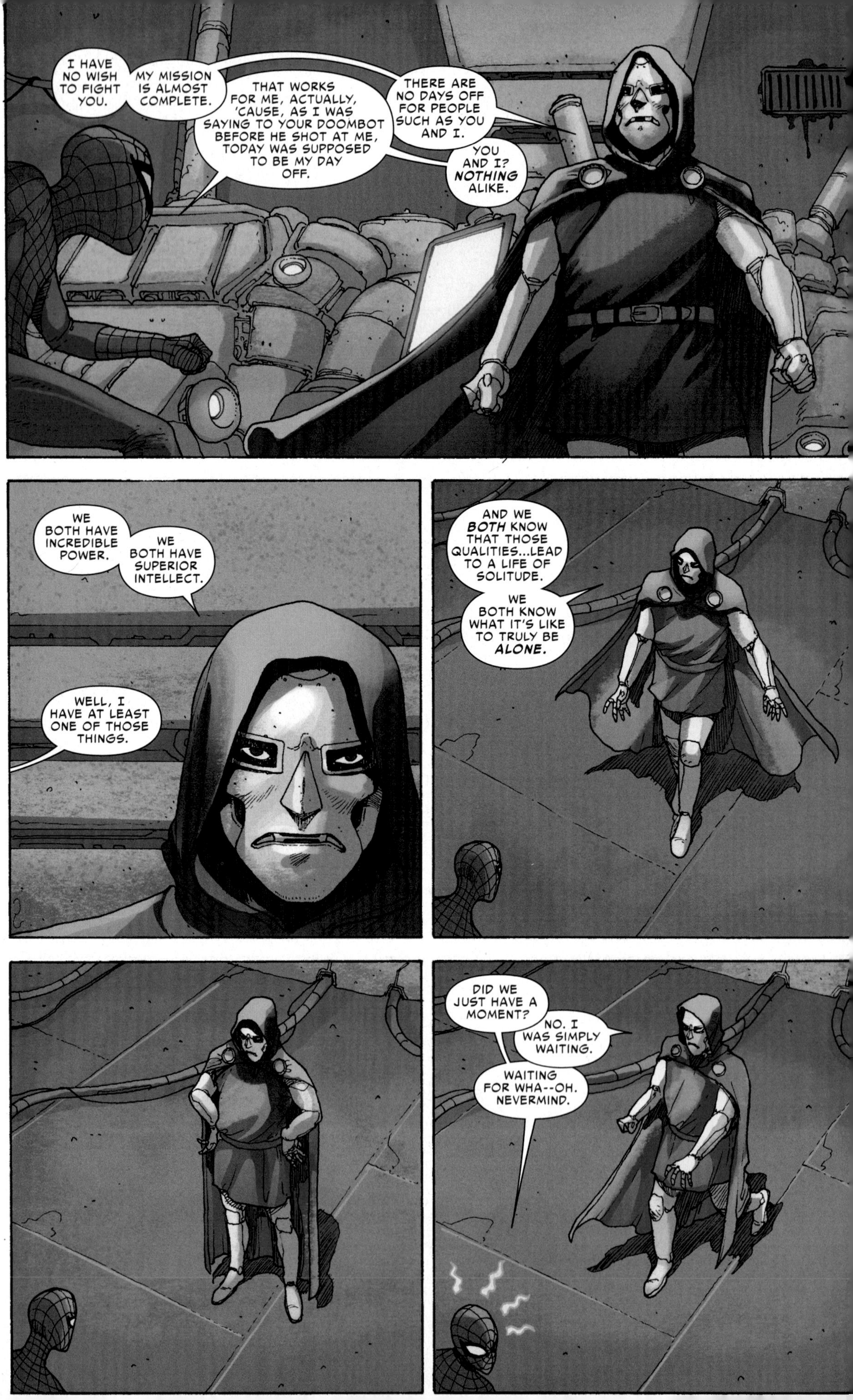
I HAVE NO WISH TO FIGHT YOU.
MY MISSION IS ALMOST COMPLETE.
THAT WORKS FOR ME, ACTUALLY, 'CAUSE, AS I WAS SAYING TO YOUR DOOMBOT BEFORE HE SHOT AT ME, TODAY WAS SUPPOSED TO BE MY DAY OFF.
THERE ARE NO DAYS OFF FOR PEOPLE SUCH AS YOU AND I.
YOU AND I? NOTHING ALIKE.
WE BOTH HAVE INCREDIBLE POWER.
WE BOTH HAVE SUPERIOR INTELLECT.
WELL, I HAVE AT LEAST ONE OF THOSE THINGS.
AND WE BOTH KNOW THAT THOSE QUALITIES...LEAD TO A LIFE OF SOLITUDE.
WE BOTH KNOW WHAT IT'S LIKE TO TRULY BE ALONE.
DID WE JUST HAVE A MOMENT?
NO. I WAS SIMPLY WAITING.
WAITING FOR WHA--OH. NEVERMIND.

I'M GUESSING YOUR WISH TO "NOT FIGHT ME" HAS BEEN REVOKED?
I WOULD NOT DEIGN TO FIGHT YOU, CHILD.
LOOK, I DON'T WANT TO TELL YOU HOW TO BE AN EVIL SOCIOPATH, BUT YOUR "ROCK 'EM, SOCK 'EM" BOTS NEED WORK. THEY ARE *WAY* TOO EASY TO--
PUNCH
GAH!
SCRATCH THAT. THESE ARE GREAT. THAT DEGREE IN DOOMOLOGY IS TOTALLY WORKING FOR YOU, DOOMSTER.
TOO MANY...
...GOTTA GET OUTTA HERE.
GOTTA--
KRATHOOM

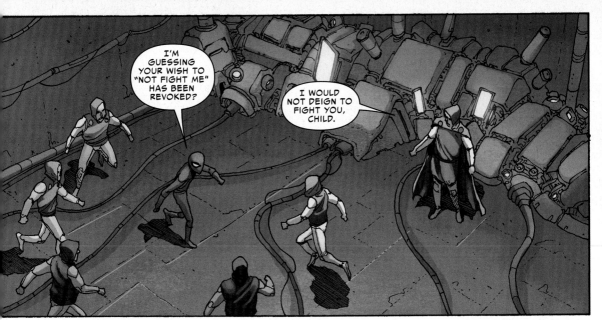

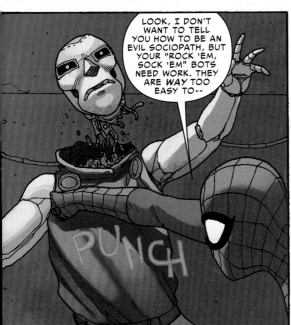

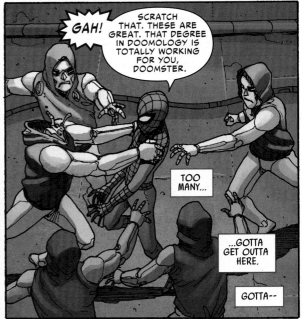

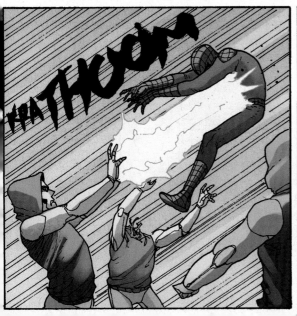

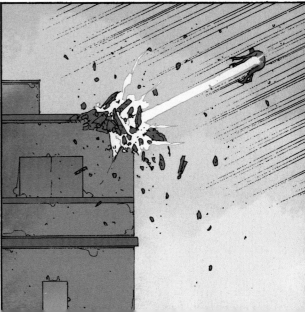

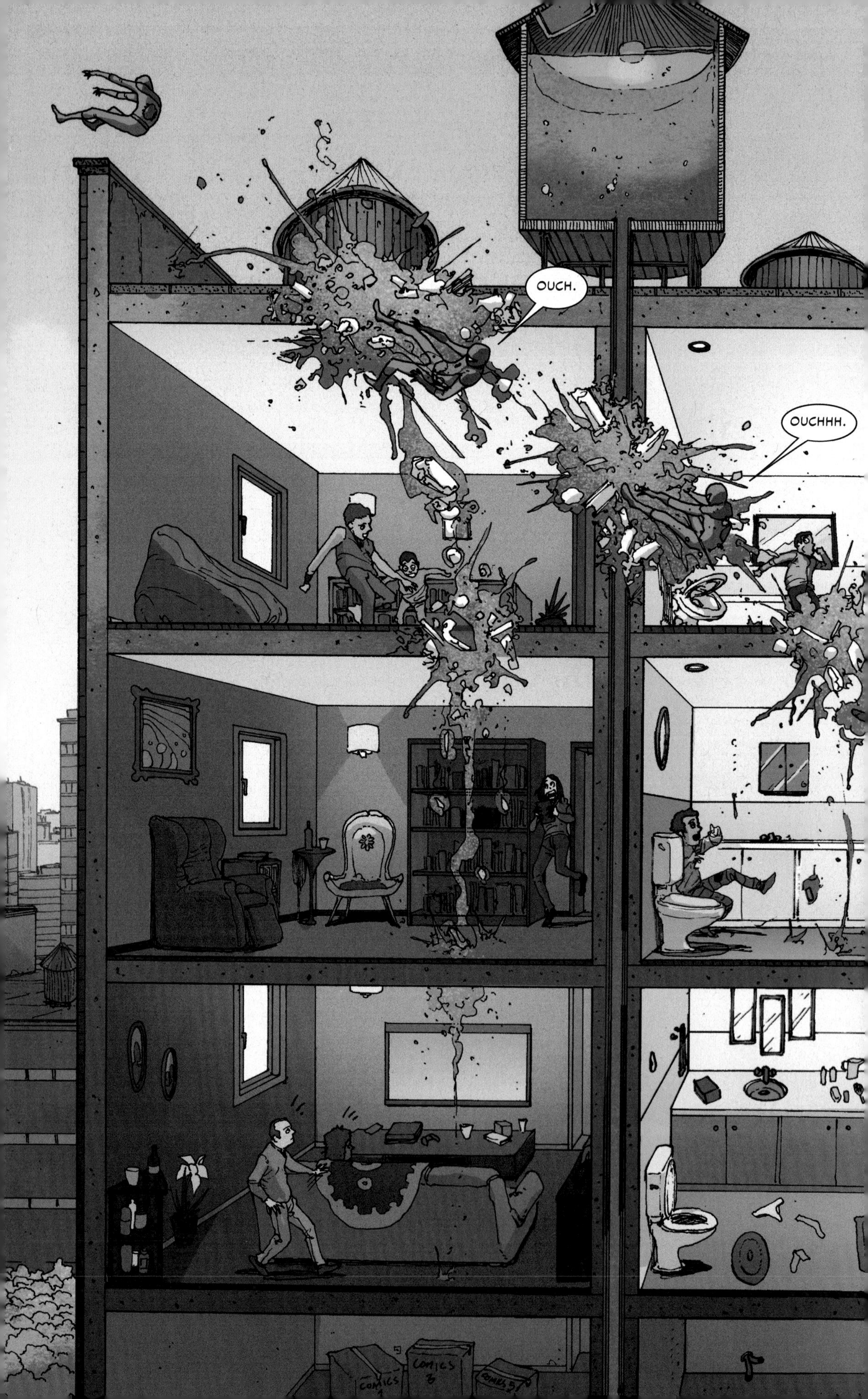
OUCH.
OUCHHH.

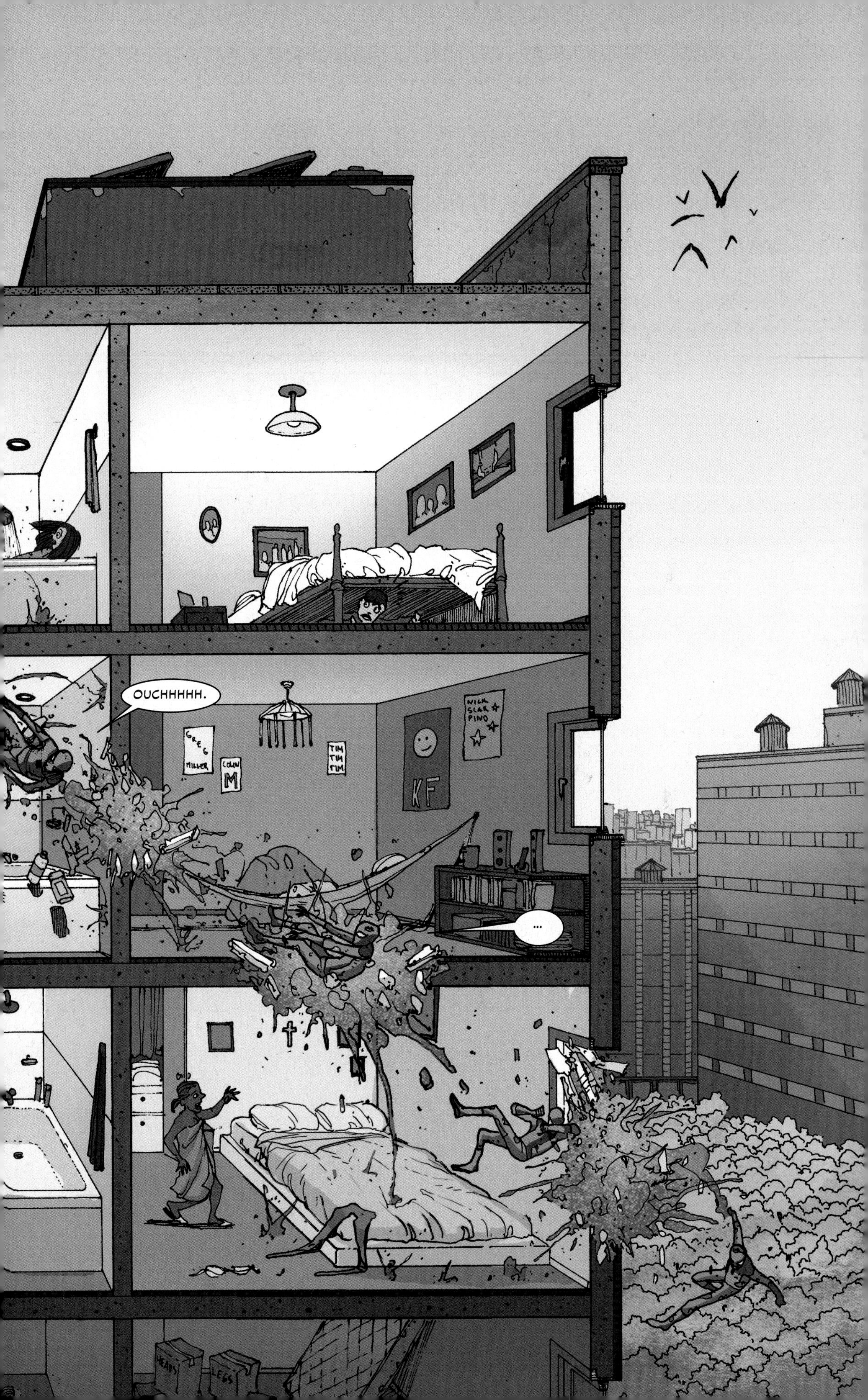
OUCHHHHH.
...

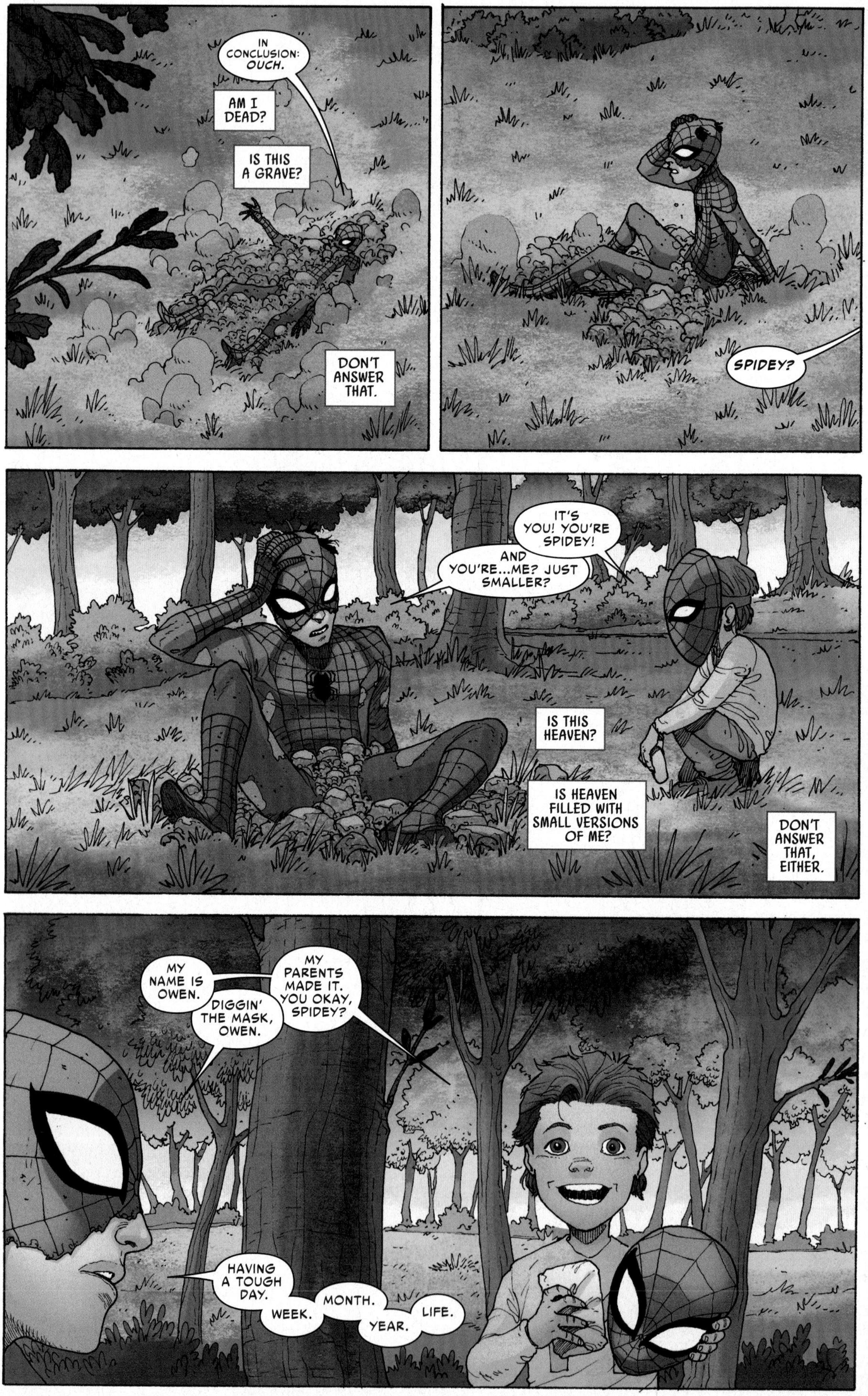
IN CONCLUSION: OUCH.
AM I DEAD?
IS THIS A GRAVE?
DON'T ANSWER THAT.
SPIDEY?
IT'S YOU! YOU'RE SPIDEY!
AND YOU'RE...ME? JUST SMALLER?
IS THIS HEAVEN?
IS HEAVEN FILLED WITH SMALL VERSIONS OF ME?
DON'T ANSWER THAT, EITHER.
MY NAME IS OWEN.
MY PARENTS MADE IT. YOU OKAY, SPIDEY?
DIGGIN' THE MASK, OWEN.
HAVING A TOUGH DAY.
WEEK.
MONTH.
YEAR.
LIFE.

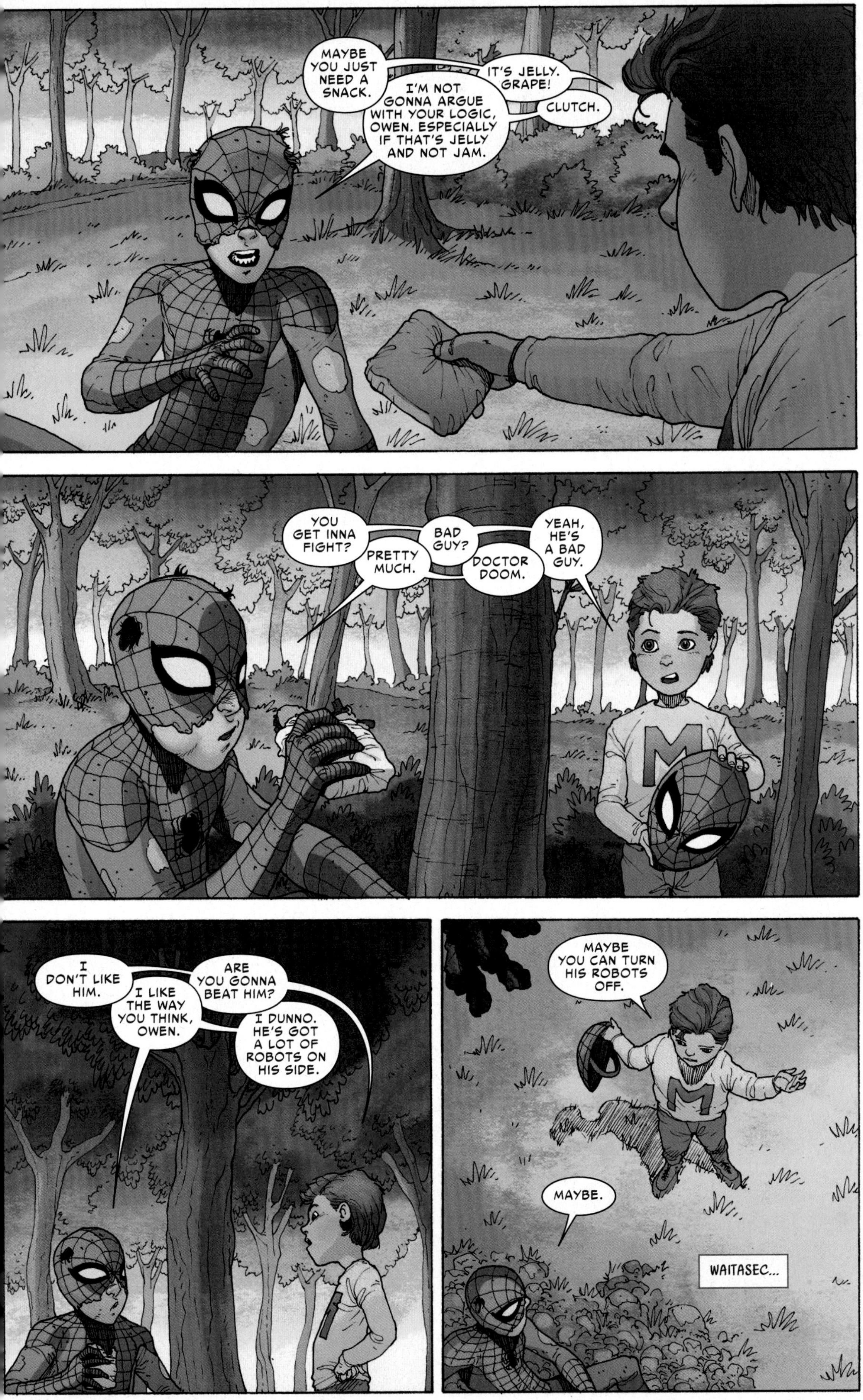

MAYBE YOU JUST NEED A SNACK.
IT'S JELLY. GRAPE!
I'M NOT GONNA ARGUE WITH YOUR LOGIC, OWEN. ESPECIALLY IF THAT'S JELLY AND NOT JAM.
CLUTCH.
YOU GET INNA FIGHT?
PRETTY MUCH.
BAD GUY?
DOCTOR DOOM.
YEAH, HE'S A BAD GUY.
I DON'T LIKE HIM.
I LIKE THE WAY YOU THINK, OWEN.
ARE YOU GONNA BEAT HIM?
I DUNNO. HE'S GOT A LOT OF ROBOTS ON HIS SIDE.
MAYBE YOU CAN TURN HIS ROBOTS OFF.
MAYBE.
WAITASEC...

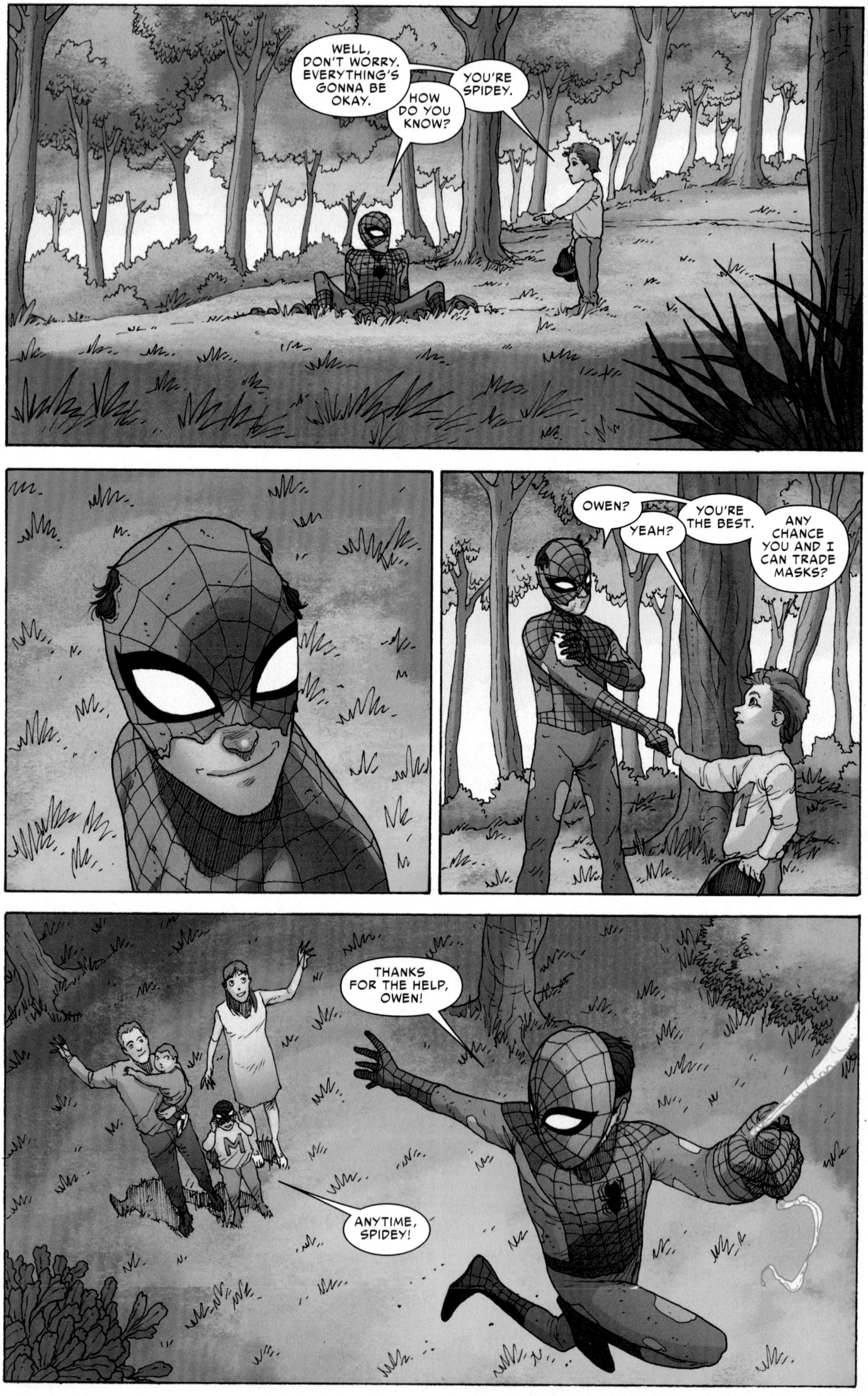
WELL, DON'T WORRY. EVERYTHING'S GONNA BE OKAY.
HOW DO YOU KNOW?
YOU'RE SPIDEY.
OWEN?
YEAH?
YOU'RE THE BEST.
ANY CHANCE YOU AND I CAN TRADE MASKS?
THANKS FOR THE HELP, OWEN!
ANYTIME, SPIDEY!

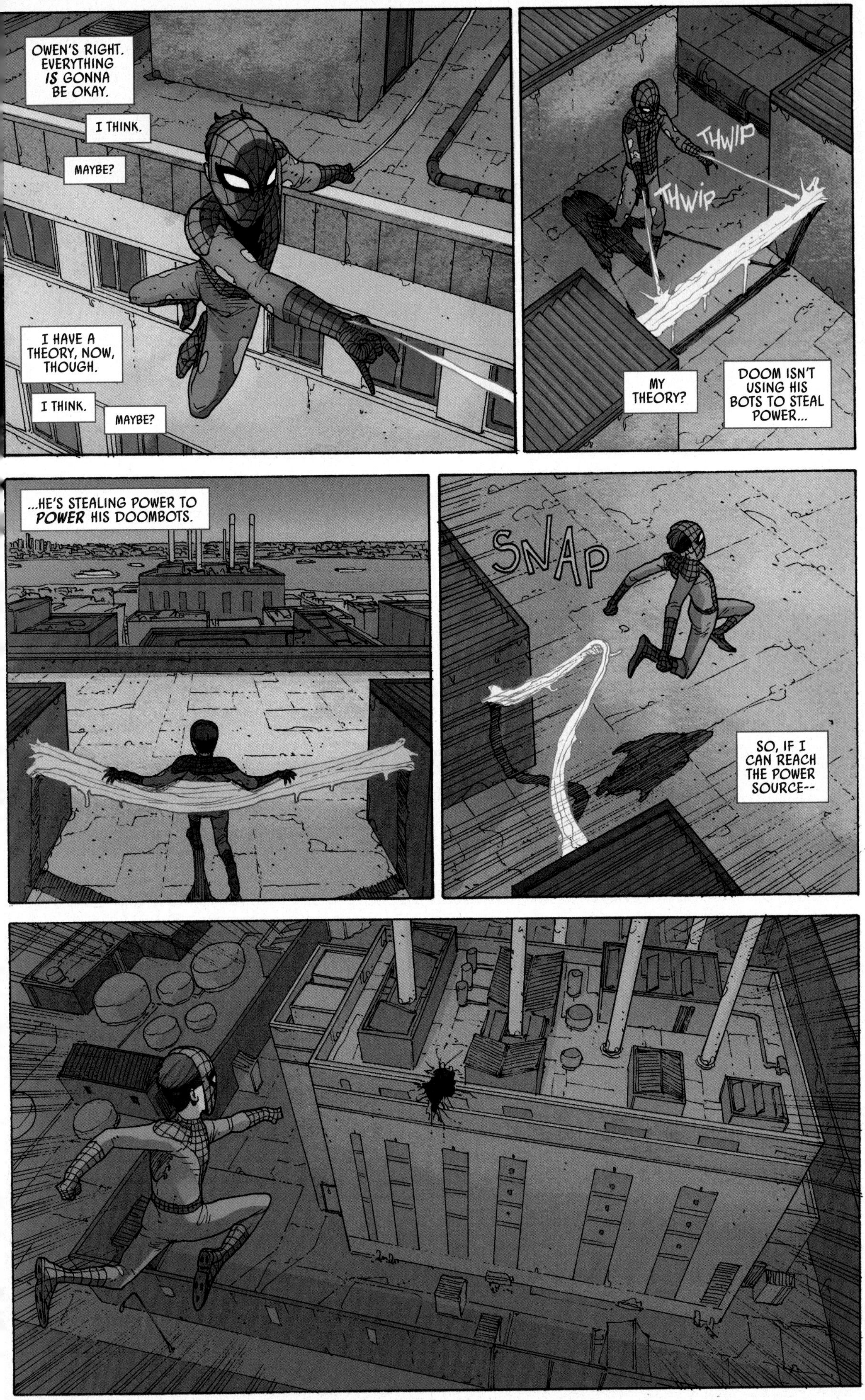
OWEN'S RIGHT. EVERYTHING *IS* GONNA BE OKAY.
I THINK.
MAYBE?
I HAVE A THEORY, NOW, THOUGH.
I THINK.
MAYBE?
THWIP
THWIP
MY THEORY?
DOOM ISN'T USING HIS BOTS TO STEAL POWER...
...HE'S STEALING POWER TO *POWER* HIS DOOMBOTS.
SNAP
SO, IF I CAN REACH THE POWER SOURCE--

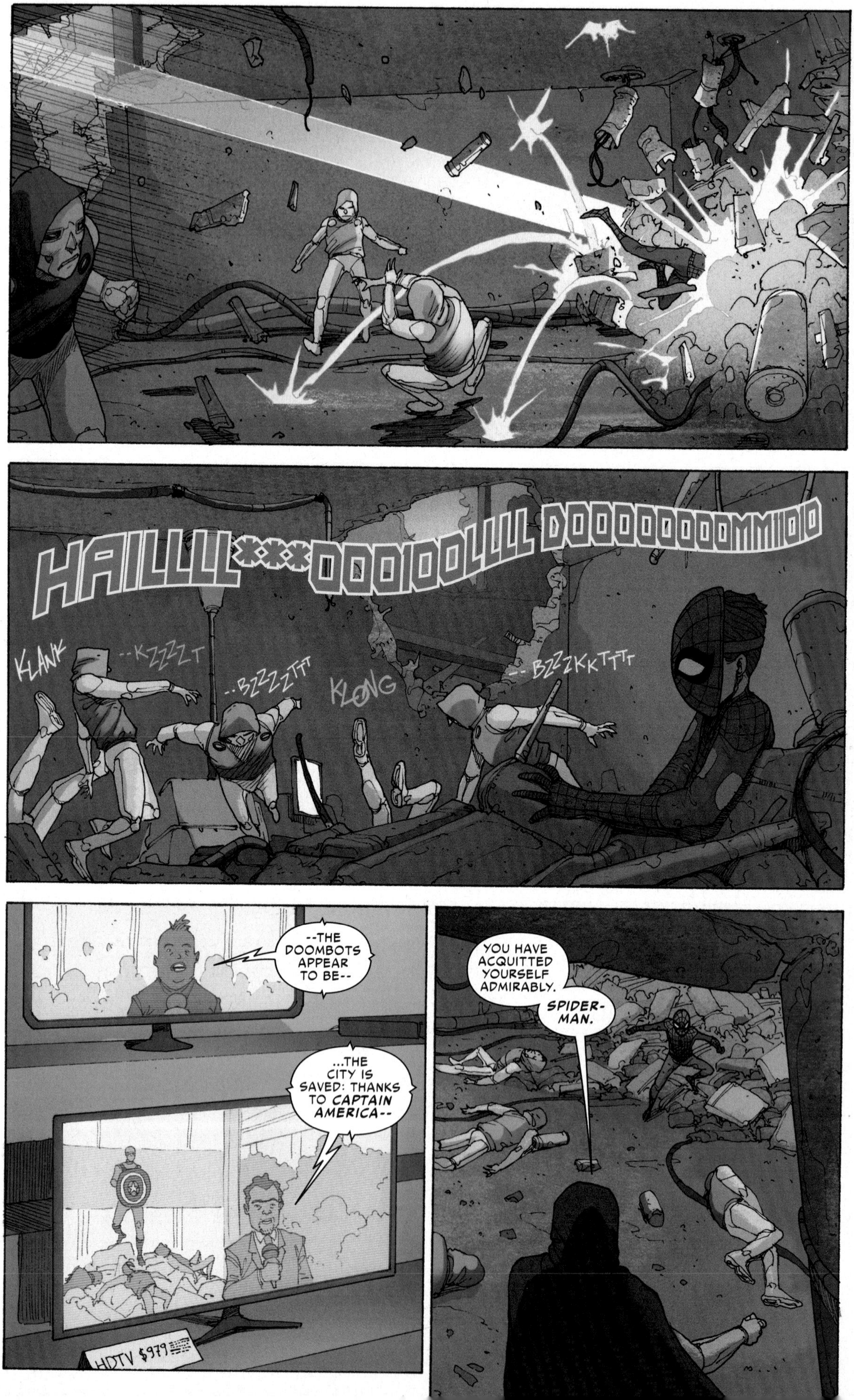
HAILLLL***DOOIOOLLLL DOOOOOOOOMMIIOIO
KLANK
--KZZZZT
--BZZZZTTT
KLONG
--BZZZKKTTTT
--THE DOOMBOTS APPEAR TO BE--
...THE CITY IS SAVED: THANKS TO CAPTAIN AMERICA--
HDTV $979
YOU HAVE ACQUITTED YOURSELF ADMIRABLY.
SPIDER-MAN.

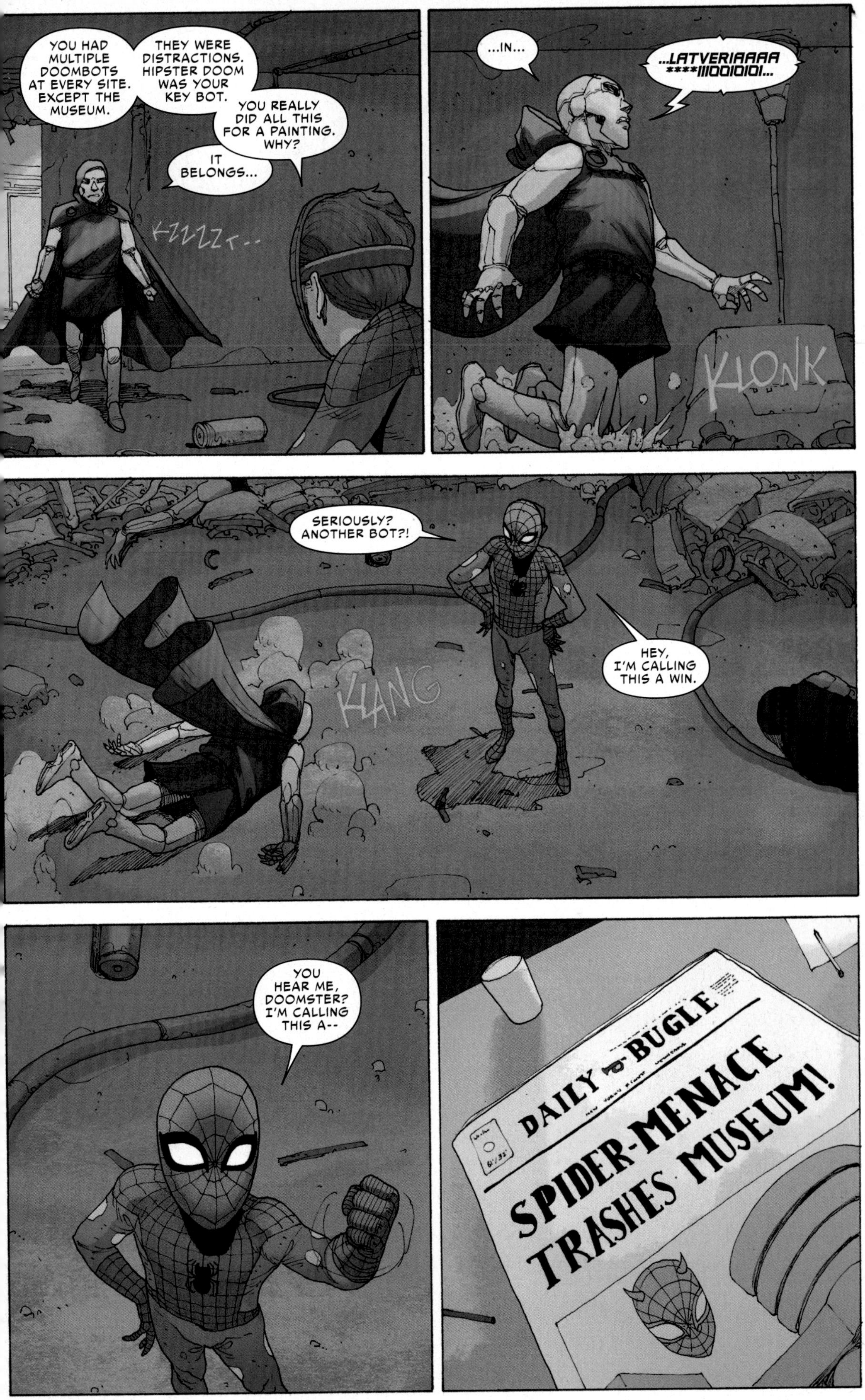
YOU HAD MULTIPLE DOOMBOTS AT EVERY SITE. EXCEPT THE MUSEUM.
THEY WERE DISTRACTIONS. HIPSTER DOOM WAS YOUR KEY BOT.
YOU REALLY DID ALL THIS FOR A PAINTING. WHY?
IT BELONGS...
KZZZZT...
...IN...
...LATVERIAAAA ****1110010101...
KLONK
SERIOUSLY? ANOTHER BOT?!
KLANG
HEY, I'M CALLING THIS A WIN.
YOU HEAR ME, DOOMSTER? I'M CALLING THIS A--
DAILY BUGLE
SPIDER-MENACE TRASHES MUSEUM!

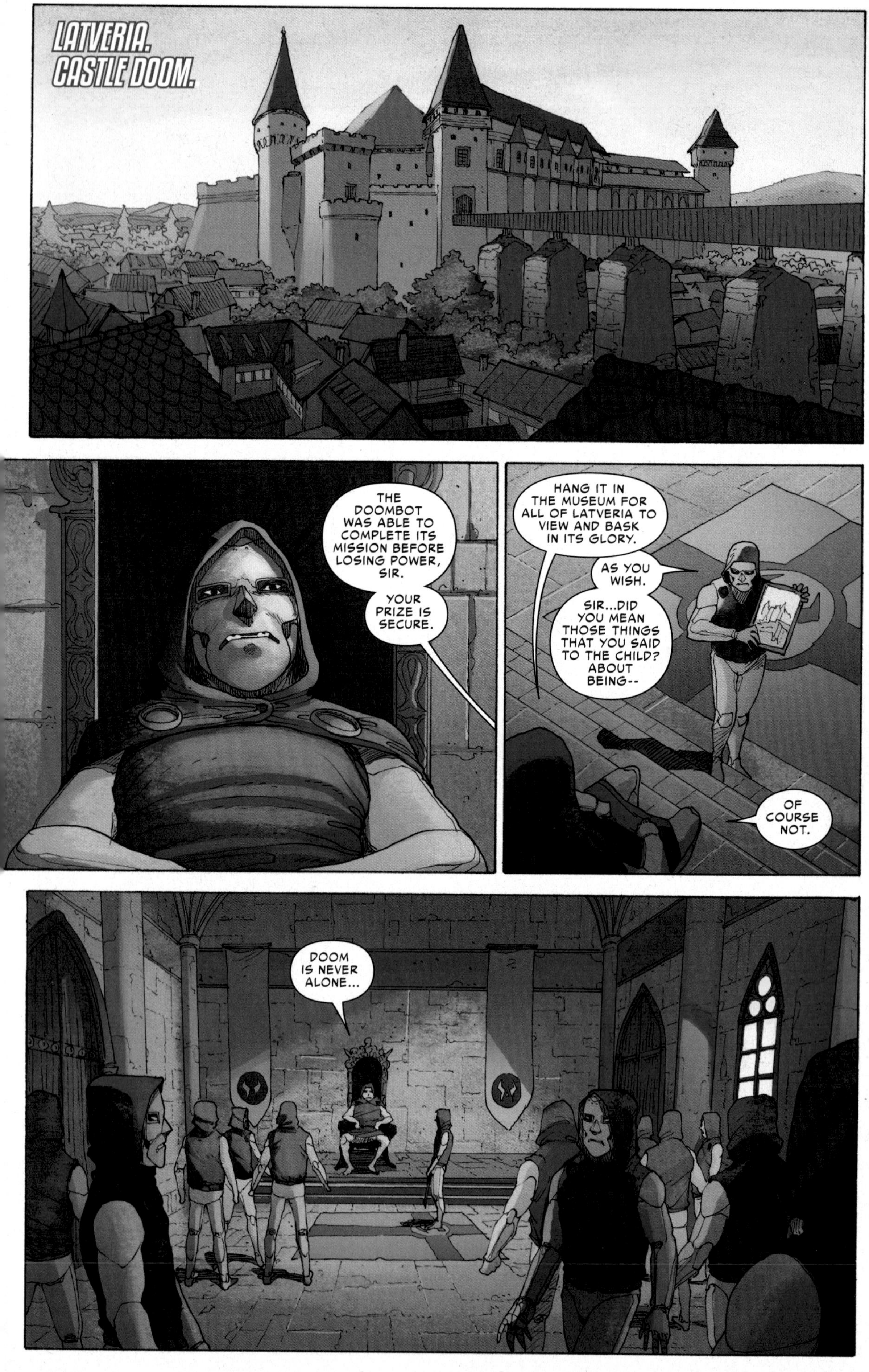
LATVERIA. CASTLE DOOM.
THE DOOMBOT WAS ABLE TO COMPLETE ITS MISSION BEFORE LOSING POWER, SIR.
YOUR PRIZE IS SECURE.
HANG IT IN THE MUSEUM FOR ALL OF LATVERIA TO VIEW AND BASK IN ITS GLORY.
AS YOU WISH.
SIR...DID YOU MEAN THOSE THINGS THAT YOU SAID TO THE CHILD? ABOUT BEING--
OF COURSE NOT.
DOOM IS NEVER ALONE...

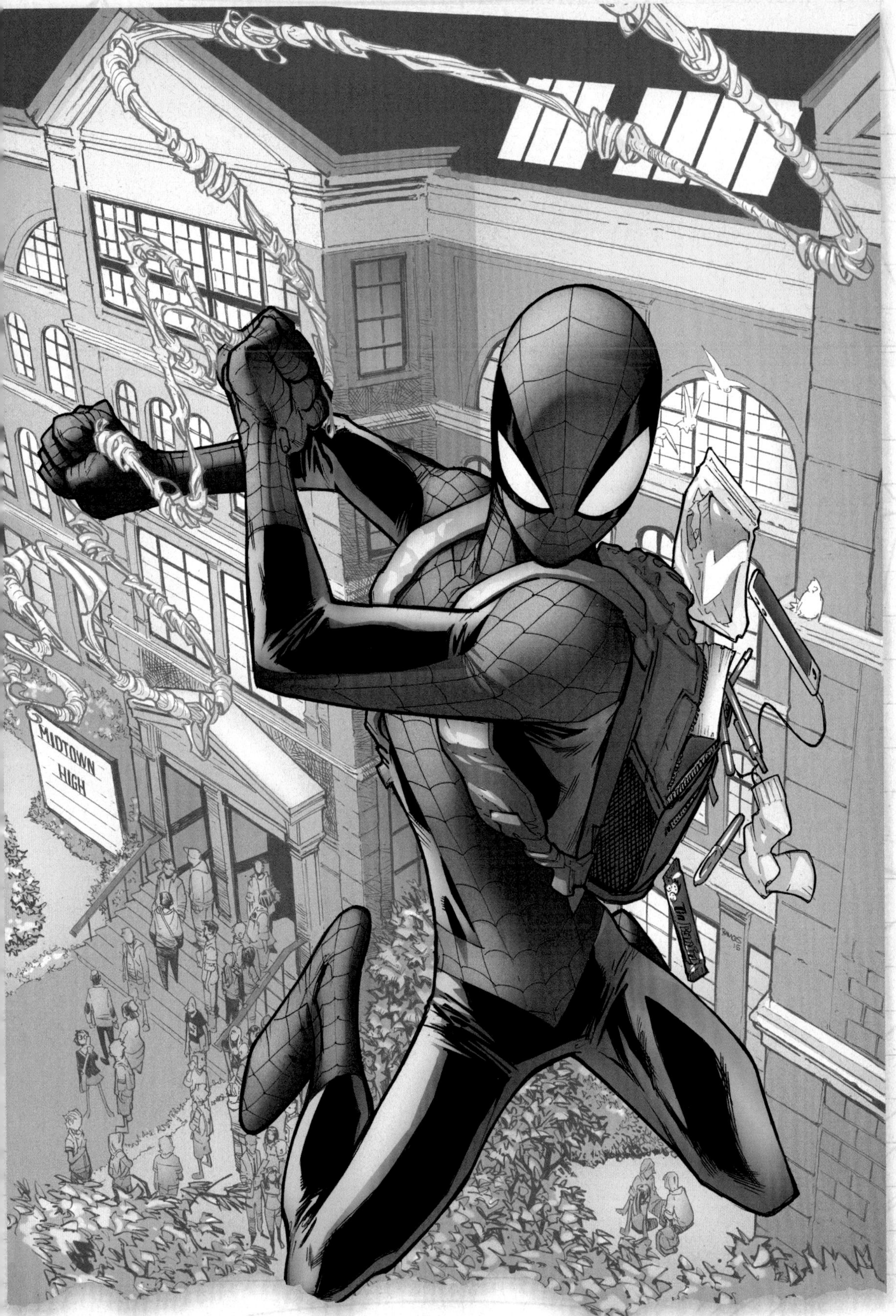
MIDTOWN HIGH

HUMBERTO RAMOS & EDGAR DELGADO
1 VARIANT

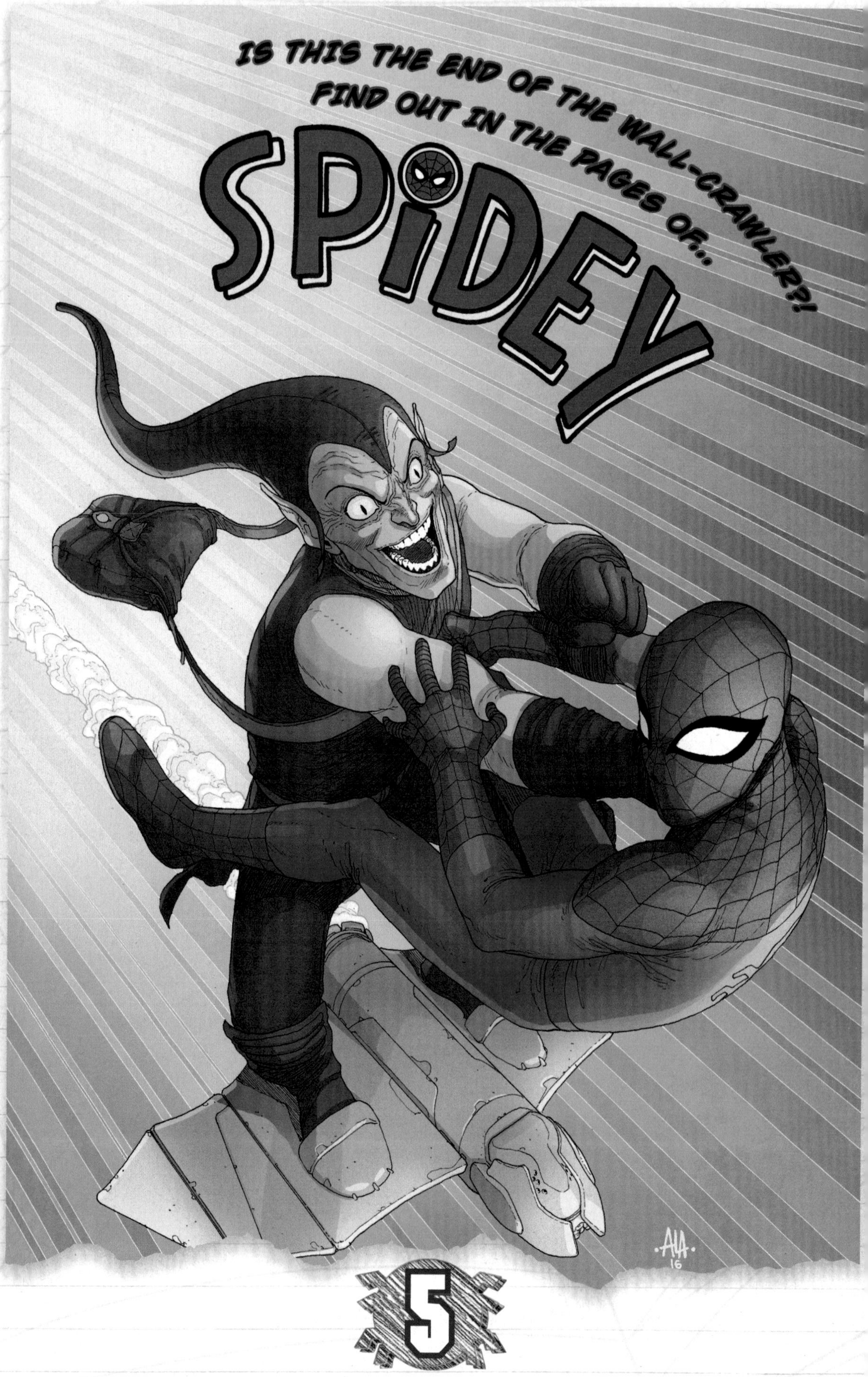
IS THIS THE END OF THE WALL-CRAWLER?!
FIND OUT IN THE PAGES OF...
SPIDEY

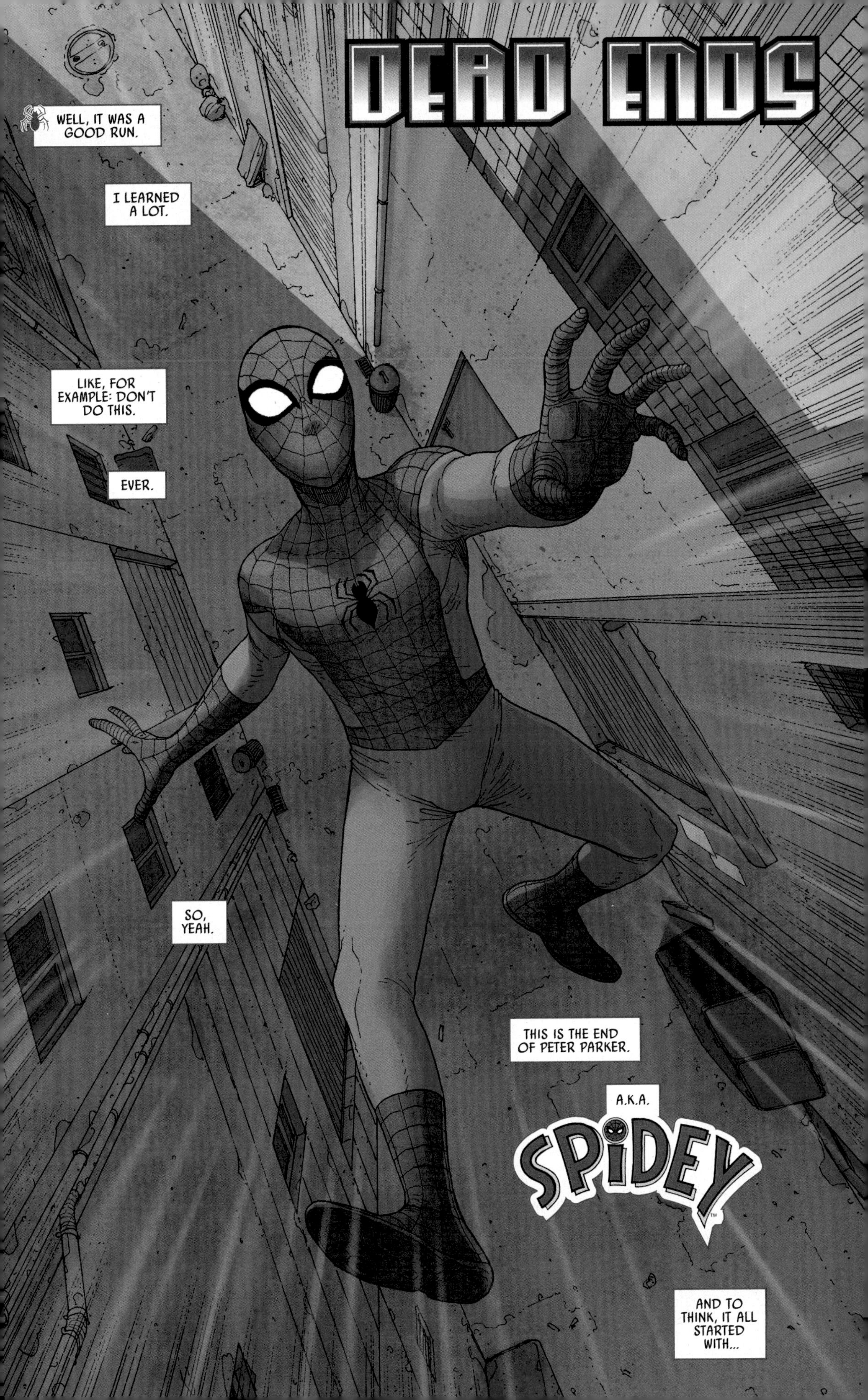
DEAD ENDS
WELL, IT WAS A GOOD RUN.
I LEARNED A LOT.
LIKE, FOR EXAMPLE: DON'T DO THIS.
EVER.
SO, YEAH.
THIS IS THE END OF PETER PARKER.
A.K.A.
SPIDEY™
AND TO THINK, IT ALL STARTED WITH...

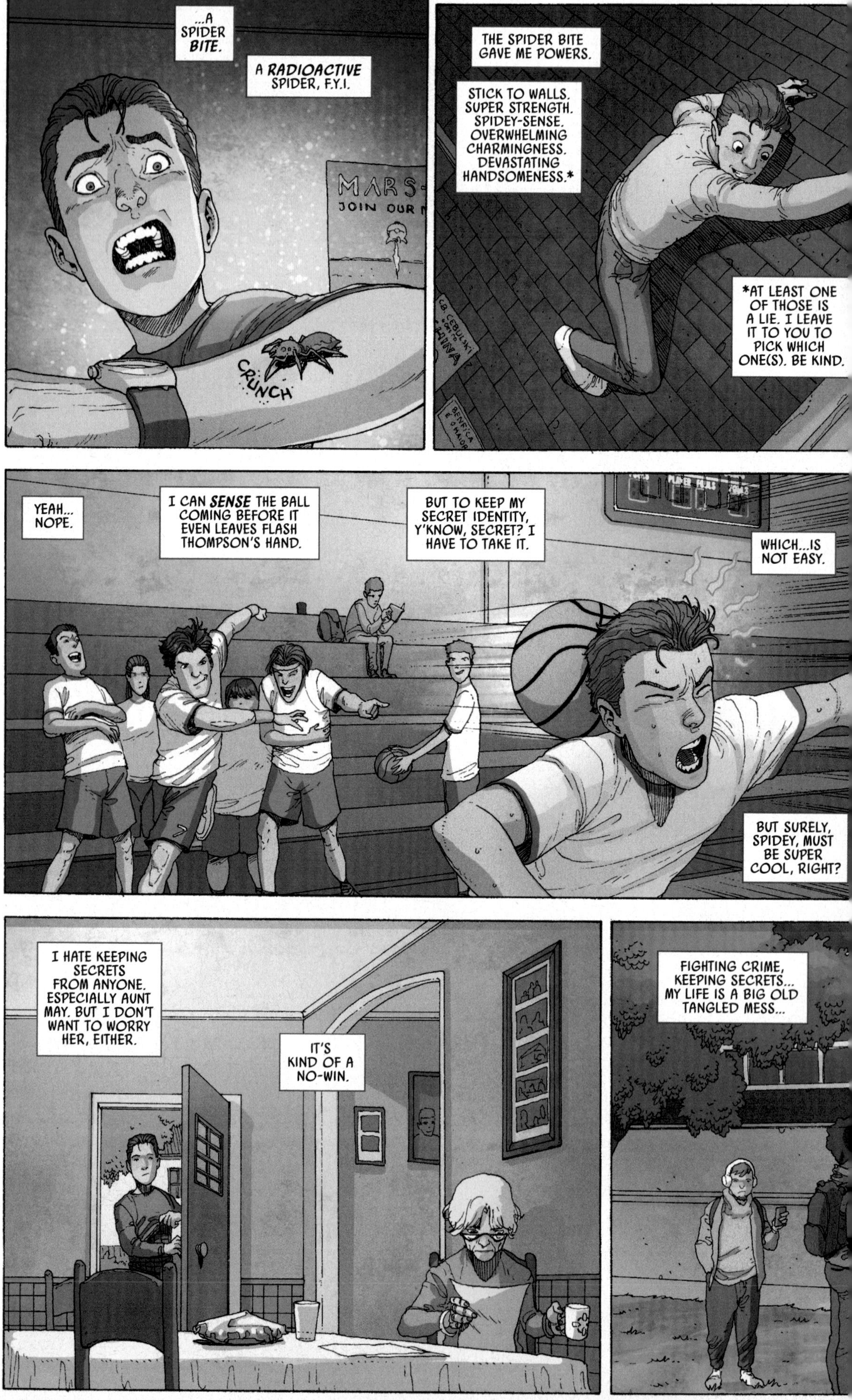

...A SPIDER BITE.
A RADIOACTIVE SPIDER, F.Y.I.
CRUNCH
THE SPIDER BITE GAVE ME POWERS.
STICK TO WALLS. SUPER STRENGTH. SPIDEY-SENSE. OVERWHELMING CHARMINGNESS. DEVASTATING HANDSOMENESS.*
*AT LEAST ONE OF THOSE IS A LIE. I LEAVE IT TO YOU TO PICK WHICH ONE(S). BE KIND.
YEAH... NOPE.
I CAN SENSE THE BALL COMING BEFORE IT EVEN LEAVES FLASH THOMPSON'S HAND.
BUT TO KEEP MY SECRET IDENTITY, Y'KNOW, SECRET? I HAVE TO TAKE IT.
WHICH...IS NOT EASY.
BUT SURELY, SPIDEY, MUST BE SUPER COOL, RIGHT?
I HATE KEEPING SECRETS FROM ANYONE. ESPECIALLY AUNT MAY. BUT I DON'T WANT TO WORRY HER, EITHER.
IT'S KIND OF A NO-WIN.
FIGHTING CRIME, KEEPING SECRETS... MY LIFE IS A BIG OLD TANGLED MESS...

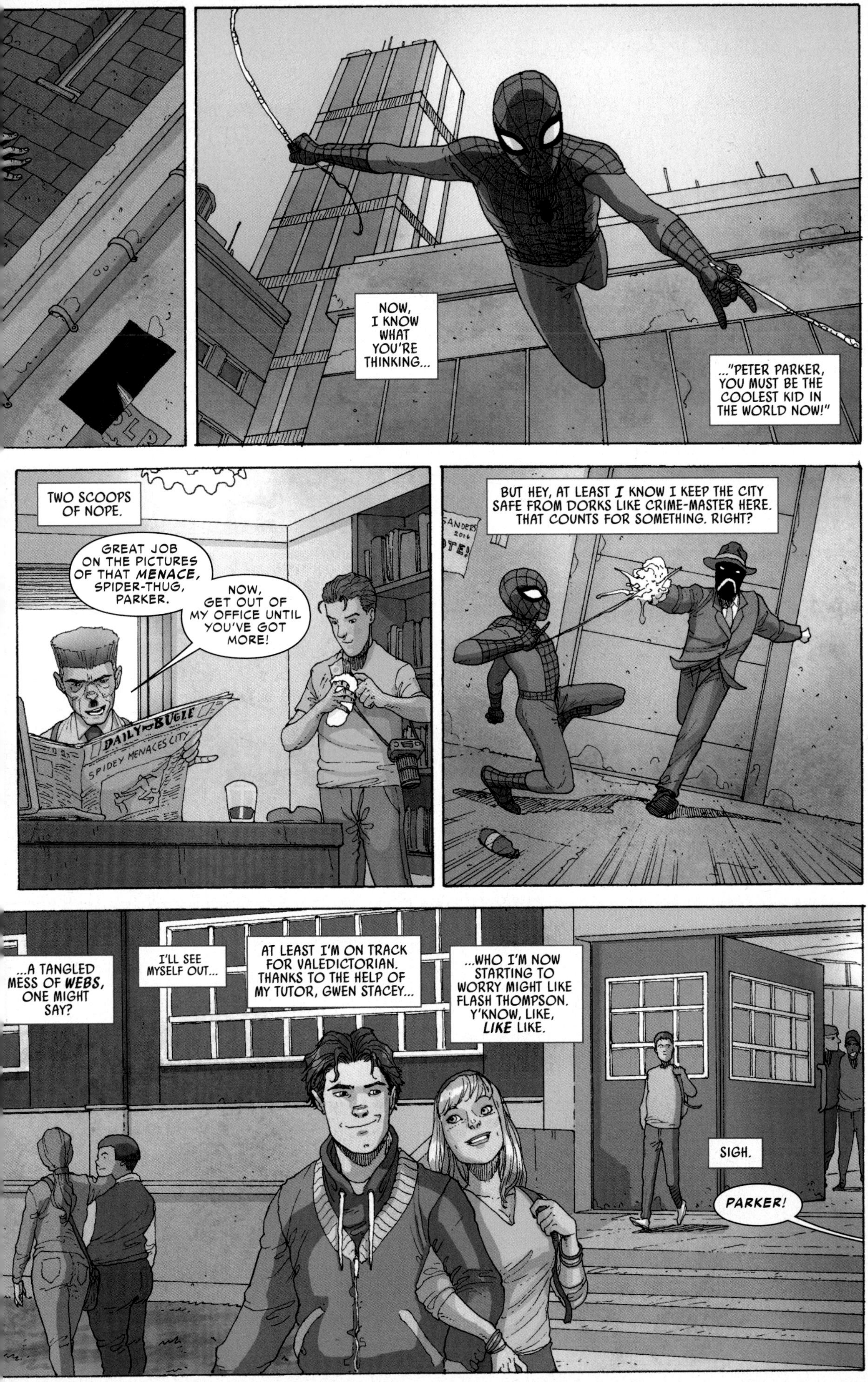
NOW, I KNOW WHAT YOU'RE THINKING...
..."PETER PARKER, YOU MUST BE THE COOLEST KID IN THE WORLD NOW!"
TWO SCOOPS OF NOPE.
GREAT JOB ON THE PICTURES OF THAT MENACE, SPIDER-THUG, PARKER.
NOW, GET OUT OF MY OFFICE UNTIL YOU'VE GOT MORE!
DAILY BUGLE
SPIDEY MENACES CITY
BUT HEY, AT LEAST I KNOW I KEEP THE CITY SAFE FROM DORKS LIKE CRIME-MASTER HERE. THAT COUNTS FOR SOMETHING. RIGHT?
SANDERS 2016
...A TANGLED MESS OF WEBS, ONE MIGHT SAY?
I'LL SEE MYSELF OUT...
AT LEAST I'M ON TRACK FOR VALEDICTORIAN. THANKS TO THE HELP OF MY TUTOR, GWEN STACEY...
...WHO I'M NOW STARTING TO WORRY MIGHT LIKE FLASH THOMPSON. Y'KNOW, LIKE, LIKE LIKE.
SIGH.
PARKER!

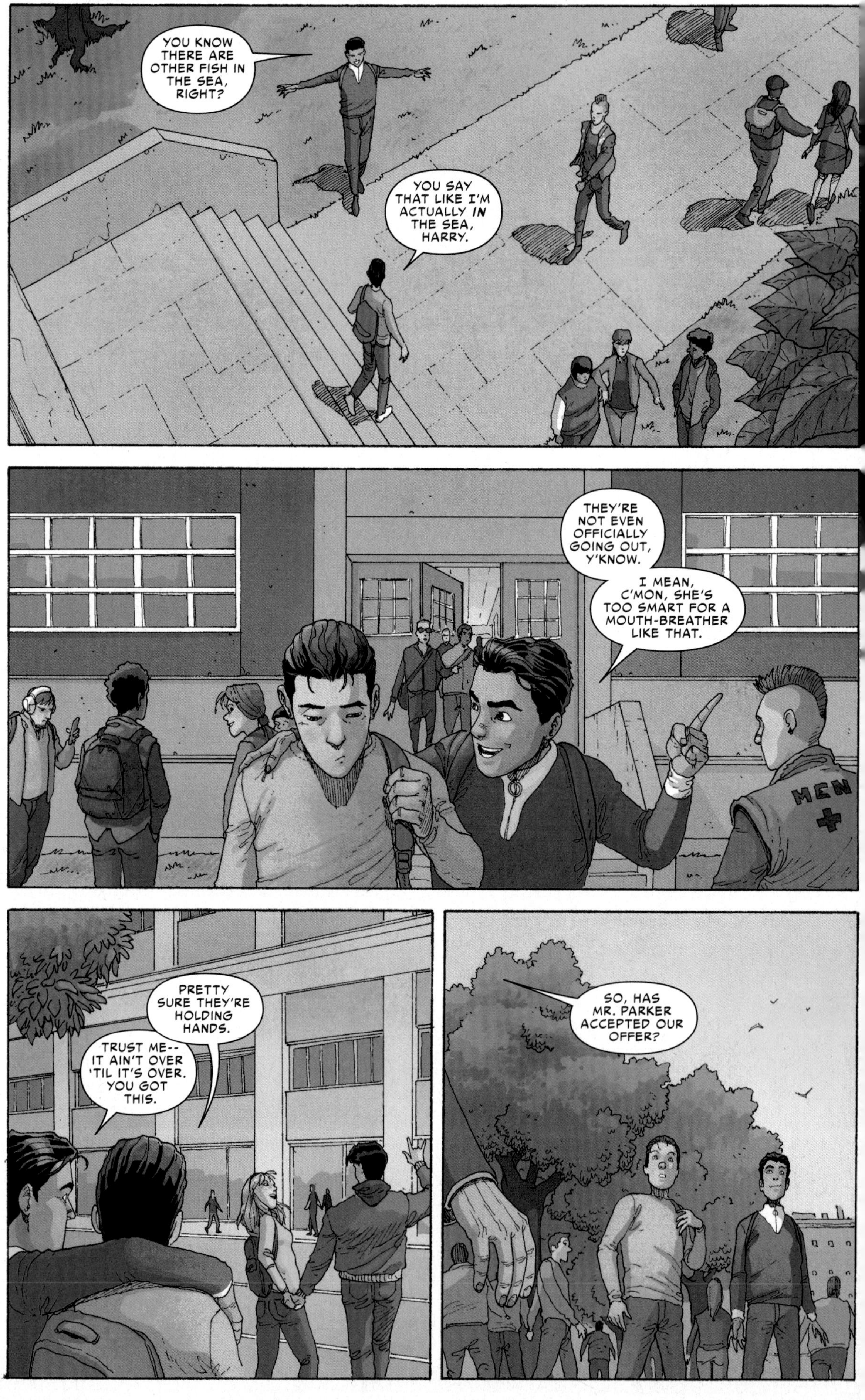
YOU KNOW THERE ARE OTHER FISH IN THE SEA, RIGHT?
YOU SAY THAT LIKE I'M ACTUALLY *IN* THE SEA, HARRY.
THEY'RE NOT EVEN OFFICIALLY GOING OUT, Y'KNOW.
I MEAN, C'MON, SHE'S TOO SMART FOR A MOUTH-BREATHER LIKE THAT.
MEN
PRETTY SURE THEY'RE HOLDING HANDS.
TRUST ME-- IT AIN'T OVER 'TIL IT'S OVER. YOU GOT THIS.
SO, HAS MR. PARKER ACCEPTED OUR OFFER?

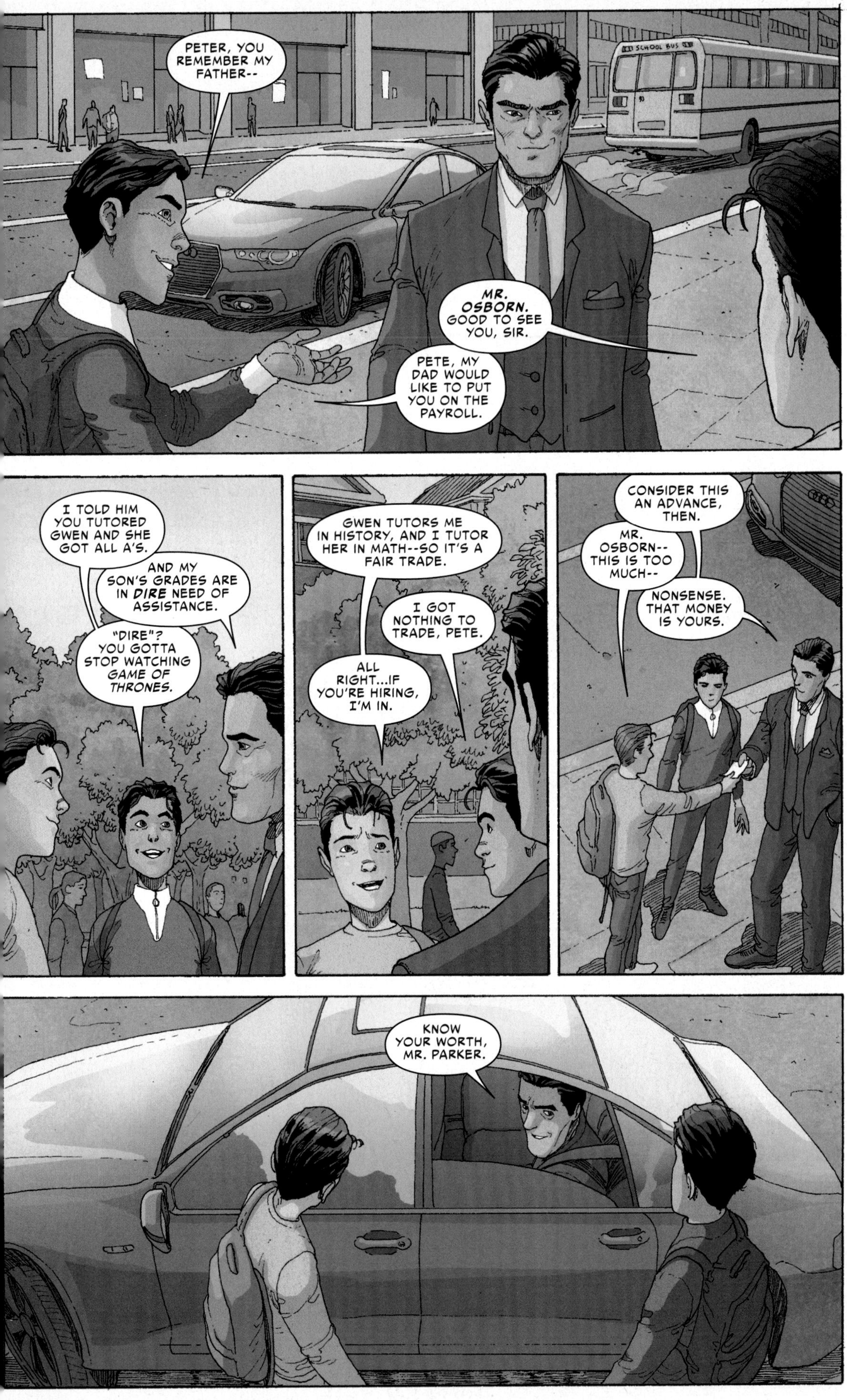
PETER, YOU REMEMBER MY FATHER--
MR. OSBORN. GOOD TO SEE YOU, SIR.
PETE, MY DAD WOULD LIKE TO PUT YOU ON THE PAYROLL.
I TOLD HIM YOU TUTORED GWEN AND SHE GOT ALL A'S.
AND MY SON'S GRADES ARE IN DIRE NEED OF ASSISTANCE.
"DIRE"? YOU GOTTA STOP WATCHING GAME OF THRONES.
GWEN TUTORS ME IN HISTORY, AND I TUTOR HER IN MATH--SO IT'S A FAIR TRADE.
I GOT NOTHING TO TRADE, PETE.
ALL RIGHT...IF YOU'RE HIRING, I'M IN.
CONSIDER THIS AN ADVANCE, THEN.
MR. OSBORN-- THIS IS TOO MUCH--
NONSENSE. THAT MONEY IS YOURS.
KNOW YOUR WORTH, MR. PARKER.

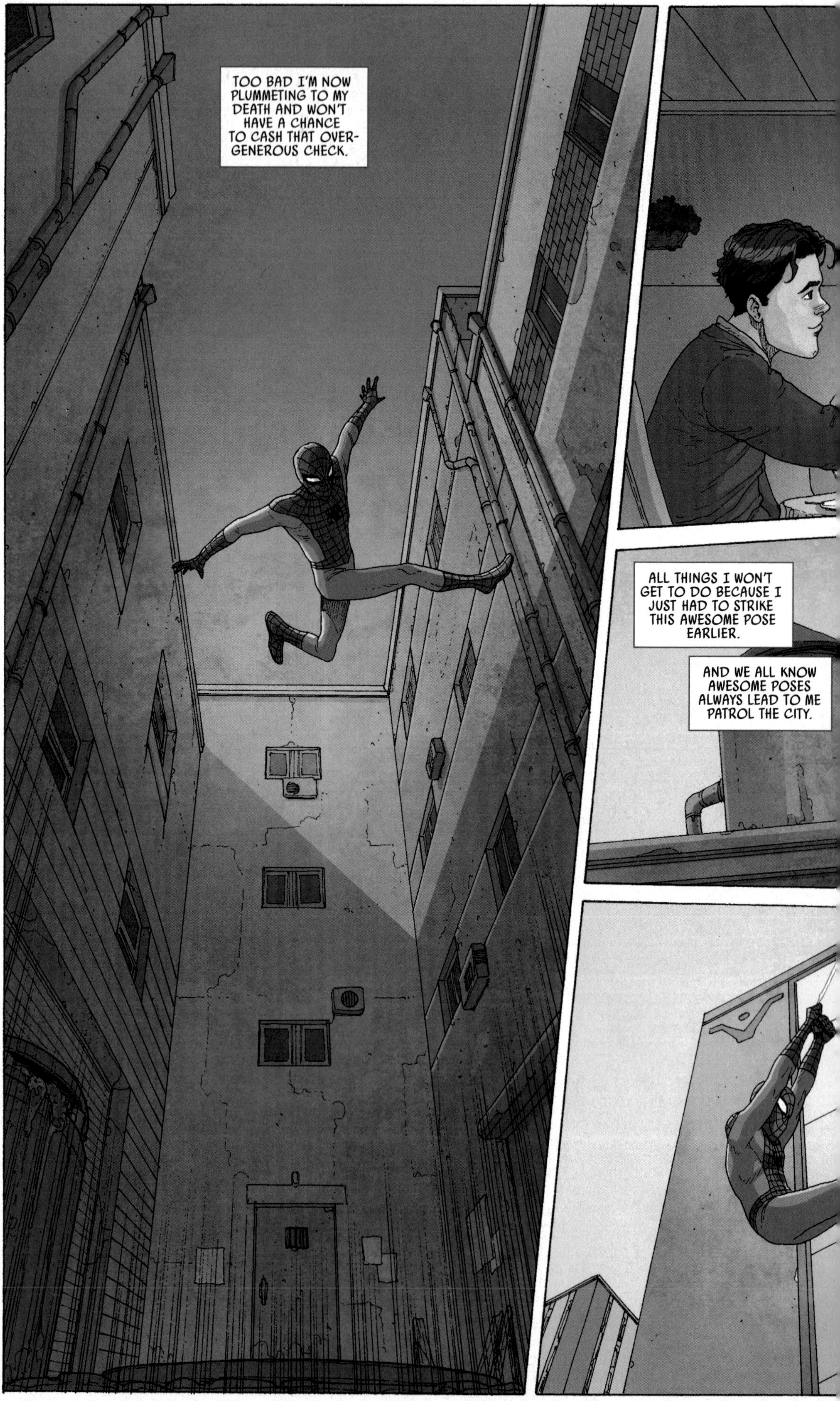
TOO BAD I'M NOW PLUMMETING TO MY DEATH AND WON'T HAVE A CHANCE TO CASH THAT OVER-GENEROUS CHECK.
ALL THINGS I WON'T GET TO DO BECAUSE I JUST HAD TO STRIKE THIS AWESOME POSE EARLIER.
AND WE ALL KNOW AWESOME POSES ALWAYS LEAD TO ME PATROL THE CITY.

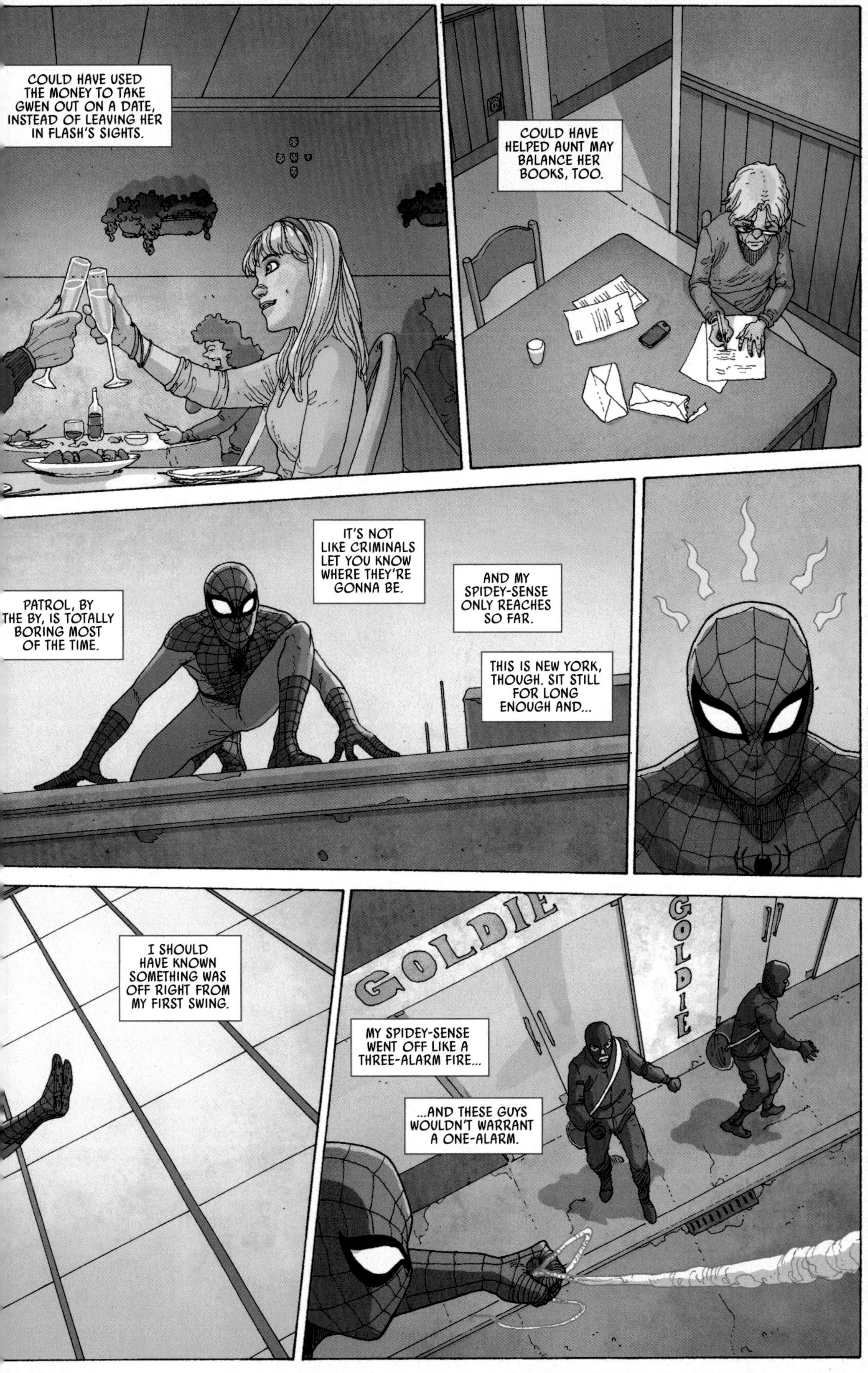
COULD HAVE USED THE MONEY TO TAKE GWEN OUT ON A DATE, INSTEAD OF LEAVING HER IN FLASH'S SIGHTS.
COULD HAVE HELPED AUNT MAY BALANCE HER BOOKS, TOO.
PATROL, BY THE BY, IS TOTALLY BORING MOST OF THE TIME.
IT'S NOT LIKE CRIMINALS LET YOU KNOW WHERE THEY'RE GONNA BE.
AND MY SPIDEY-SENSE ONLY REACHES SO FAR.
THIS IS NEW YORK, THOUGH. SIT STILL FOR LONG ENOUGH AND...
I SHOULD HAVE KNOWN SOMETHING WAS OFF RIGHT FROM MY FIRST SWING.
GOLDIE
GOLDIE
MY SPIDEY-SENSE WENT OFF LIKE A THREE-ALARM FIRE...
...AND THESE GUYS WOULDN'T WARRANT A ONE-ALARM.

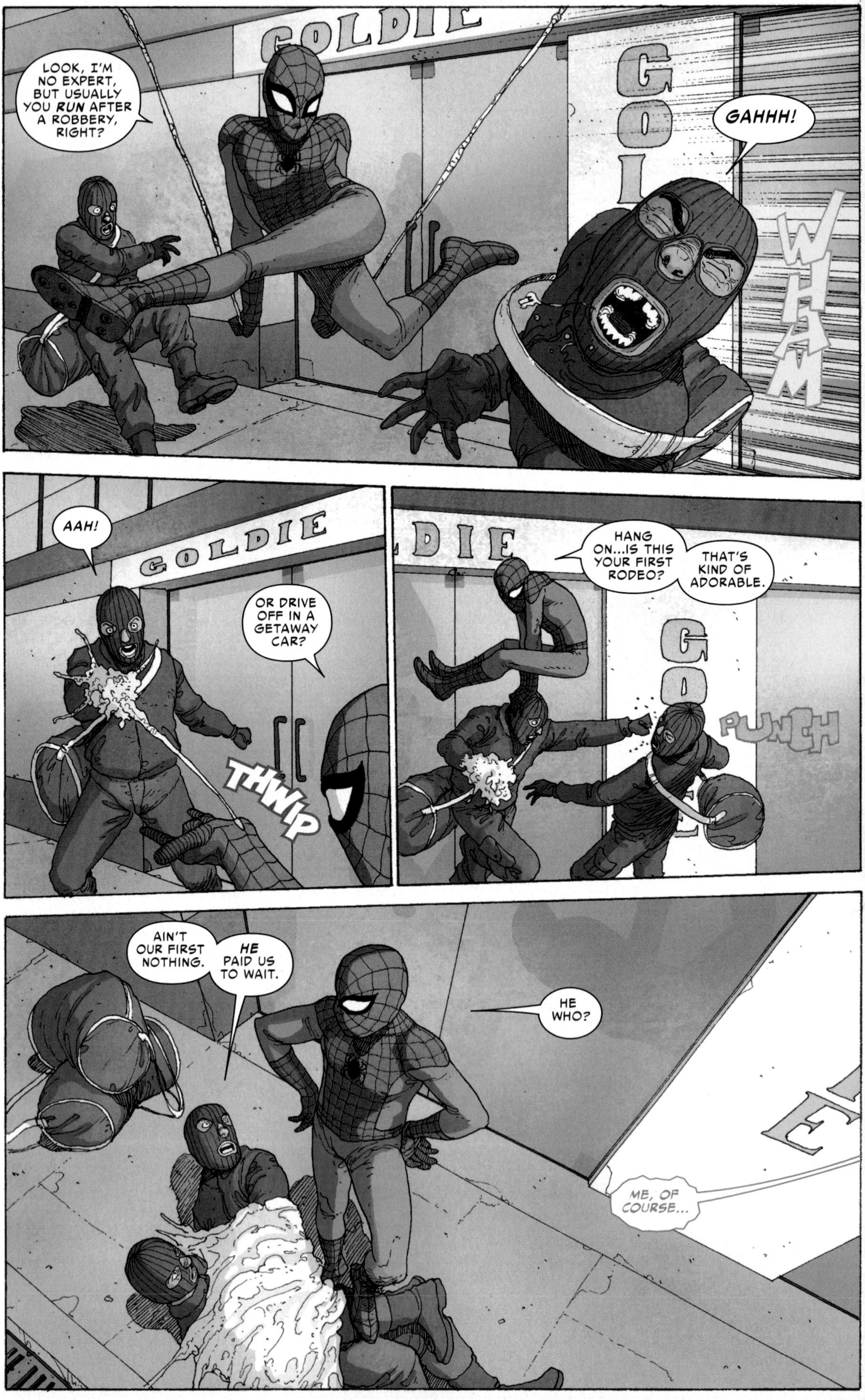
GOLDIE
LOOK, I'M NO EXPERT, BUT USUALLY YOU *RUN* AFTER A ROBBERY, RIGHT?
GAHHH!
WHAM
AAH!
GOLDIE
OR DRIVE OFF IN A GETAWAY CAR?
THWIP
HANG ON...IS THIS YOUR FIRST RODEO?
THAT'S KIND OF ADORABLE.
PUNCH
AIN'T OUR FIRST NOTHING.
HE PAID US TO WAIT.
HE WHO?
ME, OF COURSE...

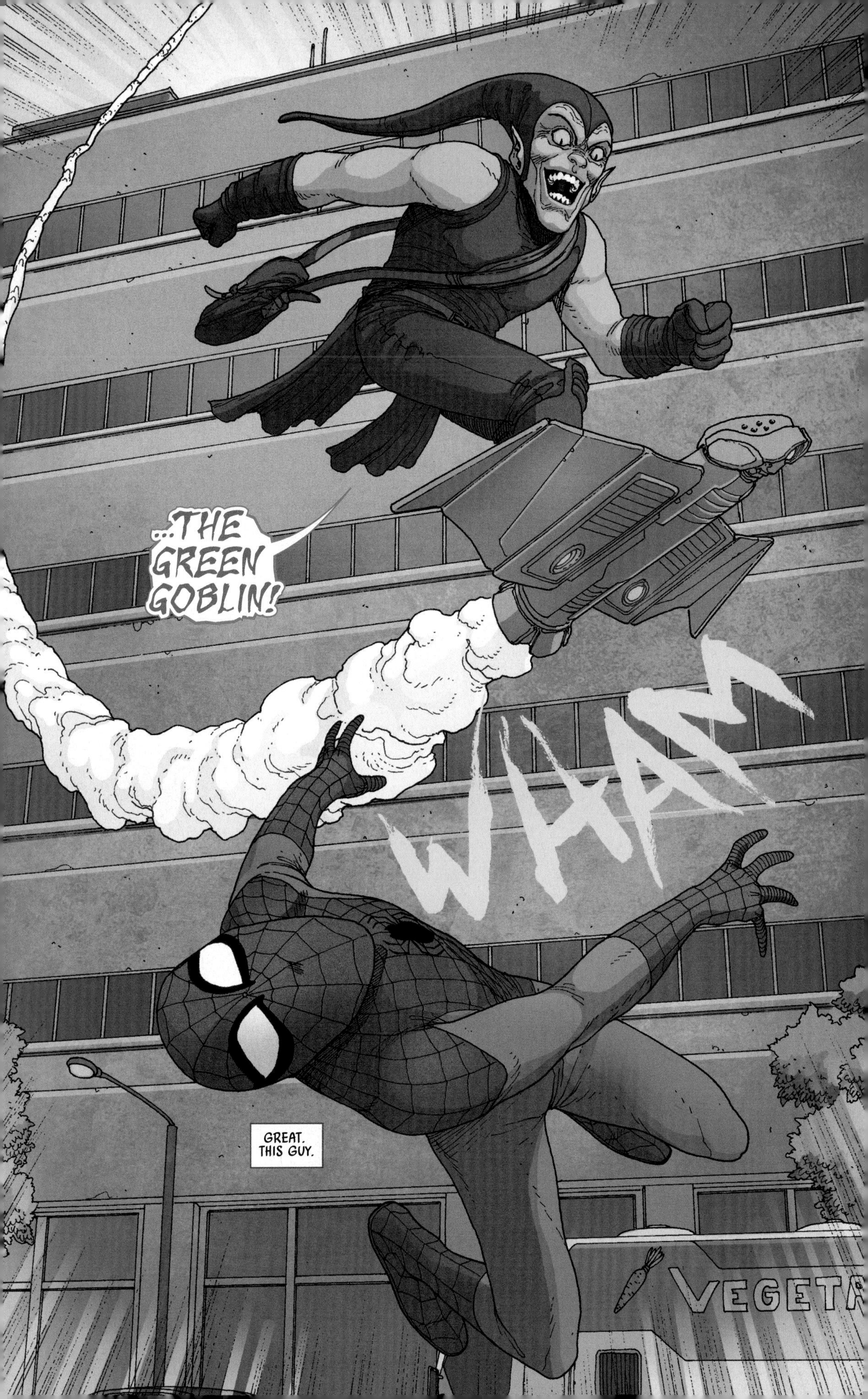
...THE GREEN GOBLIN!
WHAM
GREAT. THIS GUY.
VEGETA

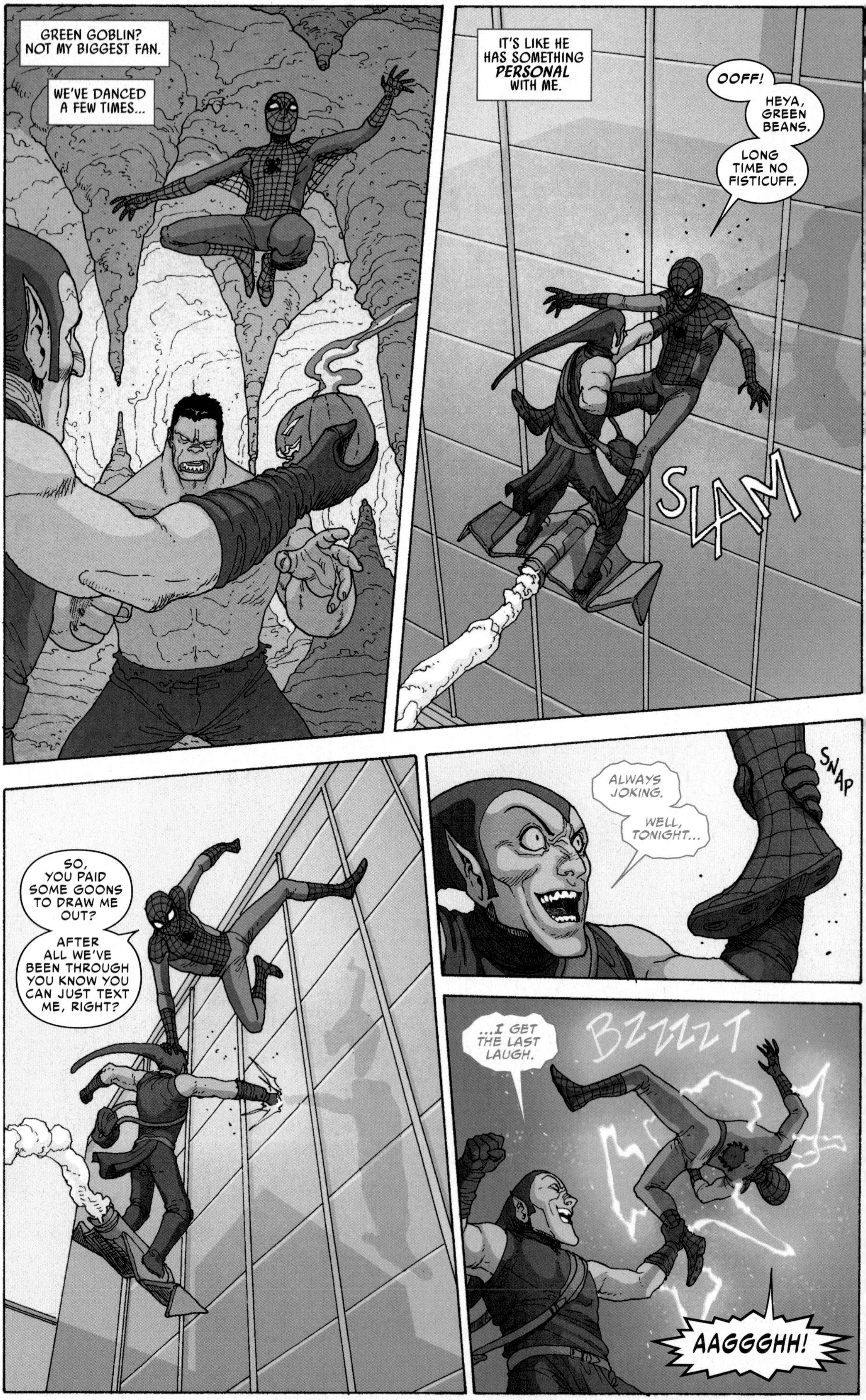
GREEN GOBLIN? NOT MY BIGGEST FAN.
WE'VE DANCED A FEW TIMES...
IT'S LIKE HE HAS SOMETHING *PERSONAL* WITH ME.
OOFF!
HEYA, GREEN BEANS.
LONG TIME NO FISTICUFF.
SLAM
SO, YOU PAID SOME GOONS TO DRAW ME OUT?
AFTER ALL WE'VE BEEN THROUGH YOU KNOW YOU CAN JUST TEXT ME, RIGHT?
SNAP
ALWAYS JOKING.
WELL, TONIGHT...
...I GET THE LAST LAUGH.
BZZZZZT
AAGGGHH!

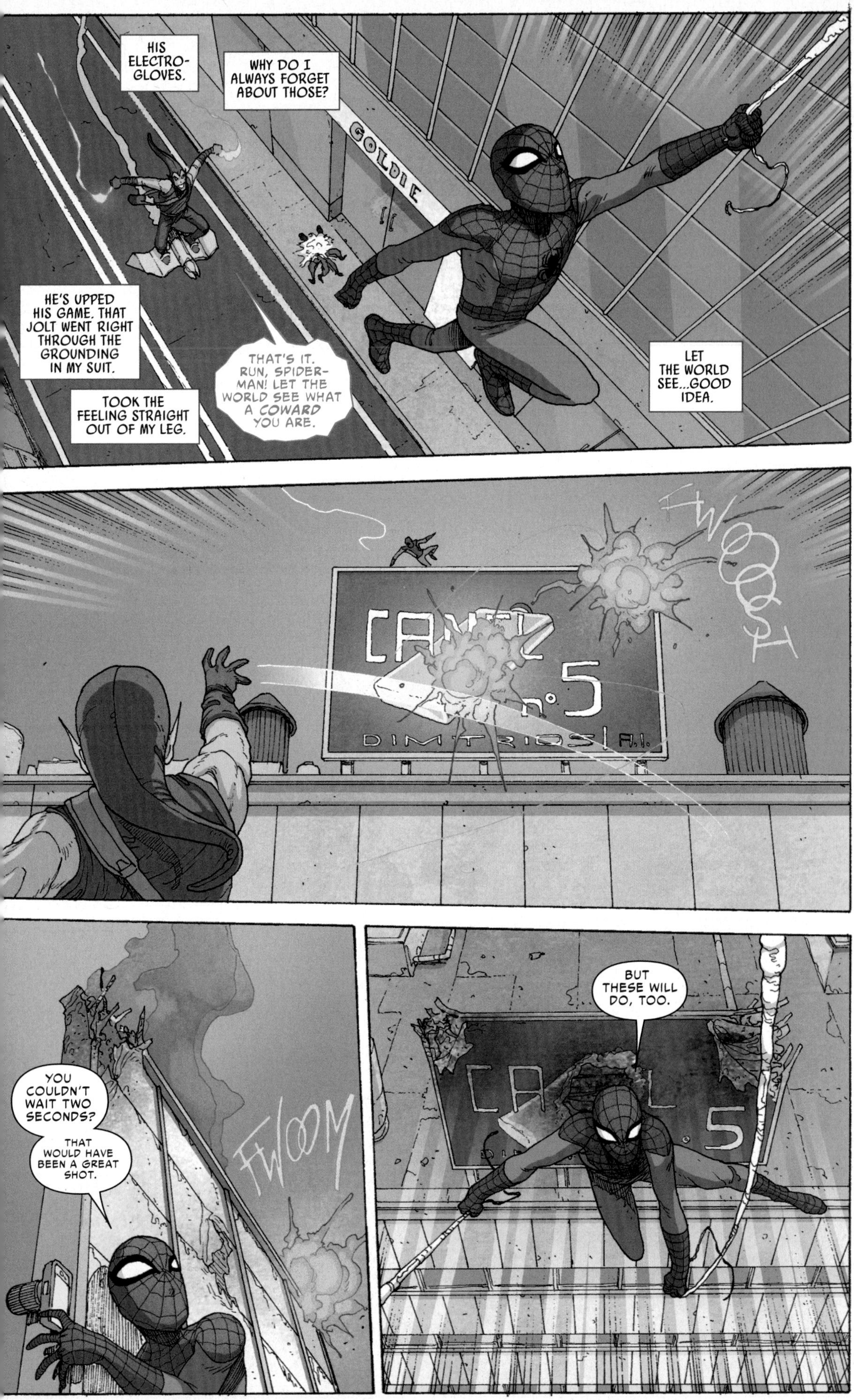
HIS ELECTRO-GLOVES.
WHY DO I ALWAYS FORGET ABOUT THOSE?
GOLDIE
HE'S UPPED HIS GAME. THAT JOLT WENT RIGHT THROUGH THE GROUNDING IN MY SUIT.
TOOK THE FEELING STRAIGHT OUT OF MY LEG.
THAT'S IT. RUN, SPIDER-MAN! LET THE WORLD SEE WHAT A COWARD YOU ARE.
LET THE WORLD SEE...GOOD IDEA.
FWOOOSH
CAREZ n°5
DIMITRIOS|A.I.
YOU COULDN'T WAIT TWO SECONDS?
THAT WOULD HAVE BEEN A GREAT SHOT.
FWOOM
BUT THESE WILL DO, TOO.

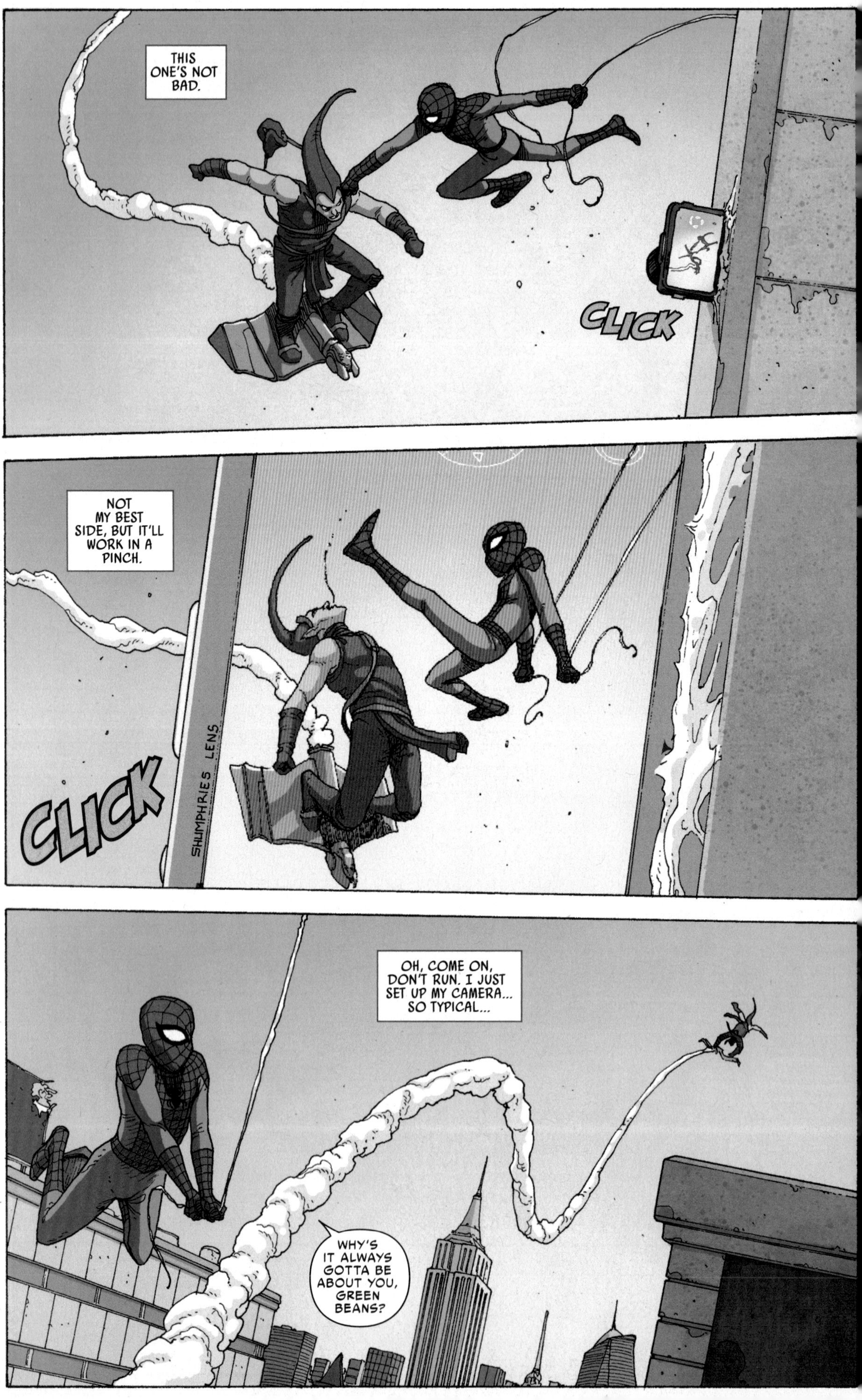
THIS ONE'S NOT BAD.
CLICK
NOT MY BEST SIDE, BUT IT'LL WORK IN A PINCH.
SHUMPHRIES LENS
CLICK
OH, COME ON, DON'T RUN. I JUST SET UP MY CAMERA... SO TYPICAL...
WHY'S IT ALWAYS GOTTA BE ABOUT YOU, GREEN BEANS?

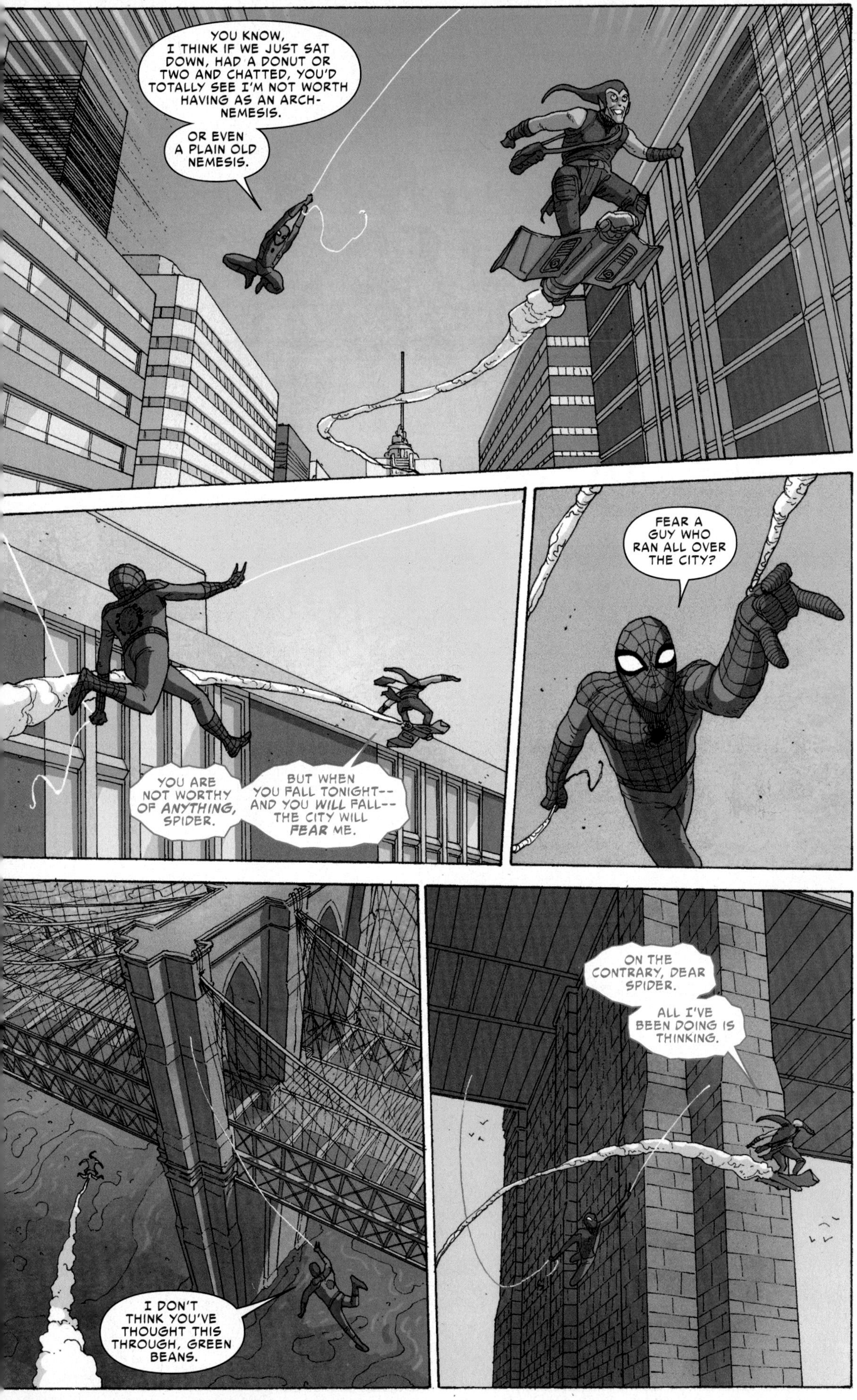
YOU KNOW, I THINK IF WE JUST SAT DOWN, HAD A DONUT OR TWO AND CHATTED, YOU'D TOTALLY SEE I'M NOT WORTH HAVING AS AN ARCH-NEMESIS.
OR EVEN A PLAIN OLD NEMESIS.
YOU ARE NOT WORTHY OF *ANYTHING*, SPIDER.
BUT WHEN YOU FALL TONIGHT-- AND YOU *WILL* FALL-- THE CITY WILL *FEAR* ME.
FEAR A GUY WHO RAN ALL OVER THE CITY?
I DON'T THINK YOU'VE THOUGHT THIS THROUGH, GREEN BEANS.
ON THE CONTRARY, DEAR SPIDER.
ALL I'VE BEEN DOING IS THINKING.

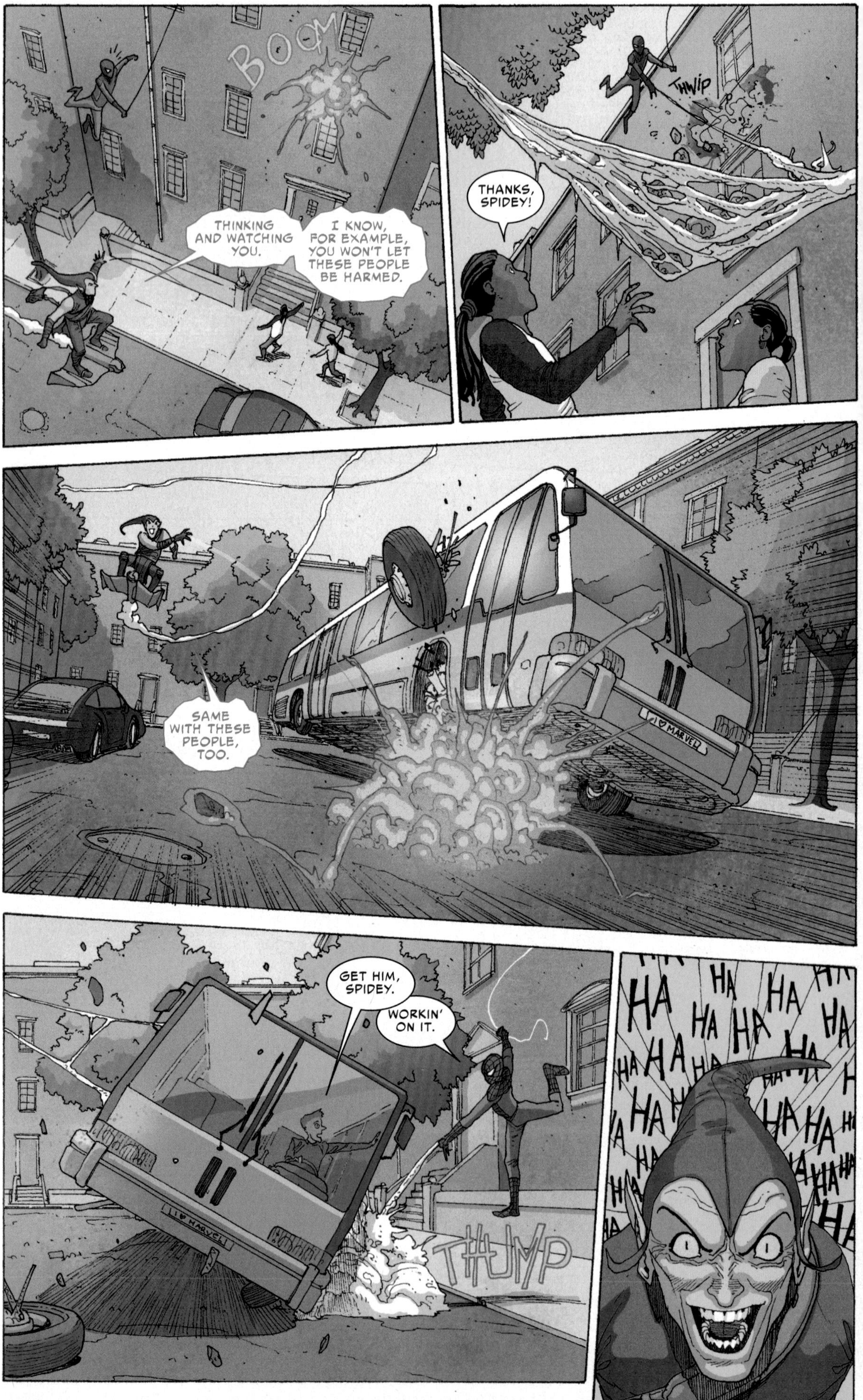
BOOM
THINKING AND WATCHING YOU.
I KNOW, FOR EXAMPLE, YOU WON'T LET THESE PEOPLE BE HARMED.
THWIP
THANKS, SPIDEY!
SAME WITH THESE PEOPLE, TOO.
I ♥ MARVEL
GET HIM, SPIDEY.
WORKIN' ON IT.
THUMP
I ♥ MARVEL
HA HA HA HA HA HA HA HA HA HA HA HA HA HA HA HA HA HA HA HA HA

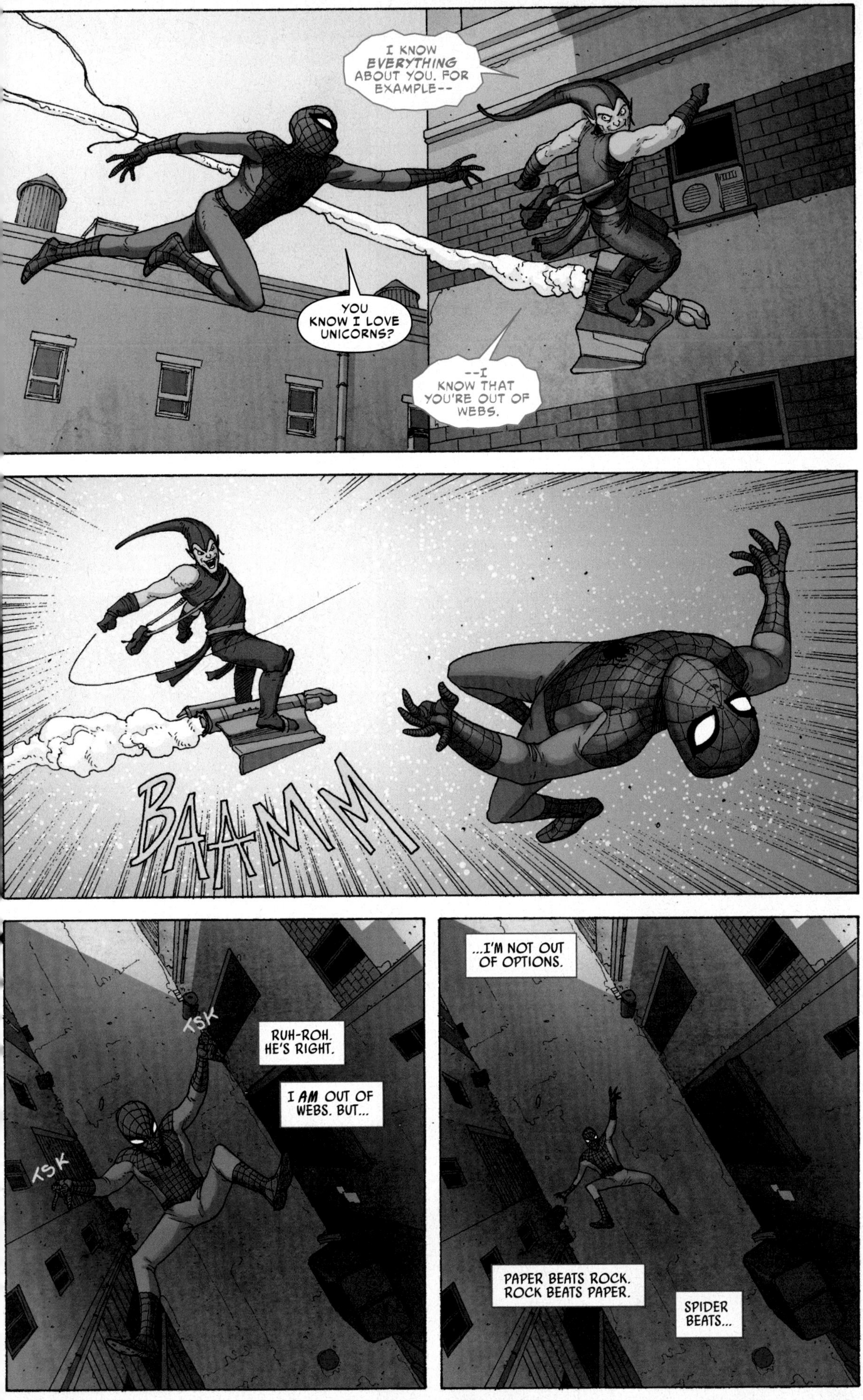

I KNOW *EVERYTHING* ABOUT YOU. FOR EXAMPLE--
YOU KNOW I LOVE UNICORNS?
--I KNOW THAT YOU'RE OUT OF WEBS.
BAAMM
RUH-ROH. HE'S RIGHT.
TSK
TSK
I *AM* OUT OF WEBS. BUT...
...I'M NOT OUT OF OPTIONS.
PAPER BEATS ROCK. ROCK BEATS PAPER.
SPIDER BEATS...

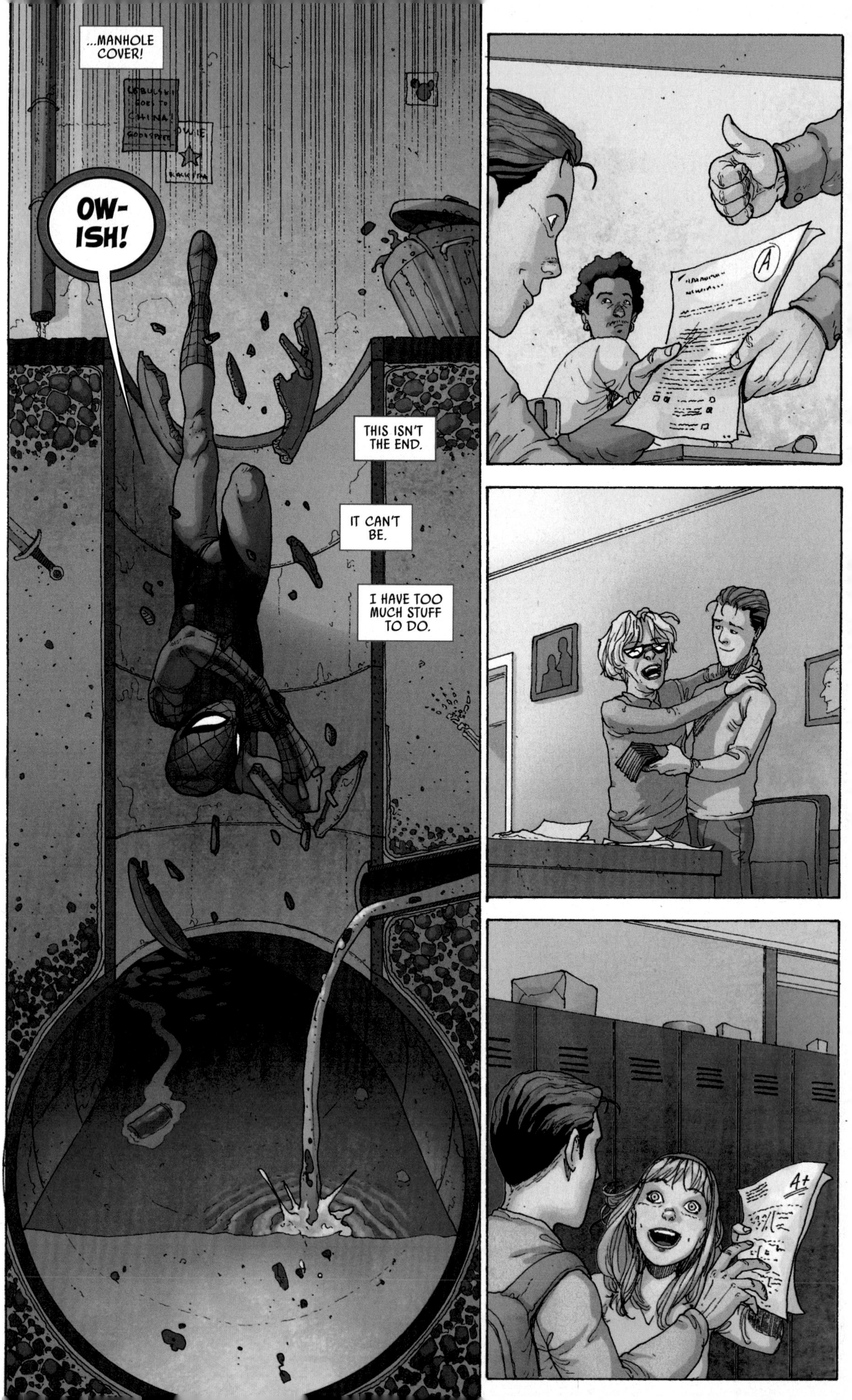
...MANHOLE COVER!
OW-ISH!
THIS ISN'T THE END.
IT CAN'T BE.
I HAVE TOO MUCH STUFF TO DO.
A
A+

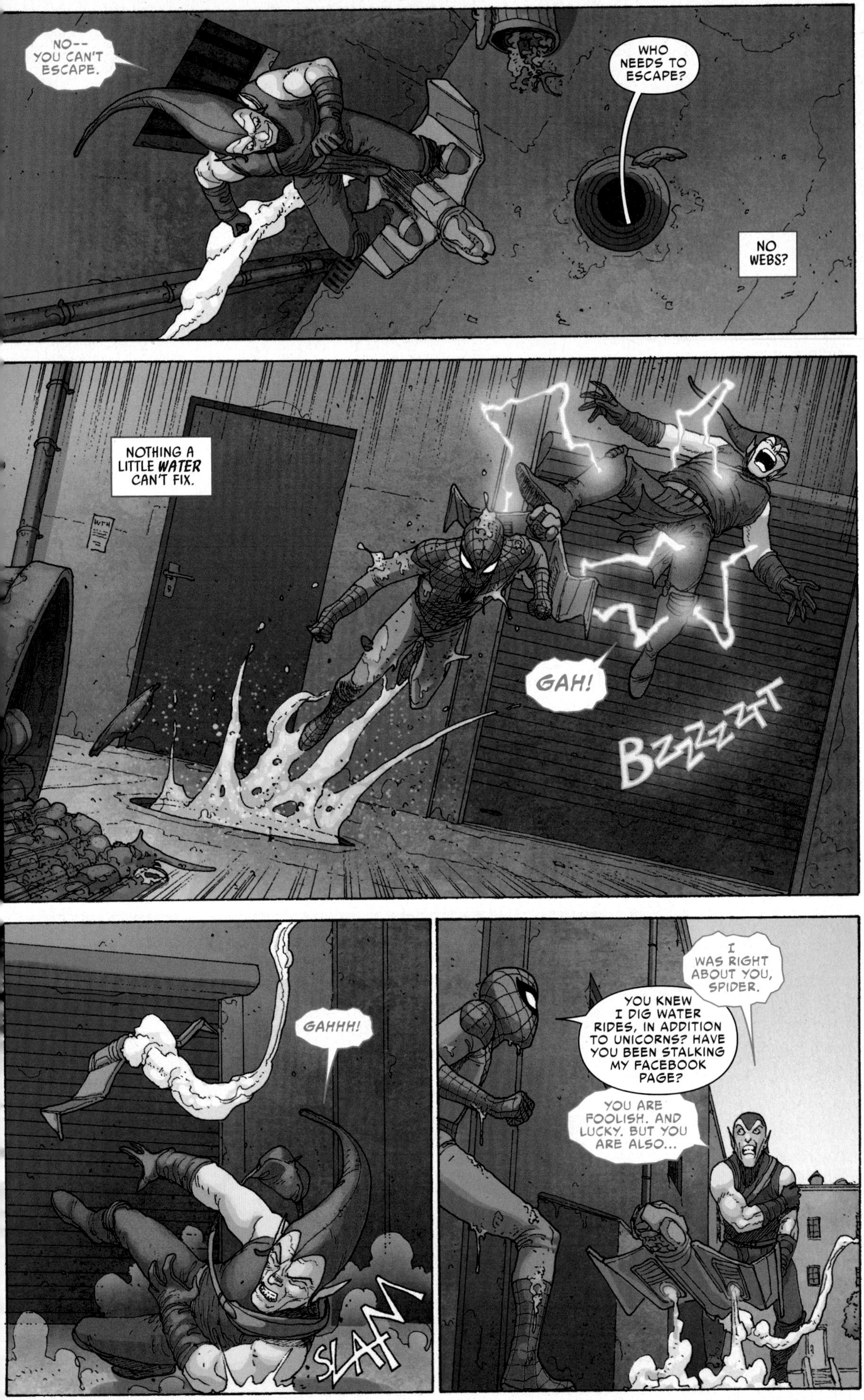
NO-- YOU CAN'T ESCAPE.
WHO NEEDS TO ESCAPE?
NO WEBS?
NOTHING A LITTLE WATER CAN'T FIX.
GAH!
BZZZZZT
GAHHH!
SLAM
I WAS RIGHT ABOUT YOU, SPIDER.
YOU KNEW I DIG WATER RIDES, IN ADDITION TO UNICORNS? HAVE YOU BEEN STALKING MY FACEBOOK PAGE?
YOU ARE FOOLISH. AND LUCKY. BUT YOU ARE ALSO...

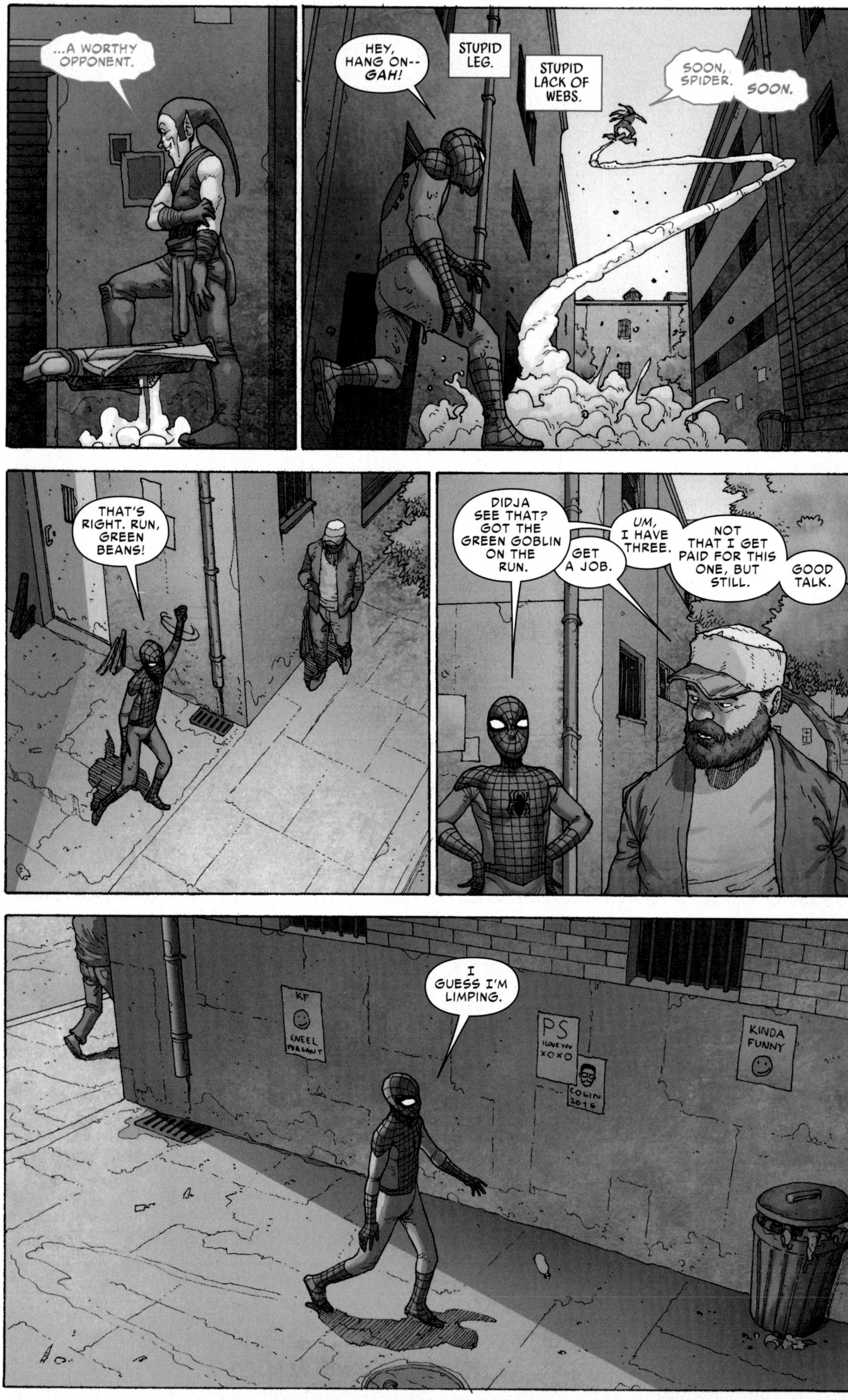

...A WORTHY OPPONENT.
HEY, HANG ON-- GAH!
STUPID LEG.
STUPID LACK OF WEBS.
SOON, SPIDER.
SOON.
THAT'S RIGHT. RUN, GREEN BEANS!
DIDJA SEE THAT? GOT THE GREEN GOBLIN ON THE RUN.
GET A JOB.
UM, I HAVE THREE.
NOT THAT I GET PAID FOR THIS ONE, BUT STILL.
GOOD TALK.
I GUESS I'M LIMPING.
KF
KNEEL PEASANT
PS
I LOVE YOU
XOXO
COLIN 2015
KINDA FUNNY

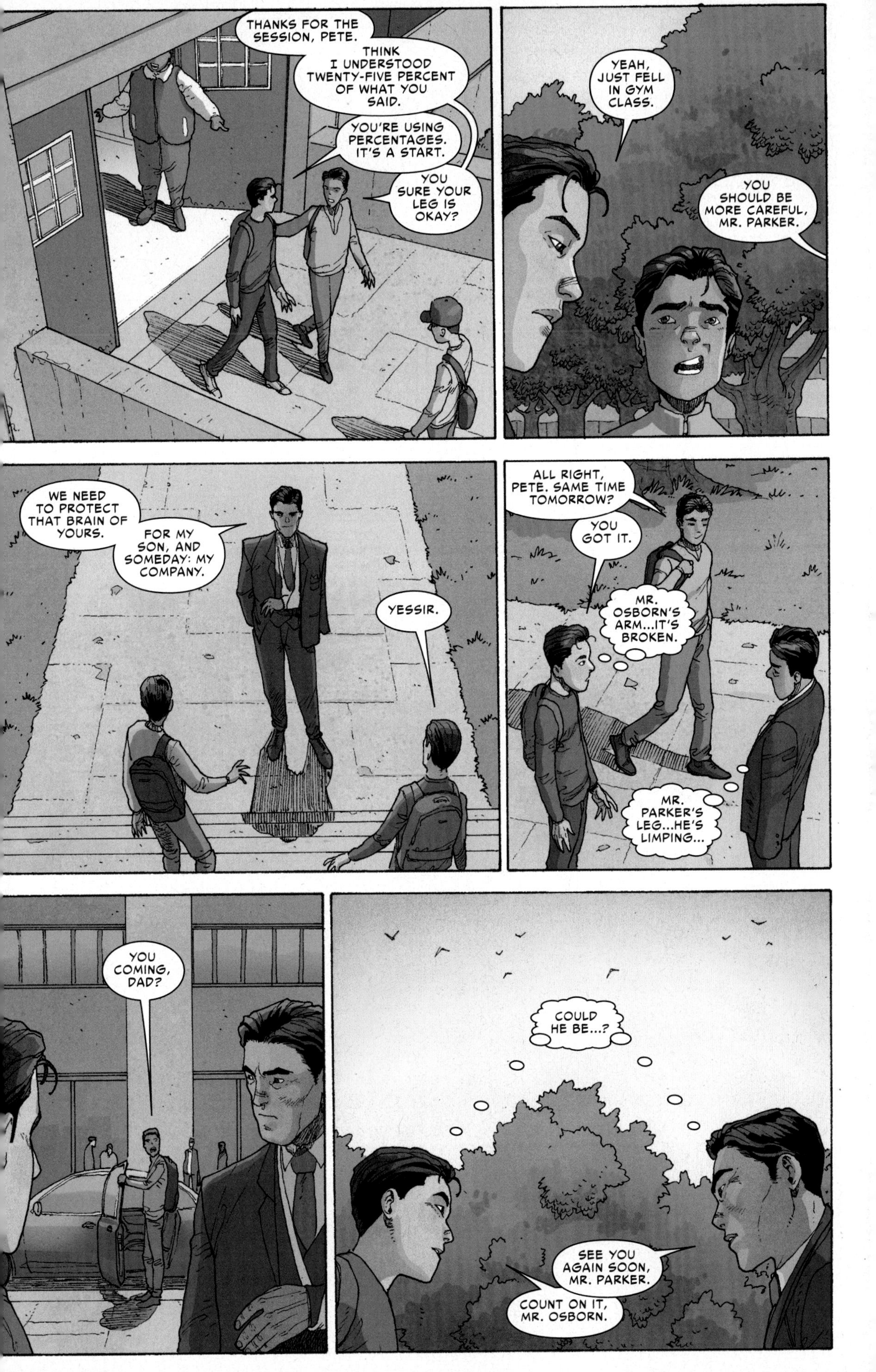
THANKS FOR THE SESSION, PETE.
THINK I UNDERSTOOD TWENTY-FIVE PERCENT OF WHAT YOU SAID.
YOU'RE USING PERCENTAGES. IT'S A START.
YOU SURE YOUR LEG IS OKAY?
YEAH, JUST FELL IN GYM CLASS.
YOU SHOULD BE MORE CAREFUL, MR. PARKER.
WE NEED TO PROTECT THAT BRAIN OF YOURS.
FOR MY SON, AND SOMEDAY: MY COMPANY.
YESSIR.
ALL RIGHT, PETE. SAME TIME TOMORROW?
YOU GOT IT.
MR. OSBORN'S ARM...IT'S BROKEN.
MR. PARKER'S LEG...HE'S LIMPING...
YOU COMING, DAD?
COULD HE BE...?
SEE YOU AGAIN SOON, MR. PARKER.
COUNT ON IT, MR. OSBORN.

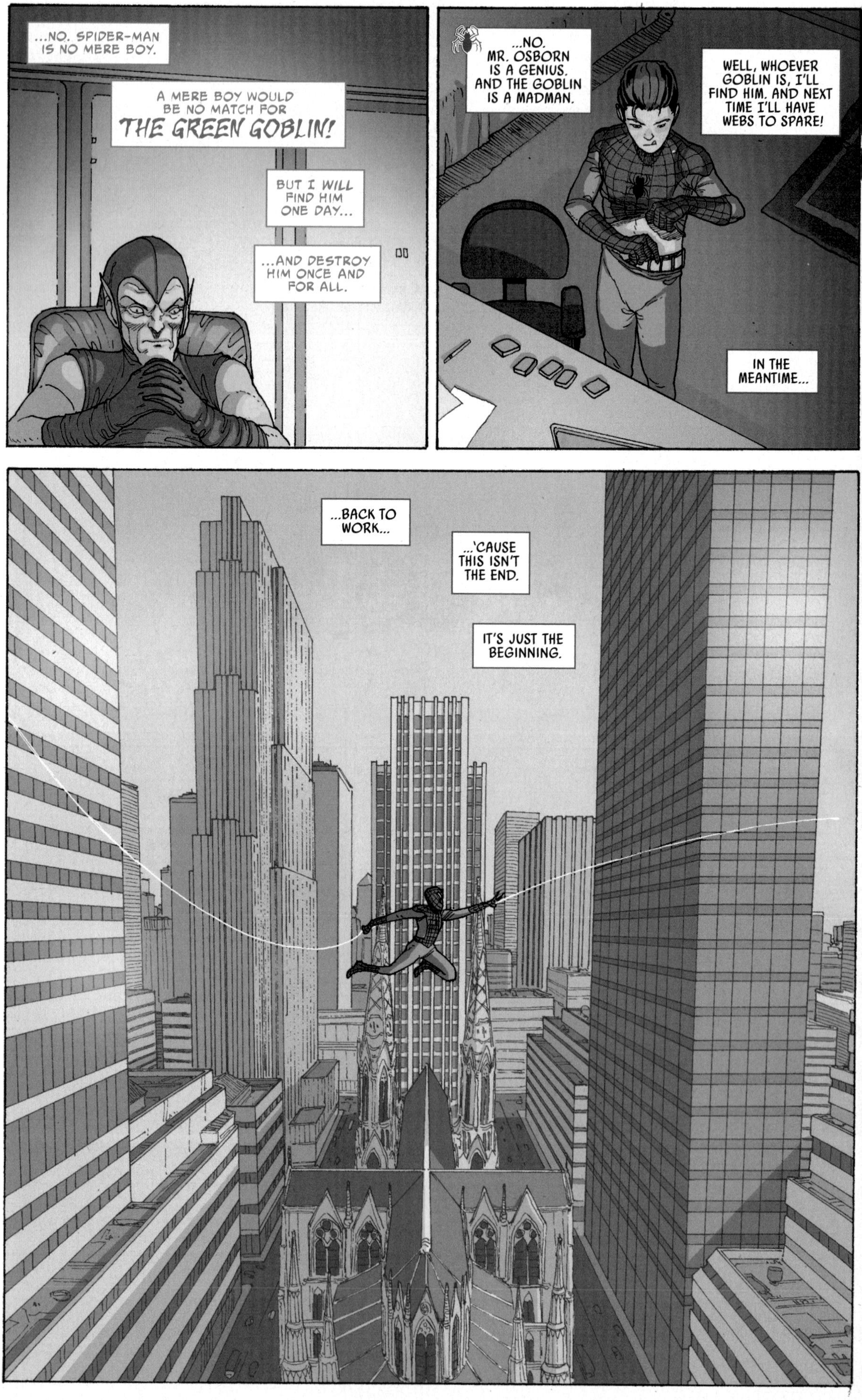

...NO. SPIDER-MAN IS NO MERE BOY.
A MERE BOY WOULD BE NO MATCH FOR THE GREEN GOBLIN!
BUT I WILL FIND HIM ONE DAY...
...AND DESTROY HIM ONCE AND FOR ALL.
...NO. MR. OSBORN IS A GENIUS. AND THE GOBLIN IS A MADMAN.
WELL, WHOEVER GOBLIN IS, I'LL FIND HIM. AND NEXT TIME I'LL HAVE WEBS TO SPARE!
IN THE MEANTIME...
...BACK TO WORK...
...'CAUSE THIS ISN'T THE END.
IT'S JUST THE BEGINNING.

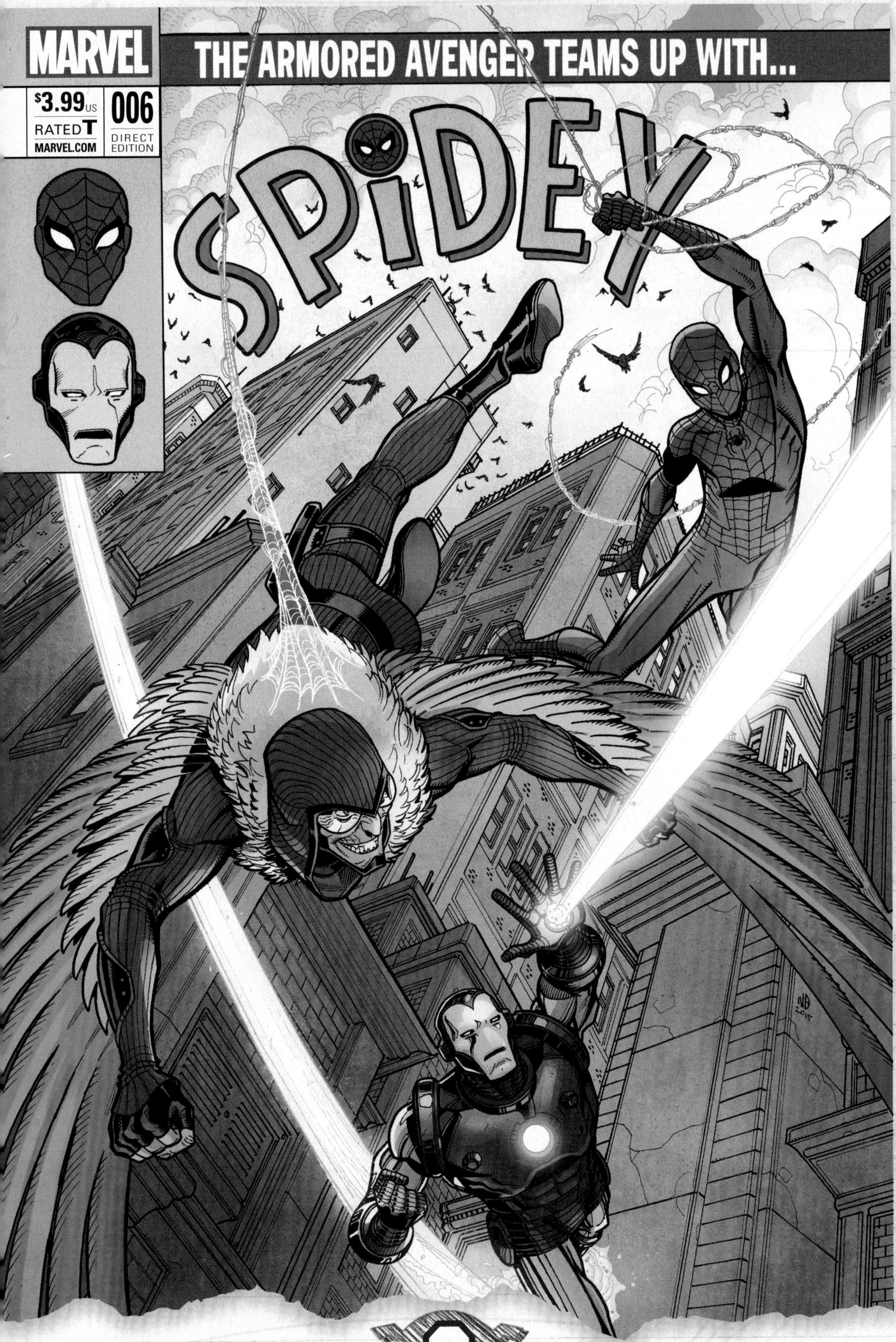
MARVEL
THE ARMORED AVENGER TEAMS UP WITH...
$3.99 US
006
RATED T
MARVEL.COM
DIRECT EDITION
SPIDEY

6

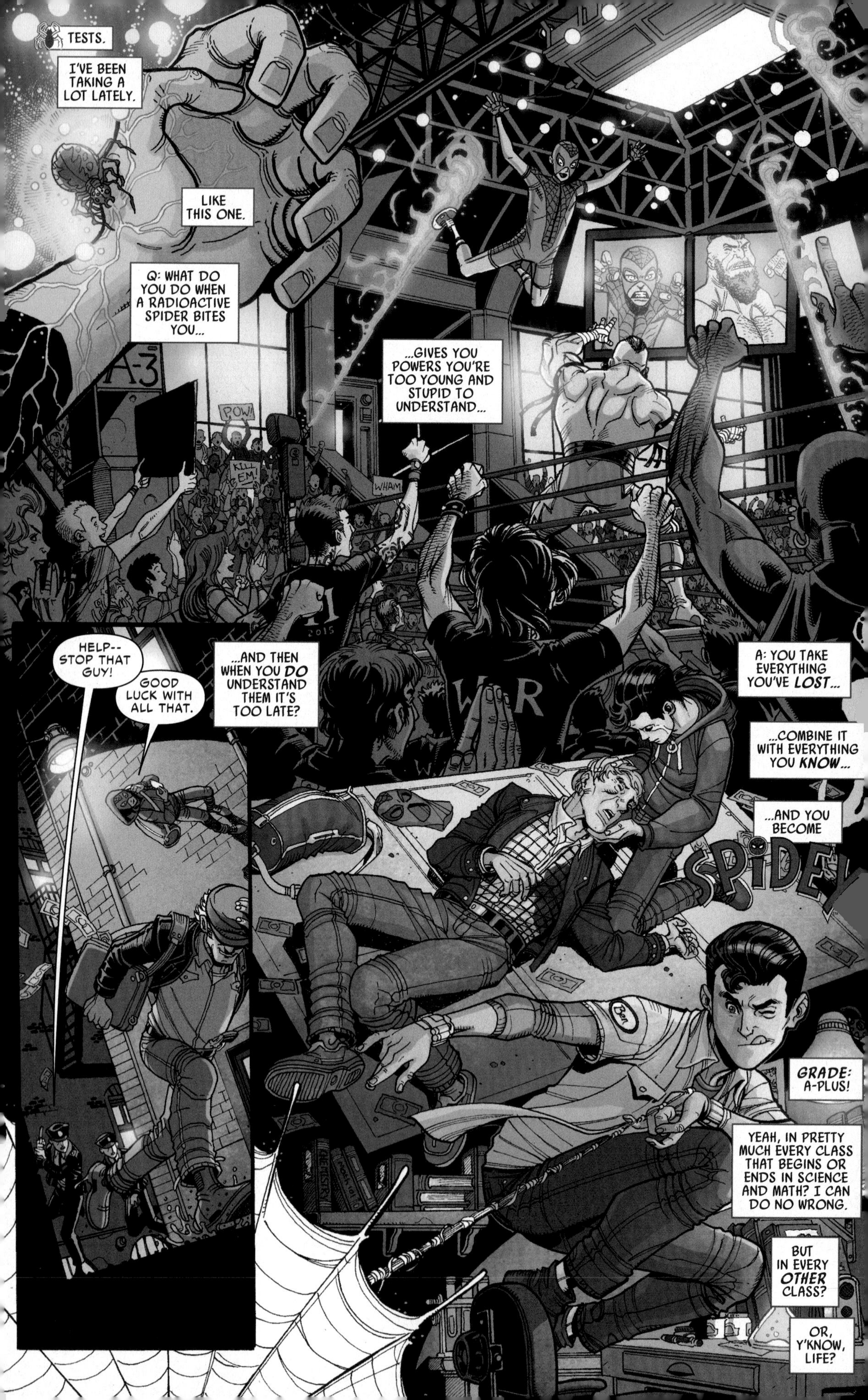
TESTS.
I'VE BEEN TAKING A LOT LATELY.
LIKE THIS ONE.
Q: WHAT DO YOU DO WHEN A RADIOACTIVE SPIDER BITES YOU...
...GIVES YOU POWERS YOU'RE TOO YOUNG AND STUPID TO UNDERSTAND...
A-3
POW!
KILL 'EM!
WHAM
HELP-- STOP THAT GUY!
GOOD LUCK WITH ALL THAT.
...AND THEN WHEN YOU *DO* UNDERSTAND THEM IT'S TOO LATE?
A: YOU TAKE EVERYTHING YOU'VE *LOST*...
...COMBINE IT WITH EVERYTHING YOU *KNOW*...
...AND YOU BECOME
SPIDEY
GRADE: A-PLUS!
YEAH, IN PRETTY MUCH EVERY CLASS THAT BEGINS OR ENDS IN SCIENCE AND MATH? I CAN DO NO WRONG.
BUT IN EVERY *OTHER* CLASS?
OR, Y'KNOW, LIFE?

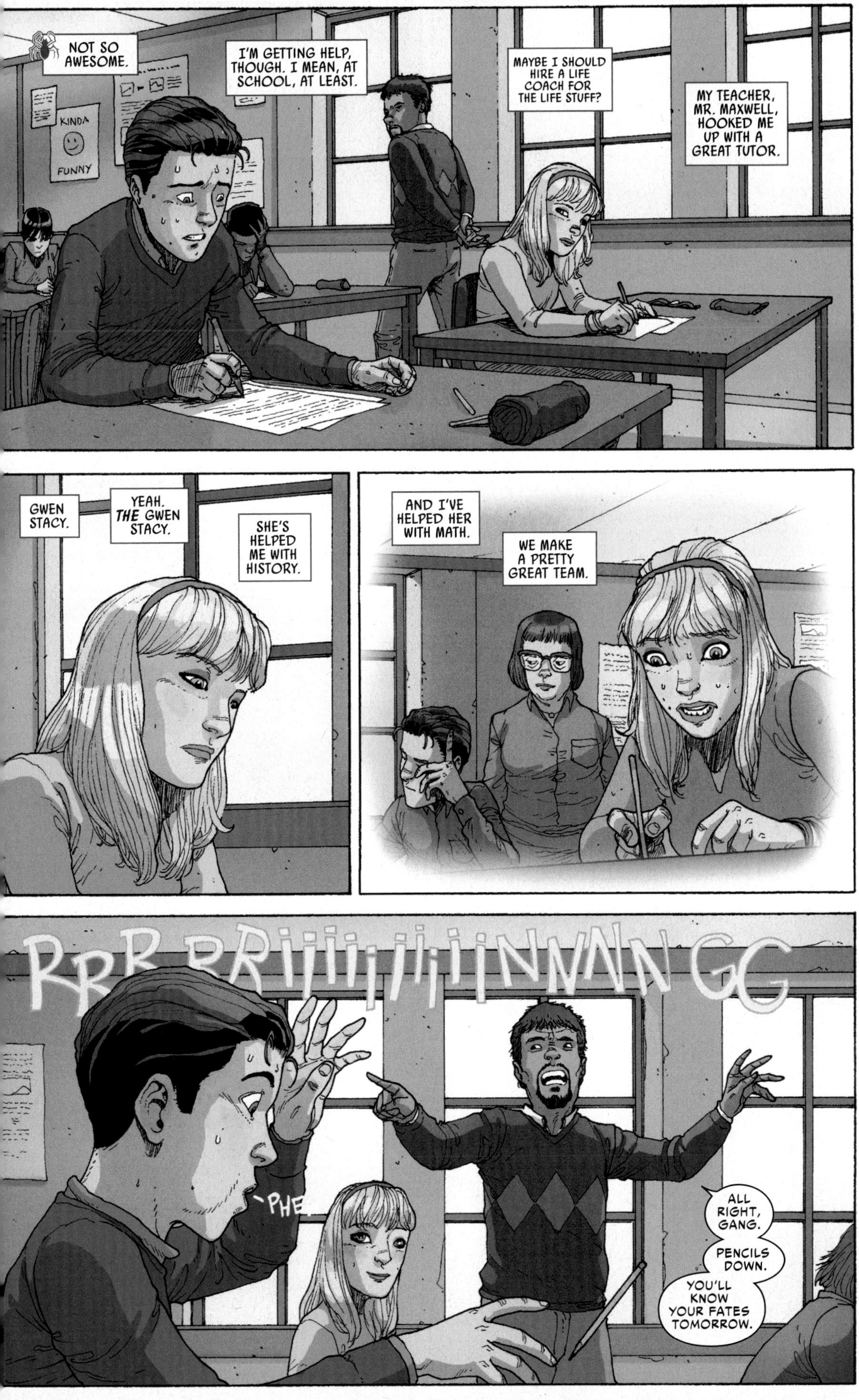
NOT SO AWESOME.
I'M GETTING HELP, THOUGH. I MEAN, AT SCHOOL, AT LEAST.
MAYBE I SHOULD HIRE A LIFE COACH FOR THE LIFE STUFF?
MY TEACHER, MR. MAXWELL, HOOKED ME UP WITH A GREAT TUTOR.
KINDA
FUNNY
GWEN STACY.
YEAH. THE GWEN STACY.
SHE'S HELPED ME WITH HISTORY.
AND I'VE HELPED HER WITH MATH.
WE MAKE A PRETTY GREAT TEAM.
RRR RRIIIIIIIIIINNNN GG
PHEW
ALL RIGHT, GANG.
PENCILS DOWN.
YOU'LL KNOW YOUR FATES TOMORROW.

SO? I MEAN, I FINISHED. THAT'S A GOOD START.

I'M SURE YOU DID GREAT, PETER. YOU HAVE, LIKE, THE WORLD'S GREATEST TUTOR.

WORLD'S GREATEST TUTOR. WORLD'S GREATEST *EVERYTHING*.

KEEP IT TOGETHER, PETER. PACE YOURSELF.

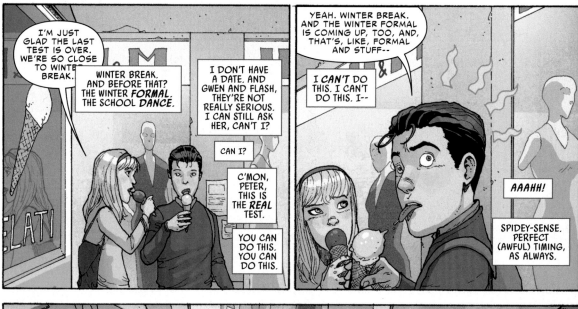

I'M JUST GLAD THE LAST TEST IS OVER. WE'RE SO CLOSE TO WINTER BREAK.

WINTER BREAK. AND BEFORE THAT? THE WINTER *FORMAL*. THE SCHOOL *DANCE*.

I DON'T HAVE A DATE. AND GWEN AND FLASH, THEY'RE NOT REALLY SERIOUS. I CAN STILL ASK HER, CAN'T I?

CAN I?

C'MON, PETER, THIS IS THE *REAL* TEST.

YOU CAN DO THIS. YOU CAN DO THIS.

YEAH. WINTER BREAK. AND THE WINTER FORMAL IS COMING UP, TOO, AND, THAT'S, LIKE, FORMAL AND STUFF--

I *CAN'T* DO THIS. I CAN'T DO THIS. I--

AAAHH!

SPIDEY-SENSE. PERFECT (AWFUL) TIMING, AS ALWAYS.

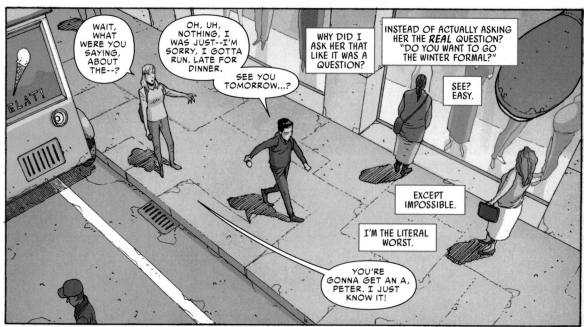

WAIT, WHAT WERE YOU SAYING, ABOUT THE--?

OH, UH, NOTHING, I WAS JUST--I'M SORRY, I GOTTA RUN. LATE FOR DINNER.

SEE YOU TOMORROW...?

WHY DID I ASK HER THAT LIKE IT WAS A QUESTION?

INSTEAD OF ACTUALLY ASKING HER THE *REAL* QUESTION? "DO YOU WANT TO GO THE WINTER FORMAL?"

SEE? EASY.

EXCEPT IMPOSSIBLE.

I'M THE LITERAL WORST.

YOU'RE GONNA GET AN A, PETER. I JUST KNOW IT!

Q: HOW DO YOU ASK A GIRL OUT?

A:...

GRADE: EPIC FAIL.

ZOMBIES THE MOVIE

WHY IS THIS SO HARD?

"DO YOU WANT TO GO TO THE WINTER FORMAL?"

IT *SOUNDS* EASY. IN MY HEAD ANYWAY.

MAYBE I SHOULD TRY IT OUT LOUD.

DO YOU WANT TO GO TO THE WINTER FORMAL?

(TERRIBLE)

DO *YOU* WANT TO GO TO THE WINTER FORMAL?

(WORSE)

BREAK-IN. WHAT BUILDING IS THIS?

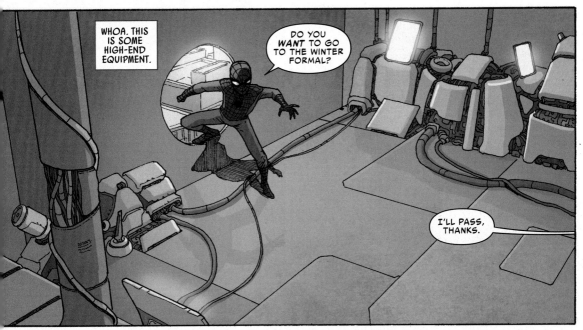

WHOA. THIS IS SOME HIGH-END EQUIPMENT.

DO YOU *WANT* TO GO TO THE WINTER FORMAL?

I'LL PASS, THANKS.

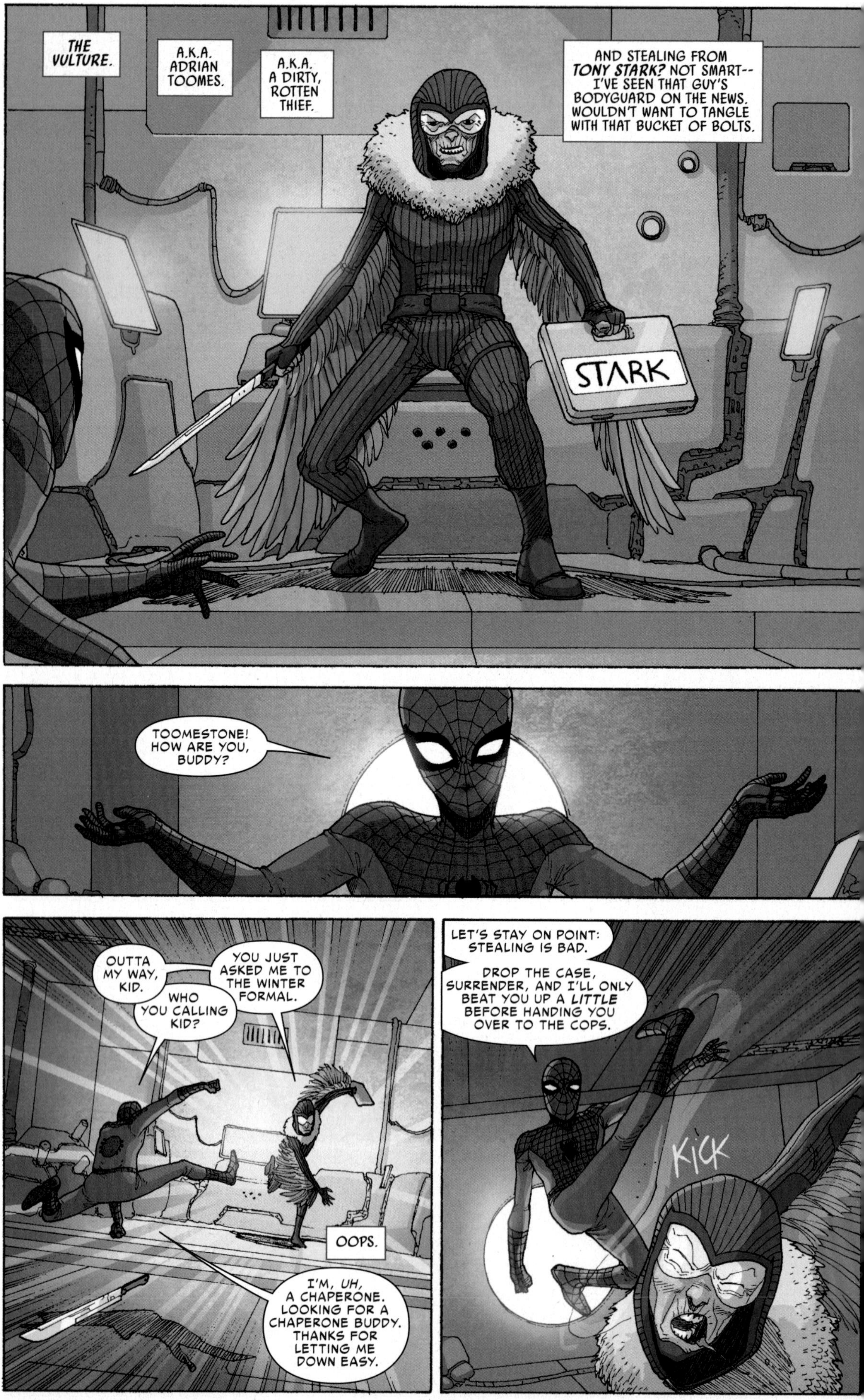

THE VULTURE.
A.K.A. ADRIAN TOOMES.
A.K.A. A DIRTY, ROTTEN THIEF.
AND STEALING FROM TONY STARK? NOT SMART-- I'VE SEEN THAT GUY'S BODYGUARD ON THE NEWS. WOULDN'T WANT TO TANGLE WITH THAT BUCKET OF BOLTS.
STARK
TOOMESTONE! HOW ARE YOU, BUDDY?
OUTTA MY WAY, KID.
YOU JUST ASKED ME TO THE WINTER FORMAL.
WHO YOU CALLING KID?
OOPS.
I'M, UH, A CHAPERONE. LOOKING FOR A CHAPERONE BUDDY. THANKS FOR LETTING ME DOWN EASY.
LET'S STAY ON POINT: STEALING IS BAD.
DROP THE CASE, SURRENDER, AND I'LL ONLY BEAT YOU UP A LITTLE BEFORE HANDING YOU OVER TO THE COPS.
KICK

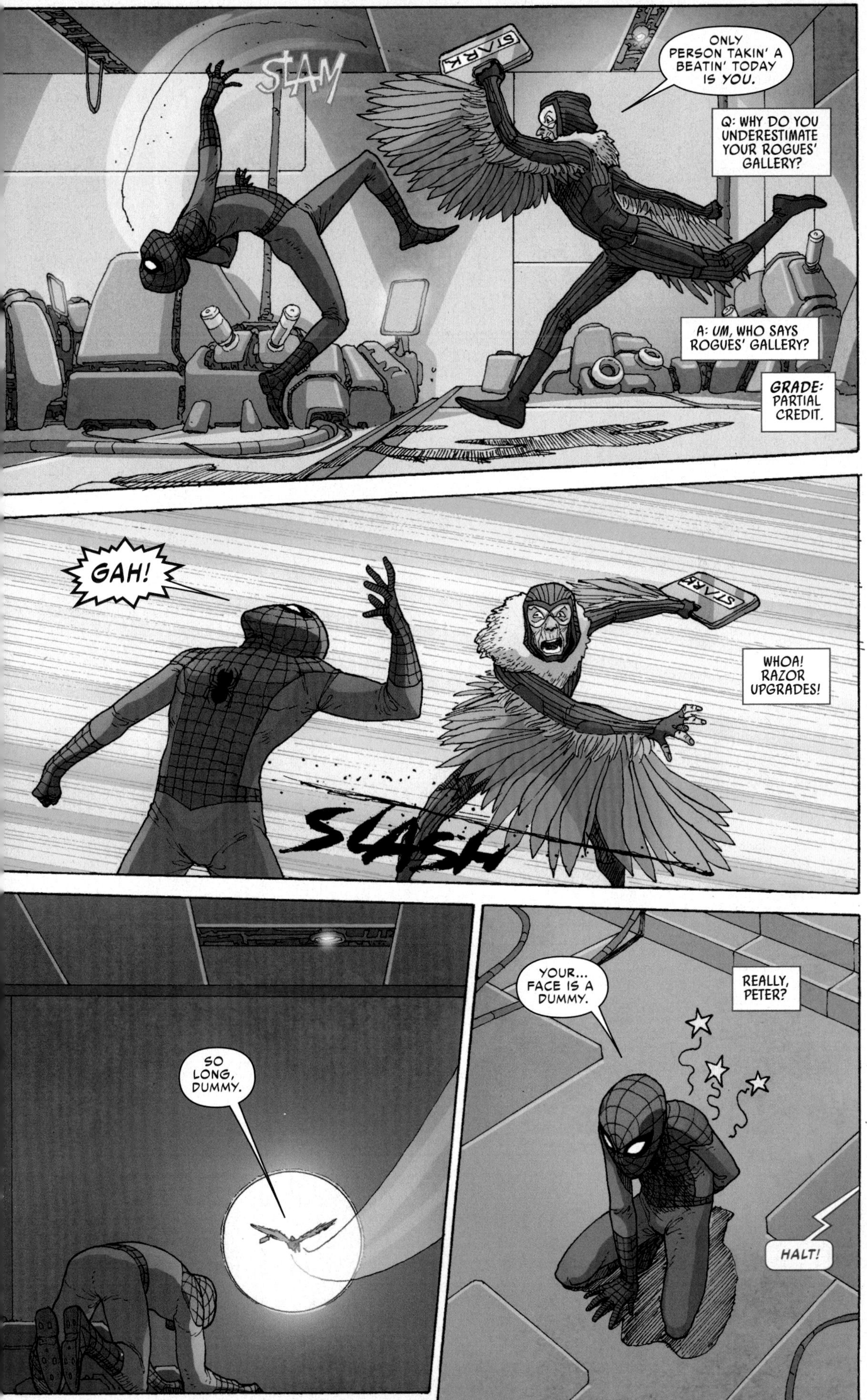
SLAM
STARK
ONLY PERSON TAKIN' A BEATIN' TODAY IS YOU.
Q: WHY DO YOU UNDERESTIMATE YOUR ROGUES' GALLERY?
A: UM, WHO SAYS ROGUES' GALLERY?
GRADE: PARTIAL CREDIT.
GAH!
STARK
WHOA! RAZOR UPGRADES!
SLASH
SO LONG, DUMMY.
YOUR... FACE IS A DUMMY.
REALLY, PETER?
HALT!

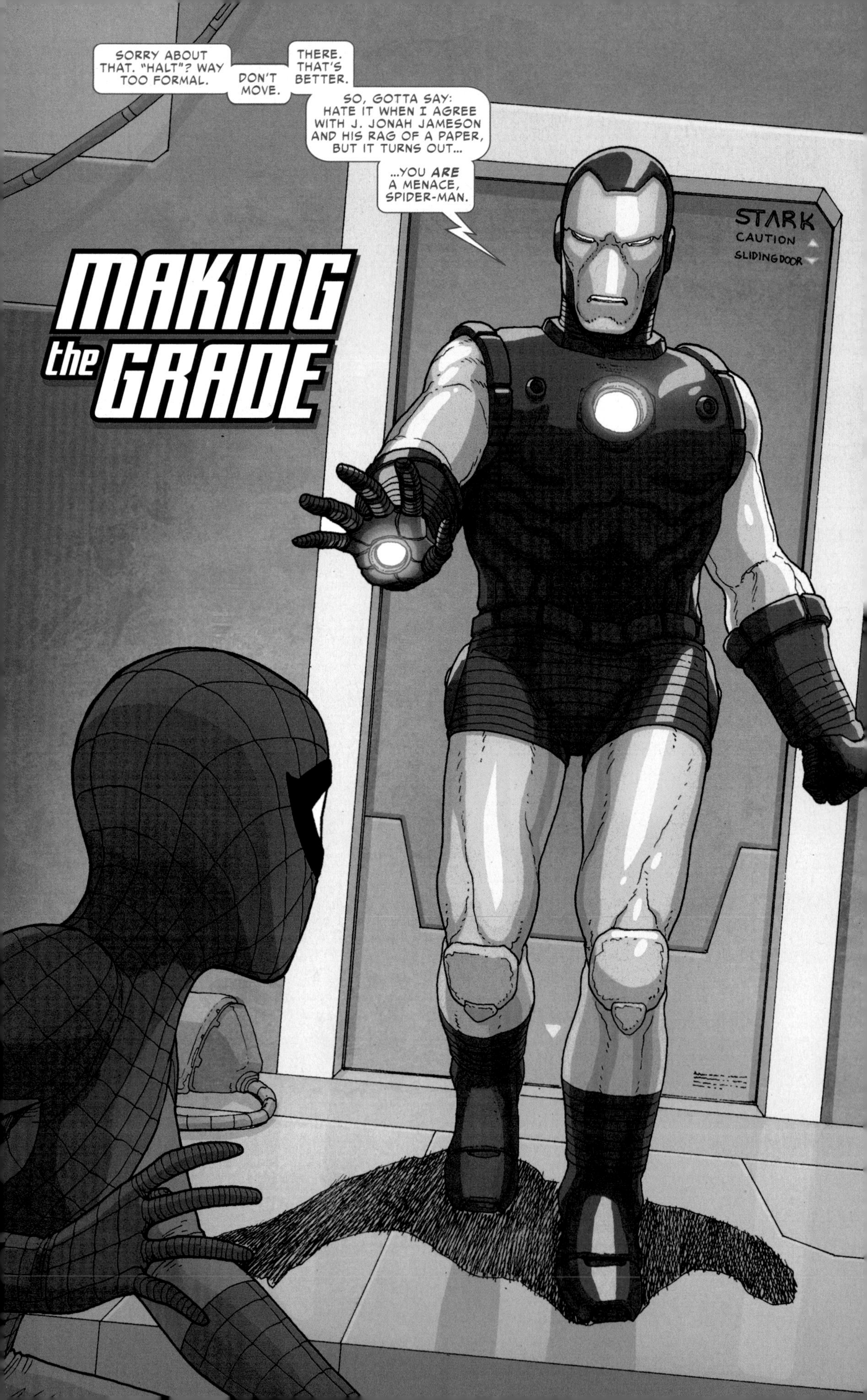
SORRY ABOUT THAT. "HALT"? WAY TOO FORMAL.
DON'T MOVE.
THERE. THAT'S BETTER.
SO, GOTTA SAY: HATE IT WHEN I AGREE WITH J. JONAH JAMESON AND HIS RAG OF A PAPER, BUT IT TURNS OUT...
...YOU ARE A MENACE, SPIDER-MAN.
STARK
CAUTION
SLIDING DOOR
MAKING the GRADE

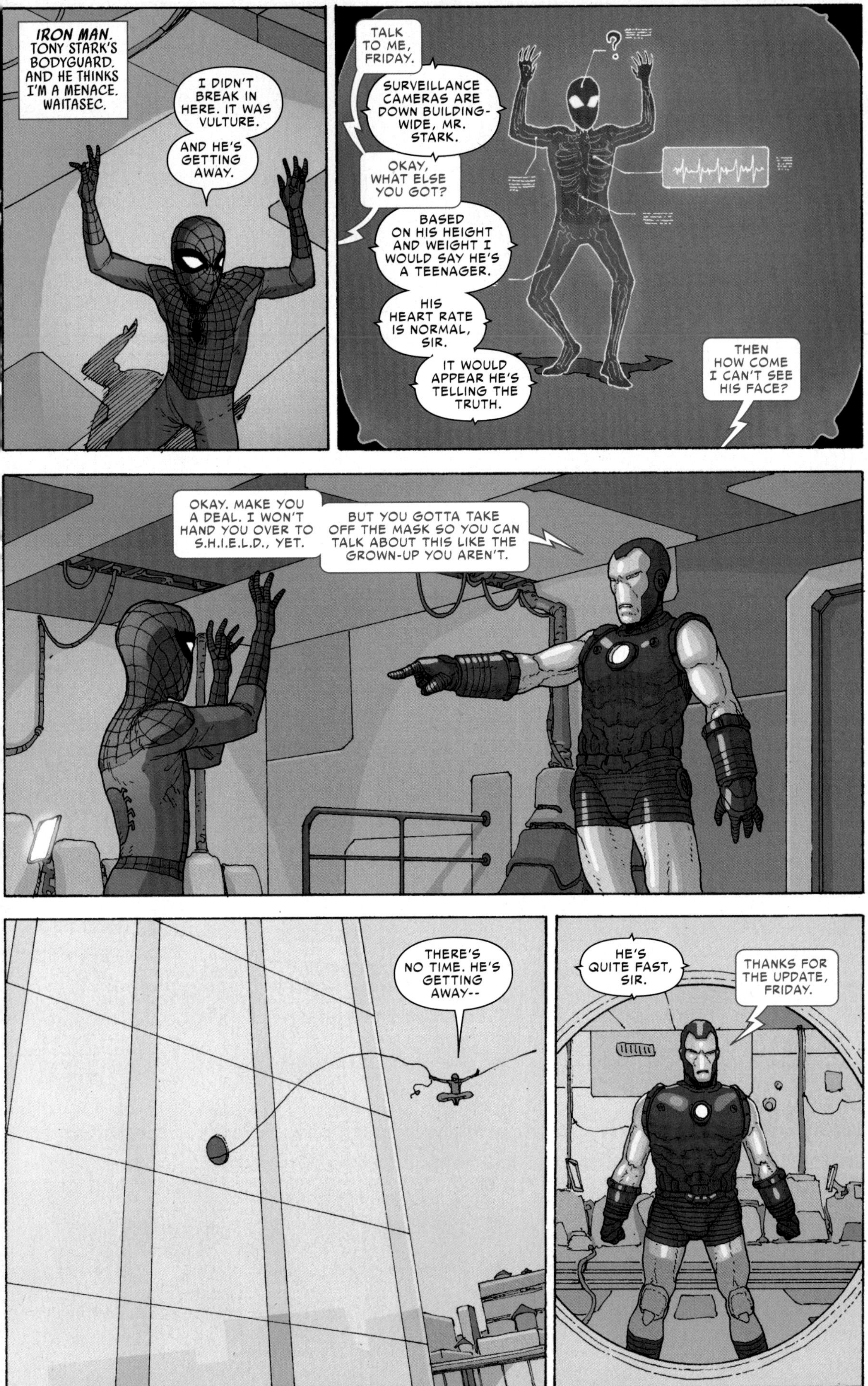

IRON MAN. TONY STARK'S BODYGUARD. AND HE THINKS I'M A MENACE. WAITASEC.
I DIDN'T BREAK IN HERE. IT WAS VULTURE.
AND HE'S GETTING AWAY.
TALK TO ME, FRIDAY.
SURVEILLANCE CAMERAS ARE DOWN BUILDING-WIDE, MR. STARK.
OKAY, WHAT ELSE YOU GOT?
BASED ON HIS HEIGHT AND WEIGHT I WOULD SAY HE'S A TEENAGER.
HIS HEART RATE IS NORMAL, SIR.
IT WOULD APPEAR HE'S TELLING THE TRUTH.
THEN HOW COME I CAN'T SEE HIS FACE?
OKAY. MAKE YOU A DEAL. I WON'T HAND YOU OVER TO S.H.I.E.L.D., YET.
BUT YOU GOTTA TAKE OFF THE MASK SO YOU CAN TALK ABOUT THIS LIKE THE GROWN-UP YOU AREN'T.
THERE'S NO TIME. HE'S GETTING AWAY--
HE'S QUITE FAST, SIR.
THANKS FOR THE UPDATE, FRIDAY.

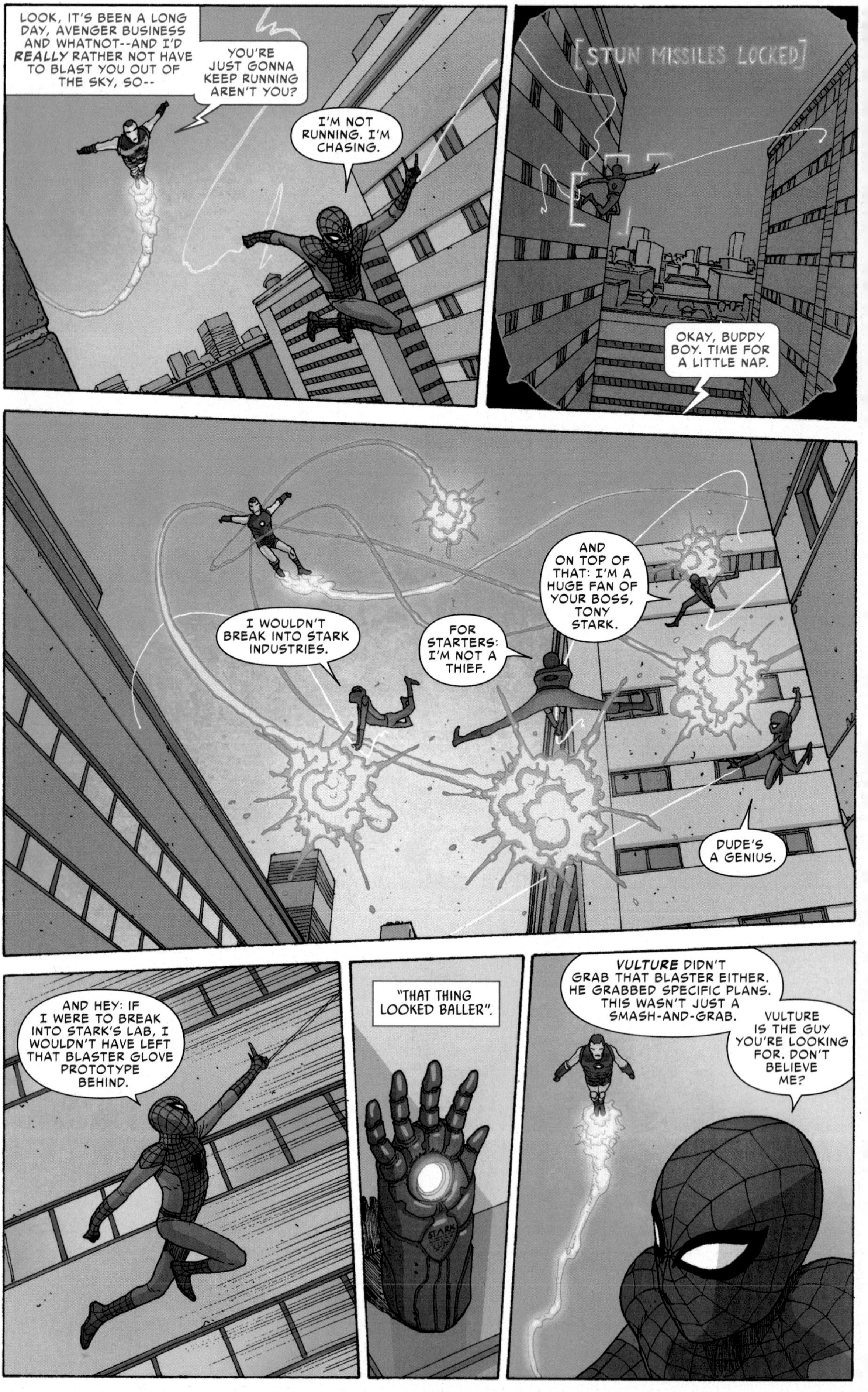
LOOK, IT'S BEEN A LONG DAY, AVENGER BUSINESS AND WHATNOT--AND I'D REALLY RATHER NOT HAVE TO BLAST YOU OUT OF THE SKY, SO--
YOU'RE JUST GONNA KEEP RUNNING AREN'T YOU?
I'M NOT RUNNING. I'M CHASING.
[STUN MISSILES LOCKED]
OKAY, BUDDY BOY. TIME FOR A LITTLE NAP.
I WOULDN'T BREAK INTO STARK INDUSTRIES.
FOR STARTERS: I'M NOT A THIEF.
AND ON TOP OF THAT: I'M A HUGE FAN OF YOUR BOSS, TONY STARK.
DUDE'S A GENIUS.
AND HEY: IF I WERE TO BREAK INTO STARK'S LAB, I WOULDN'T HAVE LEFT THAT BLASTER GLOVE PROTOTYPE BEHIND.
"THAT THING LOOKED BALLER".
STARK
VULTURE DIDN'T GRAB THAT BLASTER EITHER. HE GRABBED SPECIFIC PLANS. THIS WASN'T JUST A SMASH-AND-GRAB.
VULTURE IS THE GUY YOU'RE LOOKING FOR. DON'T BELIEVE ME?

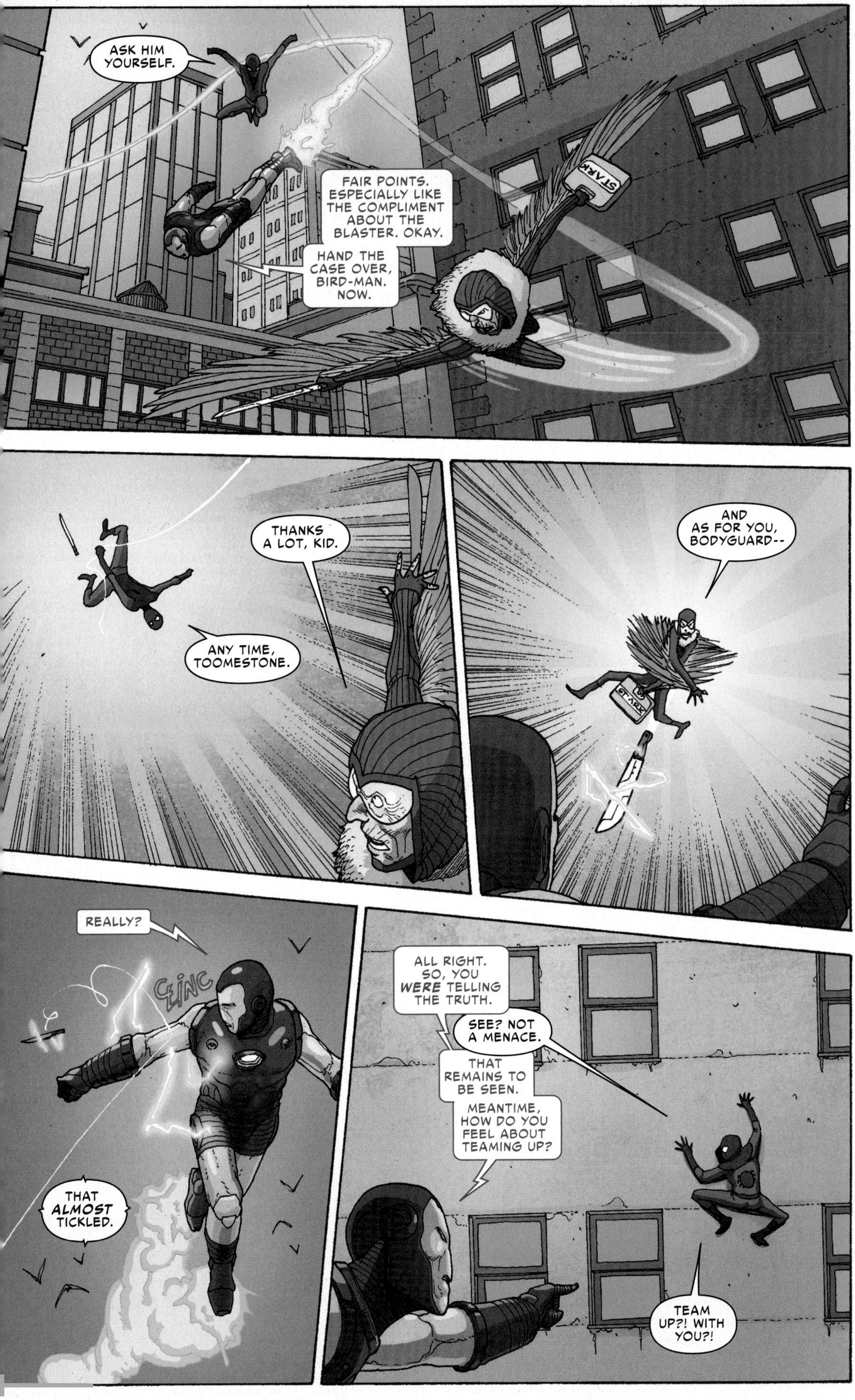
ASK HIM YOURSELF.
FAIR POINTS. ESPECIALLY LIKE THE COMPLIMENT ABOUT THE BLASTER. OKAY.
HAND THE CASE OVER, BIRD-MAN. NOW.
STARK
THANKS A LOT, KID.
ANY TIME, TOOMESTONE.
AND AS FOR YOU, BODYGUARD--
STARK
REALLY?
CLINC
THAT *ALMOST* TICKLED.
ALL RIGHT. SO, YOU *WERE* TELLING THE TRUTH.
SEE? NOT A MENACE.
THAT REMAINS TO BE SEEN.
MEANTIME, HOW DO YOU FEEL ABOUT TEAMING UP?
TEAM UP?! WITH YOU?!

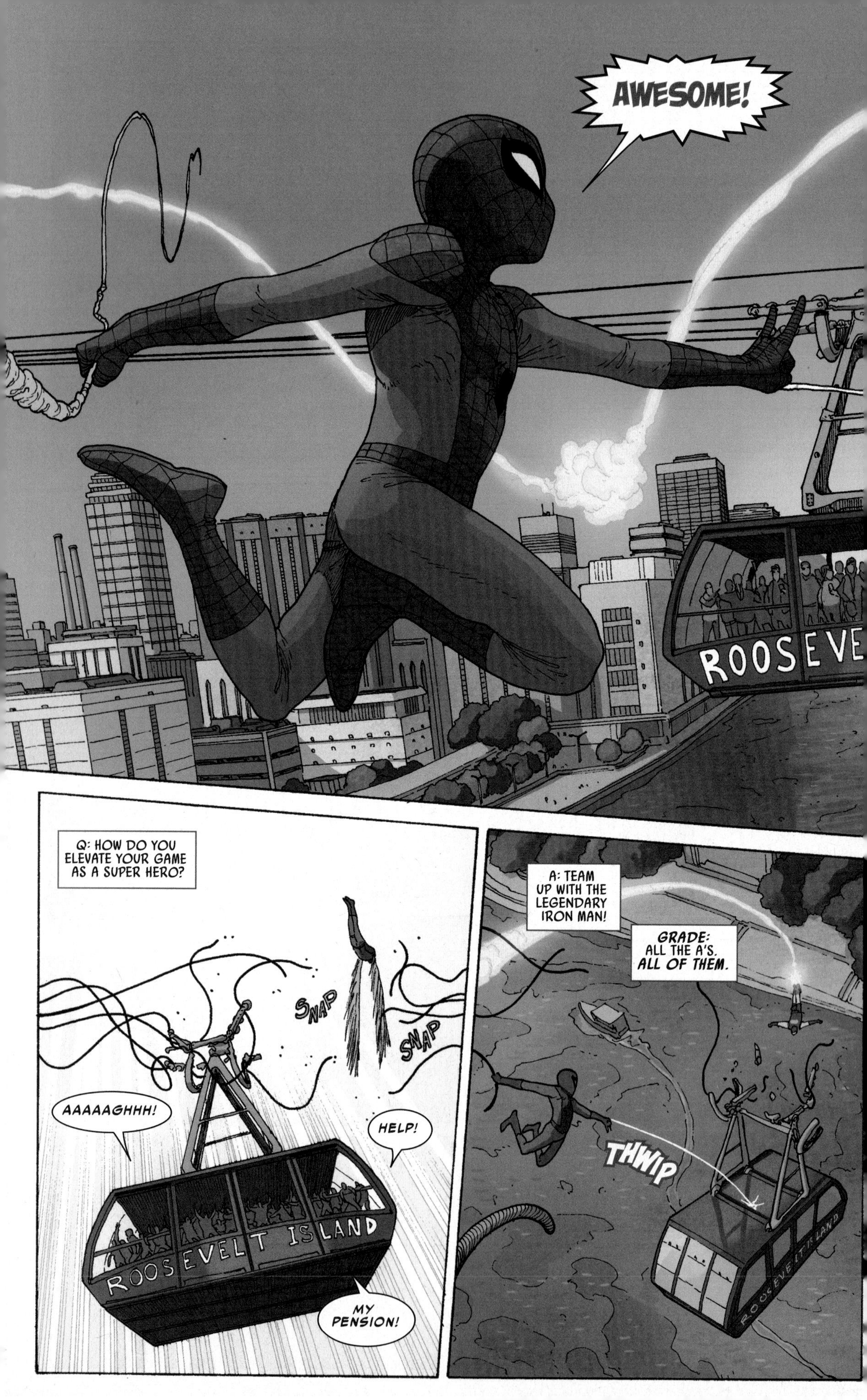
AWESOME!
ROOSEVE
Q: HOW DO YOU ELEVATE YOUR GAME AS A SUPER HERO?
SNAP
SNAP
AAAAAGHHH!
HELP!
ROOSEVELT ISLAND
MY PENSION!
A: TEAM UP WITH THE LEGENDARY IRON MAN!
GRADE: ALL THE A'S. ALL OF THEM.
THWIP
ROOSEVELT ISLAND

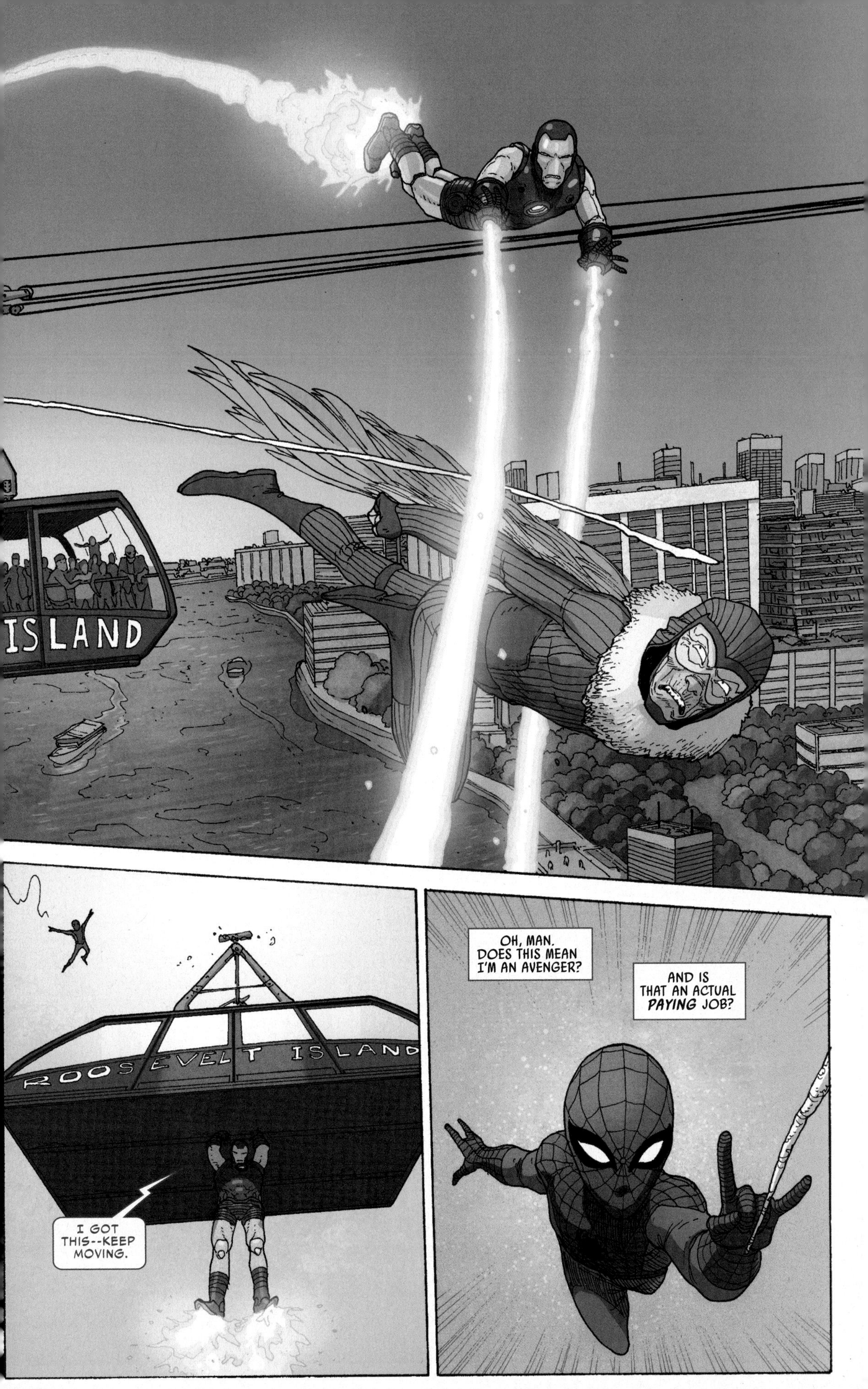
ISLAND
ROOSEVELT ISLAND
I GOT THIS--KEEP MOVING.
OH, MAN. DOES THIS MEAN I'M AN AVENGER?
AND IS THAT AN ACTUAL PAYING JOB?

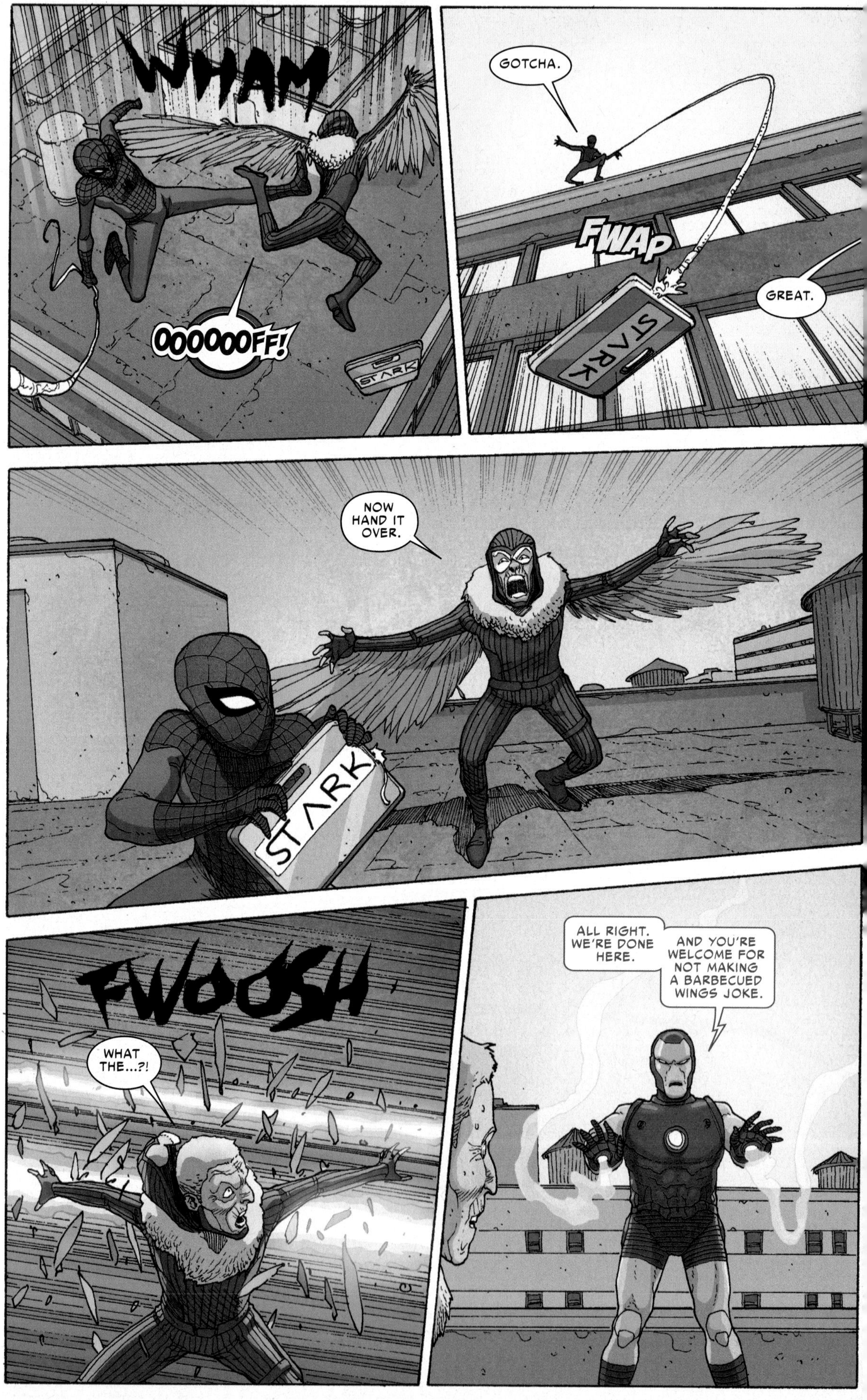
WHAM
OOOOOOFF!
STARK
GOTCHA.
FWAP
GREAT.
STARK
NOW HAND IT OVER.
STARK
FWOOSH
WHAT THE...?!
ALL RIGHT. WE'RE DONE HERE.
AND YOU'RE WELCOME FOR NOT MAKING A BARBECUED WINGS JOKE.

AGENT COULSON. HE'S ALL YOURS.

ALWAYS A PLEASURE, IRON MAN.

SHIELD 0357

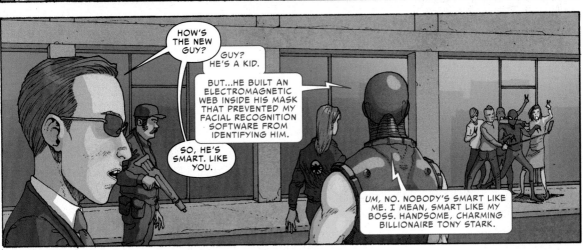

HOW'S THE NEW GUY?

GUY? HE'S A KID.

BUT...HE BUILT AN ELECTROMAGNETIC WEB INSIDE HIS MASK THAT PREVENTED MY FACIAL RECOGNITION SOFTWARE FROM IDENTIFYING HIM.

SO, HE'S SMART. LIKE YOU.

UM, NO. NOBODY'S SMART LIKE ME. I MEAN, SMART LIKE MY BOSS. HANDSOME, CHARMING BILLIONAIRE TONY STARK.

SO, WE KEEP AN EYE ON THE KID, OR DO I TAKE HIM IN, TOO?

HE'S A KID. GO AWAY.

HEY, GANG. MIND IF I BORROW THE MENACE?

WAIT, WHAT--I'M NOT--

ROOF TALK. LET'S GO. C'MON.

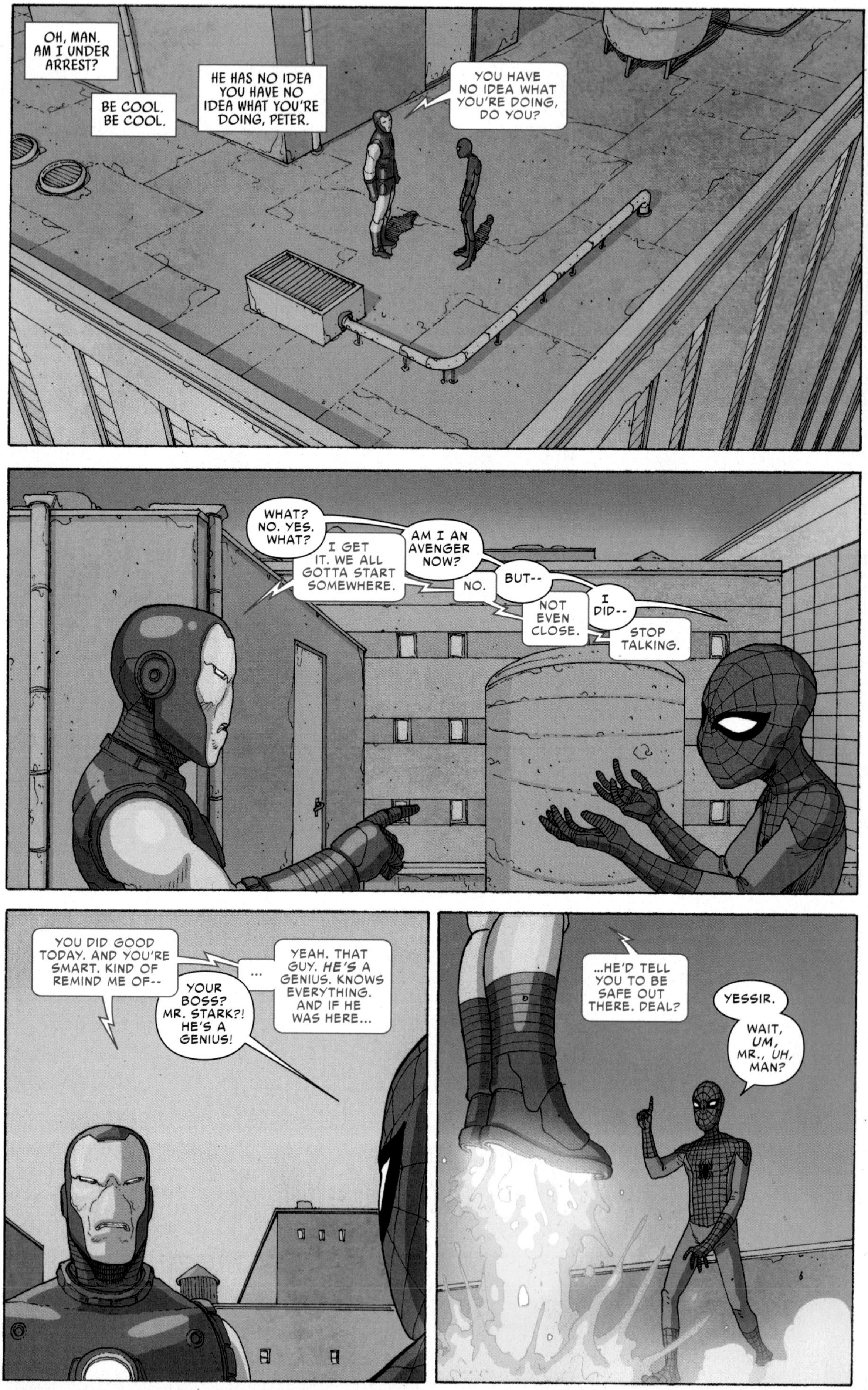
OH, MAN. AM I UNDER ARREST?
BE COOL. BE COOL.
HE HAS NO IDEA YOU HAVE NO IDEA WHAT YOU'RE DOING, PETER.
YOU HAVE NO IDEA WHAT YOU'RE DOING, DO YOU?
WHAT? NO. YES. WHAT?
I GET IT. WE ALL GOTTA START SOMEWHERE.
AM I AN AVENGER NOW?
NO.
BUT--
NOT EVEN CLOSE.
I DID--
STOP TALKING.
YOU DID GOOD TODAY. AND YOU'RE SMART. KIND OF REMIND ME OF--
YOUR BOSS? MR. STARK?! HE'S A GENIUS!
...
YEAH. THAT GUY. HE'S A GENIUS. KNOWS EVERYTHING. AND IF HE WAS HERE...
...HE'D TELL YOU TO BE SAFE OUT THERE. DEAL?
YESSIR.
WAIT, UM, MR., UH, MAN?

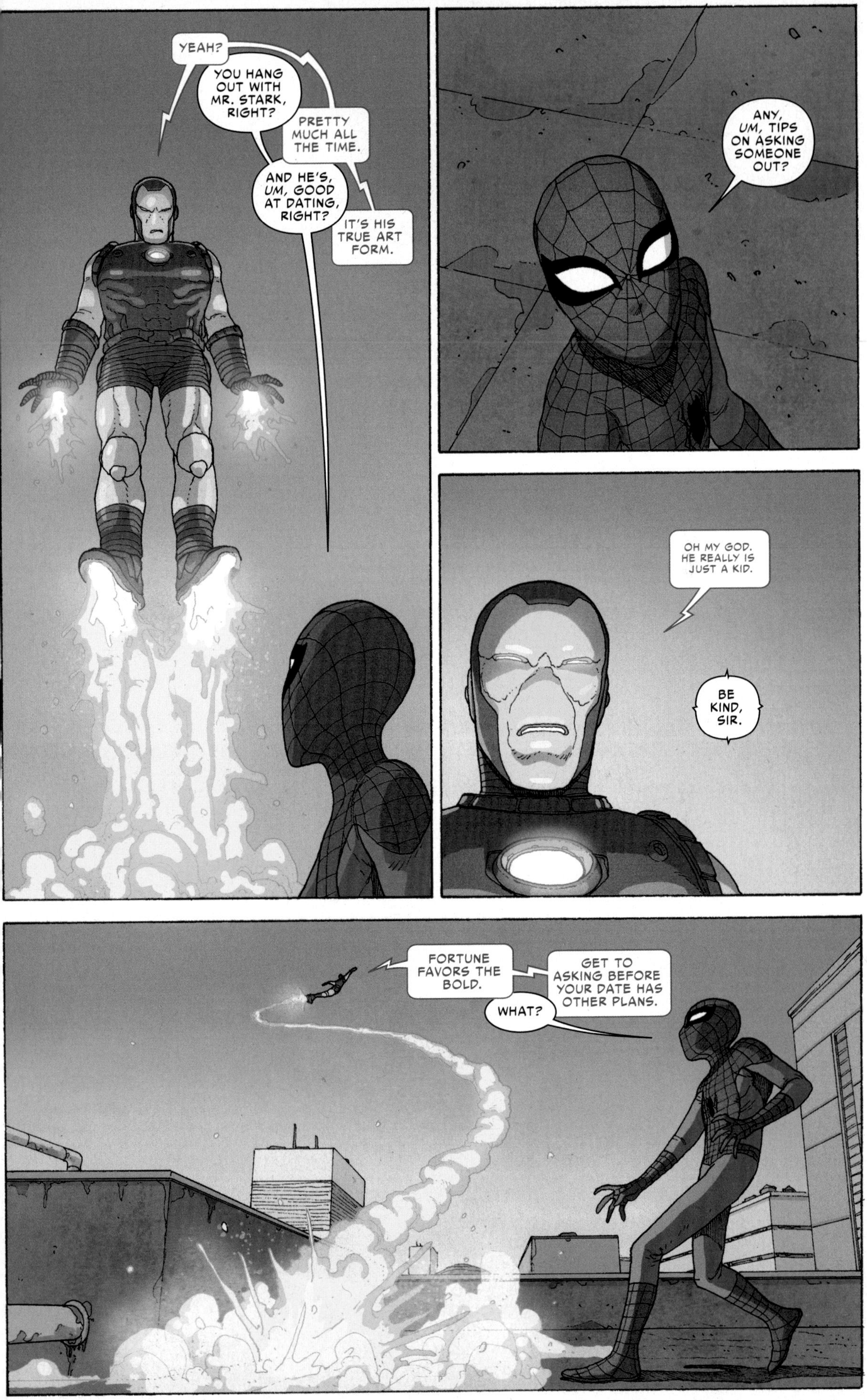
YEAH?
YOU HANG OUT WITH MR. STARK, RIGHT?
PRETTY MUCH ALL THE TIME.
AND HE'S, UM, GOOD AT DATING, RIGHT?
IT'S HIS TRUE ART FORM.
ANY, UM, TIPS ON ASKING SOMEONE OUT?
OH MY GOD. HE REALLY IS JUST A KID.
BE KIND, SIR.
FORTUNE FAVORS THE BOLD.
GET TO ASKING BEFORE YOUR DATE HAS OTHER PLANS.
WHAT?

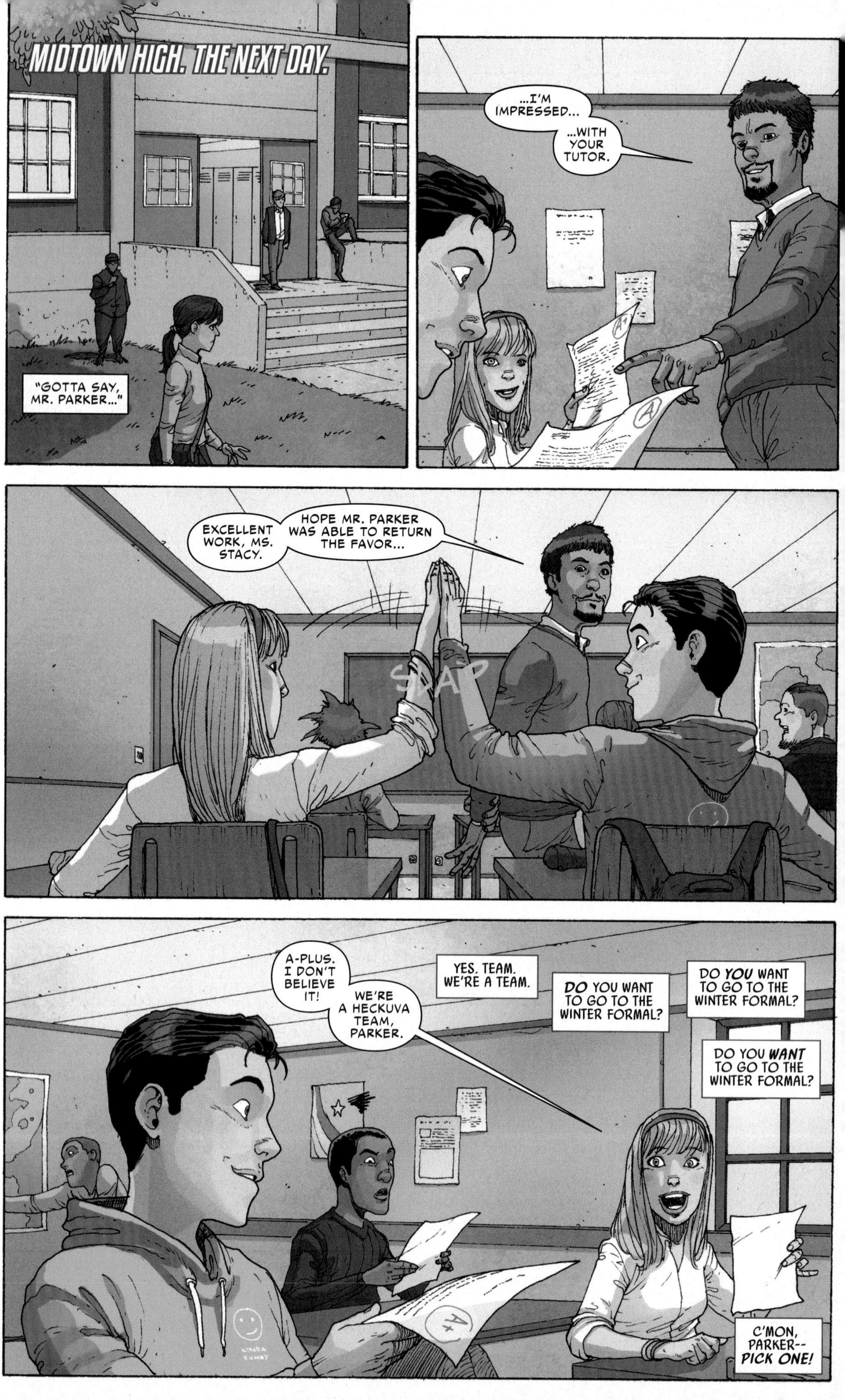
MIDTOWN HIGH. THE NEXT DAY.
"GOTTA SAY, MR. PARKER..."
...I'M IMPRESSED...
...WITH YOUR TUTOR.
EXCELLENT WORK, MS. STACY.
HOPE MR. PARKER WAS ABLE TO RETURN THE FAVOR...
SLAP
A-PLUS. I DON'T BELIEVE IT!
WE'RE A HECKUVA TEAM, PARKER.
YES. TEAM. WE'RE A TEAM.
DO YOU WANT TO GO TO THE WINTER FORMAL?
DO ***YOU*** WANT TO GO TO THE WINTER FORMAL?
DO YOU ***WANT*** TO GO TO THE WINTER FORMAL?
C'MON, PARKER-- ***PICK ONE!***

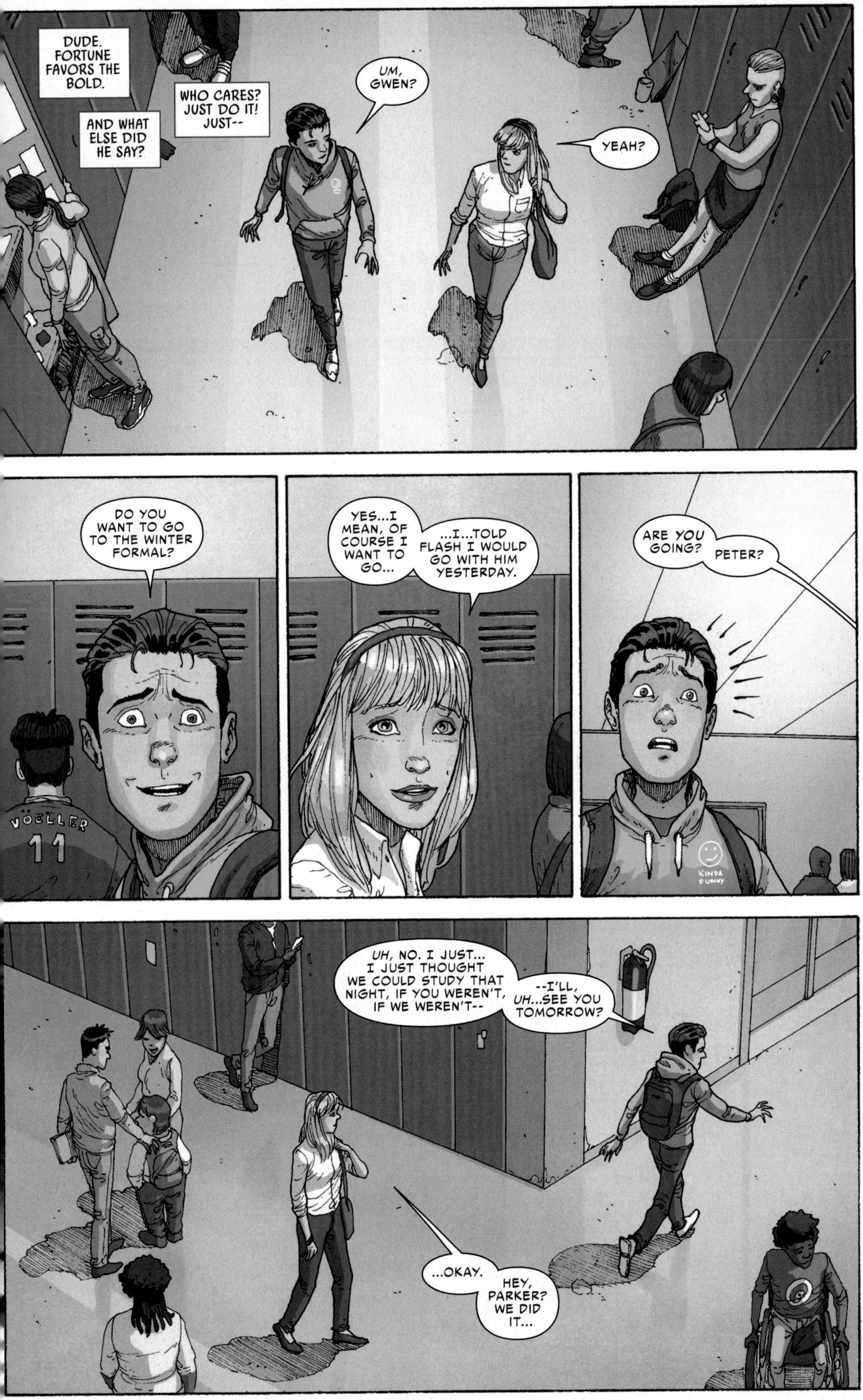
DUDE. FORTUNE FAVORS THE BOLD.
AND WHAT ELSE DID HE SAY?
WHO CARES? JUST DO IT! JUST--
UM, GWEN?
YEAH?
DO YOU WANT TO GO TO THE WINTER FORMAL?
VOELLER
11
YES...I MEAN, OF COURSE I WANT TO GO...
...I...TOLD FLASH I WOULD GO WITH HIM YESTERDAY.
ARE YOU GOING?
PETER?
KINDA FUNNY
UH, NO. I JUST... I JUST THOUGHT WE COULD STUDY THAT NIGHT, IF YOU WEREN'T, IF WE WEREN'T--
--I'LL, UH...SEE YOU TOMORROW?
...OKAY.
HEY, PARKER? WE DID IT...

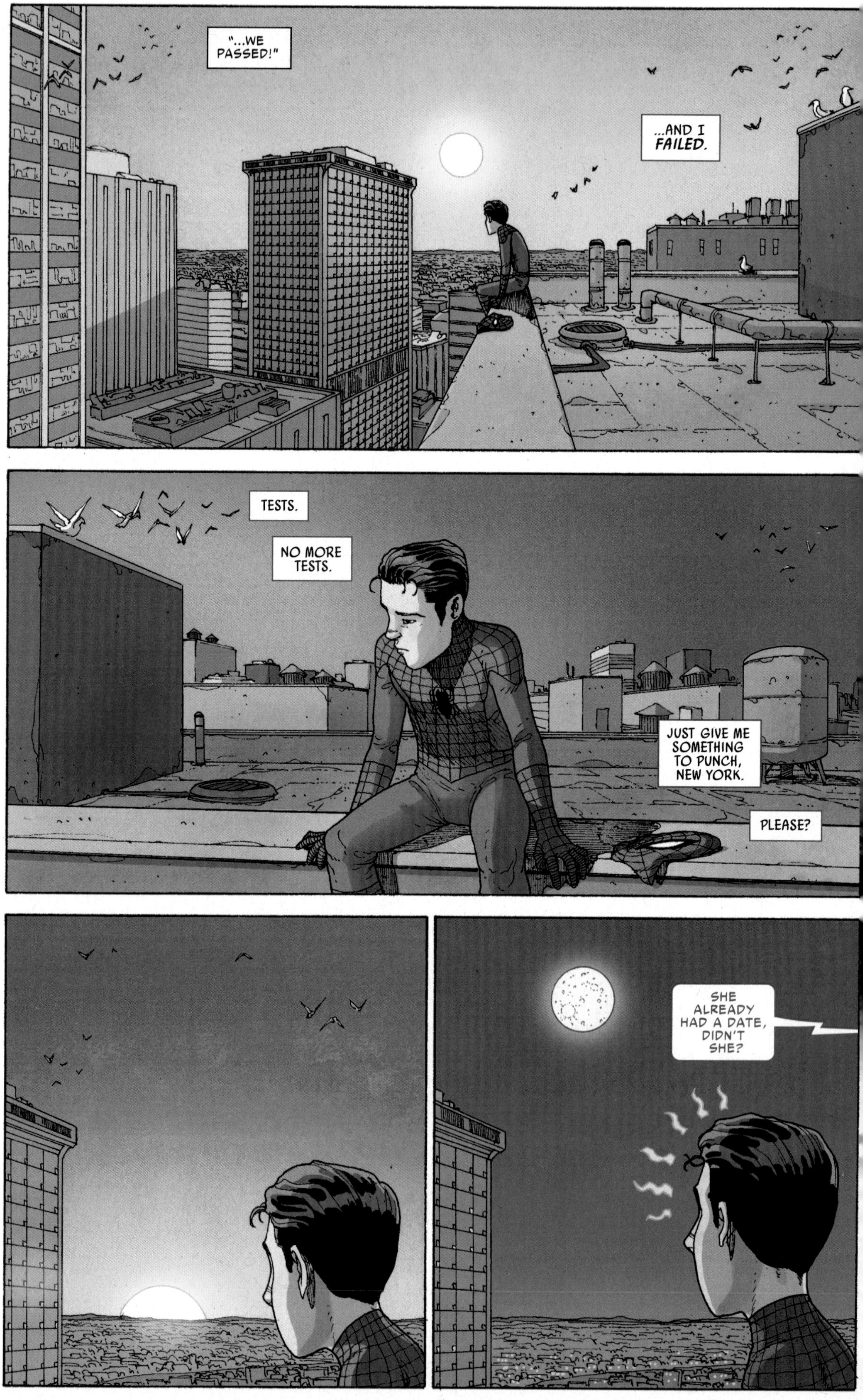
"...WE PASSED!"
...AND I *FAILED*.
TESTS.
NO MORE TESTS.
JUST GIVE ME SOMETHING TO PUNCH, NEW YORK.
PLEASE?
SHE ALREADY HAD A DATE, DIDN'T SHE?

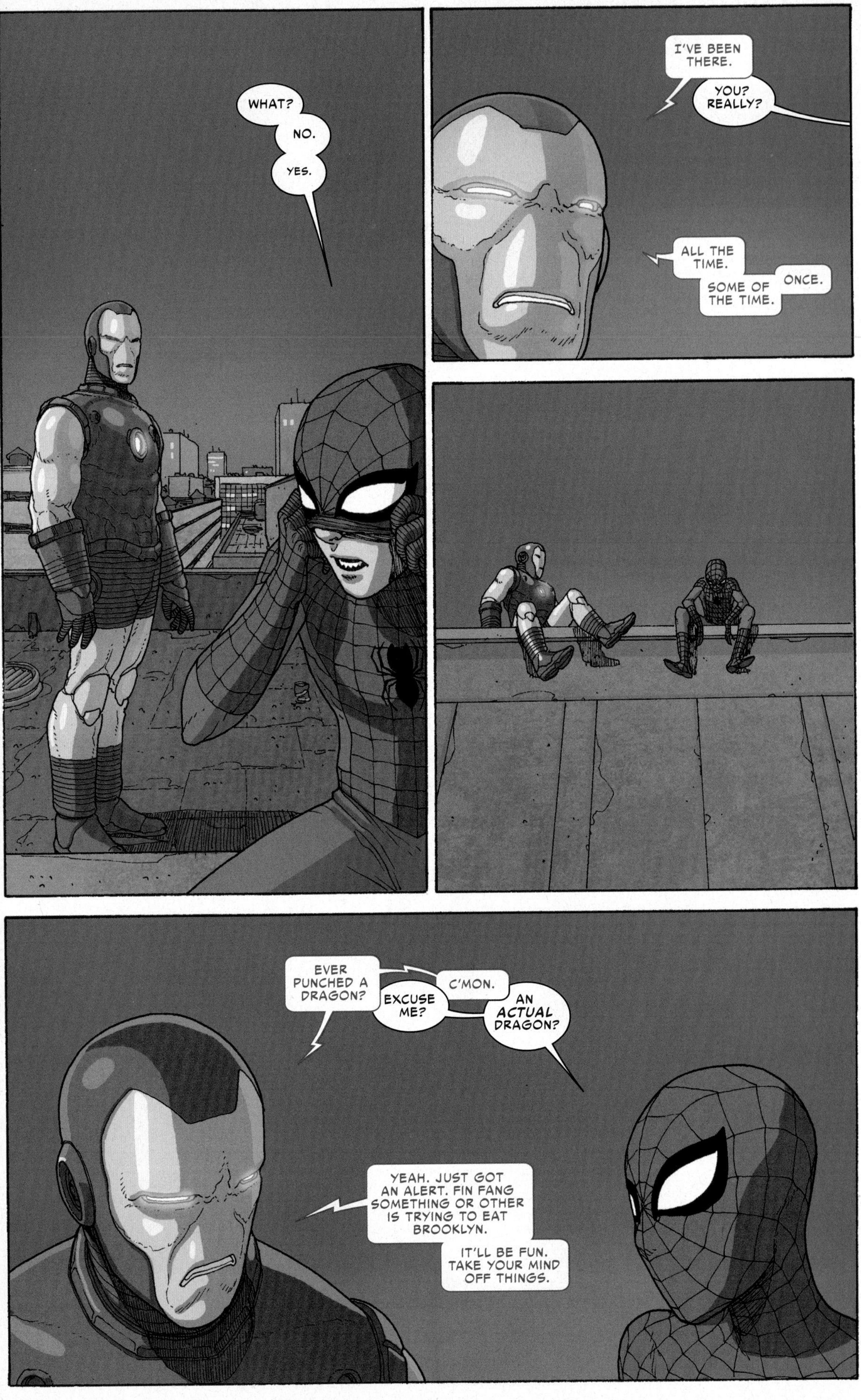

WHAT?
NO.
YES.
I'VE BEEN THERE.
YOU? REALLY?
ALL THE TIME.
SOME OF THE TIME.
ONCE.
EVER PUNCHED A DRAGON?
EXCUSE ME?
C'MON.
AN *ACTUAL* DRAGON?
YEAH. JUST GOT AN ALERT. FIN FANG SOMETHING OR OTHER IS TRYING TO EAT BROOKLYN.
IT'LL BE FUN. TAKE YOUR MIND OFF THINGS.

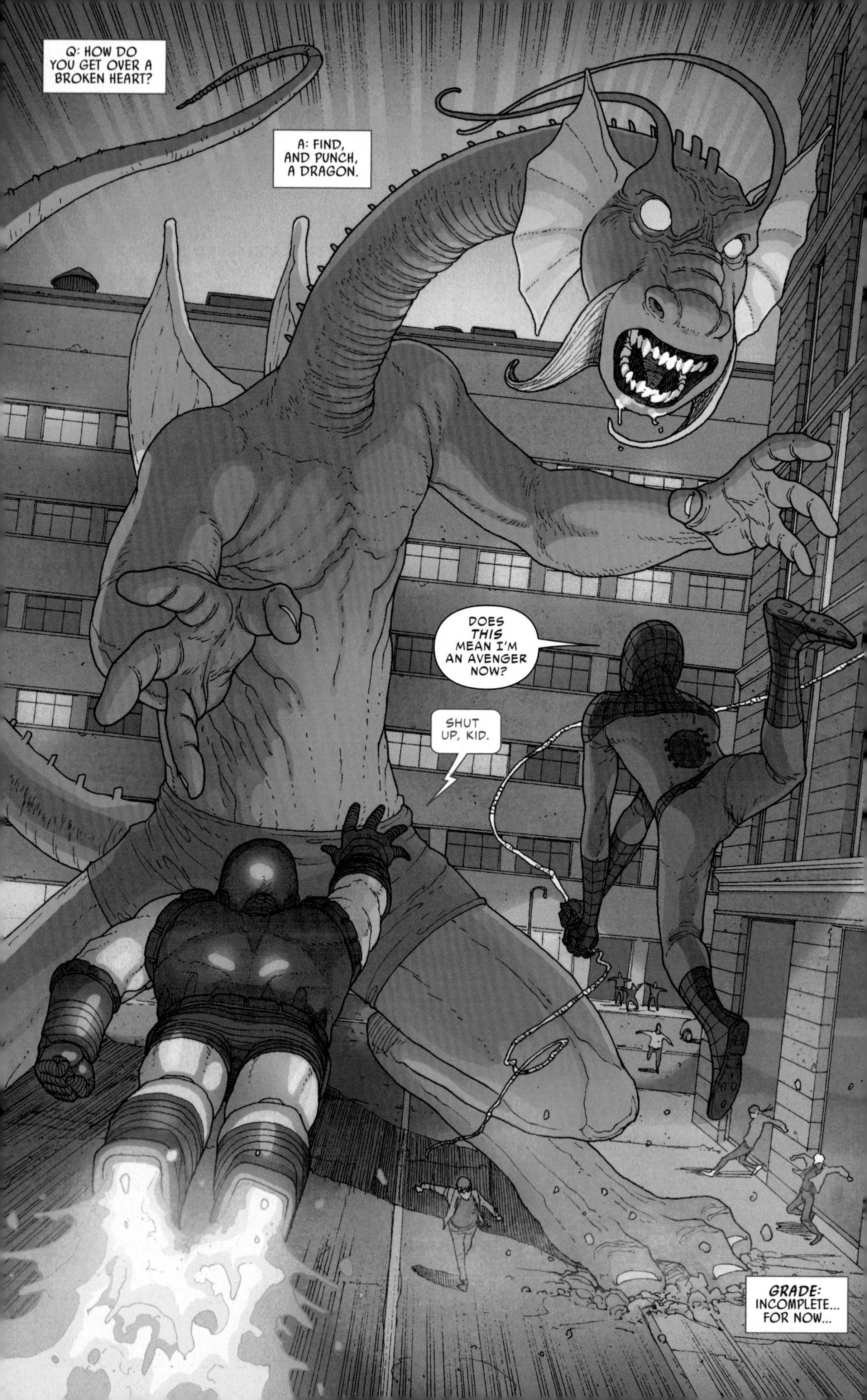
Q: HOW DO YOU GET OVER A BROKEN HEART?
A: FIND, AND PUNCH, A DRAGON.
DOES *THIS* MEAN I'M AN AVENGER NOW?
SHUT UP, KID.
GRADE: INCOMPLETE... FOR NOW...

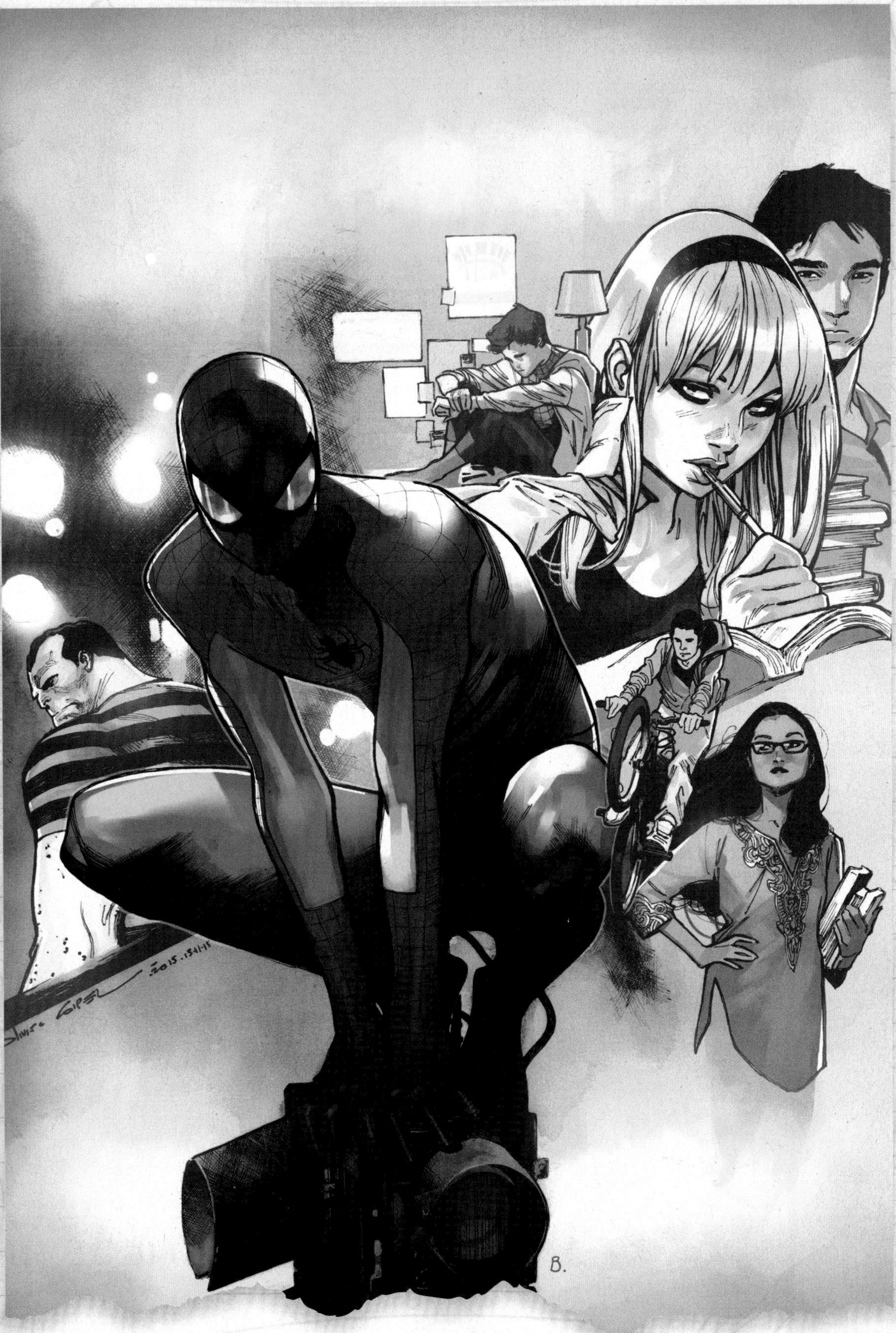

OLIVIER COIPEL
2 VARIANT

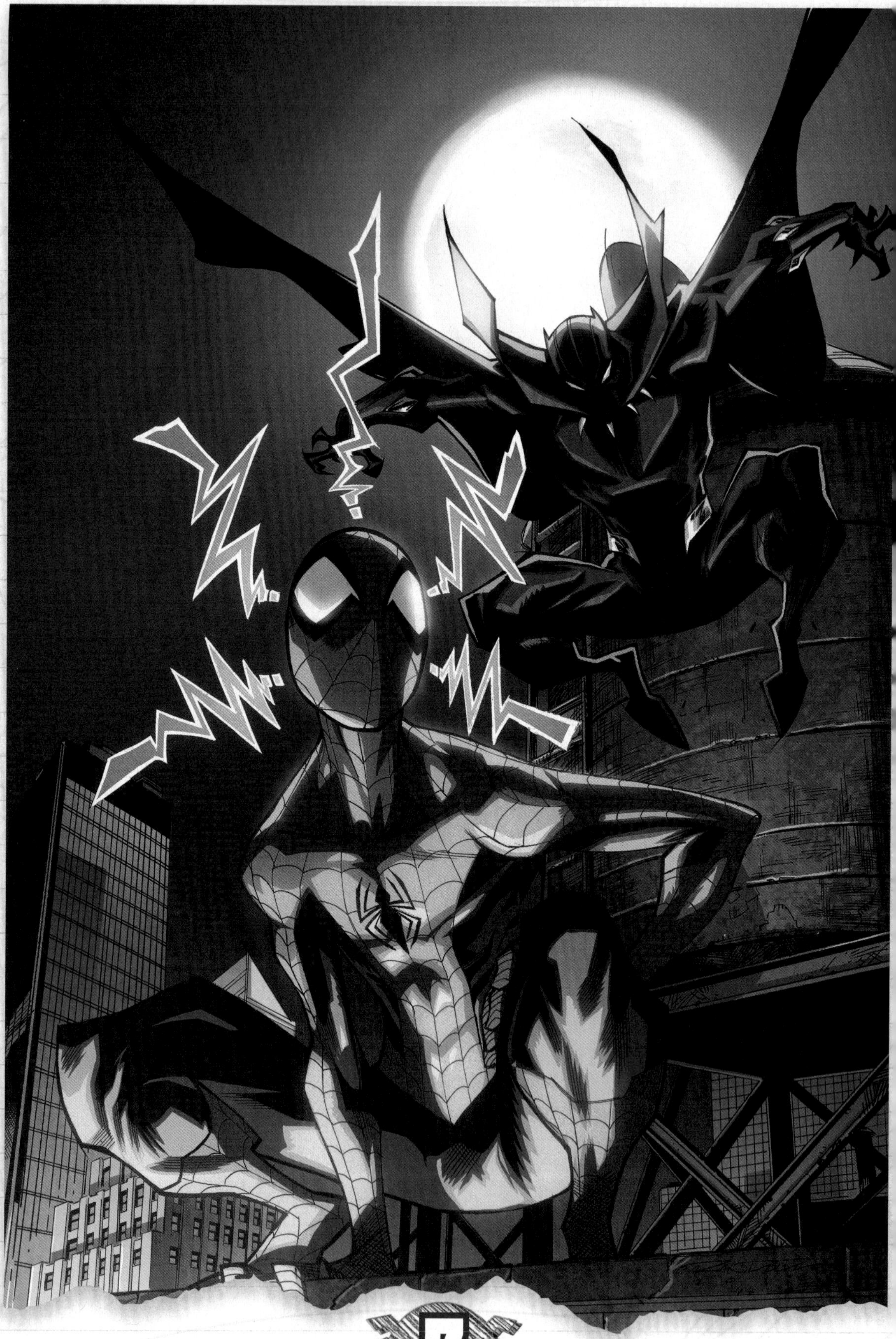

7

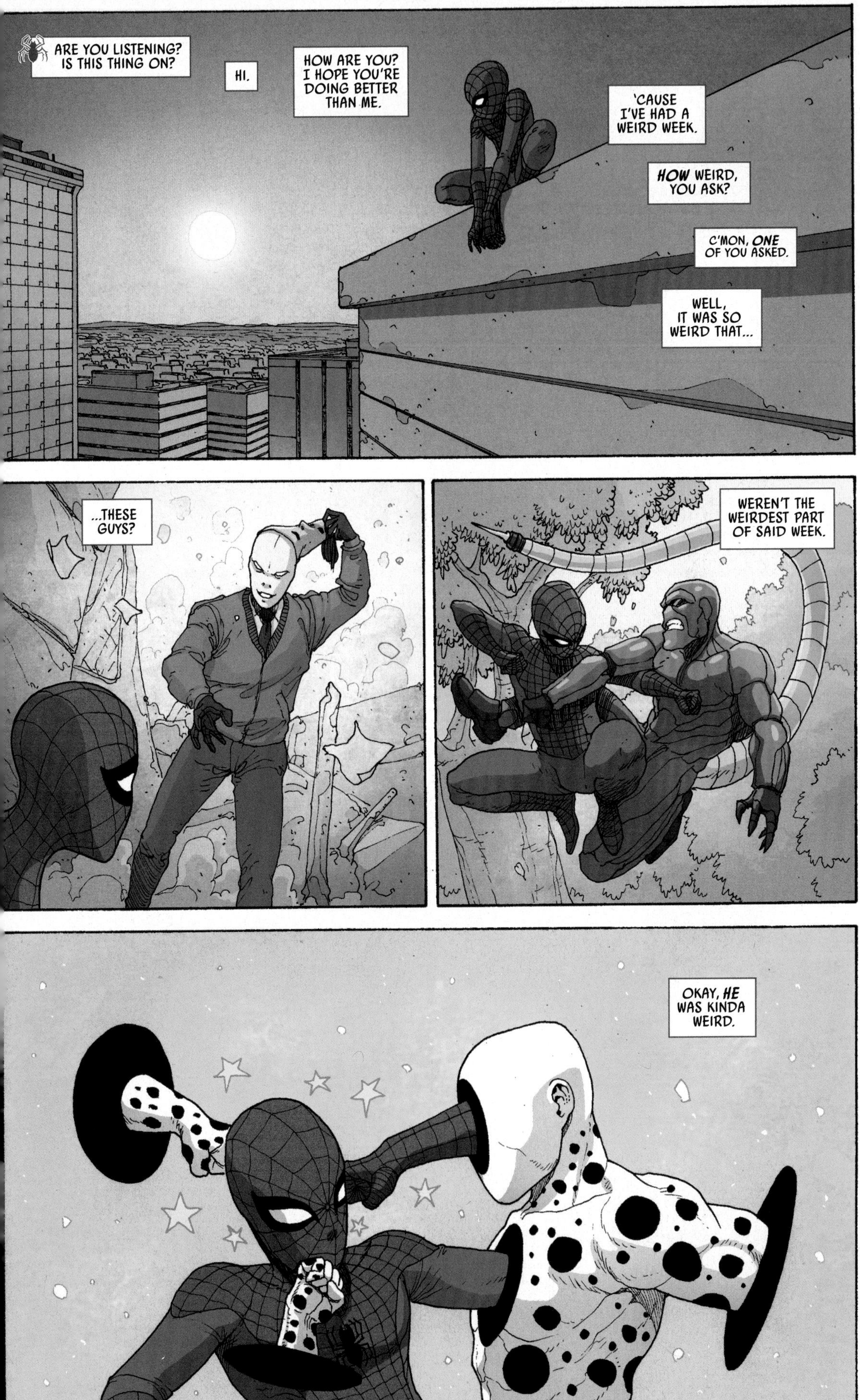
ARE YOU LISTENING? IS THIS THING ON?
HI.
HOW ARE YOU? I HOPE YOU'RE DOING BETTER THAN ME.
'CAUSE I'VE HAD A WEIRD WEEK.
HOW WEIRD, YOU ASK?
C'MON, ONE OF YOU ASKED.
WELL, IT WAS SO WEIRD THAT...
...THESE GUYS?
WEREN'T THE WEIRDEST PART OF SAID WEEK.
OKAY, HE WAS KINDA WEIRD.

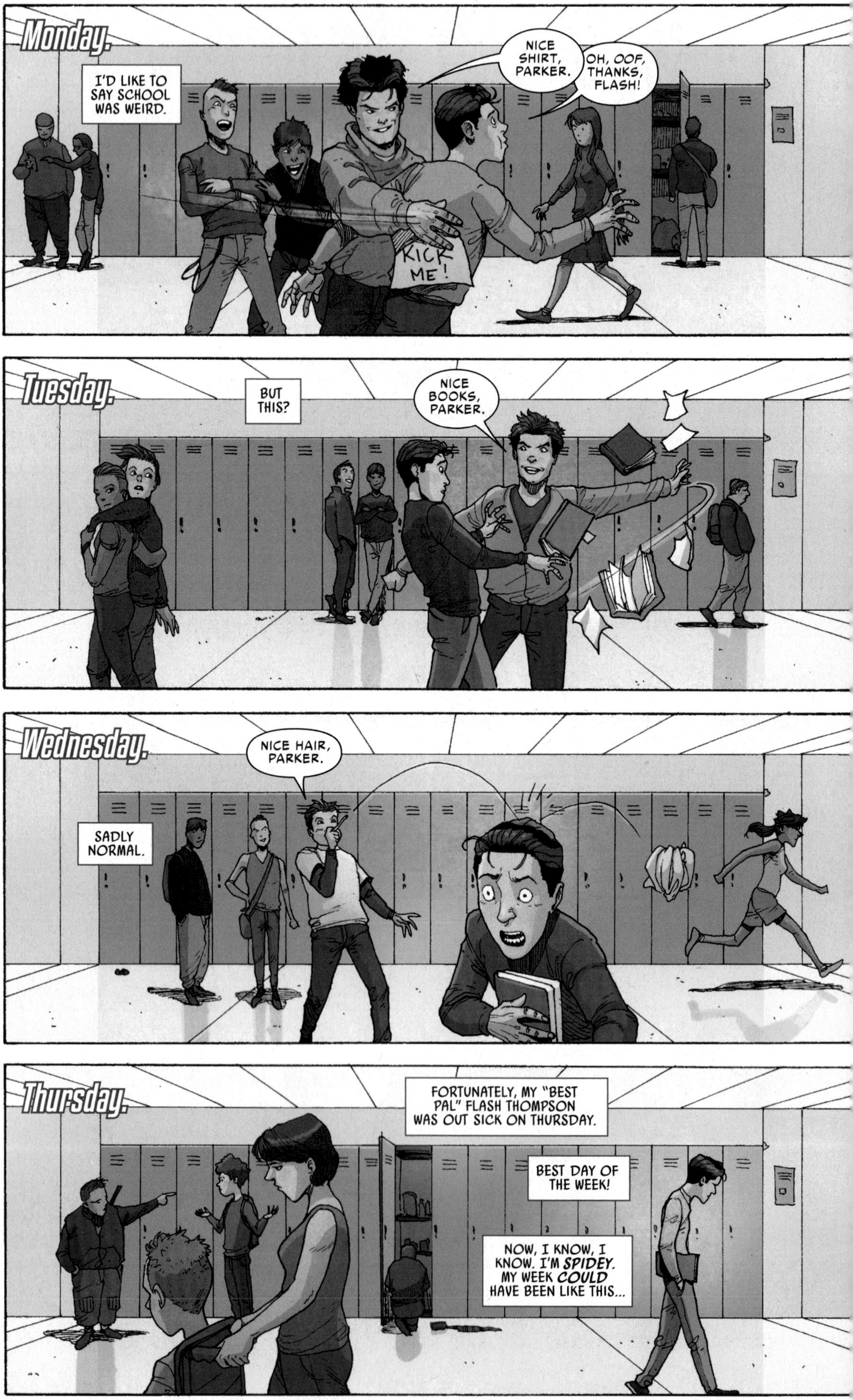

Monday.
I'D LIKE TO SAY SCHOOL WAS WEIRD.
NICE SHIRT, PARKER.
OH, OOF, THANKS, FLASH!
KICK ME!
Tuesday.
BUT THIS?
NICE BOOKS, PARKER.
Wednesday.
SADLY NORMAL.
NICE HAIR, PARKER.
Thursday.
FORTUNATELY, MY "BEST PAL" FLASH THOMPSON WAS OUT SICK ON THURSDAY.
BEST DAY OF THE WEEK!
NOW, I KNOW, I KNOW. I'M SPIDEY. MY WEEK COULD HAVE BEEN LIKE THIS...

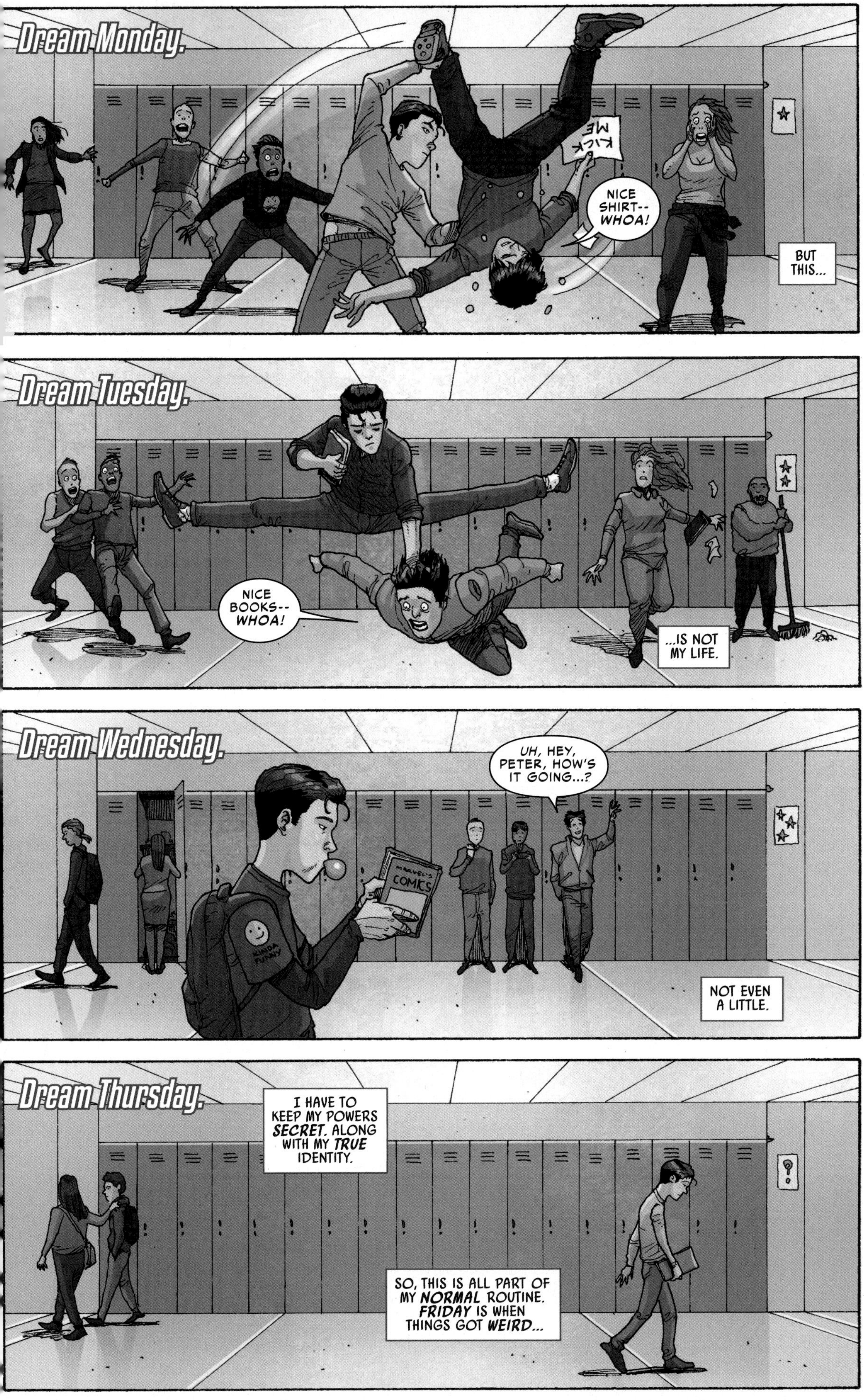
Dream Monday.
KICK ME
NICE SHIRT--WHOA!
BUT THIS...
Dream Tuesday.
NICE BOOKS--WHOA!
...IS NOT MY LIFE.
Dream Wednesday.
UH, HEY, PETER, HOW'S IT GOING...?
MARVEL'S COMICS
KINDA FUNNY
NOT EVEN A LITTLE.
Dream Thursday.
I HAVE TO KEEP MY POWERS SECRET. ALONG WITH MY TRUE IDENTITY.
SO, THIS IS ALL PART OF MY NORMAL ROUTINE. FRIDAY IS WHEN THINGS GOT WEIRD...

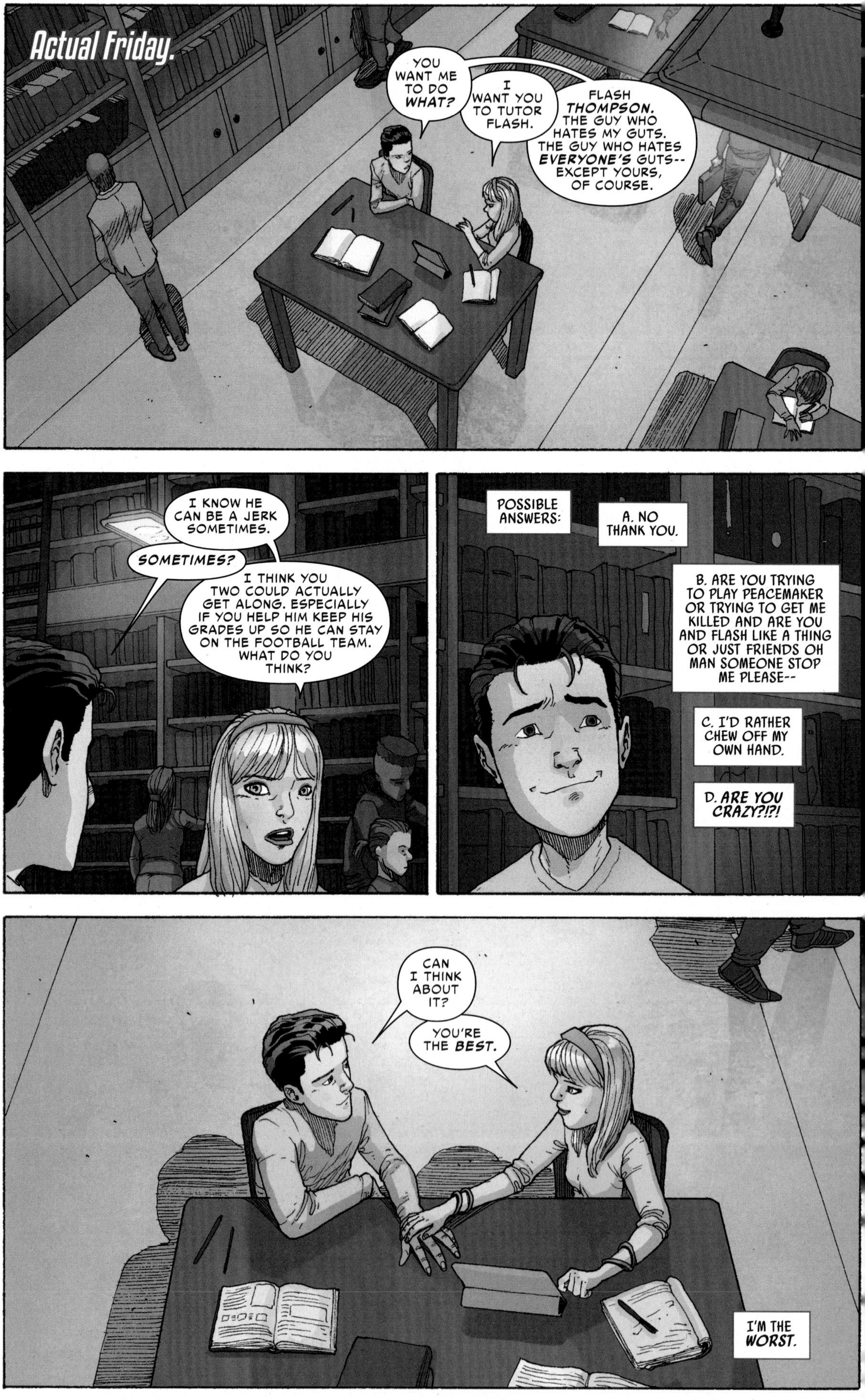

Actual Friday.
YOU WANT ME TO DO WHAT?
I WANT YOU TO TUTOR FLASH.
FLASH THOMPSON. THE GUY WHO HATES MY GUTS. THE GUY WHO HATES EVERYONE'S GUTS-- EXCEPT YOURS, OF COURSE.
I KNOW HE CAN BE A JERK SOMETIMES.
SOMETIMES?
I THINK YOU TWO COULD ACTUALLY GET ALONG. ESPECIALLY IF YOU HELP HIM KEEP HIS GRADES UP SO HE CAN STAY ON THE FOOTBALL TEAM. WHAT DO YOU THINK?
POSSIBLE ANSWERS:
A. NO THANK YOU.
B. ARE YOU TRYING TO PLAY PEACEMAKER OR TRYING TO GET ME KILLED AND ARE YOU AND FLASH LIKE A THING OR JUST FRIENDS OH MAN SOMEONE STOP ME PLEASE--
C. I'D RATHER CHEW OFF MY OWN HAND.
D. ARE YOU CRAZY?!?!
CAN I THINK ABOUT IT?
YOU'RE THE BEST.
I'M THE WORST.

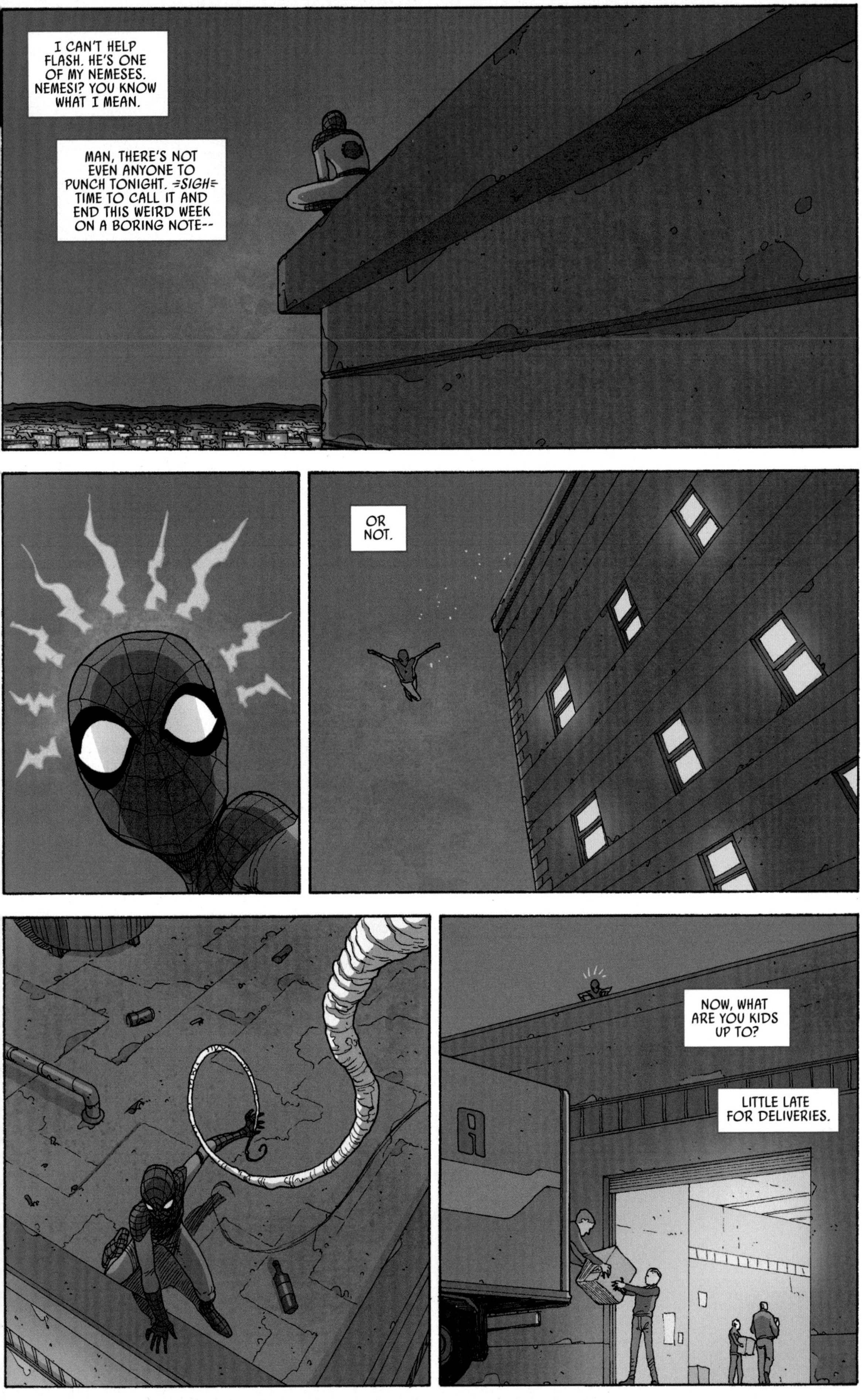
I CAN'T HELP FLASH. HE'S ONE OF MY NEMESES. NEMESI? YOU KNOW WHAT I MEAN.
MAN, THERE'S NOT EVEN ANYONE TO PUNCH TONIGHT. =SIGH= TIME TO CALL IT AND END THIS WEIRD WEEK ON A BORING NOTE--
OR NOT.
NOW, WHAT ARE YOU KIDS UP TO?
LITTLE LATE FOR DELIVERIES.

OKAY, LET'S TAKE A PEEK AND SEE--

UM, IS IT JUST ME...

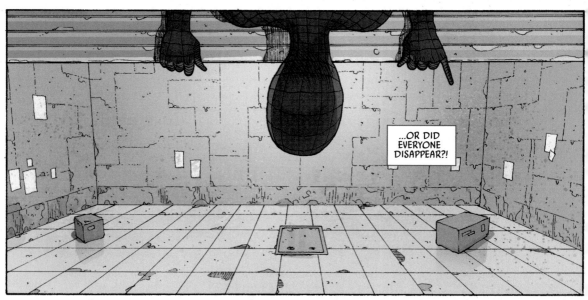

...OR DID EVERYONE DISAPPEAR?!

TRAP DOOR...? AWESOME.

I MEAN, IT'S PROBABLY A HORRIBLE NIGHTMARE DOWN THERE, BUT STILL. TRAP DOOR!

WORK WITH ME, PEOPLE.

THIS IS ONE OF THE MANY TIMES IN MY SHORT, PERHAPS ABOUT-TO-END, CAREER THAT I WISH I COULD CALL FOR BACKUP.

'CAUSE DOWN THERE...

...ARE A LOT OF FACES TO PUNCH.

BETTER GET CRACKING. IT'S NOT LIKE THEY'RE GOING TO PUNCH THEMSELVES.

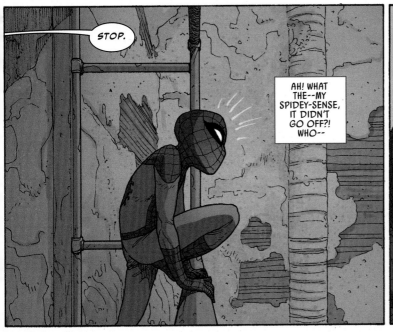

STOP.

AH! WHAT THE--MY SPIDEY-SENSE, IT DIDN'T GO OFF?! WHO--

OH. THAT EXPLAINS IT.

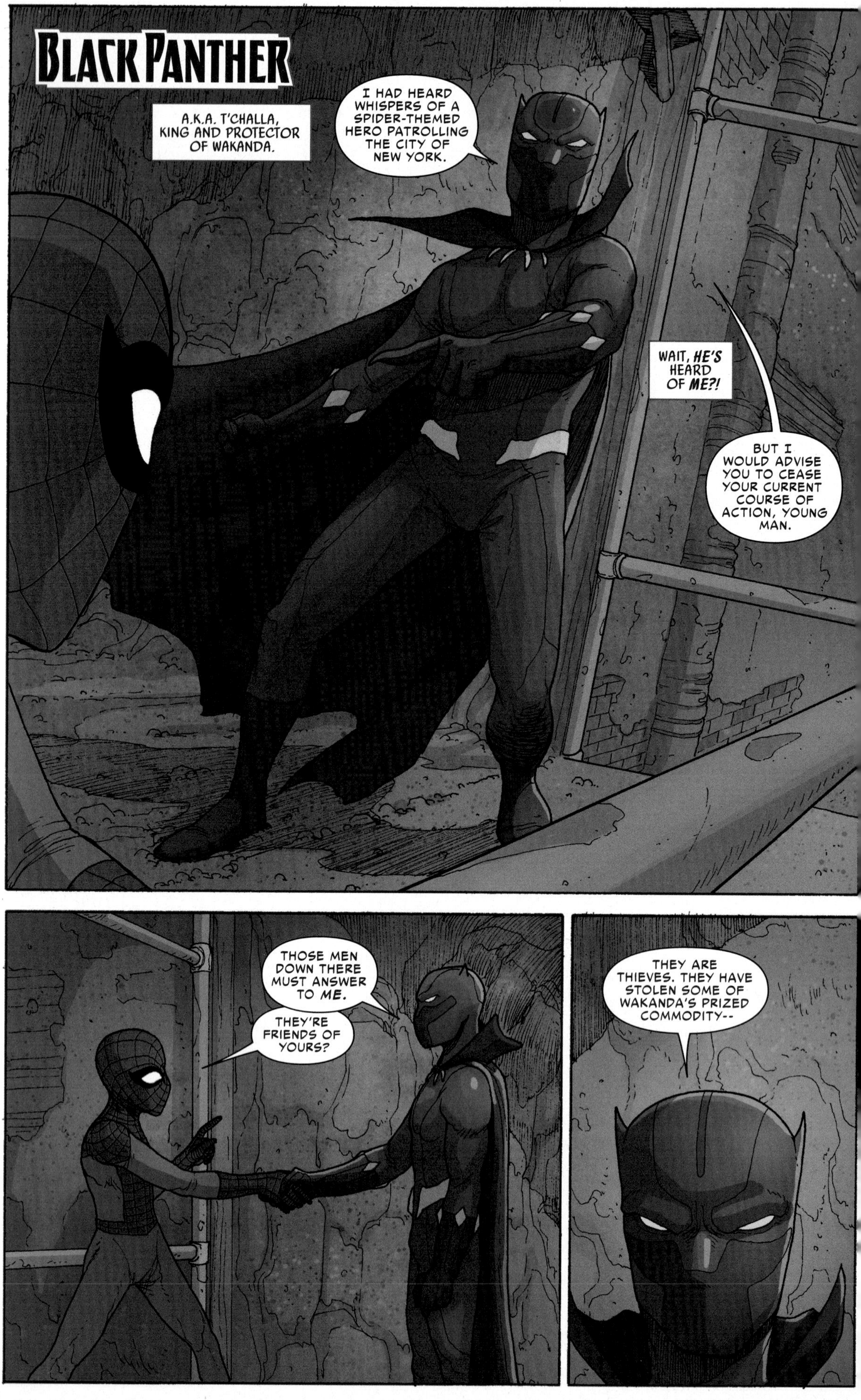
BLACK PANTHER
A.K.A. T'CHALLA, KING AND PROTECTOR OF WAKANDA.
I HAD HEARD WHISPERS OF A SPIDER-THEMED HERO PATROLLING THE CITY OF NEW YORK.
WAIT, HE'S HEARD OF ME?!
BUT I WOULD ADVISE YOU TO CEASE YOUR CURRENT COURSE OF ACTION, YOUNG MAN.
THOSE MEN DOWN THERE MUST ANSWER TO ME.
THEY'RE FRIENDS OF YOURS?
THEY ARE THIEVES. THEY HAVE STOLEN SOME OF WAKANDA'S PRIZED COMMODITY--

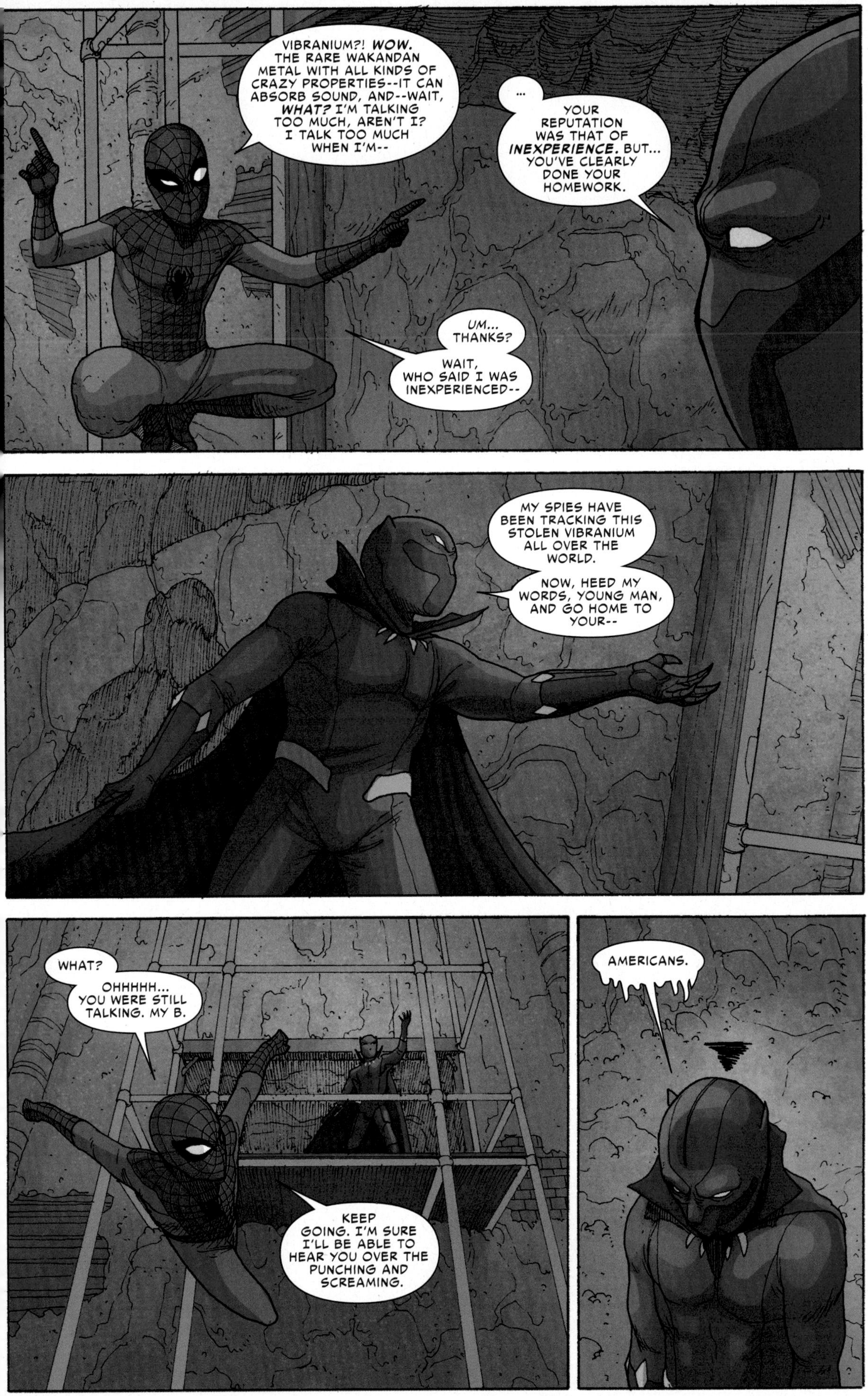
VIBRANIUM?! WOW. THE RARE WAKANDAN METAL WITH ALL KINDS OF CRAZY PROPERTIES--IT CAN ABSORB SOUND, AND--WAIT, WHAT? I'M TALKING TOO MUCH, AREN'T I? I TALK TOO MUCH WHEN I'M--
...
YOUR REPUTATION WAS THAT OF INEXPERIENCE. BUT... YOU'VE CLEARLY DONE YOUR HOMEWORK.
UM... THANKS?
WAIT, WHO SAID I WAS INEXPERIENCED--
MY SPIES HAVE BEEN TRACKING THIS STOLEN VIBRANIUM ALL OVER THE WORLD.
NOW, HEED MY WORDS, YOUNG MAN, AND GO HOME TO YOUR--
WHAT?
OHHHHH... YOU WERE STILL TALKING. MY B.
KEEP GOING. I'M SURE I'LL BE ABLE TO HEAR YOU OVER THE PUNCHING AND SCREAMING.
AMERICANS.

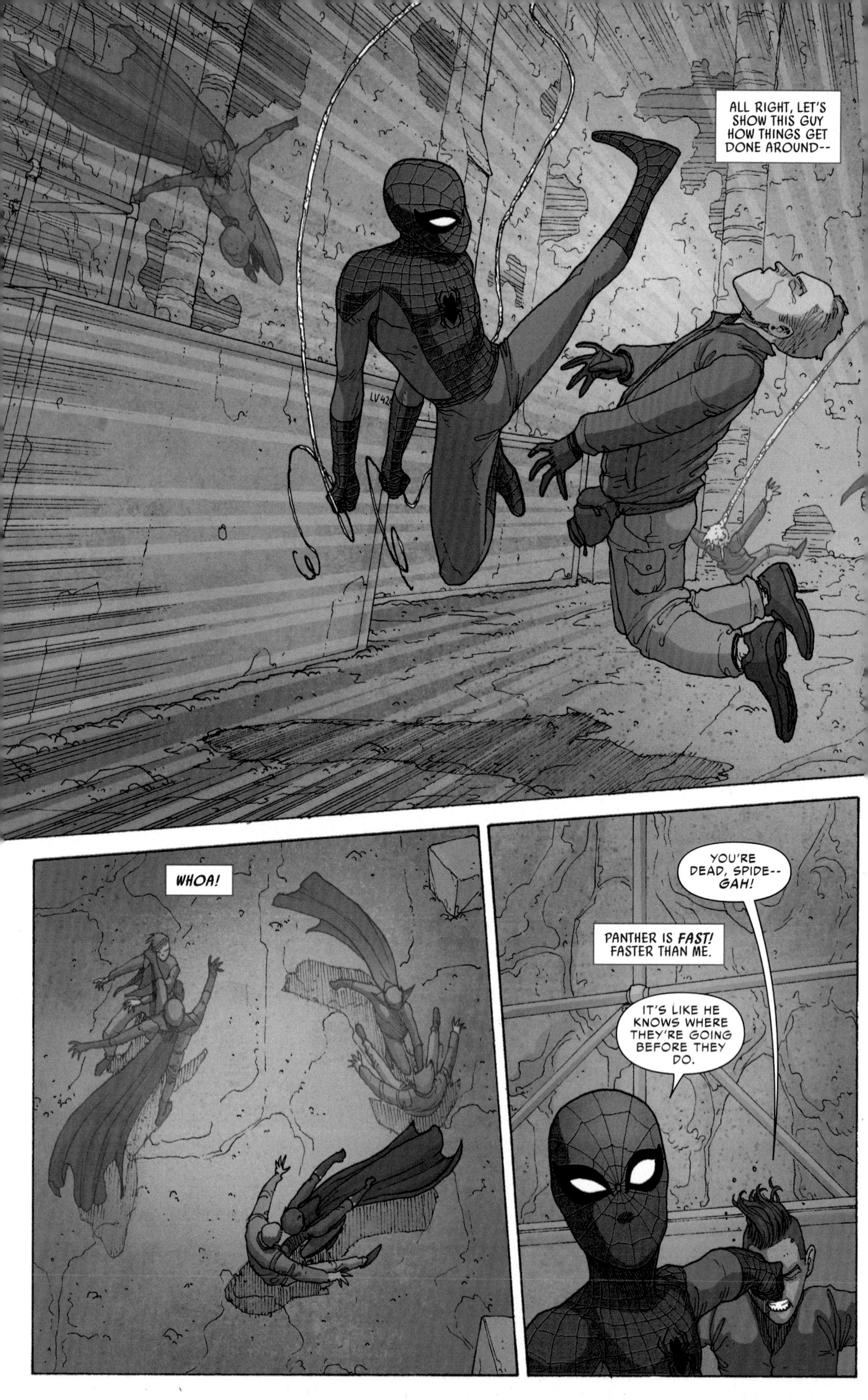
ALL RIGHT, LET'S SHOW THIS GUY HOW THINGS GET DONE AROUND--
LV424
WHOA!
YOU'RE DEAD, SPIDE-- GAH!
PANTHER IS FAST! FASTER THAN ME.
IT'S LIKE HE KNOWS WHERE THEY'RE GOING BEFORE THEY DO.

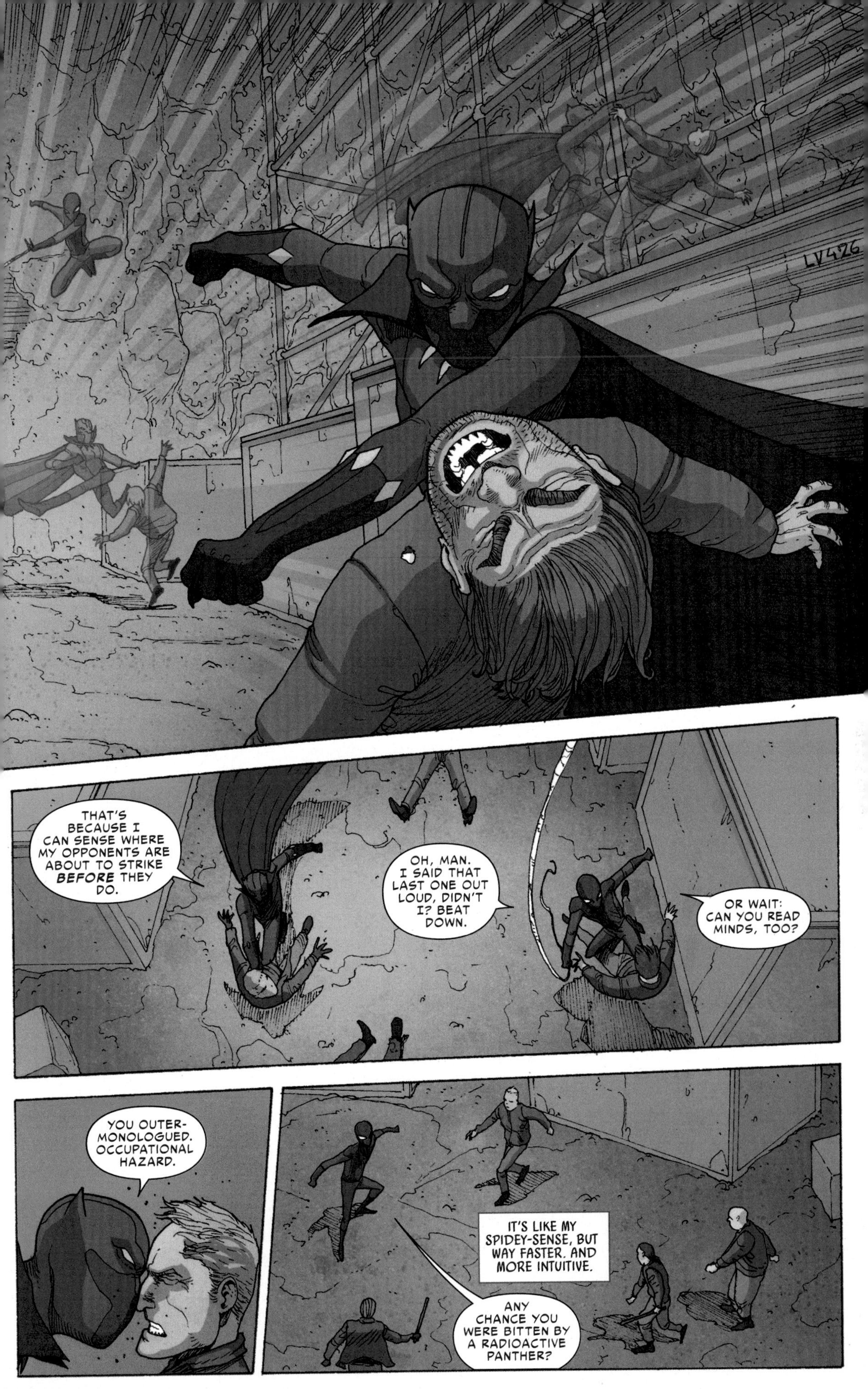
LV426
THAT'S BECAUSE I CAN SENSE WHERE MY OPPONENTS ARE ABOUT TO STRIKE *BEFORE* THEY DO.
OH, MAN. I SAID THAT LAST ONE OUT LOUD, DIDN'T I? BEAT DOWN.
OR WAIT: CAN YOU READ MINDS, TOO?
YOU OUTER-MONOLOGUED. OCCUPATIONAL HAZARD.
IT'S LIKE MY SPIDEY-SENSE, BUT WAY FASTER. AND MORE INTUITIVE.
ANY CHANCE YOU WERE BITTEN BY A RADIOACTIVE PANTHER?

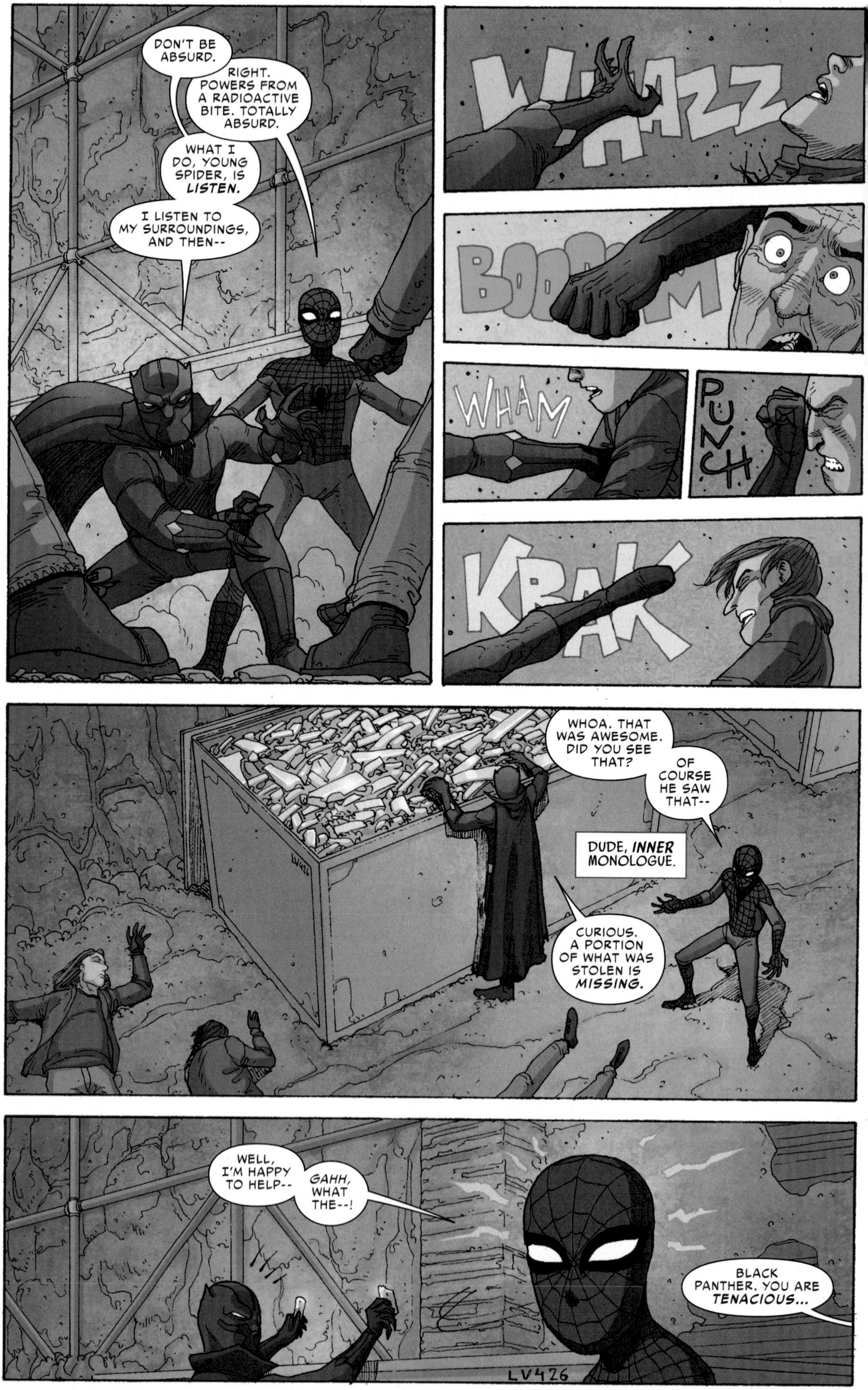
DON'T BE ABSURD.
RIGHT. POWERS FROM A RADIOACTIVE BITE. TOTALLY ABSURD.
WHAT I DO, YOUNG SPIDER, IS *LISTEN.*
I LISTEN TO MY SURROUNDINGS, AND THEN--
WHAZZ
WHAM
PUNCH
KRAK
WHOA. THAT WAS AWESOME. DID YOU SEE THAT?
OF COURSE HE SAW THAT--
DUDE, *INNER* MONOLOGUE.
CURIOUS. A PORTION OF WHAT WAS STOLEN IS *MISSING.*
WELL, I'M HAPPY TO HELP--
GAHH, WHAT THE--!
BLACK PANTHER. YOU ARE *TENACIOUS...*
LV426

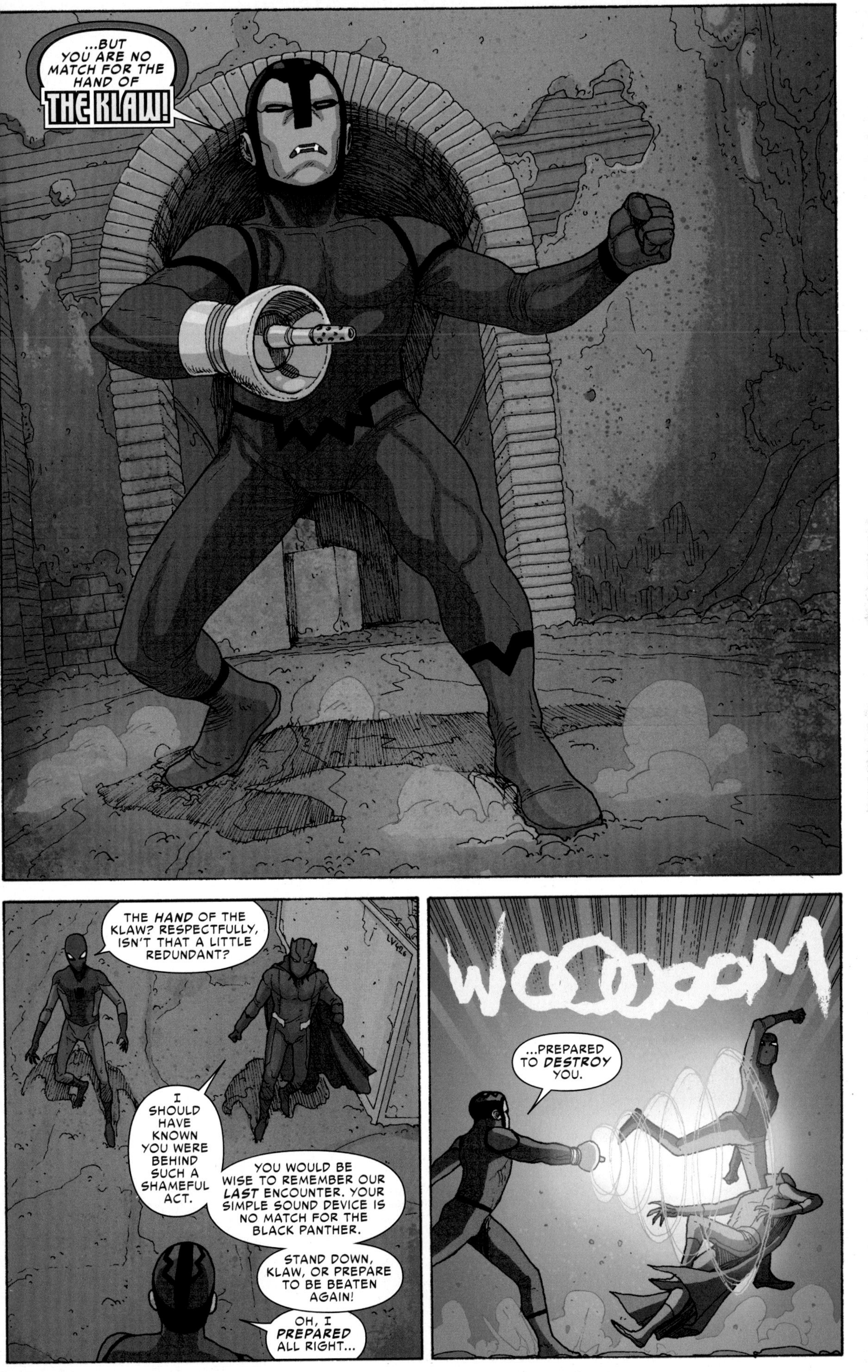
...BUT YOU ARE NO MATCH FOR THE HAND OF THE KLAW!
THE HAND OF THE KLAW? RESPECTFULLY, ISN'T THAT A LITTLE REDUNDANT?
I SHOULD HAVE KNOWN YOU WERE BEHIND SUCH A SHAMEFUL ACT.
YOU WOULD BE WISE TO REMEMBER OUR LAST ENCOUNTER. YOUR SIMPLE SOUND DEVICE IS NO MATCH FOR THE BLACK PANTHER.
STAND DOWN, KLAW, OR PREPARE TO BE BEATEN AGAIN!
OH, I PREPARED ALL RIGHT...
WOOOOOOM
...PREPARED TO DESTROY YOU.

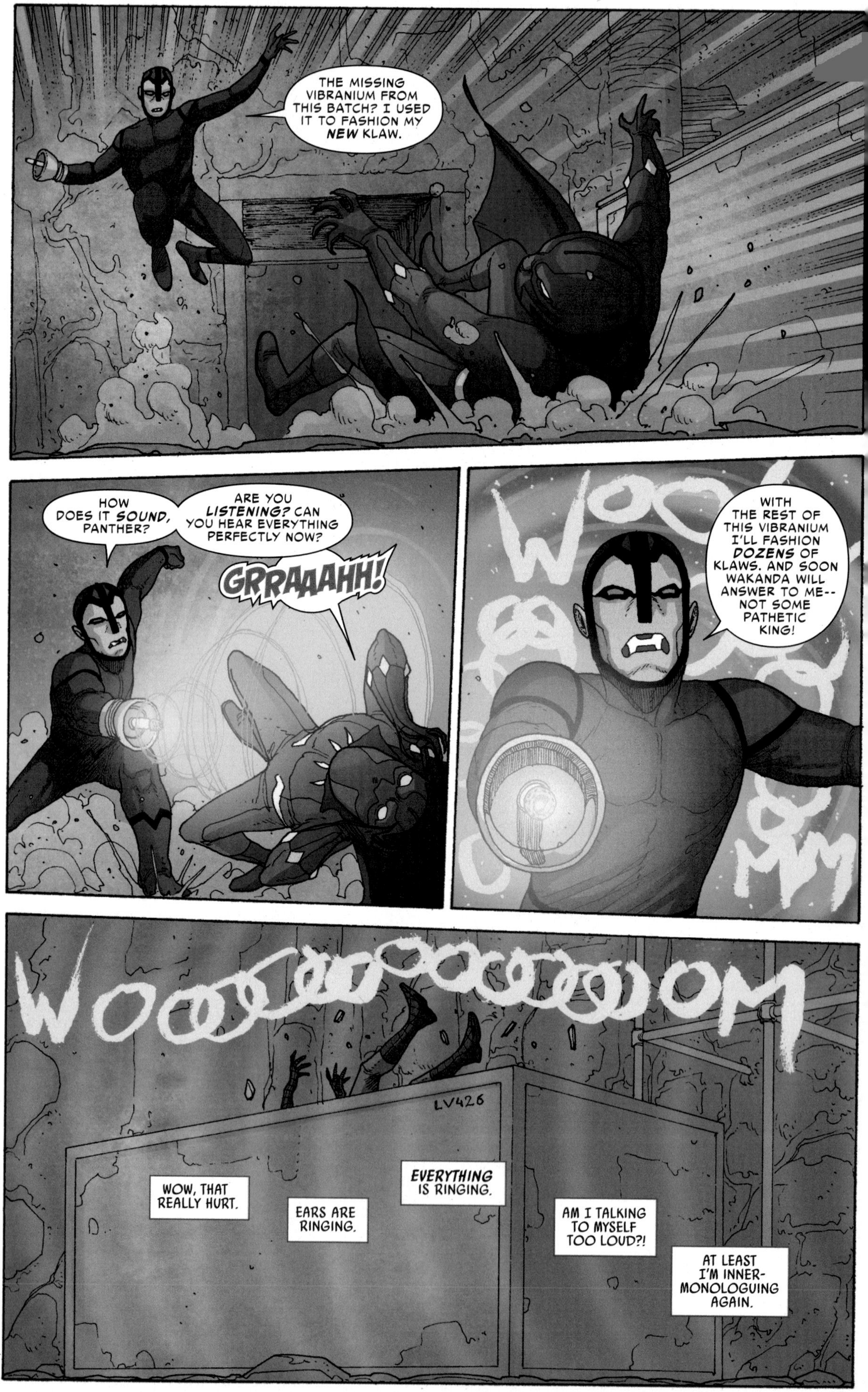
THE MISSING VIBRANIUM FROM THIS BATCH? I USED IT TO FASHION MY NEW KLAW.
HOW DOES IT SOUND, PANTHER?
ARE YOU LISTENING? CAN YOU HEAR EVERYTHING PERFECTLY NOW?
GRRAAAHH!
WITH THE REST OF THIS VIBRANIUM I'LL FASHION DOZENS OF KLAWS. AND SOON WAKANDA WILL ANSWER TO ME-- NOT SOME PATHETIC KING!
WOOOOOOOOOOOOOM
LV426
WOW, THAT REALLY HURT.
EARS ARE RINGING.
EVERYTHING IS RINGING.
AM I TALKING TO MYSELF TOO LOUD?!
AT LEAST I'M INNER-MONOLOGUING AGAIN.

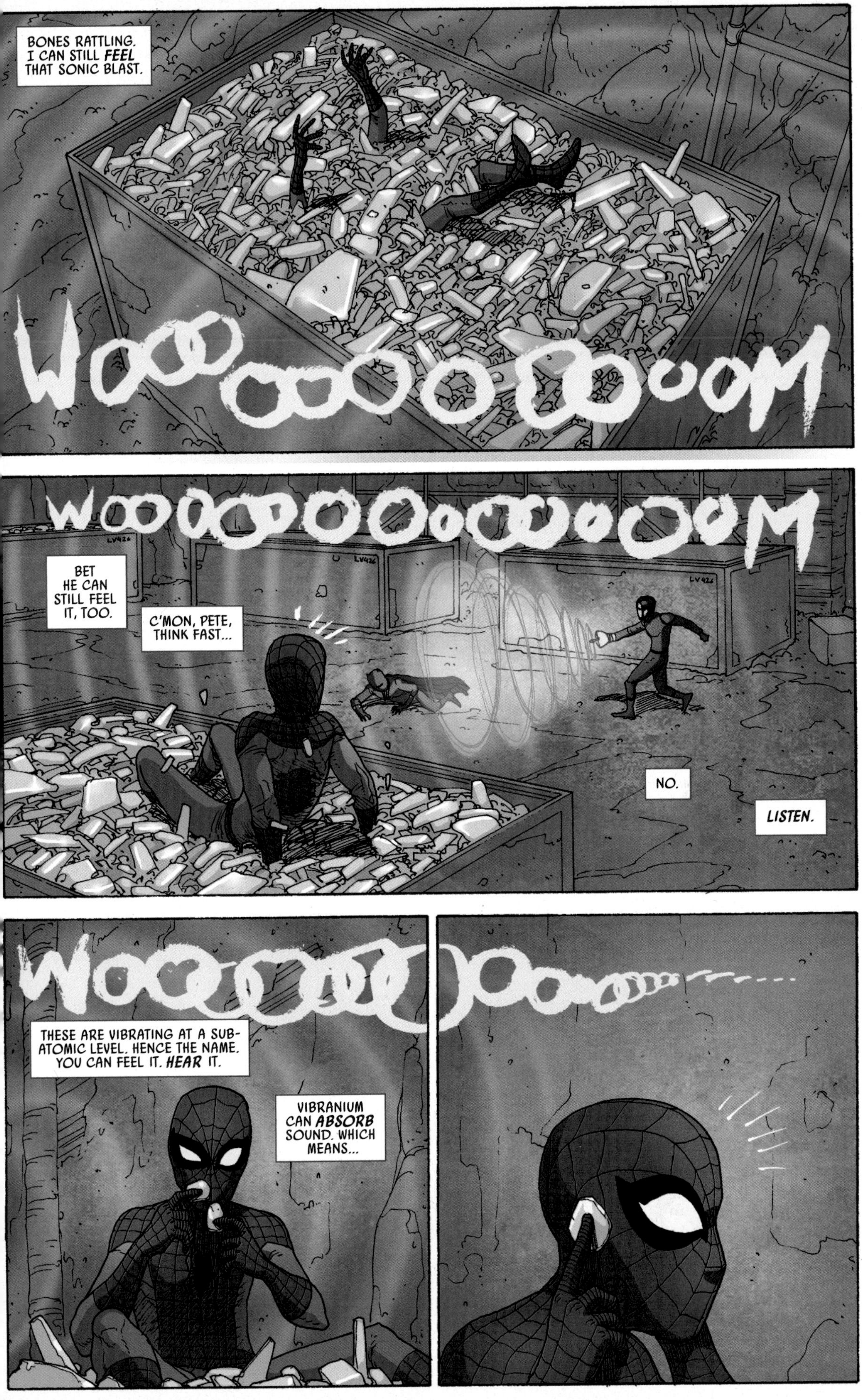
BONES RATTLING. I CAN STILL FEEL THAT SONIC BLAST.
WOOOOOOOOOOM
WOOOOOOOOOOOOM
BET HE CAN STILL FEEL IT, TOO.
C'MON, PETE, THINK FAST...
NO.
LISTEN.
WOOOOOOOOOO...
THESE ARE VIBRATING AT A SUB-ATOMIC LEVEL. HENCE THE NAME. YOU CAN FEEL IT. HEAR IT.
VIBRANIUM CAN ABSORB SOUND. WHICH MEANS...

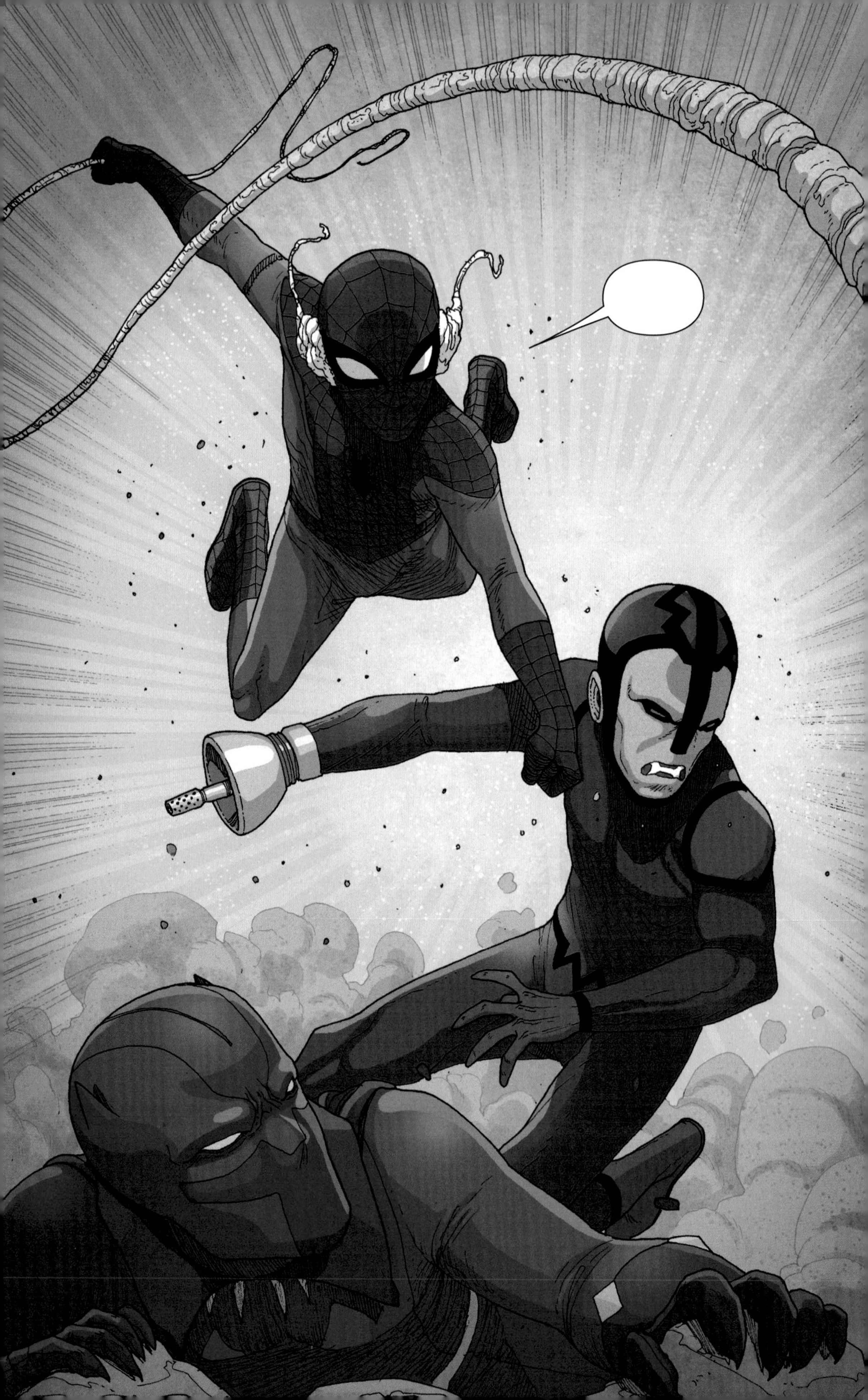

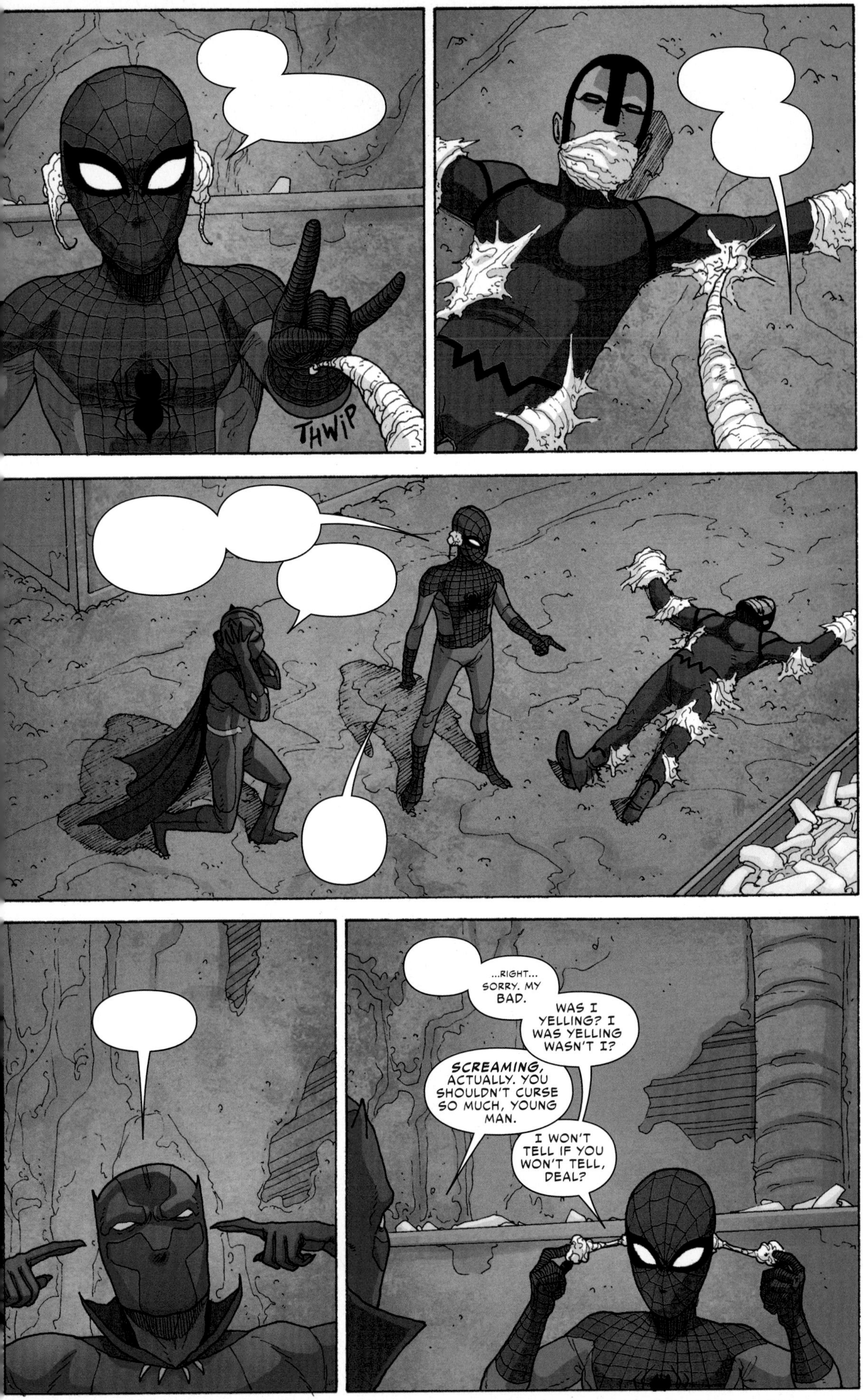
THWIP
...RIGHT... SORRY. MY BAD.
WAS I YELLING? I WAS YELLING WASN'T I?
SCREAMING, ACTUALLY. YOU SHOULDN'T CURSE SO MUCH, YOUNG MAN.
I WON'T TELL IF YOU WON'T TELL, DEAL?

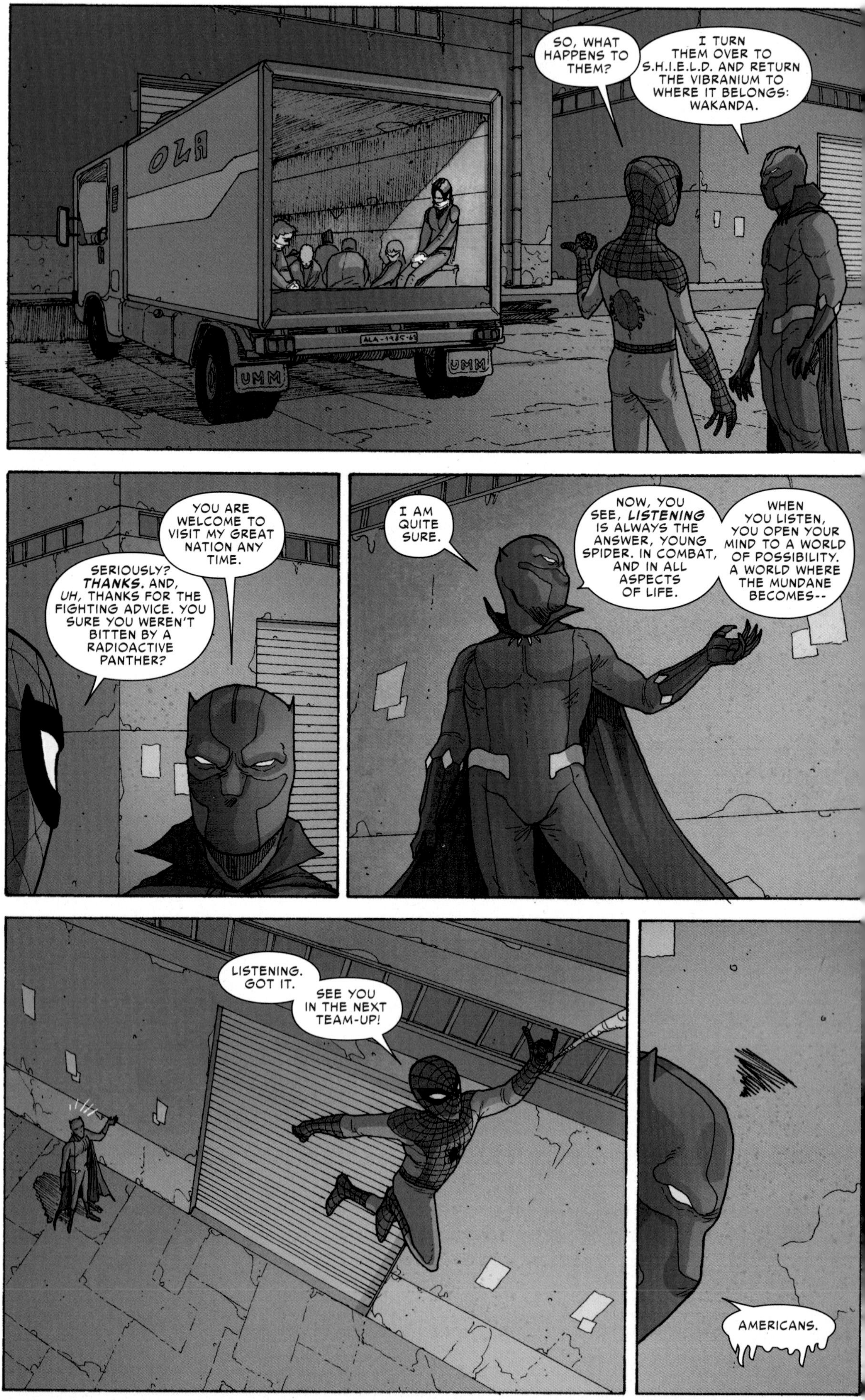

OLA
ALA-1985-61
UMM
UMM
SO, WHAT HAPPENS TO THEM?
I TURN THEM OVER TO S.H.I.E.L.D. AND RETURN THE VIBRANIUM TO WHERE IT BELONGS: WAKANDA.
YOU ARE WELCOME TO VISIT MY GREAT NATION ANY TIME.
SERIOUSLY? THANKS. AND, UH, THANKS FOR THE FIGHTING ADVICE. YOU SURE YOU WEREN'T BITTEN BY A RADIOACTIVE PANTHER?
I AM QUITE SURE.
NOW, YOU SEE, LISTENING IS ALWAYS THE ANSWER, YOUNG SPIDER. IN COMBAT, AND IN ALL ASPECTS OF LIFE.
WHEN YOU LISTEN, YOU OPEN YOUR MIND TO A WORLD OF POSSIBILITY. A WORLD WHERE THE MUNDANE BECOMES--
LISTENING. GOT IT.
SEE YOU IN THE NEXT TEAM-UP!
AMERICANS.

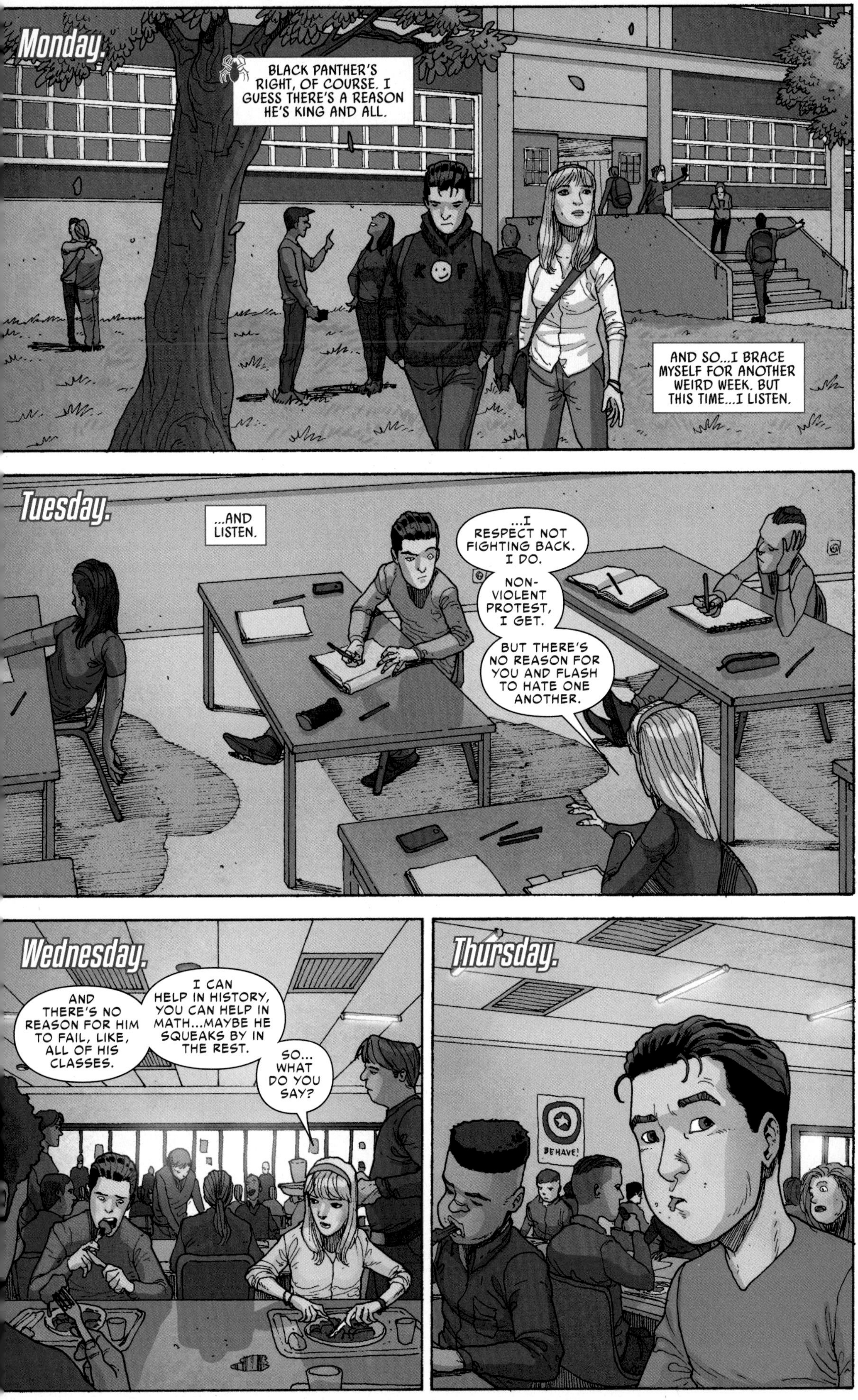
Monday.
BLACK PANTHER'S RIGHT, OF COURSE. I GUESS THERE'S A REASON HE'S KING AND ALL.
K F
AND SO...I BRACE MYSELF FOR ANOTHER WEIRD WEEK. BUT THIS TIME...I LISTEN.
Tuesday.
...AND LISTEN.
...I RESPECT NOT FIGHTING BACK. I DO.
NON-VIOLENT PROTEST, I GET.
BUT THERE'S NO REASON FOR YOU AND FLASH TO HATE ONE ANOTHER.
Wednesday.
AND THERE'S NO REASON FOR HIM TO FAIL, LIKE, ALL OF HIS CLASSES.
I CAN HELP IN HISTORY, YOU CAN HELP IN MATH...MAYBE HE SQUEAKS BY IN THE REST.
SO... WHAT DO YOU SAY?
Thursday.
BEHAVE!

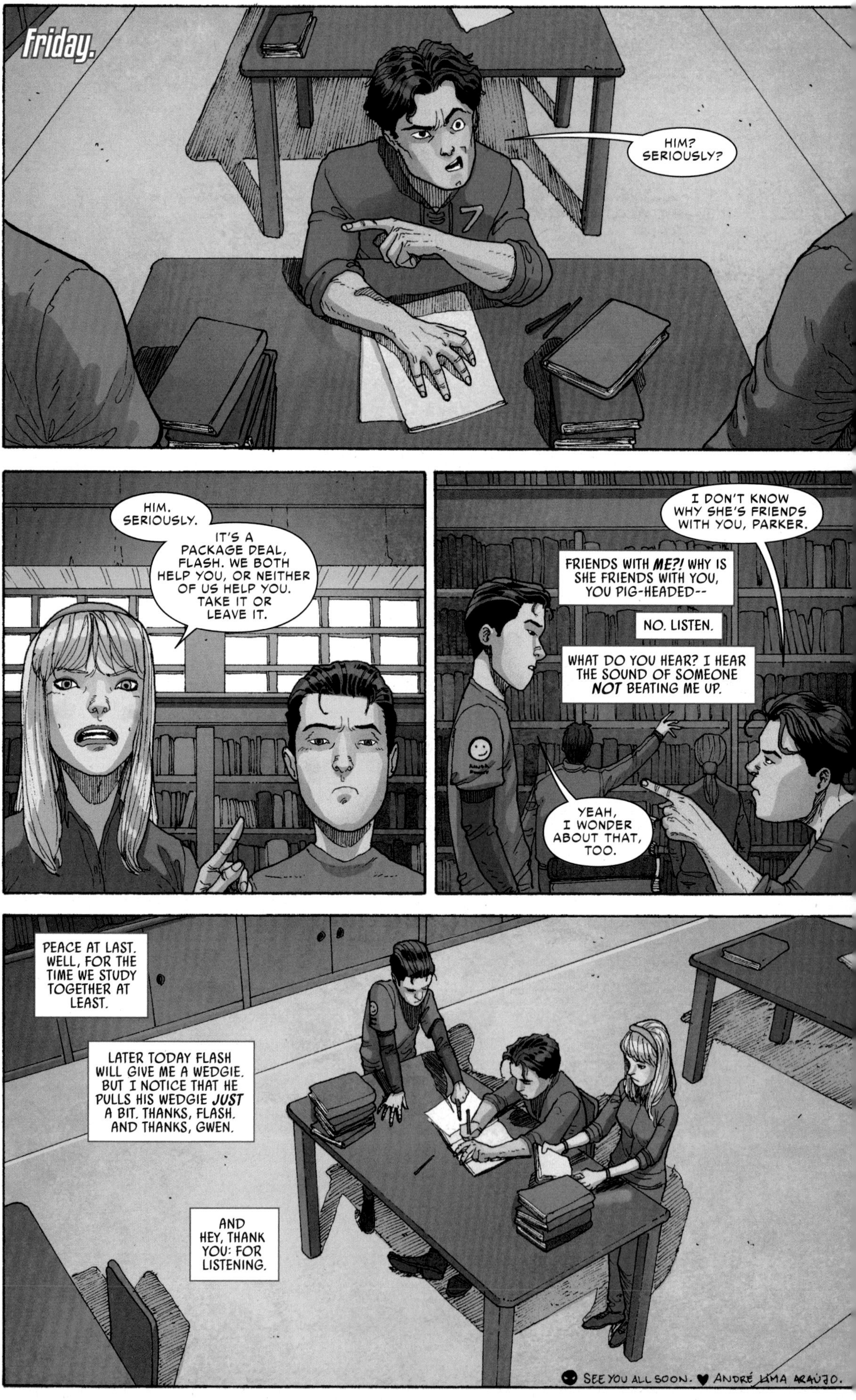
Friday.
HIM? SERIOUSLY?
HIM. SERIOUSLY.
IT'S A PACKAGE DEAL, FLASH. WE BOTH HELP YOU, OR NEITHER OF US HELP YOU. TAKE IT OR LEAVE IT.
I DON'T KNOW WHY SHE'S FRIENDS WITH YOU, PARKER.
FRIENDS WITH ME?! WHY IS SHE FRIENDS WITH YOU, YOU PIG-HEADED--
NO. LISTEN.
WHAT DO YOU HEAR? I HEAR THE SOUND OF SOMEONE NOT BEATING ME UP.
YEAH, I WONDER ABOUT THAT, TOO.
PEACE AT LAST. WELL, FOR THE TIME WE STUDY TOGETHER AT LEAST.
LATER TODAY FLASH WILL GIVE ME A WEDGIE. BUT I NOTICE THAT HE PULLS HIS WEDGIE JUST A BIT. THANKS, FLASH. AND THANKS, GWEN.
AND HEY, THANK YOU: FOR LISTENING.
SEE YOU ALL SOON. ♥ ANDRÉ LIMA ARAÚJO.

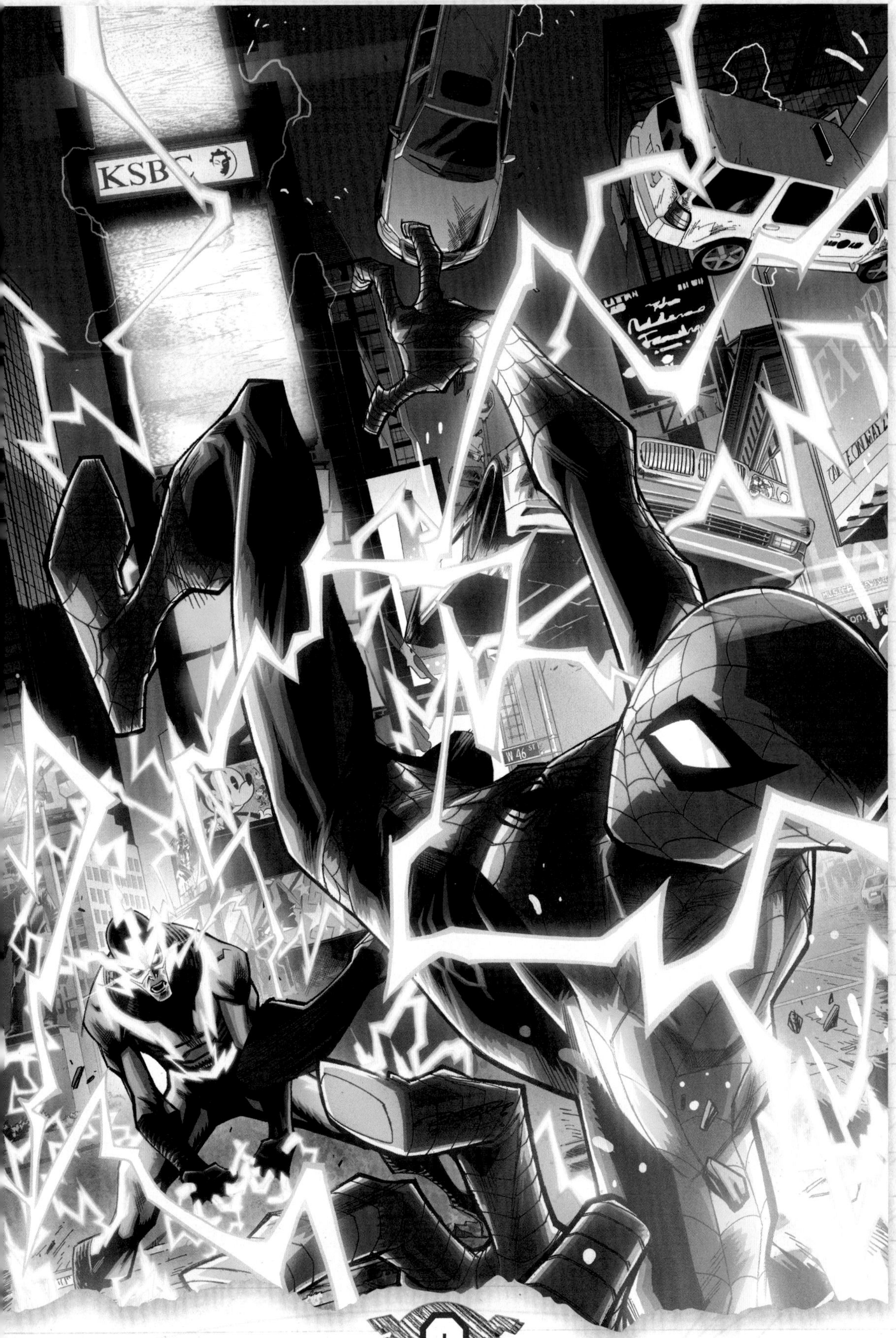
KSBC
W 46 ST

8

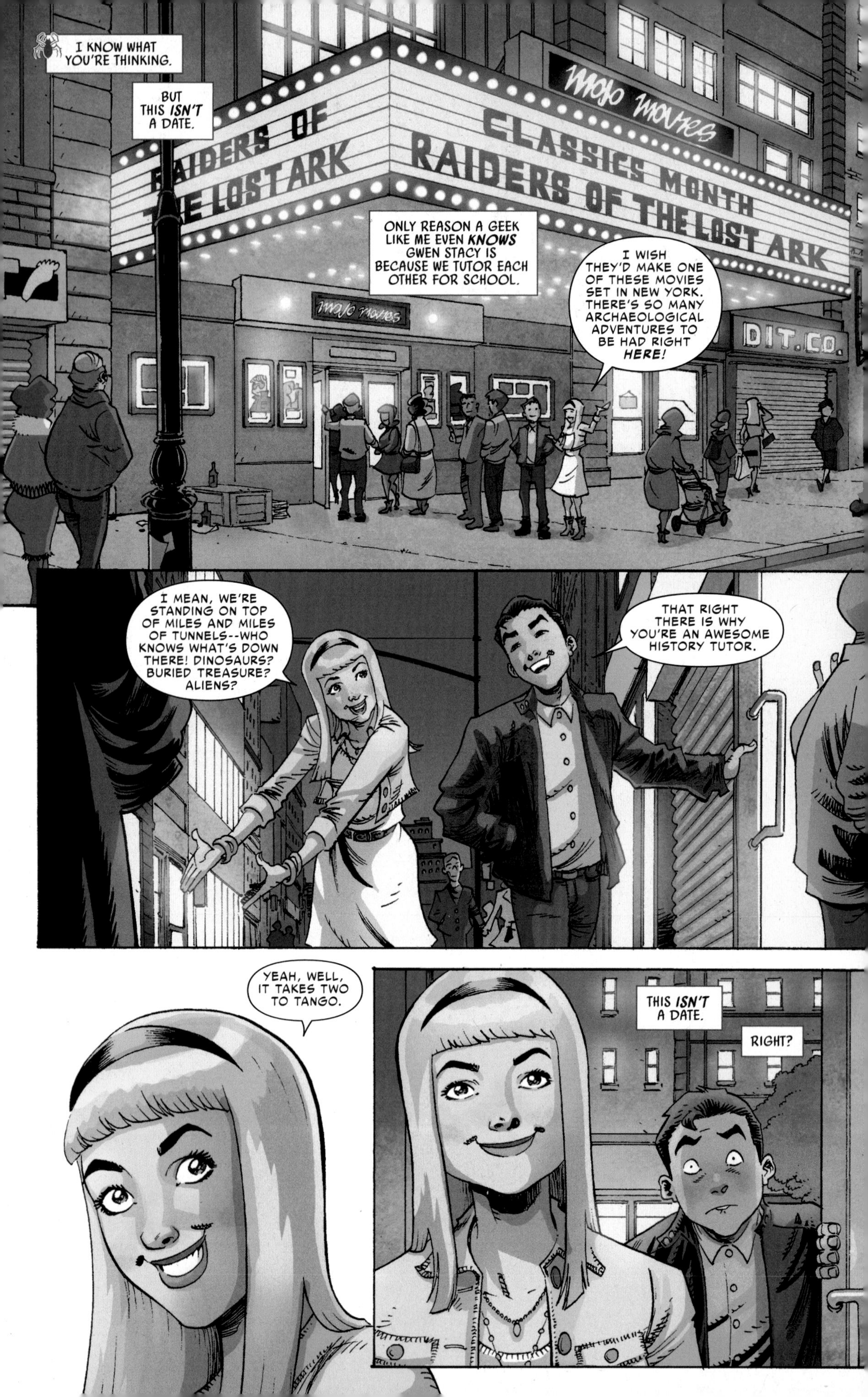
I KNOW WHAT YOU'RE THINKING.
BUT THIS *ISN'T* A DATE.
MOJO MOVIES
CLASSICS MONTH
RAIDERS OF THE LOST ARK
RAIDERS OF THE LOST ARK
ONLY REASON A GEEK LIKE ME EVEN *KNOWS* GWEN STACY IS BECAUSE WE TUTOR EACH OTHER FOR SCHOOL.
I WISH THEY'D MAKE ONE OF THESE MOVIES SET IN NEW YORK. THERE'S SO MANY ARCHAEOLOGICAL ADVENTURES TO BE HAD RIGHT *HERE!*
MOJO MOVIES
DIT. CO.
I MEAN, WE'RE STANDING ON TOP OF MILES AND MILES OF TUNNELS--WHO KNOWS WHAT'S DOWN THERE! DINOSAURS? BURIED TREASURE? ALIENS?
THAT RIGHT THERE IS WHY YOU'RE AN AWESOME HISTORY TUTOR.
YEAH, WELL, IT TAKES TWO TO TANGO.
THIS *ISN'T* A DATE.
RIGHT?

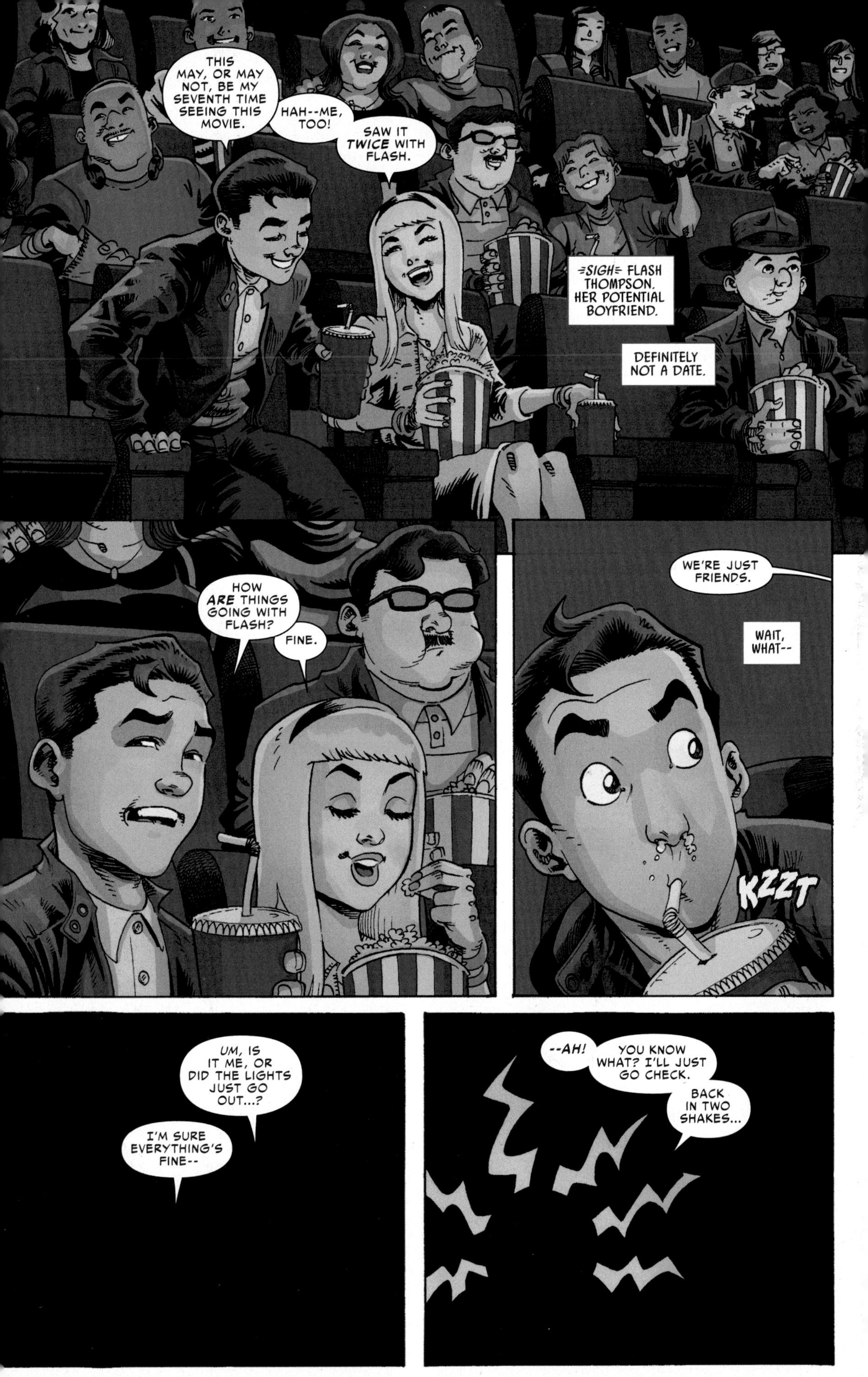
THIS MAY, OR MAY NOT, BE MY SEVENTH TIME SEEING THIS MOVIE.
HAH--ME, TOO!
SAW IT TWICE WITH FLASH.
=SIGH= FLASH THOMPSON. HER POTENTIAL BOYFRIEND.
DEFINITELY NOT A DATE.
HOW ARE THINGS GOING WITH FLASH?
FINE.
WE'RE JUST FRIENDS.
WAIT, WHAT--
KZZT
UM, IS IT ME, OR DID THE LIGHTS JUST GO OUT...?
I'M SURE EVERYTHING'S FINE--
--AH!
YOU KNOW WHAT? I'LL JUST GO CHECK.
BACK IN TWO SHAKES...

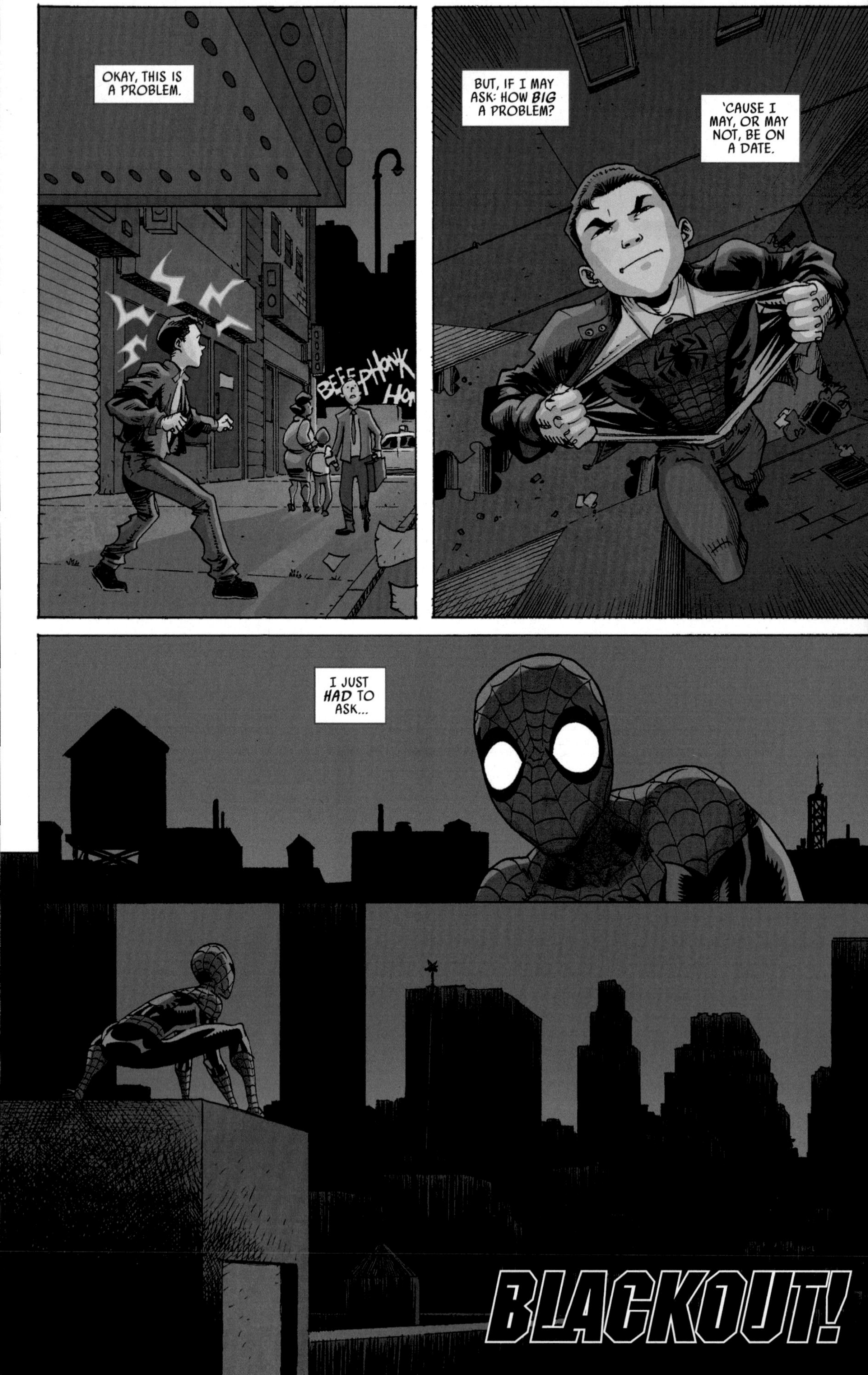
OKAY, THIS IS A PROBLEM.
BEEEEP HONK HON
BUT, IF I MAY ASK: HOW BIG A PROBLEM?
'CAUSE I MAY, OR MAY NOT, BE ON A DATE.
I JUST HAD TO ASK...
BLACKOUT!

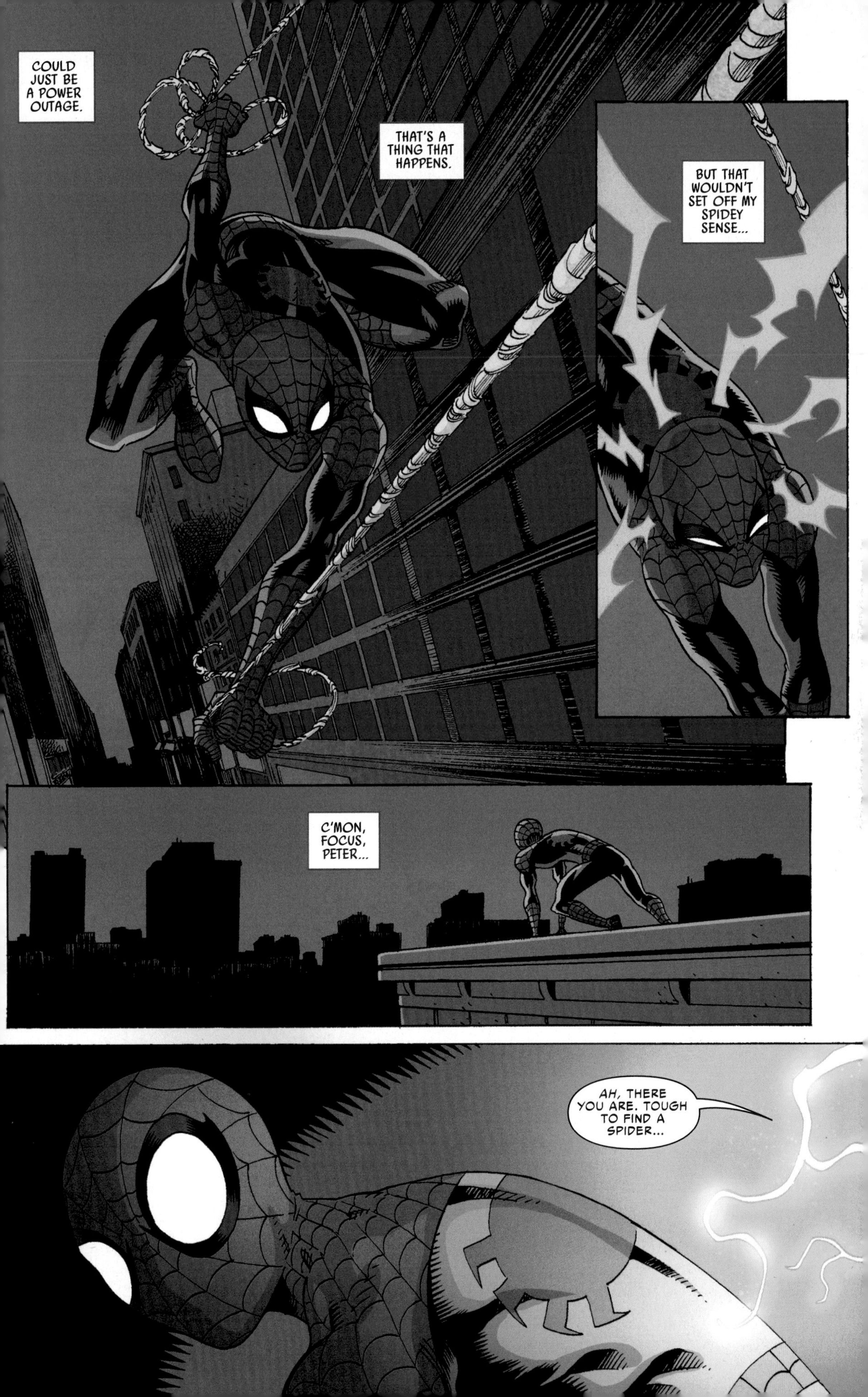
COULD JUST BE A POWER OUTAGE.
THAT'S A THING THAT HAPPENS.
BUT THAT WOULDN'T SET OFF MY SPIDEY SENSE...
C'MON, FOCUS, PETER...
AH, THERE YOU ARE. TOUGH TO FIND A SPIDER...

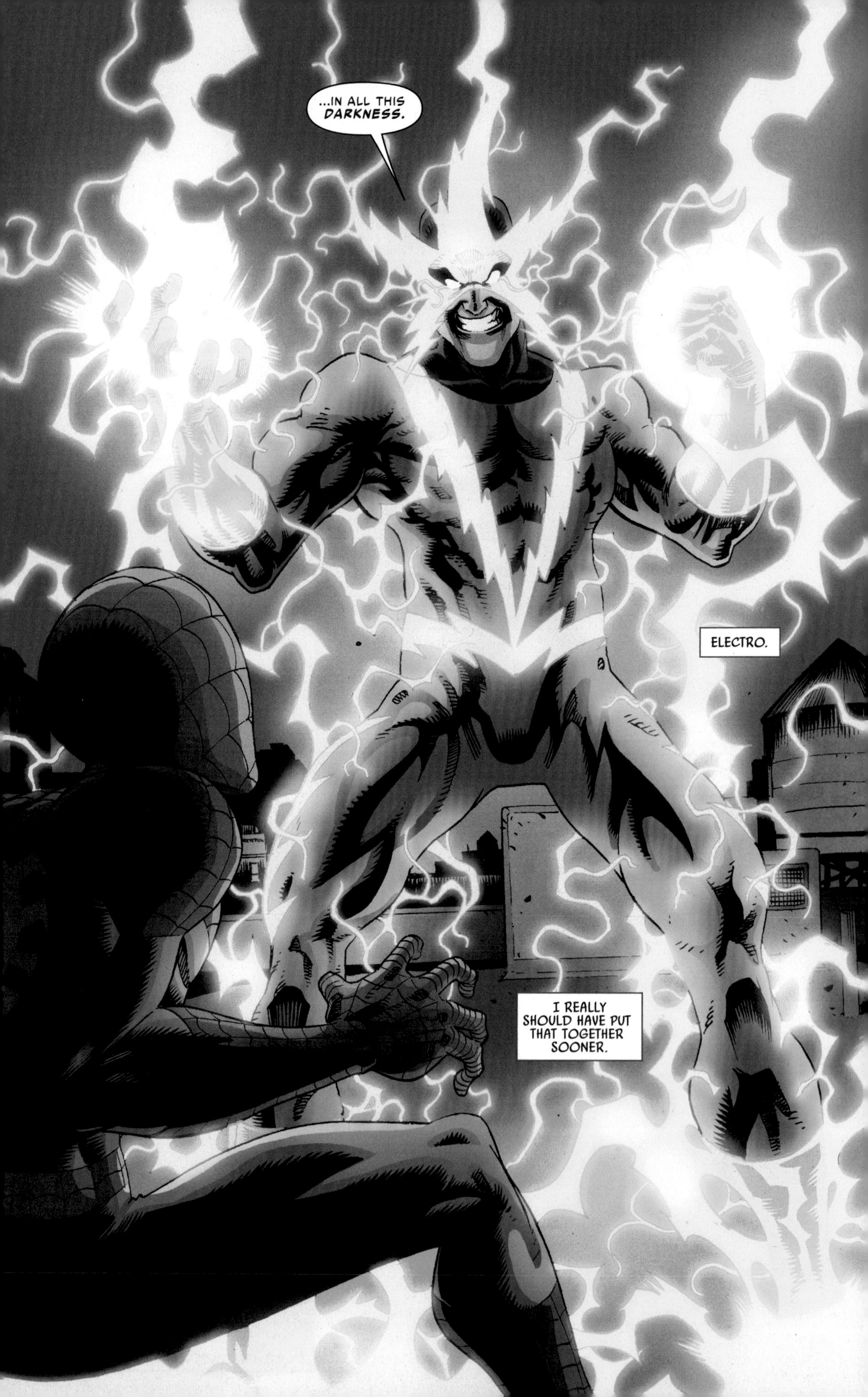
...IN ALL THIS DARKNESS.
ELECTRO.
I REALLY SHOULD HAVE PUT THAT TOGETHER SOONER.

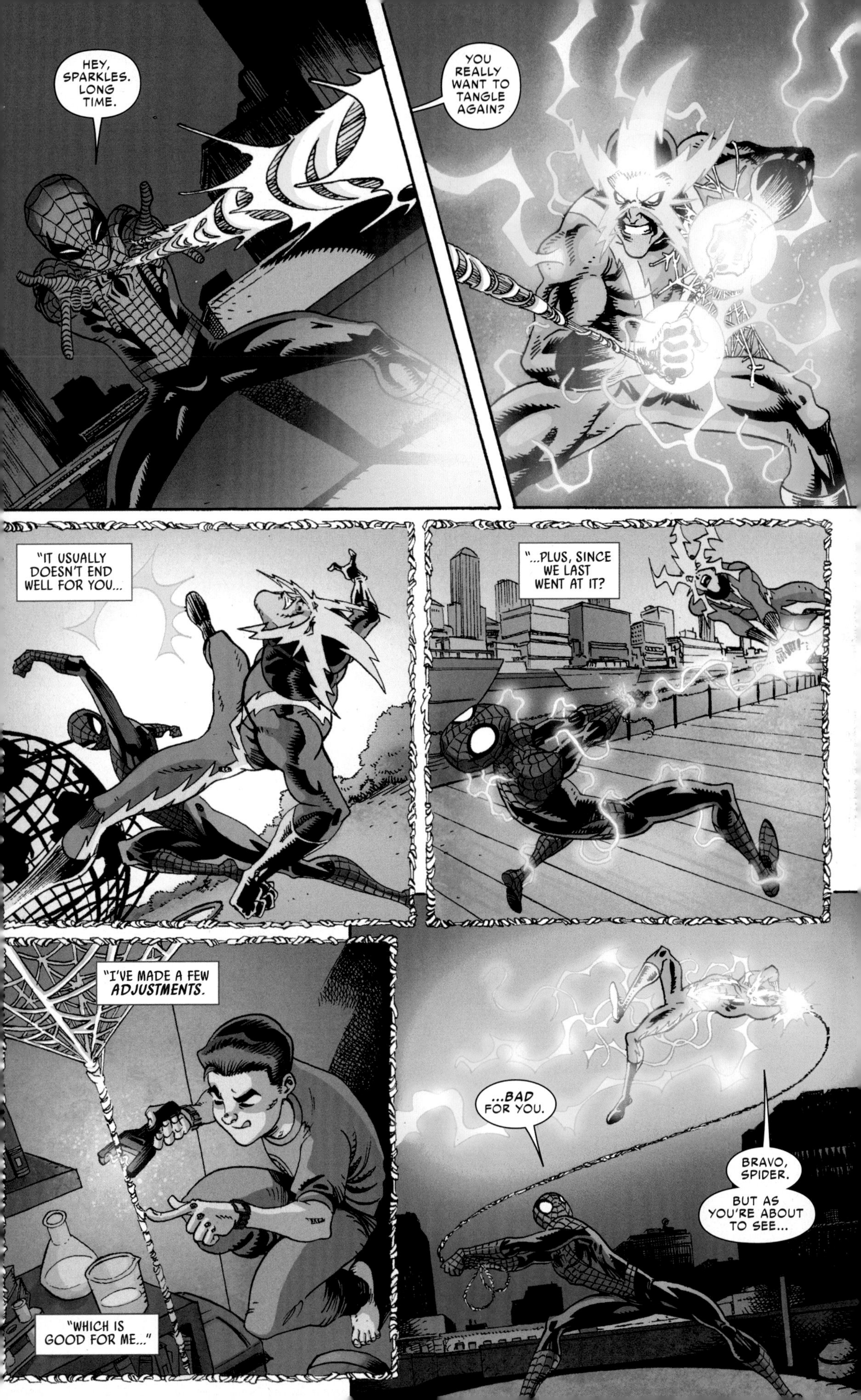
HEY, SPARKLES. LONG TIME.
YOU REALLY WANT TO TANGLE AGAIN?
"IT USUALLY DOESN'T END WELL FOR YOU...
"...PLUS, SINCE WE LAST WENT AT IT?
"I'VE MADE A FEW ADJUSTMENTS.
"WHICH IS GOOD FOR ME..."
...BAD FOR YOU.
BRAVO, SPIDER.
BUT AS YOU'RE ABOUT TO SEE...

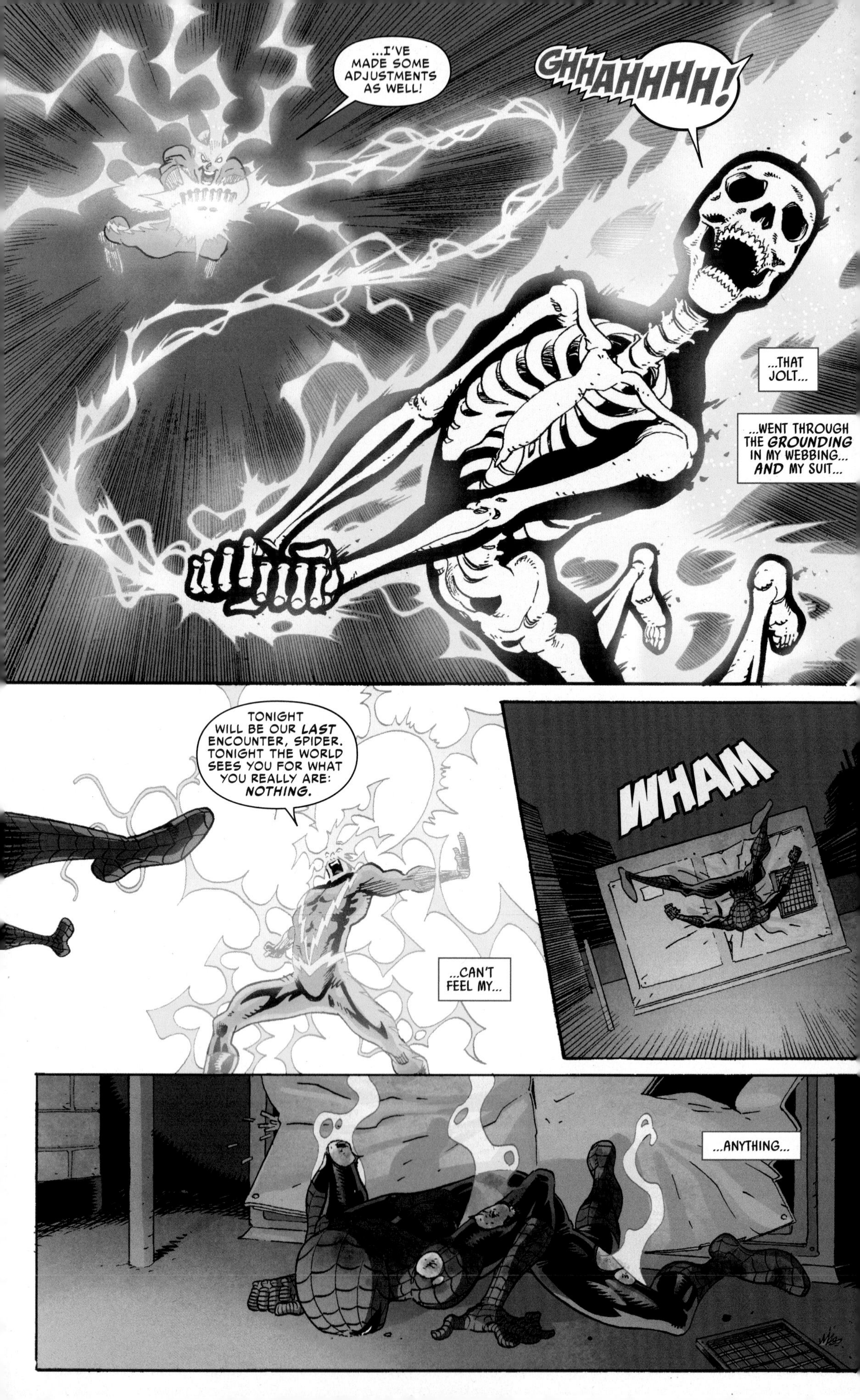
...I'VE MADE SOME ADJUSTMENTS AS WELL!
GHHAHHHH!
...THAT JOLT...
...WENT THROUGH THE GROUNDING IN MY WEBBING... AND MY SUIT...
TONIGHT WILL BE OUR LAST ENCOUNTER, SPIDER. TONIGHT THE WORLD SEES YOU FOR WHAT YOU REALLY ARE: NOTHING.
WHAM
...CAN'T FEEL MY...
...ANYTHING...

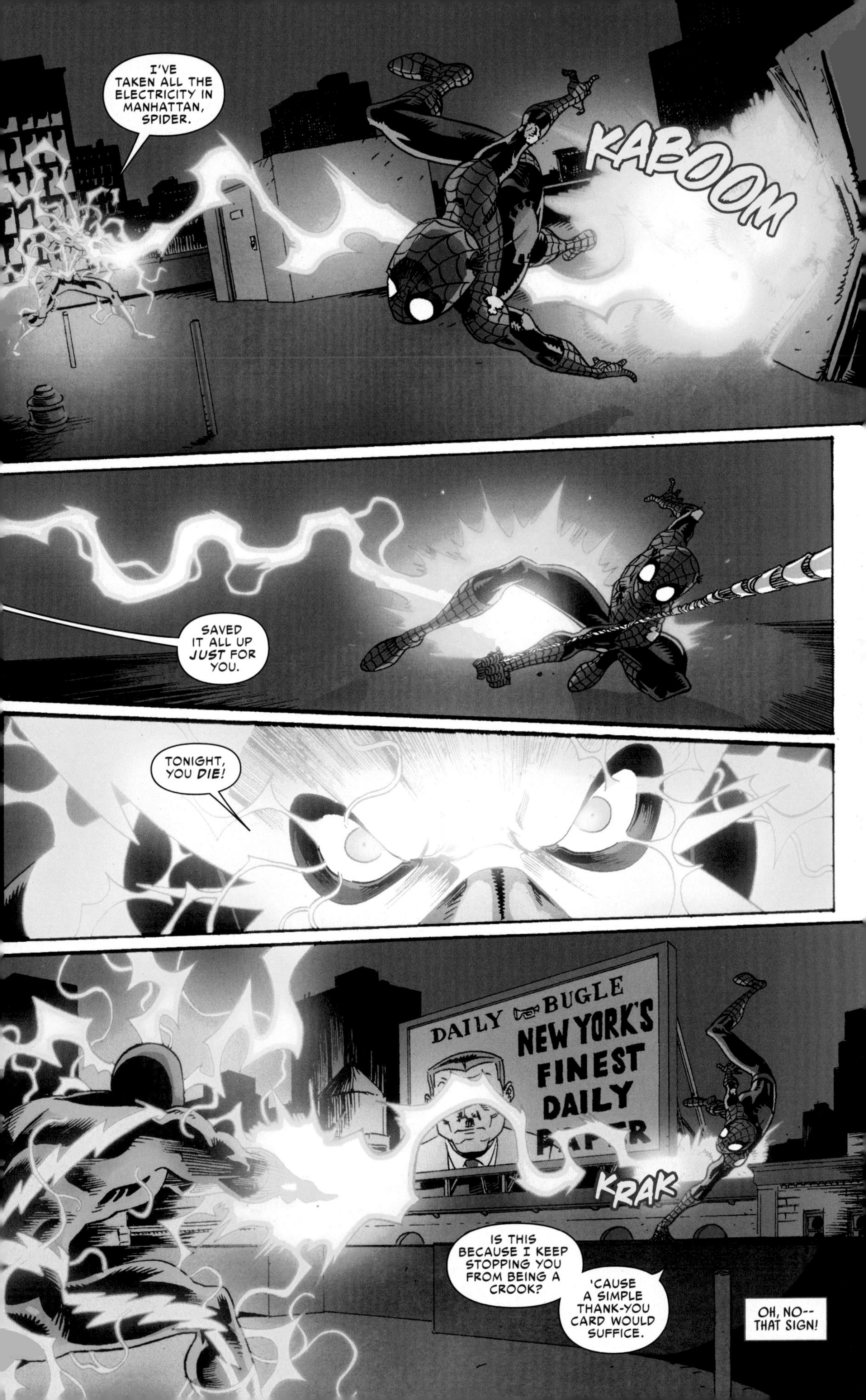
I'VE TAKEN ALL THE ELECTRICITY IN MANHATTAN, SPIDER.
KABOOM
SAVED IT ALL UP JUST FOR YOU.
TONIGHT, YOU DIE!
DAILY BUGLE
NEW YORK'S FINEST DAILY
KRAK
IS THIS BECAUSE I KEEP STOPPING YOU FROM BEING A CROOK?
'CAUSE A SIMPLE THANK-YOU CARD WOULD SUFFICE.
OH, NO-- THAT SIGN!

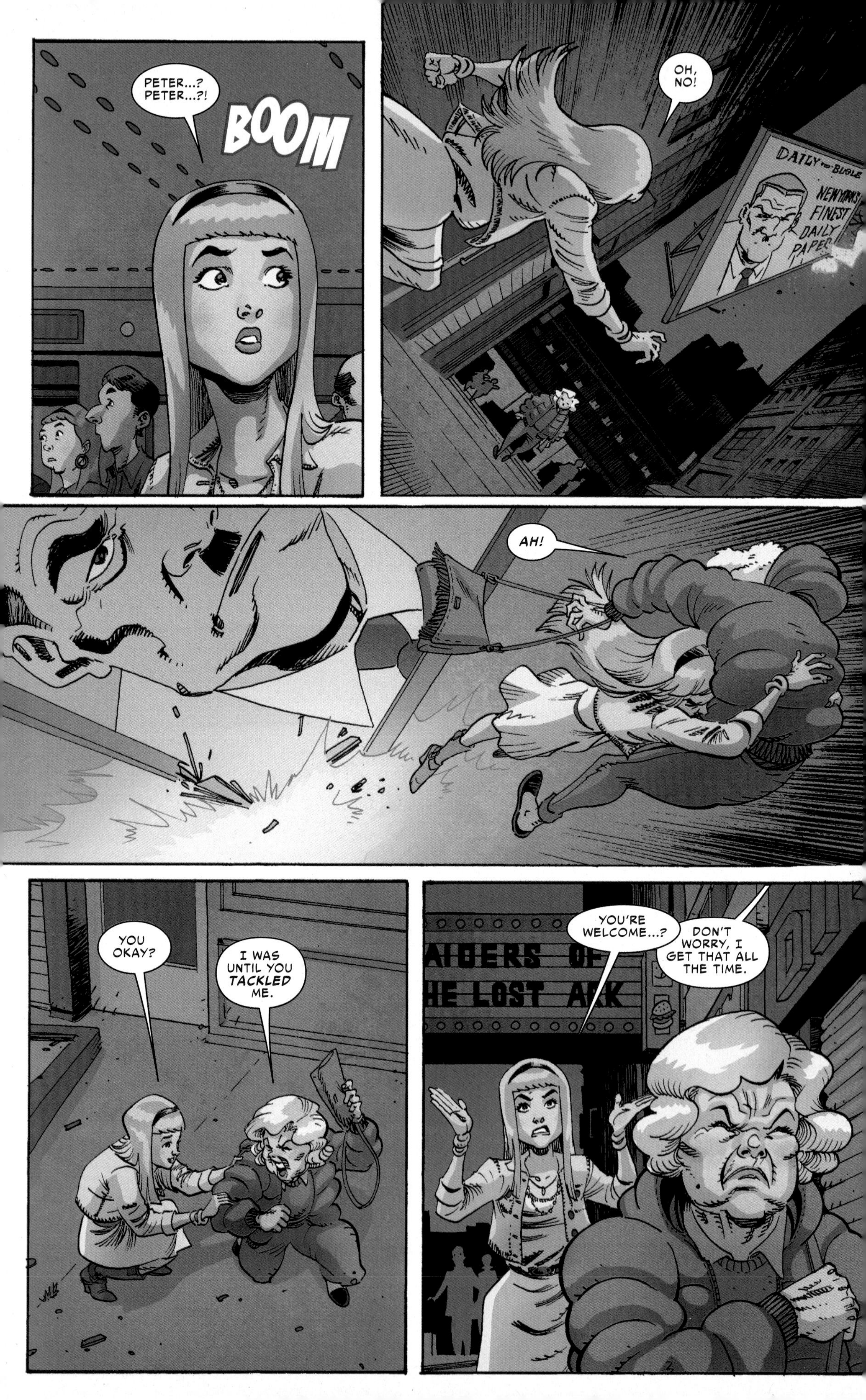
PETER...?
PETER...?!
BOOM
OH, NO!
DAILY BUGLE
NEW YORK'S FINEST DAILY PAPER
AH!
YOU OKAY?
I WAS UNTIL YOU *TACKLED* ME.
AIDERS OF
HE LOST ARK
YOU'RE WELCOME...?
DON'T WORRY, I GET THAT ALL THE TIME.

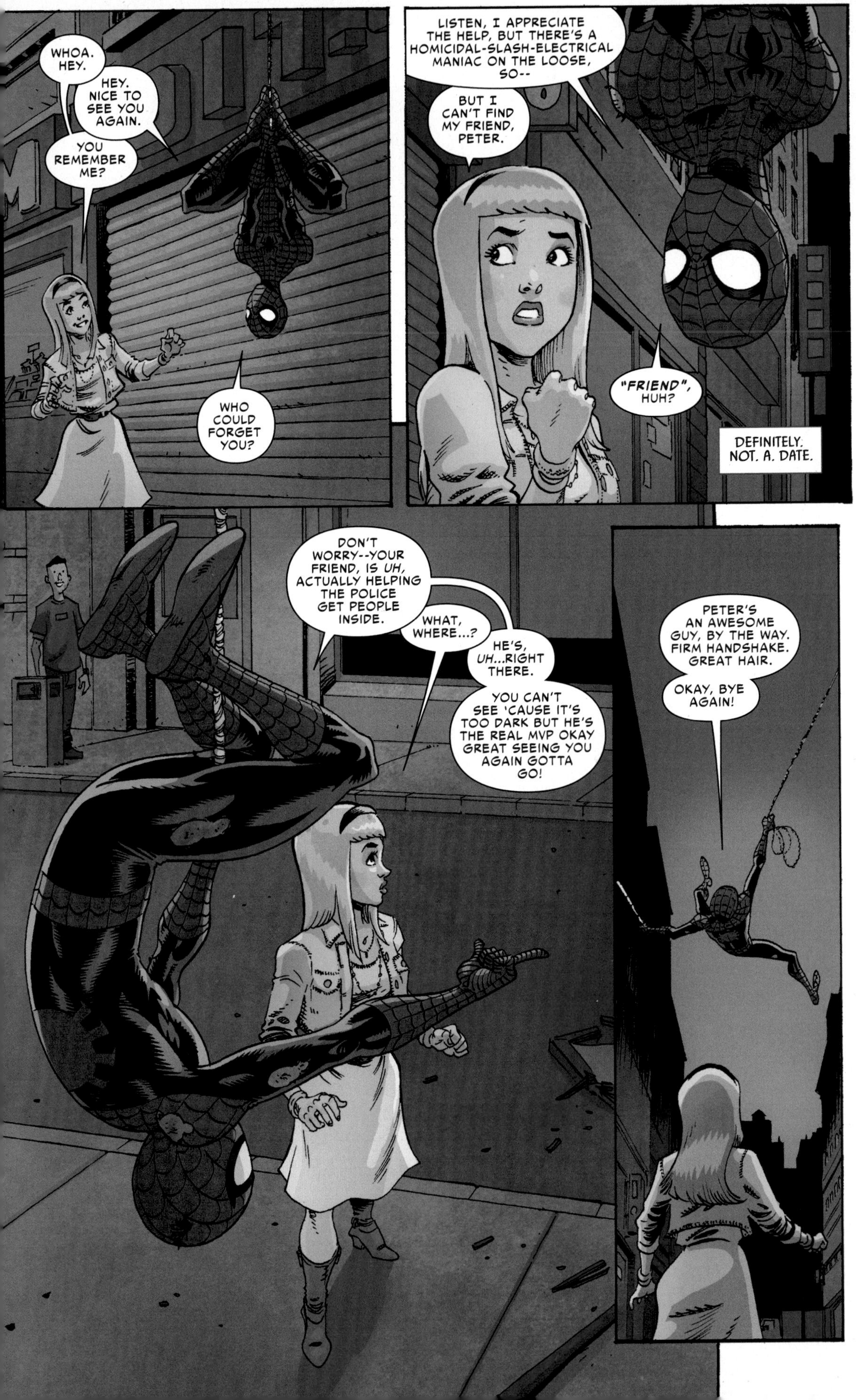
WHOA. HEY.
HEY. NICE TO SEE YOU AGAIN.
YOU REMEMBER ME?
WHO COULD FORGET YOU?
LISTEN, I APPRECIATE THE HELP, BUT THERE'S A HOMICIDAL-SLASH-ELECTRICAL MANIAC ON THE LOOSE, SO--
BUT I CAN'T FIND MY FRIEND, PETER.
"FRIEND", HUH?
DEFINITELY. NOT. A. DATE.
DON'T WORRY--YOUR FRIEND, IS UH, ACTUALLY HELPING THE POLICE GET PEOPLE INSIDE.
WHAT, WHERE...?
HE'S, UH...RIGHT THERE.
YOU CAN'T SEE 'CAUSE IT'S TOO DARK BUT HE'S THE REAL MVP OKAY GREAT SEEING YOU AGAIN GOTTA GO!
PETER'S AN AWESOME GUY, BY THE WAY. FIRM HANDSHAKE. GREAT HAIR.
OKAY, BYE AGAIN!

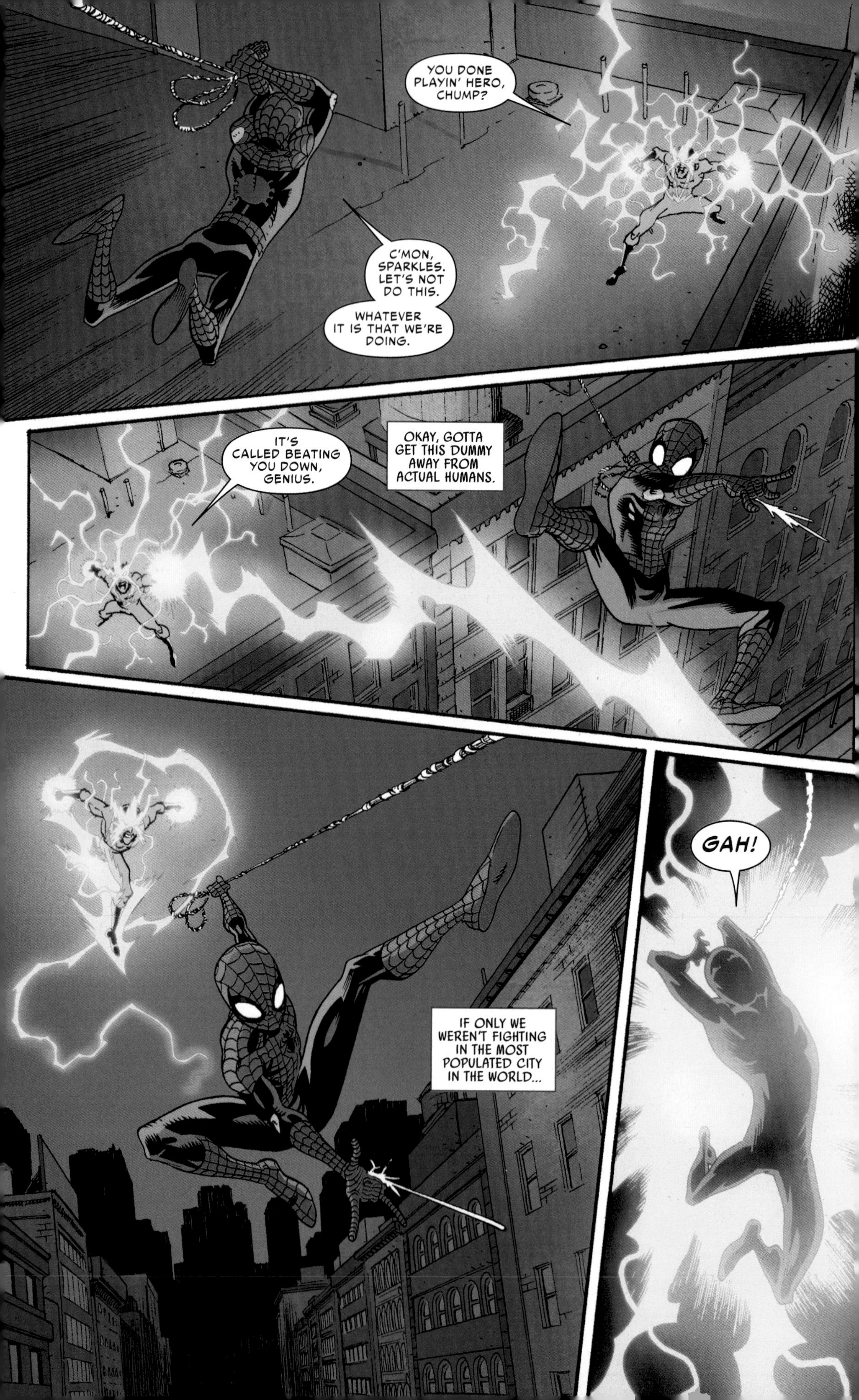
YOU DONE PLAYIN' HERO, CHUMP?
C'MON, SPARKLES. LET'S NOT DO THIS.
WHATEVER IT IS THAT WE'RE DOING.
IT'S CALLED BEATING YOU DOWN, GENIUS.
OKAY, GOTTA GET THIS DUMMY AWAY FROM ACTUAL HUMANS.
IF ONLY WE WEREN'T FIGHTING IN THE MOST POPULATED CITY IN THE WORLD...
GAH!

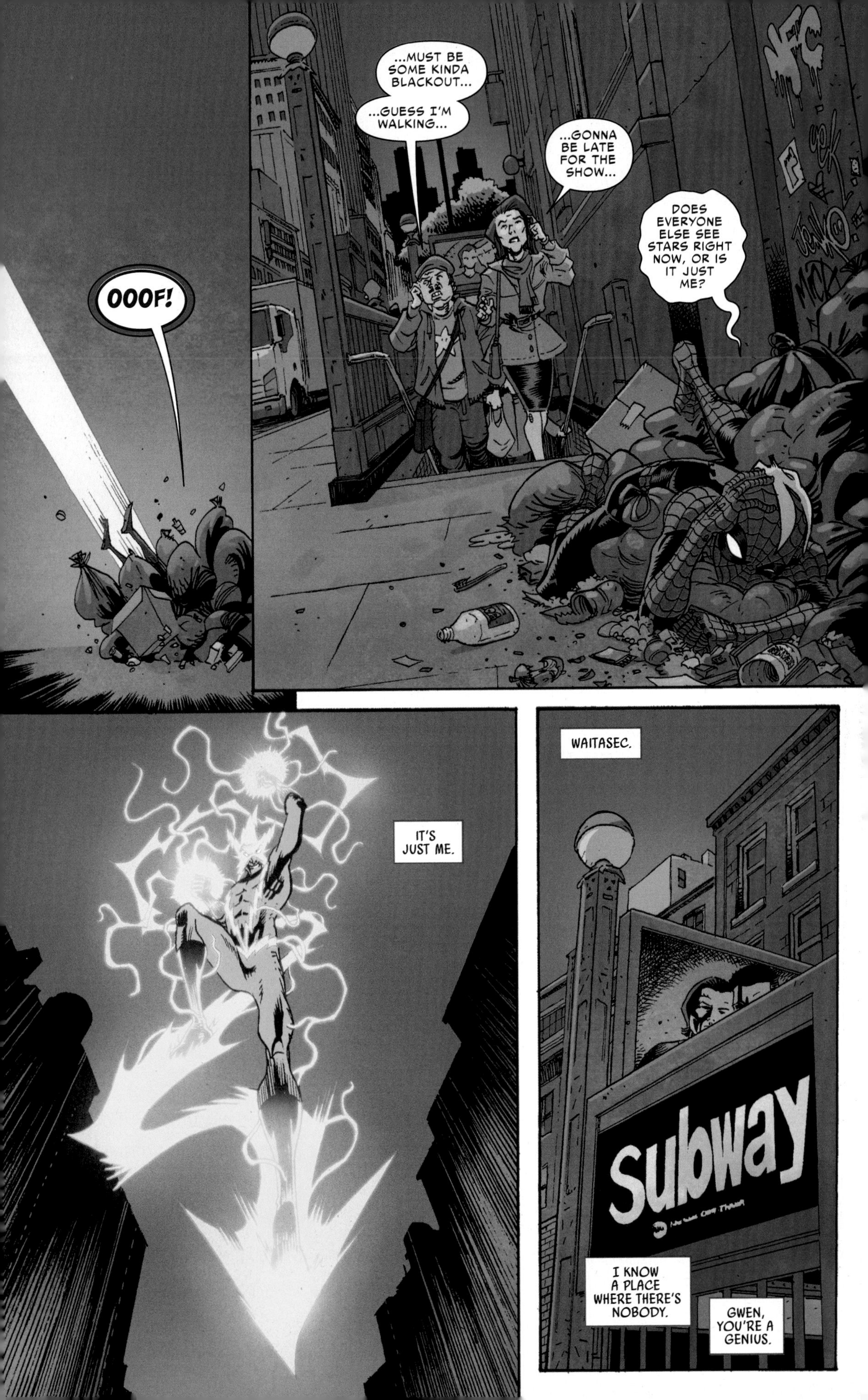
OOOF!
...MUST BE SOME KINDA BLACKOUT...
...GUESS I'M WALKING...
...GONNA BE LATE FOR THE SHOW...
DOES EVERYONE ELSE SEE STARS RIGHT NOW, OR IS IT JUST ME?
IT'S JUST ME.
WAITASEC.
Subway
I KNOW A PLACE WHERE THERE'S NOBODY.
GWEN, YOU'RE A GENIUS.

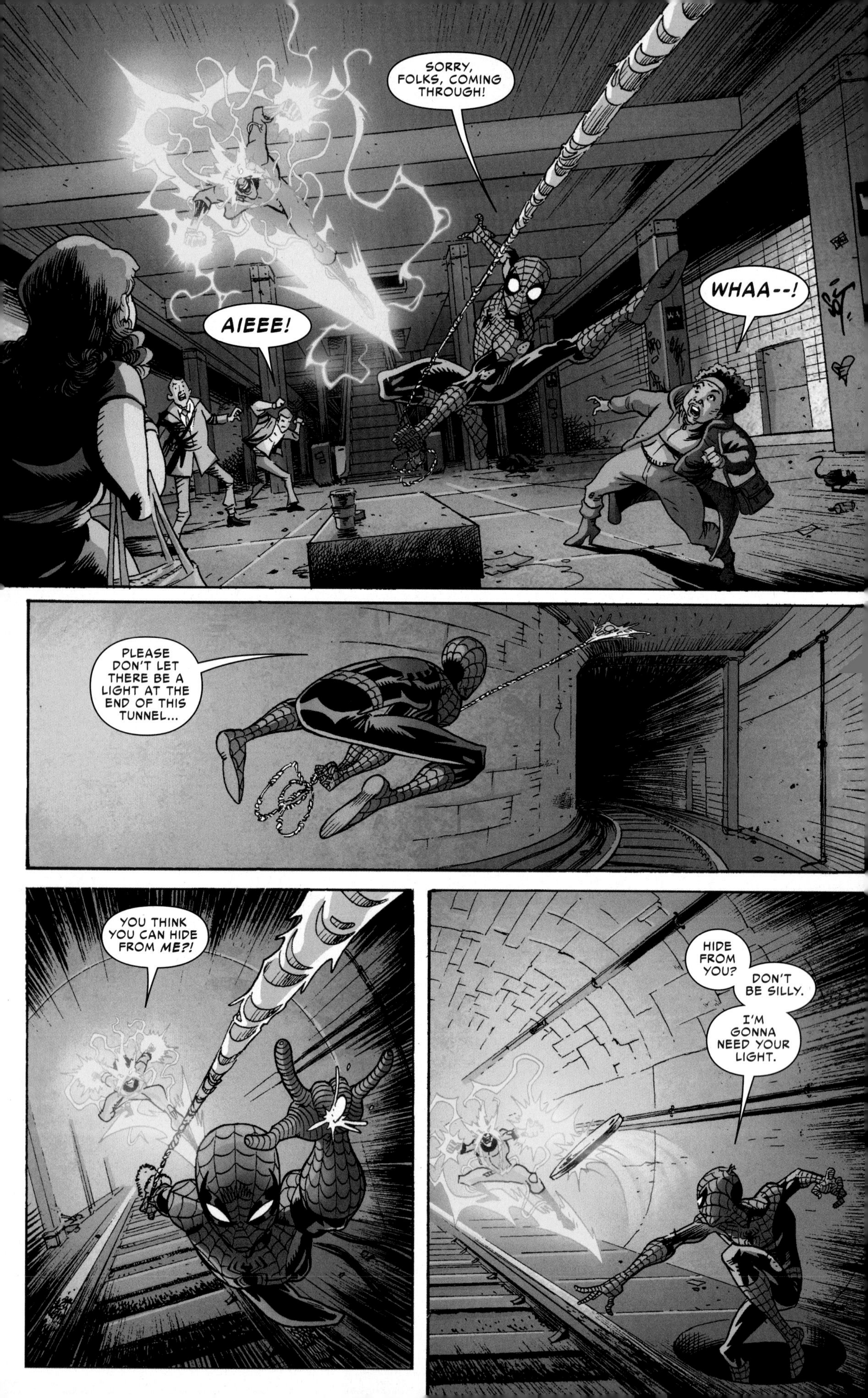
SORRY, FOLKS, COMING THROUGH!
AIEEE!
WHAA--!
PLEASE DON'T LET THERE BE A LIGHT AT THE END OF THIS TUNNEL...
YOU THINK YOU CAN HIDE FROM *ME?!*
HIDE FROM YOU?
DON'T BE SILLY.
I'M GONNA NEED YOUR LIGHT.

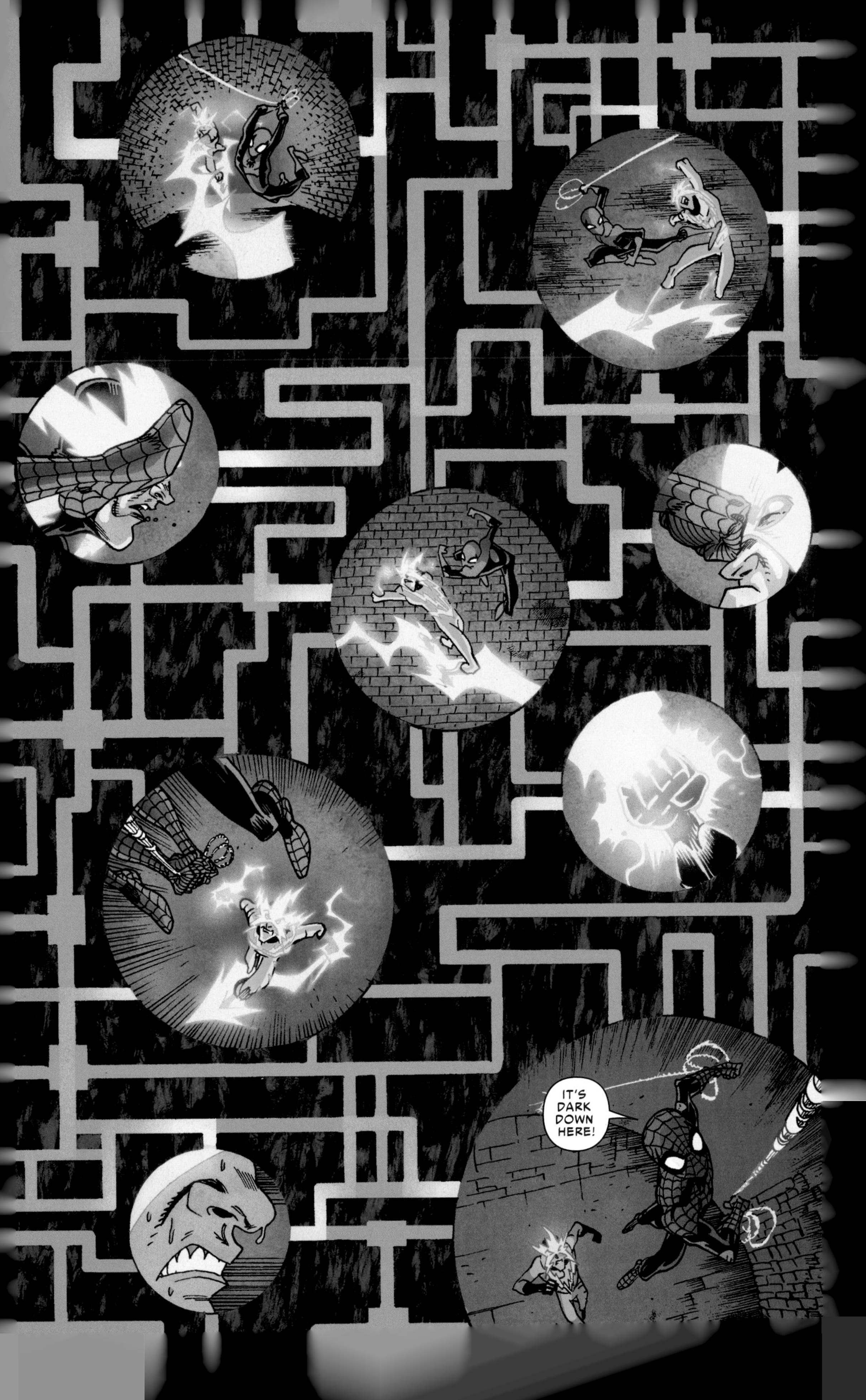
IT'S DARK DOWN HERE!

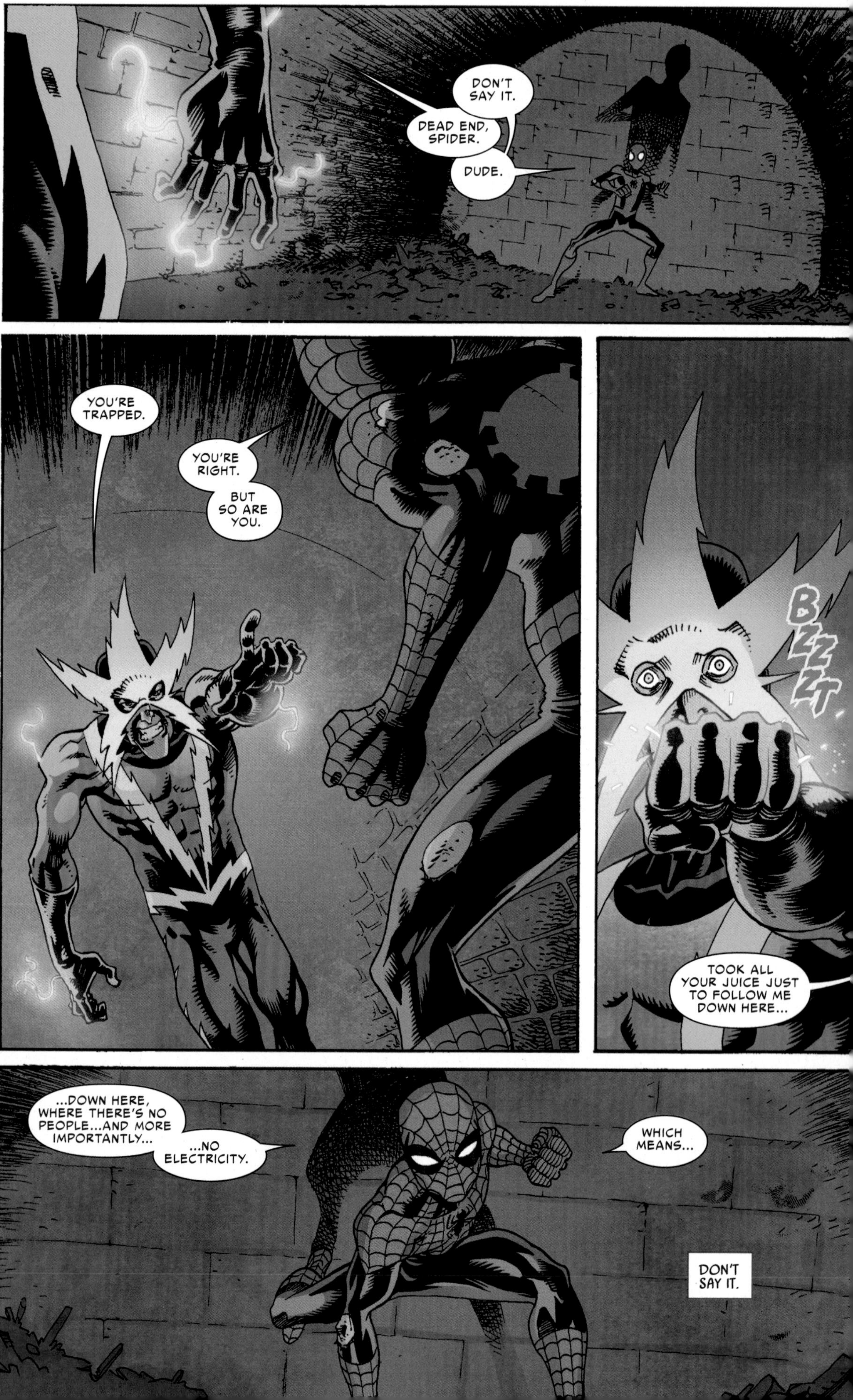
DON'T SAY IT.
DEAD END, SPIDER.
DUDE.
YOU'RE TRAPPED.
YOU'RE RIGHT.
BUT SO ARE YOU.
BZZZT
TOOK ALL YOUR JUICE JUST TO FOLLOW ME DOWN HERE...
...DOWN HERE, WHERE THERE'S NO PEOPLE...AND MORE IMPORTANTLY...
...NO ELECTRICITY.
WHICH MEANS...
DON'T SAY IT.

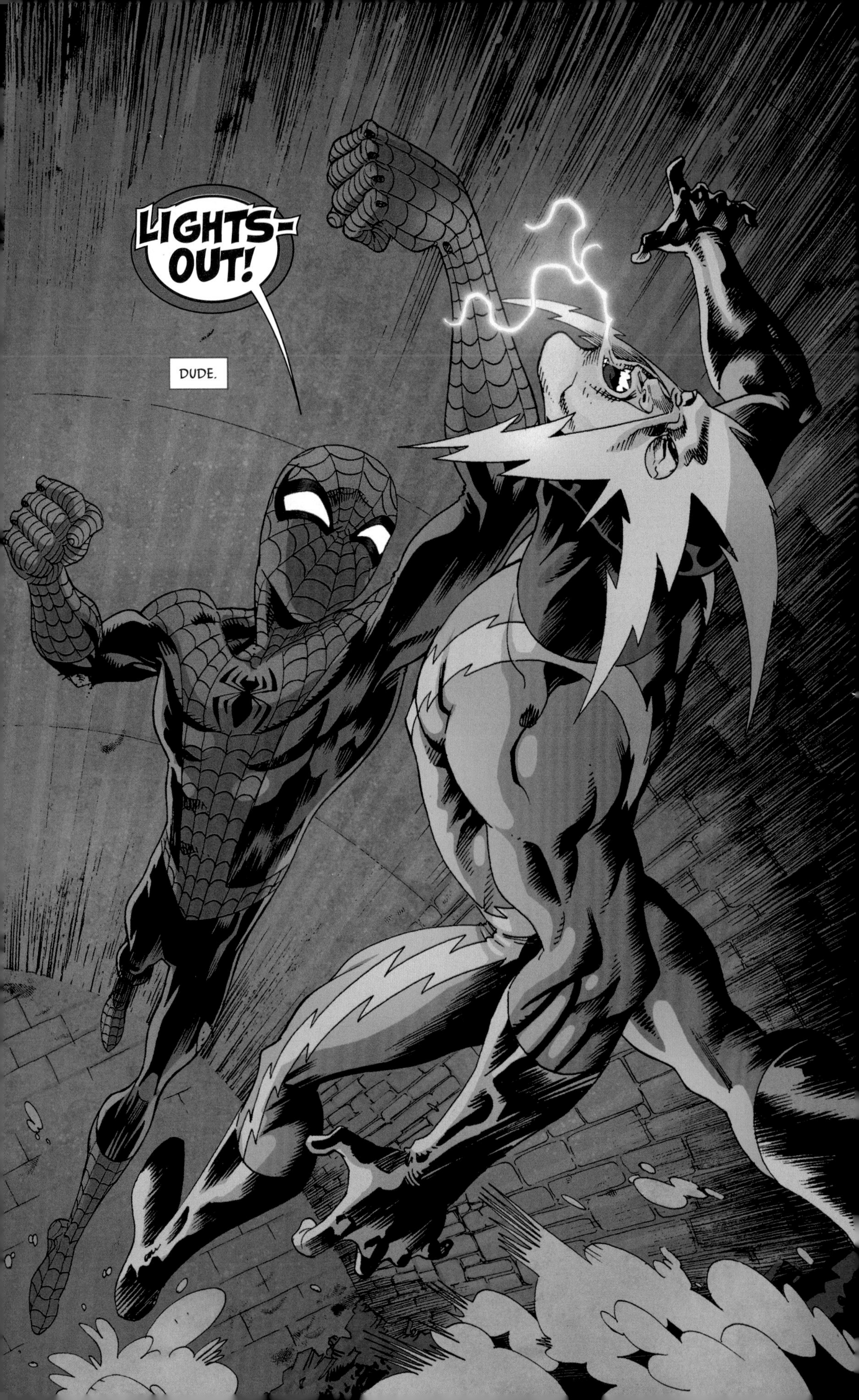
LIGHTS-OUT!
DUDE.

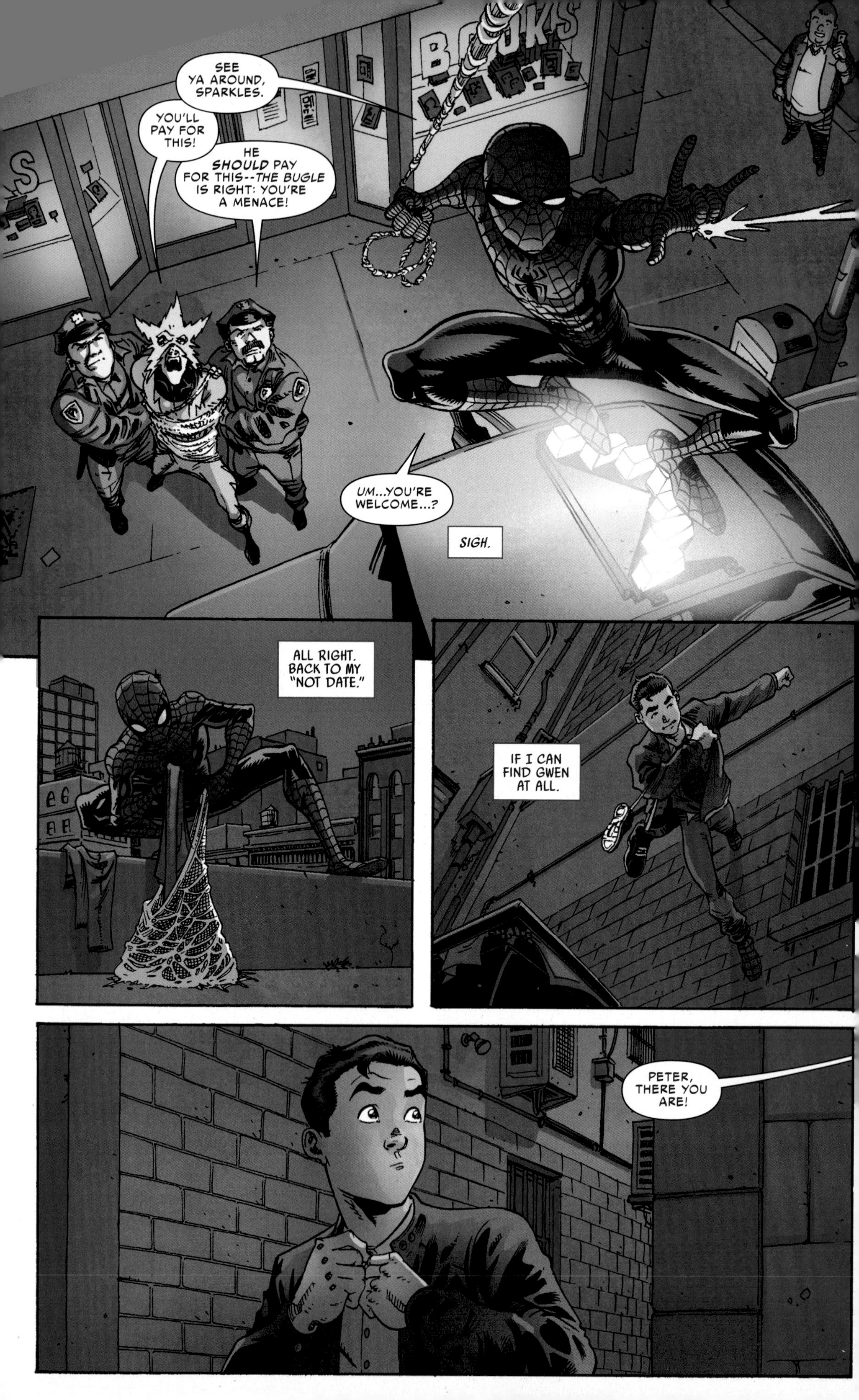
SEE YA AROUND, SPARKLES.
YOU'LL PAY FOR THIS!
HE *SHOULD* PAY FOR THIS--*THE BUGLE* IS RIGHT: YOU'RE A MENACE!
UM...YOU'RE WELCOME...?
SIGH.
BOOKS
ALL RIGHT. BACK TO MY "NOT DATE."
IF I CAN FIND GWEN AT ALL.
PETER, THERE YOU ARE!

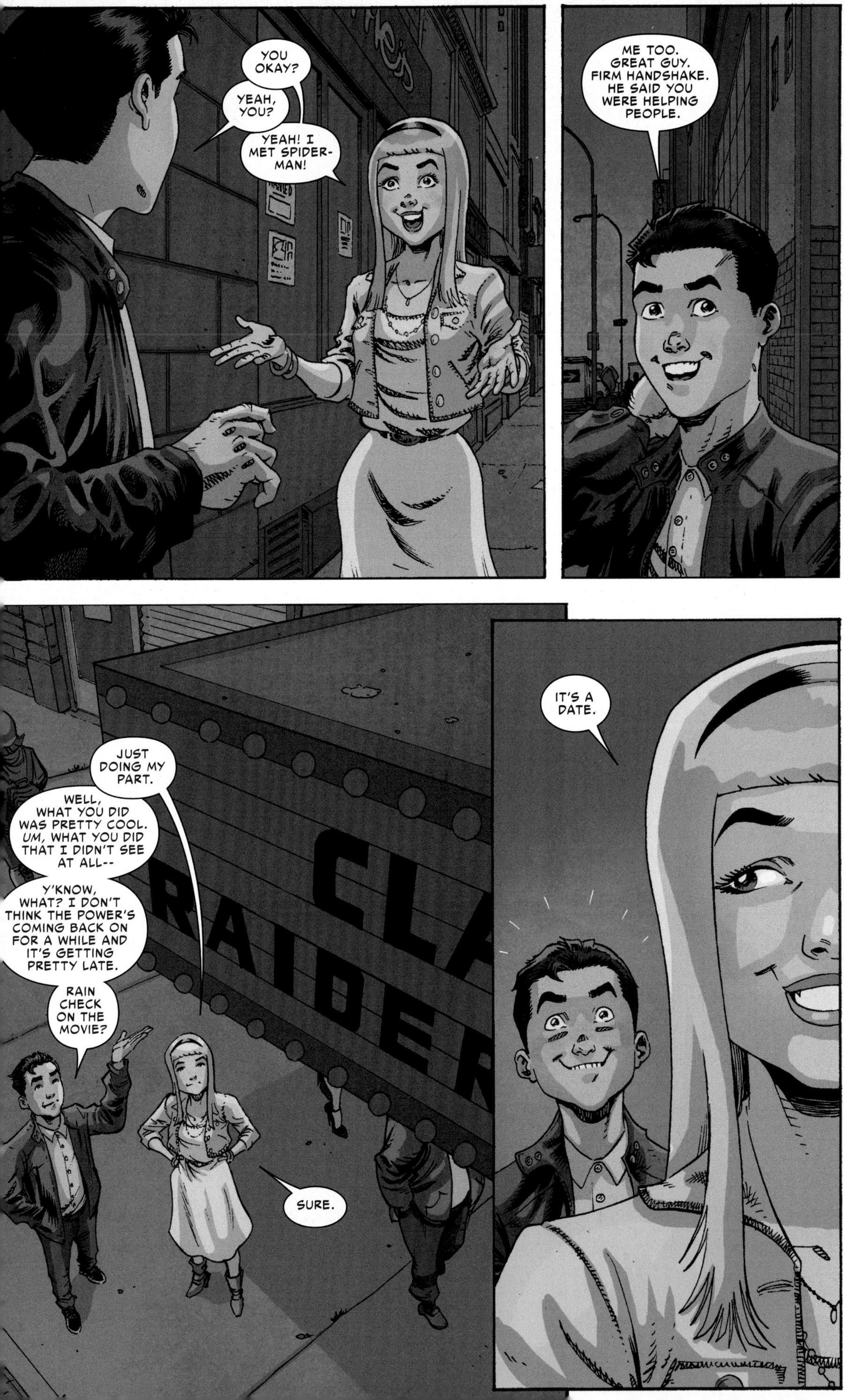

YOU OKAY?
YEAH, YOU?
YEAH! I MET SPIDER-MAN!
ME TOO. GREAT GUY. FIRM HANDSHAKE. HE SAID YOU WERE HELPING PEOPLE.
JUST DOING MY PART.
WELL, WHAT YOU DID WAS PRETTY COOL. UM, WHAT YOU DID THAT I DIDN'T SEE AT ALL--
Y'KNOW, WHAT? I DON'T THINK THE POWER'S COMING BACK ON FOR A WHILE AND IT'S GETTING PRETTY LATE.
RAIN CHECK ON THE MOVIE?
SURE.
CLA
RAIDER
IT'S A DATE.

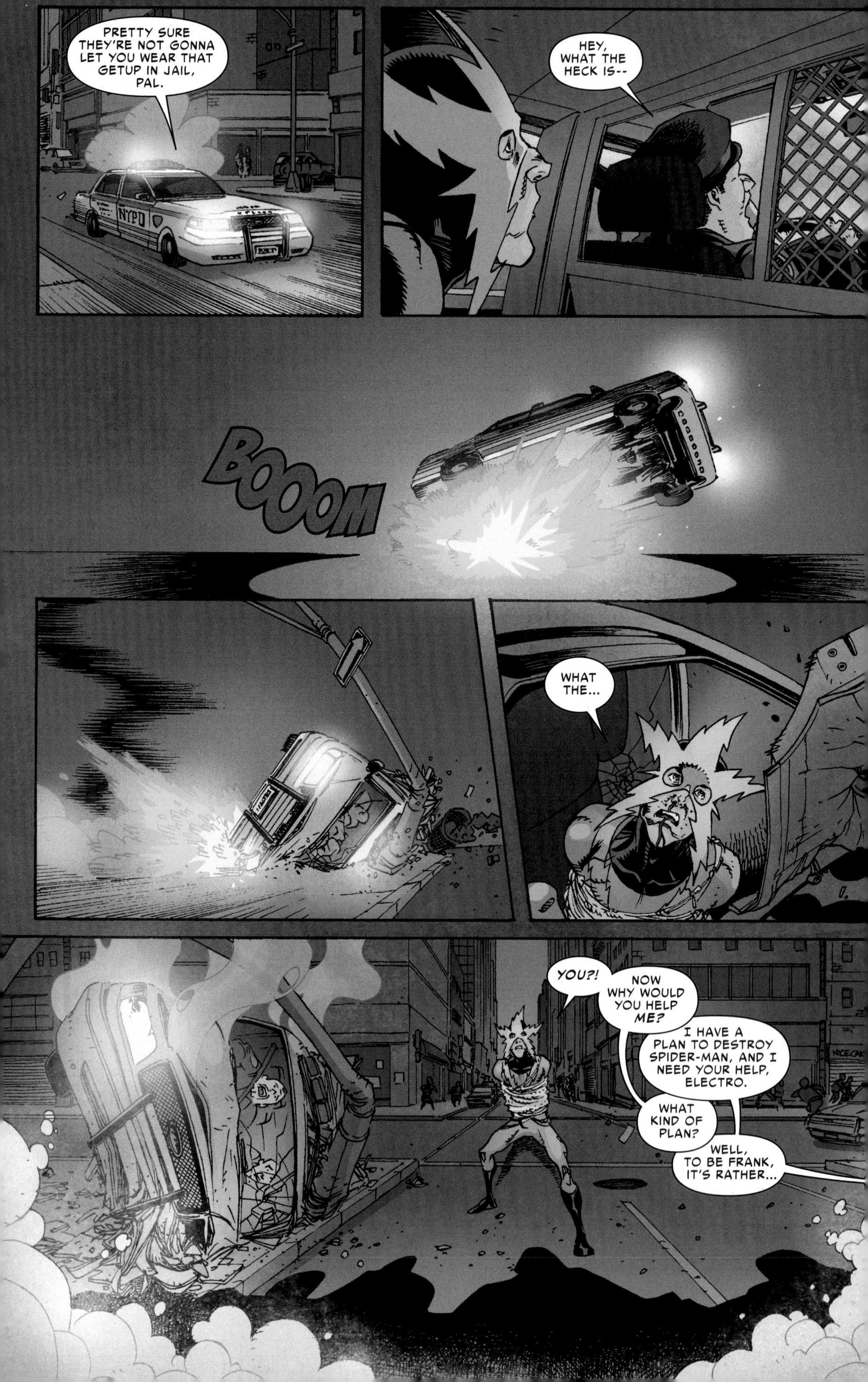
PRETTY SURE THEY'RE NOT GONNA LET YOU WEAR THAT GETUP IN JAIL, PAL.
HEY, WHAT THE HECK IS--
BOOOM
WHAT THE...
YOU?!
NOW WHY WOULD YOU HELP ME?
I HAVE A PLAN TO DESTROY SPIDER-MAN, AND I NEED YOUR HELP, ELECTRO.
WHAT KIND OF PLAN?
WELL, TO BE FRANK, IT'S RATHER...

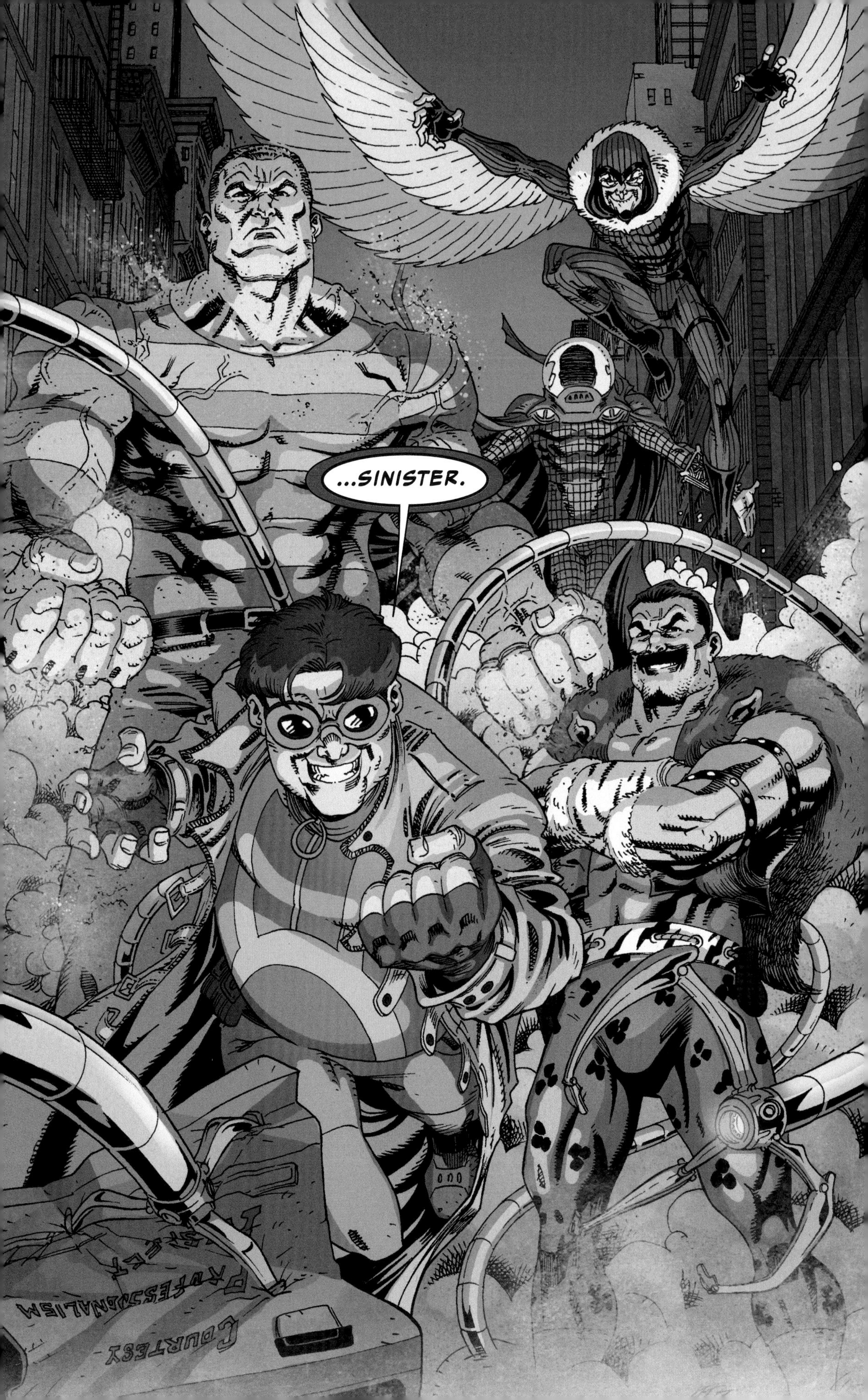
...SINISTER.

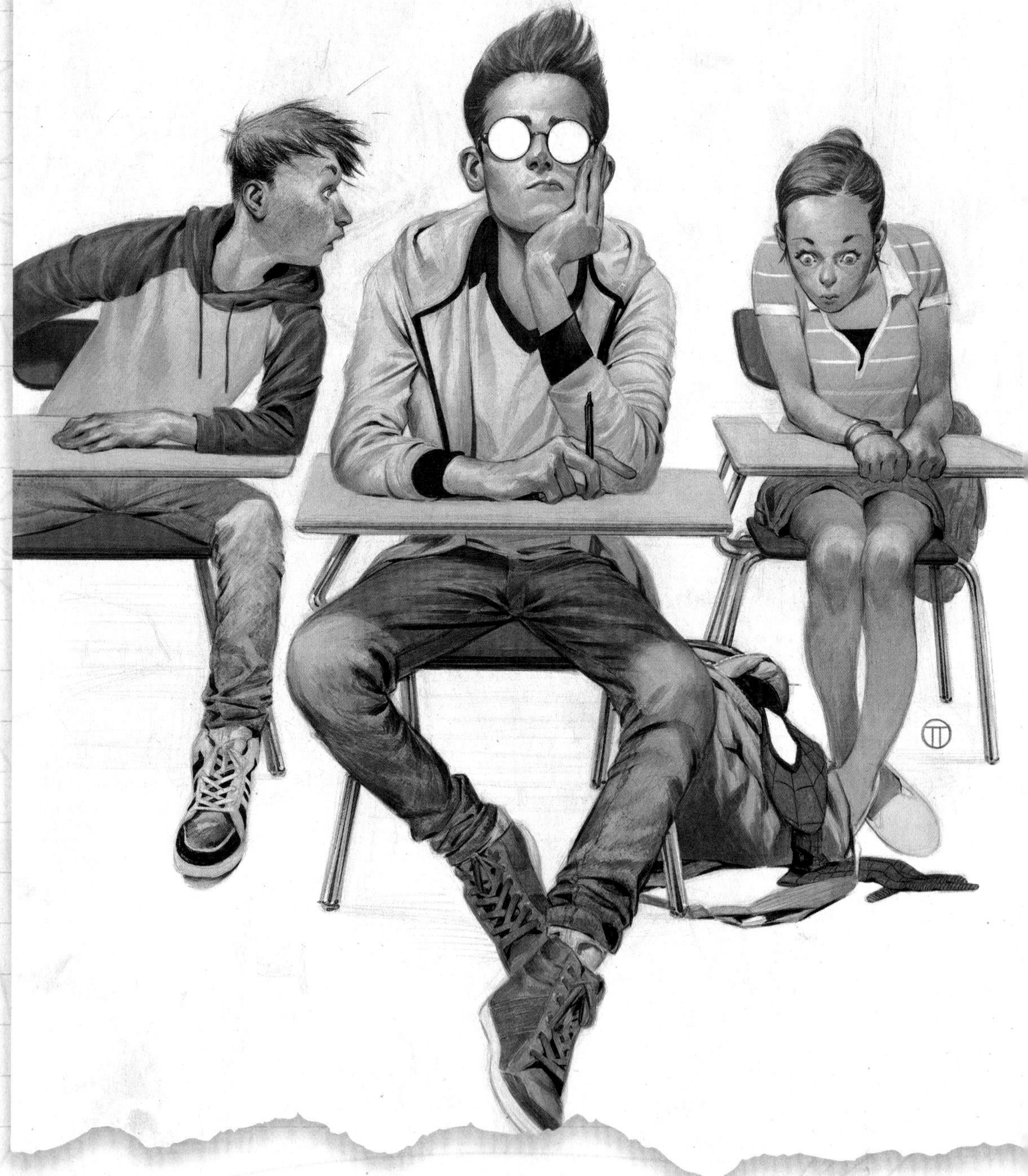

JULIAN TOTINO TEDESCO
3 VARIANT

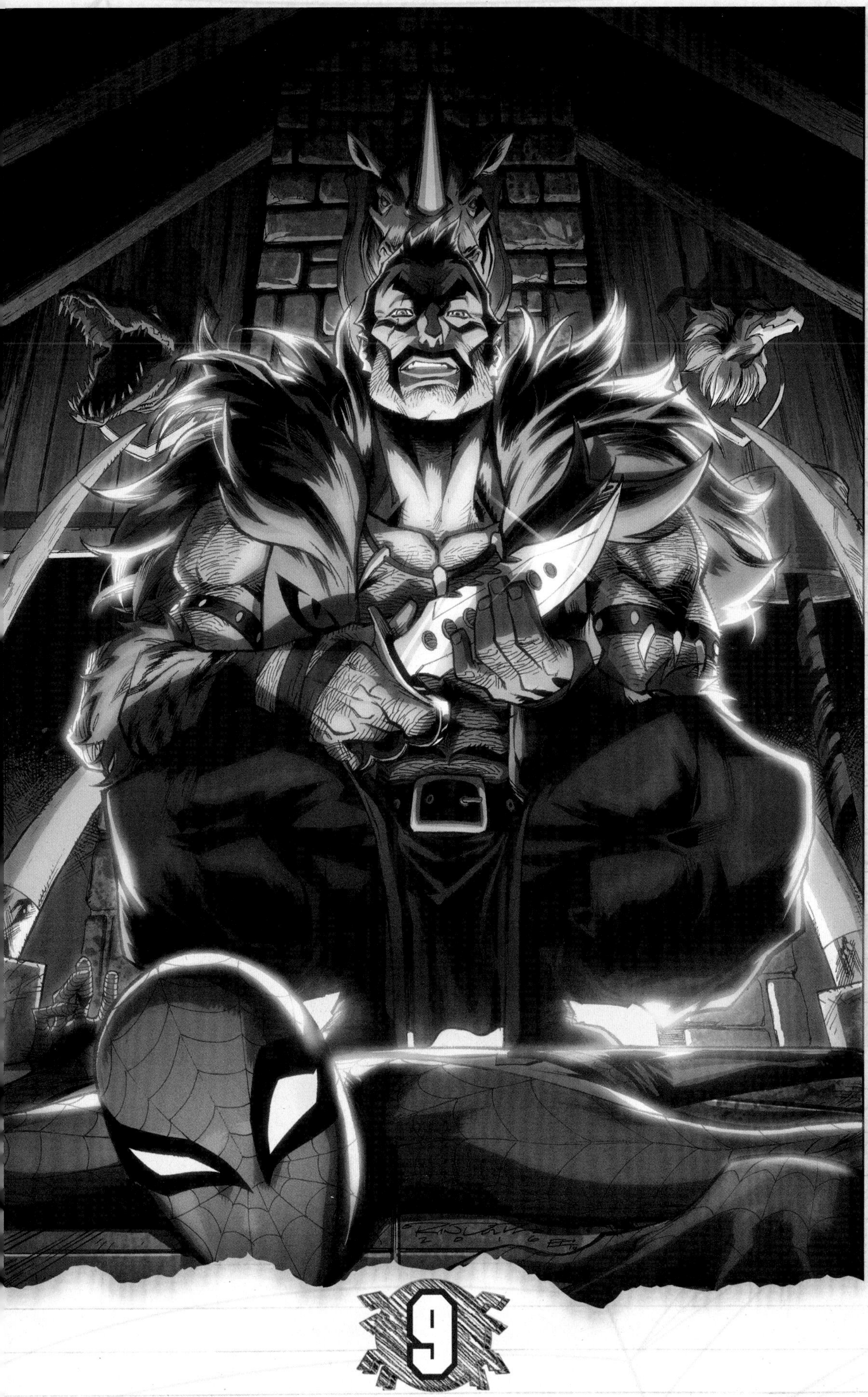

9

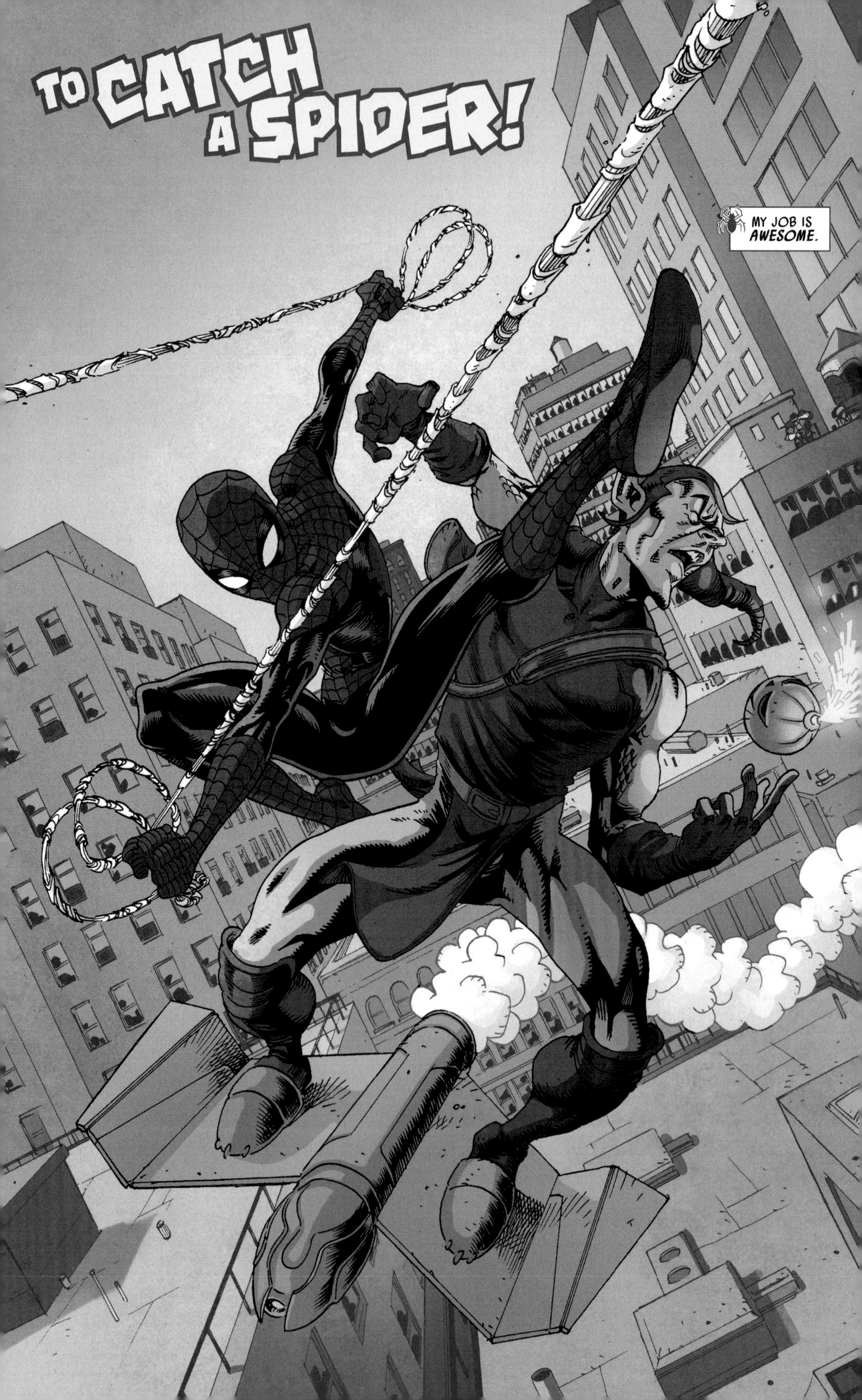
TO CATCH A SPIDER!
MY JOB IS AWESOME.

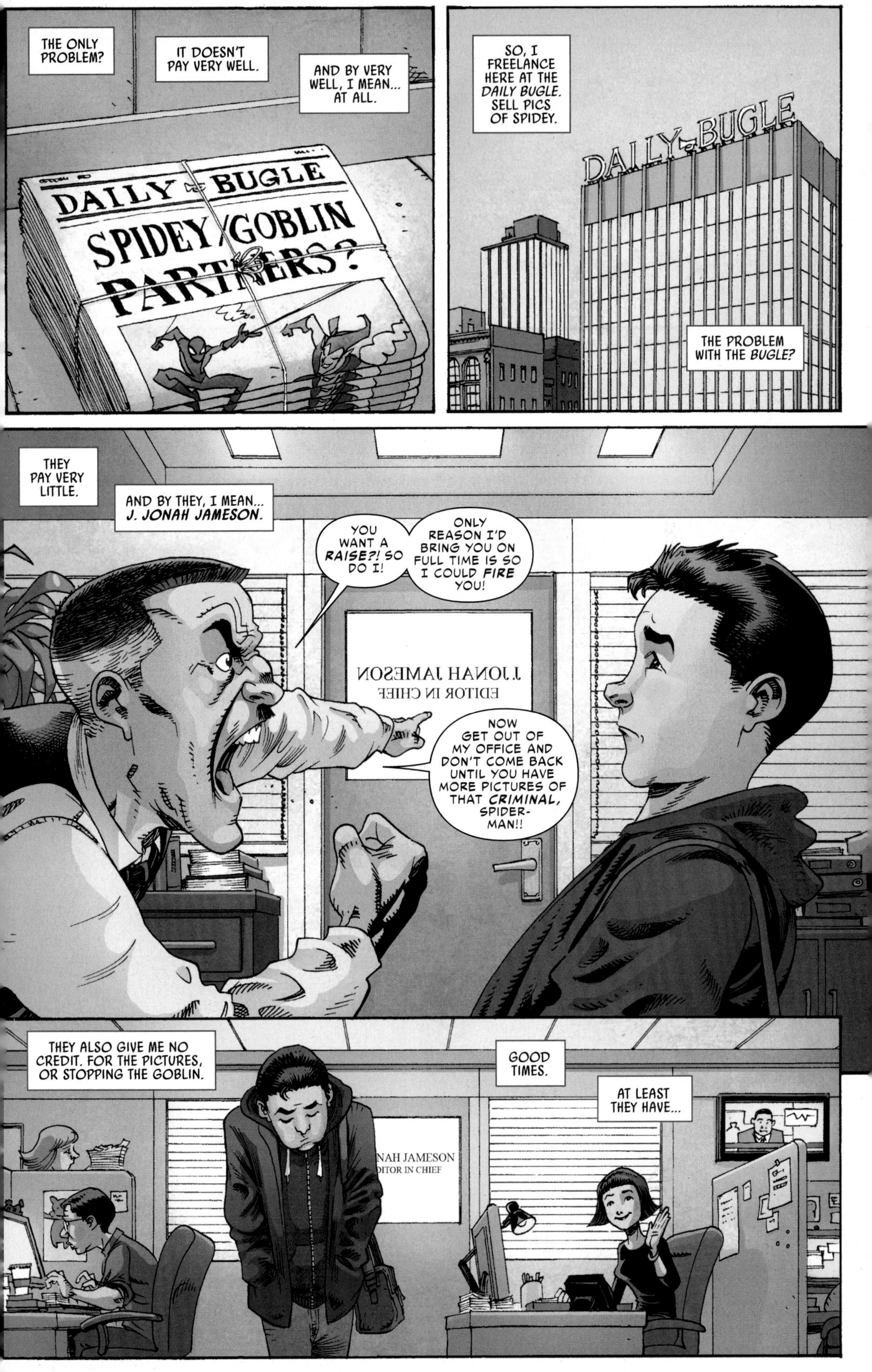

THE ONLY PROBLEM?
IT DOESN'T PAY VERY WELL.
AND BY VERY WELL, I MEAN... AT ALL.
DAILY BUGLE
SPIDEY/GOBLIN PARTNERS?
SO, I FREELANCE HERE AT THE *DAILY BUGLE*. SELL PICS OF SPIDEY.
DAILY BUGLE
THE PROBLEM WITH THE *BUGLE?*
THEY PAY VERY LITTLE.
AND BY THEY, I MEAN... ***J. JONAH JAMESON.***
YOU WANT A ***RAISE?!*** SO DO I!
ONLY REASON I'D BRING YOU ON FULL TIME IS SO I COULD ***FIRE*** YOU!
NOW GET OUT OF MY OFFICE AND DON'T COME BACK UNTIL YOU HAVE MORE PICTURES OF THAT ***CRIMINAL***, SPIDER-MAN!!
THEY ALSO GIVE ME NO CREDIT. FOR THE PICTURES, OR STOPPING THE GOBLIN.
GOOD TIMES.
AT LEAST THEY HAVE...

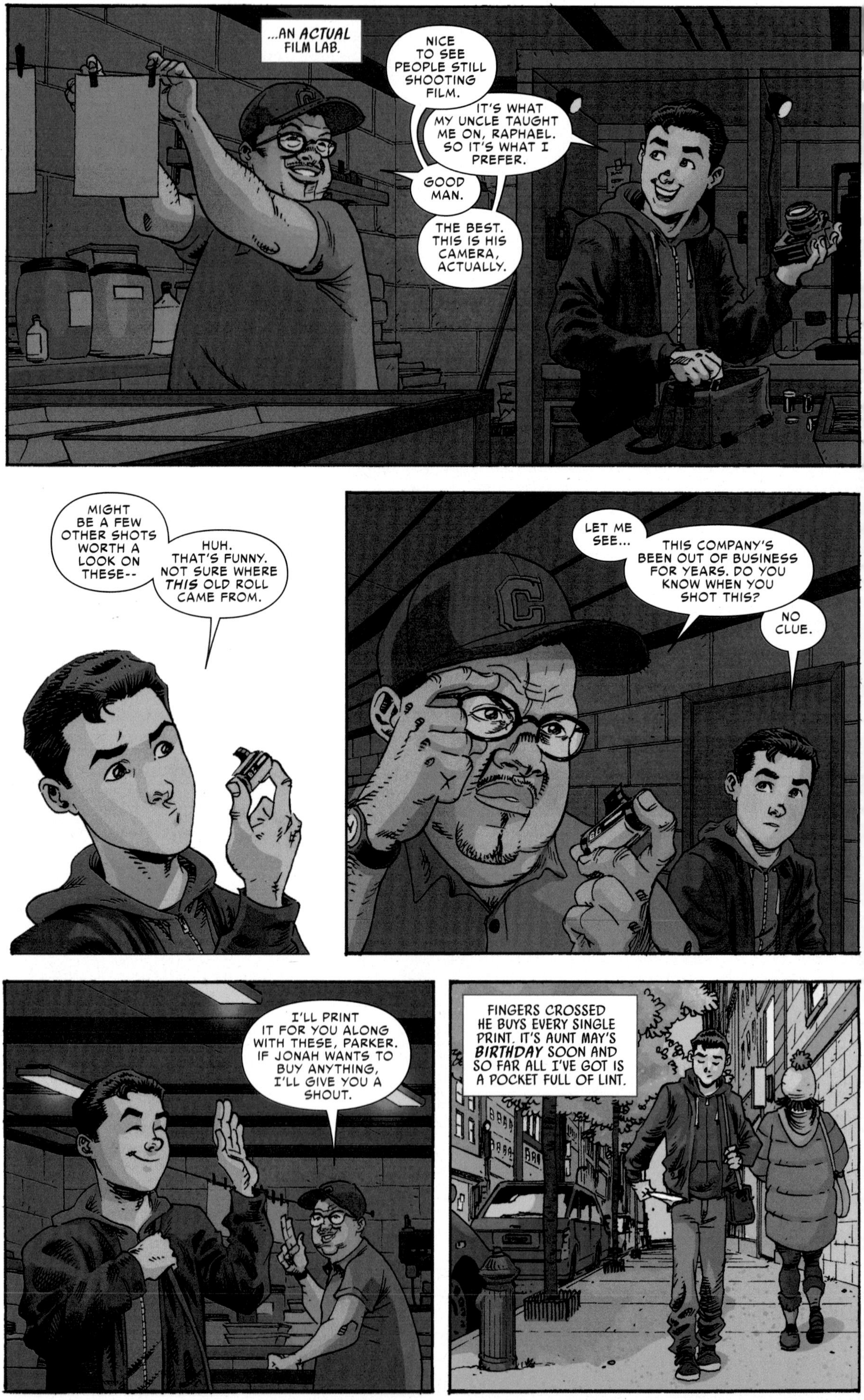
...AN *ACTUAL* FILM LAB.
NICE TO SEE PEOPLE STILL SHOOTING FILM.
IT'S WHAT MY UNCLE TAUGHT ME ON, RAPHAEL. SO IT'S WHAT I PREFER.
GOOD MAN.
THE BEST. THIS IS HIS CAMERA, ACTUALLY.
MIGHT BE A FEW OTHER SHOTS WORTH A LOOK ON THESE--
HUH. THAT'S FUNNY. NOT SURE WHERE *THIS* OLD ROLL CAME FROM.
LET ME SEE...
THIS COMPANY'S BEEN OUT OF BUSINESS FOR YEARS. DO YOU KNOW WHEN YOU SHOT THIS?
NO CLUE.
I'LL PRINT IT FOR YOU ALONG WITH THESE, PARKER. IF JONAH WANTS TO BUY ANYTHING, I'LL GIVE YOU A SHOUT.
FINGERS CROSSED HE BUYS EVERY SINGLE PRINT. IT'S AUNT MAY'S *BIRTHDAY* SOON AND SO FAR ALL I'VE GOT IS A POCKET FULL OF LINT.

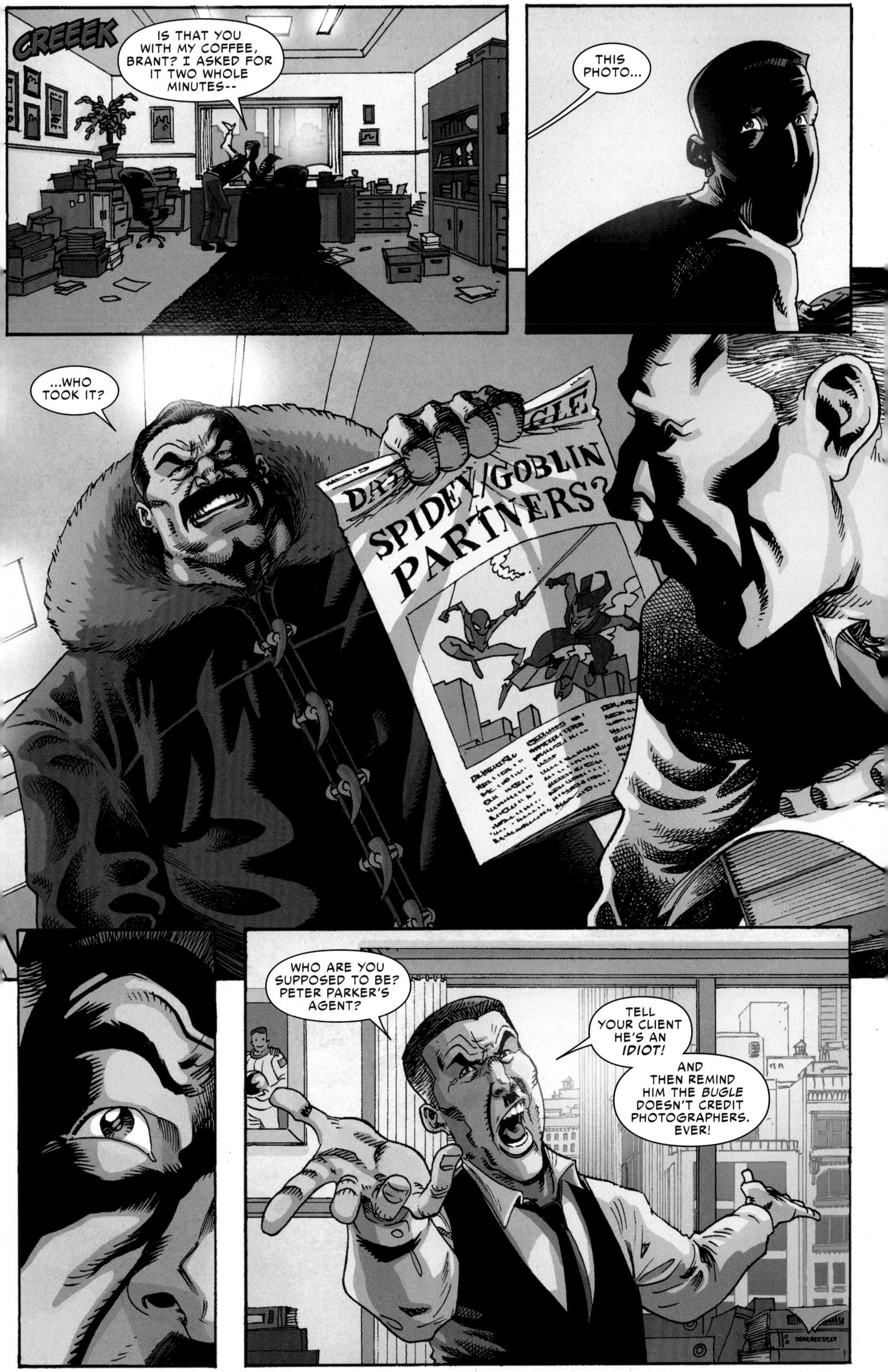
CREEEK
IS THAT YOU WITH MY COFFEE, BRANT? I ASKED FOR IT TWO WHOLE MINUTES--
THIS PHOTO...
...WHO TOOK IT?
SPIDEY/GOBLIN PARTNERS?
WHO ARE YOU SUPPOSED TO BE? PETER PARKER'S AGENT?
TELL YOUR CLIENT HE'S AN *IDIOT!*
AND THEN REMIND HIM THE *BUGLE* DOESN'T CREDIT PHOTOGRAPHERS. EVER!

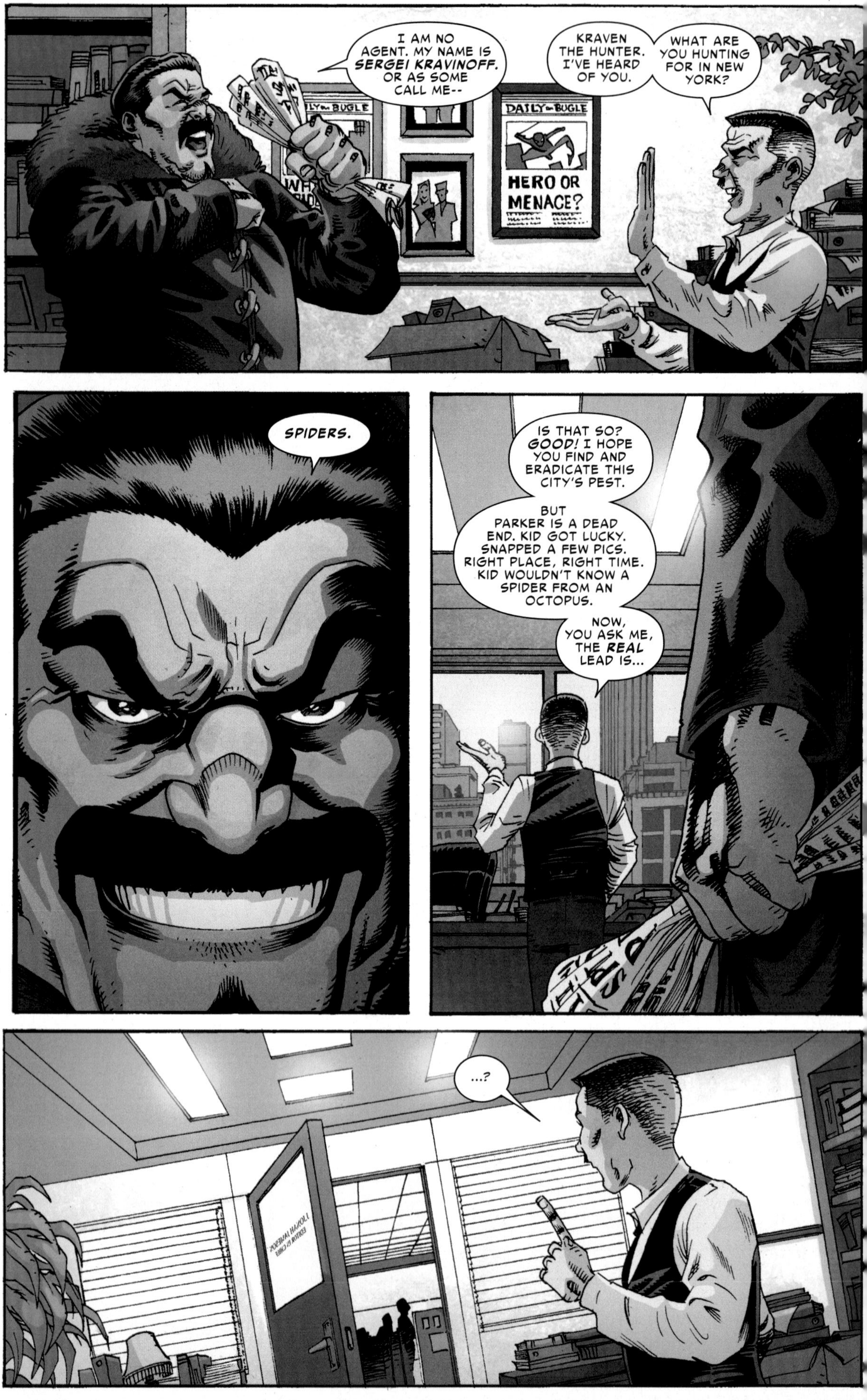
I AM NO AGENT. MY NAME IS SERGEI KRAVINOFF. OR AS SOME CALL ME--
KRAVEN THE HUNTER. I'VE HEARD OF YOU.
WHAT ARE YOU HUNTING FOR IN NEW YORK?
DAILY BUGLE
HERO OR MENACE?
SPIDERS.
IS THAT SO? GOOD! I HOPE YOU FIND AND ERADICATE THIS CITY'S PEST.
BUT PARKER IS A DEAD END. KID GOT LUCKY. SNAPPED A FEW PICS. RIGHT PLACE, RIGHT TIME. KID WOULDN'T KNOW A SPIDER FROM AN OCTOPUS.
NOW, YOU ASK ME, THE REAL LEAD IS...
...?

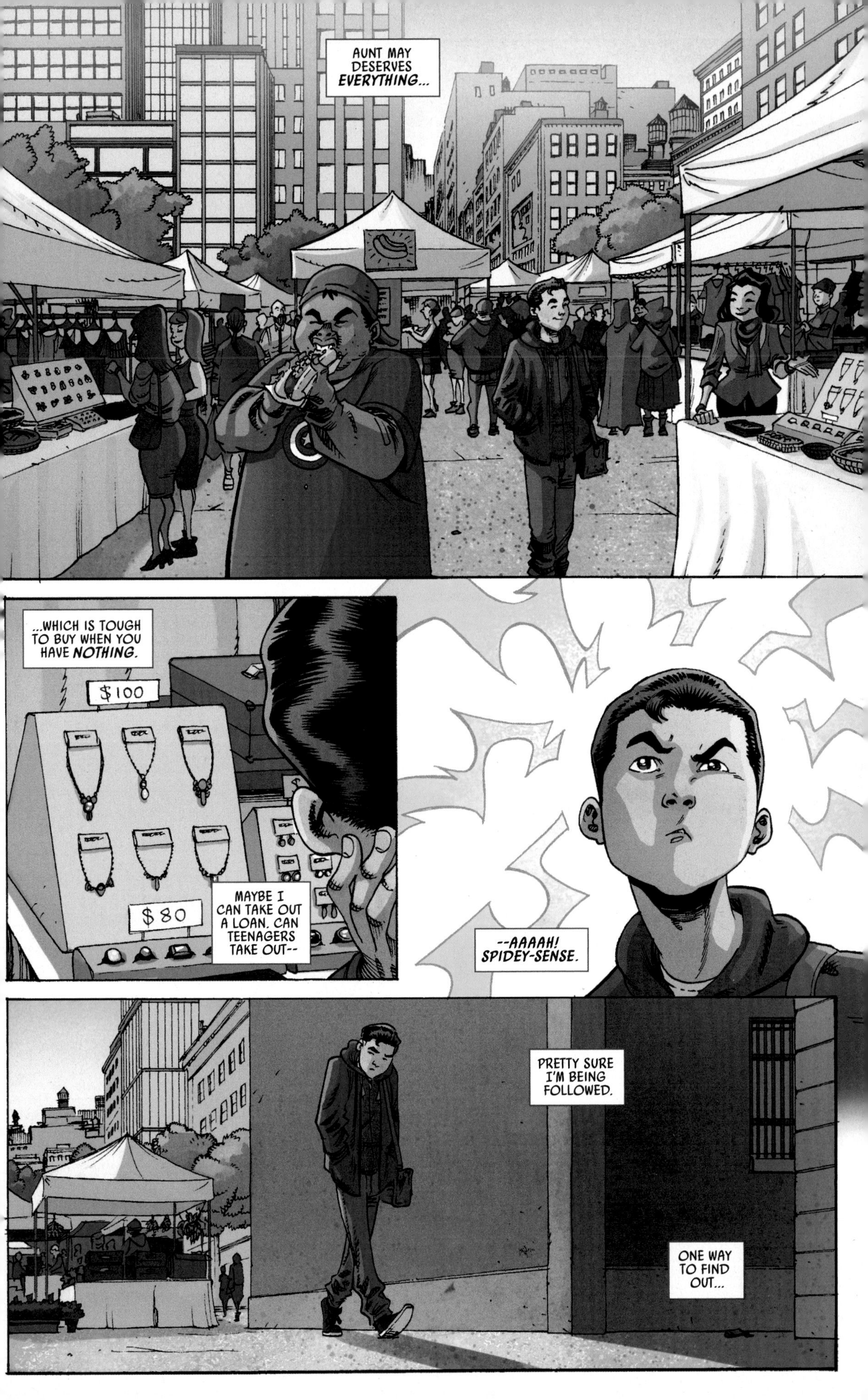
AUNT MAY DESERVES *EVERYTHING*...
...WHICH IS TOUGH TO BUY WHEN YOU HAVE *NOTHING*.
$100
$80
MAYBE I CAN TAKE OUT A LOAN. CAN TEENAGERS TAKE OUT--
--AAAAH! SPIDEY-SENSE.
PRETTY SURE I'M BEING FOLLOWED.
ONE WAY TO FIND OUT...

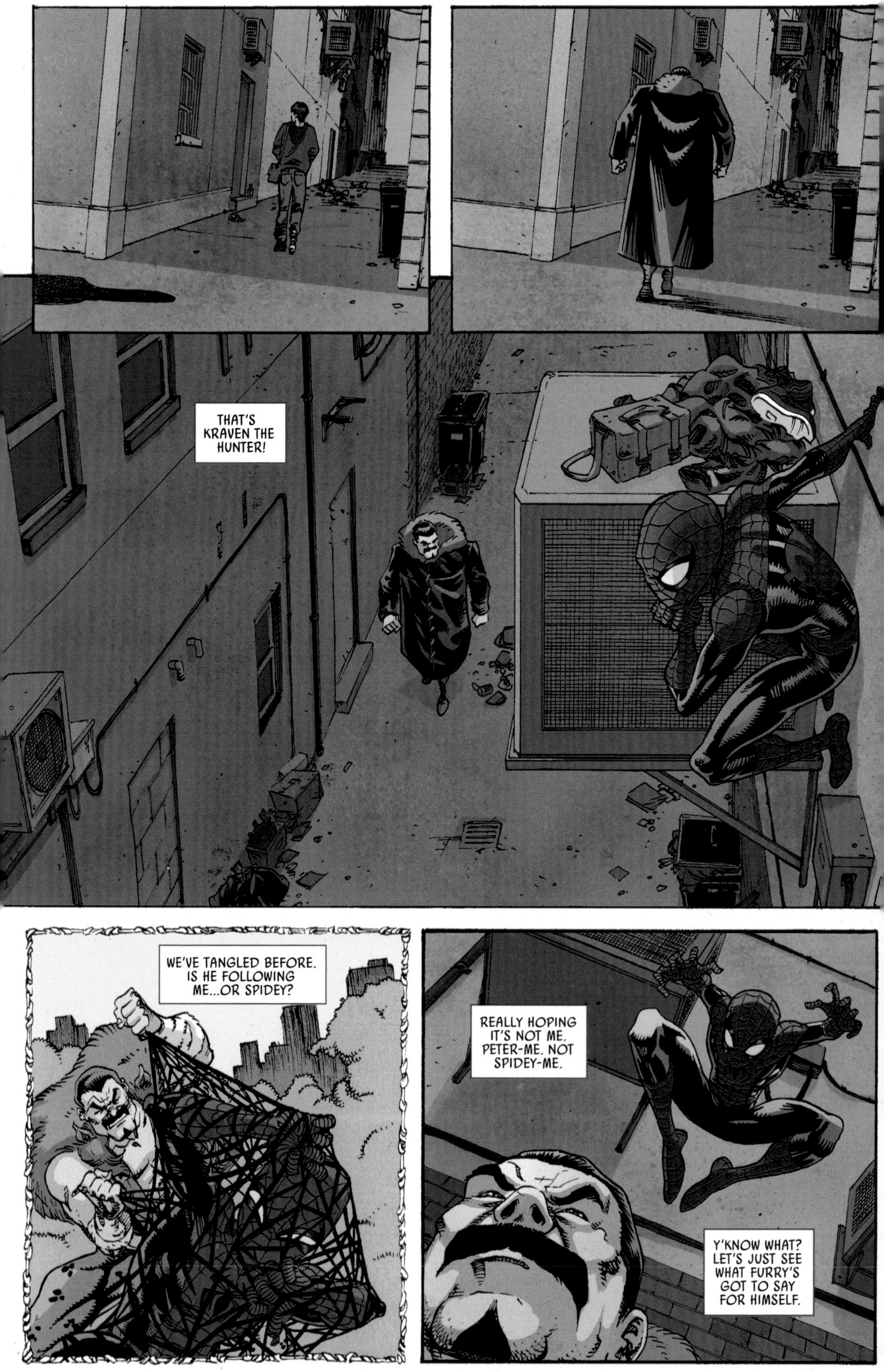
THAT'S KRAVEN THE HUNTER!
WE'VE TANGLED BEFORE. IS HE FOLLOWING ME...OR SPIDEY?
REALLY HOPING IT'S NOT ME. PETER-ME. NOT SPIDEY-ME.
Y'KNOW WHAT? LET'S JUST SEE WHAT FURRY'S GOT TO SAY FOR HIMSELF.

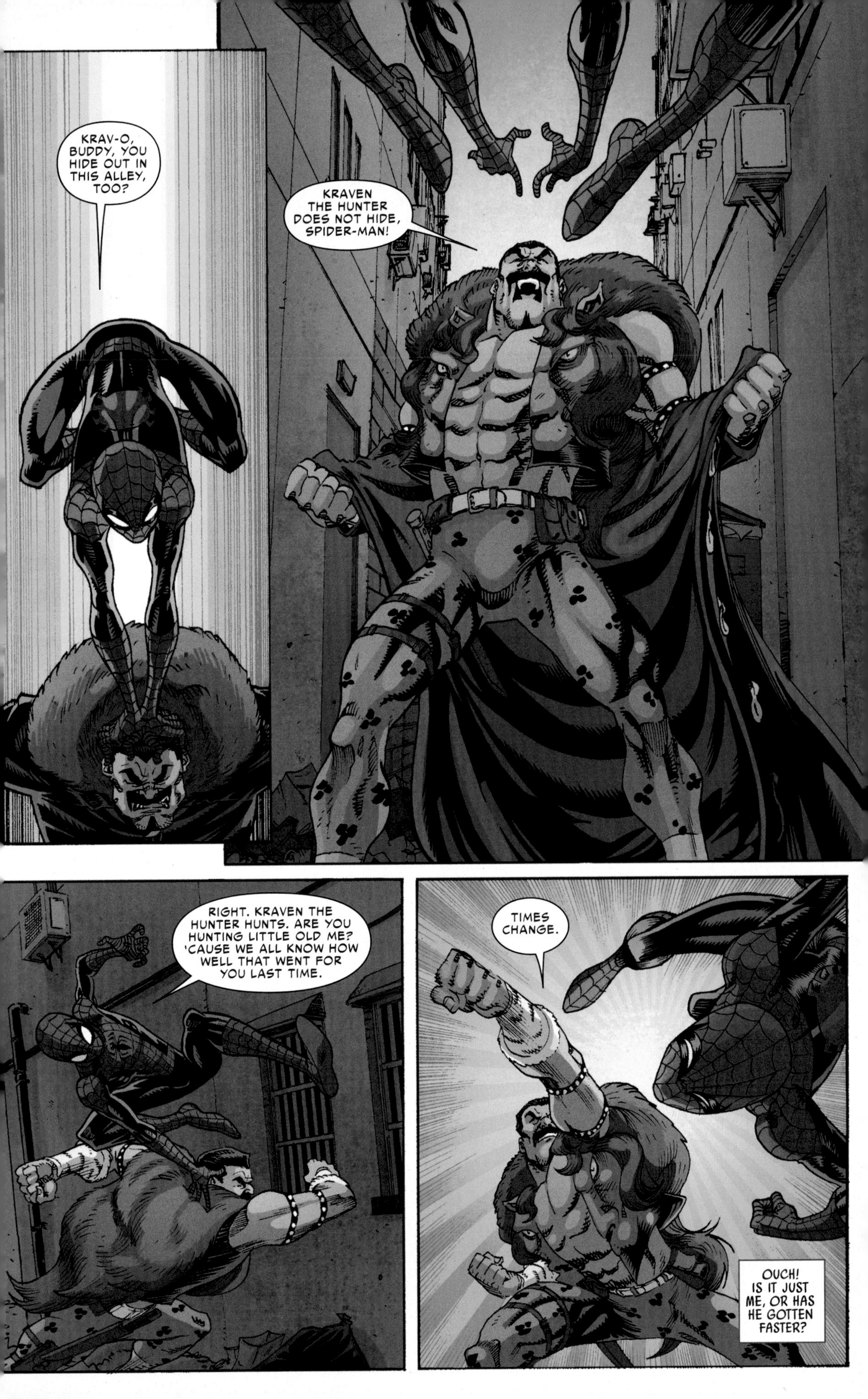
KRAV-O, BUDDY, YOU HIDE OUT IN THIS ALLEY, TOO?
KRAVEN THE HUNTER DOES NOT HIDE, SPIDER-MAN!
RIGHT. KRAVEN THE HUNTER HUNTS. ARE YOU HUNTING LITTLE OLD ME? 'CAUSE WE ALL KNOW HOW WELL THAT WENT FOR YOU LAST TIME.
TIMES CHANGE.
OUCH! IS IT JUST ME, OR HAS HE GOTTEN FASTER?

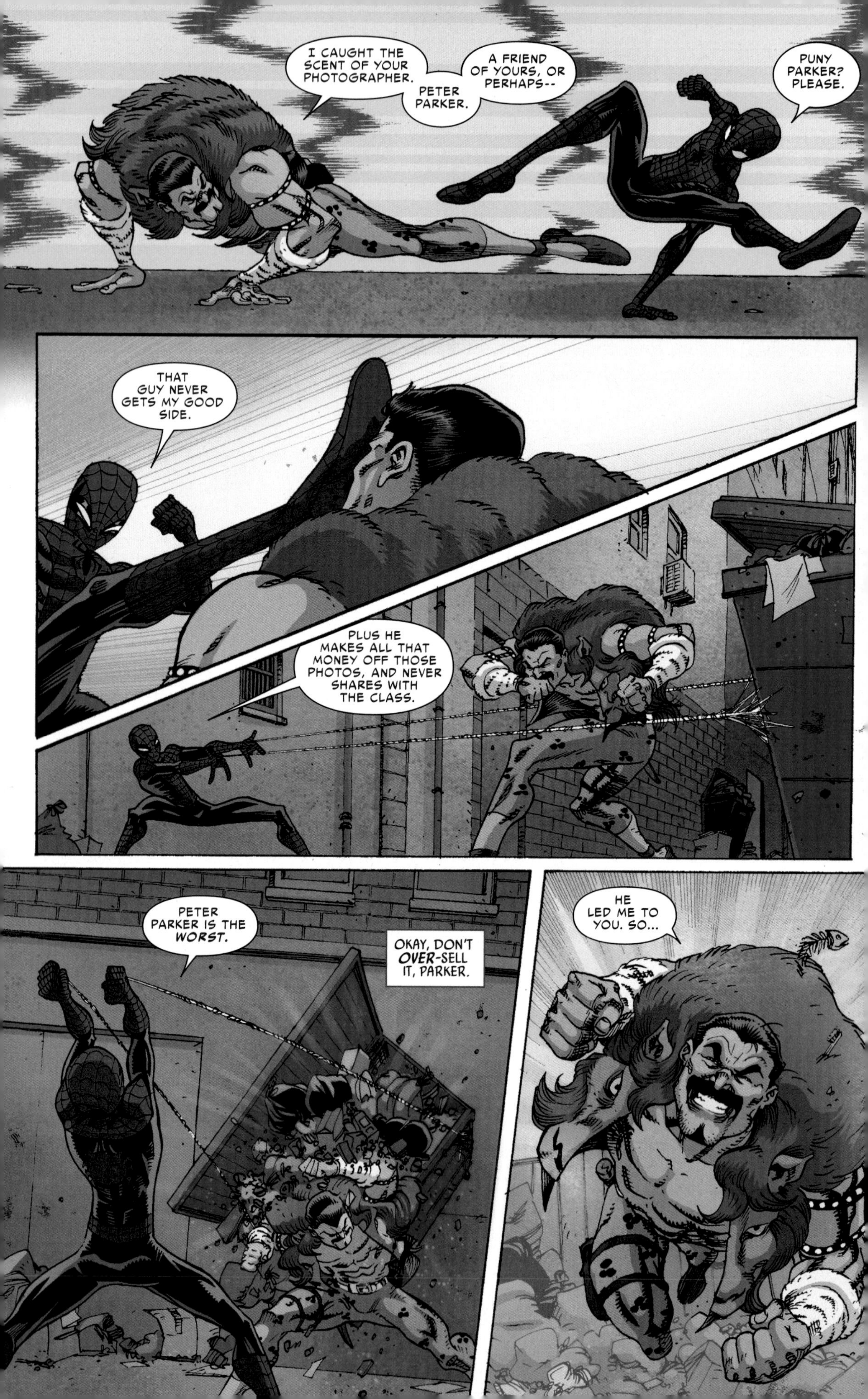
I CAUGHT THE SCENT OF YOUR PHOTOGRAPHER.
PETER PARKER.
A FRIEND OF YOURS, OR PERHAPS--
PUNY PARKER? PLEASE.
THAT GUY NEVER GETS MY GOOD SIDE.
PLUS HE MAKES ALL THAT MONEY OFF THOSE PHOTOS, AND NEVER SHARES WITH THE CLASS.
PETER PARKER IS THE *WORST.*
OKAY, DON'T *OVER*-SELL IT, PARKER.
HE LED ME TO YOU. SO...

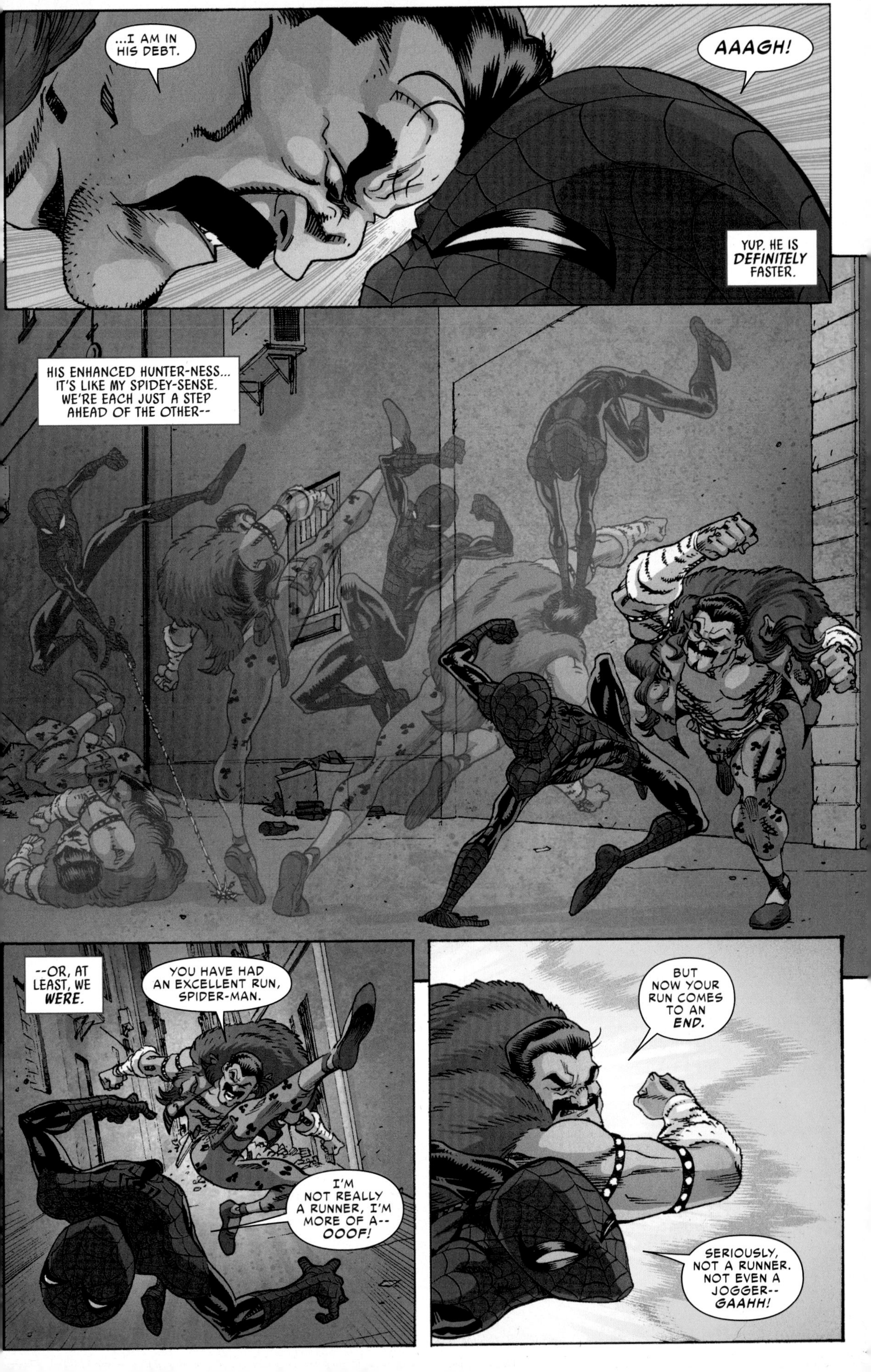
...I AM IN HIS DEBT.
AAAGH!
YUP. HE IS DEFINITELY FASTER.
HIS ENHANCED HUNTER-NESS... IT'S LIKE MY SPIDEY-SENSE. WE'RE EACH JUST A STEP AHEAD OF THE OTHER--
--OR, AT LEAST, WE WERE.
YOU HAVE HAD AN EXCELLENT RUN, SPIDER-MAN.
I'M NOT REALLY A RUNNER, I'M MORE OF A-- OOOF!
BUT NOW YOUR RUN COMES TO AN END.
SERIOUSLY, NOT A RUNNER. NOT EVEN A JOGGER-- GAAHH!

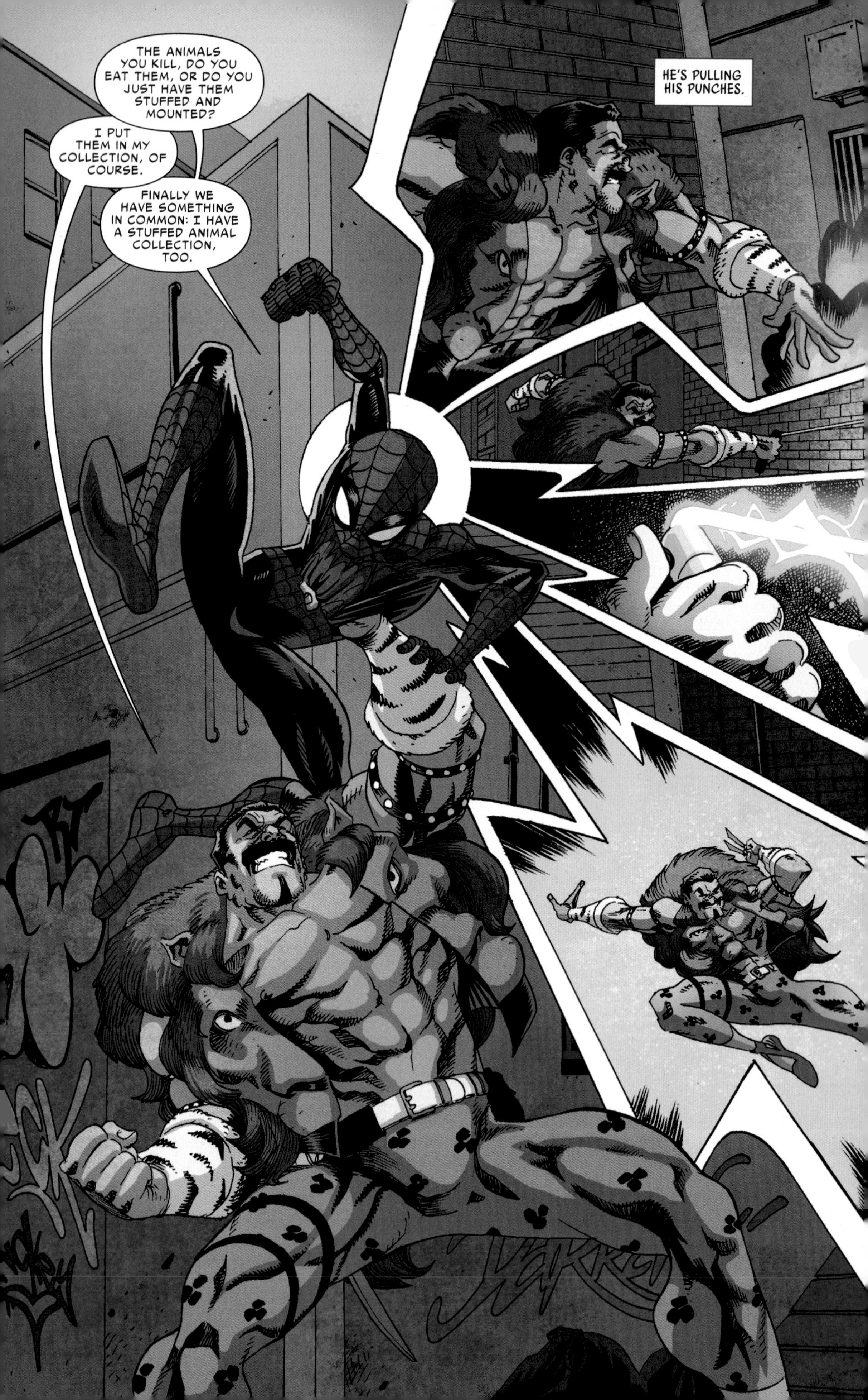
THE ANIMALS YOU KILL, DO YOU EAT THEM, OR DO YOU JUST HAVE THEM STUFFED AND MOUNTED?
I PUT THEM IN MY COLLECTION, OF COURSE.
FINALLY WE HAVE SOMETHING IN COMMON: I HAVE A STUFFED ANIMAL COLLECTION, TOO.
HE'S PULLING HIS PUNCHES.

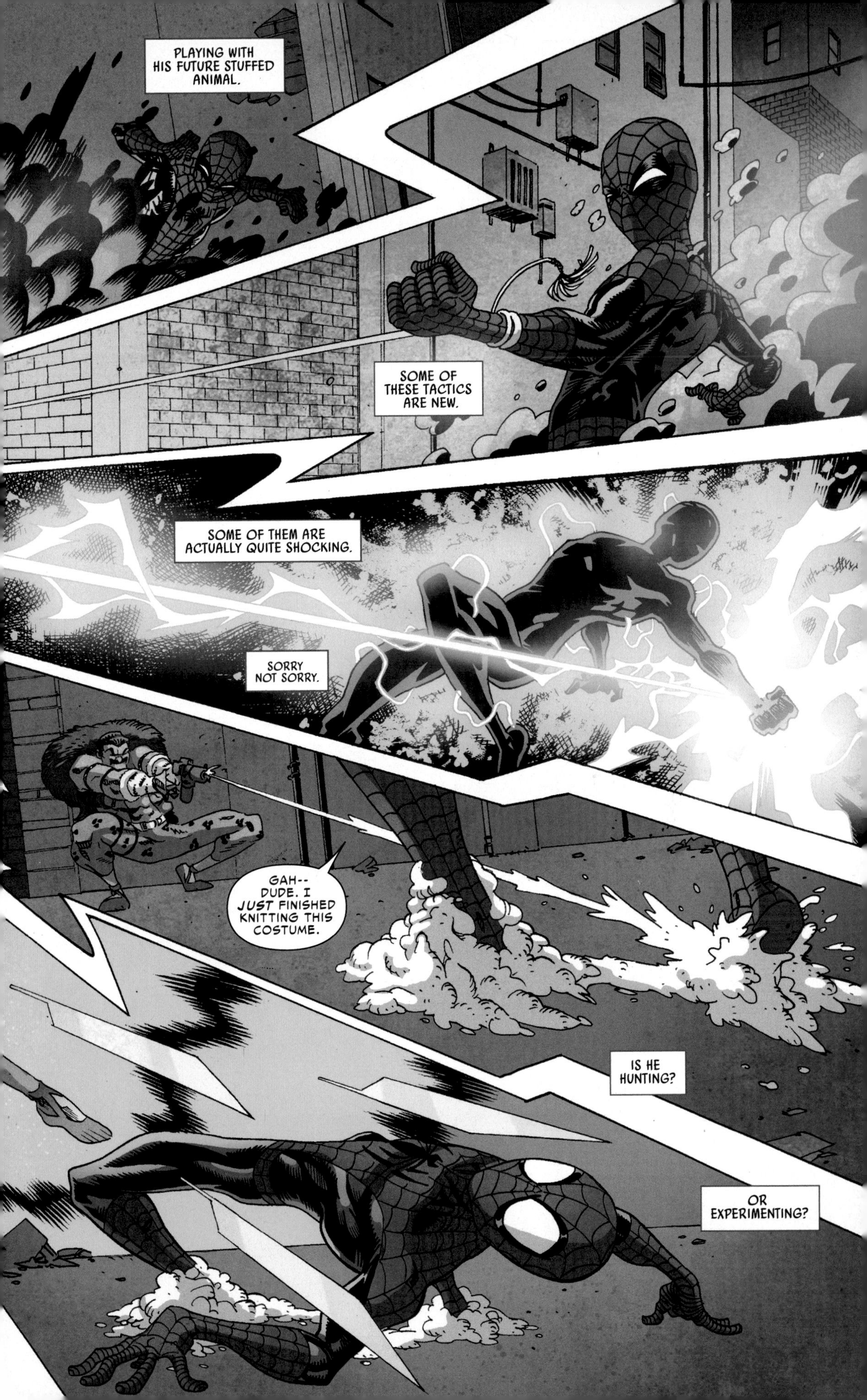
PLAYING WITH HIS FUTURE STUFFED ANIMAL.
SOME OF THESE TACTICS ARE NEW.
SOME OF THEM ARE ACTUALLY QUITE SHOCKING.
SORRY NOT SORRY.
GAH-- DUDE. I JUST FINISHED KNITTING THIS COSTUME.
IS HE HUNTING?
OR EXPERIMENTING?

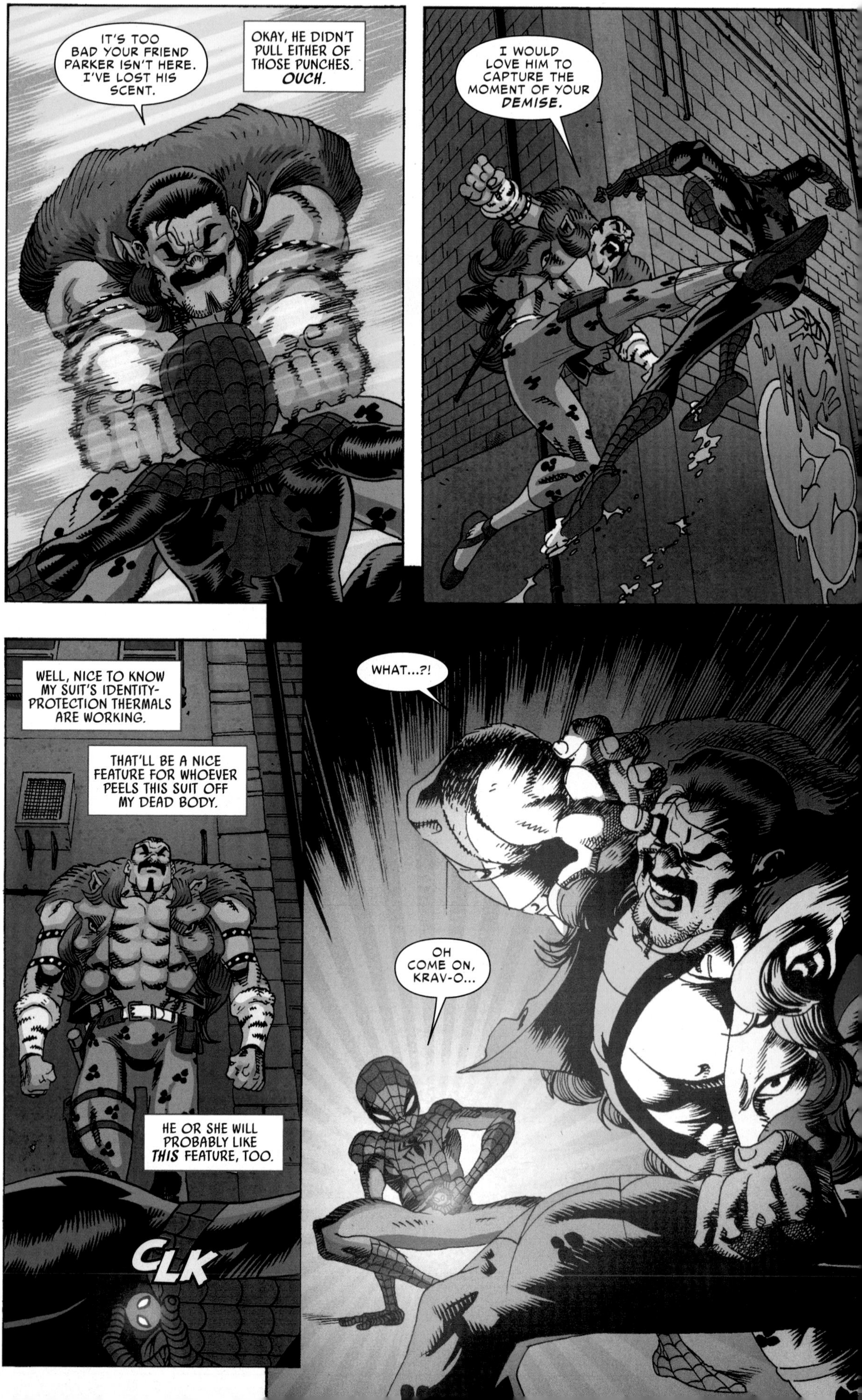
IT'S TOO BAD YOUR FRIEND PARKER ISN'T HERE. I'VE LOST HIS SCENT.
OKAY, HE DIDN'T PULL EITHER OF THOSE PUNCHES. OUCH.
I WOULD LOVE HIM TO CAPTURE THE MOMENT OF YOUR DEMISE.
WELL, NICE TO KNOW MY SUIT'S IDENTITY-PROTECTION THERMALS ARE WORKING.
THAT'LL BE A NICE FEATURE FOR WHOEVER PEELS THIS SUIT OFF MY DEAD BODY.
HE OR SHE WILL PROBABLY LIKE THIS FEATURE, TOO.
CLK
WHAT...?!
OH COME ON, KRAV-O...

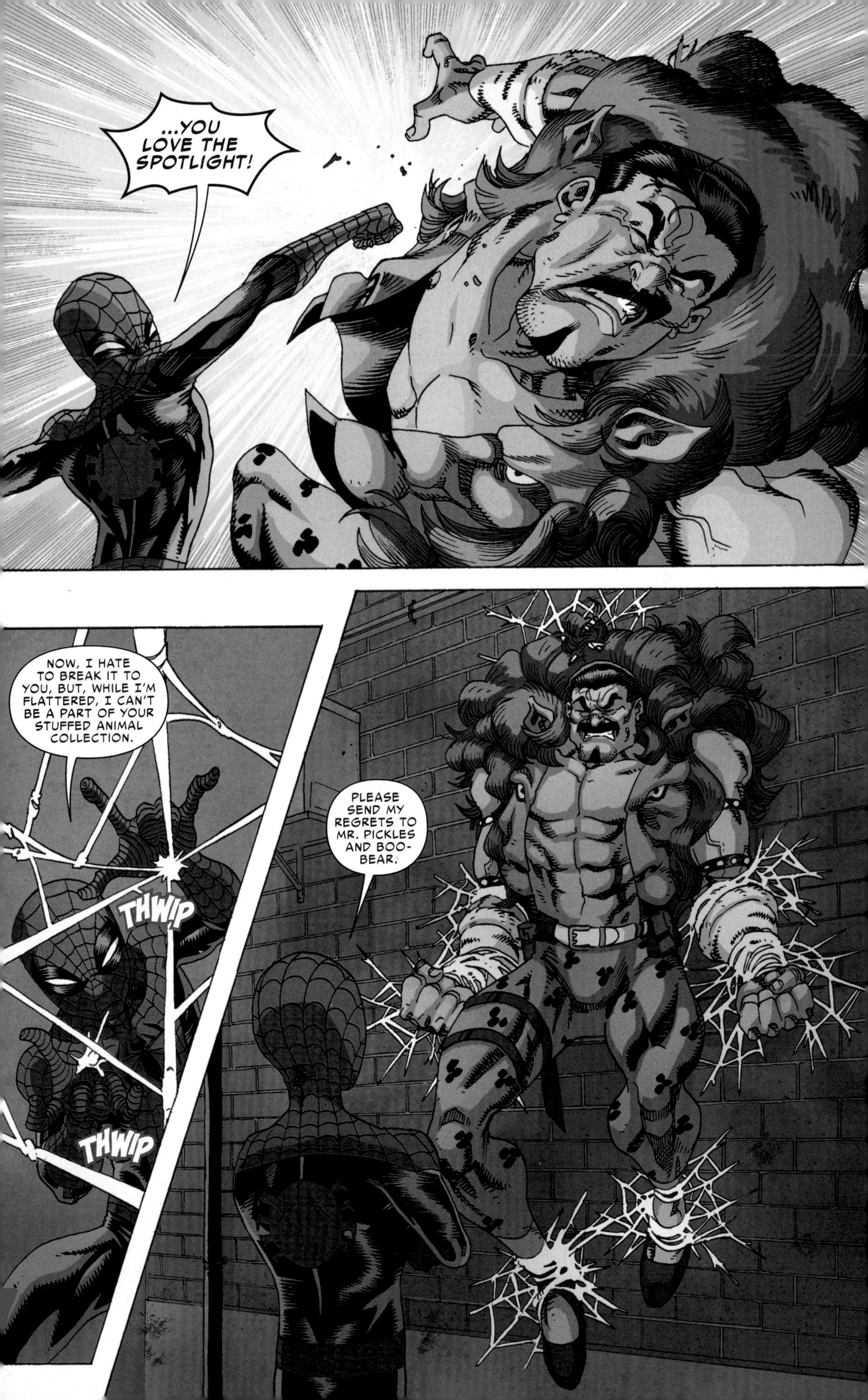
...YOU LOVE THE SPOTLIGHT!
NOW, I HATE TO BREAK IT TO YOU, BUT, WHILE I'M FLATTERED, I CAN'T BE A PART OF YOUR STUFFED ANIMAL COLLECTION.
THWIP
THWIP
PLEASE SEND MY REGRETS TO MR. PICKLES AND BOO-BEAR.

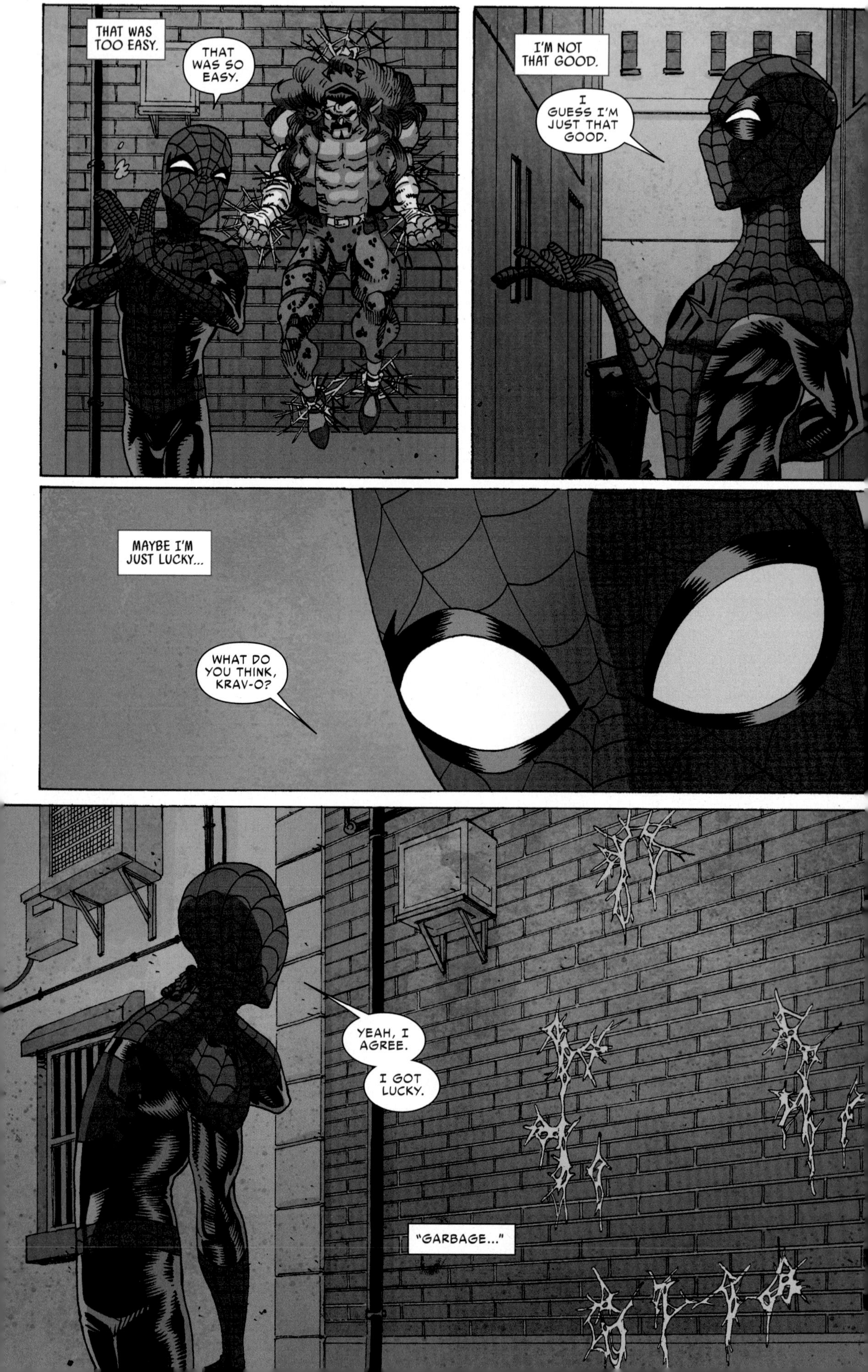
THAT WAS TOO EASY.
THAT WAS SO EASY.
I'M NOT THAT GOOD.
I GUESS I'M JUST THAT GOOD.
MAYBE I'M JUST LUCKY...
WHAT DO YOU THINK, KRAV-O?
YEAH, I AGREE.
I GOT LUCKY.
"GARBAGE..."

...GARBAGE. MORE GARBAGE.

WHERE'S THE KRAVEN FIGHT?

SIR?

SOME KIDS POSTED BLURRY PHOTOS ON THE INTERNETS. WHERE ARE THE PHOTOS FROM *THAT*, PARKER? KRAVEN TRIED TO RID THIS CITY OF THAT MENACE AND YOU MISSED IT?!

KRAVEN THOUGHT PETER BAILED...SO NO PHOTOS THIS TIME. NO PHOTOS, NO MONEY. NO MONEY, NO GIFT FOR AUNT MAY. AND ONCE AGAIN...

GUESS I BLEW IT, SIR.

GO CHECK IN WITH RAPHAEL, SEE IF HE FOUND ANYTHING ELSE ON YOUR FILM!

I'M NOT PAYING FOR ANY OF THIS GARBAGE!

JOHAH JAMESON
EDITOR IN CHIEF

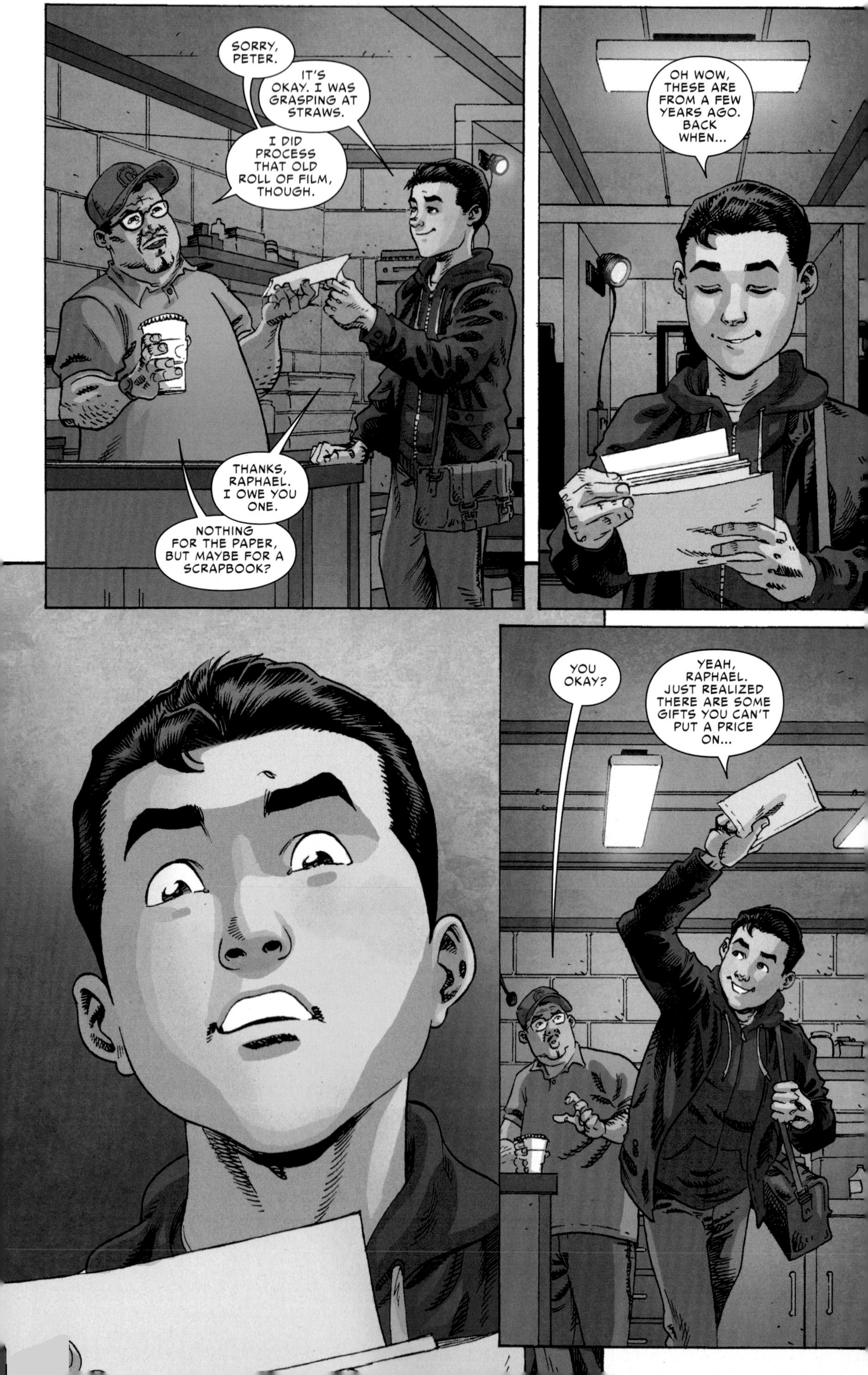
SORRY, PETER.
IT'S OKAY. I WAS GRASPING AT STRAWS.
I DID PROCESS THAT OLD ROLL OF FILM, THOUGH.
THANKS, RAPHAEL. I OWE YOU ONE.
NOTHING FOR THE PAPER, BUT MAYBE FOR A SCRAPBOOK?
OH WOW, THESE ARE FROM A FEW YEARS AGO. BACK WHEN...
YOU OKAY?
YEAH, RAPHAEL. JUST REALIZED THERE ARE SOME GIFTS YOU CAN'T PUT A PRICE ON...

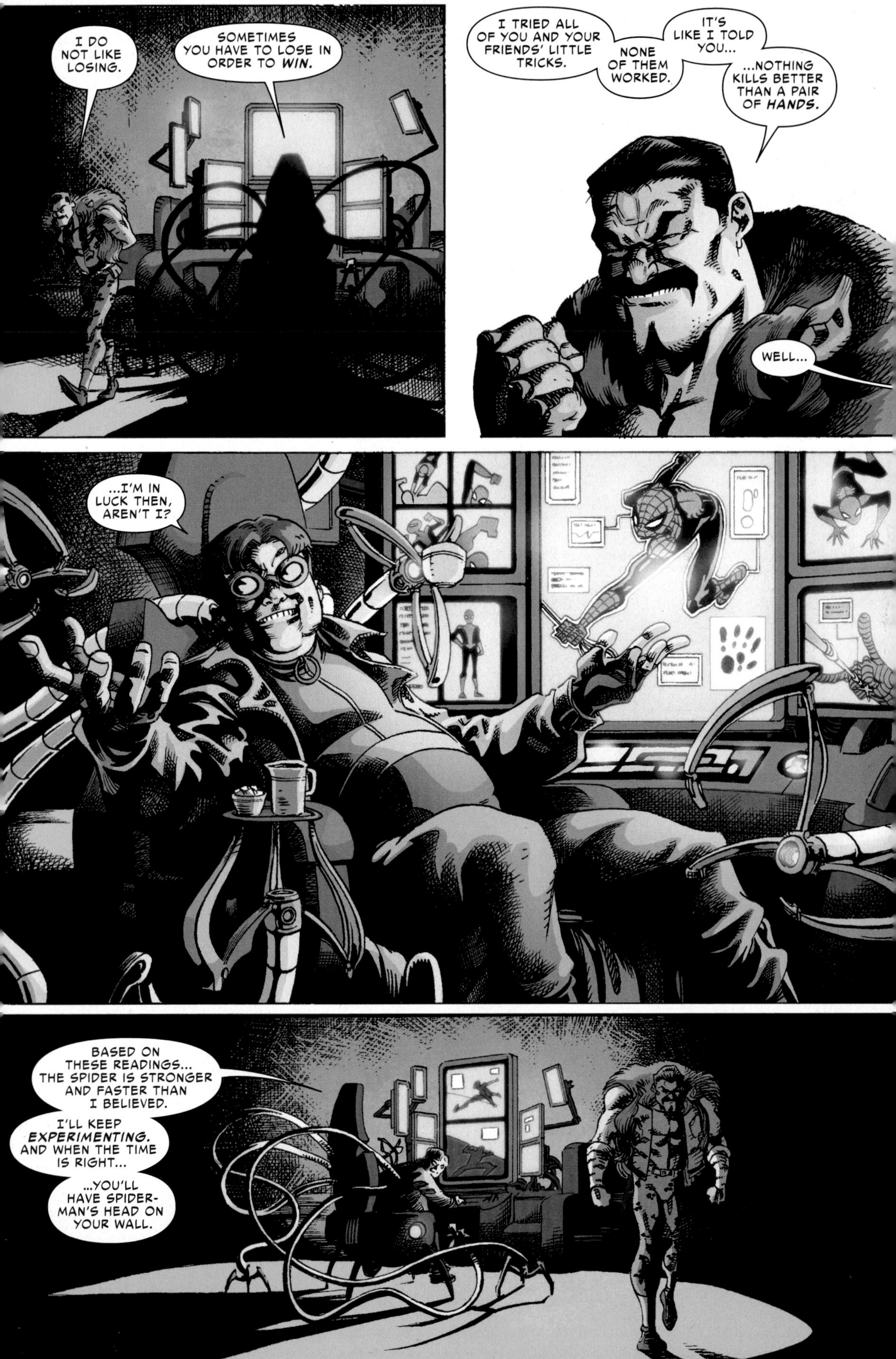
I DO NOT LIKE LOSING.
SOMETIMES YOU HAVE TO LOSE IN ORDER TO *WIN.*
I TRIED ALL OF YOU AND YOUR FRIENDS' LITTLE TRICKS.
NONE OF THEM WORKED.
IT'S LIKE I TOLD YOU...
...NOTHING KILLS BETTER THAN A PAIR OF *HANDS.*
WELL...
...I'M IN LUCK THEN, AREN'T I?
BASED ON THESE READINGS... THE SPIDER IS STRONGER AND FASTER THAN I BELIEVED.
I'LL KEEP *EXPERIMENTING.* AND WHEN THE TIME IS RIGHT...
...YOU'LL HAVE SPIDER-MAN'S HEAD ON YOUR WALL.

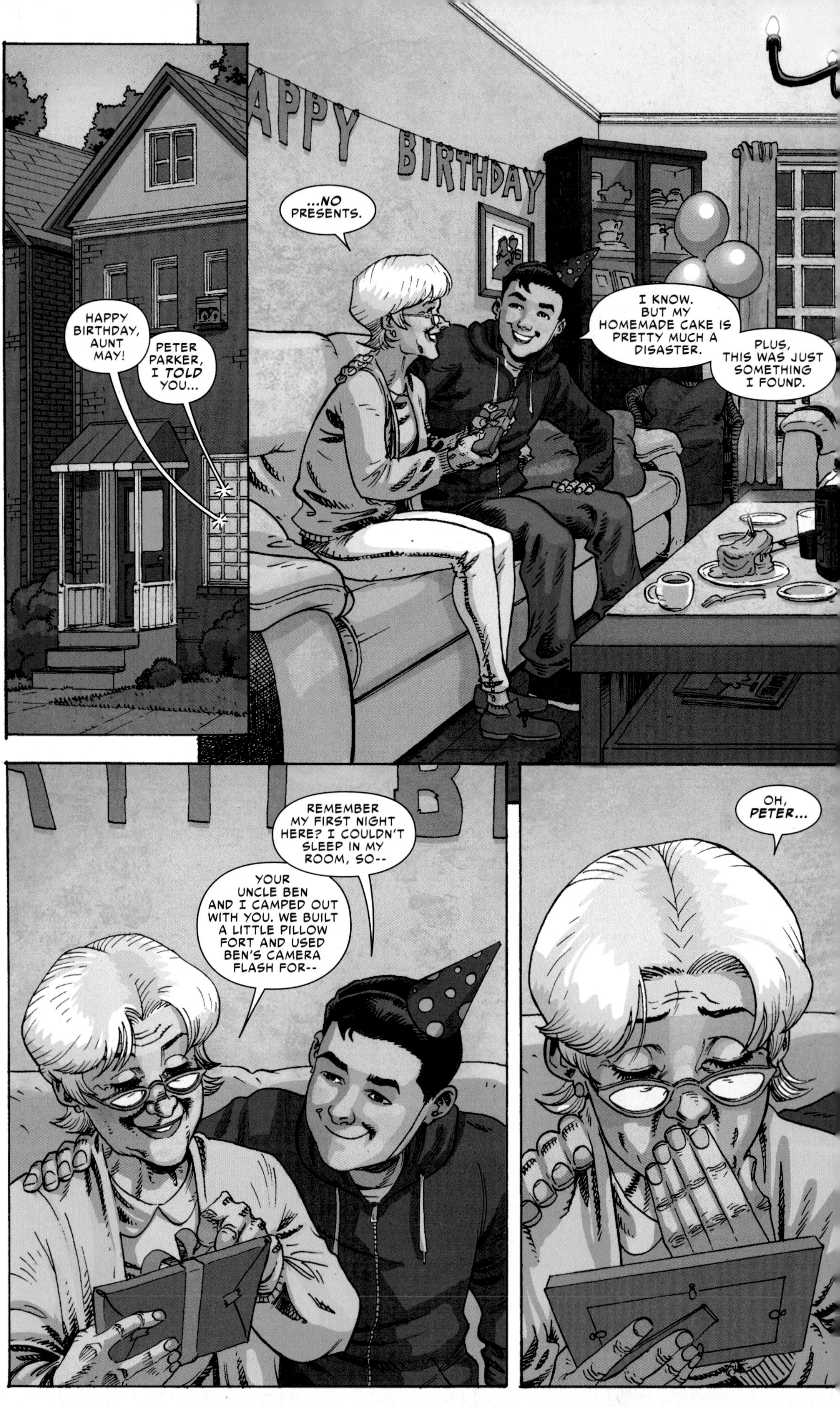
HAPPY BIRTHDAY, AUNT MAY!
PETER PARKER, I TOLD YOU...
HAPPY BIRTHDAY
...NO PRESENTS.
I KNOW. BUT MY HOMEMADE CAKE IS PRETTY MUCH A DISASTER.
PLUS, THIS WAS JUST SOMETHING I FOUND.
REMEMBER MY FIRST NIGHT HERE? I COULDN'T SLEEP IN MY ROOM, SO--
YOUR UNCLE BEN AND I CAMPED OUT WITH YOU. WE BUILT A LITTLE PILLOW FORT AND USED BEN'S CAMERA FLASH FOR--
OH, PETER...

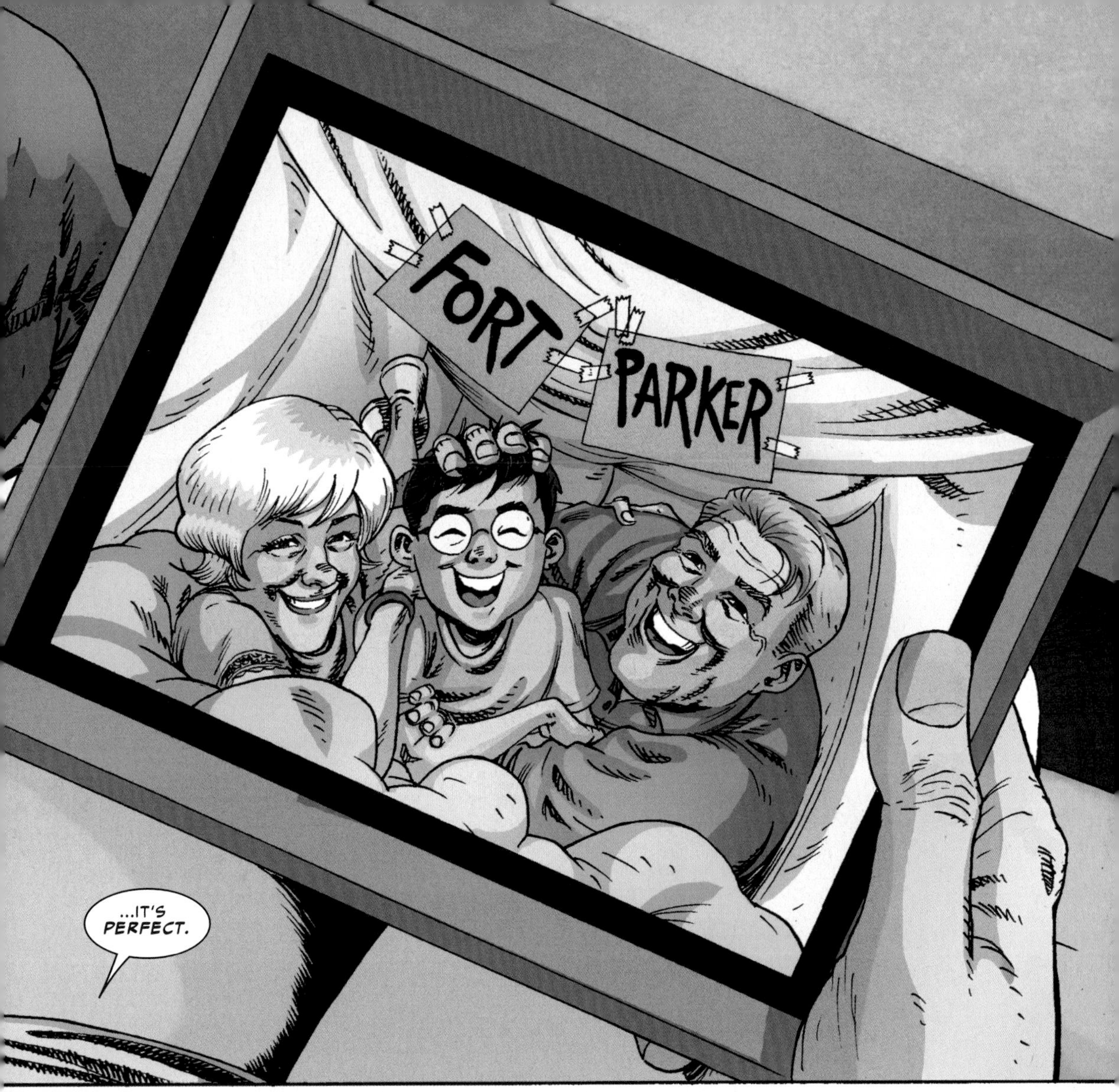
FORT
PARKER
...IT'S PERFECT.

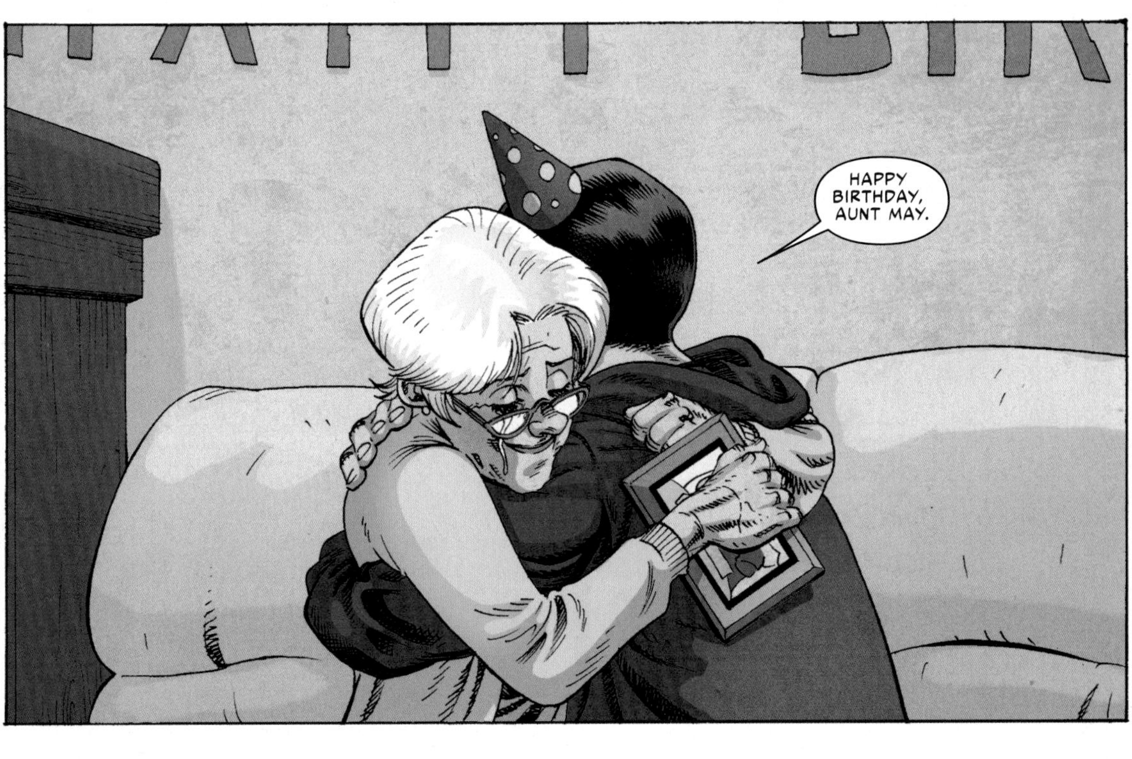
HAPPY BIRTHDAY, AUNT MAY.

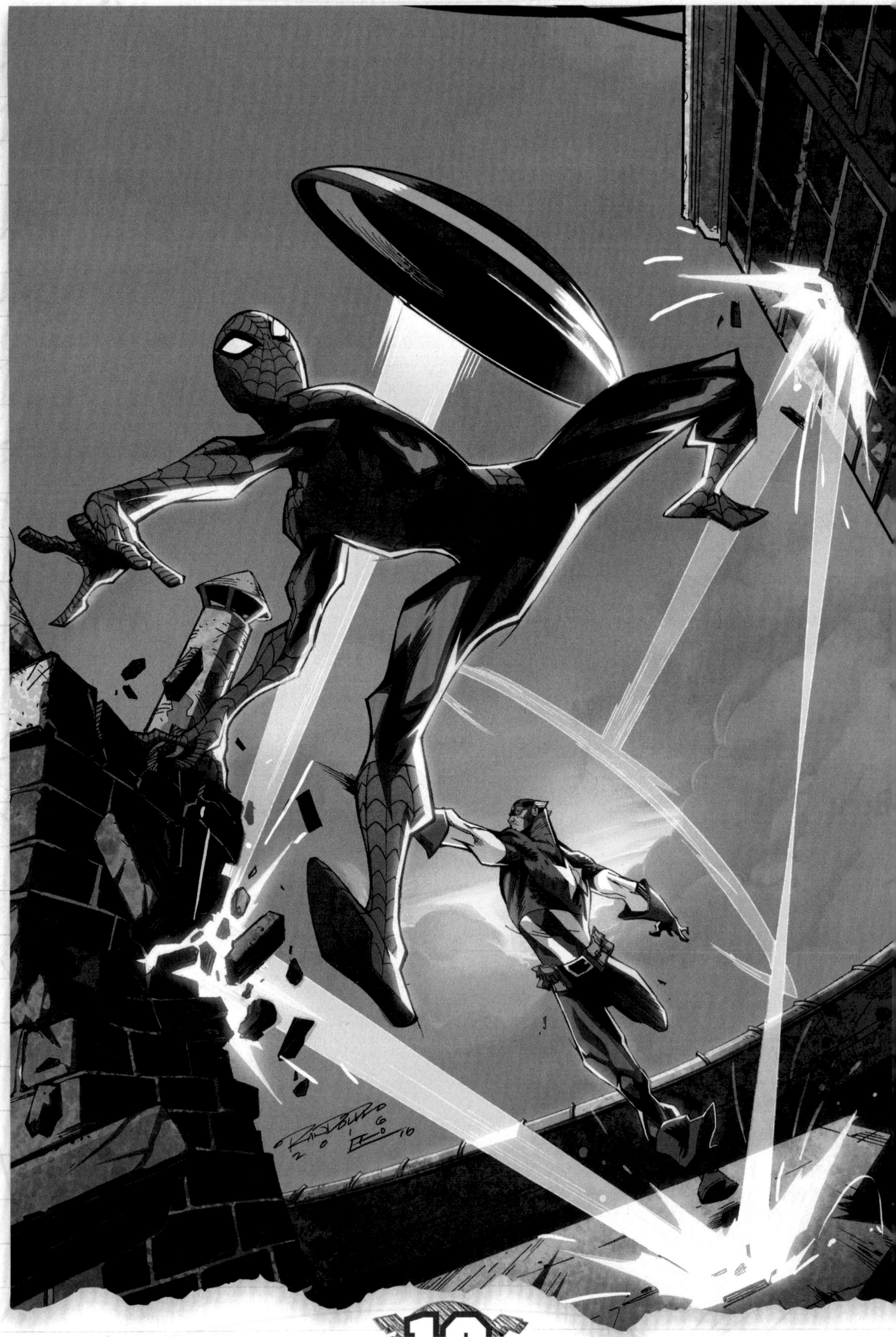

10

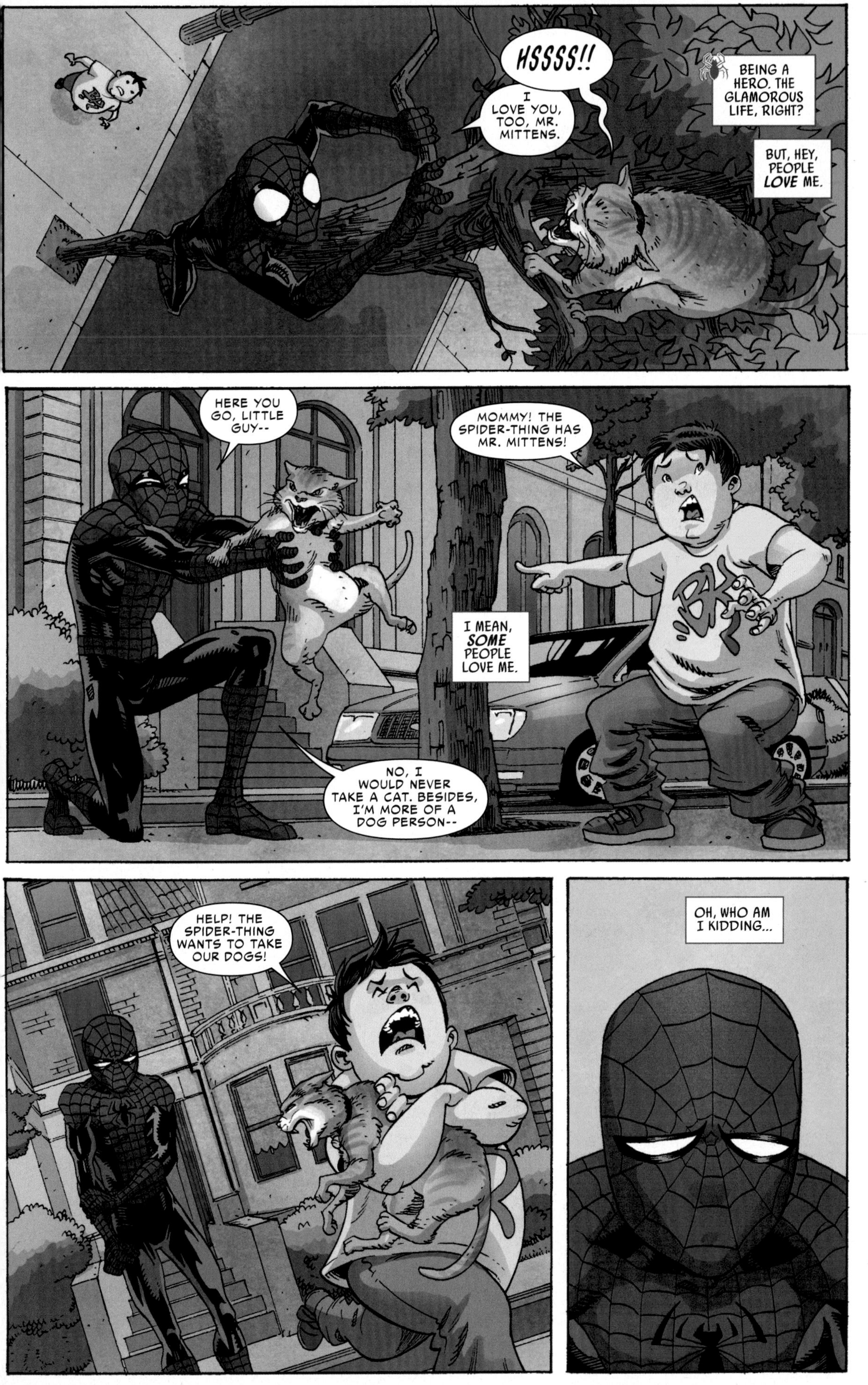
HSSSS!!
I LOVE YOU, TOO, MR. MITTENS.
BEING A HERO. THE GLAMOROUS LIFE, RIGHT?
BUT, HEY, PEOPLE LOVE ME.
HERE YOU GO, LITTLE GUY--
MOMMY! THE SPIDER-THING HAS MR. MITTENS!
I MEAN, SOME PEOPLE LOVE ME.
NO, I WOULD NEVER TAKE A CAT. BESIDES, I'M MORE OF A DOG PERSON--
HELP! THE SPIDER-THING WANTS TO TAKE OUR DOGS!
OH, WHO AM I KIDDING...

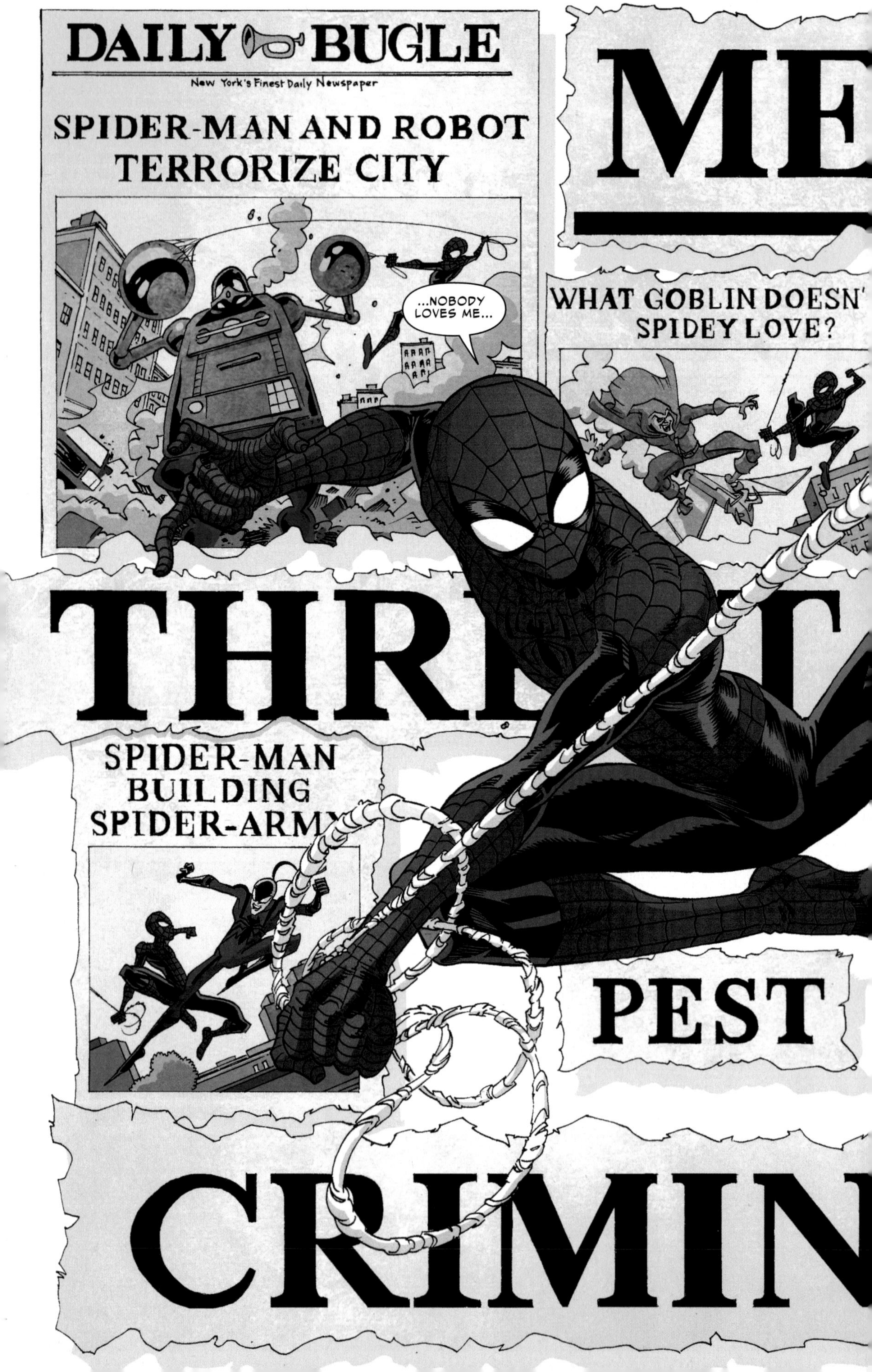
DAILY BUGLE
New York's Finest Daily Newspaper
SPIDER-MAN AND ROBOT TERRORIZE CITY
...NOBODY LOVES ME...
ME
WHAT GOBLIN DOESN'
SPIDEY LOVE?
THR
SPIDER-MAN BUILDING SPIDER-ARMY
PEST
CRIMIN

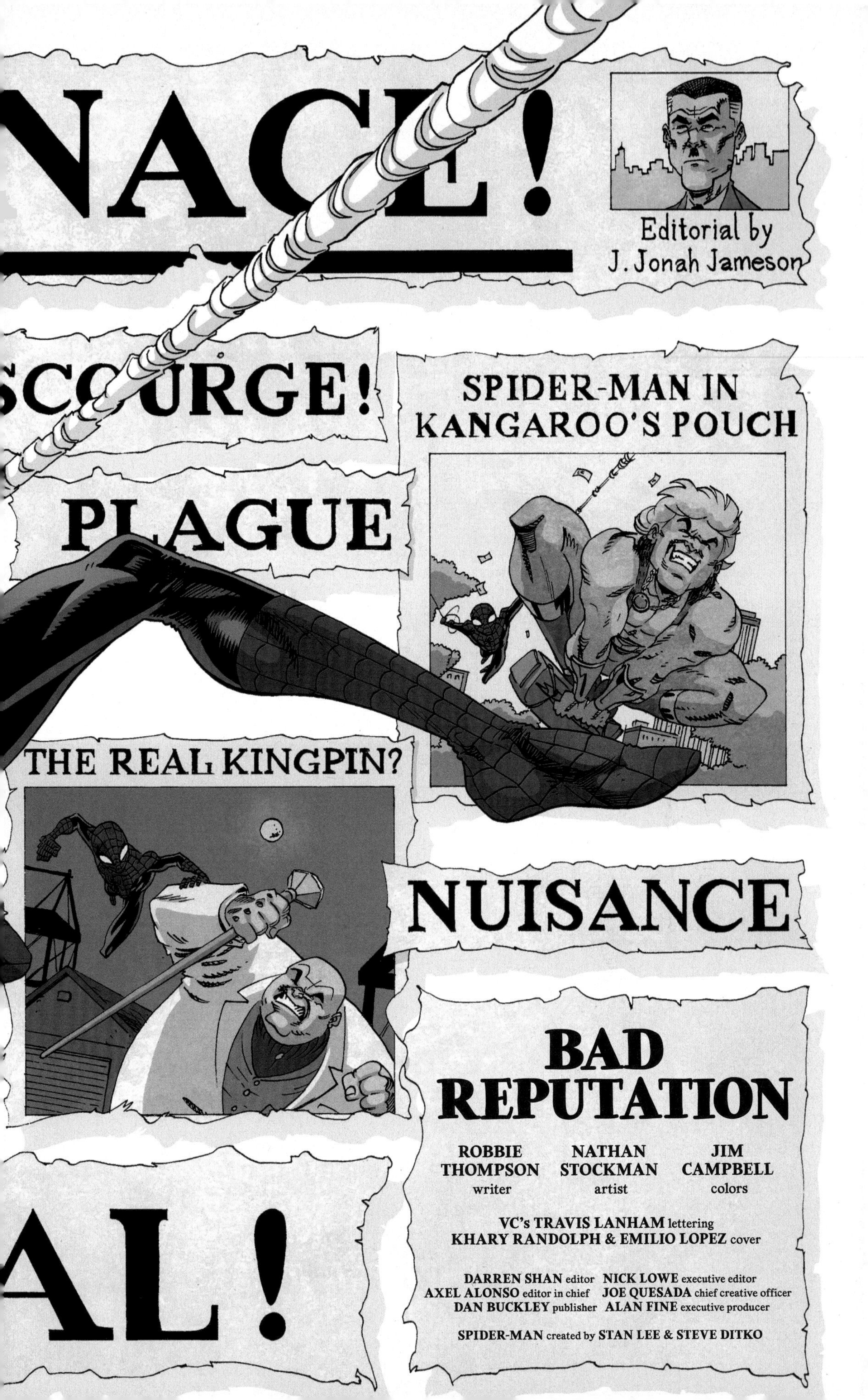

NACE!
Editorial by J. Jonah Jameson
SCOURGE!
SPIDER-MAN IN KANGAROO'S POUCH
PLAGUE
THE REAL KINGPIN?
NUISANCE
AL!
BAD REPUTATION
ROBBIE THOMPSON writer
NATHAN STOCKMAN artist
JIM CAMPBELL colors
VC's TRAVIS LANHAM lettering
KHARY RANDOLPH & EMILIO LOPEZ cover
DARREN SHAN editor
NICK LOWE executive editor
AXEL ALONSO editor in chief
JOE QUESADA chief creative officer
DAN BUCKLEY publisher
ALAN FINE executive producer
SPIDER-MAN created by STAN LEE & STEVE DITKO

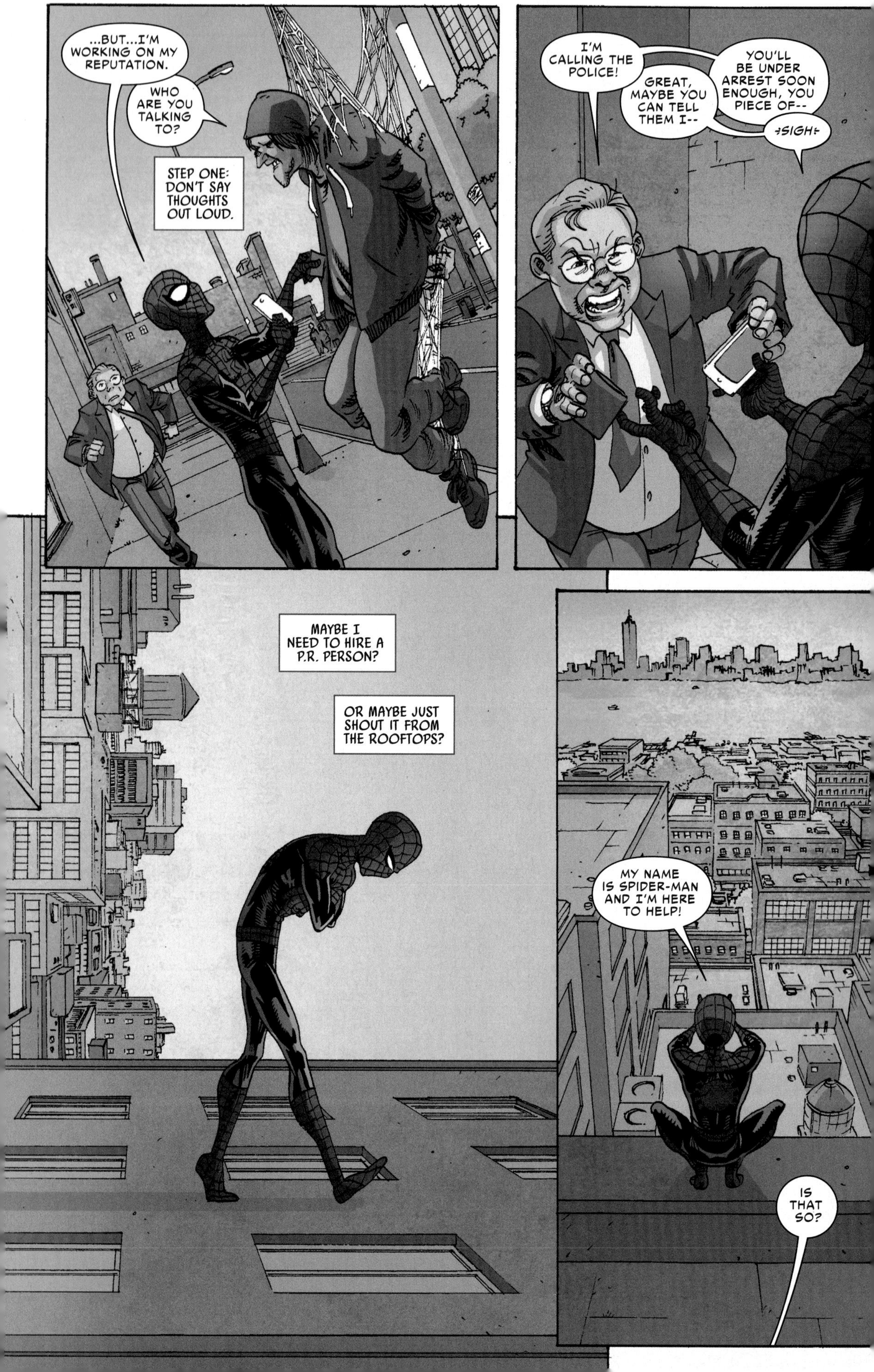
...BUT...I'M WORKING ON MY REPUTATION.
WHO ARE YOU TALKING TO?
STEP ONE: DON'T SAY THOUGHTS OUT LOUD.
I'M CALLING THE POLICE!
GREAT, MAYBE YOU CAN TELL THEM I--
YOU'LL BE UNDER ARREST SOON ENOUGH, YOU PIECE OF--
SIGH
MAYBE I NEED TO HIRE A P.R. PERSON?
OR MAYBE JUST SHOUT IT FROM THE ROOFTOPS?
MY NAME IS SPIDER-MAN AND I'M HERE TO HELP!
IS THAT SO?

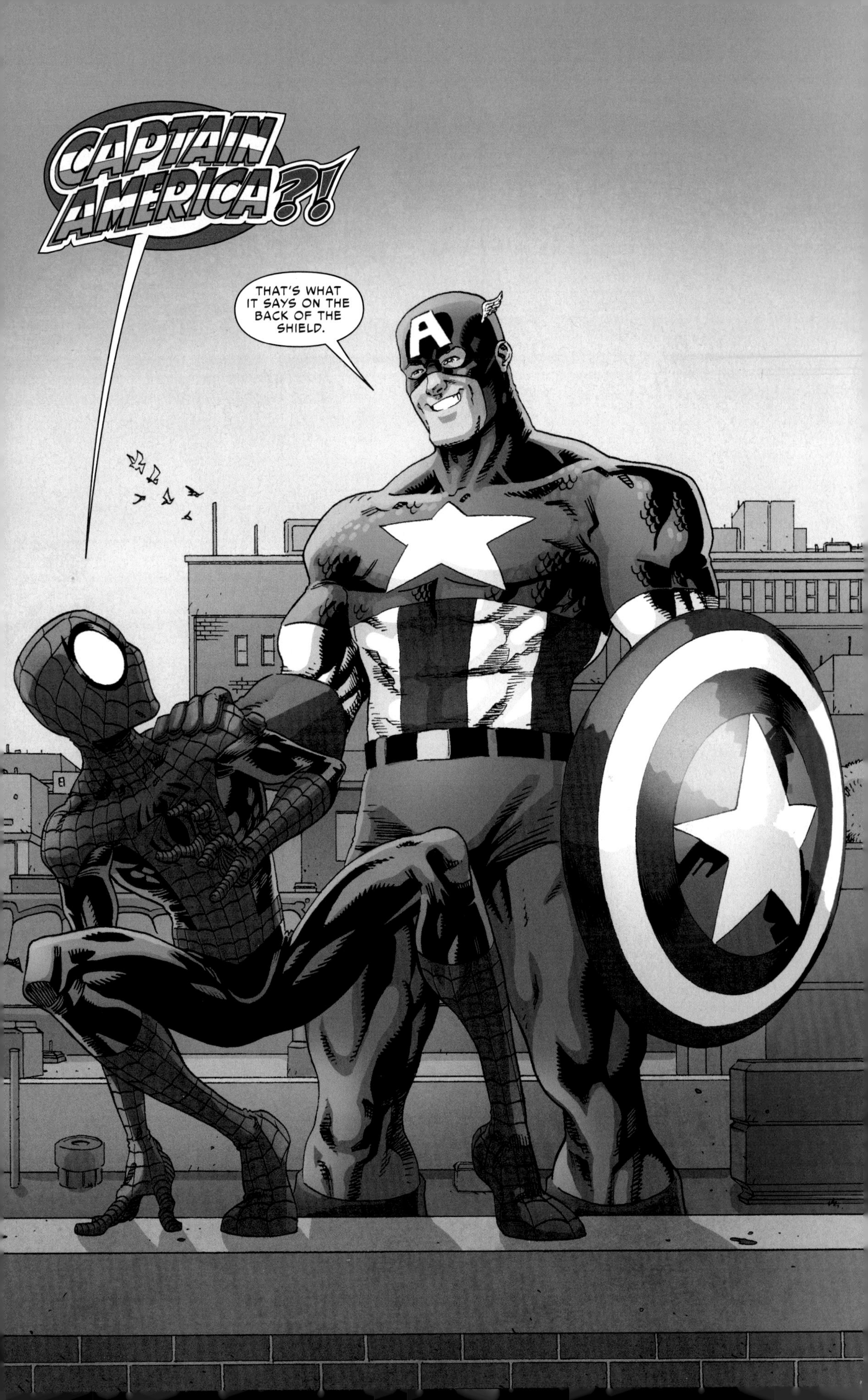
CAPTAIN AMERICA?!
THAT'S WHAT IT SAYS ON THE BACK OF THE SHIELD.

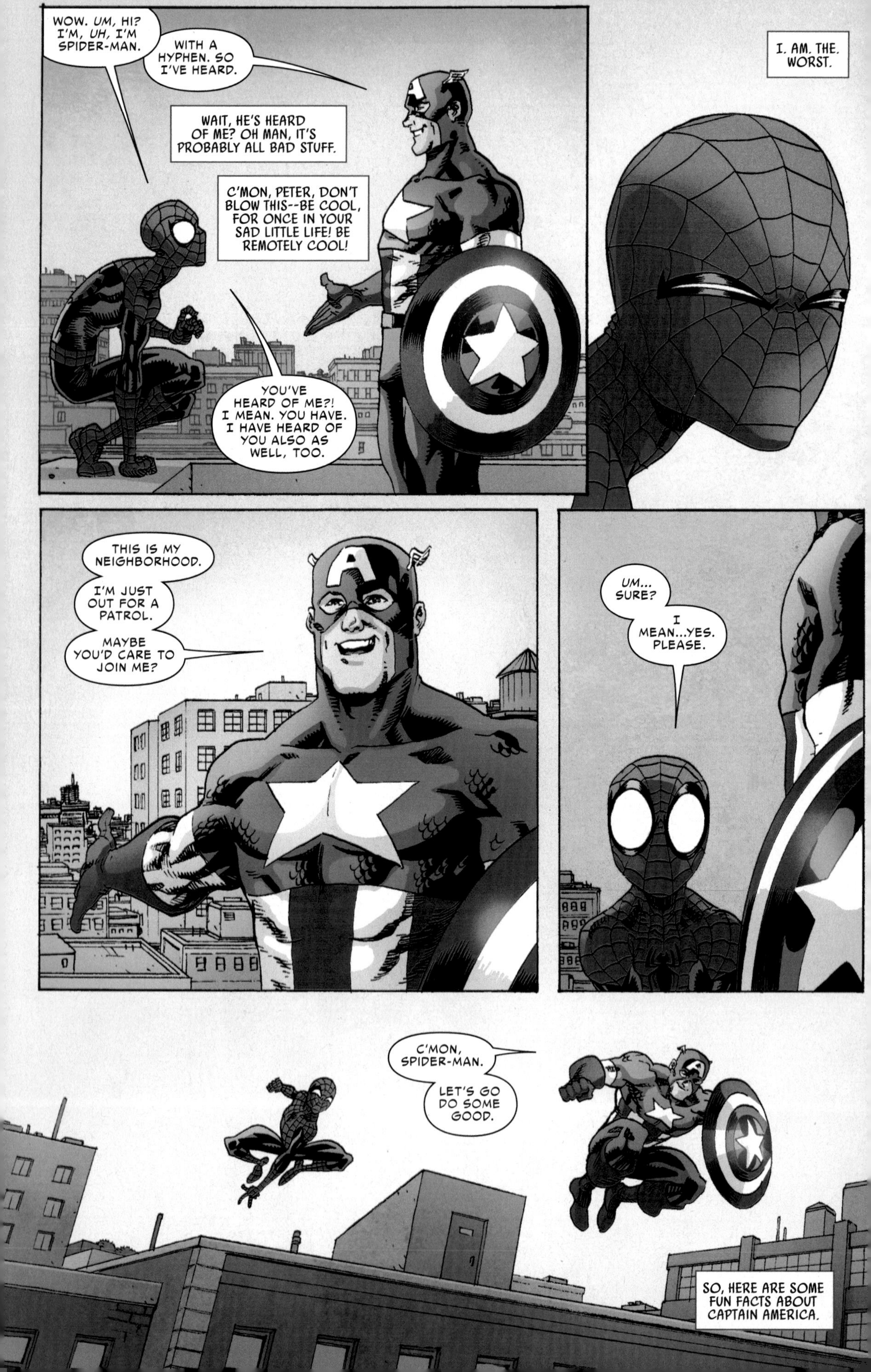

WOW. *UM*, HI? I'M, *UH*, I'M SPIDER-MAN.
WITH A HYPHEN. SO I'VE HEARD.
WAIT, HE'S HEARD OF ME? OH MAN, IT'S PROBABLY ALL BAD STUFF.
C'MON, PETER, DON'T BLOW THIS--BE COOL, FOR ONCE IN YOUR SAD LITTLE LIFE! BE REMOTELY COOL!
YOU'VE HEARD OF ME?! I MEAN. YOU HAVE. I HAVE HEARD OF YOU ALSO AS WELL, TOO.
I. AM. THE. WORST.
THIS IS MY NEIGHBORHOOD.
I'M JUST OUT FOR A PATROL.
MAYBE YOU'D CARE TO JOIN ME?
UM... SURE?
I MEAN...YES. PLEASE.
C'MON, SPIDER-MAN.
LET'S GO DO SOME GOOD.
SO, HERE ARE SOME FUN FACTS ABOUT CAPTAIN AMERICA.

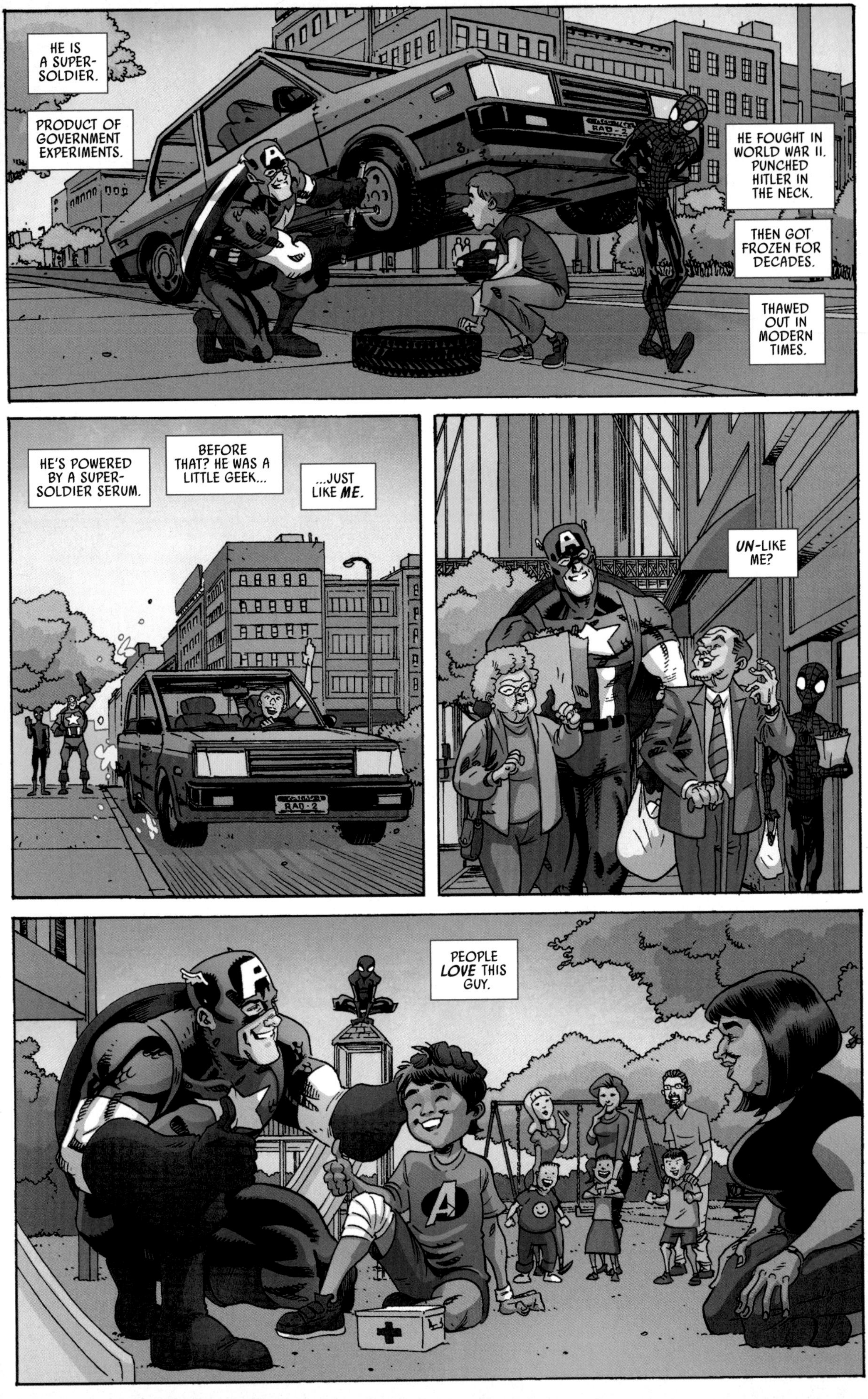
HE IS A SUPER-SOLDIER.
PRODUCT OF GOVERNMENT EXPERIMENTS.
HE FOUGHT IN WORLD WAR II. PUNCHED HITLER IN THE NECK.
THEN GOT FROZEN FOR DECADES.
THAWED OUT IN MODERN TIMES.
RAD-2
HE'S POWERED BY A SUPER-SOLDIER SERUM.
BEFORE THAT? HE WAS A LITTLE GEEK...
...JUST LIKE *ME.*
RAD-2
UN-LIKE ME?
PEOPLE *LOVE* THIS GUY.

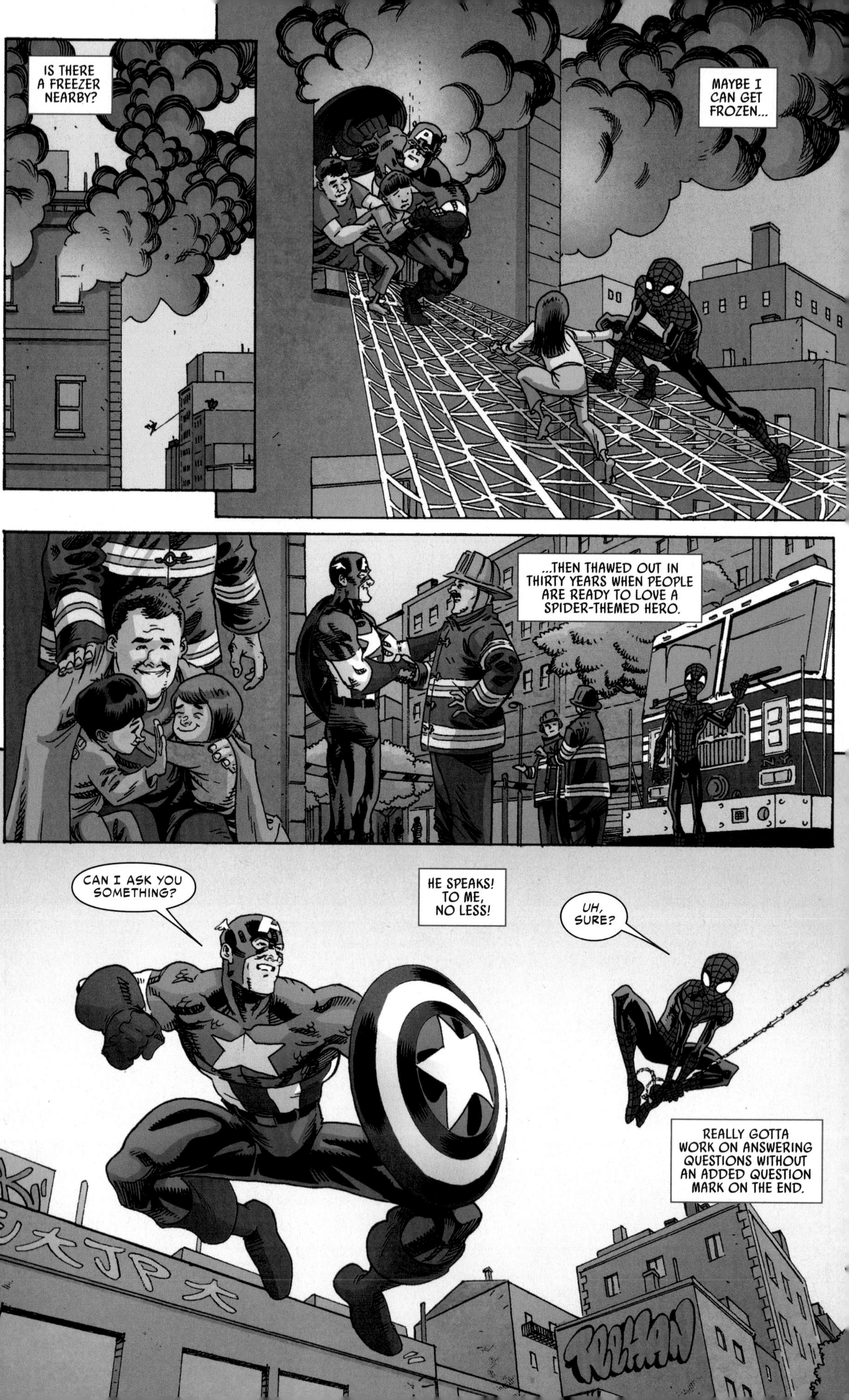
IS THERE A FREEZER NEARBY?
MAYBE I CAN GET FROZEN...
...THEN THAWED OUT IN THIRTY YEARS WHEN PEOPLE ARE READY TO LOVE A SPIDER-THEMED HERO.
CAN I ASK YOU SOMETHING?
HE SPEAKS! TO ME, NO LESS!
UH, SURE?
REALLY GOTTA WORK ON ANSWERING QUESTIONS WITHOUT AN ADDED QUESTION MARK ON THE END.

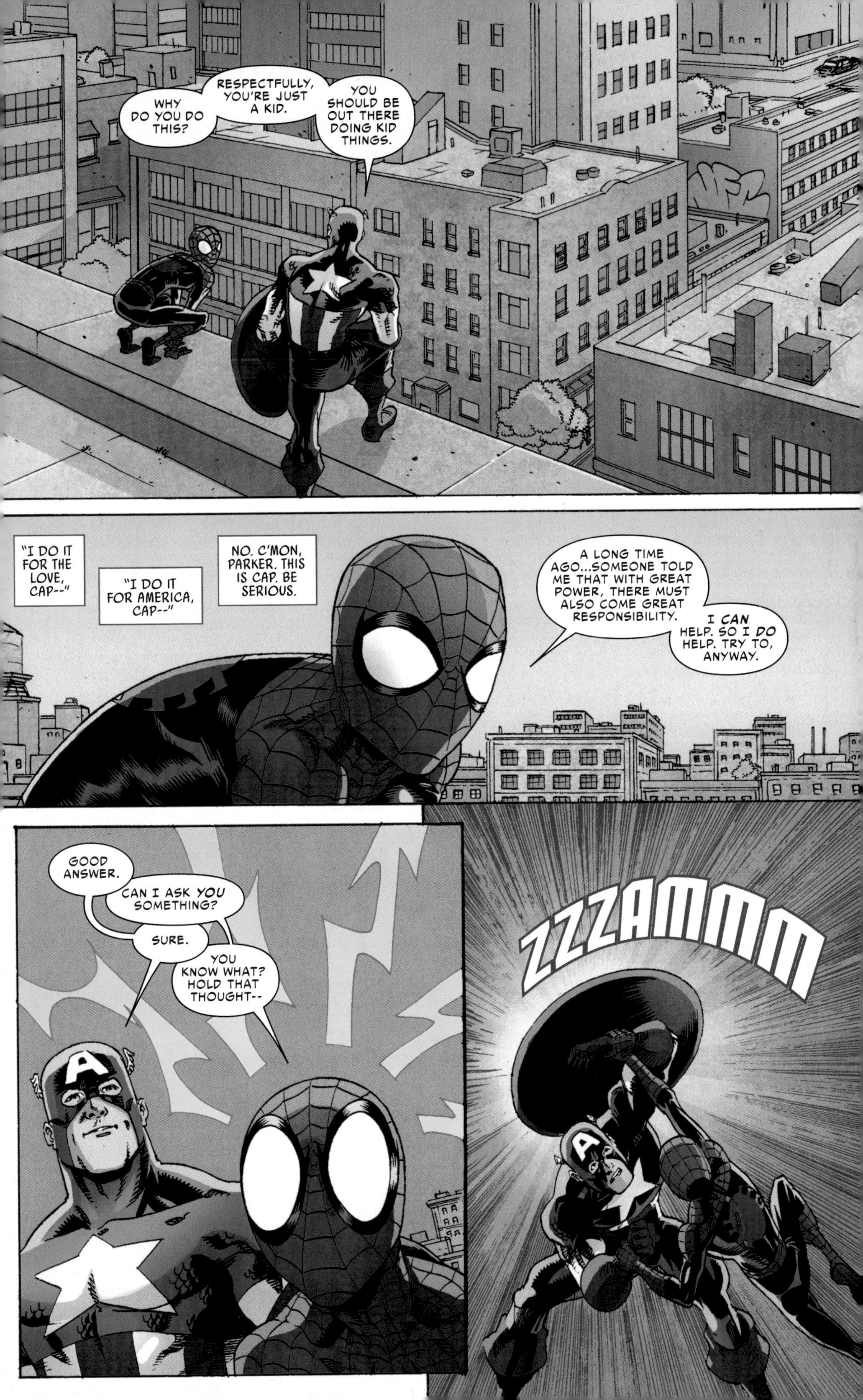
WHY DO YOU DO THIS?
RESPECTFULLY, YOU'RE JUST A KID.
YOU SHOULD BE OUT THERE DOING KID THINGS.
"I DO IT FOR THE LOVE, CAP--"
"I DO IT FOR AMERICA, CAP--"
NO. C'MON, PARKER. THIS IS CAP. BE SERIOUS.
A LONG TIME AGO...SOMEONE TOLD ME THAT WITH GREAT POWER, THERE MUST ALSO COME GREAT RESPONSIBILITY.
I CAN HELP. SO I DO HELP. TRY TO, ANYWAY.
GOOD ANSWER.
CAN I ASK YOU SOMETHING?
SURE.
YOU KNOW WHAT? HOLD THAT THOUGHT--
ZZZAMMMM

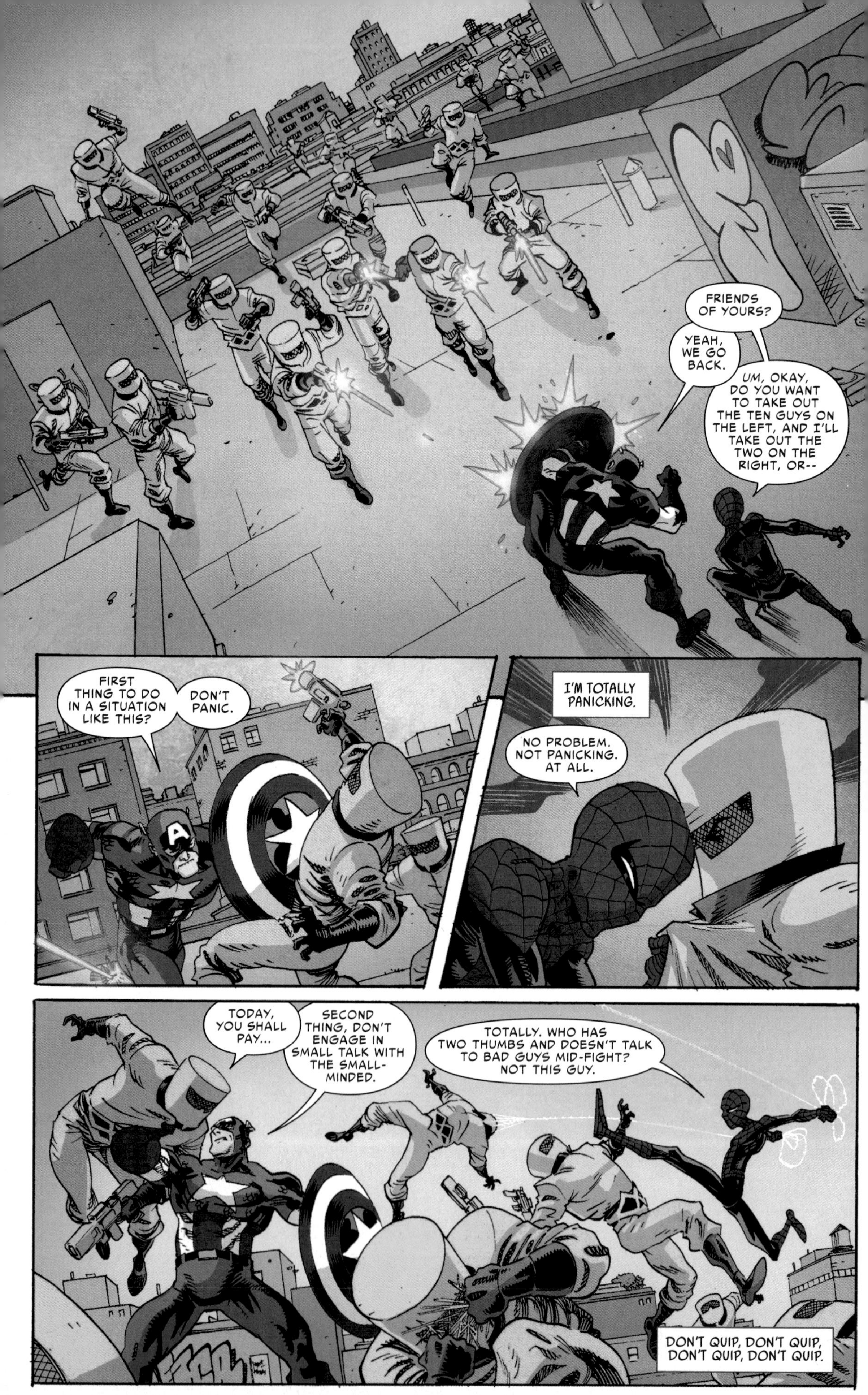
FRIENDS OF YOURS?
YEAH, WE GO BACK.
UM, OKAY, DO YOU WANT TO TAKE OUT THE TEN GUYS ON THE LEFT, AND I'LL TAKE OUT THE TWO ON THE RIGHT, OR--
FIRST THING TO DO IN A SITUATION LIKE THIS?
DON'T PANIC.
I'M TOTALLY PANICKING.
NO PROBLEM. NOT PANICKING. AT ALL.
TODAY, YOU SHALL PAY...
SECOND THING, DON'T ENGAGE IN SMALL TALK WITH THE SMALL-MINDED.
TOTALLY. WHO HAS TWO THUMBS AND DOESN'T TALK TO BAD GUYS MID-FIGHT? NOT THIS GUY.
DON'T QUIP, DON'T QUIP, DON'T QUIP, DON'T QUIP.

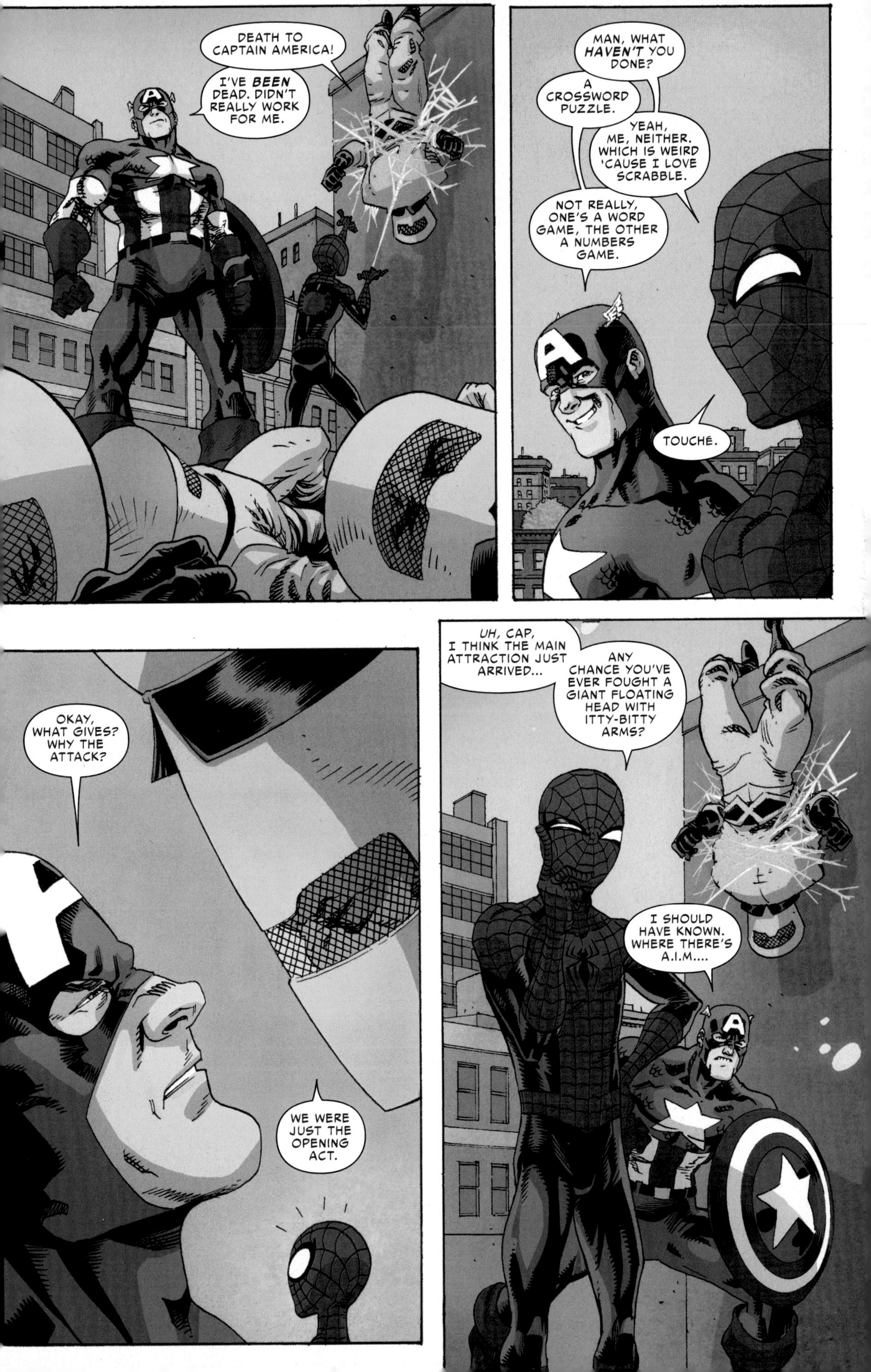
DEATH TO CAPTAIN AMERICA!
I'VE **BEEN** DEAD. DIDN'T REALLY WORK FOR ME.
MAN, WHAT ***HAVEN'T*** YOU DONE?
A CROSSWORD PUZZLE.
YEAH, ME, NEITHER. WHICH IS WEIRD 'CAUSE I LOVE SCRABBLE.
NOT REALLY, ONE'S A WORD GAME, THE OTHER A NUMBERS GAME.
TOUCHÉ.
OKAY, WHAT GIVES? WHY THE ATTACK?
WE WERE JUST THE OPENING ACT.
UH, CAP, I THINK THE MAIN ATTRACTION JUST ARRIVED...
ANY CHANCE YOU'VE EVER FOUGHT A GIANT FLOATING HEAD WITH ITTY-BITTY ARMS?
I SHOULD HAVE KNOWN. WHERE THERE'S A.I.M....

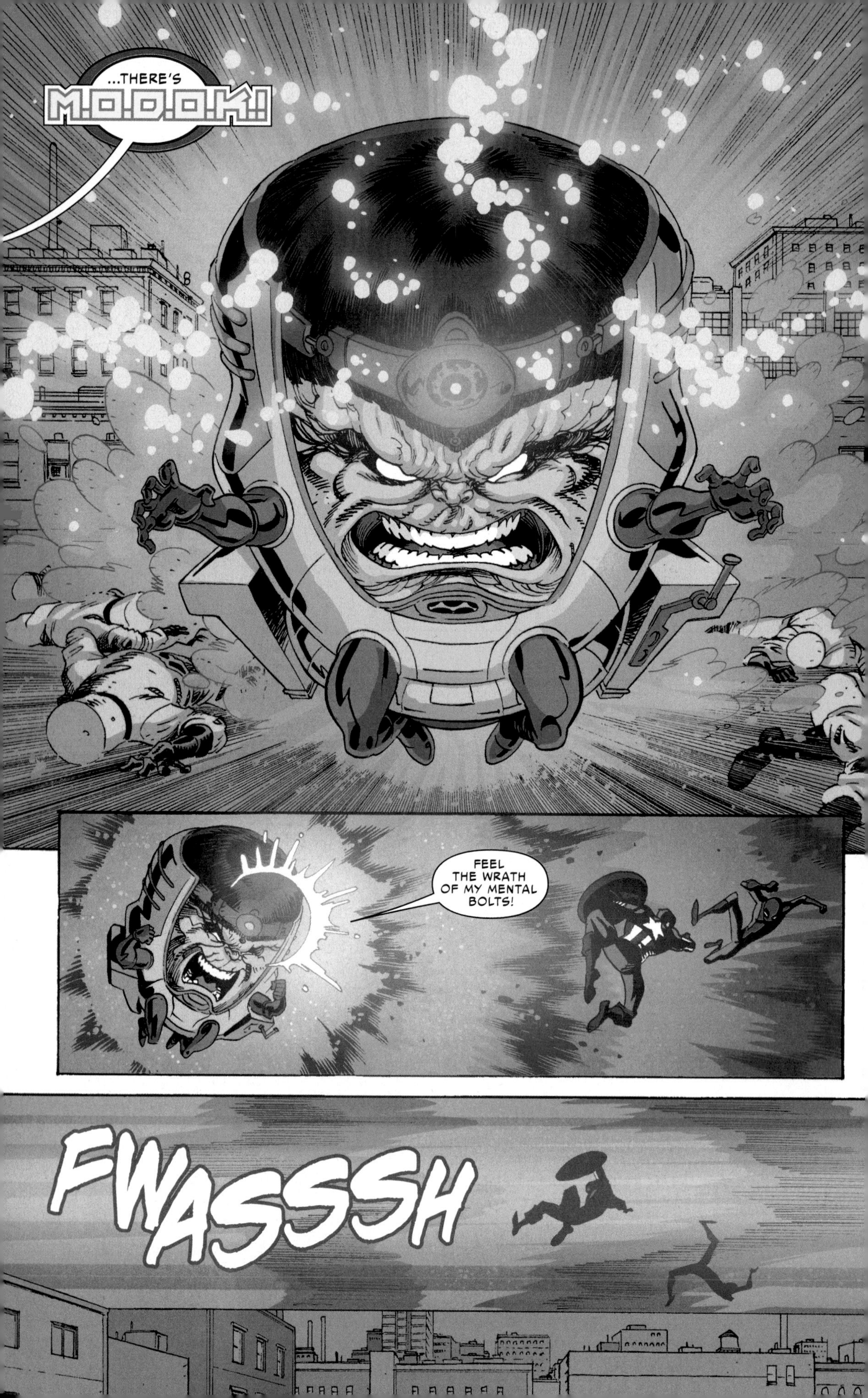
...THERE'S
M.O.D.O.K.!
FEEL THE WRATH OF MY MENTAL BOLTS!
FWASSSH

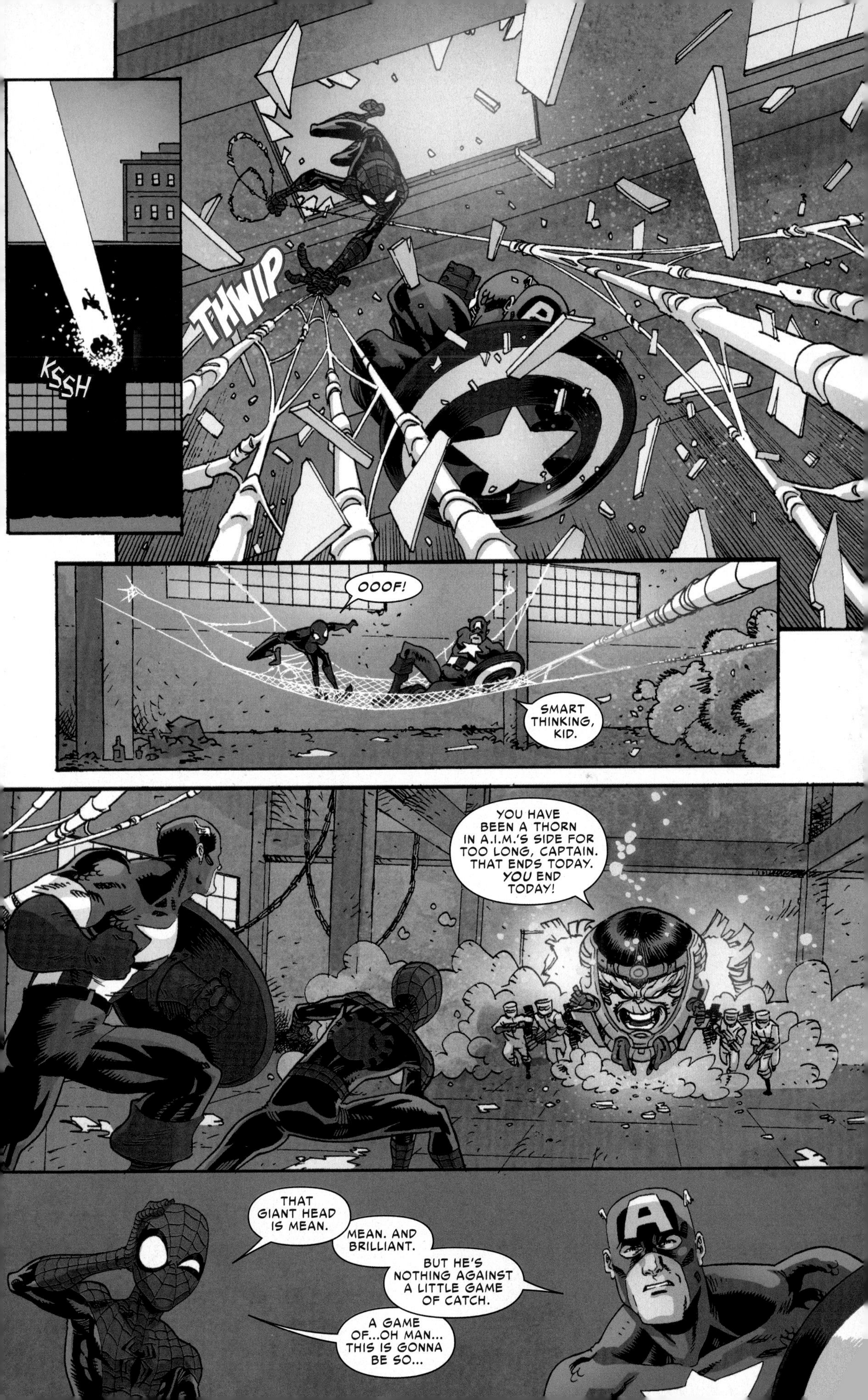
KSSH
THWIP
OOOF!
SMART THINKING, KID.
YOU HAVE BEEN A THORN IN A.I.M.'S SIDE FOR TOO LONG, CAPTAIN. THAT ENDS TODAY. *YOU* END TODAY!
THAT GIANT HEAD IS MEAN.
MEAN. AND BRILLIANT.
BUT HE'S NOTHING AGAINST A LITTLE GAME OF CATCH.
A GAME OF...OH MAN... THIS IS GONNA BE SO...

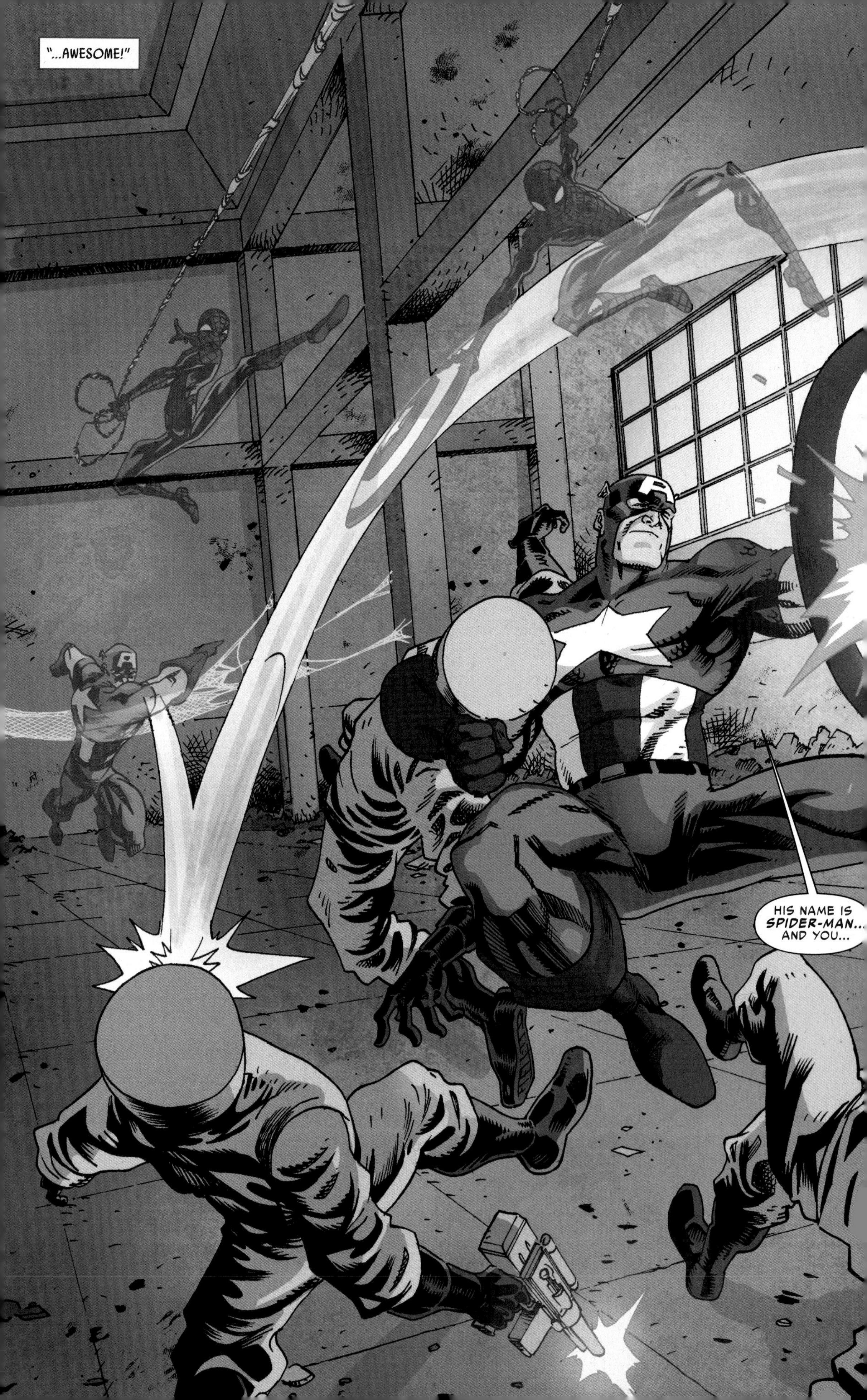
"...AWESOME!"
HIS NAME IS SPIDER-MAN... AND YOU...

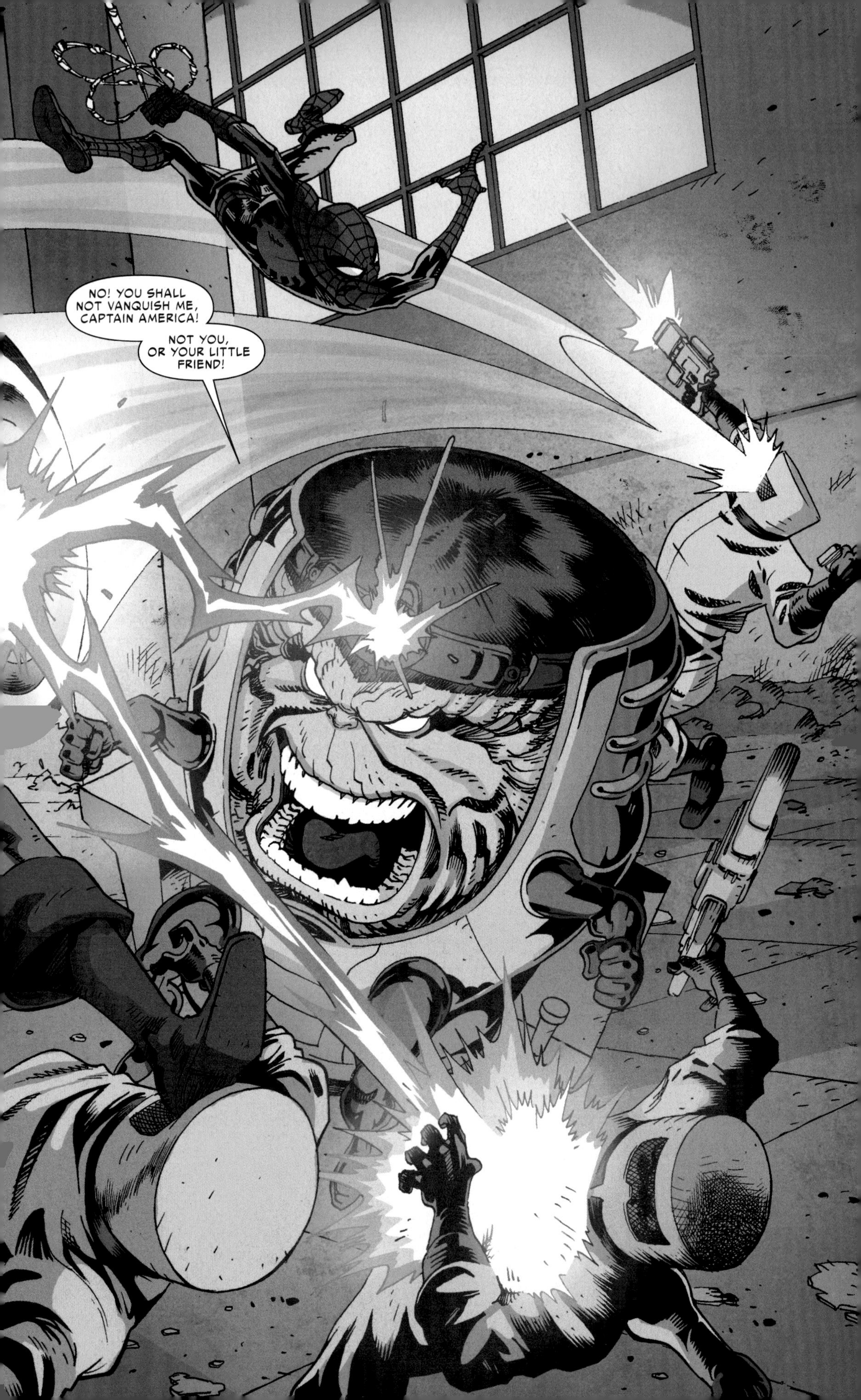
NO! YOU SHALL NOT VANQUISH ME, CAPTAIN AMERICA!
NOT YOU, OR YOUR LITTLE FRIEND!

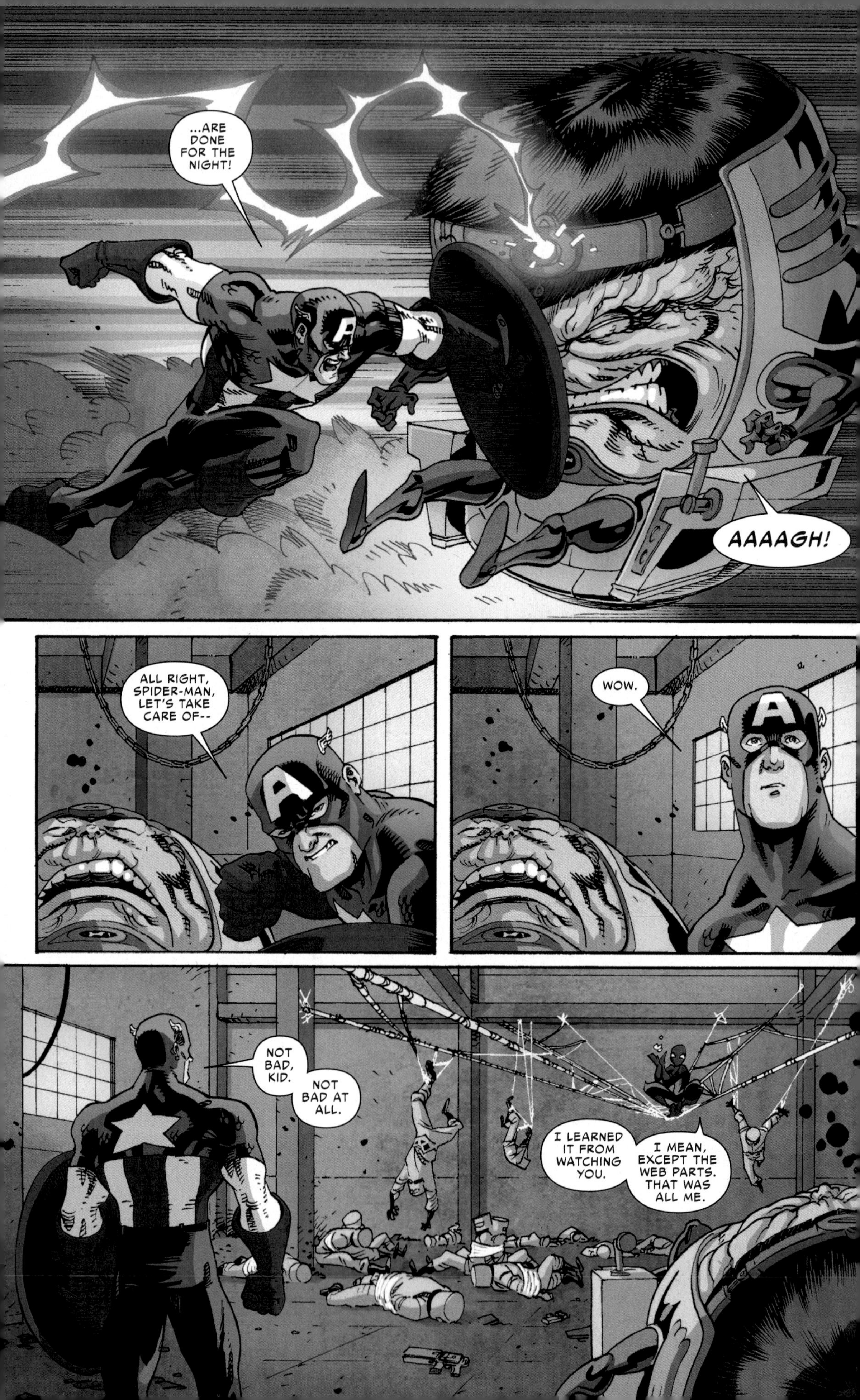
...ARE DONE FOR THE NIGHT!
AAAAGH!
ALL RIGHT, SPIDER-MAN, LET'S TAKE CARE OF--
WOW.
NOT BAD, KID.
NOT BAD AT ALL.
I LEARNED IT FROM WATCHING YOU.
I MEAN, EXCEPT THE WEB PARTS. THAT WAS ALL ME.

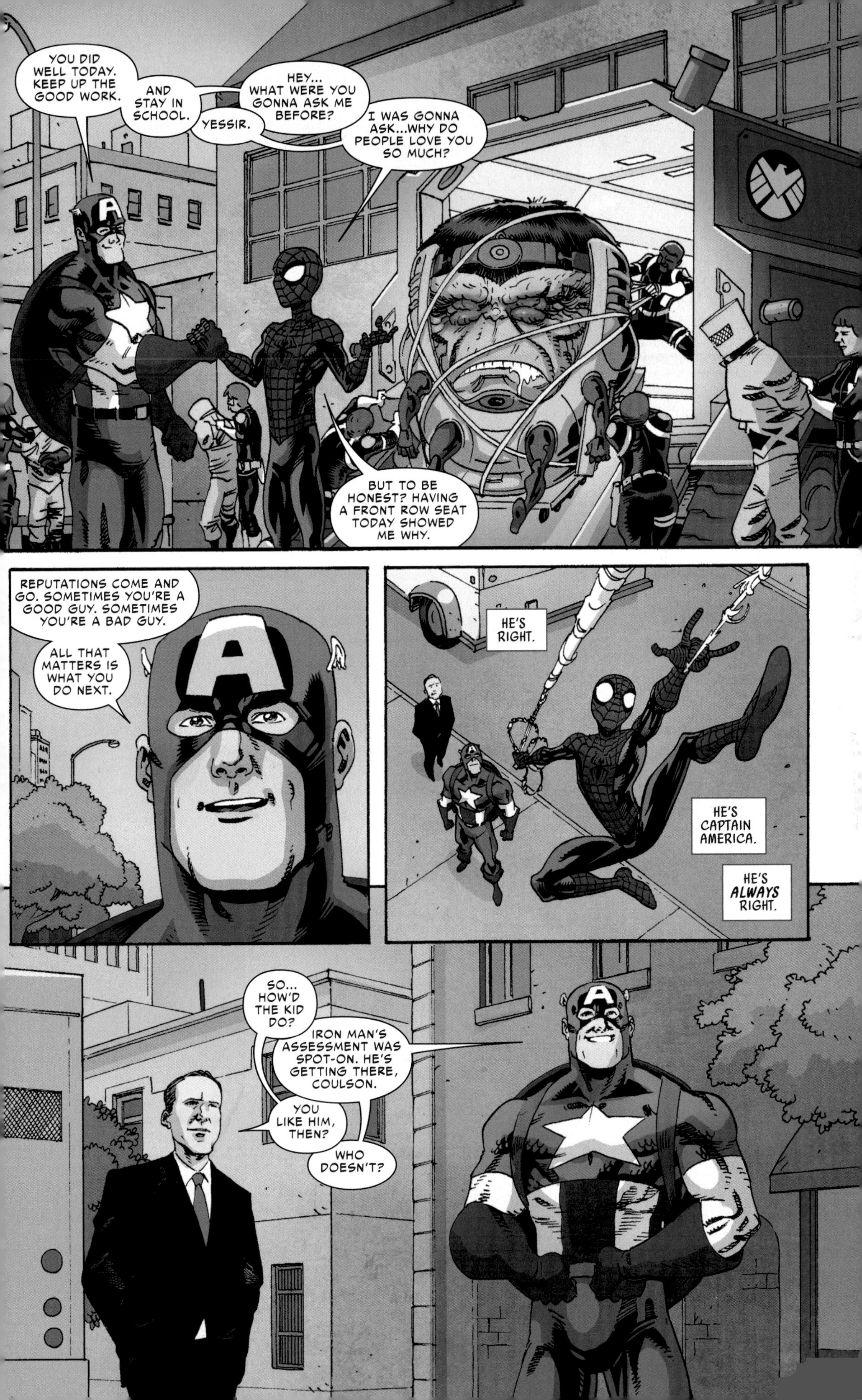

YOU DID WELL TODAY. KEEP UP THE GOOD WORK.
AND STAY IN SCHOOL.
YESSIR.
HEY... WHAT WERE YOU GONNA ASK ME BEFORE?
I WAS GONNA ASK...WHY DO PEOPLE LOVE YOU SO MUCH?
BUT TO BE HONEST? HAVING A FRONT ROW SEAT TODAY SHOWED ME WHY.
REPUTATIONS COME AND GO. SOMETIMES YOU'RE A GOOD GUY. SOMETIMES YOU'RE A BAD GUY.
ALL THAT MATTERS IS WHAT YOU DO NEXT.
HE'S RIGHT.
HE'S CAPTAIN AMERICA.
HE'S *ALWAYS* RIGHT.
SO... HOW'D THE KID DO?
IRON MAN'S ASSESSMENT WAS SPOT-ON. HE'S GETTING THERE, COULSON.
YOU LIKE HIM, THEN?
WHO DOESN'T?

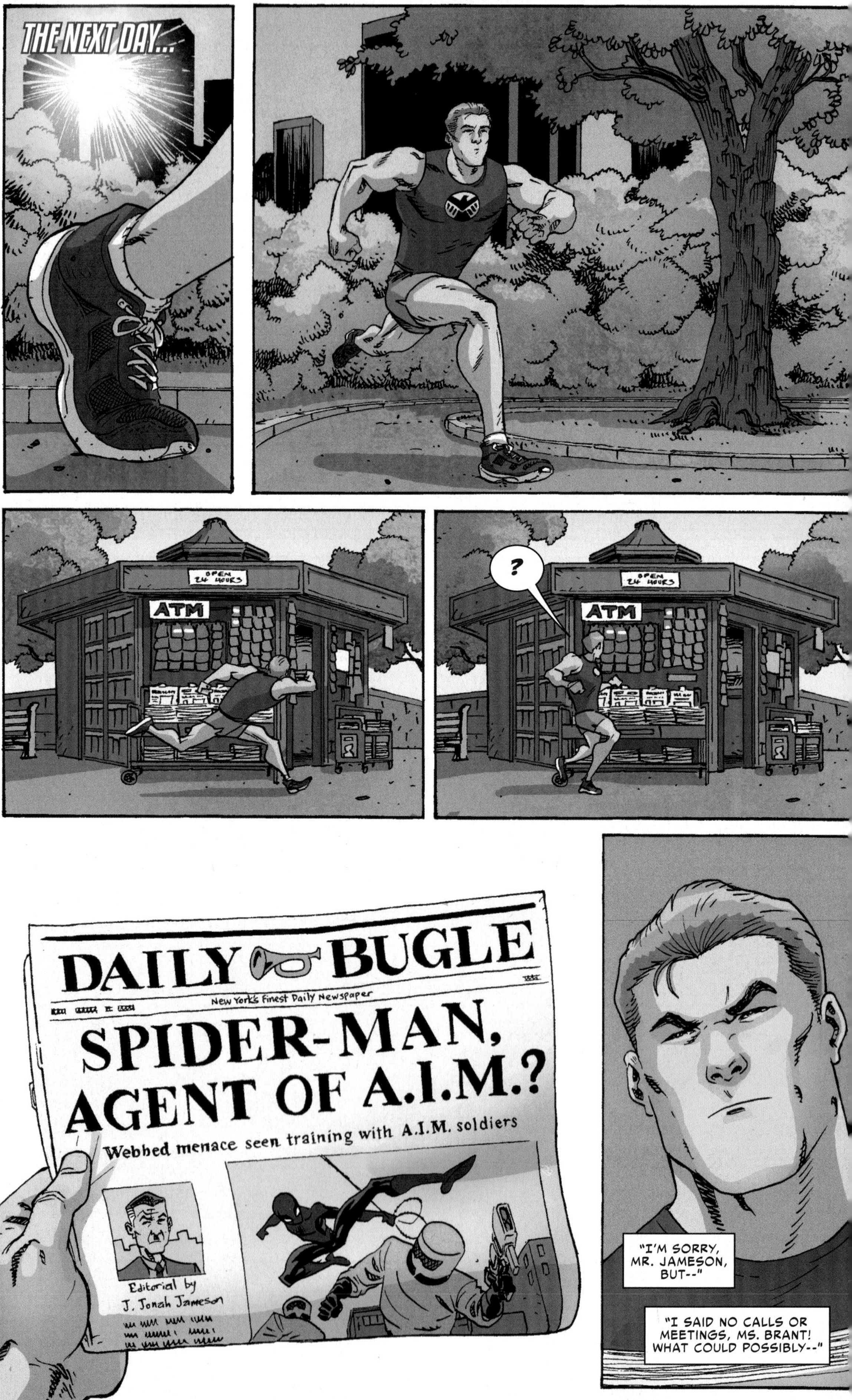
THE NEXT DAY...
OPEN 24 HOURS
ATM
?
DAILY BUGLE
New York's Finest Daily Newspaper
SPIDER-MAN, AGENT OF A.I.M.?
Webbed menace seen training with A.I.M. soldiers
Editorial by J. Jonah Jameson
"I'M SORRY, MR. JAMESON, BUT--"
"I SAID NO CALLS OR MEETINGS, MS. BRANT! WHAT COULD POSSIBLY--"

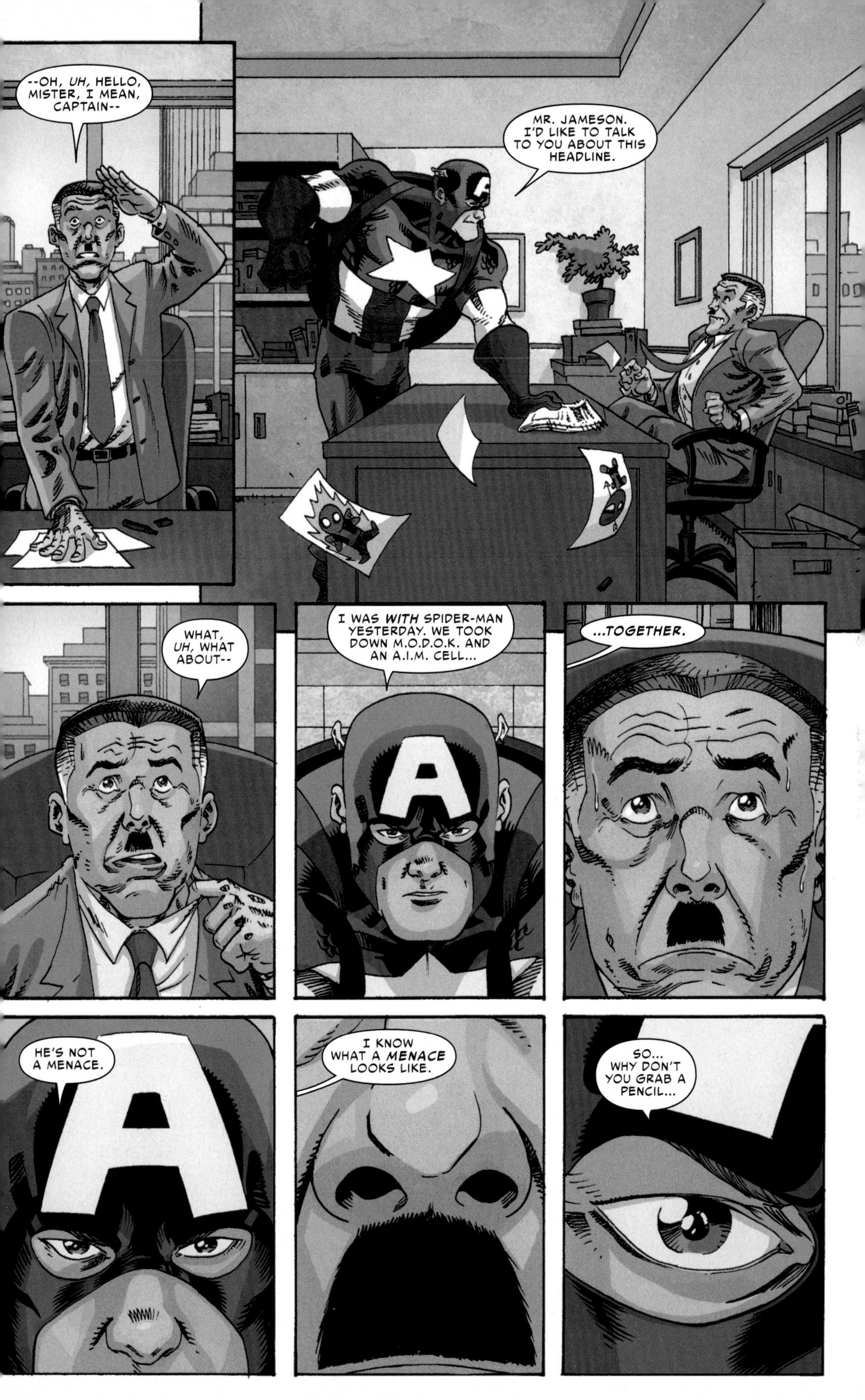
--OH, UH, HELLO, MISTER, I MEAN, CAPTAIN--
MR. JAMESON. I'D LIKE TO TALK TO YOU ABOUT THIS HEADLINE.
WHAT, UH, WHAT ABOUT--
I WAS WITH SPIDER-MAN YESTERDAY. WE TOOK DOWN M.O.D.O.K. AND AN A.I.M. CELL...
...TOGETHER.
HE'S NOT A MENACE.
I KNOW WHAT A MENACE LOOKS LIKE.
SO... WHY DON'T YOU GRAB A PENCIL...

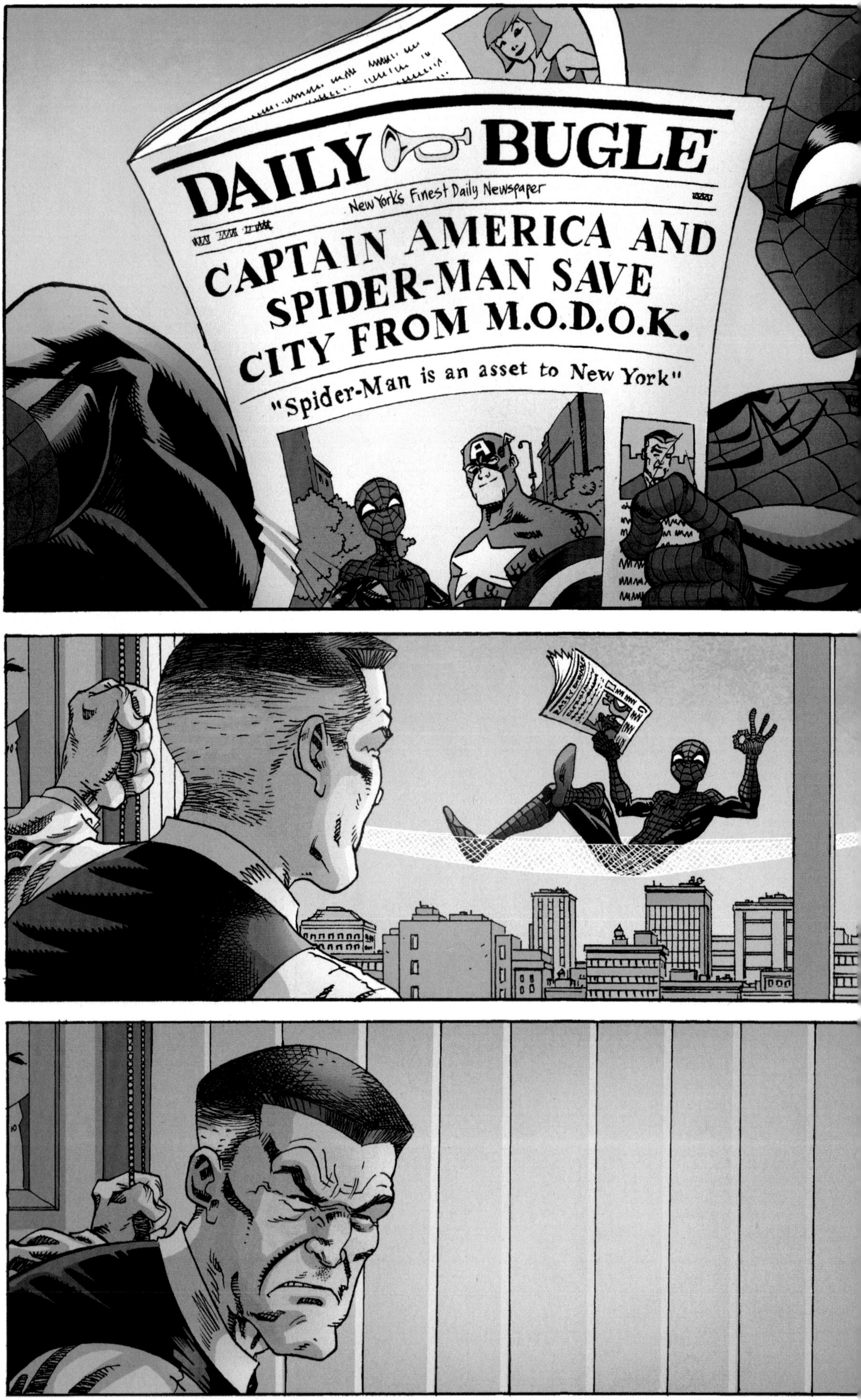
DAILY BUGLE
New York's Finest Daily Newspaper
CAPTAIN AMERICA AND SPIDER-MAN SAVE CITY FROM M.O.D.O.K.
"Spider-Man is an asset to New York"

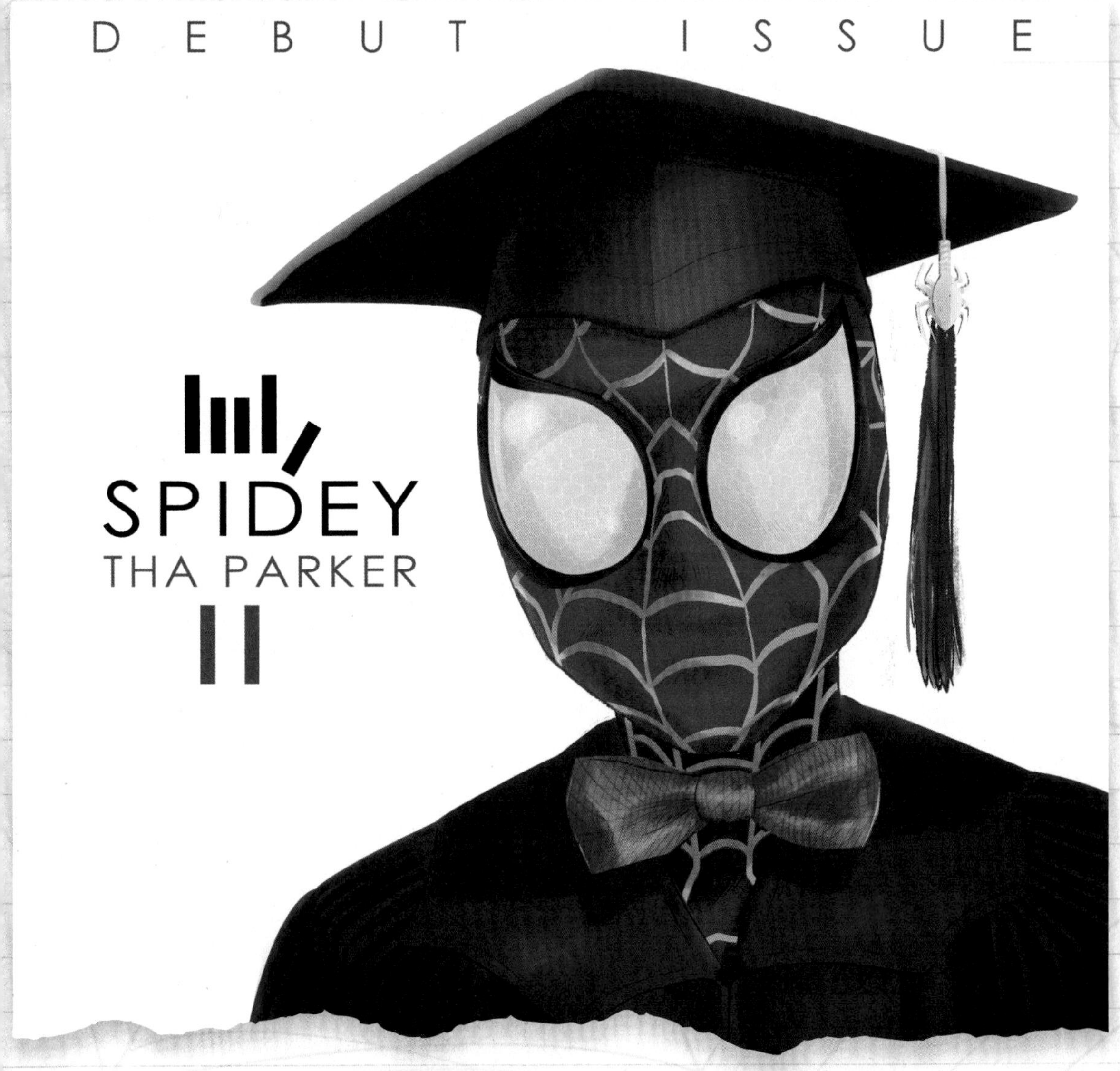
DEBUT ISSUE
SPIDEY
THA PARKER

GYIMAH GARIBA
1 HIP-HOP VARIANT

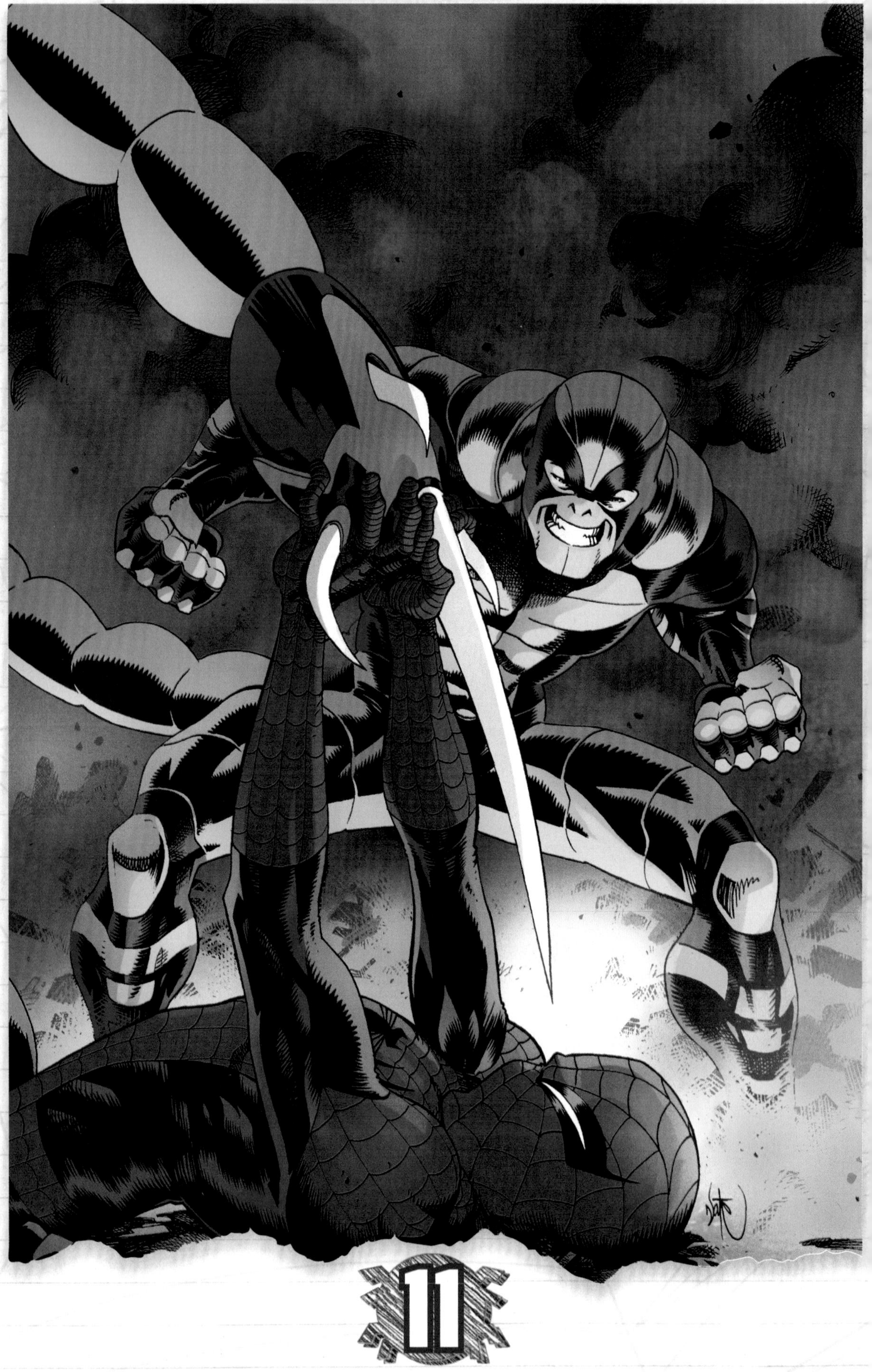

11

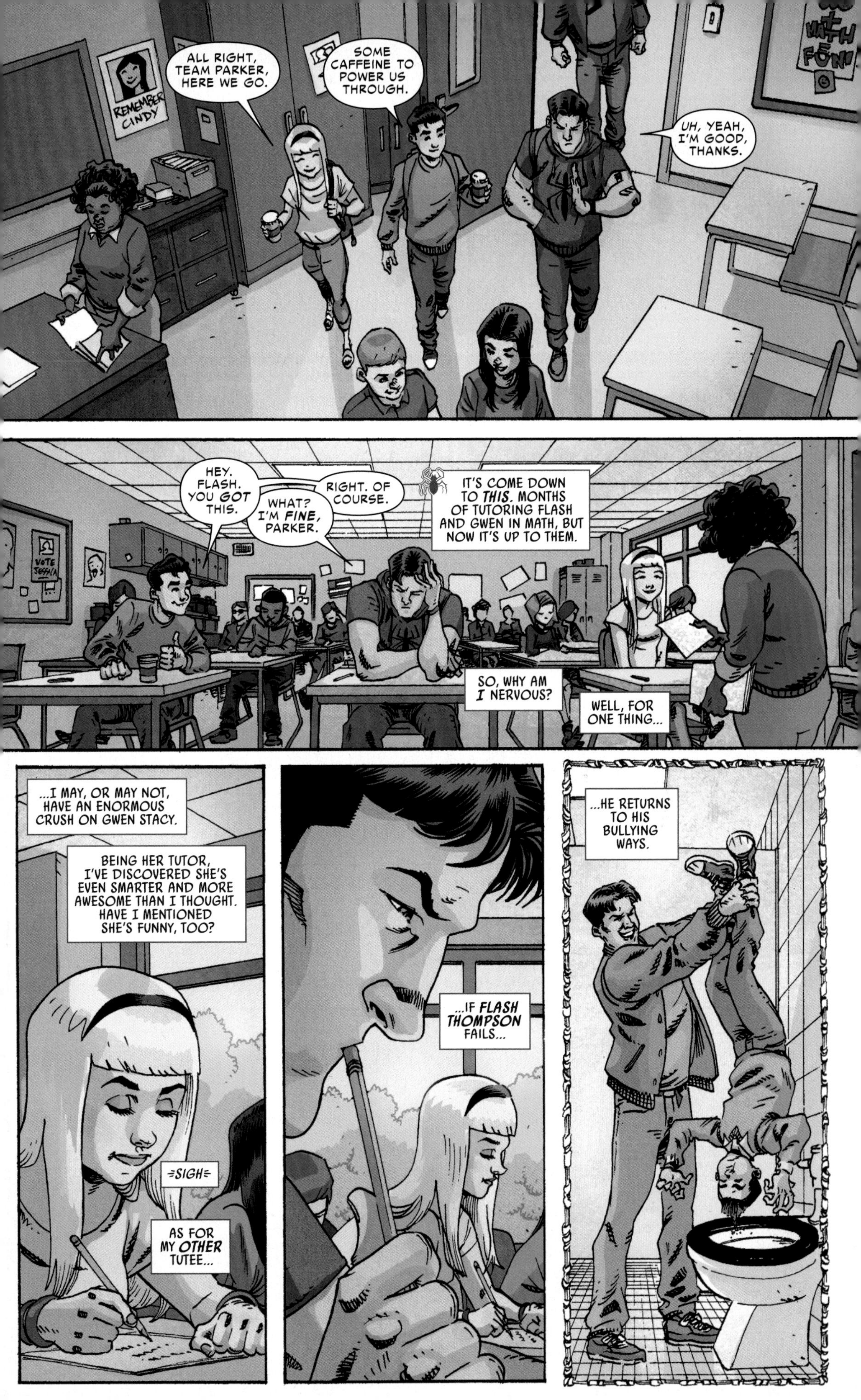
REMEMBER CINDY
ALL RIGHT, TEAM PARKER, HERE WE GO.
SOME CAFFEINE TO POWER US THROUGH.
UH, YEAH, I'M GOOD, THANKS.
HEY. FLASH. YOU GOT THIS.
WHAT? I'M FINE, PARKER.
RIGHT. OF COURSE.
IT'S COME DOWN TO THIS. MONTHS OF TUTORING FLASH AND GWEN IN MATH, BUT NOW IT'S UP TO THEM.
SO, WHY AM I NERVOUS?
WELL, FOR ONE THING...
...I MAY, OR MAY NOT, HAVE AN ENORMOUS CRUSH ON GWEN STACY.
BEING HER TUTOR, I'VE DISCOVERED SHE'S EVEN SMARTER AND MORE AWESOME THAN I THOUGHT. HAVE I MENTIONED SHE'S FUNNY, TOO?
SIGH
AS FOR MY OTHER TUTEE...
...IF FLASH THOMPSON FAILS...
...HE RETURNS TO HIS BULLYING WAYS.

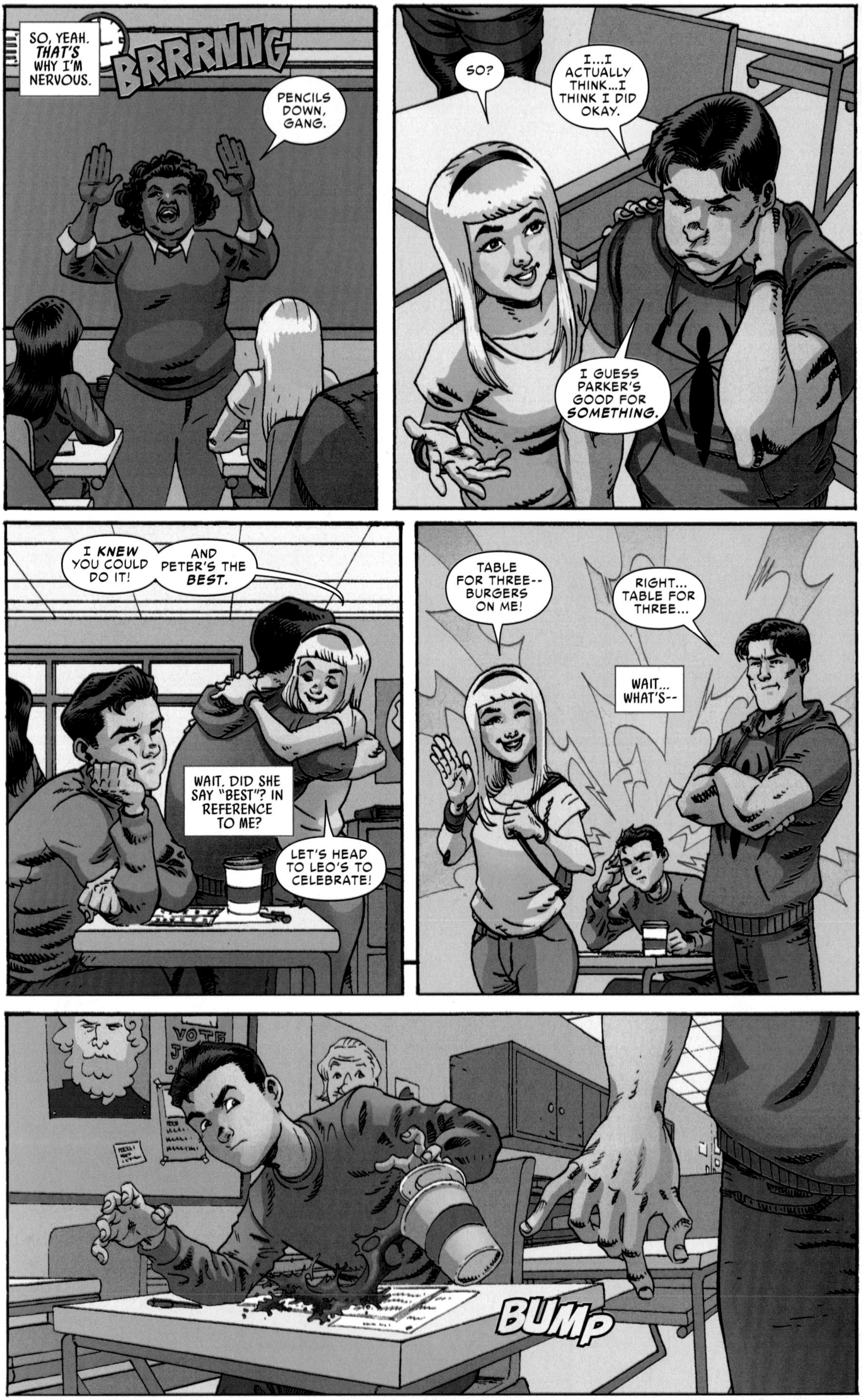

SO, YEAH. *THAT'S* WHY I'M NERVOUS.
BRRRNNG
PENCILS DOWN, GANG.
SO?
I...I ACTUALLY THINK...I THINK I DID OKAY.
I GUESS PARKER'S GOOD FOR *SOMETHING*.
I *KNEW* YOU COULD DO IT!
AND PETER'S THE *BEST*.
WAIT. DID SHE SAY "BEST"? IN REFERENCE TO ME?
LET'S HEAD TO LEO'S TO CELEBRATE!
TABLE FOR THREE-- BURGERS ON ME!
RIGHT... TABLE FOR THREE...
WAIT... WHAT'S--
VOTE
BUMP

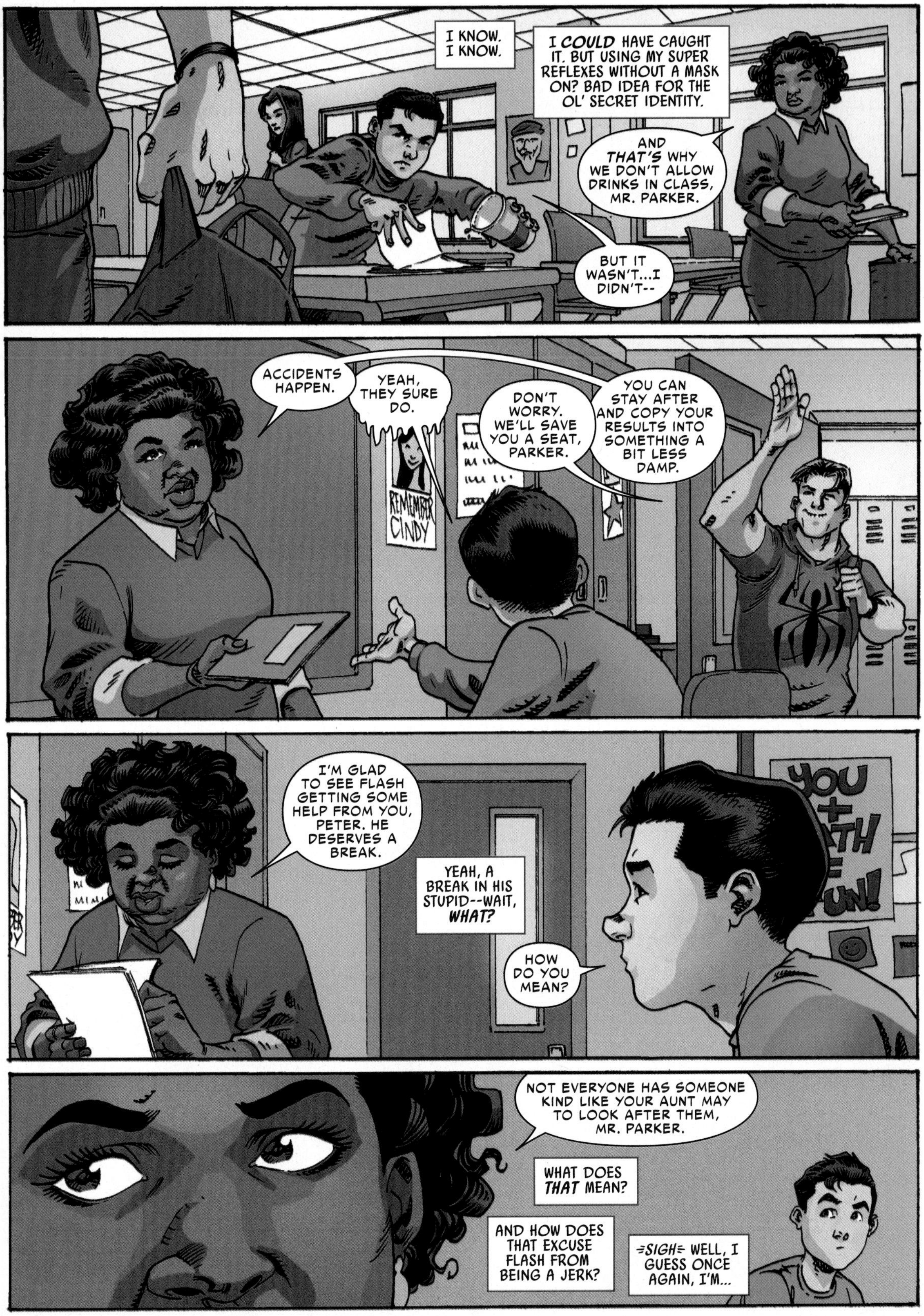
I KNOW. I KNOW.
I COULD HAVE CAUGHT IT. BUT USING MY SUPER REFLEXES WITHOUT A MASK ON? BAD IDEA FOR THE OL' SECRET IDENTITY.
AND THAT'S WHY WE DON'T ALLOW DRINKS IN CLASS, MR. PARKER.
BUT IT WASN'T...I DIDN'T--
ACCIDENTS HAPPEN.
YEAH, THEY SURE DO.
YOU CAN STAY AFTER AND COPY YOUR RESULTS INTO SOMETHING A BIT LESS DAMP.
DON'T WORRY. WE'LL SAVE YOU A SEAT, PARKER.
REMEMBER CINDY
I'M GLAD TO SEE FLASH GETTING SOME HELP FROM YOU, PETER. HE DESERVES A BREAK.
YEAH, A BREAK IN HIS STUPID--WAIT, WHAT?
HOW DO YOU MEAN?
NOT EVERYONE HAS SOMEONE KIND LIKE YOUR AUNT MAY TO LOOK AFTER THEM, MR. PARKER.
WHAT DOES THAT MEAN?
AND HOW DOES THAT EXCUSE FLASH FROM BEING A JERK?
=SIGH= WELL, I GUESS ONCE AGAIN, I'M...

MISSING OUT

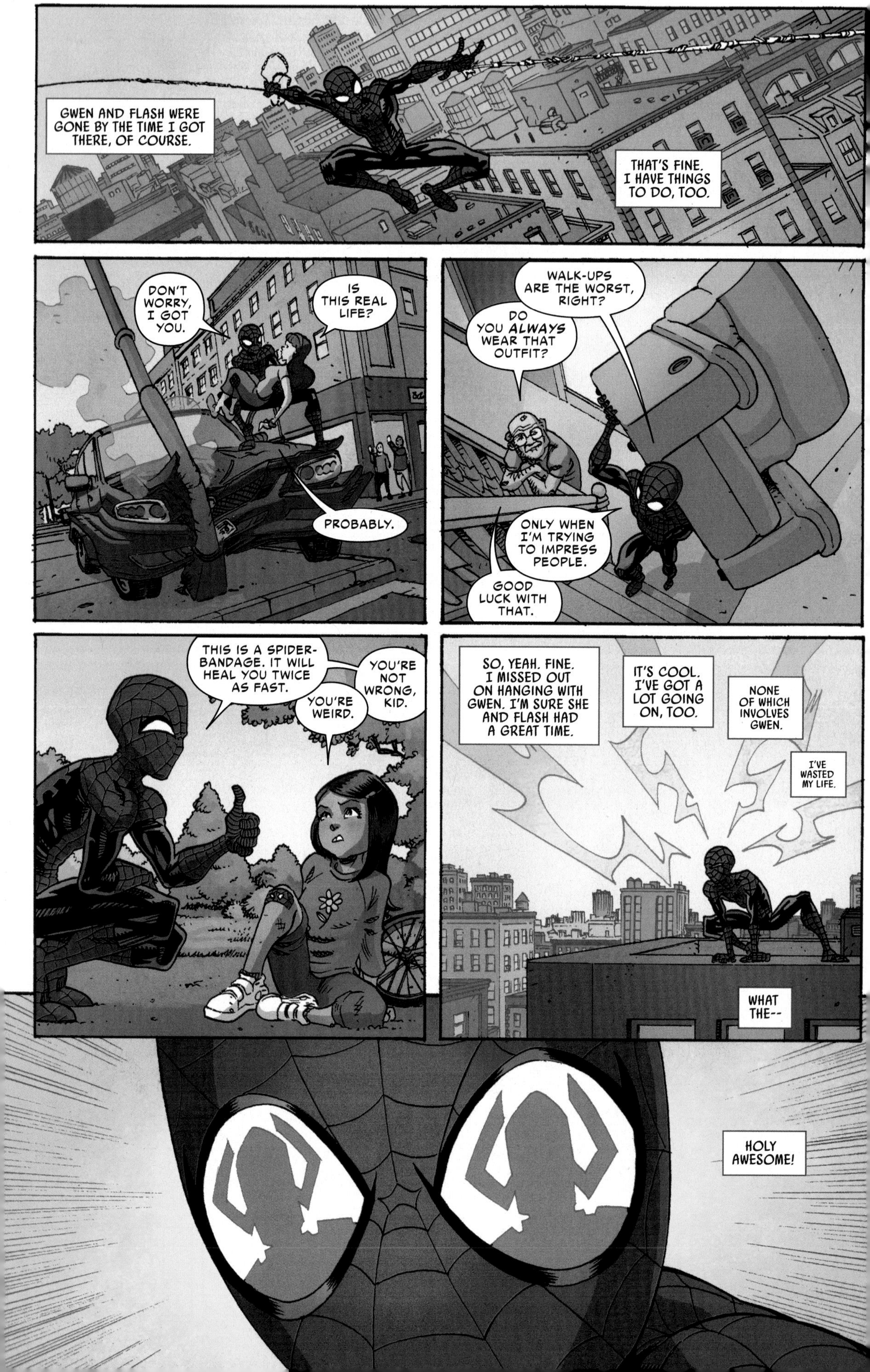
GWEN AND FLASH WERE GONE BY THE TIME I GOT THERE, OF COURSE.
THAT'S FINE. I HAVE THINGS TO DO, TOO.
DON'T WORRY, I GOT YOU.
IS THIS REAL LIFE?
PROBABLY.
WALK-UPS ARE THE WORST, RIGHT?
DO YOU ALWAYS WEAR THAT OUTFIT?
ONLY WHEN I'M TRYING TO IMPRESS PEOPLE.
GOOD LUCK WITH THAT.
THIS IS A SPIDER-BANDAGE. IT WILL HEAL YOU TWICE AS FAST.
YOU'RE WEIRD.
YOU'RE NOT WRONG, KID.
SO, YEAH. FINE. I MISSED OUT ON HANGING WITH GWEN. I'M SURE SHE AND FLASH HAD A GREAT TIME.
IT'S COOL. I'VE GOT A LOT GOING ON, TOO.
NONE OF WHICH INVOLVES GWEN.
I'VE WASTED MY LIFE.
WHAT THE--
HOLY AWESOME!

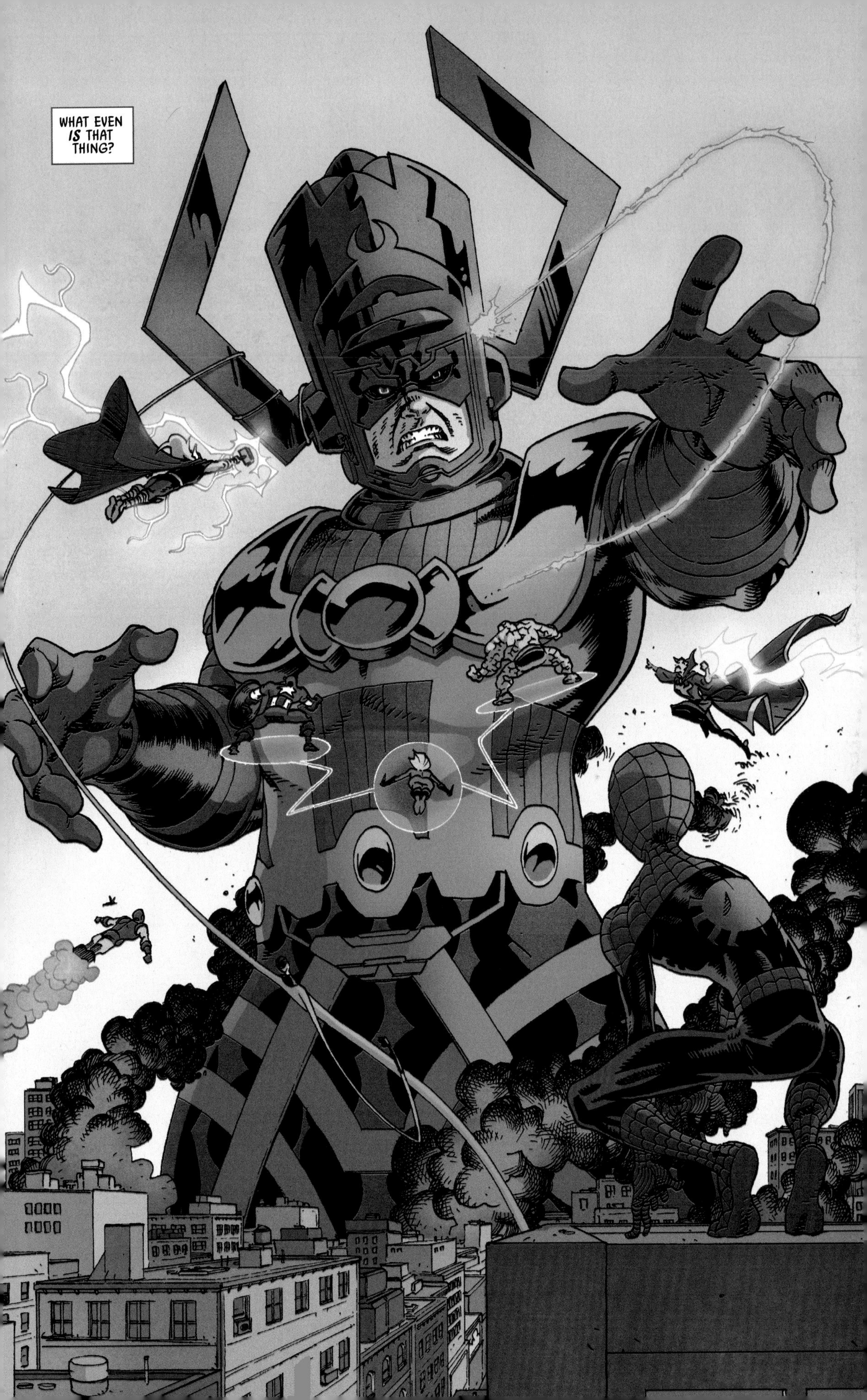
WHAT EVEN IS THAT THING?

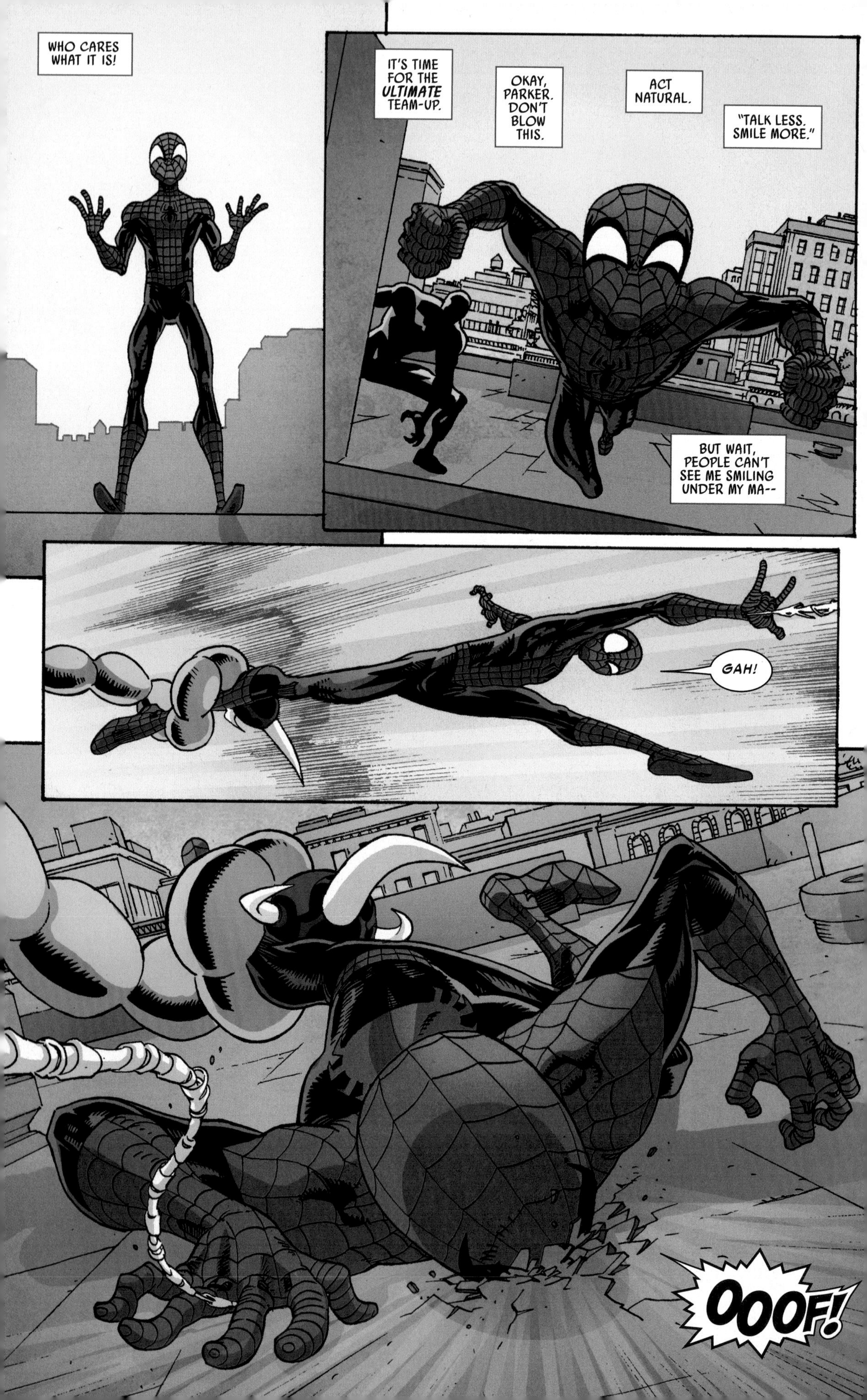

WHO CARES WHAT IT IS!
IT'S TIME FOR THE ULTIMATE TEAM-UP.
OKAY, PARKER. DON'T BLOW THIS.
ACT NATURAL.
"TALK LESS. SMILE MORE."
BUT WAIT, PEOPLE CAN'T SEE ME SMILING UNDER MY MA--
GAH!
OOOF!

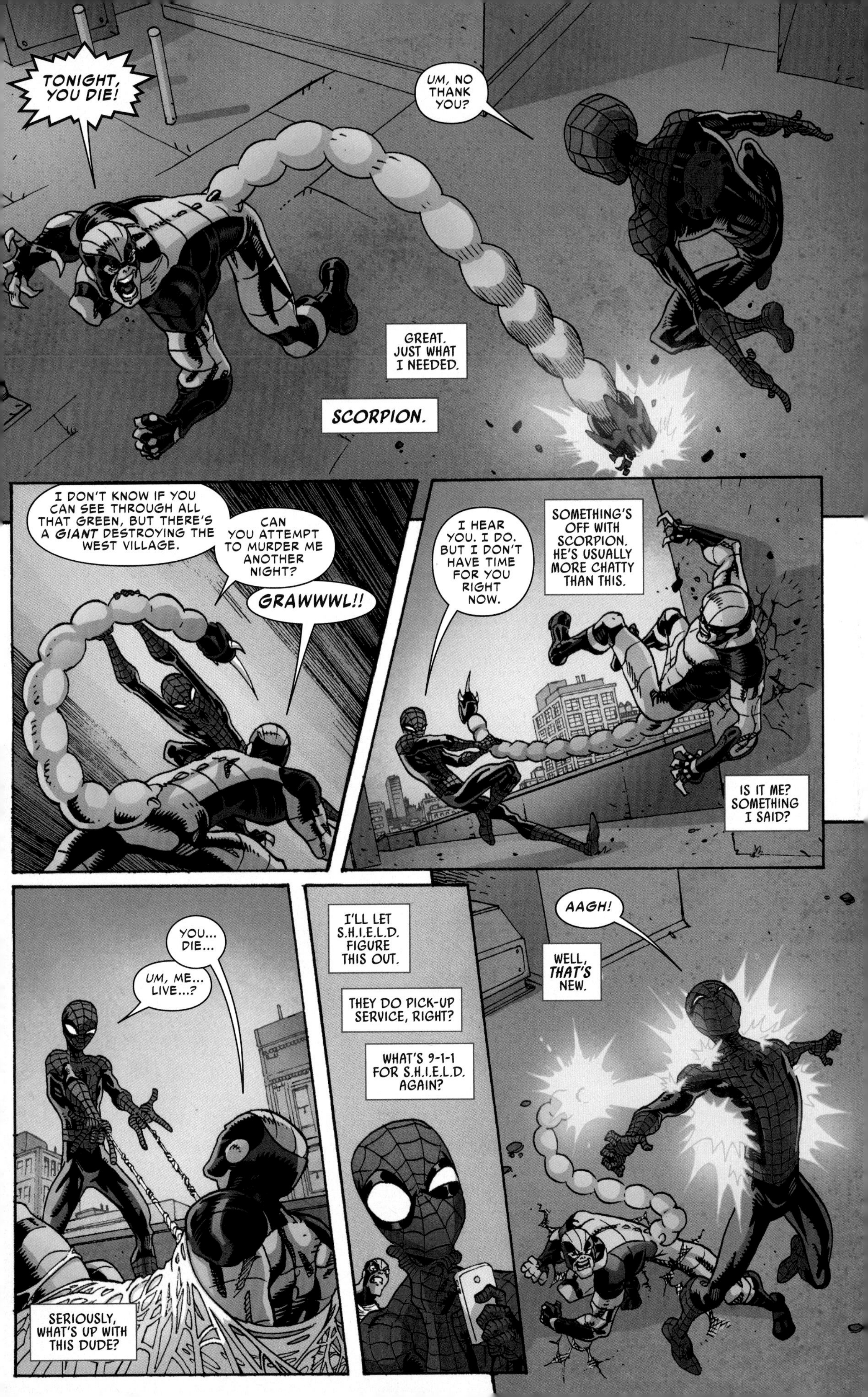
TONIGHT, YOU DIE!
UM, NO THANK YOU?
GREAT. JUST WHAT I NEEDED.
SCORPION.
I DON'T KNOW IF YOU CAN SEE THROUGH ALL THAT GREEN, BUT THERE'S A GIANT DESTROYING THE WEST VILLAGE.
CAN YOU ATTEMPT TO MURDER ME ANOTHER NIGHT?
GRAWWWL!!
I HEAR YOU. I DO. BUT I DON'T HAVE TIME FOR YOU RIGHT NOW.
SOMETHING'S OFF WITH SCORPION. HE'S USUALLY MORE CHATTY THAN THIS.
IS IT ME? SOMETHING I SAID?
YOU... DIE...
UM, ME... LIVE...?
SERIOUSLY, WHAT'S UP WITH THIS DUDE?
I'LL LET S.H.I.E.L.D. FIGURE THIS OUT.
THEY DO PICK-UP SERVICE, RIGHT?
WHAT'S 9-1-1 FOR S.H.I.E.L.D. AGAIN?
AAGH!
WELL, THAT'S NEW.

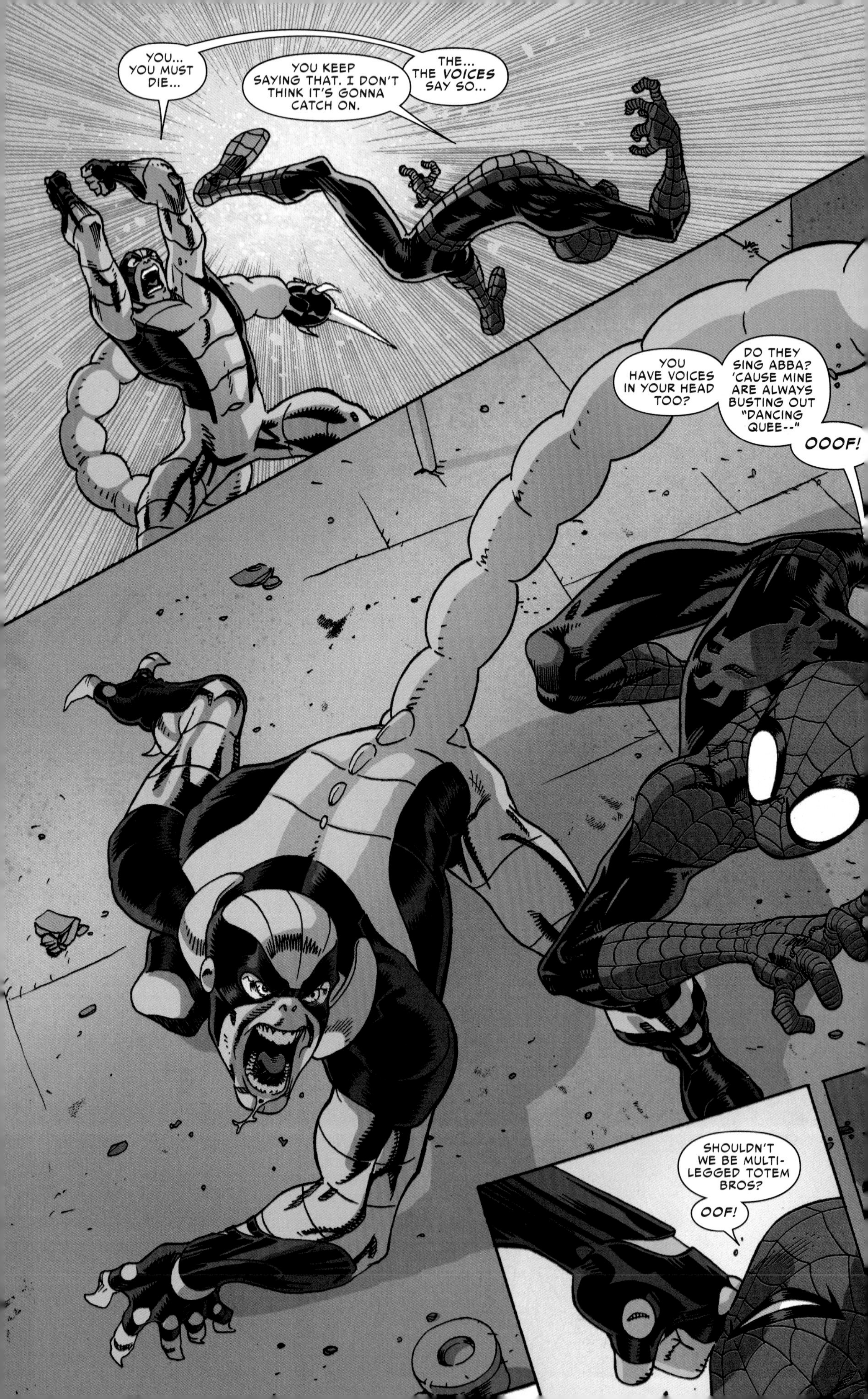
YOU... YOU MUST DIE...
YOU KEEP SAYING THAT. I DON'T THINK IT'S GONNA CATCH ON.
THE... THE *VOICES* SAY SO...
YOU HAVE VOICES IN YOUR HEAD TOO?
DO THEY SING ABBA? 'CAUSE MINE ARE ALWAYS BUSTING OUT "DANCING QUEE--"
OOOF!
SHOULDN'T WE BE MULTI-LEGGED TOTEM BROS?
OOF!

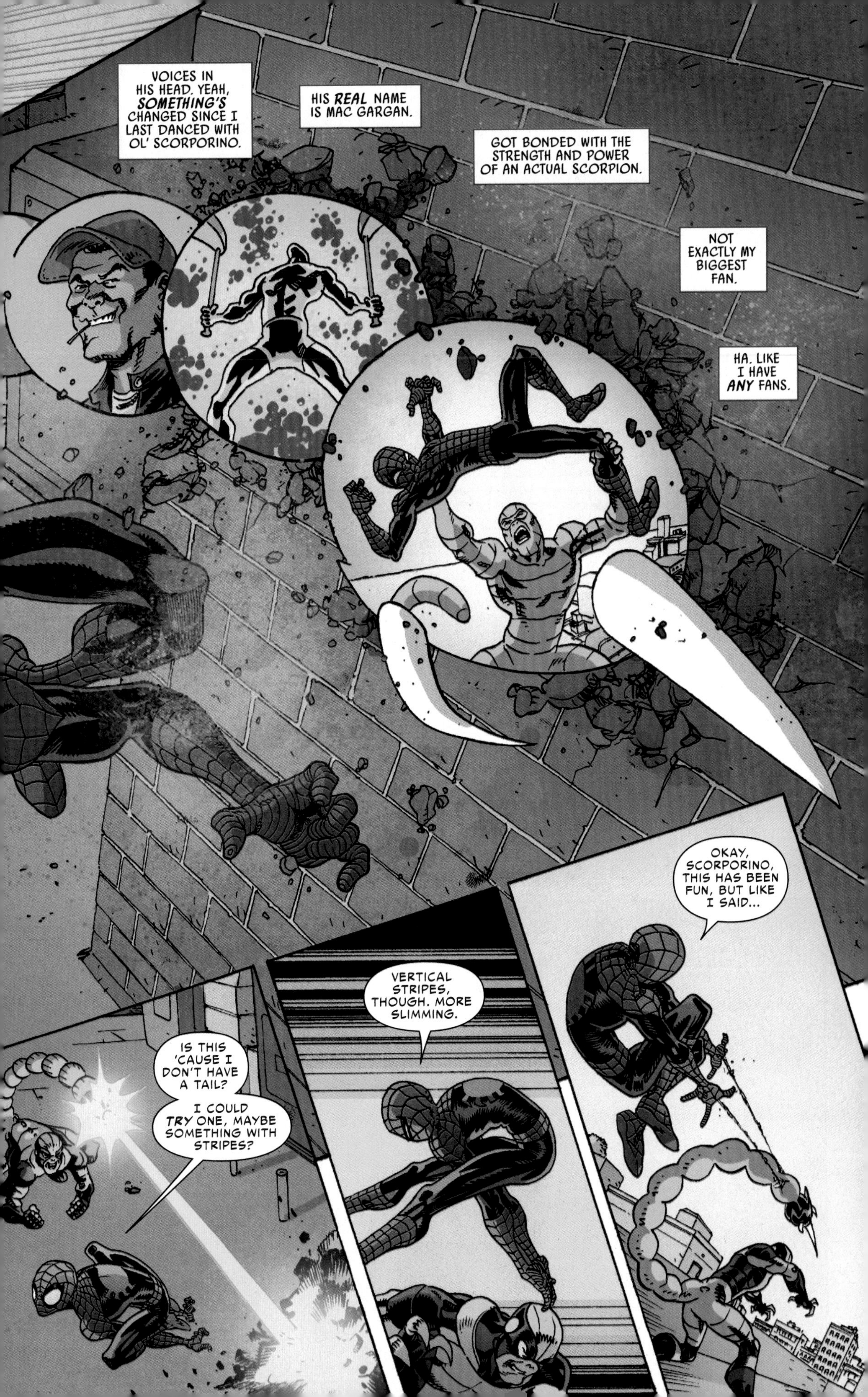
VOICES IN HIS HEAD. YEAH, SOMETHING'S CHANGED SINCE I LAST DANCED WITH OL' SCORPORINO.
HIS REAL NAME IS MAC GARGAN.
GOT BONDED WITH THE STRENGTH AND POWER OF AN ACTUAL SCORPION.
NOT EXACTLY MY BIGGEST FAN.
HA. LIKE I HAVE ANY FANS.
IS THIS 'CAUSE I DON'T HAVE A TAIL?
I COULD TRY ONE, MAYBE SOMETHING WITH STRIPES?
VERTICAL STRIPES, THOUGH. MORE SLIMMING.
OKAY, SCORPORINO, THIS HAS BEEN FUN, BUT LIKE I SAID...

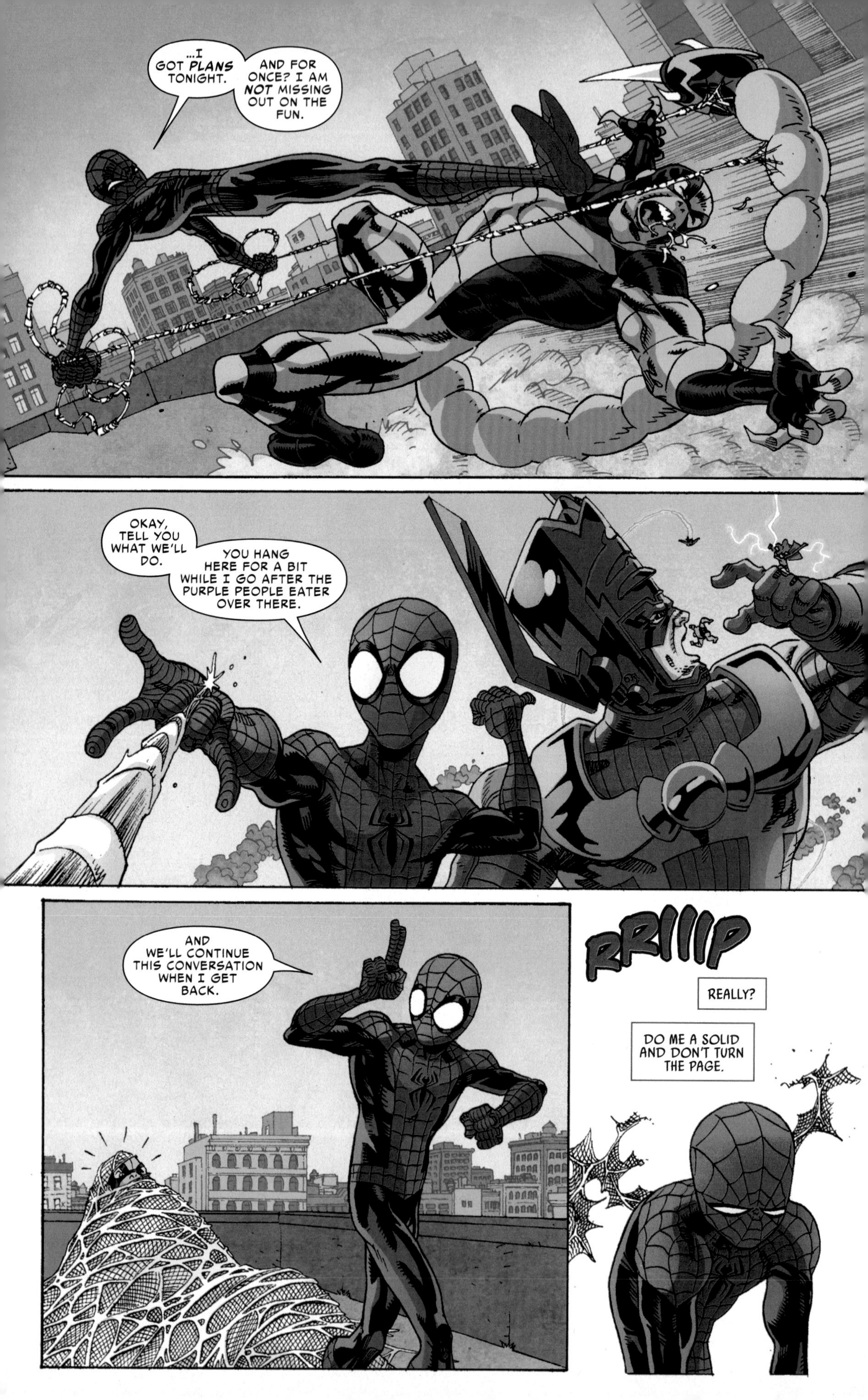
...I GOT PLANS TONIGHT.
AND FOR ONCE? I AM NOT MISSING OUT ON THE FUN.
OKAY, TELL YOU WHAT WE'LL DO.
YOU HANG HERE FOR A BIT WHILE I GO AFTER THE PURPLE PEOPLE EATER OVER THERE.
AND WE'LL CONTINUE THIS CONVERSATION WHEN I GET BACK.
RRIIIP
REALLY?
DO ME A SOLID AND DON'T TURN THE PAGE.

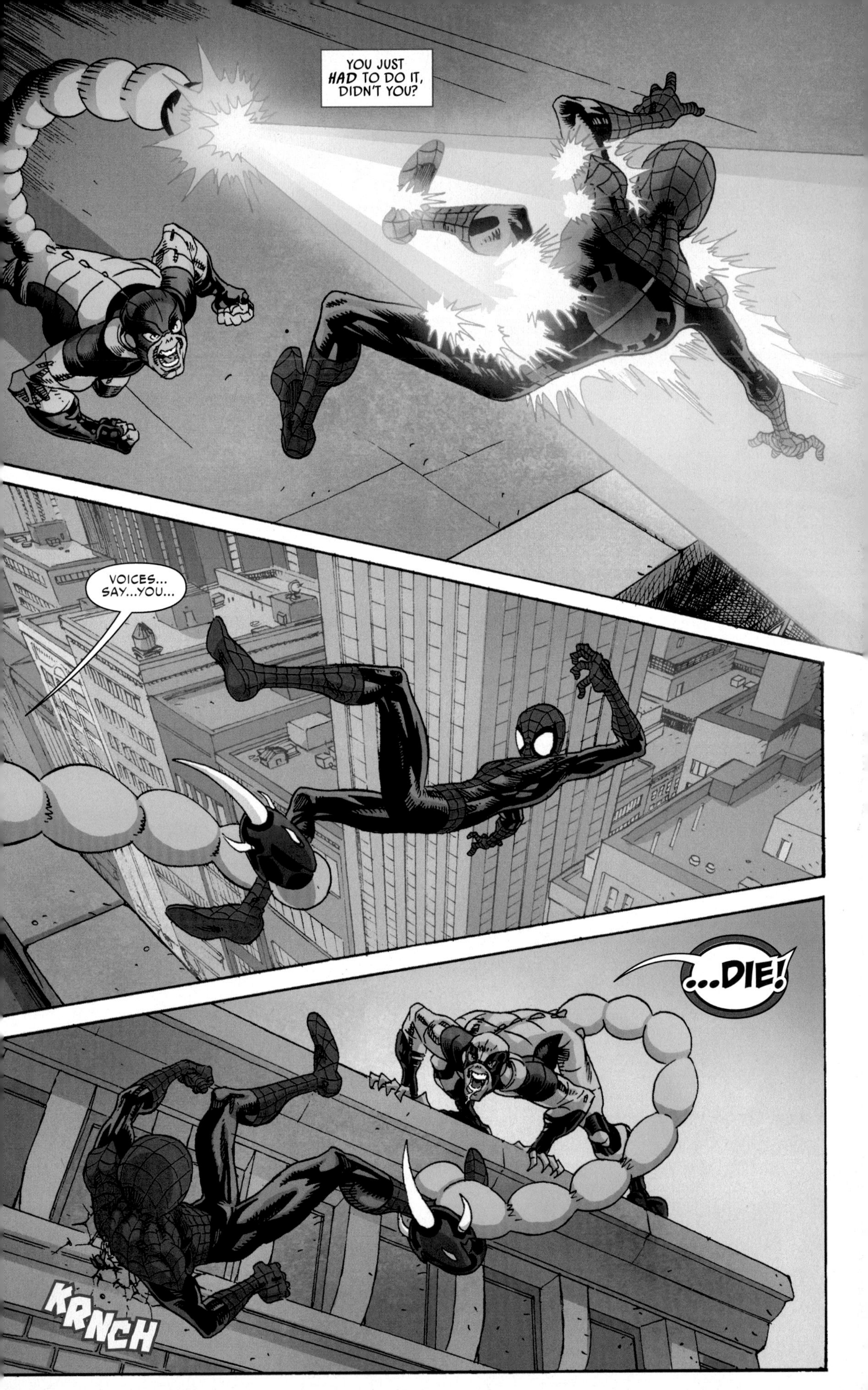

YOU JUST HAD TO DO IT, DIDN'T YOU?
VOICES... SAY...YOU...
...DIE!
KRNCH

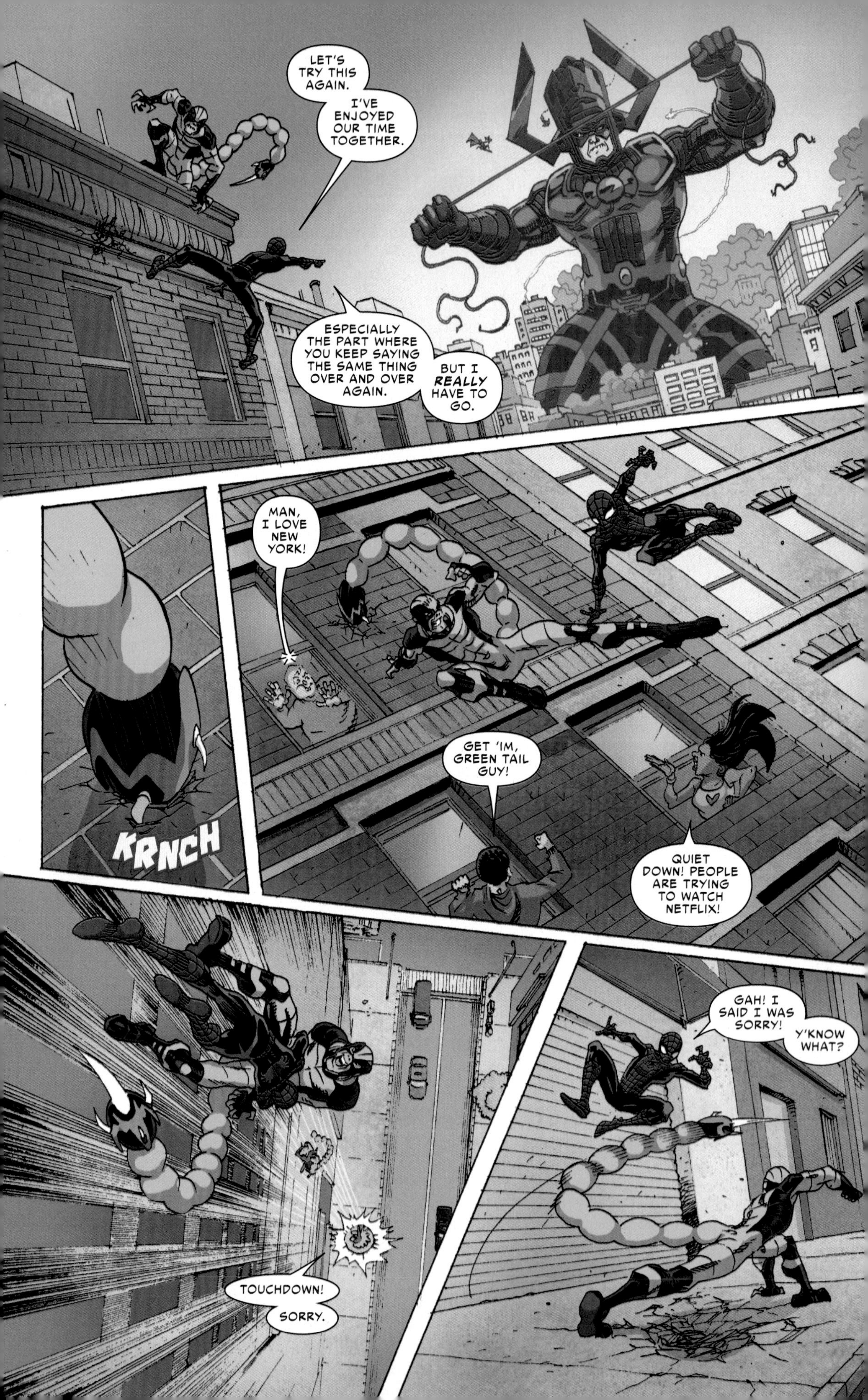
LET'S TRY THIS AGAIN.
I'VE ENJOYED OUR TIME TOGETHER.
ESPECIALLY THE PART WHERE YOU KEEP SAYING THE SAME THING OVER AND OVER AGAIN.
BUT I *REALLY* HAVE TO GO.
KRNCH
MAN, I LOVE NEW YORK!
GET 'IM, GREEN TAIL GUY!
QUIET DOWN! PEOPLE ARE TRYING TO WATCH NETFLIX!
TOUCHDOWN!
SORRY.
GAH! I SAID I WAS SORRY!
Y'KNOW WHAT?

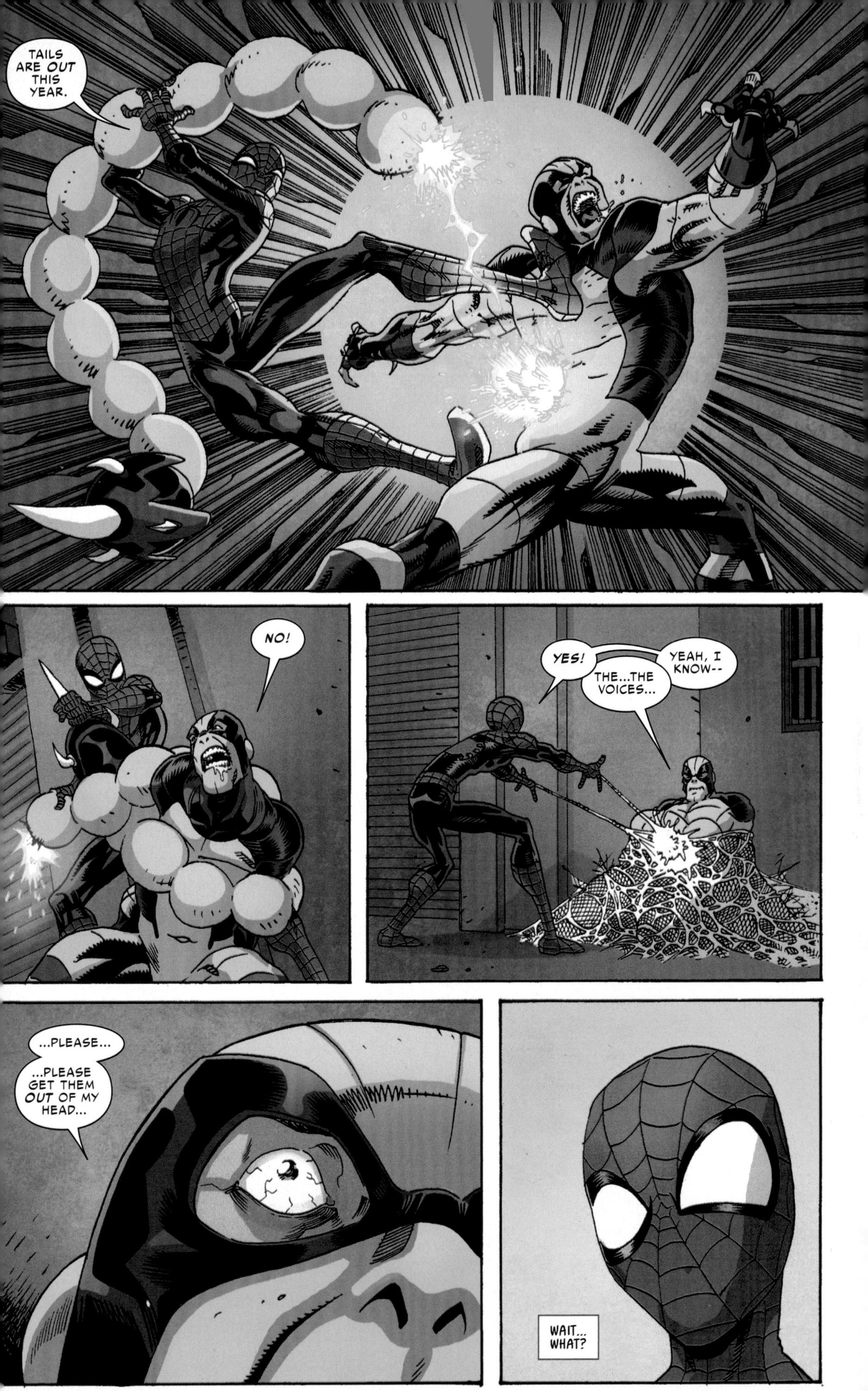
TAILS ARE OUT THIS YEAR.
NO!
YES!
YEAH, I KNOW--
THE...THE VOICES...
...PLEASE...
...PLEASE GET THEM OUT OF MY HEAD...
WAIT... WHAT?

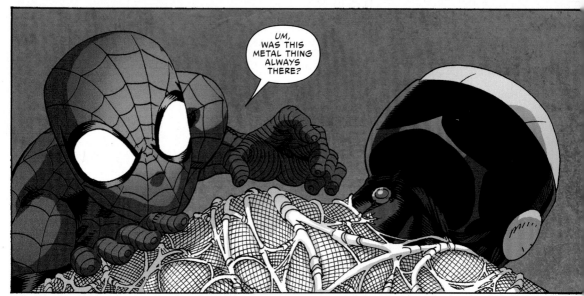

UM, WAS THIS METAL THING ALWAYS THERE?

AAAGH!

THANK... THANK YOU...

WHAT THE--

PERFECT. IT SELF-DESTRUCTED.

NOTHING OMINOUS ABOUT THAT.

NOPE. NOT EVEN A LITTLE BIT.

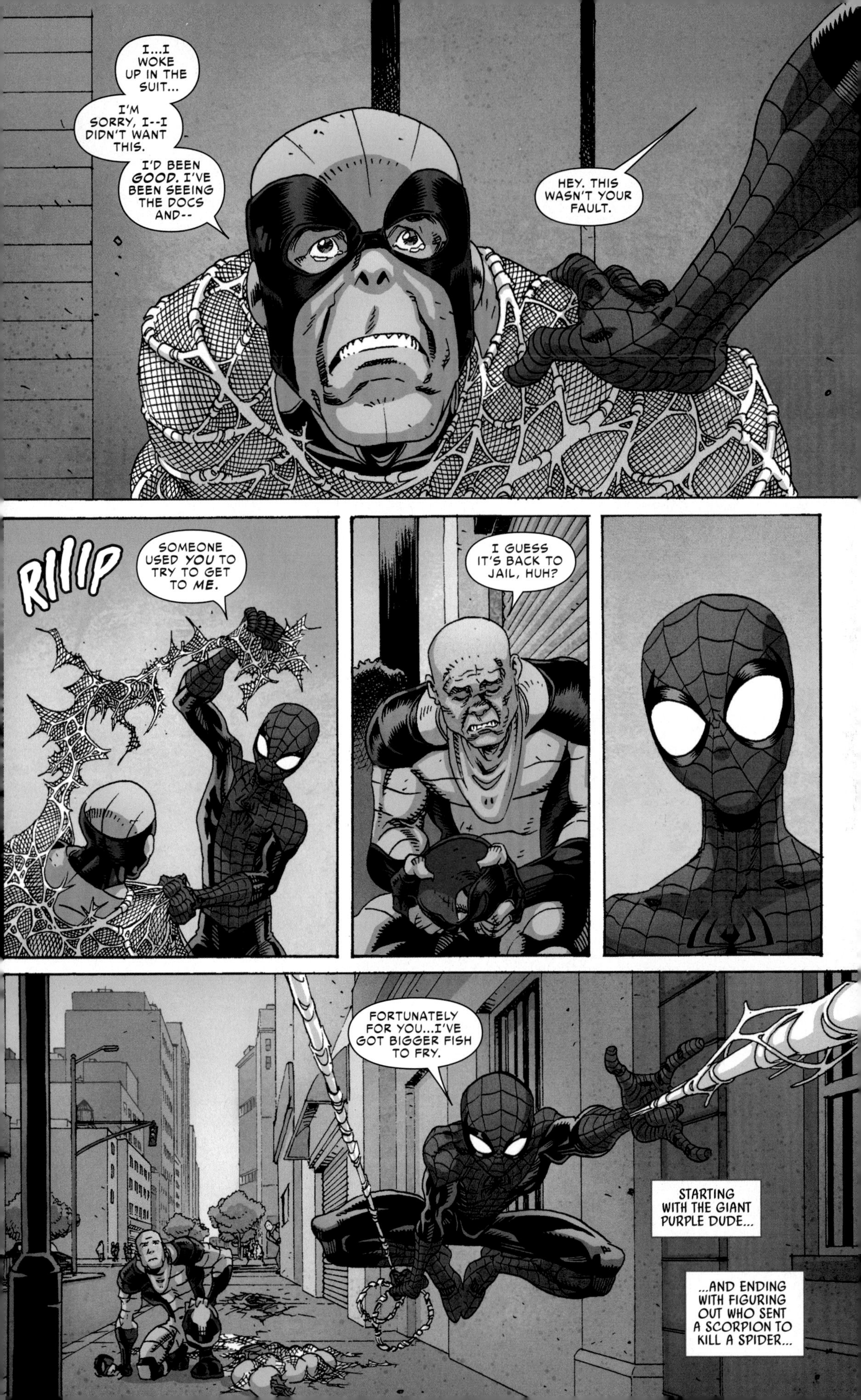
I...I WOKE UP IN THE SUIT...
I'M SORRY, I--I DIDN'T WANT THIS.
I'D BEEN GOOD. I'VE BEEN SEEING THE DOCS AND--
HEY. THIS WASN'T YOUR FAULT.
RIIIP
SOMEONE USED YOU TO TRY TO GET TO ME.
I GUESS IT'S BACK TO JAIL, HUH?
FORTUNATELY FOR YOU...I'VE GOT BIGGER FISH TO FRY.
STARTING WITH THE GIANT PURPLE DUDE...
...AND ENDING WITH FIGURING OUT WHO SENT A SCORPION TO KILL A SPIDER...

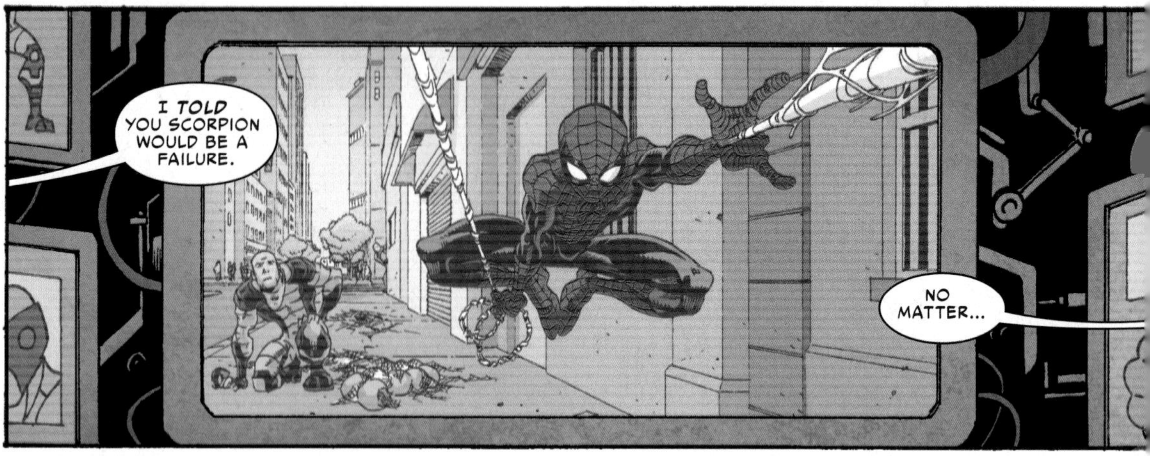
I TOLD YOU SCORPION WOULD BE A FAILURE.
NO MATTER...
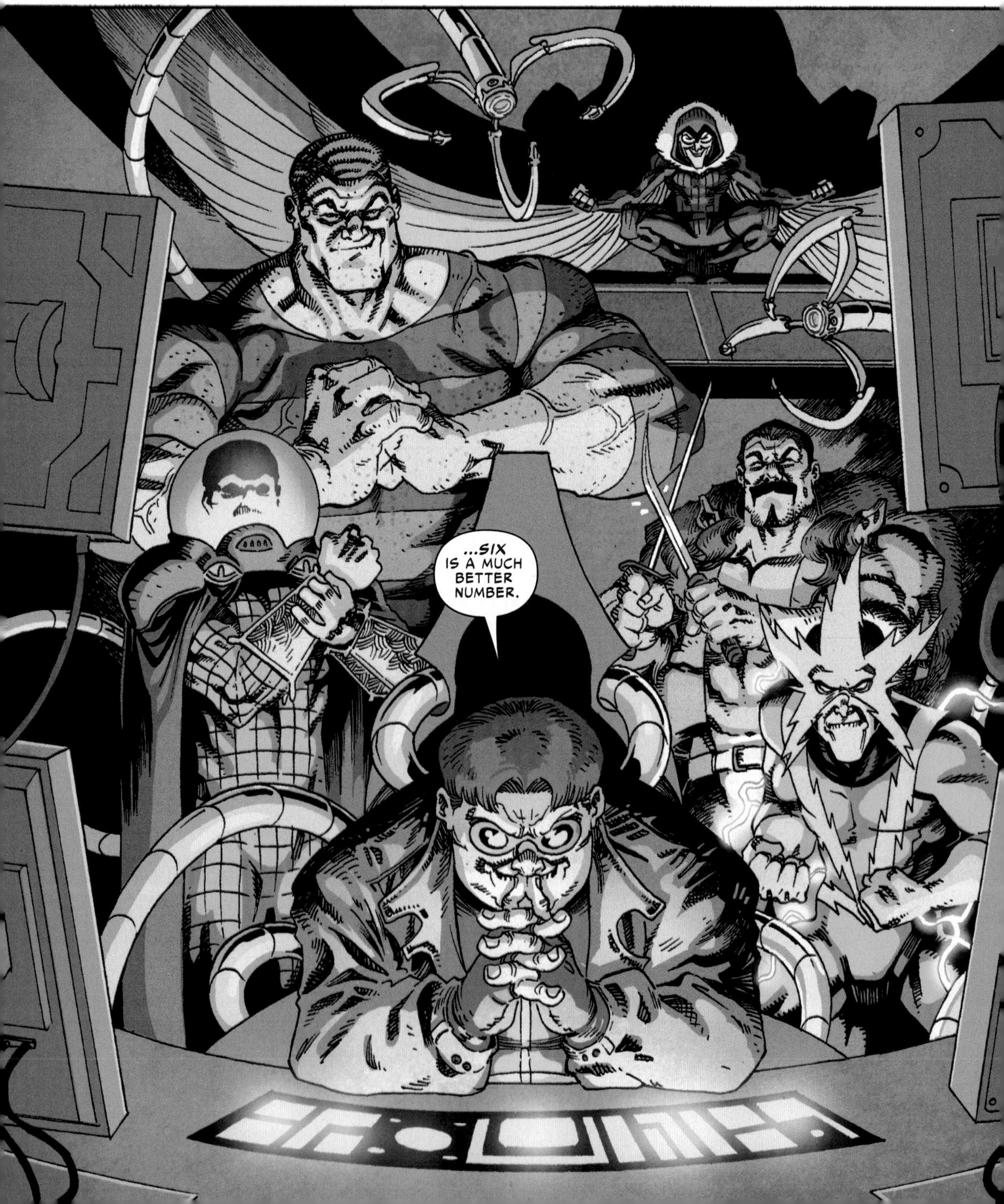
...SIX IS A MUCH BETTER NUMBER.

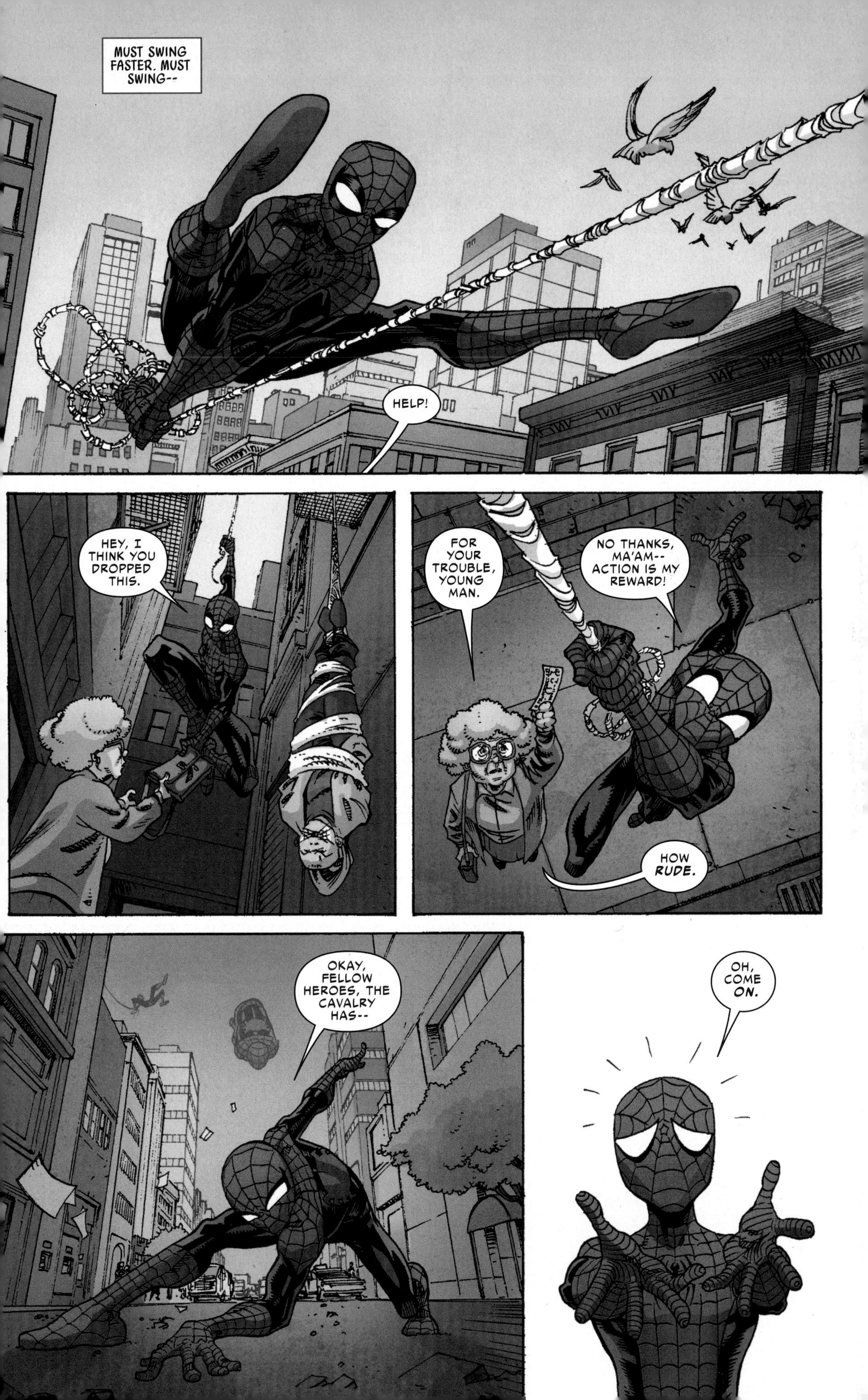
MUST SWING FASTER. MUST SWING--
HELP!
HEY, I THINK YOU DROPPED THIS.
FOR YOUR TROUBLE, YOUNG MAN.
NO THANKS, MA'AM-- ACTION IS MY REWARD!
HOW RUDE.
OKAY, FELLOW HEROES, THE CAVALRY HAS--
OH, COME ON.

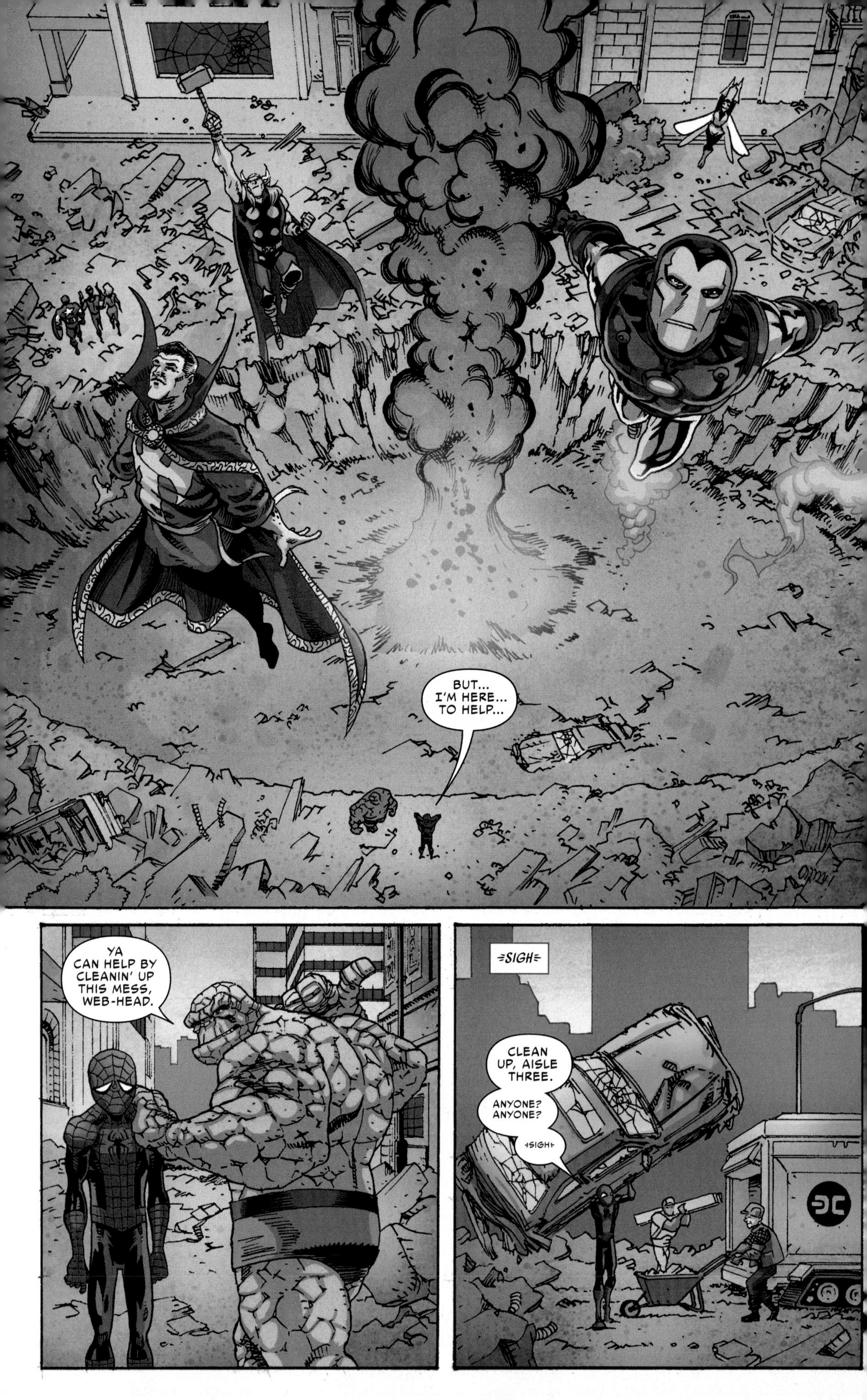
BUT... I'M HERE... TO HELP...
YA CAN HELP BY CLEANIN' UP THIS MESS, WEB-HEAD.
SIGH
CLEAN UP, AISLE THREE.
ANYONE? ANYONE?
SIGH

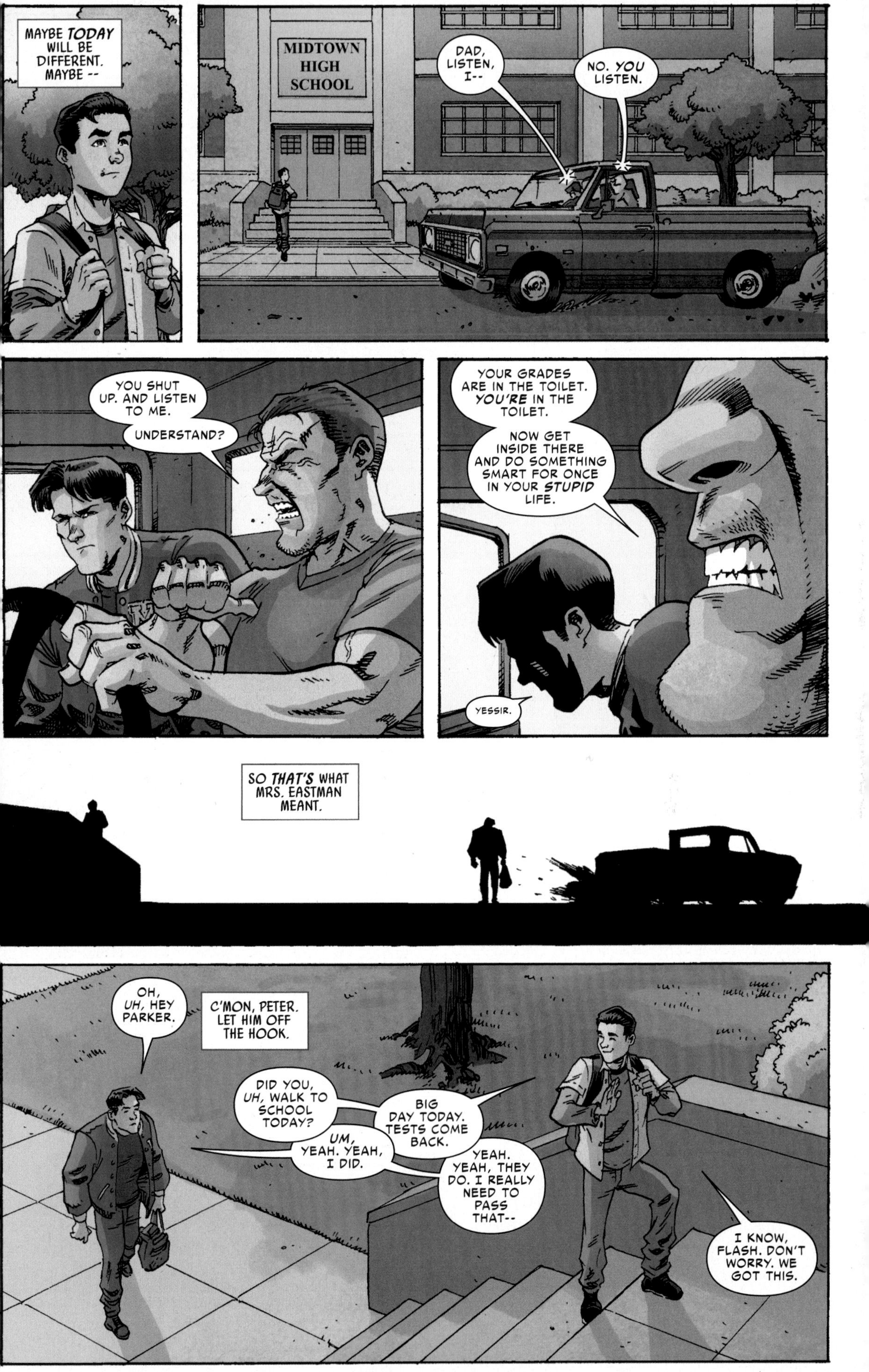
MAYBE TODAY WILL BE DIFFERENT. MAYBE --
MIDTOWN HIGH SCHOOL
DAD, LISTEN, I--
NO. YOU LISTEN.
YOU SHUT UP. AND LISTEN TO ME.
UNDERSTAND?
YOUR GRADES ARE IN THE TOILET. YOU'RE IN THE TOILET.
NOW GET INSIDE THERE AND DO SOMETHING SMART FOR ONCE IN YOUR STUPID LIFE.
YESSIR.
SO THAT'S WHAT MRS. EASTMAN MEANT.
OH, UH, HEY PARKER.
C'MON, PETER. LET HIM OFF THE HOOK.
DID YOU, UH, WALK TO SCHOOL TODAY?
UM, YEAH. YEAH, I DID.
BIG DAY TODAY. TESTS COME BACK.
YEAH. YEAH, THEY DO. I REALLY NEED TO PASS THAT--
I KNOW, FLASH. DON'T WORRY. WE GOT THIS.

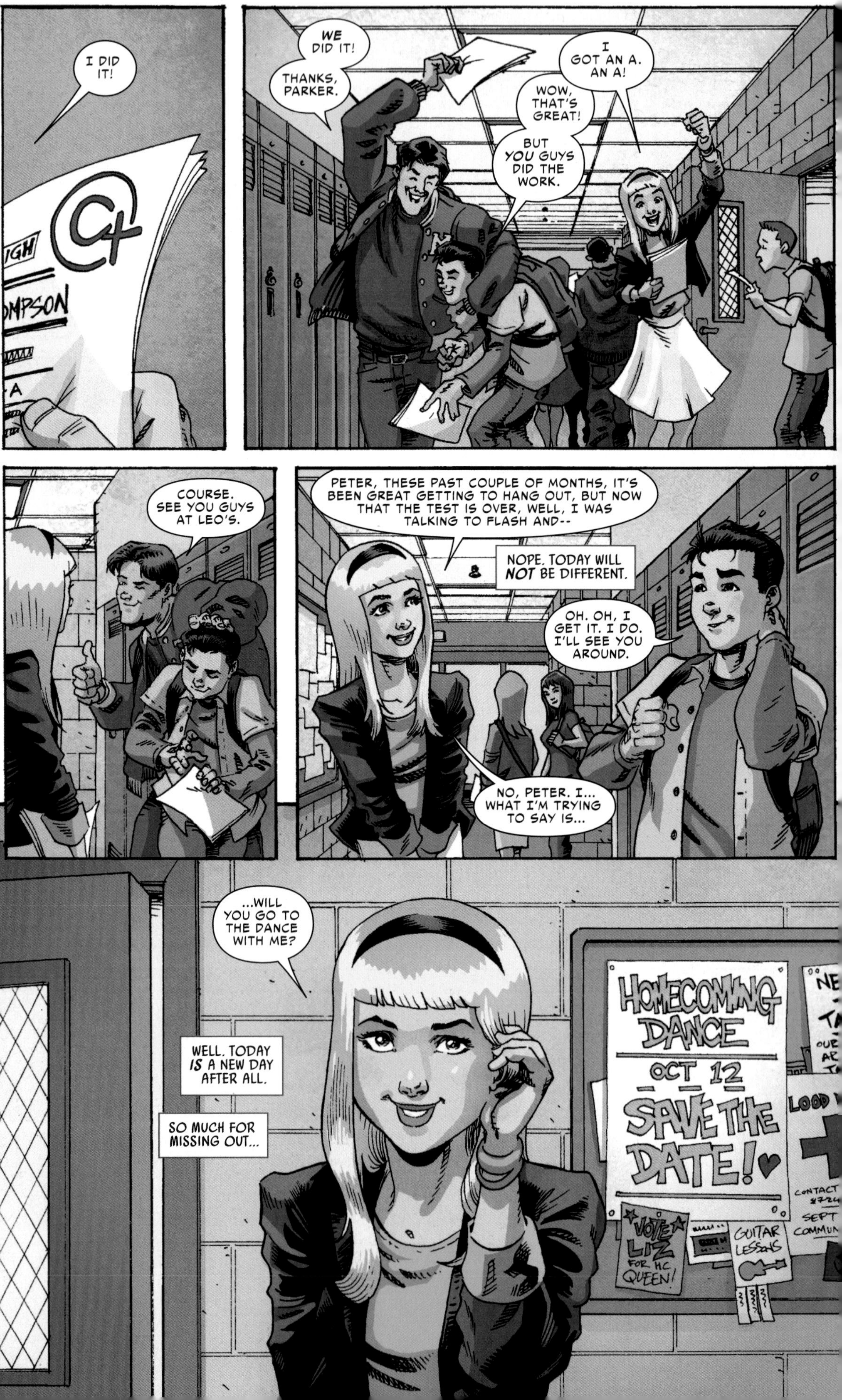
I DID IT!
WE DID IT!
THANKS, PARKER.
I GOT AN A. AN A!
WOW, THAT'S GREAT!
BUT YOU GUYS DID THE WORK.
COURSE. SEE YOU GUYS AT LEO'S.
PETER, THESE PAST COUPLE OF MONTHS, IT'S BEEN GREAT GETTING TO HANG OUT, BUT NOW THAT THE TEST IS OVER, WELL, I WAS TALKING TO FLASH AND--
NOPE. TODAY WILL NOT BE DIFFERENT.
OH. OH, I GET IT. I DO. I'LL SEE YOU AROUND.
NO, PETER. I... WHAT I'M TRYING TO SAY IS...
...WILL YOU GO TO THE DANCE WITH ME?
WELL. TODAY IS A NEW DAY AFTER ALL.
SO MUCH FOR MISSING OUT...
HOMECOMING DANCE
OCT 12
SAVE THE DATE!
VOTE LIZ FOR H.C. QUEEN!
GUITAR LESSONS

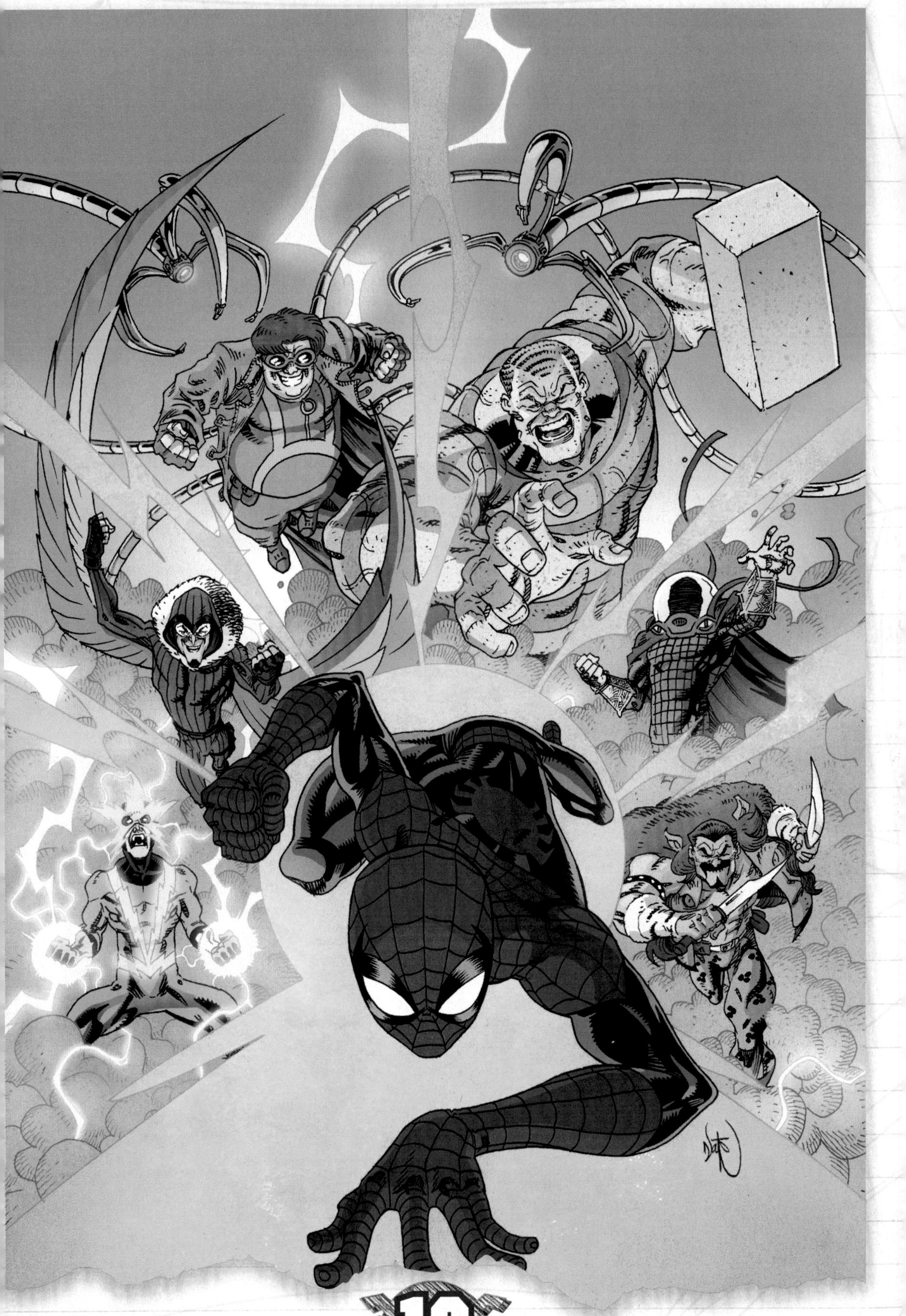

12

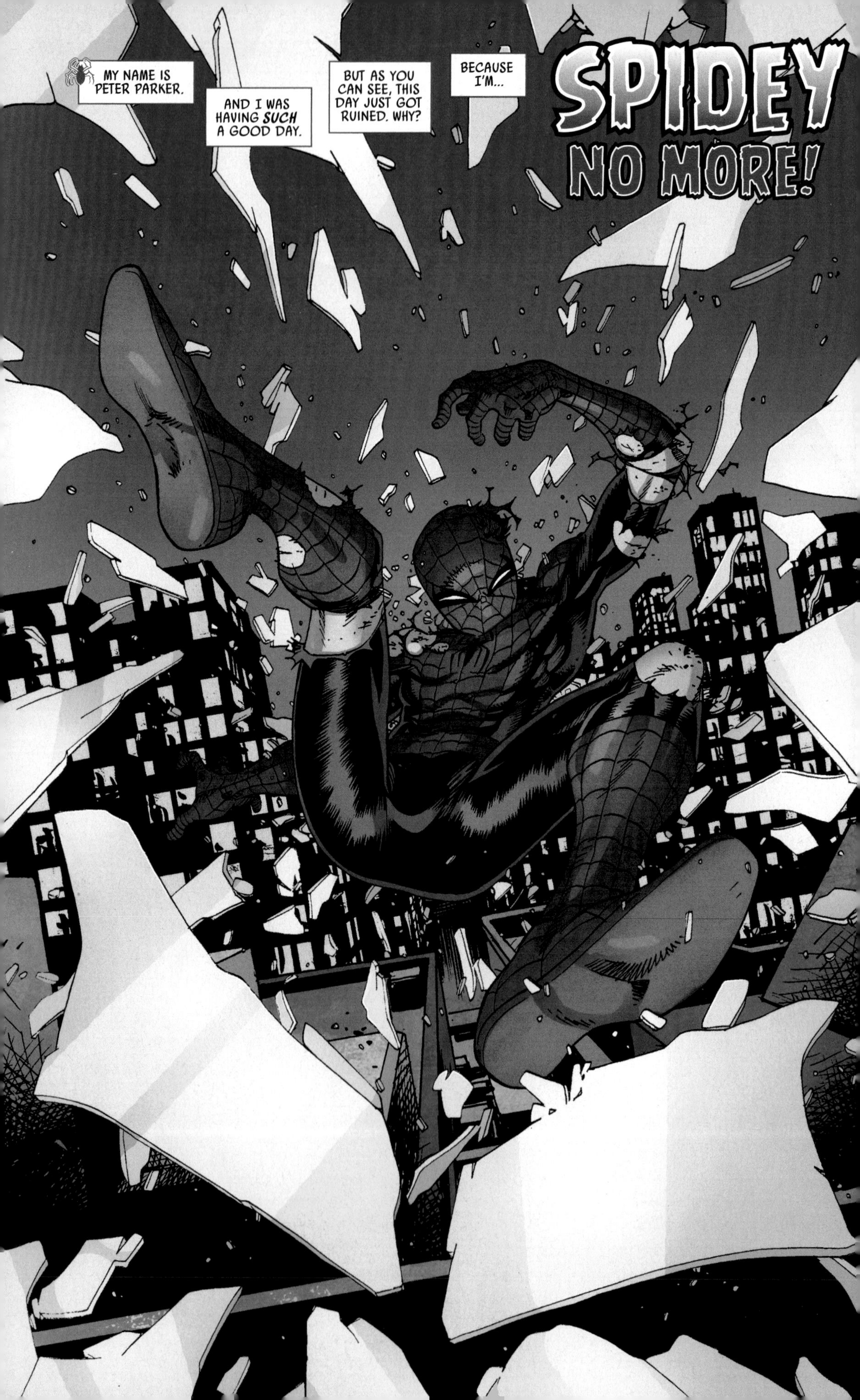
MY NAME IS PETER PARKER.
AND I WAS HAVING SUCH A GOOD DAY.
BUT AS YOU CAN SEE, THIS DAY JUST GOT RUINED. WHY?
BECAUSE I'M...
SPIDEY NO MORE!

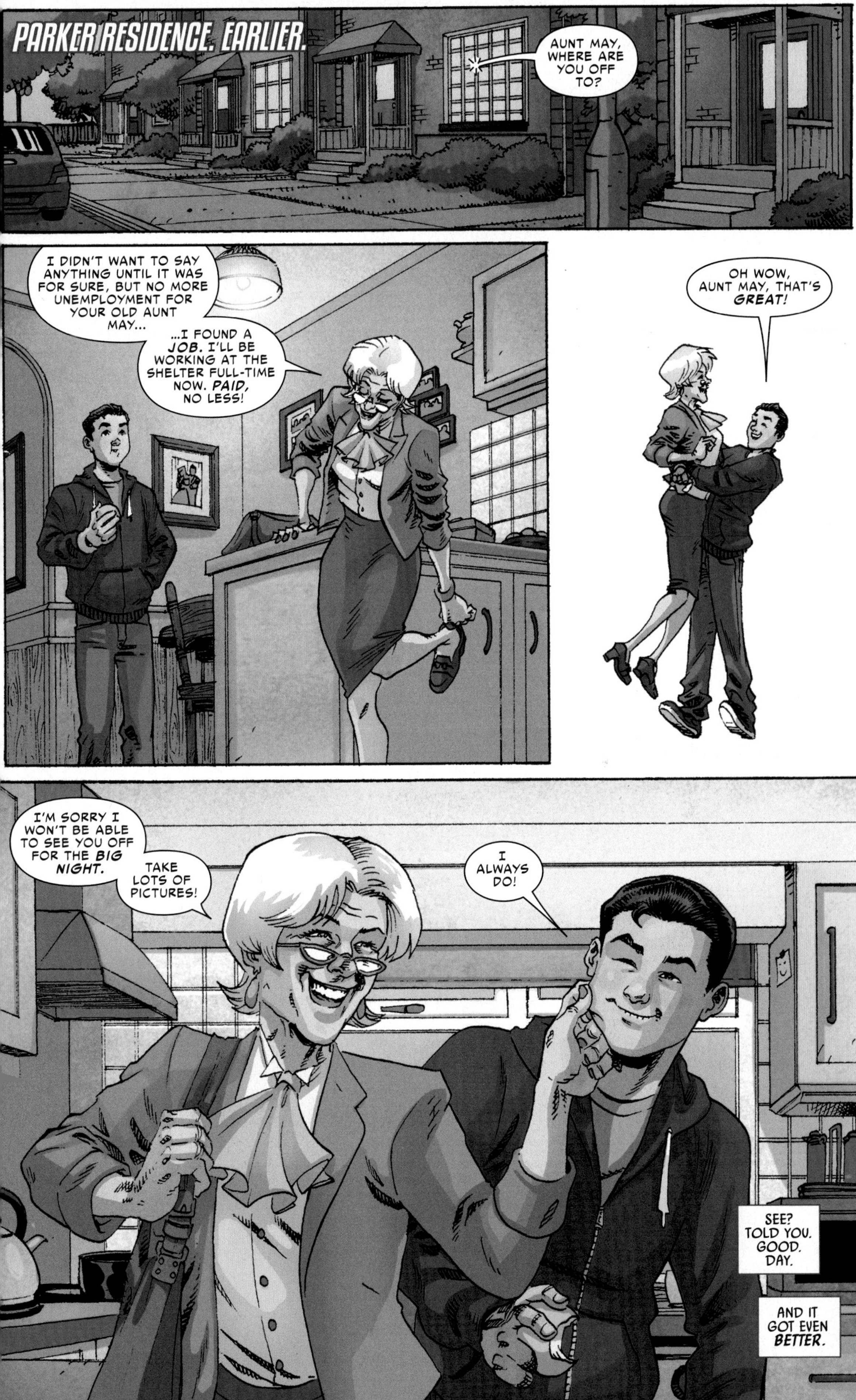
PARKER RESIDENCE. EARLIER.
AUNT MAY, WHERE ARE YOU OFF TO?
I DIDN'T WANT TO SAY ANYTHING UNTIL IT WAS FOR SURE, BUT NO MORE UNEMPLOYMENT FOR YOUR OLD AUNT MAY...
...I FOUND A JOB. I'LL BE WORKING AT THE SHELTER FULL-TIME NOW. PAID, NO LESS!
OH WOW, AUNT MAY, THAT'S GREAT!
I'M SORRY I WON'T BE ABLE TO SEE YOU OFF FOR THE BIG NIGHT.
TAKE LOTS OF PICTURES!
I ALWAYS DO!
SEE? TOLD YOU. GOOD. DAY.
AND IT GOT EVEN BETTER.

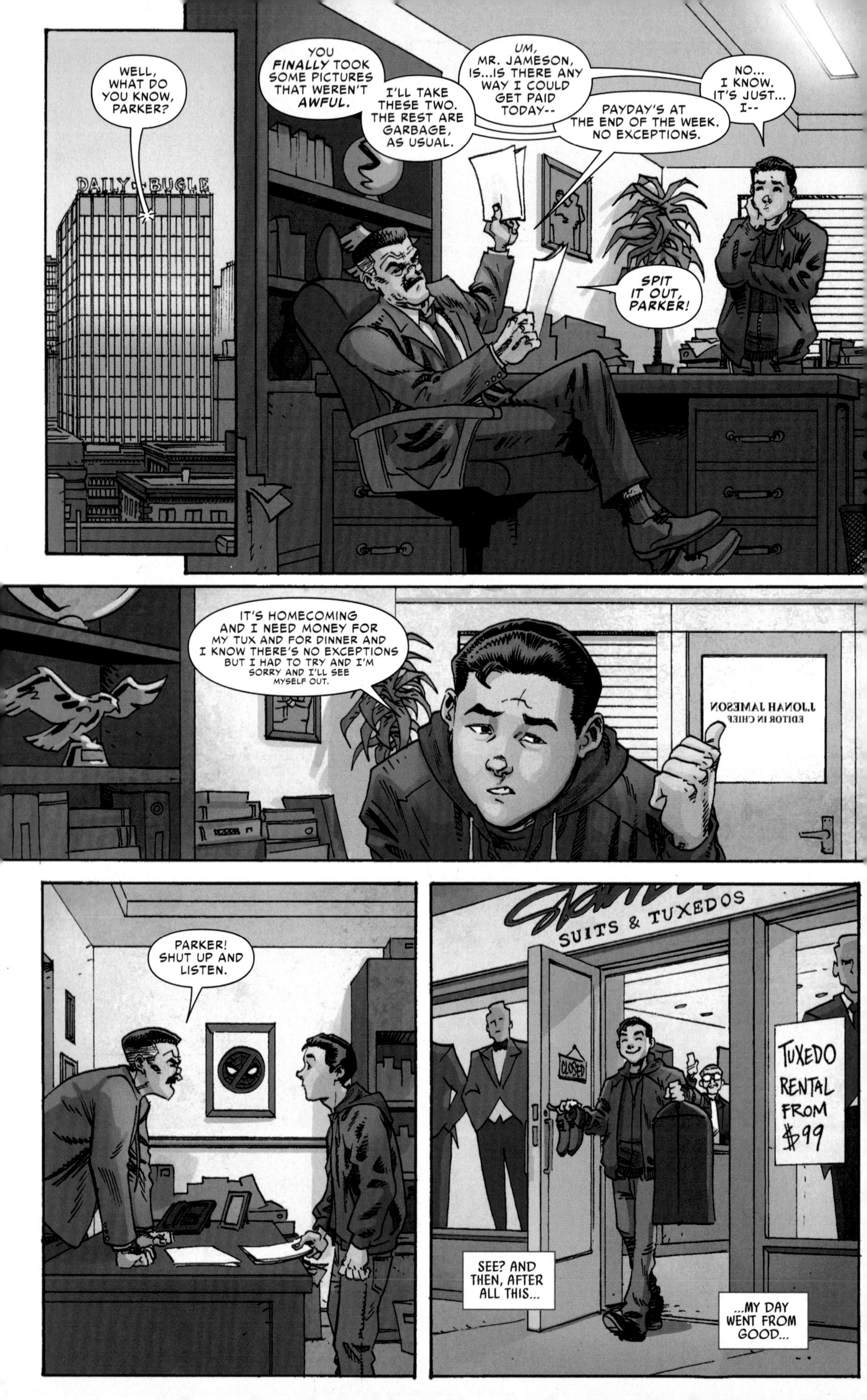
WELL, WHAT DO YOU KNOW, PARKER?
DAILY BUGLE
YOU FINALLY TOOK SOME PICTURES THAT WEREN'T AWFUL.
I'LL TAKE THESE TWO. THE REST ARE GARBAGE, AS USUAL.
UM, MR. JAMESON, IS...IS THERE ANY WAY I COULD GET PAID TODAY--
PAYDAY'S AT THE END OF THE WEEK. NO EXCEPTIONS.
NO... I KNOW. IT'S JUST... I--
SPIT IT OUT, PARKER!
IT'S HOMECOMING AND I NEED MONEY FOR MY TUX AND FOR DINNER AND I KNOW THERE'S NO EXCEPTIONS BUT I HAD TO TRY AND I'M SORRY AND I'LL SEE MYSELF OUT.
J. JONAH JAMESON
EDITOR IN CHIEF
PARKER! SHUT UP AND LISTEN.
SUITS & TUXEDOS
CLOSED
TUXEDO RENTAL FROM $99
SEE? AND THEN, AFTER ALL THIS...
...MY DAY WENT FROM GOOD...

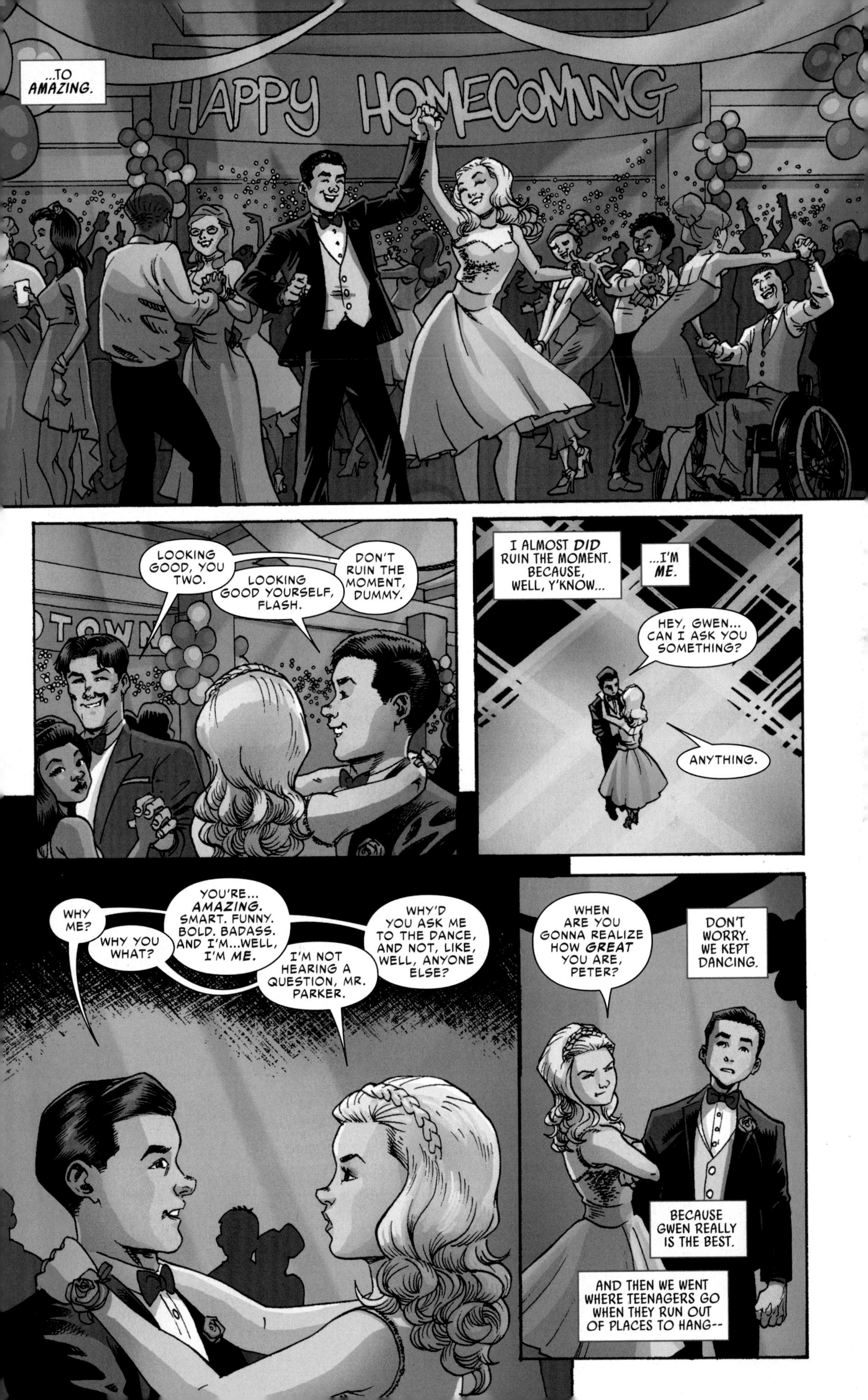
...TO AMAZING.
HAPPY HOMECOMING
LOOKING GOOD, YOU TWO.
DON'T RUIN THE MOMENT, DUMMY.
LOOKING GOOD YOURSELF, FLASH.
I ALMOST DID RUIN THE MOMENT. BECAUSE, WELL, Y'KNOW...
...I'M ME.
HEY, GWEN... CAN I ASK YOU SOMETHING?
ANYTHING.
WHY ME?
WHY YOU WHAT?
YOU'RE... AMAZING. SMART. FUNNY. BOLD. BADASS. AND I'M...WELL, I'M ME.
I'M NOT HEARING A QUESTION, MR. PARKER.
WHY'D YOU ASK ME TO THE DANCE, AND NOT, LIKE, WELL, ANYONE ELSE?
WHEN ARE YOU GONNA REALIZE HOW GREAT YOU ARE, PETER?
DON'T WORRY. WE KEPT DANCING.
BECAUSE GWEN REALLY IS THE BEST.
AND THEN WE WENT WHERE TEENAGERS GO WHEN THEY RUN OUT OF PLACES TO HANG--

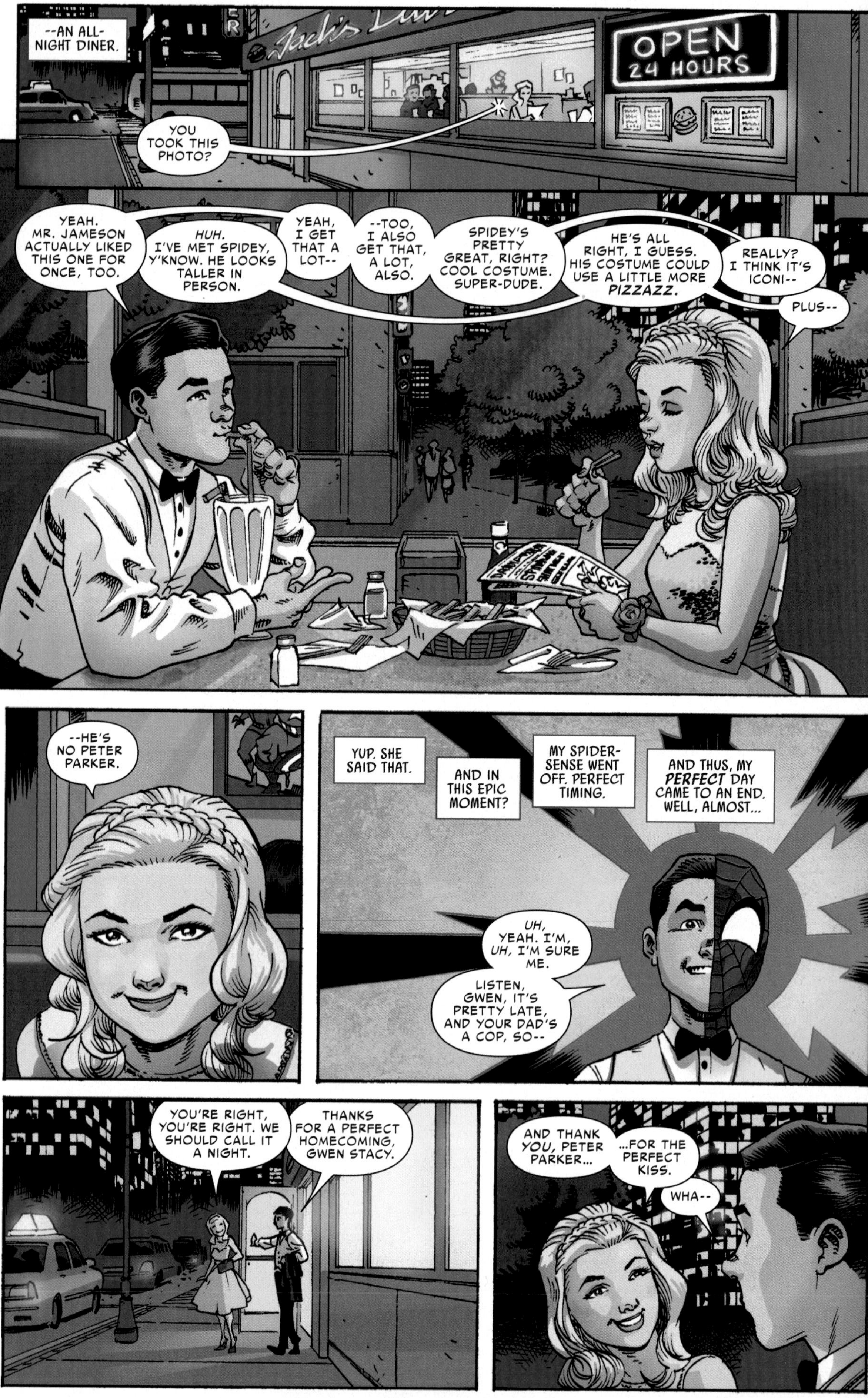
--AN ALL-NIGHT DINER.
Jack's Diner
OPEN 24 HOURS
YOU TOOK THIS PHOTO?
YEAH. MR. JAMESON ACTUALLY LIKED THIS ONE FOR ONCE, TOO.
HUH. I'VE MET SPIDEY, Y'KNOW. HE LOOKS TALLER IN PERSON.
YEAH, I GET THAT A LOT--
--TOO, I ALSO GET THAT, A LOT, ALSO.
SPIDEY'S PRETTY GREAT, RIGHT? COOL COSTUME. SUPER-DUDE.
HE'S ALL RIGHT, I GUESS. HIS COSTUME COULD USE A LITTLE MORE PIZZAZZ.
REALLY? I THINK IT'S ICONI--
PLUS--
--HE'S NO PETER PARKER.
YUP. SHE SAID THAT.
AND IN THIS EPIC MOMENT?
MY SPIDER-SENSE WENT OFF. PERFECT TIMING.
AND THUS, MY PERFECT DAY CAME TO AN END. WELL, ALMOST...
UH, YEAH. I'M, UH, I'M SURE ME.
LISTEN, GWEN, IT'S PRETTY LATE, AND YOUR DAD'S A COP, SO--
YOU'RE RIGHT, YOU'RE RIGHT. WE SHOULD CALL IT A NIGHT.
THANKS FOR A PERFECT HOMECOMING, GWEN STACY.
AND THANK YOU, PETER PARKER...
...FOR THE PERFECT KISS.
WHA--

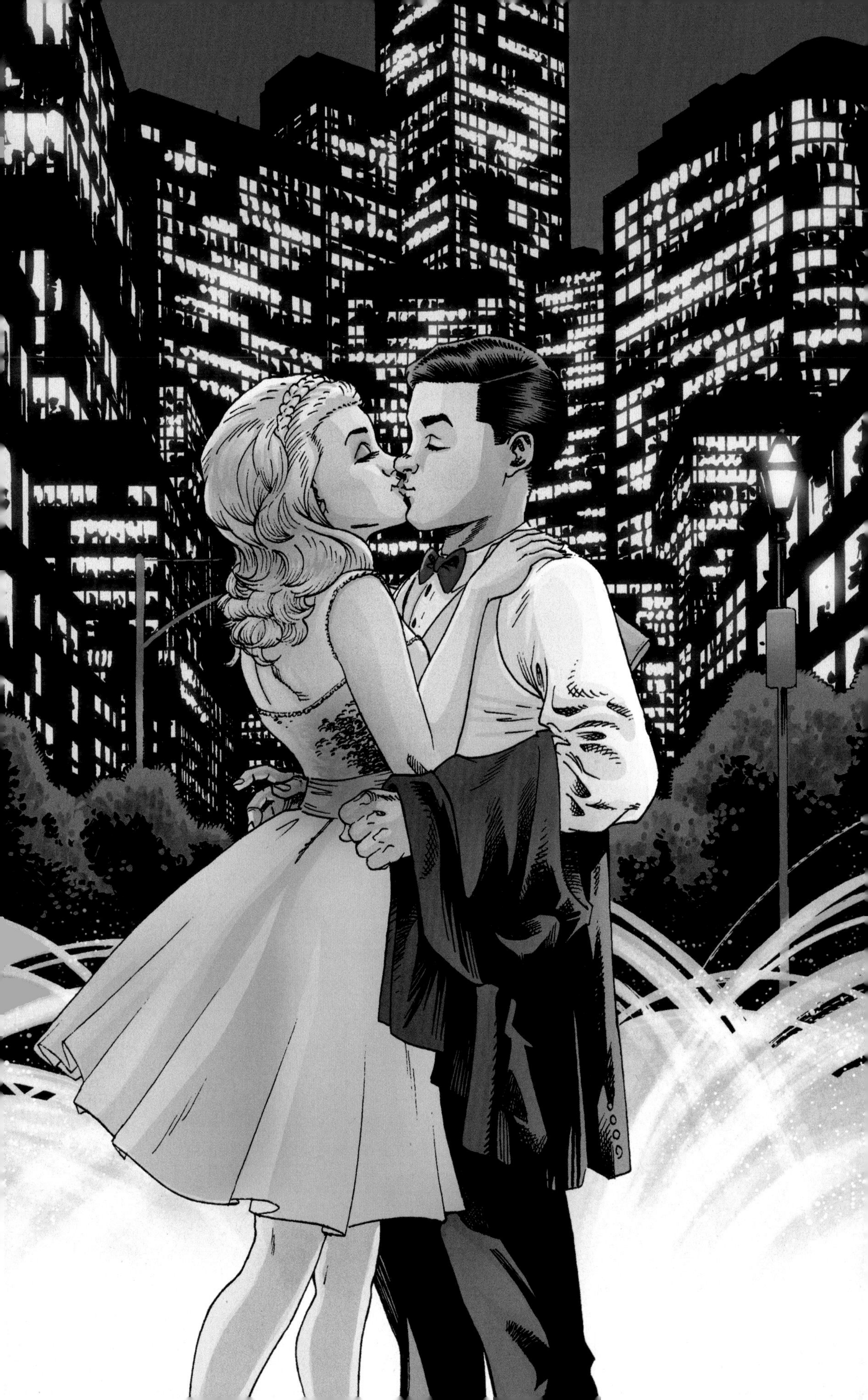

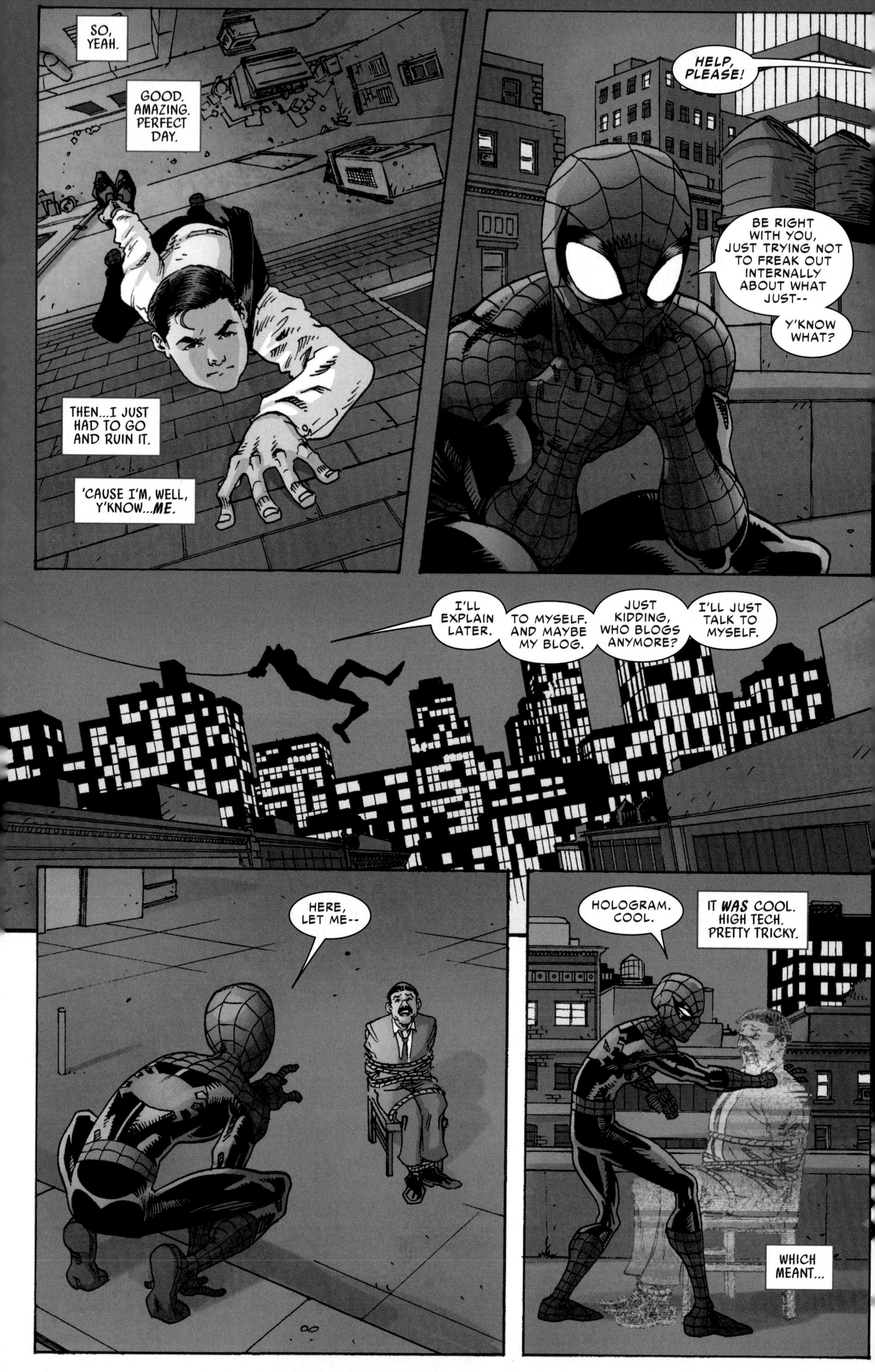
SO, YEAH.
GOOD. AMAZING. PERFECT DAY.
THEN...I JUST HAD TO GO AND RUIN IT.
'CAUSE I'M, WELL, Y'KNOW...*ME.*
HELP, PLEASE!
BE RIGHT WITH YOU, JUST TRYING NOT TO FREAK OUT INTERNALLY ABOUT WHAT JUST--
Y'KNOW WHAT?
I'LL EXPLAIN LATER.
TO MYSELF. AND MAYBE MY BLOG.
JUST KIDDING, WHO BLOGS ANYMORE?
I'LL JUST TALK TO MYSELF.
HERE, LET ME--
HOLOGRAM. COOL.
IT *WAS* COOL. HIGH TECH. PRETTY TRICKY.
WHICH MEANT...

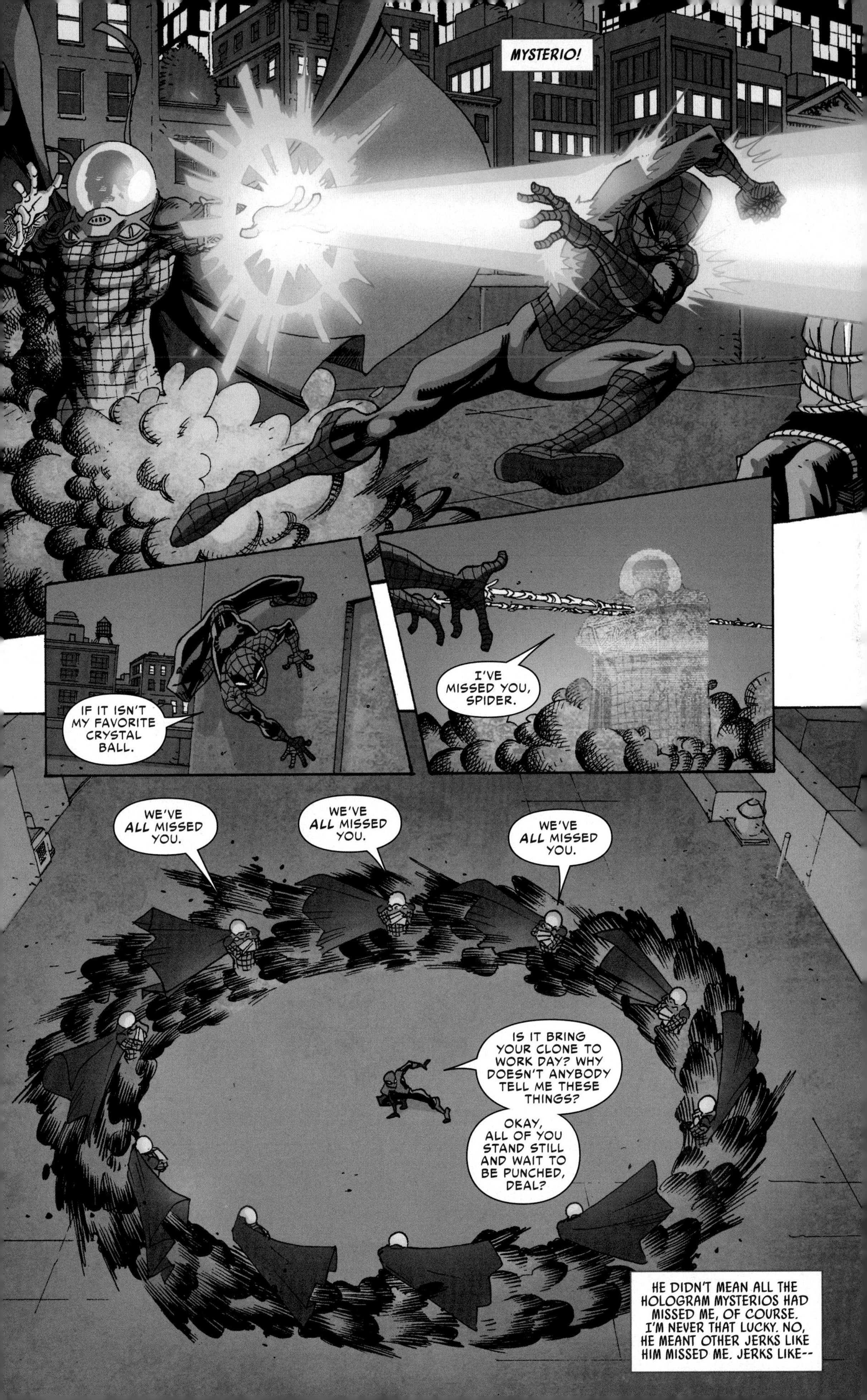
MYSTERIO!
IF IT ISN'T MY FAVORITE CRYSTAL BALL.
I'VE MISSED YOU, SPIDER.
WE'VE ALL MISSED YOU.
WE'VE ALL MISSED YOU.
WE'VE ALL MISSED YOU.
IS IT BRING YOUR CLONE TO WORK DAY? WHY DOESN'T ANYBODY TELL ME THESE THINGS?
OKAY, ALL OF YOU STAND STILL AND WAIT TO BE PUNCHED, DEAL?
HE DIDN'T MEAN ALL THE HOLOGRAM MYSTERIOS HAD MISSED ME, OF COURSE. I'M NEVER THAT LUCKY. NO, HE MEANT OTHER JERKS LIKE HIM MISSED ME. JERKS LIKE--

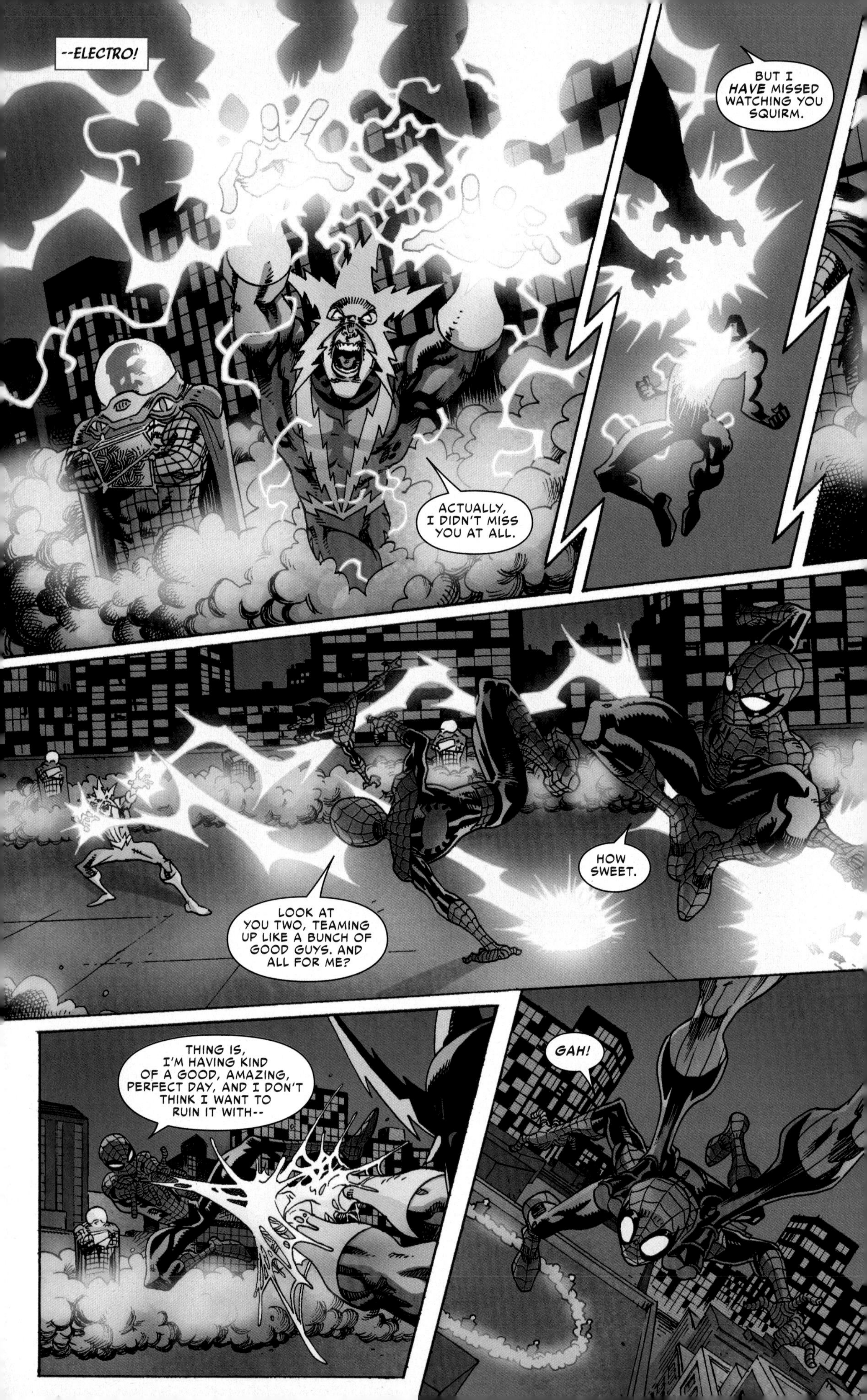
--ELECTRO!
ACTUALLY, I DIDN'T MISS YOU AT ALL.
BUT I HAVE MISSED WATCHING YOU SQUIRM.
LOOK AT YOU TWO, TEAMING UP LIKE A BUNCH OF GOOD GUYS. AND ALL FOR ME?
HOW SWEET.
THING IS, I'M HAVING KIND OF A GOOD, AMAZING, PERFECT DAY, AND I DON'T THINK I WANT TO RUIN IT WITH--
GAH!

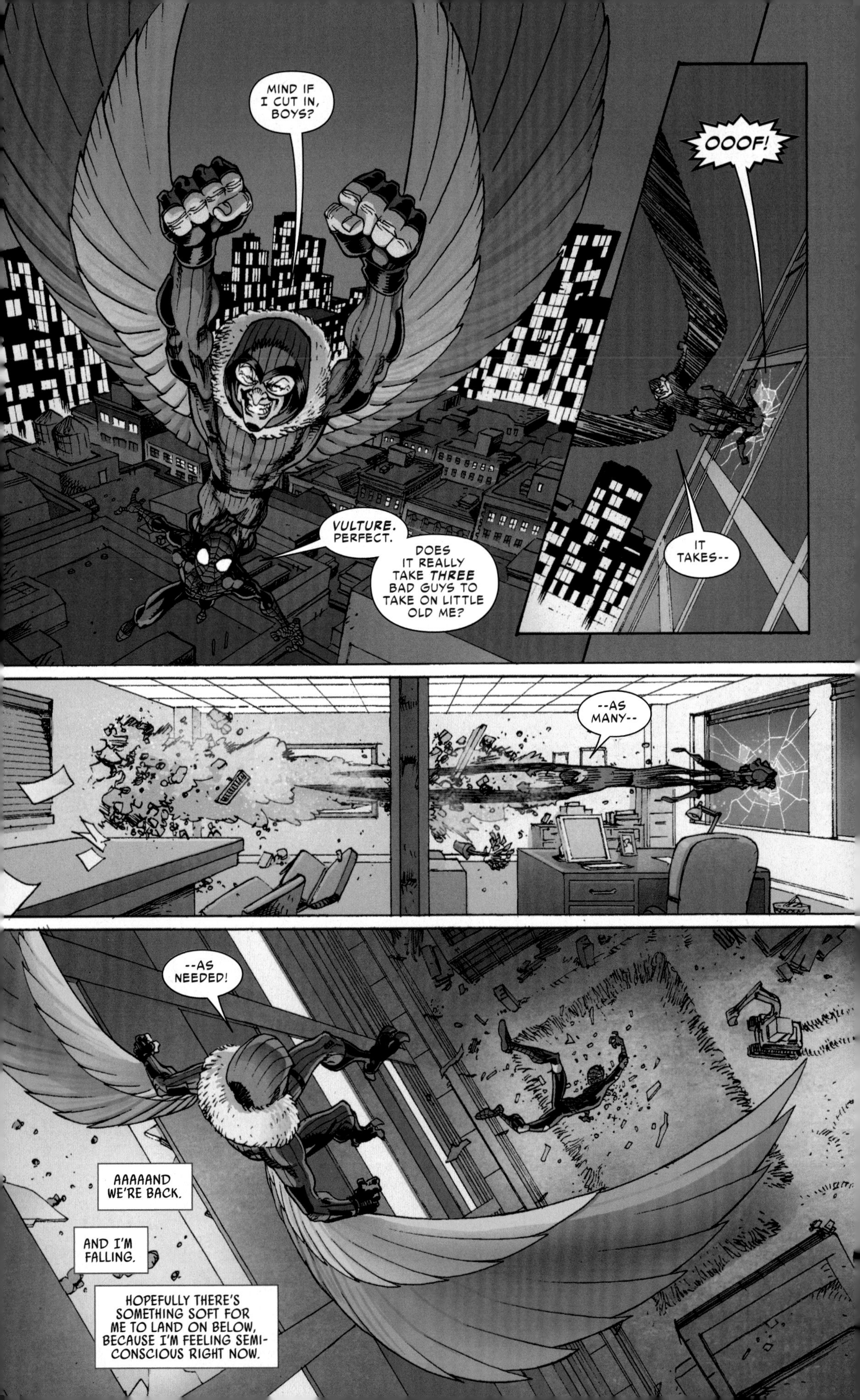
MIND IF I CUT IN, BOYS?
VULTURE. PERFECT.
DOES IT REALLY TAKE *THREE* BAD GUYS TO TAKE ON LITTLE OLD ME?
OOOF!
IT TAKES--
--AS MANY--
--AS NEEDED!
AAAAAND WE'RE BACK.
AND I'M FALLING.
HOPEFULLY THERE'S SOMETHING SOFT FOR ME TO LAND ON BELOW, BECAUSE I'M FEELING SEMI-CONSCIOUS RIGHT NOW.

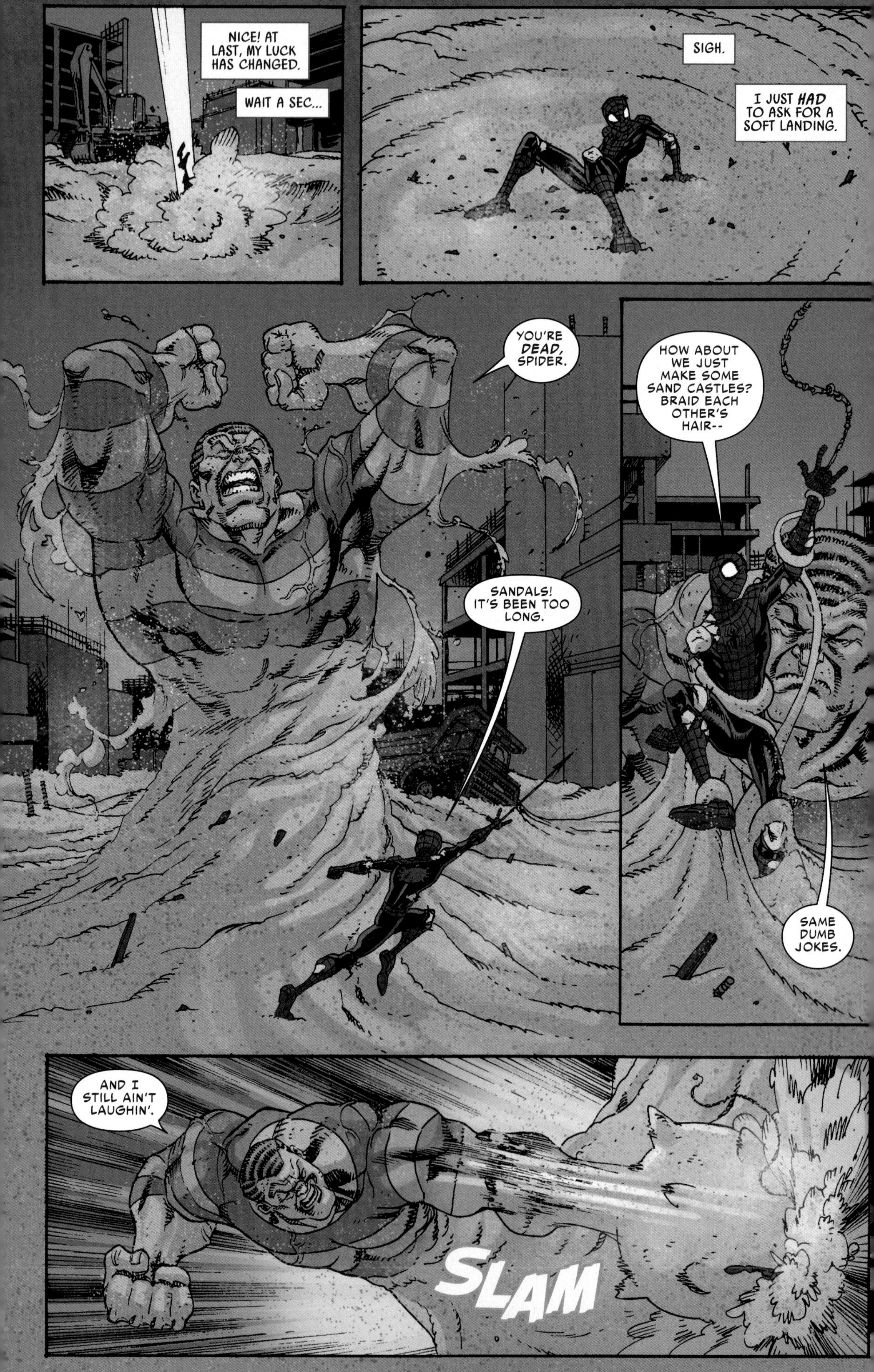
NICE! AT LAST, MY LUCK HAS CHANGED.
WAIT A SEC...
SIGH.
I JUST HAD TO ASK FOR A SOFT LANDING.
YOU'RE DEAD, SPIDER.
SANDALS! IT'S BEEN TOO LONG.
HOW ABOUT WE JUST MAKE SOME SAND CASTLES? BRAID EACH OTHER'S HAIR--
SAME DUMB JOKES.
AND I STILL AIN'T LAUGHIN'.
SLAM

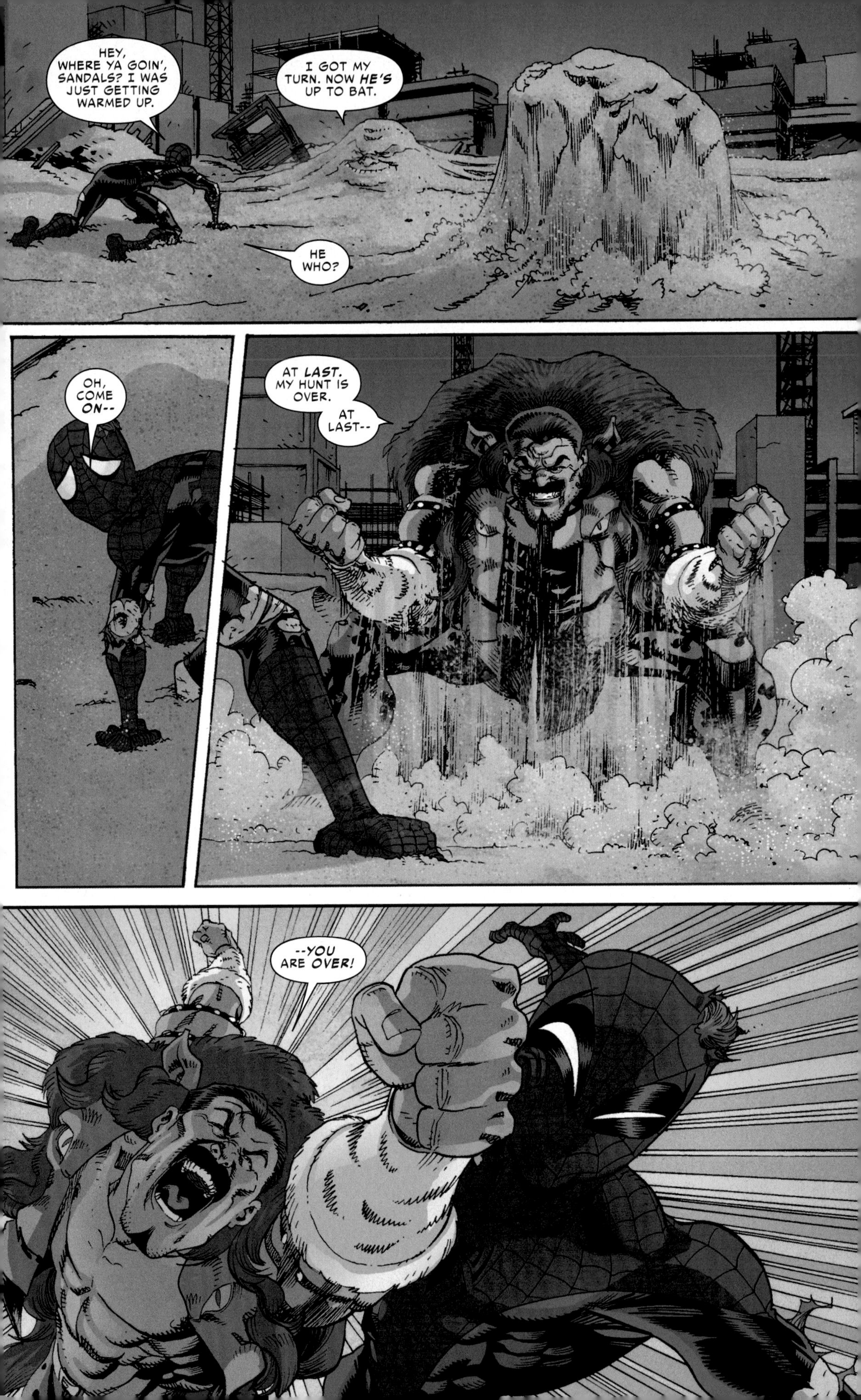
HEY, WHERE YA GOIN', SANDALS? I WAS JUST GETTING WARMED UP.
I GOT MY TURN. NOW HE'S UP TO BAT.
HE WHO?
OH, COME ON--
AT LAST. MY HUNT IS OVER.
AT LAST--
--YOU ARE OVER!

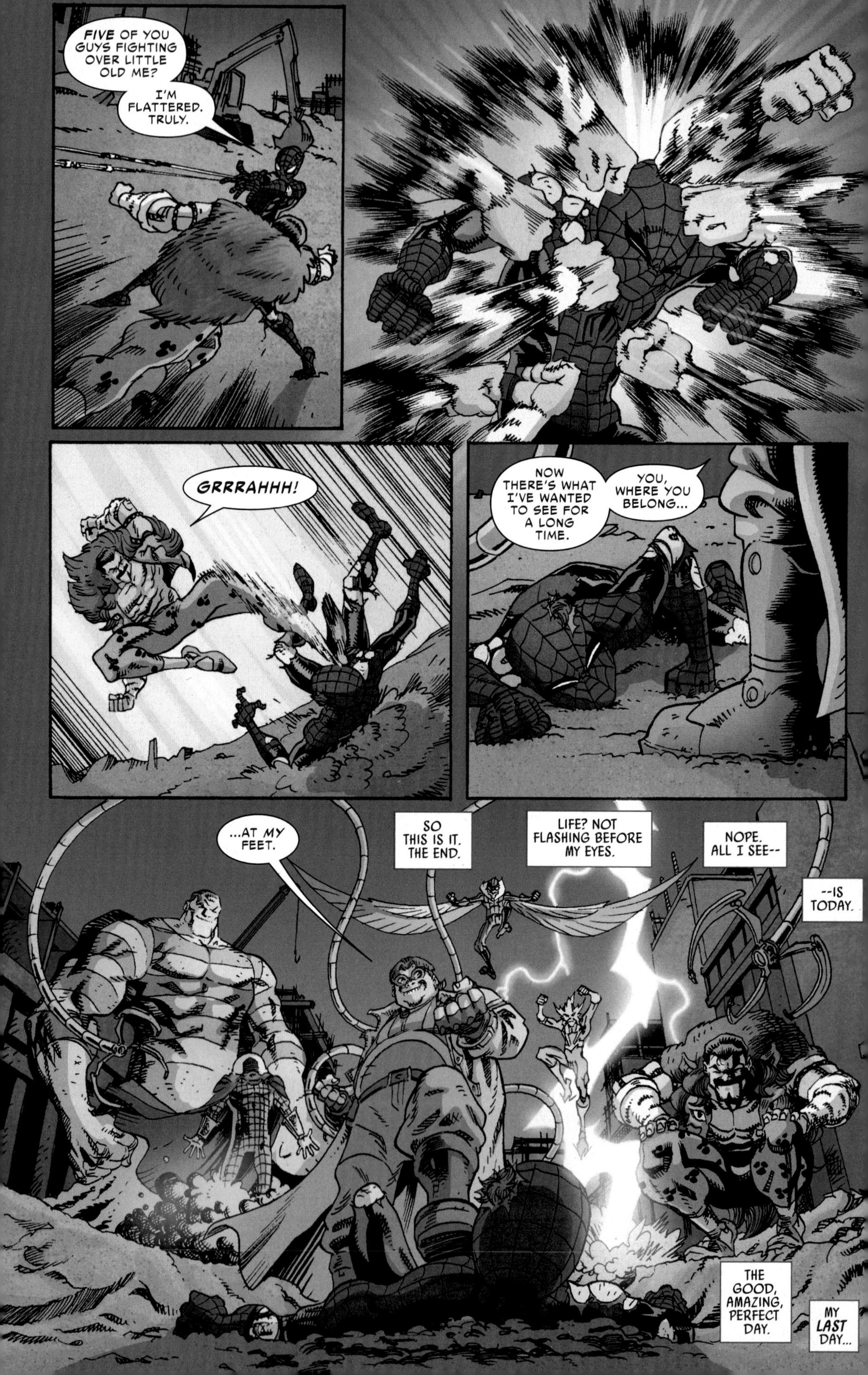
FIVE OF YOU GUYS FIGHTING OVER LITTLE OLD ME?
I'M FLATTERED. TRULY.
GRRRAHHH!
NOW THERE'S WHAT I'VE WANTED TO SEE FOR A LONG TIME.
YOU, WHERE YOU BELONG...
...AT MY FEET.
SO THIS IS IT. THE END.
LIFE? NOT FLASHING BEFORE MY EYES.
NOPE. ALL I SEE--
--IS TODAY.
THE GOOD, AMAZING, PERFECT DAY.
MY LAST DAY...

...AND ALL ITS PERFECT MOMENTS.
YOU ASKED ME WHY YOU? I'LL TELL YOU, PETER PARKER. SURE, YOU'RE SMART...
...AND TALENTED...
...AND SWEET...
...BUT MOST OF ALL? NO MATTER WHAT LIFE PUTS IN YOUR WAY? NO MATTER WHAT THE OBSTACLE?
YOU ALWAYS KEEP MOVING FORWARD. USUALLY WITH A DUMB JOKE AT YOUR SIDE, BUT YOU NEVER GIVE UP.
I ADMIRE THAT.
I LOVE THAT.
NEVER GIVE UP.
DUMB JOKES.
YUP...

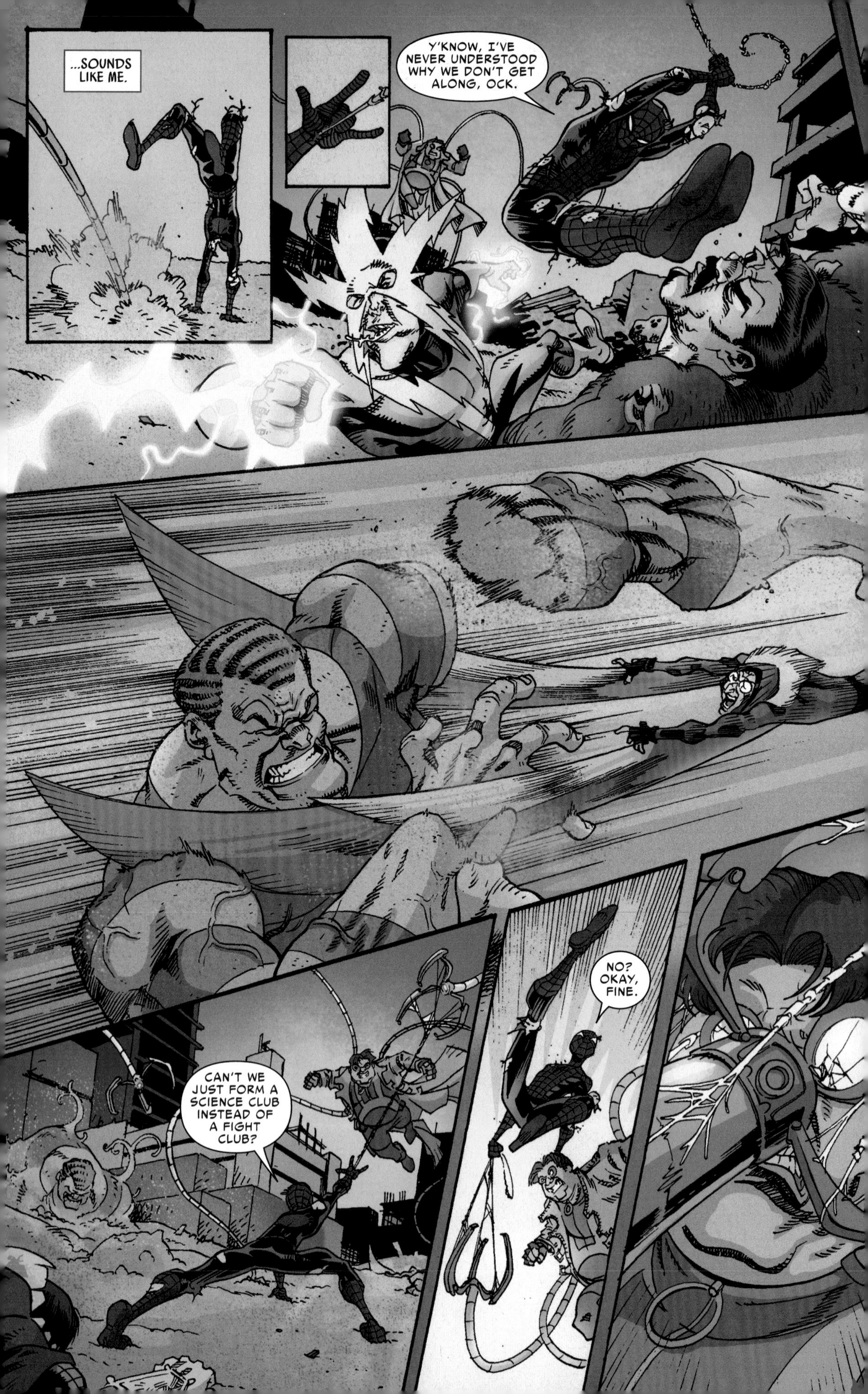
...SOUNDS LIKE ME.
Y'KNOW, I'VE NEVER UNDERSTOOD WHY WE DON'T GET ALONG, OCK.
CAN'T WE JUST FORM A SCIENCE CLUB INSTEAD OF A FIGHT CLUB?
NO? OKAY, FINE.

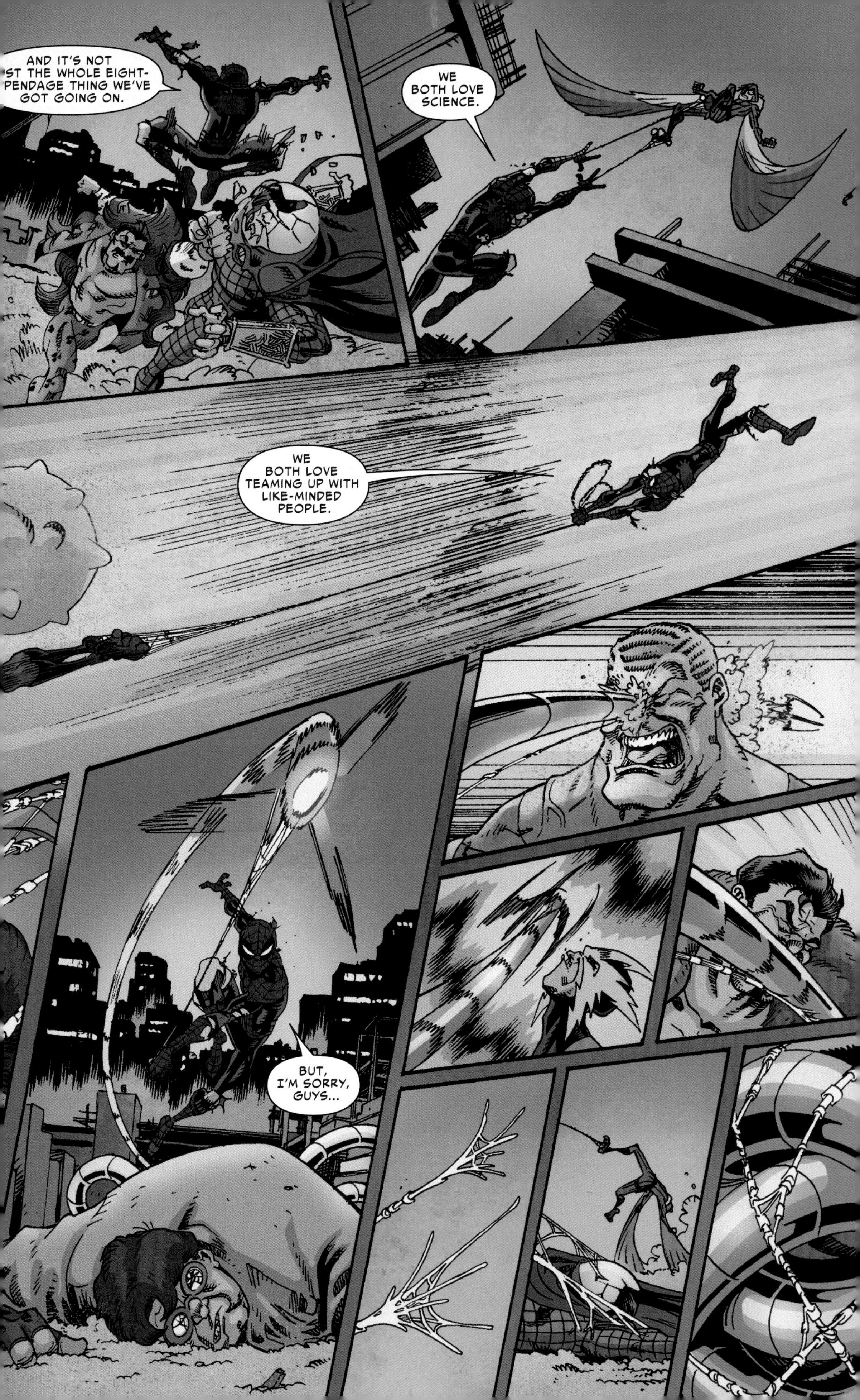
AND IT'S NOT
ST THE WHOLE EIGHT-
PENDAGE THING WE'VE
GOT GOING ON.
WE
BOTH LOVE
SCIENCE.
WE
BOTH LOVE
TEAMING UP WITH
LIKE-MINDED
PEOPLE.
BUT,
I'M SORRY,
GUYS...

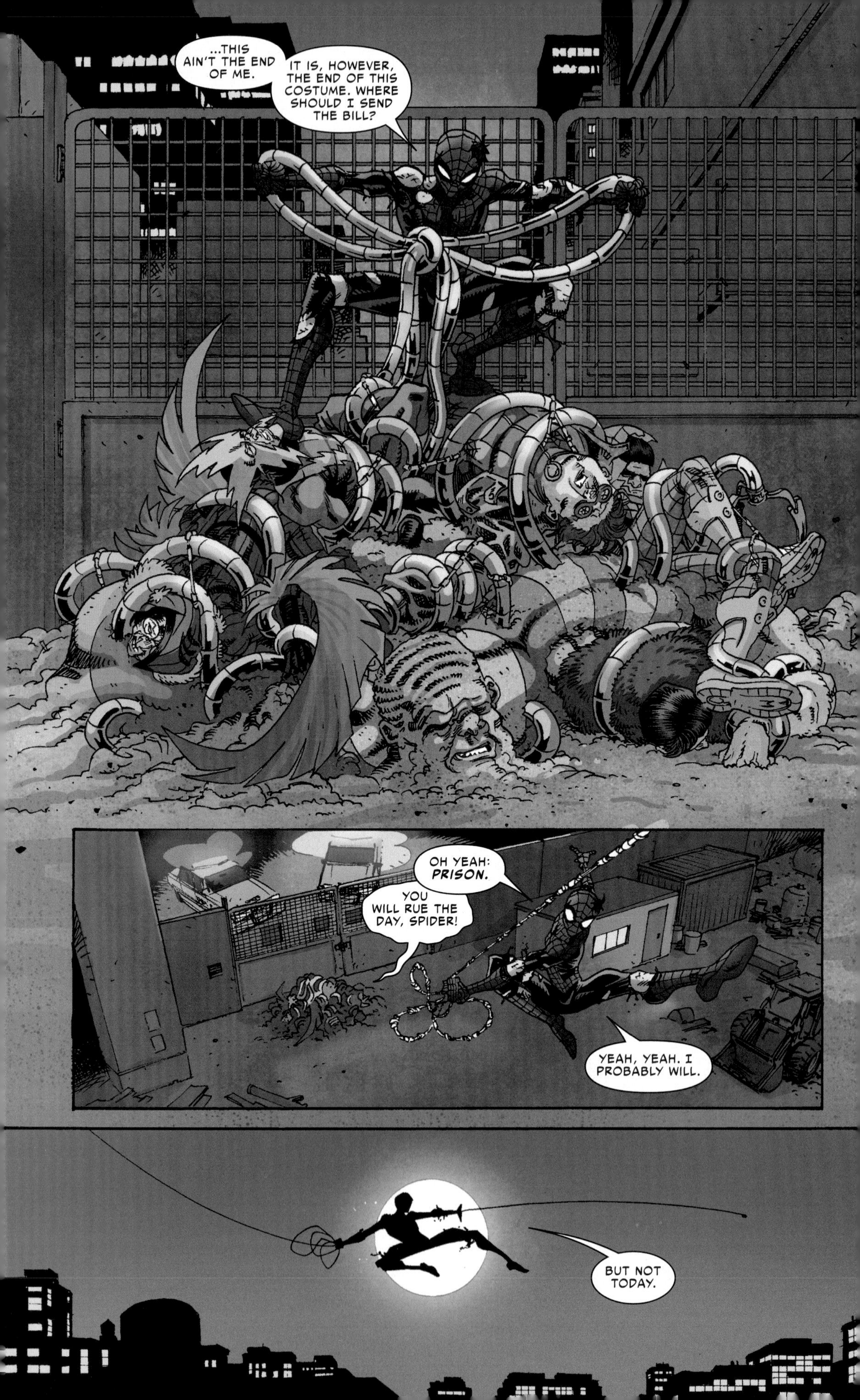
...THIS AIN'T THE END OF ME.
IT IS, HOWEVER, THE END OF THIS COSTUME. WHERE SHOULD I SEND THE BILL?
OH YEAH: *PRISON.*
YOU WILL RUE THE DAY, SPIDER!
YEAH, YEAH. I PROBABLY WILL.
BUT NOT TODAY.

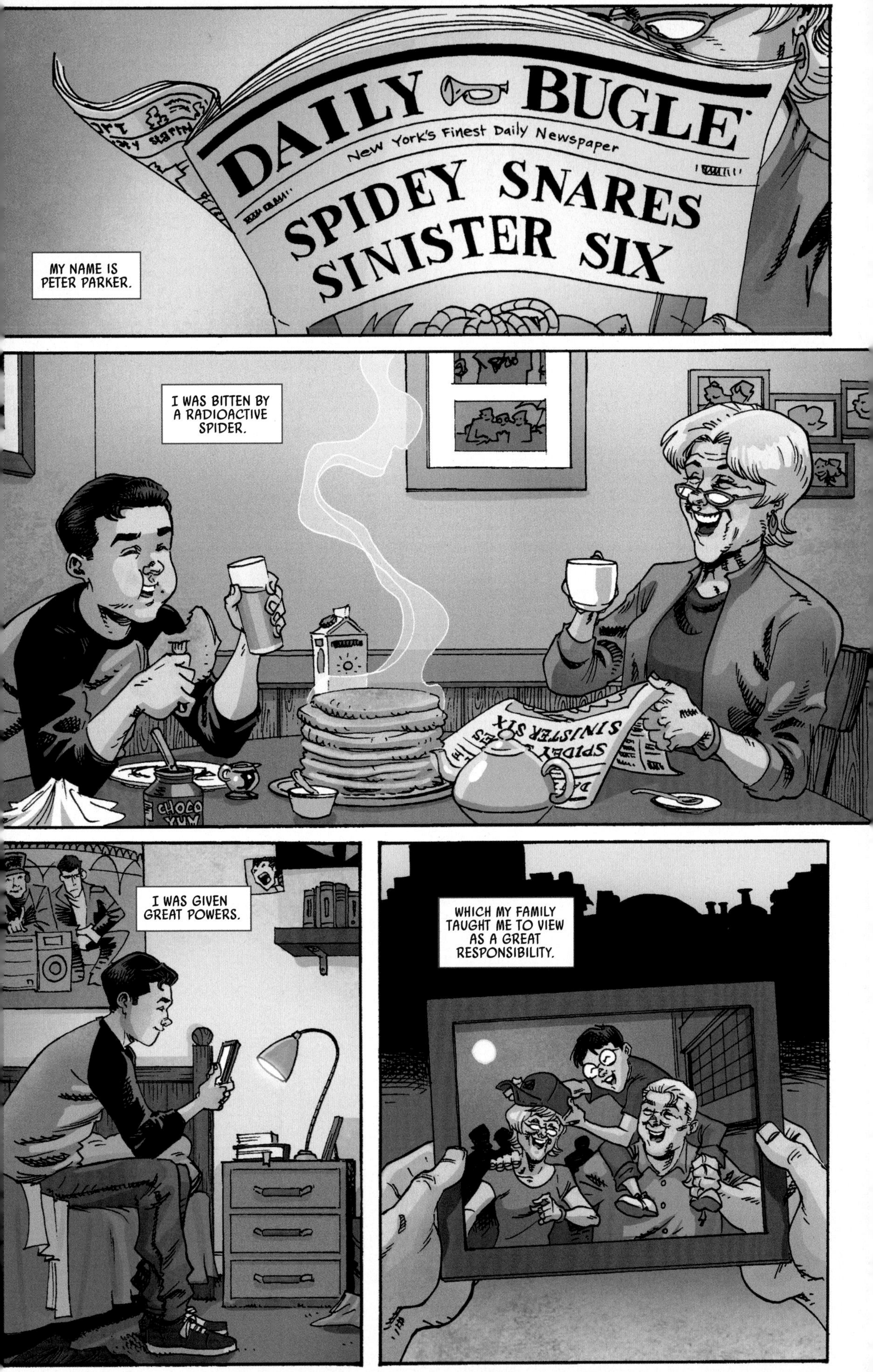
DAILY BUGLE
New York's Finest Daily Newspaper
SPIDEY SNARES SINISTER SIX
MY NAME IS PETER PARKER.
I WAS BITTEN BY A RADIOACTIVE SPIDER.
CHOCO YUM
I WAS GIVEN GREAT POWERS.
WHICH MY FAMILY TAUGHT ME TO VIEW AS A GREAT RESPONSIBILITY.

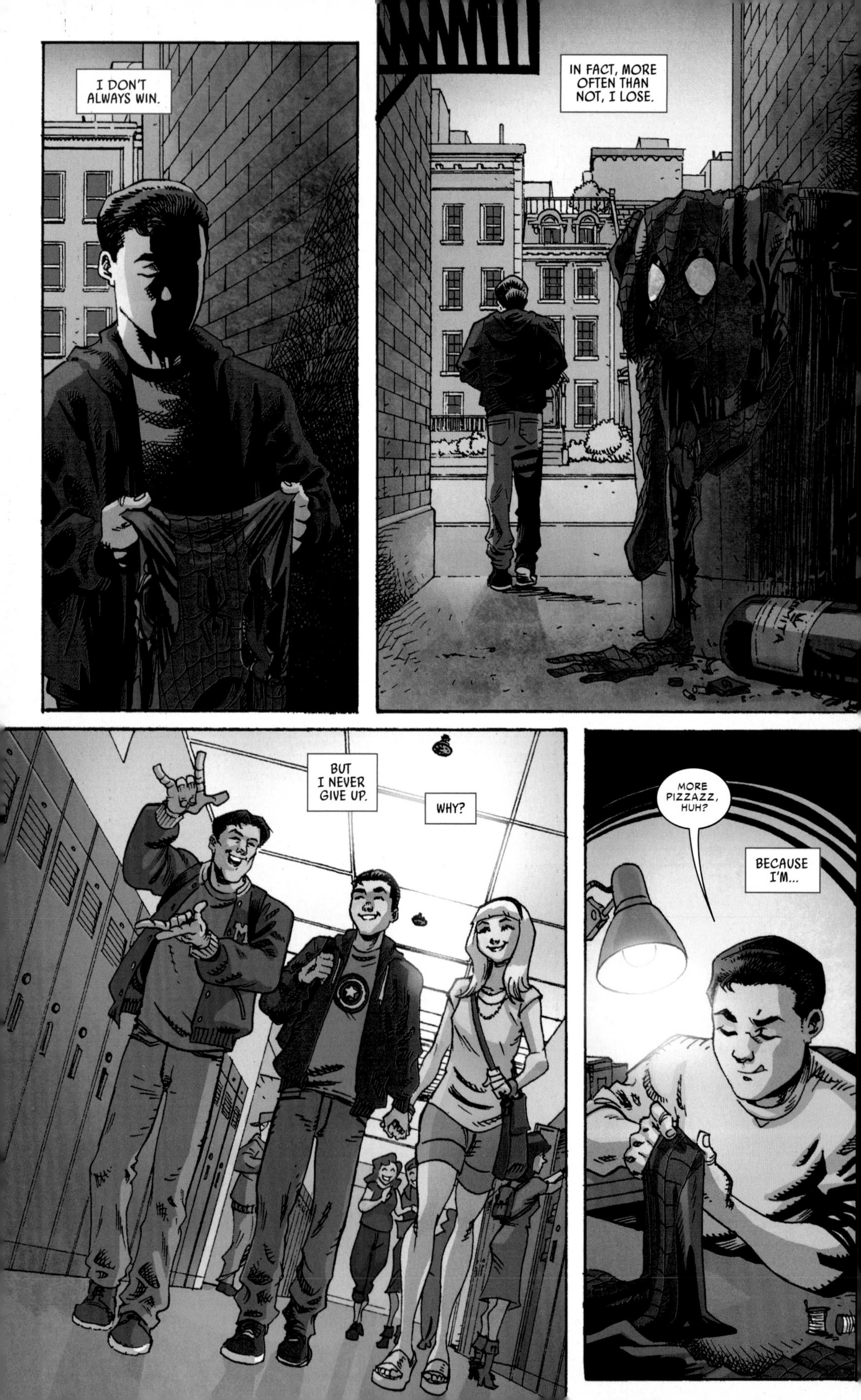

I DON'T ALWAYS WIN.
IN FACT, MORE OFTEN THAN NOT, I LOSE.
BUT I NEVER GIVE UP.
WHY?
MORE PIZZAZZ, HUH?
BECAUSE I'M...

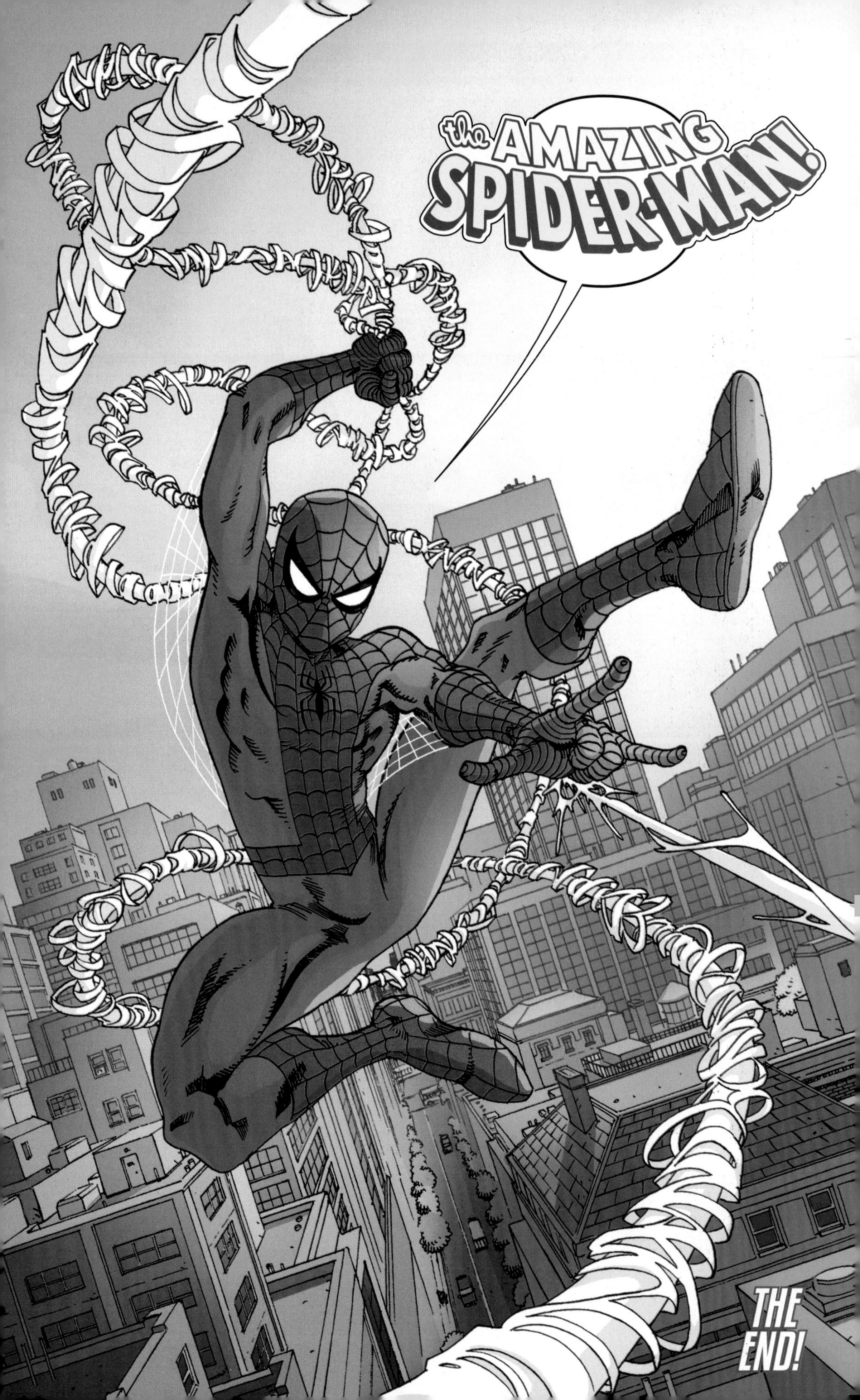
the AMAZING SPIDER-MAN!
THE END!

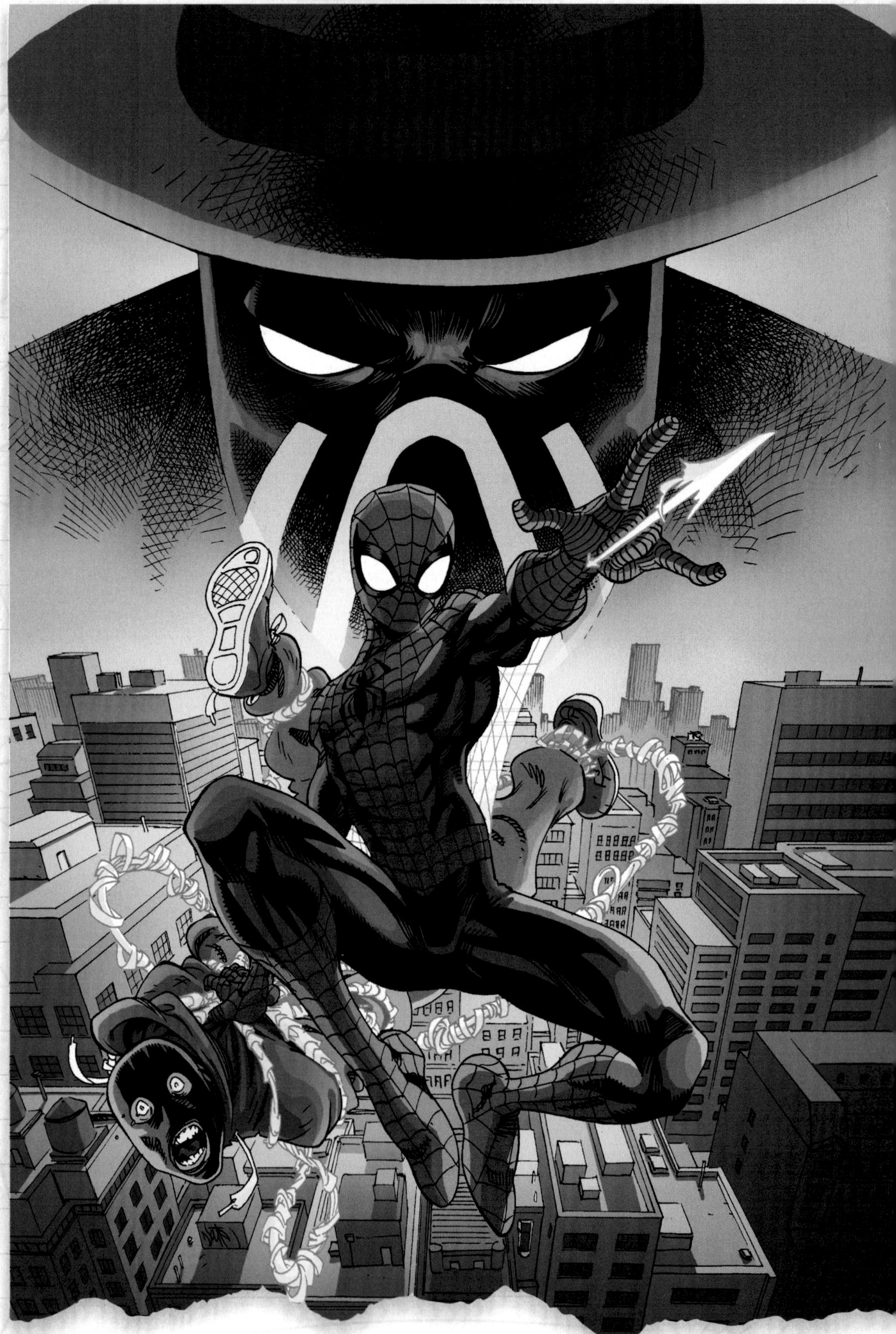

SPIDER-MAN: MASTER PLAN

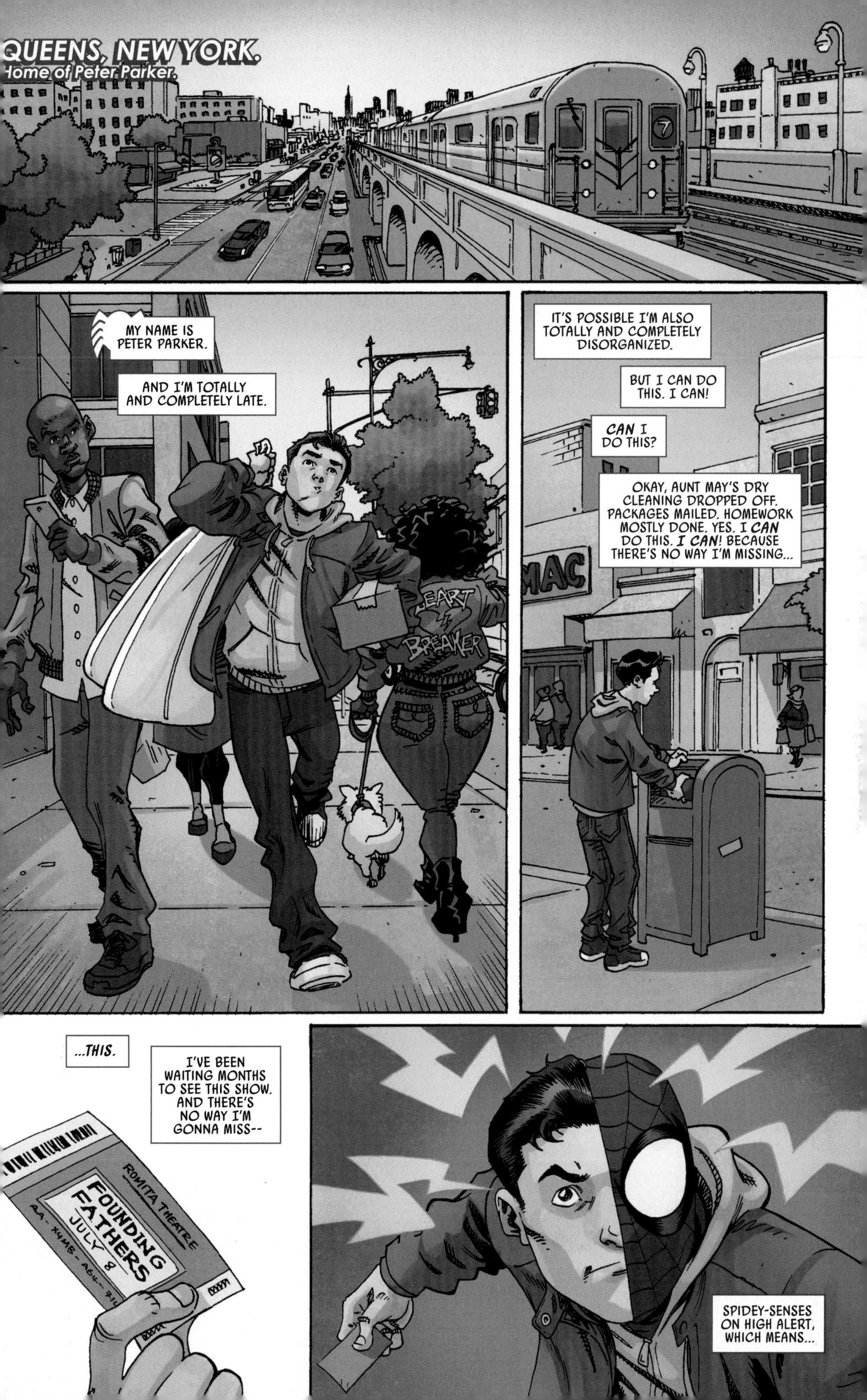
QUEENS, NEW YORK.
Home of Peter Parker.
MY NAME IS PETER PARKER.
AND I'M TOTALLY AND COMPLETELY LATE.
HEART BREAKER
IT'S POSSIBLE I'M ALSO TOTALLY AND COMPLETELY DISORGANIZED.
BUT I CAN DO THIS. I CAN!
CAN I DO THIS?
OKAY, AUNT MAY'S DRY CLEANING DROPPED OFF. PACKAGES MAILED. HOMEWORK MOSTLY DONE. YES. I CAN DO THIS. I CAN! BECAUSE THERE'S NO WAY I'M MISSING...
...THIS.
I'VE BEEN WAITING MONTHS TO SEE THIS SHOW. AND THERE'S NO WAY I'M GONNA MISS--
ROMITA THEATRE
FOUNDING FATHERS
JULY 8
SPIDEY-SENSES ON HIGH ALERT, WHICH MEANS...

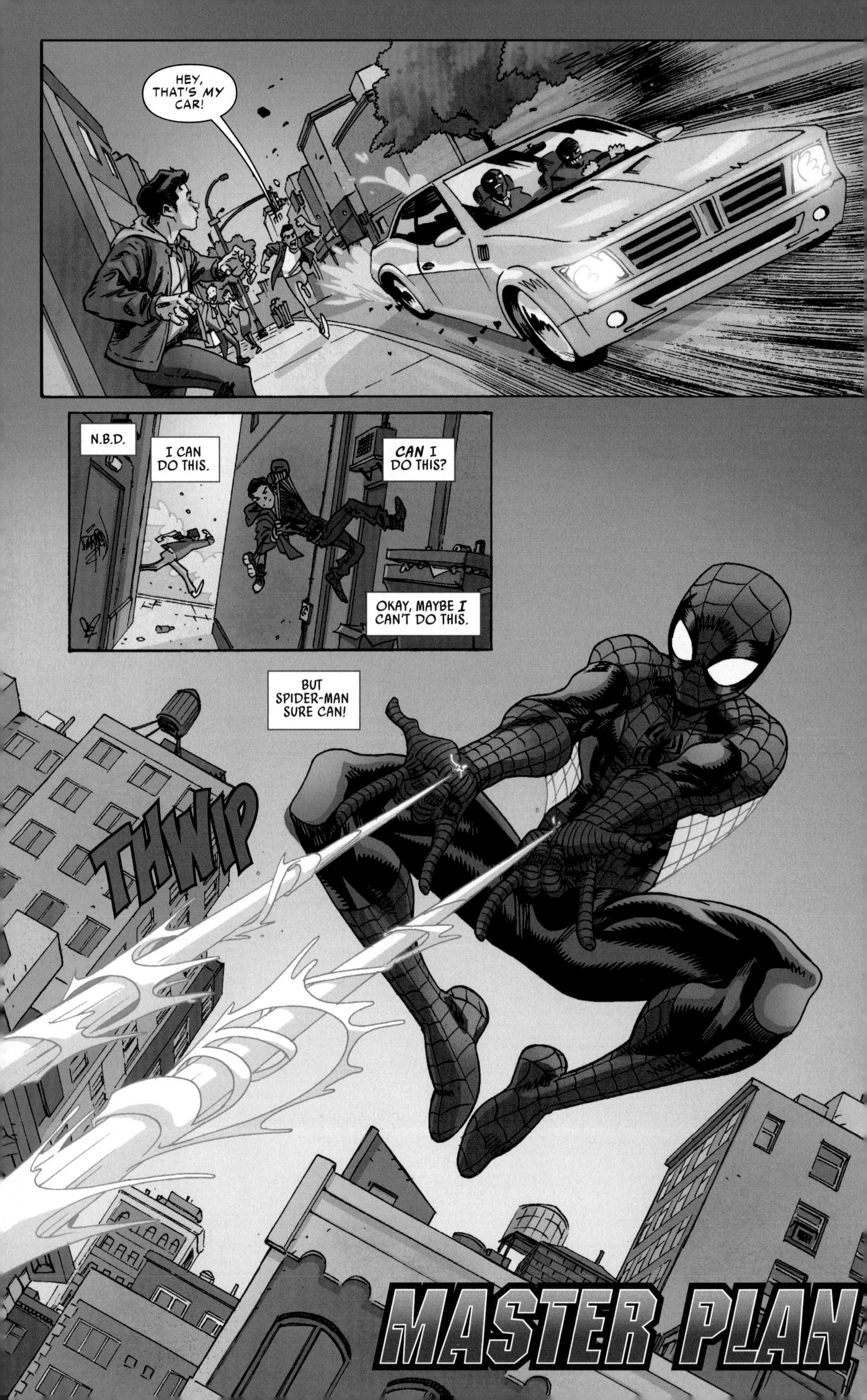
HEY, THAT'S MY CAR!
N.B.D.
I CAN DO THIS.
CAN I DO THIS?
OKAY, MAYBE I CAN'T DO THIS.
BUT SPIDER-MAN SURE CAN!
THWIP
MASTER PLAN

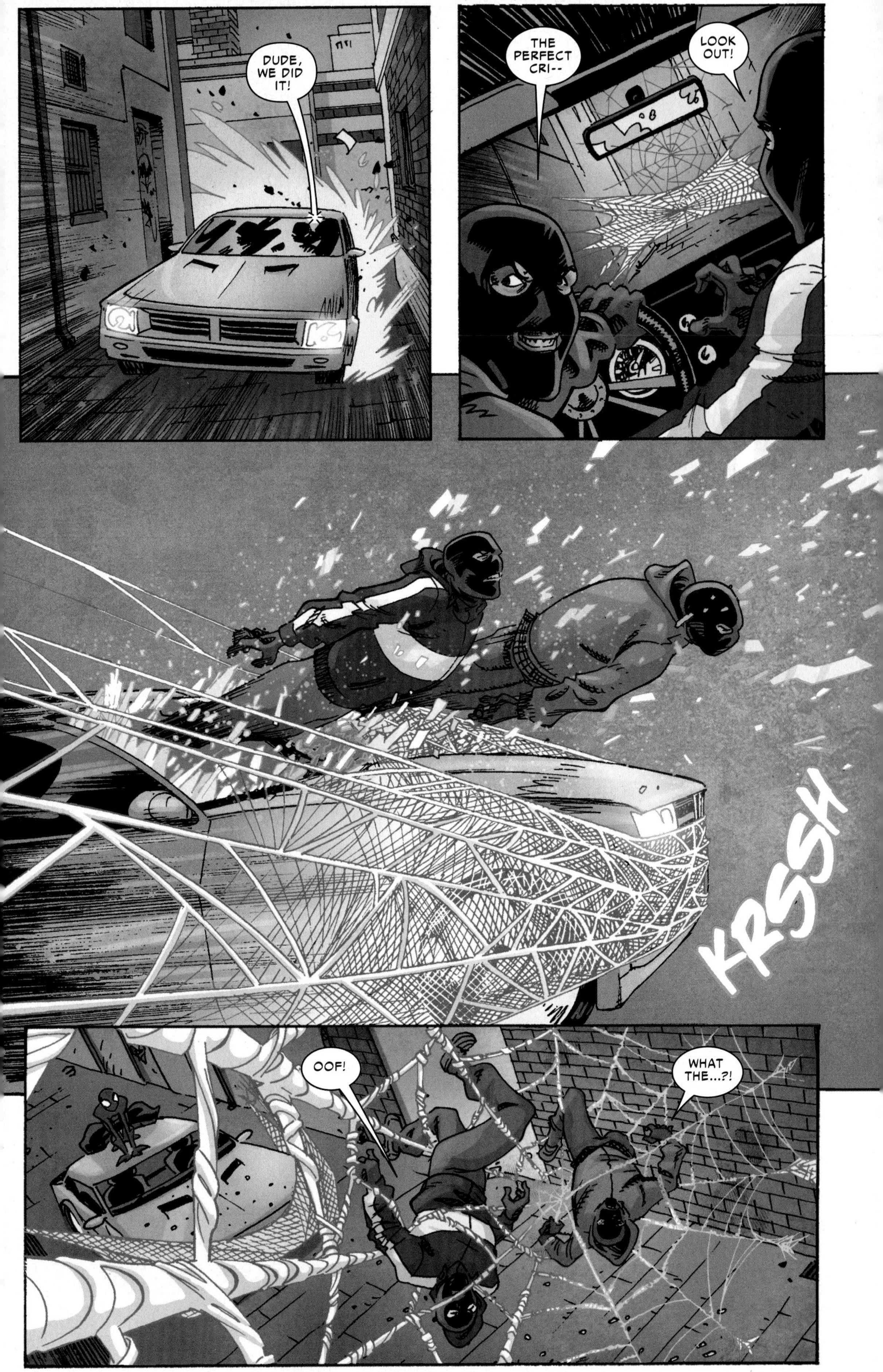
DUDE, WE DID IT!
THE PERFECT CRI--
LOOK OUT!
KRSSH
OOF!
WHAT THE...?!

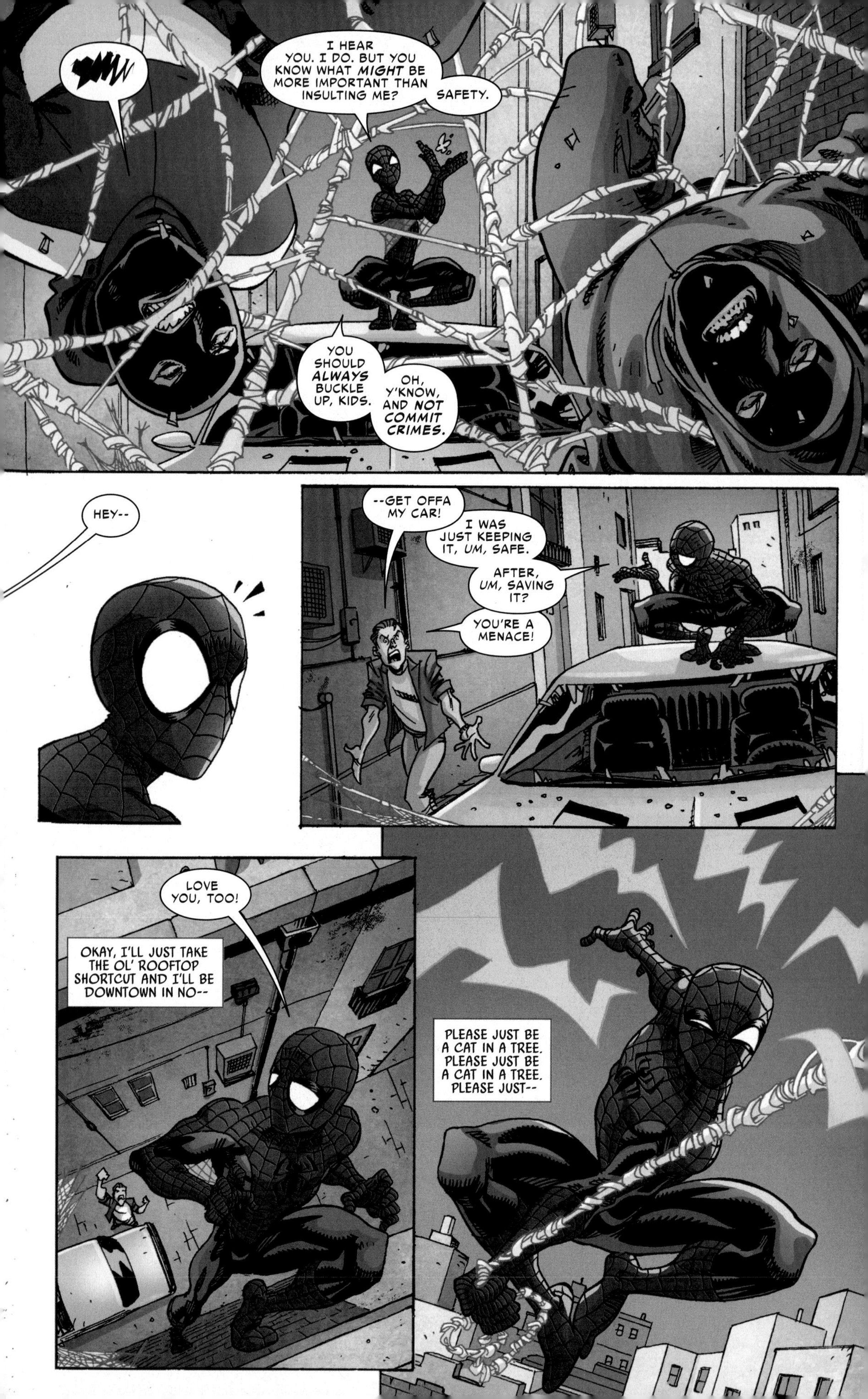
I HEAR YOU. I DO. BUT YOU KNOW WHAT MIGHT BE MORE IMPORTANT THAN INSULTING ME?
SAFETY.
YOU SHOULD ALWAYS BUCKLE UP, KIDS.
OH, Y'KNOW, AND NOT COMMIT CRIMES.
HEY--
--GET OFFA MY CAR!
I WAS JUST KEEPING IT, UM, SAFE.
AFTER, UM, SAVING IT?
YOU'RE A MENACE!
LOVE YOU, TOO!
OKAY, I'LL JUST TAKE THE OL' ROOFTOP SHORTCUT AND I'LL BE DOWNTOWN IN NO--
PLEASE JUST BE A CAT IN A TREE. PLEASE JUST BE A CAT IN A TREE. PLEASE JUST--

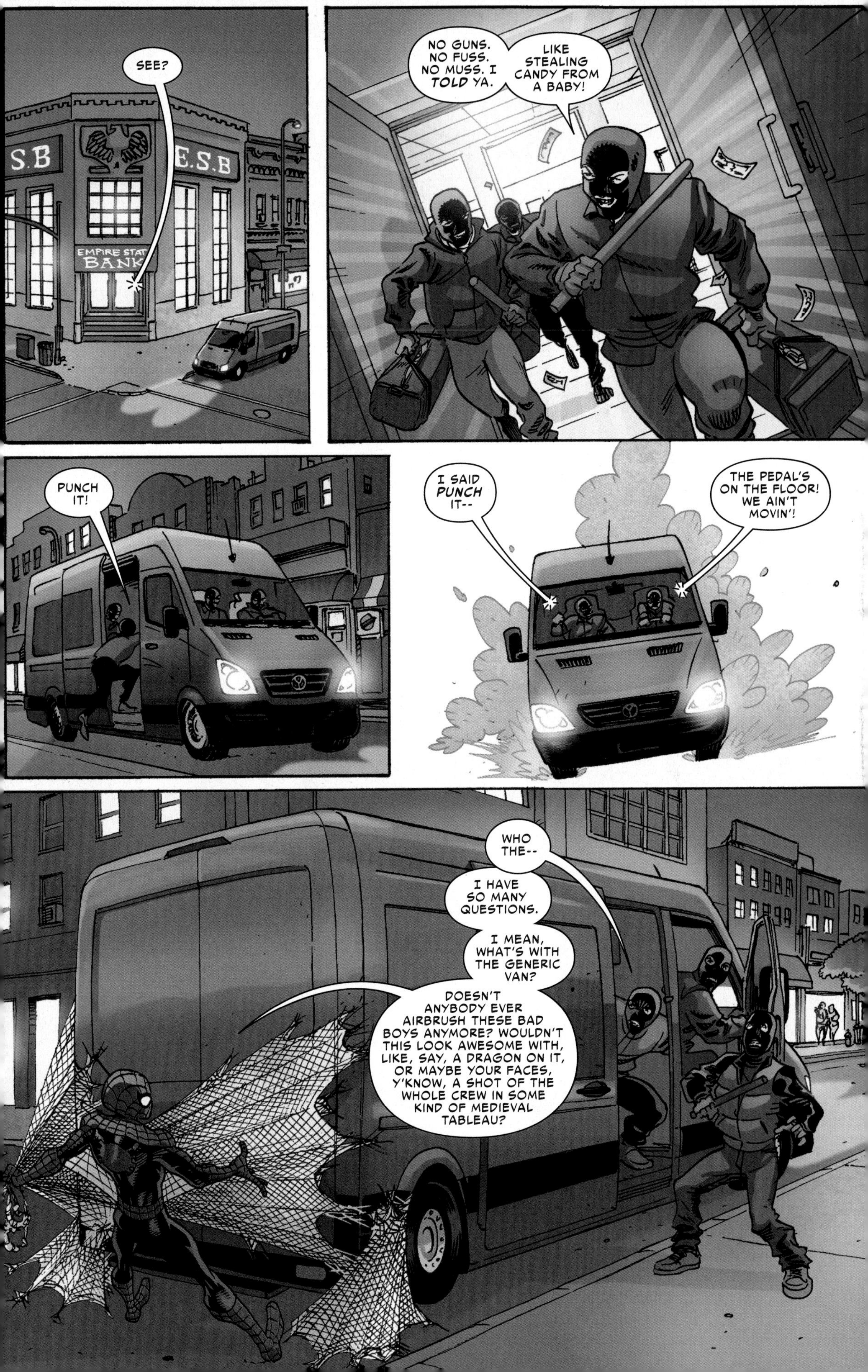
SEE?
S.B
E.S.B
EMPIRE STATE BANK
NO GUNS. NO FUSS. NO MUSS. I TOLD YA.
LIKE STEALING CANDY FROM A BABY!
PUNCH IT!
I SAID PUNCH IT--
THE PEDAL'S ON THE FLOOR! WE AIN'T MOVIN'!
WHO THE--
I HAVE SO MANY QUESTIONS.
I MEAN, WHAT'S WITH THE GENERIC VAN?
DOESN'T ANYBODY EVER AIRBRUSH THESE BAD BOYS ANYMORE? WOULDN'T THIS LOOK AWESOME WITH, LIKE, SAY, A DRAGON ON IT, OR MAYBE YOUR FACES, Y'KNOW, A SHOT OF THE WHOLE CREW IN SOME KIND OF MEDIEVAL TABLEAU?

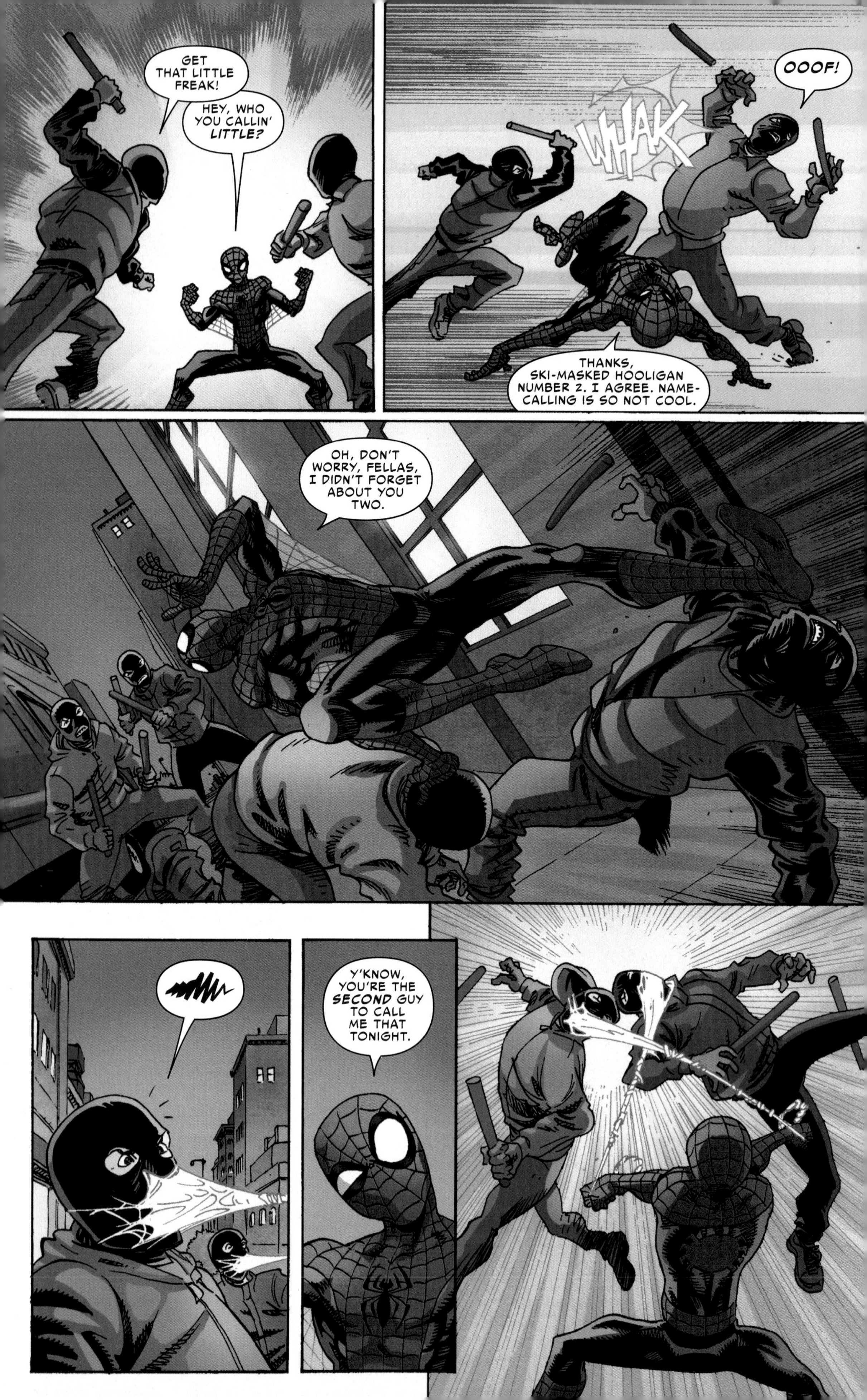
GET THAT LITTLE FREAK!
HEY, WHO YOU CALLIN' *LITTLE?*
WHAK
OOOF!
THANKS, SKI-MASKED HOOLIGAN NUMBER 2. I AGREE. NAME-CALLING IS SO NOT COOL.
OH, DON'T WORRY, FELLAS, I DIDN'T FORGET ABOUT YOU TWO.
Y'KNOW, YOU'RE THE **SECOND** GUY TO CALL ME THAT TONIGHT.

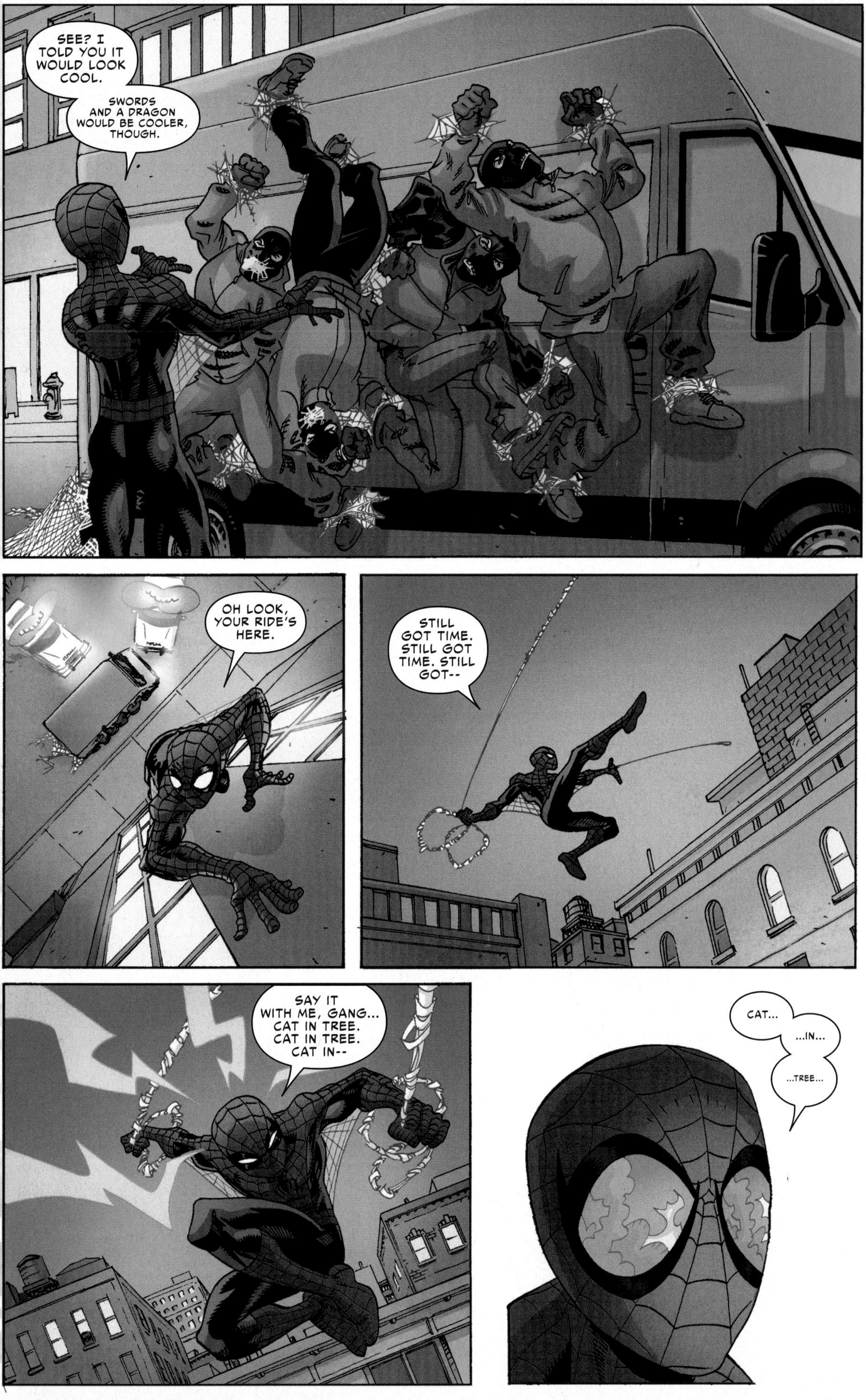
SEE? I TOLD YOU IT WOULD LOOK COOL.
SWORDS AND A DRAGON WOULD BE COOLER, THOUGH.
OH LOOK, YOUR RIDE'S HERE.
STILL GOT TIME. STILL GOT TIME. STILL GOT--
SAY IT WITH ME, GANG... CAT IN TREE. CAT IN TREE. CAT IN--
CAT...
...IN...
...TREE...

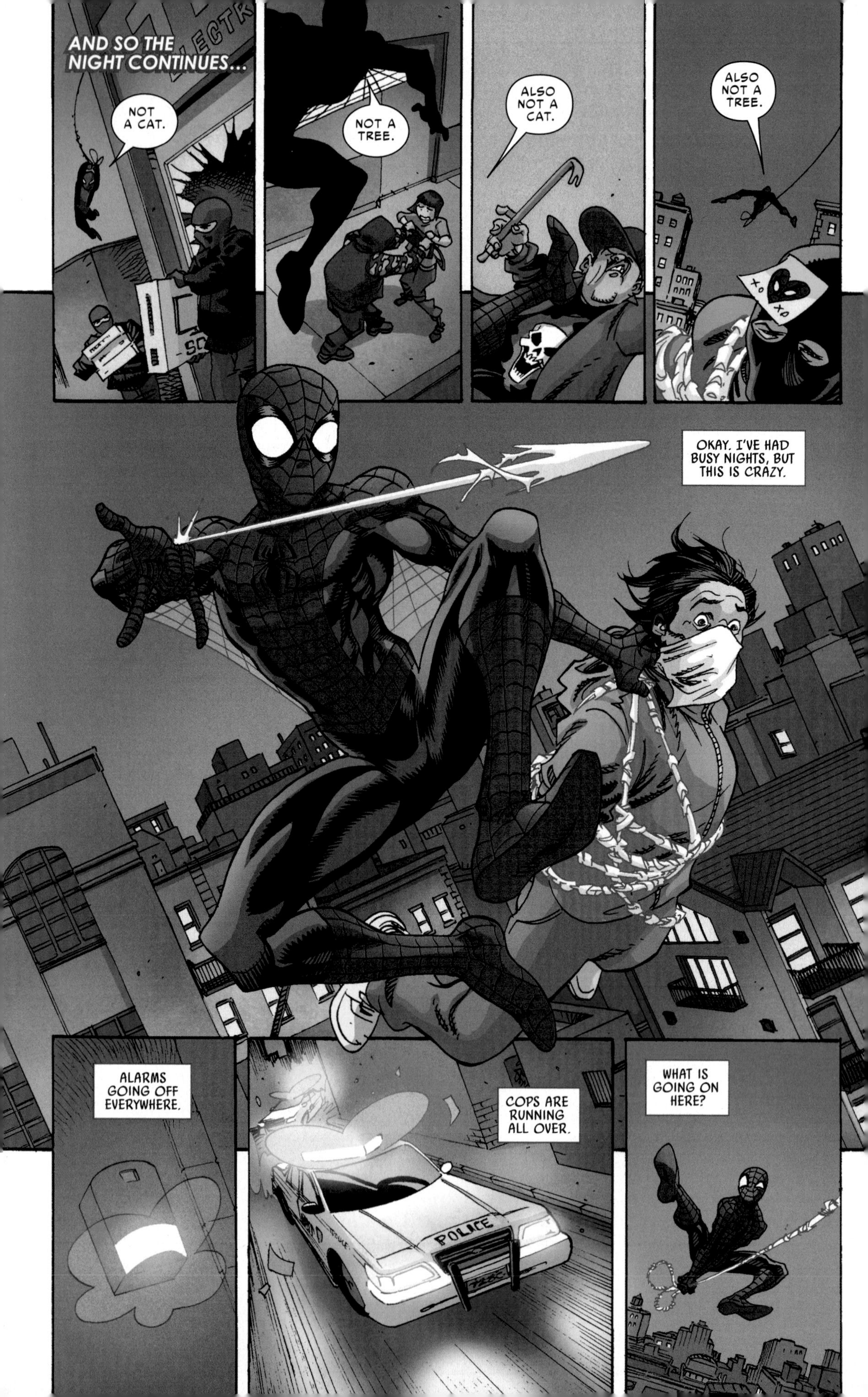

AND SO THE NIGHT CONTINUES...
NOT A CAT.
NOT A TREE.
ALSO NOT A CAT.
ALSO NOT A TREE.
OKAY. I'VE HAD BUSY NIGHTS, BUT THIS IS CRAZY.
ALARMS GOING OFF EVERYWHERE.
COPS ARE RUNNING ALL OVER.
WHAT IS GOING ON HERE?

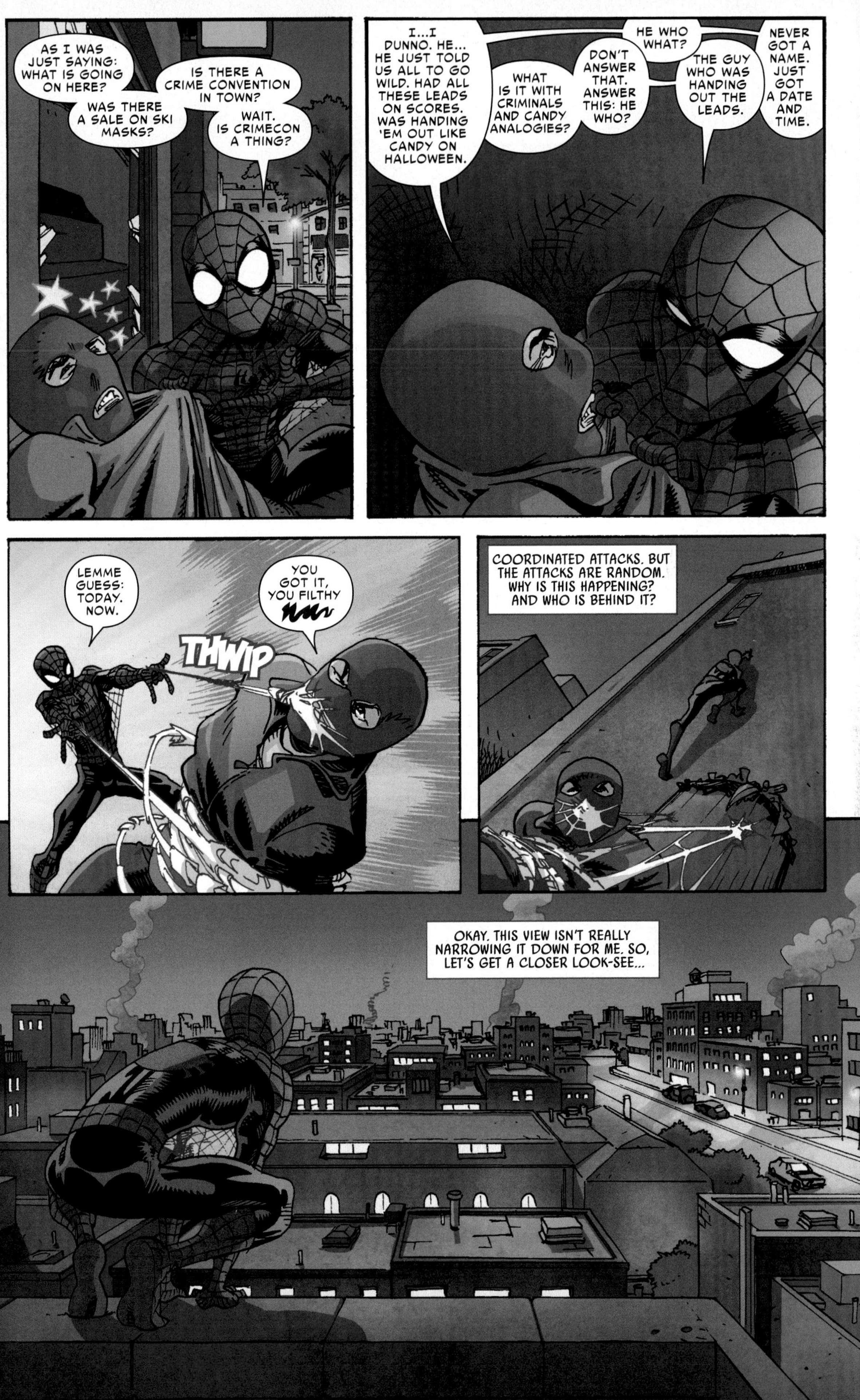
AS I WAS JUST SAYING: WHAT IS GOING ON HERE?
WAS THERE A SALE ON SKI MASKS?
IS THERE A CRIME CONVENTION IN TOWN?
WAIT. IS CRIMECON A THING?
I...I DUNNO. HE... HE JUST TOLD US ALL TO GO WILD. HAD ALL THESE LEADS ON SCORES. WAS HANDING 'EM OUT LIKE CANDY ON HALLOWEEN.
WHAT IS IT WITH CRIMINALS AND CANDY ANALOGIES?
DON'T ANSWER THAT. ANSWER THIS: HE WHO?
HE WHO WHAT?
THE GUY WHO WAS HANDING OUT THE LEADS.
NEVER GOT A NAME. JUST GOT A DATE AND TIME.
LEMME GUESS: TODAY. NOW.
YOU GOT IT, YOU FILTHY
THWIP
COORDINATED ATTACKS. BUT THE ATTACKS ARE RANDOM. WHY IS THIS HAPPENING? AND WHO IS BEHIND IT?
OKAY. THIS VIEW ISN'T REALLY NARROWING IT DOWN FOR ME. SO, LET'S GET A CLOSER LOOK-SEE...

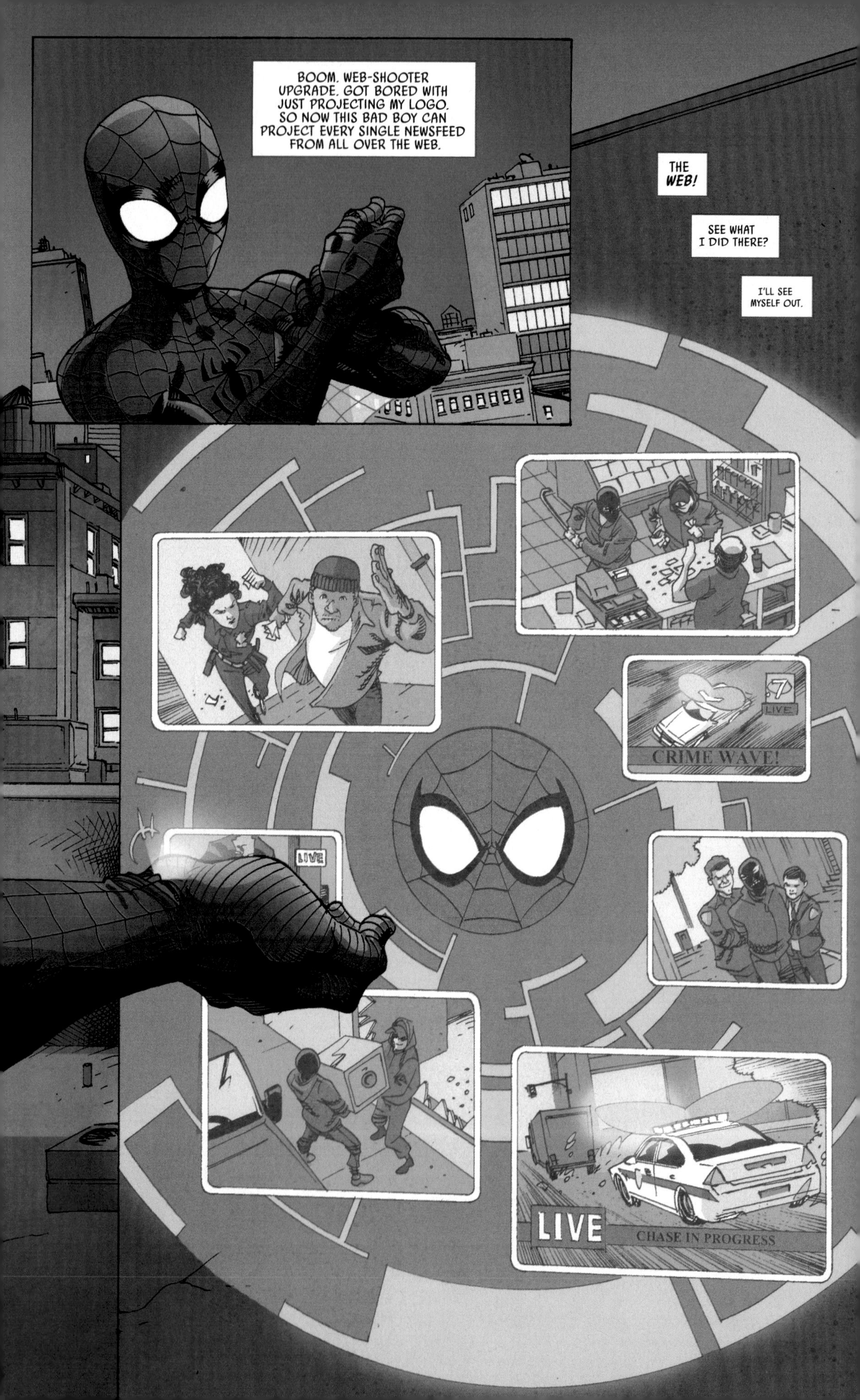
BOOM. WEB-SHOOTER UPGRADE. GOT BORED WITH JUST PROJECTING MY LOGO. SO NOW THIS BAD BOY CAN PROJECT EVERY SINGLE NEWSFEED FROM ALL OVER THE WEB.
THE WEB!
SEE WHAT I DID THERE?
I'LL SEE MYSELF OUT.
7
LIVE
CRIME WAVE!
LIVE
LIVE
CHASE IN PROGRESS

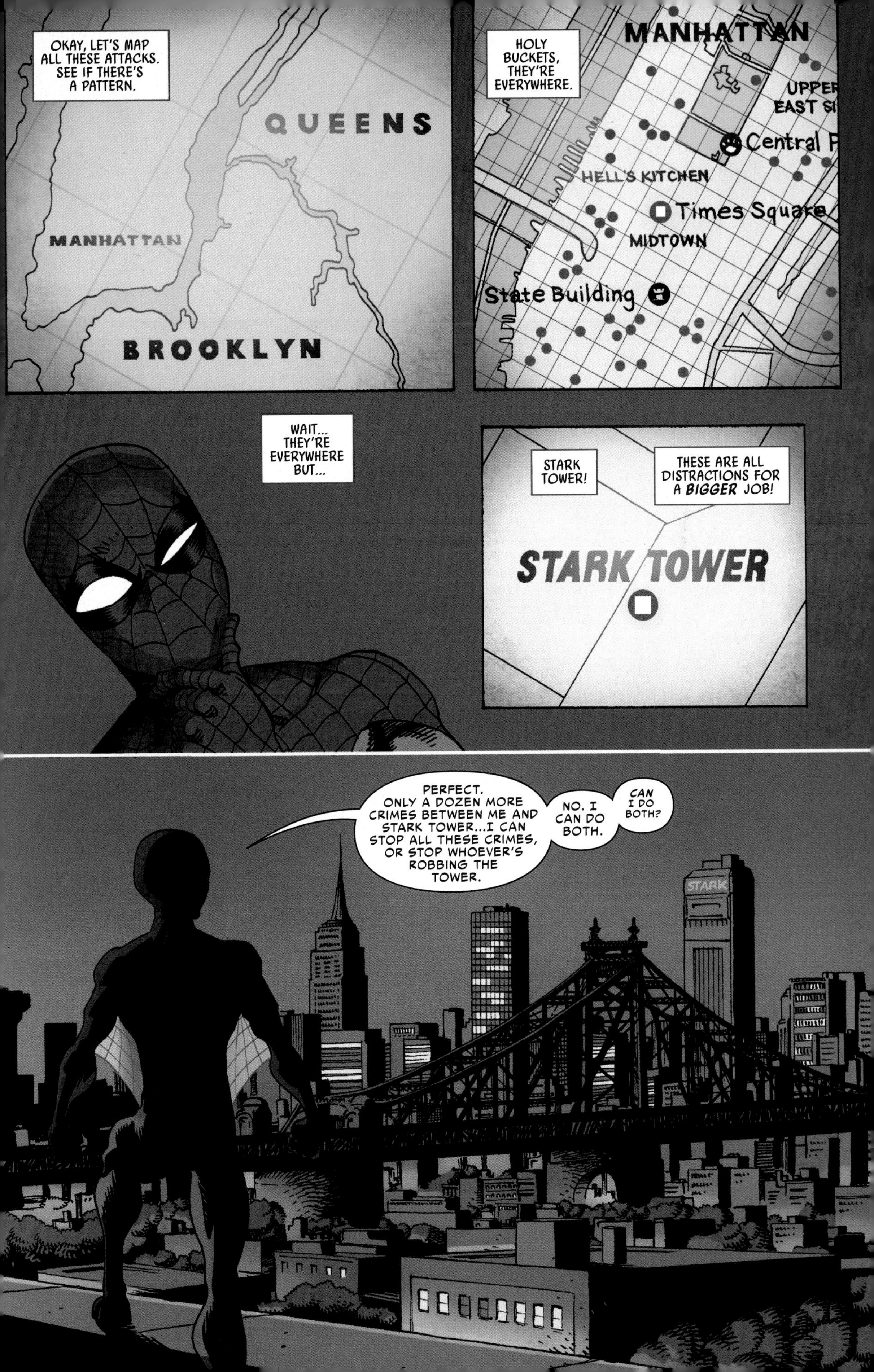
OKAY, LET'S MAP ALL THESE ATTACKS. SEE IF THERE'S A PATTERN.
QUEENS
MANHATTAN
BROOKLYN
HOLY BUCKETS, THEY'RE EVERYWHERE.
MANHATTAN
UPPER EAST SI
Central P
HELL'S KITCHEN
Times Square
MIDTOWN
State Building
WAIT... THEY'RE EVERYWHERE BUT...
STARK TOWER!
THESE ARE ALL DISTRACTIONS FOR A *BIGGER* JOB!
STARK TOWER
PERFECT. ONLY A DOZEN MORE CRIMES BETWEEN ME AND STARK TOWER...I CAN STOP ALL THESE CRIMES, OR STOP WHOEVER'S ROBBING THE TOWER.
CAN I DO BOTH?
NO. I CAN DO BOTH.
STARK

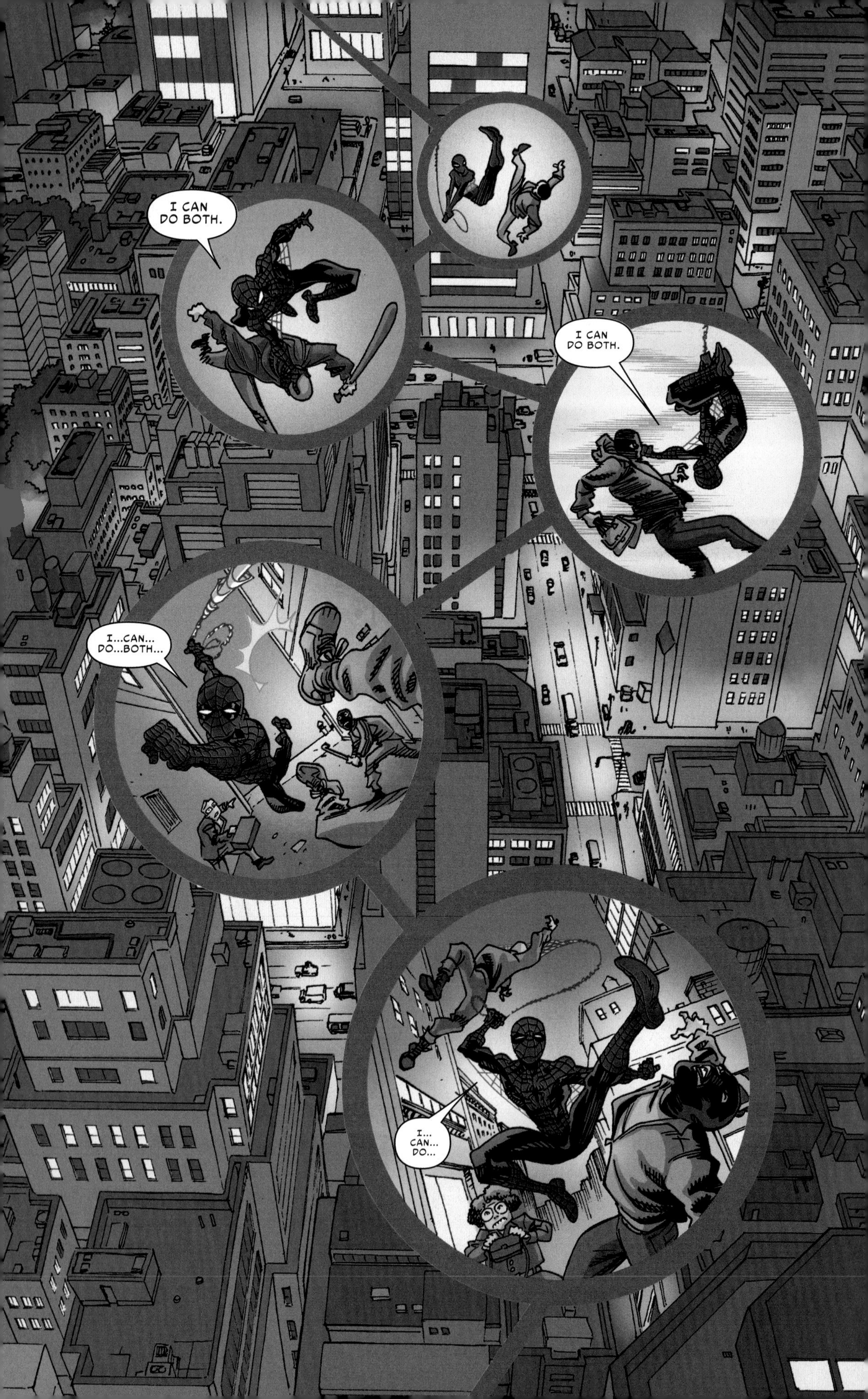
I CAN DO BOTH.
I CAN DO BOTH.
I...CAN... DO...BOTH...
I... CAN... DO...

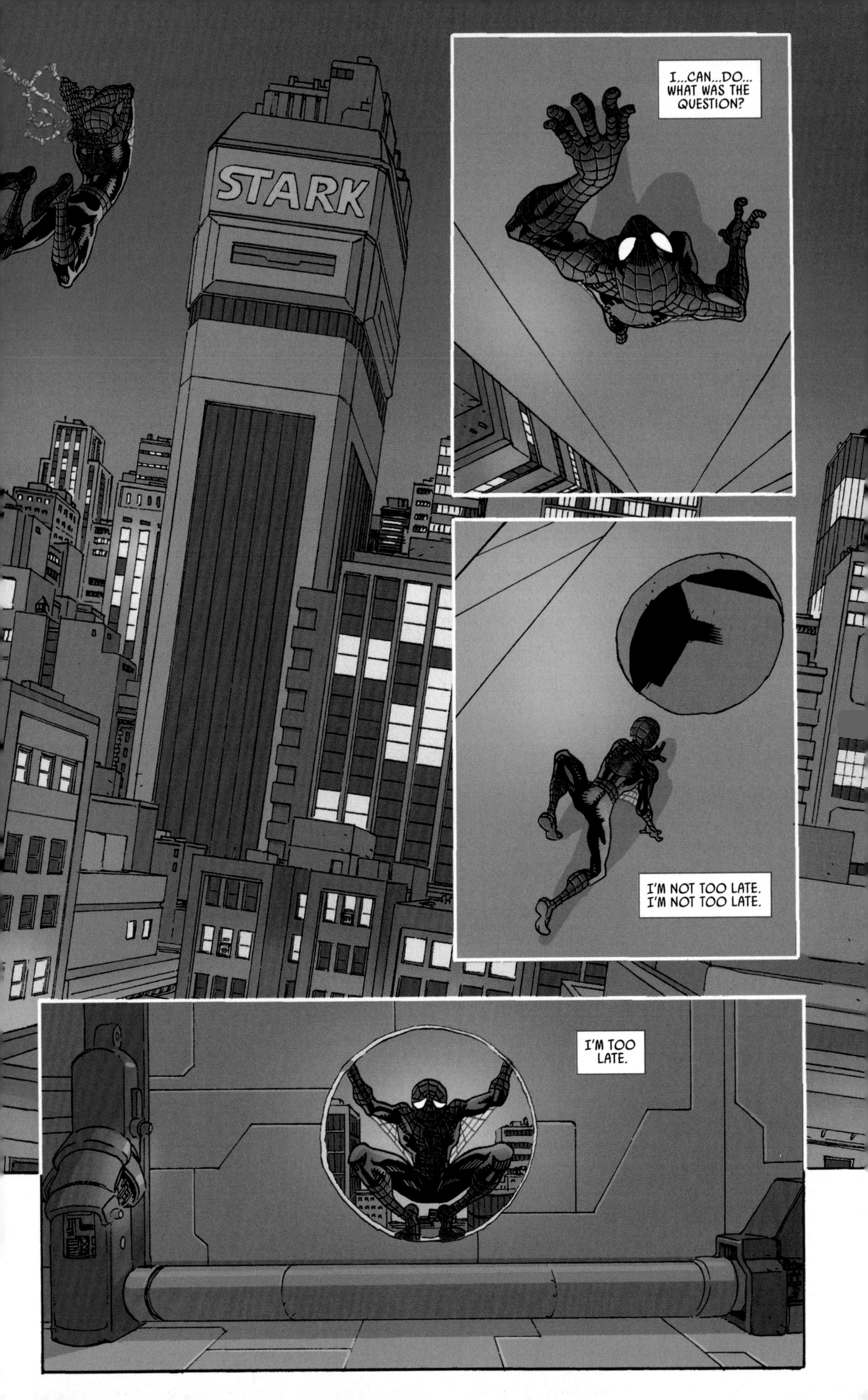
I...CAN...DO...
WHAT WAS THE
QUESTION?
I'M NOT TOO LATE.
I'M NOT TOO LATE.
I'M TOO
LATE.

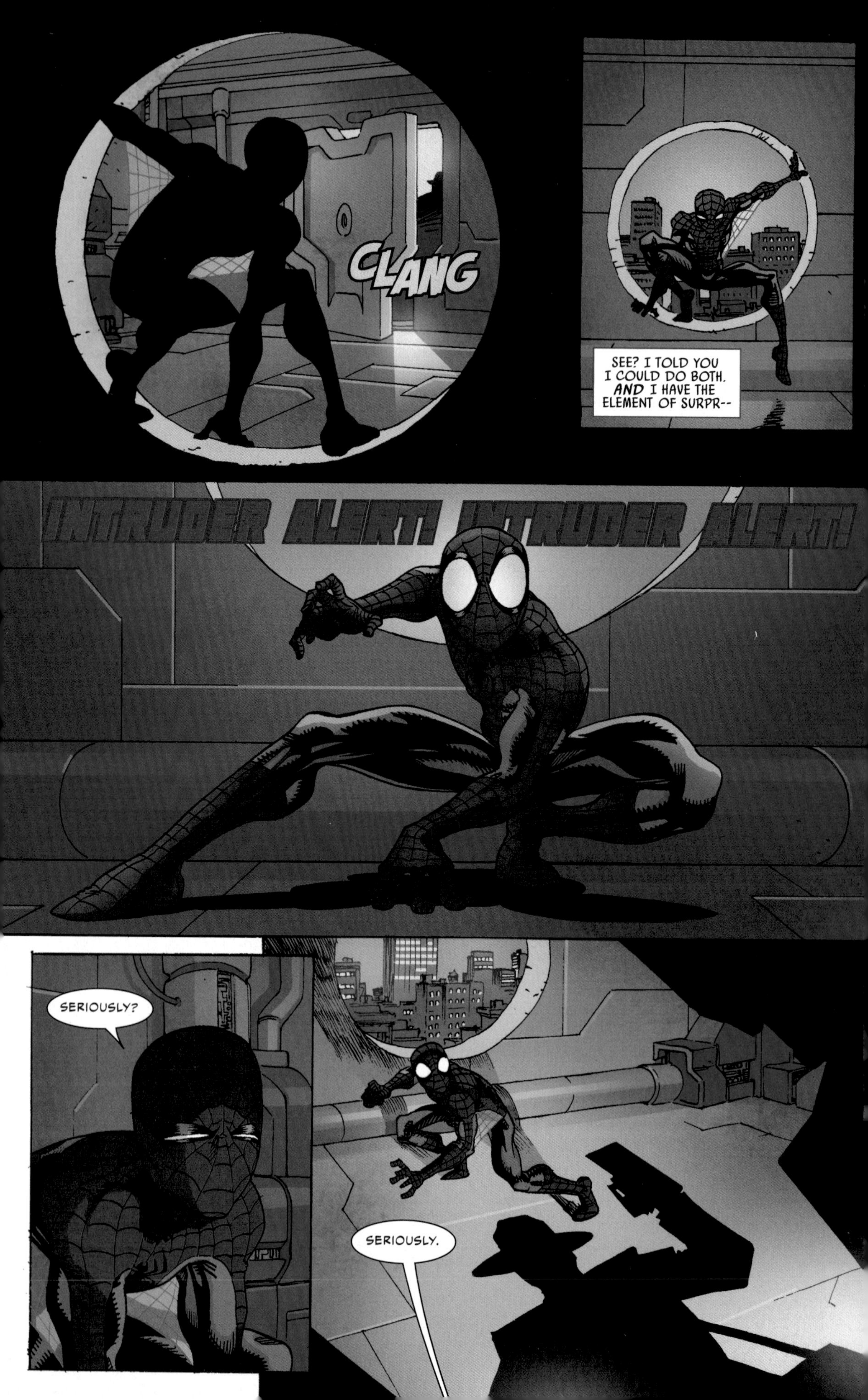
CLANG
SEE? I TOLD YOU I COULD DO BOTH. AND I HAVE THE ELEMENT OF SURPR--
INTRUDER ALERT! INTRUDER ALERT!
SERIOUSLY?
SERIOUSLY.

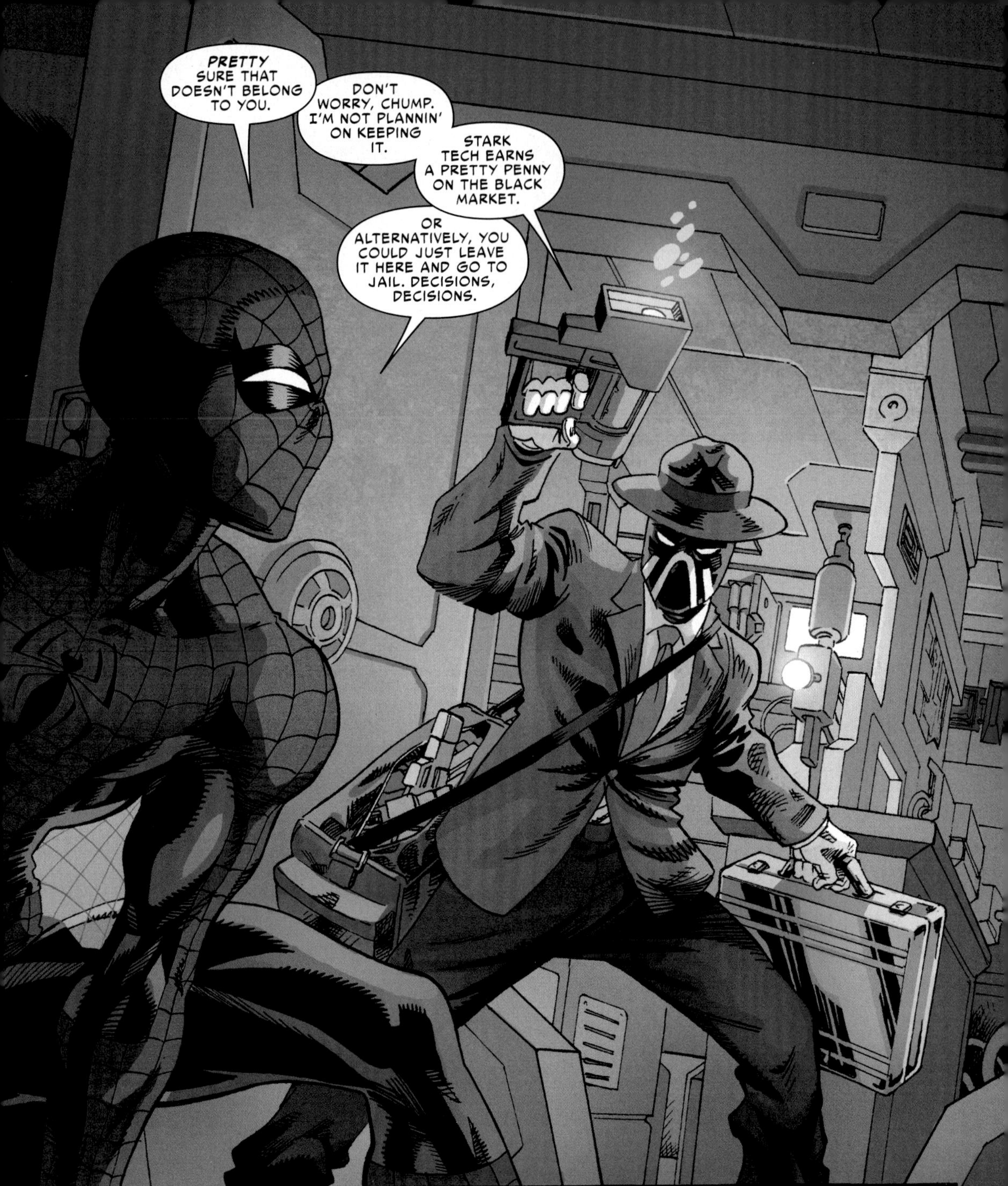
PRETTY SURE THAT DOESN'T BELONG TO YOU.
DON'T WORRY, CHUMP. I'M NOT PLANNIN' ON KEEPING IT.
STARK TECH EARNS A PRETTY PENNY ON THE BLACK MARKET.
OR ALTERNATIVELY, YOU COULD JUST LEAVE IT HERE AND GO TO JAIL. DECISIONS, DECISIONS.

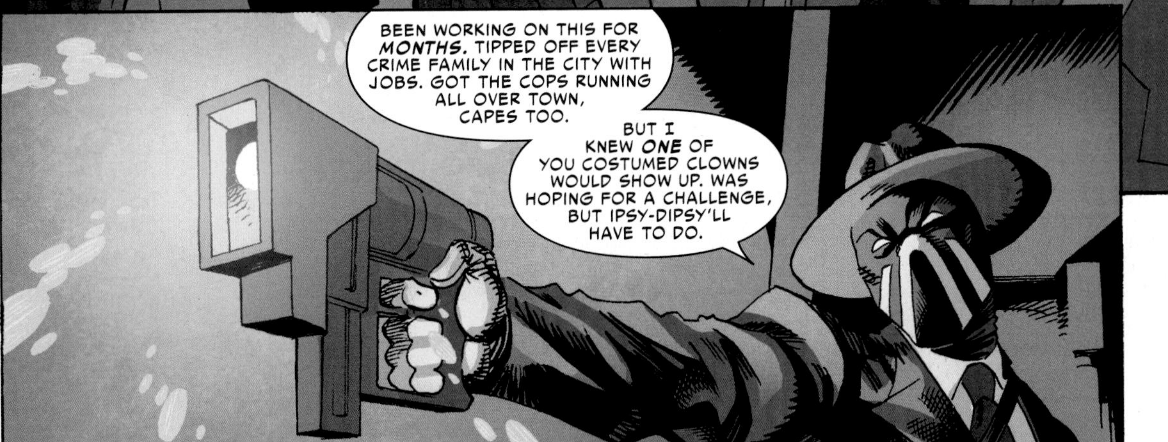
BEEN WORKING ON THIS FOR MONTHS. TIPPED OFF EVERY CRIME FAMILY IN THE CITY WITH JOBS. GOT THE COPS RUNNING ALL OVER TOWN, CAPES TOO.
BUT I KNEW ONE OF YOU COSTUMED CLOWNS WOULD SHOW UP. WAS HOPING FOR A CHALLENGE, BUT IPSY-DIPSY'LL HAVE TO DO.

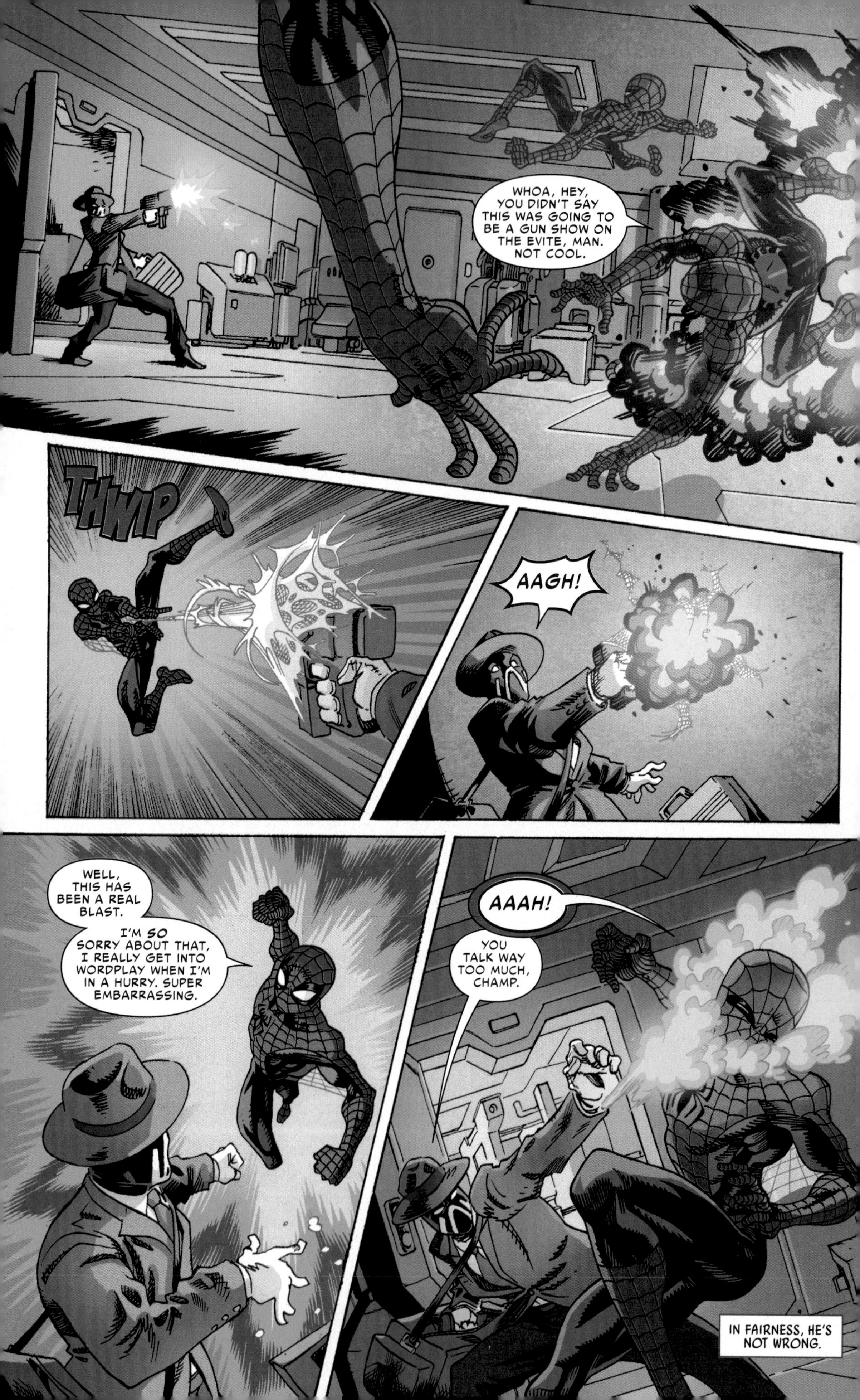
WHOA, HEY, YOU DIDN'T SAY THIS WAS GOING TO BE A GUN SHOW ON THE EVITE, MAN. NOT COOL.
THWIP
AAGH!
WELL, THIS HAS BEEN A REAL BLAST.
I'M SO SORRY ABOUT THAT, I REALLY GET INTO WORDPLAY WHEN I'M IN A HURRY. SUPER EMBARRASSING.
AAAH!
YOU TALK WAY TOO MUCH, CHAMP.
IN FAIRNESS, HE'S NOT WRONG.

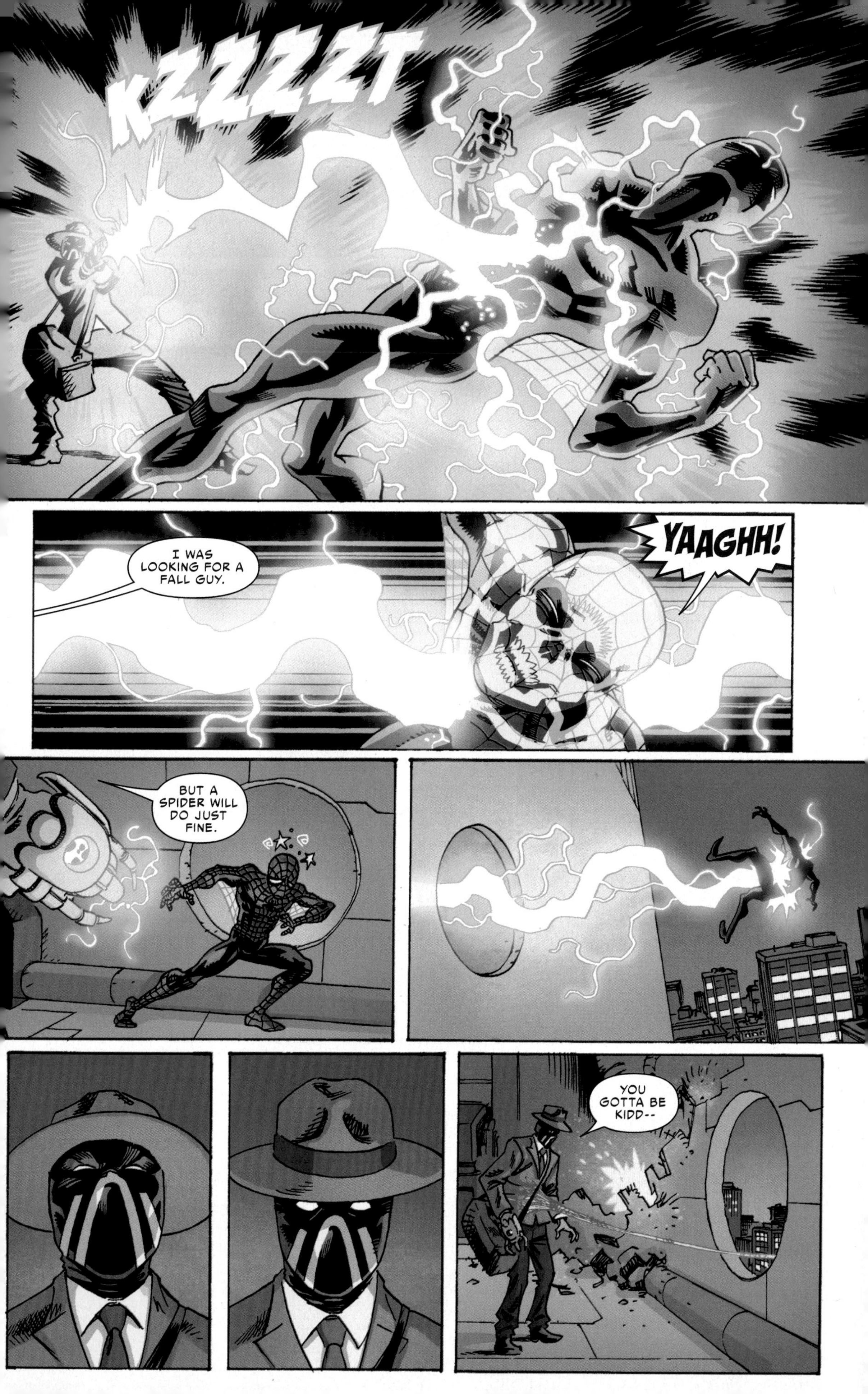
KZZZZZT
I WAS LOOKING FOR A FALL GUY.
YAAGHH!
BUT A SPIDER WILL DO JUST FINE.
YOU GOTTA BE KIDD--

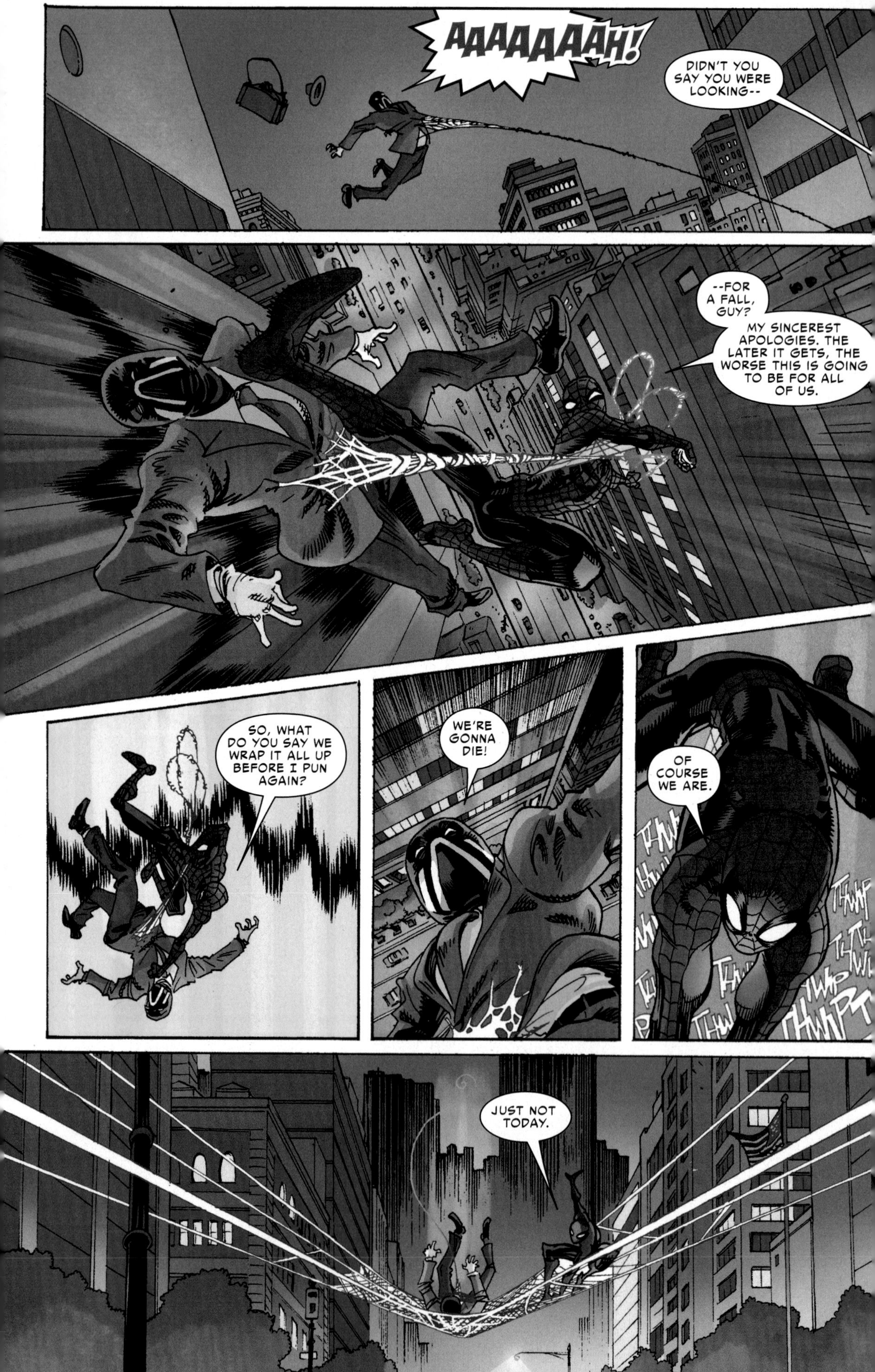
AAAAAAAH!
DIDN'T YOU SAY YOU WERE LOOKING--
--FOR A FALL, GUY?
MY SINCEREST APOLOGIES. THE LATER IT GETS, THE WORSE THIS IS GOING TO BE FOR ALL OF US.
SO, WHAT DO YOU SAY WE WRAP IT ALL UP BEFORE I PUN AGAIN?
WE'RE GONNA DIE!
OF COURSE WE ARE.
JUST NOT TODAY.

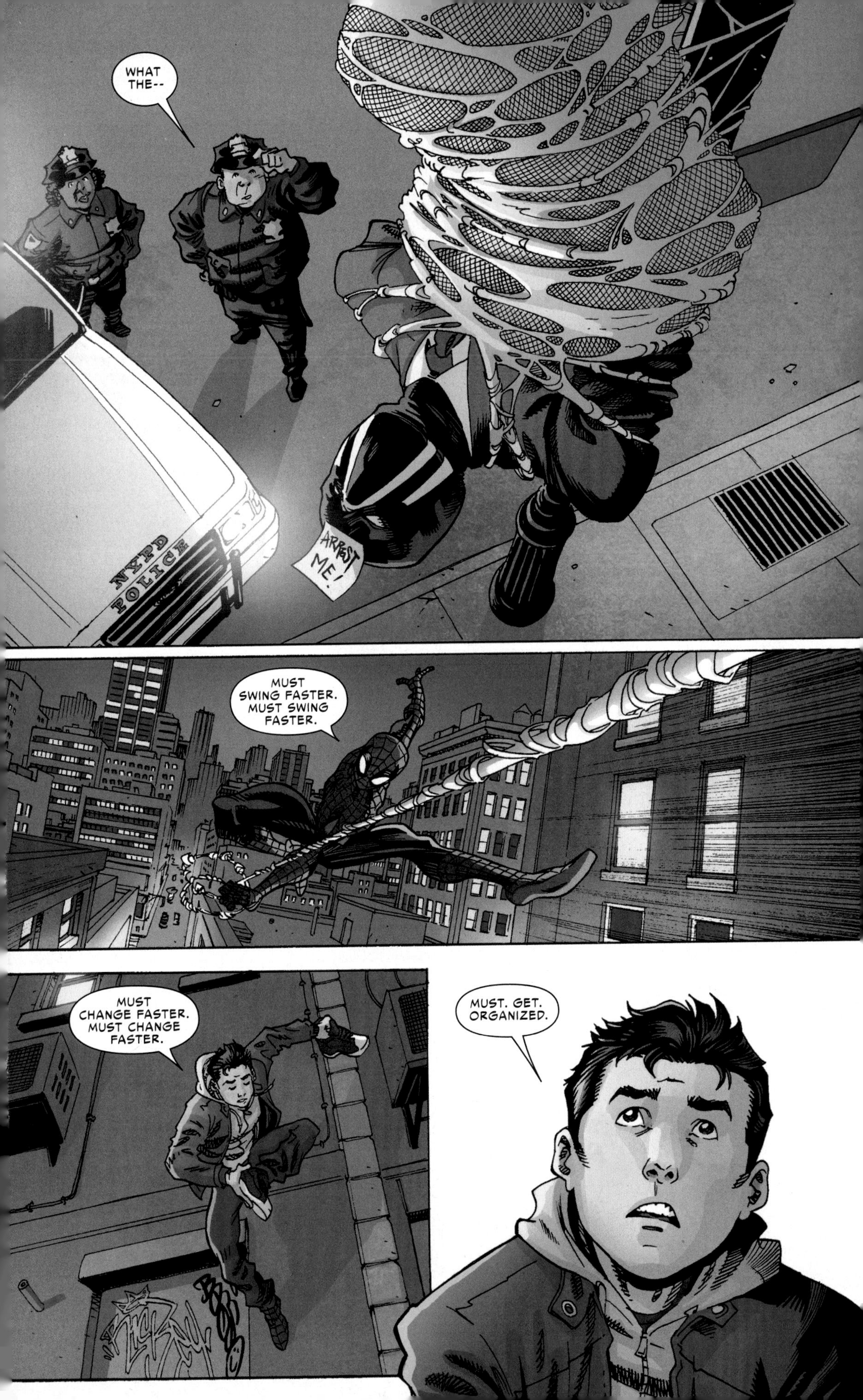
WHAT THE--
ARREST ME!
NYPD POLICE
MUST SWING FASTER. MUST SWING FASTER.
MUST CHANGE FASTER. MUST CHANGE FASTER.
MUST. GET. ORGANIZED.

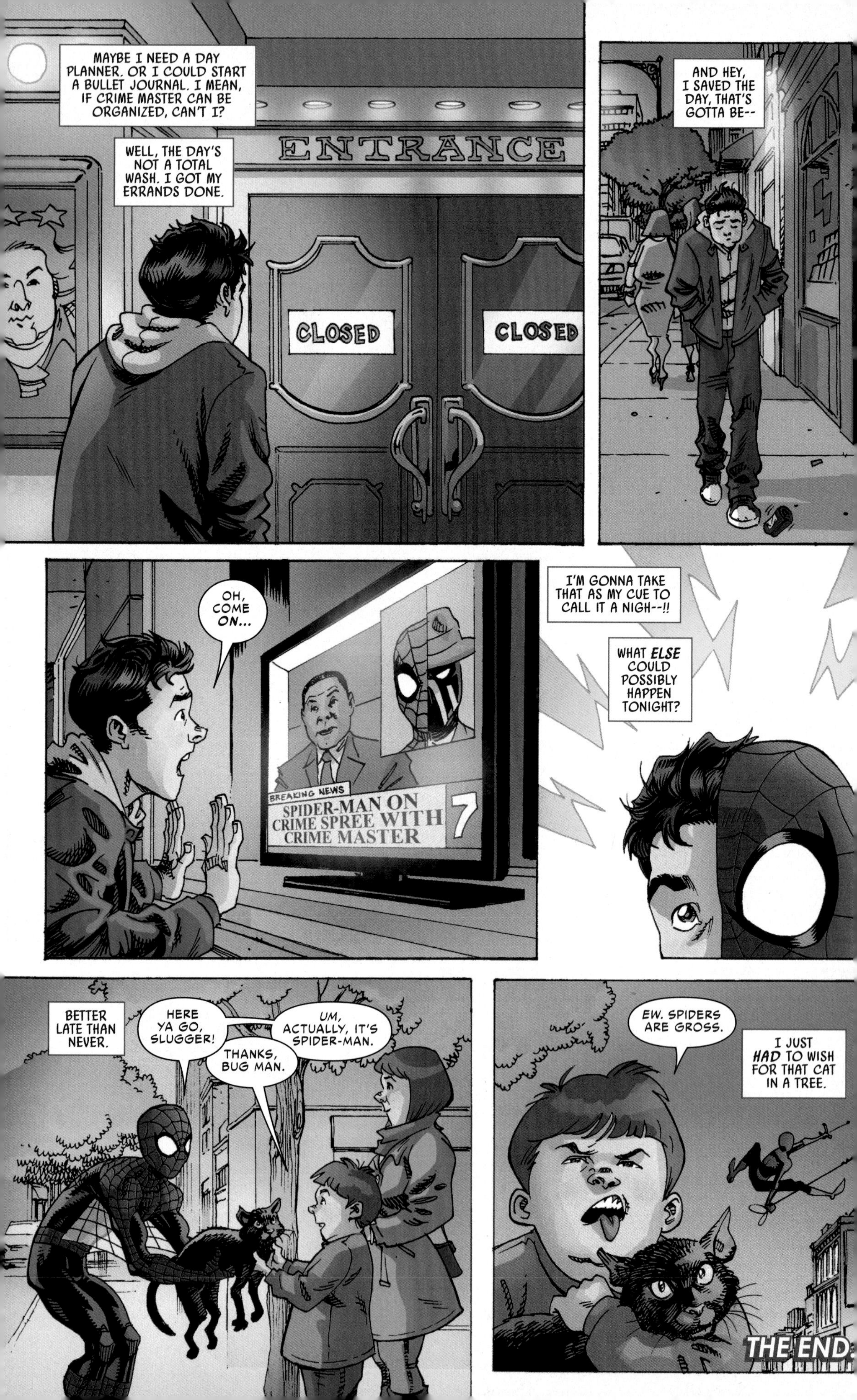
MAYBE I NEED A DAY PLANNER. OR I COULD START A BULLET JOURNAL. I MEAN, IF CRIME MASTER CAN BE ORGANIZED, CAN'T I?
WELL, THE DAY'S NOT A TOTAL WASH. I GOT MY ERRANDS DONE.
ENTRANCE
CLOSED
CLOSED
AND HEY, I SAVED THE DAY, THAT'S GOTTA BE--
OH, COME ON...
BREAKING NEWS
SPIDER-MAN ON CRIME SPREE WITH CRIME MASTER
7
I'M GONNA TAKE THAT AS MY CUE TO CALL IT A NIGH--!!
WHAT ELSE COULD POSSIBLY HAPPEN TONIGHT?
BETTER LATE THAN NEVER.
HERE YA GO, SLUGGER!
UM, ACTUALLY, IT'S SPIDER-MAN.
THANKS, BUG MAN.
EW. SPIDERS ARE GROSS.
I JUST HAD TO WISH FOR THAT CAT IN A TREE.
THE END.

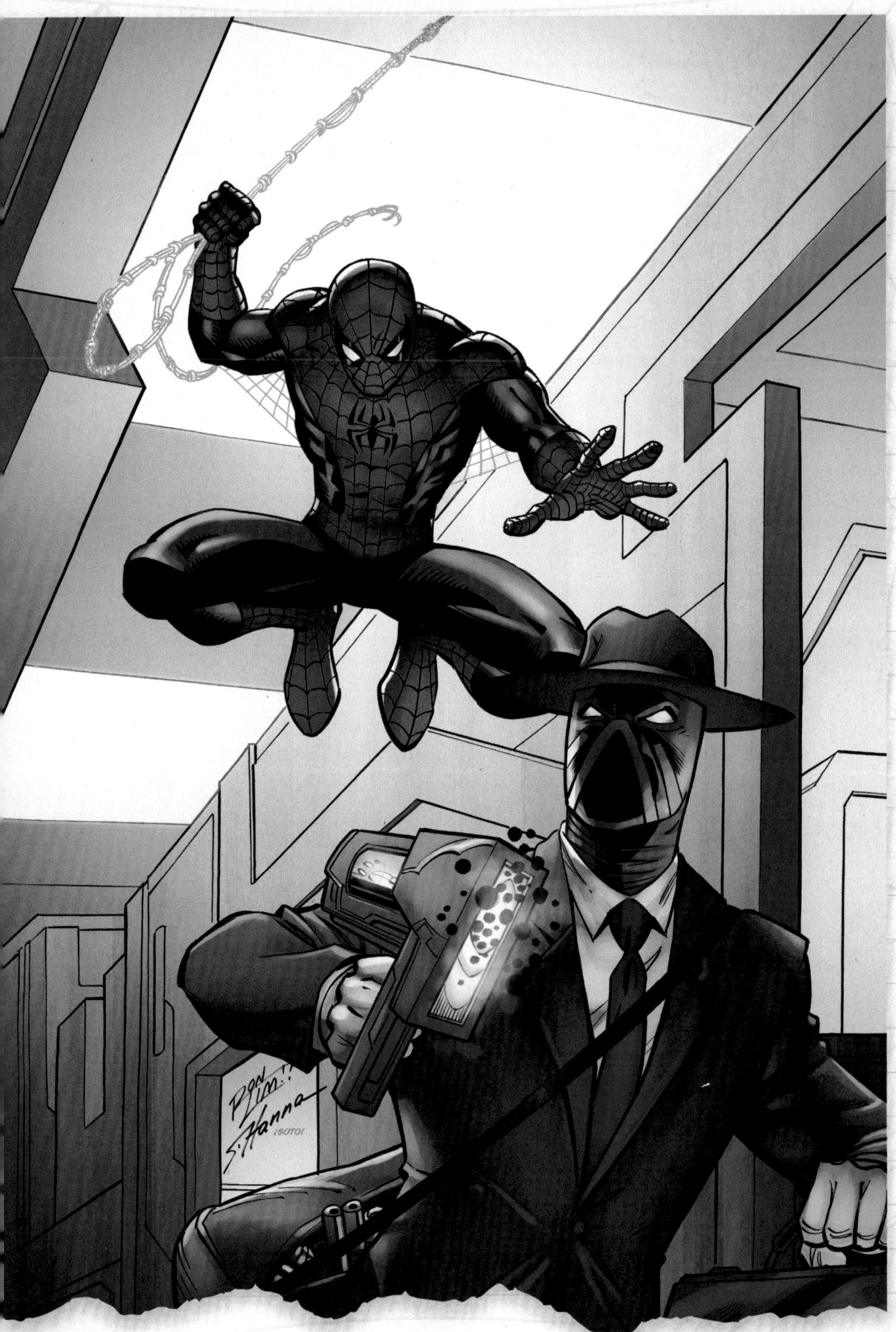

RON LIM, SCOTT HANNA & CHRIS SOTOMAYOR
SPIDER-MAN: MASTER PLAN VARIANT

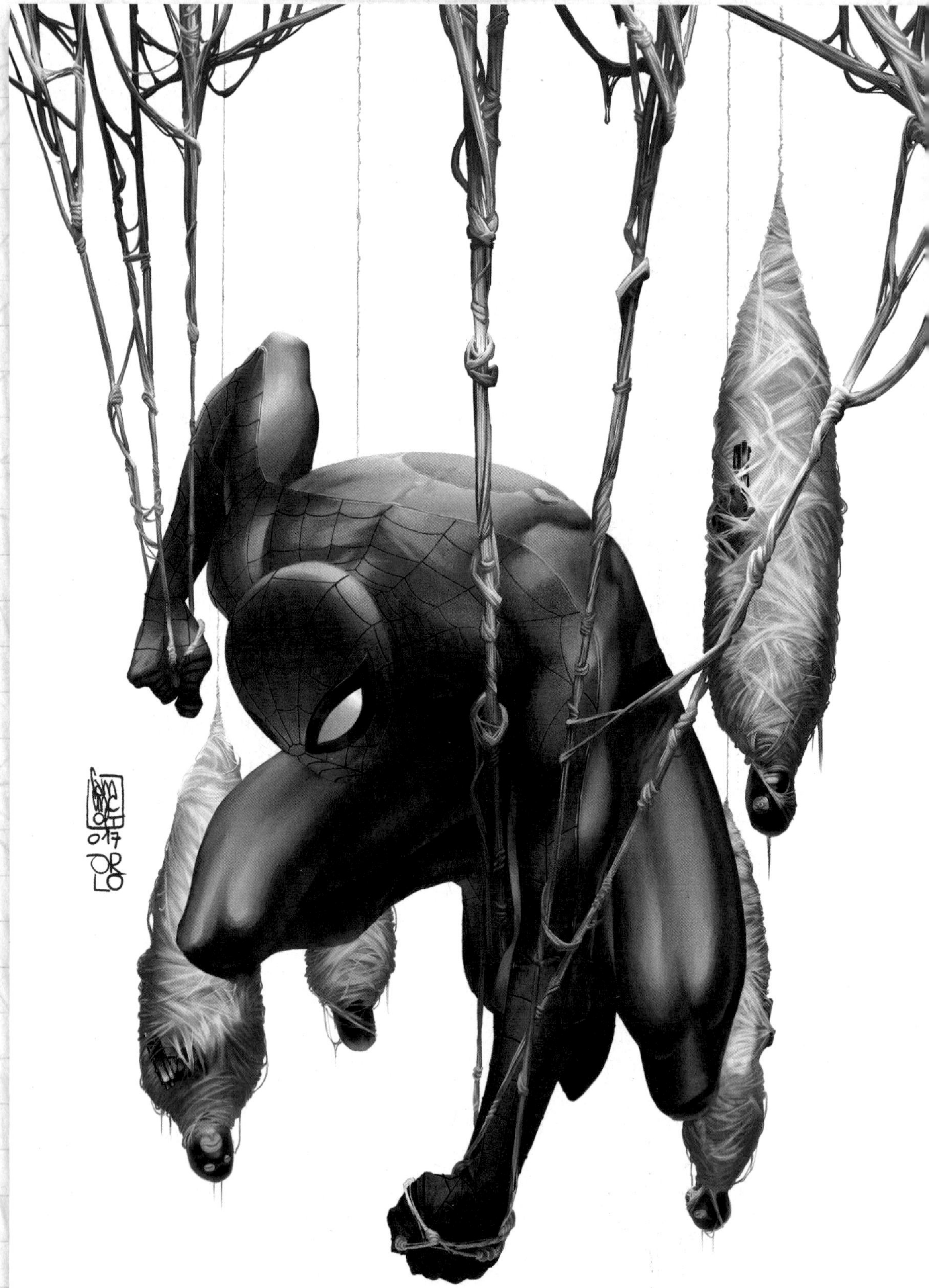

GIUSEPPE CAMUNCOLI & DANIELE ORLANDINI
SPIDER-MAN: MASTER PLAN VARIANT